THE PRIVATE JOURNALS
OF THE
LONG PARLIAMENT

2 June to 17 September 1642

THE PRIVATE JOURNALS
OF THE
LONG PARLIAMENT

2 June to 17 September 1642

EDITED BY

VERNON F. SNOW
ANNE STEELE YOUNG

Yale University Press
New Haven and London

The preparation of this volume was made possible (in part) by a grant from the Program for Editions, and publication assistance was provided by the Division of Research Programs of the National Endowment for the Humanities, an independent federal agency.

Set in Times Roman type by The Composing Room of Michigan, Inc., Grand Rapids, Michigan
Printed in the United States of America by Thomson-Shore, Dexter, Michigan

Library of Congress Cataloging-in-Publication Data
(Revised for vol. 3)

The Private Journals of the Long Parliament.

   Vol. 3–edited by Vernon F. Snow and Anne Steele Young.
   Includes bibliographical references and index.
   Contents: [1] 3 January to 5 March 1642—[2] 7 March to
1 June 1642—[3] 2 June to 17 September 1642.
   1. Great Britain. Parliament—History—Sources.
2. Great Britain—Politics and government—1642–1649—
Sources. I. Coates, Willson Havelock. II. Young, Anne Steele,
1923–   . III. Snow, Vernon F., 1924–
JN505.P74   328.41′09   81–3323
ISBN 0–300–05204–9 (v. 3)

A catalogue record for this book is available from the British Library.

The paper in this book meets the guidelines for permanence and durability of the Committee on Production Guidelines for Book Longevity of the Council on Library Resources.

10 9 8 7 6 5 4 3 2 1

CONTENTS

INTRODUCTION

> We have insensibly slid into this beginning of a civil war . . . and we scarce know how, but from paper combats, by declarations, remonstrances, protestations, votes, messages, answers, and replies, we are now come to the question of raising forces, and naming a general and officers of an army.

Thus did Bulstrode Whitelocke, MP for Great Marlow, depict England in the summer of 1642.[1] This third volume of private journals of the Long Parliament will substantiate Whitelocke's statement with the jottings of three diarists: Sir Simonds D'Ewes, MP for Sudbury; Framlingham Gawdy, MP for Thetford; and Roger Hill, MP for Bridport.[2]

The coming of the civil war in England during that summer adversely affected the quantity and quality of parliamentary diaries. No new diarists commenced writing until Walter Yonge, MP for Honiton, Devon, and uncle of Roger Hill, began his journal on 19 September 1642,[3] followed by Lawrence Whitaker, MP for Okehampton, Devon, on 8 October. Sir Thomas Peyton, having concluded his journal on 24 March, secured a leave to go to Kent and rarely returned to the parliament. Sir Ralph Verney ceased writing on 27 June, though he stayed in the house until 1643.[4] John Moore continued his journal through the opening months of the civil war, according to D'Ewes's references to it, but it was either destroyed or lost, probably after D'Ewes's death. D'Ewes also continues to refer to John Bodvel's diary, though it too has not been located. Both Framlingham Gawdy and Roger Hill continued their journals through 28 July. Thus only the persevering D'Ewes remains as a diarist, and even his journal suffers from occasional absences as well as from partisan rancor. Nevertheless, the journals of D'Ewes,

---

1. Bulstrode Whitelocke, *Memorials of the English Affairs, 1625–1660* (Oxford, 1853), I, 176.

2. D'Ewes: BL, Harl. MSS 163–64. Gawdy: BL, Add. MS 14,827. Hill: Record Office, Aylesbury, Bucks, Way MSS, AR 68/69, D/W/97/7. For further information about the diarists, see *PJ*, 1: xiii–xxi, and 2: x–xii.

3. For this reason the editors have concluded the present volume of parliamentary journals with the proceedings of 17 September.

4. Sir Ralph Verney, *Verney Papers: Notes of Proceedings in the Long Parliament*, ed. John Bruce [Camden Society] (London, 1845).

Gawdy, and Hill supply evidence and viewpoints not available from other sources, and therein lies their intrinsic value.

Through 23 July Sir Simonds D'Ewes remained true to his self-appointed mission of faithfully recording the deliberations in St. Stephen's Chapel. He wrote daily and at length either during the plenary session or shortly thereafter. He was rarely absent, but when he was, he invariably sought out another source to fill in the gaps. D'Ewes also continued to regard himself as the principal parliamentarian, procedural expert, and source for precedents and antiquarian data. He lectured his fellow MPs on points of order and was not above criticizing the Speaker and his rulings. His long and pedantic speeches must have irked many MPs.

Small wonder that on 23 July he was censured by the commons for indecorous words and forced to withdraw and beg forgiveness before reentering the house. He never fully recovered from this humiliating experience. For some time he attended less regularly and devoted less effort to his diary. Instead of taking notes in St. Stephen's Chapel, he wrote at home, relying on his memory and the records of Moore, Bodvel, and the clerk. For a month D'Ewes remained silent in the lower house, though on one occasion he persuaded Miles Corbet to put forward a motion on his behalf. Yet on 27 August he voted Aye on the resolution to adhere to the Earl of Essex and on 11 October pledged £100 for defense of the kingdom. (Most pledges by MPs had been made in early June.) Though silenced and embittered over the "fiery spirits," he remained committed to the parliamentary cause.

An analysis of D'Ewes's allies and enemies is instructive. He seems to have been in sympathy with Miles Corbet and Sir Thomas Bowyer. On 24 June both he and John Selden defended the king's right to private counsel, a right questioned by many MPs, especially the "violent spirits." On 27 August he defended Sir John Colepeper and John Pym for their attempts at reconciliation. He appears to have had a good working relationship with both the private and the official journalists. His principal antagonists, whom he referred to as the "fiery spirits," were John Glyn, John Gurdon, Denzil Holles, Henry Marten, Alexander Rigby, and particularly William Strode, the radical and militant MP from Devonshire. All of these MPs were nonaccommodationists, while D'Ewes saw himself as a parliamentary moderate, disposed to reconciliation with the king.

In fact, D'Ewes might well have become a royalist if it had not been for his strongly puritan views. He had studied Thomas Cartwright's *Catechism* while at Cambridge University, favored the reform of episcopacy, and preferred the sermons of such moderate puritan preachers as

Josias Shute, William Gouge, and Richard Byfield. His puritan commitment to daily discipline is evident in a little-known essay he wrote on religion: "All men, therefore, being [made] to give an account should live as accountants, every day casting up our reckonings, that so we may discover whether we thrive in grace or sin thrive in us."[5] Despite being deeply disturbed by the outbreak of war, he remained in the House of Commons, served on committees, and continued to record the proceedings of the house. In so doing, he disappointed his brother Richard D'Ewes, who in August 1642 invited him to join the king and fellow royalists in Nottingham.[6] D'Ewes did not return to the parliament following Pride's Purge in December 1648 and died in 1650.

Framlingham Gawdy remained in London until the end of July 1642 and continued his daily entries in his journal, occasionally relying on other members for information when he was out of the house. D'Ewes never refers the reader to Gawdy's journal as he does to Moore's; yet Gawdy often supplies information omitted by D'Ewes. Gawdy's attitude toward defense efforts is difficult to assess. He pledged £50 for defense in June but on 9 July voted against raising ten thousand men, as proposed by the committee of safety. Nevertheless, upon leaving London for Norfolk on 28 July, he assumed his duties as deputy lieutenant there. A brief note at the end of his journal indicates his return to London in 1643 and 1645. He was secluded from the parliament in Pride's Purge and died in 1655.

Roger Hill's private journal[7] continues to reveal a busy and hard-working lawyer. He was deeply committed to the cause of parliament, pledged £100 for defense in June, served on numerous committees, and was frequently occupied with legal proceedings, especially impeachments. For example, on 11 June he was named to the committee charged with drawing up an indictment against the nine peers who had absented themselves from the House of Lords. Eleven days later he was ordered to attend the judges who were examining three Irish rebels and to give them what information he had acquired. On 8 July he and seven other

5. BL, Harl. MS 227, "A Theological Discourse by Sir Simonds D'Ewes." The editors are indebted to John Ehman of the University of Rochester for permitting them to use his transcript of this manuscript.

6. James Orchard Halliwell, ed., *The Autobiography and Correspondence of Sir Simonds D'Ewes, Bart.* (London, 1845), II, 290–91.

7. Roger Hill's diary was first brought to the attention of American historians late in 1931 by Professor James Clifford of Columbia University. The diary was then in the possession of Major Roger Hill Way of Gerrards Cross, Bucks. Professor Clifford sent word of it to Professor William Haller at Columbia, who in turn informed Professor Willson H. Coates at the University of Rochester about it. Thus, after lengthy negotiations with Major Way, it was possible to include this little-known diary in the three volumes of *The Private Journals of the Long Parliament.*

MPs were ordered to attend the impeachment of the lord mayor of London in the upper house. Following the lord mayor's plea of "Not Guilty," Hill was appointed on 19 July as one of the managers in the trial. On 29 and 30 August he was named to committees for the impeachment of Lord Strange and several others.

Already a member of numerous committees, Hill was named to approximately thirty more between 3 June and 3 September. On the latter date he was given leave to go to the country. One of the most important of these committees, established after his journal concludes, was concerned with members absent from the House of Commons.[8] The fact that Hill's legal and committee activities consumed much time may account for the irregularity of his journal entries, which cease entirely on 28 July. Strangely, his committee involvements are rarely if ever mentioned in his own journals.

Some further insight into Hill's private and parliamentary concerns can be gained from his letters to his second wife, Abigail Gurdon, three of which are included at the end of this volume.[9] Hill continued as a member of parliament following Pride's Purge. During the Protectorate he became a serjeant-at-law and baron of the Exchequer. His death occurred in 1667.

II

When parliament passed the Nineteen Propositions in Westminster on 1 June 1642, King Charles was two hundred miles away in Yorkshire mustering support for his cause. He had left London in early January with his family and a small retinue and refused to return. Queen Henrietta Maria had been in the Low Countries since late February pawning the royal jewels and seeking support from her French relations. Their two sons, Charles, Prince of Wales, and James, Duke of York, were with the king in York. The king was attended by Secretary of State Sir Edward Nicholas, Edward Hyde, several other informal advisers, and a few loyal household servants and had a lifeguard of about two hundred for protection. The Privy Council was defunct for all practical purposes, for it did not meet after 8 January. Nevertheless, the king summoned most of his councillors to attend him in York, where he had established his center of government.

8. See 20 August, n. 6; and 2 September.
9. See Appendix K.

Charles remained in York until 7 July, then renewed his peregrinations in the north and midlands:[10]

July 7–11	Beverley
12	Doncaster
13	Newark
14–15	Lincoln
16–20	Beverley
21–25	Nottingham and Leicester
26	Doncaster
27–29	Beverley
July 30–Aug. 18	York
Aug. 19–21	Stoneleigh and Coventry
Aug. 22–Sept. 12	Nottingham
Sept. 13–15	Derby
16	Uttoxeter

The purpose of his travels was to enlist moral support and secure horses, ammunition, money, and manpower. He sought to enforce the commissions of array and solicited public displays of military power and loyalty as he moved through the countryside. Finally, in a symbolic medieval gesture, he raised the royal standard at Nottingham on 22 August and challenged his rebellious subjects either to lay down their arms or to prepare for war.

All of the activities of the king and his retinue were monitored by parliamentary watchdogs and reported in the lower house. Some reports were accurate, others fictitious; most provoked debate. The parliamentary diarists covered the more important deliberations concerning these royal activities and augmented the information in the official record about such events as the king's assembling of the Yorkshire gentry and yeomen on 3 June, the proposed adjournment of the Westminster courts to York, the sale of the crown jewels in the Low Countries, the local reactions to the commissions of array, and parliament's reactions to all of these events.

Much of this information came from the parliamentary committees in Yorkshire and Lincolnshire. Usually they used written communications, though occasionally a committee member appeared in person; and in

10. For 2 June–15 August, see George Poulson, *Beverlac: or, the Antiquities and History of the Town of Beverley* (London, 1829), I, 385n; for 16 August–17 September, see Edward, Earl of Clarendon, *The History of the Rebellion and Civil Wars in England*, ed. W. Dunn Macray (Oxford, 1888), II, 288–93, 300, 310; and *CSPD, 1641–43*, pp. 389–90. Other sources present minor variations in the itinerary.

early June the house sent John Rushworth to York to secure information. Intelligence came also from other sources. Reports from foreign agents and diplomats revealed the queen's activities in the Low Countries and the French attempts to send ships to the northern ports. Letters from military governors in England and Ireland gave the house logistical data. Messages from the Earl of Warwick informed the house about the state of the navy. Intercepted messages, such as one from Sir Edward Nicholas to Sir William Boswell in the Low Countries, gave the house access to royal plans and intentions.

Parliament also learned from the printed word of the king's actions and movements. Shortly after arriving in York, a royal printer began to issue broadsides and public pronouncements. The events in Hull were widely publicized. Parliamentary petitions and messages were published. In some cases a royal paper became available in printed form before it reached the recipient. To counter the king's use of the printing press, the House of Commons revitalized its committee for printing and resorted to stiff punitive measures against antiparliamentary printers. A new ordinance issued on 24 August reflected a House of Commons deeply concerned over the power of the printed word.[11]

During the early summer the Nineteen Propositions and the king's answer to them were the subject of many deliberations in the lower house. The Nineteen Propositions, following approval on 1 June, were sent to York, where they were considered by the king and his closest advisers. At the same time they were printed and distributed widely in London and throughout the kingdom. Although Charles originally intended to ignore the propositions because they were derogatory and unreasonable,[12] he was subsequently persuaded to answer them point by point. His reply, written by Lord Falkland and Sir John Colepeper, was completed by 18 June and sent to parliament, where it provoked a debate on the nature of kingship and royal authority. Yet the lower house proved to be more concerned with the king's actions than with his arguments.

Throughout the summer the commons devoted considerable time to the king's attempt to raise an army by resorting to the medieval commission of array. They questioned his authority to issue the commission, protested against each commission that the local authorities used to raise troops, and castigated those royalists who responded favorably. If the king had peaceful intentions, as he repeatedly claimed in pronouncements from York, why did he persist with acts of war? Why did he raise a

---

11. See *CJ*, II, 739.
12. See Clarendon, *History*, II, 171.

lifeguard? Why did he summon his peers to York? Why did he hold a council in York on 13 June? Why did he refuse to return to London and rule through parliament? To those members of parliament still in Westminster, these were not rhetorical questions but questions evoking much deliberation and debate.

Even as the king prepared for war, so the lower house took measures to defend parliament and the kingdom. In early June they began to order the deputy lieutenants to their counties to muster the militia. They diverted arms from Hull to the Tower of London. On 10 June they initiated the collection of pledges and contributions of "horse, money, and plate" and required each member to indicate the nature and quantity of his commitment. When some balked at this loyalty test, they were permitted to pledge to defend both "king and parliament" rather than simply "parliament."[13] On 21 June the house ordered the purchase of saltpeter. In early July parliamentary preparation increased with the appointment of the Earl of Warwick as lord admiral, the establishment of the committee of defense (safety), and the solicitation of money and horse from the respective boroughs and counties of the members. By mid-July preparations were well under way in most counties. In a controversial move on 30 July, the lower house redirected Ireland-bound troops to the service of the Earl of Essex, parliament's lord general. In addition, £100,000 intended for the committee for Irish adventurers was redirected to the committee of safety.[14]

In order to implement the militia ordinance, the leaders of the lower house initiated closer ties with the various counties and constituencies. Often they simply sent orders or logistical information by messengers to the lord or deputy lieutenants. On other occasions they commissioned MPs residing in or representing the counties to transmit information personally or to oversee military operations. Sometimes the house ordered MPs to go to their respective counties to counteract the efforts of the king to enforce the commissions of array. They in turn reported to the parliament concerning the local circumstances. Frequently these parliamentary initiatives provoked resistance or clashes between royal and parliamentary directives.[15]

The relationship between the lower house and Yorkshire continued to be unique because of the king's presence and the magazine at Hull. The

13. See 10 and 13 June.
14. See 20 June, n. 1; 16 August, n. 2; and *CJ*, II, 698.
15. For a county by county survey of these local conflicts, see Anthony Fletcher, "The Coming of War," in *Reactions to the English Civil War 1642–1649*, ed. John Morrill (London, 1982), pp. 29–38.

"watchdog" committees appointed by the commons in the spring remained in Yorkshire and Lincolnshire to observe and report the activities of the king and his supporters. Their reports to the house often evoked orders, letters, and declarations. These committees in the north linking Westminster with the provinces served as prototypes for the regional associations established for military purposes after the outbreak of the civil war. Most examples of local reactions to the militia ordinance and the commission of array can be traced through the Index.[16]

The public pronouncements of the house reflected shifting causes and rationale. Instead of subjugating the Irish rebels, soldiers were asked to engage themselves to defend the "king and parliament." The safety of both houses of parliament and of the king's person demanded a parliamentary force. True religion, laws, and liberties needed to be preserved. When some members questioned the reasons for parliament's raising an army to war against the king, as they did on 15 July, others responded with allusions to the king's two bodies, one natural and one artificial. When Selden, D'Ewes, and others questioned parliament's assumption of war-making power, their arguments were dismissed.

The possibility of a civil war was mentioned on several occasions in August by D'Ewes,[17] who attributed the danger to the "fiery and violent spirits" in the lower house. In August and September, when these MPs pressed for armed conflict in the committee of safety and the plenary sessions, much of the house followed their lead. At various times the house authorized the Speaker to issue licenses and warrants for arms and on 12 August formulated instructions for county committees to raise arms and prepare for war.[18] On 5 September the commons proposed funding military preparations by seizing the estates of delinquents. All of these early war preparations, having been approved in plenary sessions, were executed by means of orders, warrants, and licenses emanating from the Speaker.

Meanwhile the lower house maintained close ties with the Scottish Covenanters even as the king continued to communicate with the Privy Council of Scotland. The formal communications were facilitated by the commons' negotiating committee and by the Scottish commissioners who remained in London; certainly there were personal and clandestine ties as well. The house continued negotiations with the Scots over payment of the "brotherly assistance" and the deployment of Scots to

---

16. For maps illustrating the implementation of both, see Anthony Fletcher, *The Outbreak of the English Civil War* (New York, 1981), pp. 349, 357.

17. E.g., see 6, 10, 27, and 31 August.

18. See *CJ*, II, 717–18.

quell the Irish rebellion throughout the summer. In conjunction with the convening of the National Assembly of the Church of Scotland in St. Andrews on 26 July, the commons sent a declaration to the assembly appealing to the Covenanters for understanding and support, promising "a Reformation of the Church as shall be most agreeable to God's Word," and looking forward to a "firm and stable Union between the Two Kingdoms." The assembly in a detailed answer called for the abolition of English prelacy and the establishment of a single church encompassing England, Scotland, and Ireland. Parliament in turn invited the Covenanters to send delegates to the Westminster Assembly scheduled to meet in London in 1643. However, not until November 1642, after the civil war had begun, did Pym and his followers appeal to the Scots for military assistance against the king[19] in a move which culminated in the Solemn League and Covenant the following year.

III

The size and composition of the lower house changed considerably in the summer of 1642. While by-elections brought a few new faces to St. Stephen's Chapel, leaves, departures, disablements, and deaths greatly depleted the total number of qualified members by mid-September. The six newly elected MPs were: Sir William Constable, who replaced the disabled Henry Benson for Knaresborough, Yorkshire; Sir John Glanville and John Taylor, elected for Bristol after the disablement of monopolists Richard Long and Humphrey Hooke; Thomas Hanham, elected for Minehead, Somerset, in place of Alexander Luttrell, who had died in the spring; Richard Jennings, replacing his father, Sir John Jennings, who died in July while representing St. Albans, Hertfordshire; and James Scudamore, elected for Hereford in place of Richard Weaver, who had died in May.[20]

While Glanville and Constable were older men who had served in earlier parliaments, the rest were without parliamentary experience and, with the exception of Taylor, only twenty-five years of age or younger. Each of these men was elected before the outbreak of the civil war. There is clear evidence that Constable, Hanham, and Taylor took their seats before the end of 1642; it is uncertain when Jennings and

19. The declaration presented from the committee of safety appears in *LJ,* V, 430–31. For coverage of these events, see also David Stevenson, *The Scottish Revolution 1637–1644* (Newton Abbot, 1973), pp. 243–56.

20. For biographical sketches of the new MPs, see Appendix A.

Scudamore did so; and it appears that Glanville never did. Only Jennings, who was eliminated in Pride's Purge, and Constable were sympathetic to the parliamentary cause; the other four were eventually disabled.[21]

The ranks of the house were thinned during the summer by the deaths of three members and the departure of numerous MPs for a variety of reasons. In addition to Sir John Jennings, Sir Arthur Ingram died in August, and Henry Tulse died sometime during the summer. Many members were given leave for recovery of their health, family illness, the need to carry arms to their counties, or simply the desire "to go to the country." Some but not all leaves were limited to a specified length of time. The house seemingly approved these requests without question, even though the action reduced the size of the house.[22]

A second type of leave was for service to the parliament. During the summer months, particularly June, numerous MPs, many of whom were deputy lieutenants, were ordered to their respective counties to put the militia ordinance into execution. Others served the house as members of "watchdog" committees, especially those ordered to Yorkshire and Lincolnshire. A few acted as messengers to and from the king. Whatever the reason, whether personal or public, the result was the same: a sorely depleted house.

Another group of MPs, mostly royalists, absented themselves without either an excusation or a parliamentary order. These MPs were deemed delinquents and eventually suspended and/or disabled. To counter these absences, the commons devised both preventive and punitive measures: roll calls, fines, special summonses, and loyalty checks. For example, following a roll call of the house on 16 June, a committee was named both to take the excuses of absentees and to impose a £100 fine on those who failed to return within a reasonable length of time.[23] Most of the preventive measures, though temporarily successful, did not forestall the departure of those MPs loyal to the king and the royalist cause. The punitive measures probably served to preserve and stabilize Pym's leadership.

The testimony of the diarists confirms and amplifies the official *Journal* concerning attendance and absentees. Gawdy noted, for example, that on 7 June the house lacked a quorum in the late afternoon, but that on 16 June between 240 and 260 responded to the calling of the house.

21. See D. Brunton and D. H. Pennington, *Members of the Long Parliament* (Cambridge, Mass., 1954), pp. 200–45.

22. For the MPs who died or were given leave, see Appendixes A and B.

23. For the names of the absentees, see Appendix G.

Two days later D'Ewes reported a thin house. On 23 June Gawdy noted that 260 MPs voted on the king's answer to the Nineteen Propositions. The subsequent "thin" days, according to the diarists, were: 2, 5, and 26 July; 10, 20, and 30 August; 8, 12, and 15 September. On 15 September D'Ewes reported that only twenty MPs appeared for prayers and that the house lacked a quorum until 10 a.m.

The figures for the sixteen divisions between 2 June and 17 September further demonstrate the dwindling attendance:

June	3	99	July	9	170	Aug.	15	75
	11	160		19	120		17	59
	16	264		23	132		27	95
		238		26	83	Sept.	2	69
		179		28	114			
	27	69						
	30	84						

The high point on 16 June represents the day the house was called and debated its policy concerning absent members. The low point on 17 August was a vote as to whether Sir William Uvedale should be summoned to attend the house.

When special summonses, roll calls, and fines failed to forestall the dwindling attendance and the existence of a quorum became doubtful, the house was forced to take further measures. On 17 August a committee concerning absent members was named, seemingly with Roger Hill as chairman. The issue was debated in the house on several occasions. Finally in early September about sixty members were suspended until the cause of their absence could be examined, and the committee was charged with considering "which way the House may be replenished." Subsequently the house ordered that all members absent without leave should appear by Michaelmas (29 September) or face disablement.[24] Meanwhile between 4 August and 16 September forty-six members had been disabled.[25] Thus nearly 10 percent of the house was eliminated in a six-week period.

Clearly no mass exodus of royalists to the king's side was prompted by the early departures of such MPs as Sir Thomas Jermyn, Endymion Porter, and Edward Hyde. Rather there was a steady erosion of support throughout the spring and summer. Colepeper and Falkland remained in

24. See 20 August and 2 September.
25. For their names see Appendix A.

the house for a time after Hyde's departure and faithfully transmitted information to the councillors in the north. Several less well-known royalists remained after the king had raised his standard at Nottingham in late August. The names of tellers at divisions reflect those royalists who remained in the house during June: Henry Killigrew, Edmund Waller, John White (MP for Rye), Sir Robert Hatton, Sir John Strang-ways, Sir Patrick Curwen, Sir George Dalston, Sidney Godolphin, Nicholas Weston, and either Francis or Walter Lloyd. Only the names of Waller and Strangways recur as tellers in July. Most of these incipient royalists departed in July and August and were subsequently disabled. Several were Straffordians, and in two divisions they were joined by John Selden, also a Straffordian. While attracting some MPs from the fluctuating middle, the hard core remained between thirty and fifty in June and July. The eclipse of the royalist cause in the House of Commons was virtually complete by early September.

Nevertheless, sharp divisions of opinion continued long after the departure of the king's adherents. In fact, according to D'Ewes, partisan intensity increased with the disappearance of the king's party in the lower house. There were parliamentary accommodationists who strove to find some grounds for negotiating with the king and a few royal accommodationists who wanted to avoid an armed conflict. With the gradual departure of the latter group, however, the former found themselves at odds with the leaders of the war faction, such as Marten, Strode, Rigby, Cromwell, Holles, and Gurdon. In between was a large and fluctuating middle group held together by Pym and like-minded moderates. By August and September most of the partisan clashes were between the middle group and the nonaccommodationists. D'Ewes's sympathies lay with the middle group, and he was deeply disturbed over the increased factiousness and the decline of civility in the deliberations.

Since the private journals, in contrast to the official *Journal,* record the names of many speakers and motion-makers, it is possible to ascertain the principal leaders in the lower house. The most prominent MPs, based on their frequency of participation as recorded by the diarists,[26] were: John Pym, Denzil Holles, William Strode, and William Lenthall. The second most active group were:

Robert Reynolds	John Wilde
John Hampden	Sir Thomas Barrington
Oliver Cromwell	Sir Walter Erle

26. This method of evaluating is simply an index of participation and is neither definitive nor verifiable.

| Giles Green | Sir Robert Harley |
| Henry Marten | Sir Henry Vane, Jr. |

Clearly Pym remained the dominant leader through the summer of 1642, and those following him in frequency present no surprises. However, the apparent decline in participation of John Glyn, Walter Long, and Sir Philip Stapleton, all of whose names appeared more frequently during the earlier months of 1642, should be underscored. On the other hand, Robert Reynolds, through his involvement with Irish affairs, Henry Marten, as a member of the committee of safety, and Oliver Cromwell assumed more important roles than heretofore.

The increasing participation of Cromwell deserves comment. He spoke more frequently. He was named to serve on many committees, the most important being the committee for defense, charged with advancing the propositions for bringing in money, horse, and plate. On 10 June he pledged £500 for defense.[27] He was a faithful member of the commission for Irish affairs, as is evident from his attendance record. He was selected several times by the Speaker to communicate with the upper house. His record of participation in the lower house indicates, not surprisingly, particular interest in Ireland, Cambridgeshire, and military affairs.[28]

The formal organization of the lower house remained intact throughout the summer. William Lenthall continued to preside over the deliberations as Speaker of the house. Henry Elsynge, clerk, John Rushworth, his assistant, and John Hunt, sergeant at arms, all retained their positions. There is no evidence of bureaucratic proliferation despite long hours and increased business.

The powers of the Speaker, however, increased appreciably as the house prepared for war. He sometimes served as the de facto executive by enforcing orders and, as required, issuing warrants. In most cases the warrants were specific in nature: for example, on 14 June a warrant to stop the shipment of sword blades, and on 2 July a warrant to allow the Beckwiths to travel overseas. In the absence of the royal bureaucracy, the lower house improvised and established its own policies and procedure. This warrant system was, however, open to misuse, as D'Ewes

27. See *CJ*, II, 660; and Appendix F.

28. For Cromwell's career during this period, including his committee assignments, see Wilbur Cortez Abbott, *The Writings and Speeches of Oliver Cromwell* (Cambridge, Mass., 1937–47), I, 179–201. See also J. S. A. Adamson, "Oliver Cromwell and the Long Parliament," in *Oliver Cromwell and the English Revolution*, ed. John Morrill (London, 1990), pp. 54–56.

noted on several occasions. On 8 June the house authorized the Speaker to issue a blank warrant, allowing Pym to fill in the name of the person to be apprehended because the matter concerned "the safety of the commonwealth." On 19 August, when the Speaker reported that he had issued one hundred general warrants for search and seizure, he was overruled by the house and ordered to cease the issuance of such warrants, a practice prohibited in the Petition of Right. Nevertheless, on 26 August John Ashe, MP for Westbury, complained that his house had been searched by constables and other Londoners, presumably by authority of a general warrant. The lower house took his complaint seriously, for it sent for the perpetrators and established a committee to reform the abuse of the warrant system.[29]

Lenthall continued to exercise the traditional powers of the Speaker. Except when overruled by the house, he determined the legislative calendar and committee hours. There is no evidence that anyone ever took his place as Speaker pro tempore, although he stepped aside when the house met as a committee of the whole. Though ostensibly neutral, he appeared to work closely with Pym in setting the agenda. On a few occasions he took part in the deliberations, as on 15 June when he moved to expedite the tonnage and poundage bill and on 23 June when he participated in the debates over the king's answer to the Nineteen Propositions. With these few exceptions his role in the deliberations remained passive and inconspicuous.

Yet in a variety of ways Speaker Lenthall could and did influence the informal organization of the lower house. He could manage the ebb and flow of debate, recognize one MP and ignore another, and produce or withhold correspondence. He could also influence the selection of committees, appoint the tellers in a division, and select messengers to the upper house. Through these and other powers he "managed" the deliberations. He also exerted influence on messages, orders, ordinances, and bills by selecting the drafters of these legislative instruments. For example, he appointed Robert Reynolds to draft several official letters in September 1642. The journals reveal that Serjeant Wilde, Alexander Rigby, and Bulstrode Whitelocke were among those selected to draft bills and orders. There is little doubt that the Speaker, by delegating his authority to legal specialists, expedited and influenced events.

Though the Speaker had little impact on the composition of committees, he could exert influence through setting the agenda and recognizing committee chairmen in the deliberations. Committee members continued to be named by the MPs from the floor of the house, with the clerk or assistant listing the names as they were called out. Sometimes the first-named MP became the chairman and reporter. An attempt by Wilde on 21 July to propose members for a committee was opposed by William Cage and the whole house. On the other hand, occasionally committee composition was limited by specialization (for example, lawyers) or by geography (MPs from a specific jurisdiction). The committee of the whole concerned with tonnage and poundage was customarily chaired by the solicitor general, presiding from the clerk's chair.

Procedural anomalies and innovations with regard to committees sometimes appear in the private member journals. On 23 June the house resorted to a subcommittee in responding to the king's answer to the Nineteen Propositions, an infrequently used device. On 17 June Strode precipitated a procedural dispute over whether the committee for privileges was a public or private committee. The day before, the house had voted to revive the committee in order to resolve the Arundel election dispute. Strode's motion that the order be reversed was presumably on grounds that, as a private committee, it was not subject to the ordinary rules of the house. In the ensuing debate D'Ewes pointed out that all business of the house was public, especially that pertaining to elections. Strode, however, carried the day in a close vote, and the committee did not meet that afternoon. This conflict and the result further confused the distinction between public and private committees.

The informal organization of the lower house, especially the committees, changed almost daily. New crises produced new committees. Each message from the king in the north was turned over to a committee for study and reply. Many select committees lapsed without comment in the *Journal,* while others were revived or expanded to include new members. Moreover, as royalists left St. Stephen's Chapel, the balance of committee composition shifted, and little-known backbenchers began to fill the vacuum and play a larger role in the deliberations. Cromwell and others of his persuasion assumed important roles in the committees *before* they became prominent on the floor of the house. A few guideposts in the maze of committees and commissions may be helpful.

The committee system during this period mirrored the changing composition and conditions. A number of the standing and select committees continued under the same chairmen:

Accounts	John Trenchard
Customers	Giles Green
Informations	Lawrence Whitaker

Irish Adventurers	Walter Long
Navy	Giles Green
Printing	John White[30]
Scandalous Ministers	Miles Corbet
Trade	Sir Henry Vane, Sr.

Many of these committees, as the nation moved toward war, changed in function from legislative to quasi-administrative bodies. To overcome entrenched chairmen, the house added new members to old committees or established new committees. Both processes took place in the summer of 1642, so that it is sometimes difficult either to distinguish between overlapping committees or to ascertain membership.

The commission for Irish affairs, constituted in early April, continued to make most of the logistical and military decisions relating to the quelling of the Irish rebellion and the establishment of an English military force. The editors have again included the minute book of this body[31] to augment the record of the diarists and the official *Journals*. The commission continued to meet, though with decreasing frequency, in the Star Chamber and acted as the "war cabinet" through August.[32] It approved contracts, received and answered letters, planned purchases, recommended appointments, and even drafted orders. In mid-June the commission redirected the arms and ammunition at Hull to Ireland despite a royal warrant against it and in mid-July ordered Lord Lieutenant Leicester to raise four thousand volunteers to send to West Chester. Most of these activities won approval in the lower house, either before or after orders were issued.

In early August problems arose over lack of a quorum. As a temporary measure it was ordered by both houses that the commission should meet as a committee, thus requiring a smaller quorum. Then on 3 September a new select committee for Irish affairs was named to replace the commission, which met only two more times.[33] During all of these changes Pym continued to be the principal spokesman for both the commission and the new committee.

Meanwhile Irish affairs were demanding less attention than the raising of an English army to defend "king and parliament." In response to the new threat of a royalist army, the House of Commons on 6 June estab-

---

30. MP for Southwark.
31. National Library of Ireland, Dublin, MS 14,305.
32. See below, n. 39.
33. See CIA, 16 August, n. 2, and 3 September.

lished a committee for defense of the kingdom empowered to consider ways of providing "Horse, Men, and Monies" for defense and to formulate propositions to this end.[34] Even more important, however, was a new joint committee for defense of the kingdom (or committee of safety) named on 4 July. Meeting in the Court of Wards, this committee was to consider "whatever may concern the Safety of the Kingdom, the Defence of the Parliament, the Preservation of the Peace."[35] The dominant peers were Essex, Northumberland, Pembroke, Say and Sele, and Holland, while the leading commoners were Pym, Holles, and Marten. Soon after its formation this committee proposed the naming of a general (Essex) and the raising of an army.[36] Subsequently, as already noted, both money and men intended for Ireland were diverted by this increasingly powerful committee for use at home,[37] and matters concerning defense were frequently referred first to the committee of safety rather than to the House of Commons. In addition, the committee formulated numerous declarations and messages concerning defense. By early September the committee had a treasurer (Sir Gilbert Gerard) to issue pay warrants and a permanent secretary (Henry Parker) to handle messages and orders.[38] By the time the Earl of Essex left London on 9 September, the committee of safety had supplanted the commission for Irish affairs as the "war cabinet."[39]

Because both the dissemination and control of printed materials were continuing issues, in addition to the standing committee for printing two ad hoc committees were named in June. One was charged with publicizing parliamentary votes and orders, the other with preventing the printing of "scandalous pamphlets." At this time the House of Commons began printing as many as nine thousand copies of its various pronouncements and sending them out to sheriffs and constables in the provinces.[40] In late August one of the committees concerned with print-

34. See 8 and 10 June.
35. See 5 July, n. 11; and *CJ*, II, 651.
36. See 12 July.
37. See above, n. 14.
38. PRO, SP 28: 262 (Letterbook of the Committee of Safety).
39. Most of the generalizations and conclusions that Lotte Glow attributed to the committee of safety are true also for the commission for Irish affairs. Since the latter antedated the committee of safety by three months, it should be regarded as the prototype "war cabinet" for military policy and administration. The committee of safety then was the principal administrative link between the commission for Irish affairs and the committee of both kingdoms. See Lotte Glow, "The Committee of Safety," *English Historical Review*, 80 (1965): 289–313; and Wallace Notestein, "The Establishment of the Committee of Both Kingdoms," *American Historical Review*, 17 (1912): 477–95.
40. *CJ*, II, 604, 616, 624.

ing established new rules for the publication of information and penalties for violations.[41]

The official journals reveal little about the duration of the daily meetings of the lower house. Though they clearly indicate afternoon sessions, they do not include beginning and closing times. However, from the diarists, especially D'Ewes and occasionally Gawdy, it is possible to reconstruct the legislative day for June and July. Even when D'Ewes arrived after prayers, he faithfully recorded the time that the house convened. Unfortunately after 23 July he was sometimes absent or attended for only an hour and therefore no longer recorded the time of adjournment.

During the period covered by this volume, the house met every day except Sunday. On most days during June the Speaker opened the session with prayers at 8 a.m., during July between 8 and 9 a.m. In August and September the house convened later, usually between 9 and 10 a.m. The hour of adjournment varied according to the substance of the deliberations and the intensity of debate. On some days the plenary session adjourned at 1 or 2 p.m., allowing for committee meetings during the afternoon; on other days the house adjourned for dinner, then reconvened and deliberated until 7 or 8 p.m. On 23 June the prolonged debate on the king's answer to the Nineteen Propositions lasted until 9 p.m. On fast days the house did not meet until after the sermons and then only briefly to thank the preachers and arrange for future sermons.

Committees continued generally to meet during the afternoon, though a few met simultaneously with the plenary sessions, during the dinner hour, or in the early morning before prayers. The meeting places in the inner Court of Wards or the Exchequer Chamber were near St. Stephen's Chapel. Thus the schedule of plenary deliberations as well as committee meetings was indeed demanding. In fact, it was so rigorous that some members arrived late and/or departed early. Small wonder that there was at times a "thin house" or on rare occasions the lack of a quorum.

The deliberations in St. Stephen's Chapel became more heated and less decorous as the summer progressed. On 4 June, shortly before dinner, Sir Thomas Barrington was interrupted by cries to adjourn. That same day the house derided a nonmember's petition, delivered by Denzil Holles, for defeating the Irish rebels, while John Glyn "snarled" at D'Ewes. Four days later Sir John Northcote was laughed at for both the content and the delivery of his speech. In late June D'Ewes himself

41. See above, p. xii.

admitted that he "nipped" Strode in a verbal exchange. In the debates over the king's answer to the Nineteen Propositions, tempers flared, and the deliberations concerning payment to Captain Arthur Chichester's regiment on 14 June were long and agitated.

Occasionally the rules of debate were stretched or violated. On 30 June Strode spoke twice on the same subject (elections), as did Rigby on 12 September, both seemingly with the Speaker's tolerance. In addition, freedom of expression was limited during this period, as several incidents clearly indicate. On 8 June the house objected to remarks made by William Pleydell about parliament's propositions for defense; he was excused only after explaining himself. Two days later Isaac Penington, having disparaged Pleydell for refusing to subscribe either money or horses, was called into question for his remarks. When on 23 July the committee of safety presented a new declaration to the house, D'Ewes severely criticized both the procedure and the committee, averring that parts of the declaration had been copied from a printed pamphlet. He was both compelled to withdraw and censured, though upon returning to the house, he defended the principle of freedom of speech and apologized for his indiscretion.

To deal with the constant pressure of events, the house sometimes resorted to procedural technicalities and innovations. On 2 June D'Ewes pointed out in his journal that no new motion could be introduced after noon without prior approval of the majority, a rule perhaps designed to prevent surprise moves in a thin house. Four days later both houses set aside all business except that dealing with the defense of England and Ireland. On 22 June several MPs demanded that Pym cease reading letters from Hull, presumably on the grounds that only the clerk of the house could do so. On 11 July Strode, objecting to letters from Hull being read in the house, urged that such letters should be referred first to the committee of safety. Clearly the incipient royalists were not trusted by their fellow members. On 15 July D'Ewes objected when the house, prompted by Holles and Strode, attempted to amend an order passed in the House of Lords. Though Speaker Lenthall initially supported this procedural maneuver, he apparently reversed himself when D'Ewes pointed out that since the lords' orders could not be amended by the commons, a new order originating in the commons should be drafted.

Access to St. Stephen's Chapel became more limited as the summer wore on. The arrival of a senator from Hamburg on 11 August precipitated a debate over protocol and procedures, which D'Ewes recorded. Though the senator was allowed to present his credentials, the diplomatic messages were not considered until after his departure. On 4

August Serjeant Robert Hyde, MP and recorder of Salisbury, was questioned, ordered to withdraw, sent to the Tower, and subsequently disabled for advising the mayor of Salisbury to obey the king's command. The personal appeal of Sir John Colepeper to deliver a message from the king on 27 August presented the commons with another dilemma. Should the house admit him or disable him? The war party failed at that time to have him disabled by a vote of 69 to 26, which pitted Henry Marten and William Strode against Sir Robert Harley and Sir John Finch as tellers. However, the victorious majority, led by Pym, only allowed Colepeper to approach the bar and present the royal messages, thus denying him access to the floor of the house. Similarly on 5 September Lord Falkland was required to deliver the king's message at the bar.

It is also possible to detect procedural changes and anomalies in the summer deliberations. On 2 June the lower house authorized Miles Corbet, chairman of the committee concerning scandalous ministers, to proceed with an examination of a minister. The authorization was not a voice vote but, as D'Ewes noted, "the sense of the house." This device, subsequently labeled common consent, no doubt served to expedite matters. On 11 June the Ayes remained in the house during the division while the Noes went forth, even though the former carried the vote by 109 to 51. On 11 August the house departed from its traditional procedure, and members were compelled to vote individually as to whether they would "venture and hazard their lives and fortunes with the Earl of Essex, lord general." The voting took place behind closed doors, and no one was permitted to leave until he had voted. Following the Speaker's stern reproof, William Jesson changed his vote from No to Aye, and subsequently many MPs were overawed into voting Aye.

Procedures relating to the passage of bills, however, changed little. The last bill to receive the royal assent pertained to the Irish rebellion. Having received its first reading in the commons on 15 May, it was approved by the king in York on 22 June. Between 2 June and 17 September, only six new bills were read in the House of Commons, two of which had already been passed by the House of Lords. Of these six only one, the bill for tonnage and poundage, was passed by both houses and sent to the king.[42]

The king's absence from London led parliament to enact laws which lacked the royal assent, just as Richard II had promulgated ordinances approved by his council but lacking the consent of lords and commons.

---

42. For a history of these bills see Appendix C.

This medieval precedent was revived at D'Ewes's suggestion in August 1641, when Charles I was in Scotland. The lower house wished to appoint commissioners to observe the king and first issued an order to this effect. D'Ewes, while objecting to this unilateral enactment, informed the commons that an order passed by both houses had the force of law.[43] Thus did the two houses revive and revise the medieval practice. As a result parliament approved five ordinances between 20 August and 9 September 1641, a process which continued in 1641 and 1642[44] and provoked little controversy until February 1642, when its validity was challenged. At that time the militia ordinance, though rejected by the king on 28 February, was passed by both houses on 5 March. In mid-March the two houses declared that it had the force of law and "doth oblige the People, and ought to be obeyed, by the fundamental Laws of this Kingdom."[45]

This action did not resolve the matter, however, for the king continued to oppose the form and royalists began to ridicule it. During the summer the parliament, resigned to the king's reluctance to assent to any further legislation, turned more and more to enacting ordinances. For example, the house resorted to an ordinance concerning tonnage and poundage when the king refused to assent to the bill. Similarly when the commons realized that the king would not sign any of the several bills convening the Westminster Assembly of Divines, an ordinance was finally drafted in May 1643, which subsequently won the approval of both houses.[46]

The relationship between the two houses changed little, even though normal procedures often proved cumbersome. Each house had its own messengers to transmit business to the other house. Moreover, when messengers from the lords appeared, they were to be received before any new business. When D'Ewes reminded the house of this custom on 14 June, the messengers were promptly admitted. However, on 9 July the lords' messengers waited for an hour before being received. By then the upper house had adjourned for dinner.

The impeachment of the nine peers for absenting themselves from the House of Lords without leave presented the lower house with a procedural dilemma. On 11 June the commons voted that the nine lords were "suspected to further a civil war in the kingdom," and a committee

---

43. See Harl. 164, ff. 46b–48a; and *CJ*, II, 265–67.

44. For a discussion of ordinances during this period, see C. H. Firth and R. S. Rait, eds., *Acts and Ordinances of the Interregnum 1642–1660* (London, 1911), III, xiii–xvii.

45. See *PJ*, 1: 480, 513–14; and *LJ*, IV, 646.

46. See 14 July, n. 13.

was named to draw up an impeachment. When the impeachment was debated on 14 June, some members urged that the indictment include an admission of guilt and a penalty of forfeiture. D'Ewes objected on the grounds that the lower house could only accuse and never judge; a majority in the house followed his lead. Next day Denzil Holles delivered the modified impeachment to the lords "by word of mouth" but was subsequently ordered on Serjeant Wilde's motion to set it down in writing. Yet on 5 July Wilde himself delivered the impeachment of the lord mayor of London "by word of mouth," and the house immediately voted that Gurney be impeached at the bar in the upper house. Six days later the formal charges, now in written form on parchment, were presented to the lords,[47] and on 19 July the lord mayor appeared before the lords to answer them. He was subsequently tried and on 12 August was found guilty and committed to the Tower. It is noteworthy that both houses took time from their war preparations and heavy schedules to engage in the cumbersome impeachment process.

The lower house also devoted considerable time to the case of Lady Elizabeth Sedley, who had been raped by John Griffith, MP for Caernarvonshire. Griffith apparently claimed privilege from arrest and threatened to leave the country. When Lady Sedley petitioned parliament on 8 June for the right to prosecute Griffith and to secure his person, the house concurred and appointed a powerful committee[48] to consider the matter. D'Ewes reported details of the case and the committee's proceedings on 20 June and 22 July. Finally on 10 August Griffith was disabled to be a member of the house because of misconduct.

The house also considered more significant petitions. A number of them requested the appointment of lecturers to provide pious and orthodox preaching in various churches. Others from counties or towns concerned preparations for war. On several occasions appeals to the historic Petition of Right came before the lower house. On 6 June both D'Ewes and Gawdy related that the king had cited the Petition of Right in the Beckwith incident. On 23 June both the solicitor general and John Whistler alluded to it when discussing the king's answer to the Nineteen Propositions. In July and August the house, while not referring directly to the Petition of Right, approved orders against the billeting of soldiers. Even during war preparations the rights of the subject were not entirely forgotten.

---

47. *CJ*, II, 653, 664.
48. *CJ*, II, 613, 685.

IV

The achievements of the lower house during the summer of 1642 were limited, almost exclusively, to military decisions and war preparations. The Irish rebellion was being subdued by means of Scottish and English forces. The Scots troops were sent to the northern counties of Ireland under terms defined in a treaty with Scotland. Parliament continued to raise money, especially through the adventurers, for the English troops in Ireland, while the commission for Irish affairs initiated and supervised decisions concerning logistics and supply. The king concurred with these endeavors by giving the royal assent to the bill calling for the reducing of Ireland by means of subscriptions. This approval on 22 June was the last royal concurrence before the outbreak of hostilities in England.

Commons also organized an English army to defend "the king and parliament." Relying upon the authority of the militia ordinance, it sent the deputy lieutenants to the counties and called for musters of the local militia. It gained control of castles, forts, magazines, and munitions. It appointed an admiral, the Earl of Warwick, to insure control of the seas and named the Earl of Essex as lord general of the army. In addition, on 5 September the house approved a draconian method of repaying parliamentary loans through the seizure and sale of delinquents' estates. None of these deliberative actions won the approval of the king and in fact were extremely divisive in the lower house, the upper house, and the kingdom at large. They accelerated the departure of many MPs and peers either to their respective counties or to the king in the north.

The lower house continued to push for religious reforms. The bills calling for the abolition of pluralities and for the elimination of the Laudian innovations won the approval of both houses and awaited the king's signature. The bill against scandalous ministers, which had been approved by the lower house, languished in the House of Lords. The bill convening the Westminster Assembly, after much debate, was passed by both houses and transmitted to the king, who refused to concur with it. Charles I remained adamant in his rejection of religious reforms.

Parliament itself was deeply divided over the future of the church. The debates over the Westminster Assembly revealed a broad spectrum of religious opinion within both houses. There existed a "negative concurrence" against Archbishop Laud and his innovations; he remained in prison with his impeachment stalled in committee. Commons responded to a number of petitions calling for the removal or reassignment of ministers and the appointment of lecturers with puritan sympathies. However, for many members of parliament these changes were no substitute for broad-based reformation in the church.

Nor did commons resolve the deep-seated constitutional differences. The Nineteen Propositions, received by the king in early June, were rejected, and the king's answer, while offering a few concessions, precipitated heated and prolonged debates in the lower house. The "paper war" polarized opinion and rendered reconciliation unlikely if not impossible. In the final analysis the king and parliament reached a standoff over their respective constitutional powers, and each prepared to resolve the differences between them by appealing to swords rather than words. Many MPs were torn between loyalty to the monarchical system and devotion to parliament. All three of the remaining diarists continued to be committed to parliament, but in differing degrees. Gawdy rendered lukewarm assistance from a distance. Hill gave wholehearted support in the house. D'Ewes, after anguished soul-searching, remained in the house and cautiously recorded the proceedings as a passive spectator.

V

The editorial objectives and practices set forth in the first two volumes of *The Private Journals* have been continued in this volume.[49] The editors have attempted to provide an accurate and useful text of the three parliamentary journals and the Minute Book of the Commissioners for Irish Affairs, as well as appropriate annotation. As in the two earlier volumes, capitalization, punctuation, and spelling have been modernized, but grammar and syntax have not been altered.

The paragraphing in the original manuscripts has been followed. The names of members of parliament appear in capitals when they speak or take action in the house. Abbreviations have been extended without brackets except in cases of doubt. Occasional missing words have been supplied in brackets. Substantive crossed-out passages appear in the footnotes. Renditions of D'Ewes's cipher and Hill's Law French have been underlined. Hill's unrelated legal material has been omitted but noted.

The principal sources used appear in the list of Abbreviations which follows. Where there are multiple references for one printed document

---

49. See *PJ*, 1: xxix–xxxiii, and 2: xxiv–xxvi.

in the Wing *Short-Title Catalogue,* the one found in the Thomason Collection is generally cited. Though the editors have examined all the relevant documents in the Main Papers in the House of Lords Record Office, frequently the *HMC, Fifth Report,* is cited because of its greater accessibility.

Members of parliament included in Mary Frear Keeler's *The Long Parliament* have not been identified. However, there are biographical notes for seven new members in the second volume of *The Private Journals* and for six new members in this volume. Again the editors have attempted to identify those persons whose names have not occurred heretofore and to assist readers in finding their way through the maze of committees, bills, orders, ordinances, declarations, and messages.

VI

In preparing this third volume for publication, the editors have incurred numerous debts of gratitude. We are obligated to the following archives for permission to publish the private member journals: the British Library, the University of Minnesota Library, and the Buckinghamshire Record Office. We are also grateful to the Council of Trustees of the National Library of Ireland and the Keeper of Manuscripts, D. Ó Luanaigh, for permission to publish the Minute Book of the Commissioners for Irish Affairs. Many other repositories have supplied relevant materials appearing in the Introduction, footnotes, and Appendixes: the House of Lords Record Office, especially Mr. H. S. Cobb; the British Library, especially Mr. L. C. Skeat; the Public Record Office; the Bristol Record Office, especially Mr. J. S. Williams; the Buckinghamshire Record Office, especially Mr. H. A. Hanley; the John Rylands Library, especially Miss Glenis A. Matheson; the Bodleian Library; the Institute of Historical Research; the Yale Center for Parliamentary History; the University of Rochester Library, especially the Department of Rare Books; the Syracuse University Library; the Cornell University Library; and the Yale University Libraries. In addition, we have greatly benefited from being able to use the private library of the late Glenn Gray and Helen Barber Gray.

We are also indebted to the following persons for various types of assistance and courtesies: Maija Jansson and William B. Bidwell of the Yale Center for Parliamentary History; Peter Hasler of the History of Parliament Trust; Mary Frear Keeler of Hood College; J. H. Hexter of Washington University; Conrad Russell of University College, University of London; A. J. Fletcher of the University of Durham; the staff of the Department of History, University of Rochester; Kenneth Pennington, Carol Devlin, Johanna Moyer, and Robin Lamott of Syracuse University; and Elizabeth Young DeBruyne of Rochester, New York.

For various forms of financial assistance which have made possible this publication, we are obligated to the late Hilda Altschule Coates, Yale University, Syracuse University, the University of Rochester, especially the Willson H. Coates Memorial Fund, and the National Endowment for the Humanities.

Vernon F. Snow
Syracuse, New York

Anne S. Young
Rochester, New York

July 1991

ABBREVIATIONS

Add. MSS	BL, Additional Manuscripts.
AO	*Alumni Oxonienses . . . 1500–1714.* Oxford, 1891.
BL	British Library, London.
Calamy	A. G. Matthews, *Calamy Revised.* Oxford, 1934.
CAM	Mary Anne Everett Green, ed., *Calendar of the Proceedings of the Committee for the Advance of Money, 1642–1656.* 1888. Reprint. Nendeln, 1967.
CCC	Mary Anne Everett Green, ed., *Calendar of the Proceedings of the Committee for Compounding, 1643–1660.* 1889–92. Reprint. Nendeln, 1967.
CIA	Minute Book of the Commissioners for Irish Affairs.
CJ	*Journals of the House of Commons.* London, 1742–.
Coates	Willson Havelock Coates, ed., *The Journal of Sir Simonds D'Ewes.* New Haven, 1942.
CSPD	*Calendar of State Papers, Domestic Series.* London, 1857–.
CSP Ire.	*Calendar of State Papers Relating to Ireland.* London, 1870–.
CSP Ven.	*Calendar of State Papers and Manuscripts Relating to English Affairs, Existing in the Archives and Collections of Venice, and in the Other Libraries of Northern Italy.* London, 1900–.
D	Journal of Sir Simonds D'Ewes.
DNB	*Dictionary of National Biography.* London, 1967–68.
G	Journal of Framlingham Gawdy.
GEC, *Baronetage*	G. E. C[okayne], *Complete Baronetage.* Exeter, 1900–06.
GEC, *Peerage*	G. E. C[okayne], *The Complete Peerage of England, Scotland, Ireland, Great Britain, and the United Kingdom.* London, 1910–59.
H	Journal of Roger Hill.
Harl. MSS	BL, Harleian Manuscripts.
HLRO	House of Lords Record Office, London.

HMC	*Historical Manuscripts Commission.*
Keeler	Mary Frear Keeler, *The Long Parliament, 1640–41.* Philadelphia, 1954.
LJ	*Journals of the House of Lords.* London, 1767–.
M of P	*Members of Parliament. Return of the Names of every Member returned to serve in each Parliament.* London, 1878.
MP	Member of Parliament.
NED	*New English Dictionary.* Oxford, 1888–1928.
Notestein	Wallace Notestein, ed., *The Journal of Sir Simonds D'Ewes.* New Haven, 1923.
Pink MSS	Manuscripts of W. D. Pink. John Rylands Library, Manchester.
PJ, 1	Willson H. Coates, Anne Steele Young, Vernon F. Snow, eds., *The Private Journals of the Long Parliament: 3 January to 5 March 1642.* New Haven, 1982.
PJ, 2	Vernon F. Snow and Anne Steele Young, eds., *The Private Journals of the Long Parliament: 7 March to 1 June 1642.* New Haven, 1987.
PRO	Public Record Office, London.
Roy. Off.	P. R. Newman, *Royalist Officers in England and Wales, 1642–1660.* New York, 1981.
RP	*Rotuli Parliamentorum ut et Petitiones et Placita in Parliamento.* [n.p., n.d.]
Rushworth	John Rushworth, *Historical Collections of Private Passages of State.* London, 1721–22.
Sheriffs	PRO, Lists and Indexes, No. IX, *List of Sheriffs for England and Wales.* 1898. Reprint. New York, 1963.
SL	*The Statutes at Large.* London, 1769–74.
SP	State Papers, Domestic, PRO.
SR	*The Statutes of the Realm.* London, 1810–28.
VCH	*Victoria County History.*
Walker	A. G. Matthews, *Walker Revised.* Oxford, 1948.
Wing	Donald Wing, *Short-Title Catalogue . . . 1641–1700.* New York, 1972–88.

OFFICIALS

This list includes only the major offices held by MPs or others mentioned in the journals or in the annotation. It is not intended as a complete list of office-holders.

I. Parliament

Clerk of the House of Commons	Henry Elsynge
Clerk Assistant	John Rushworth
Clerk of the Parliaments	John Browne
Gentleman Usher of the Black Rod	James Maxwell
Sergeant at Arms, House of Commons	John Hunt
Speaker of the House of Commons	William Lenthall, MP

II. Central Administration

Chancellor of the Exchequer	Sir John Colepeper, MP
Chief Justice of the Common Pleas	Sir John Banks
Chief Justice of the King's Bench	Sir John Bramston
Clerk of the Crown	Thomas Willis
Comptroller of the Household	Sir Peter Wyche
Earl Marshal	Thomas Howard, Earl of Arundel and Surrey
Lieutenant of the Ordnance	Sir John Heydon
Lieutenant of the Tower	Sir John Conyers
Lord Admiral	Algernon Percy, Earl of Northumberland (to 25 June)
	Robert Rich, Earl of Warwick (from 1 July)
Lord Great Chamberlain	Robert Bertie, Earl of Lindsey
Lord Keeper of the Great Seal	Edward, Lord Littleton
Master of the Jewel House	Sir Henry Mildmay, MP
Master of the Ordnance	Mountjoy Blount, Earl of Newport
Master of the Rolls	Sir Charles Caesar
Postmaster General	Philip Burlamachi

Secretaries of State	Lucius Cary, Viscount Falkland, MP
	Sir Edward Nicholas
Solicitor General	Oliver St. John, MP
Treasurer of the Army	Sir William Uvedale, MP (to August)
	Sir Gilbert Gerard, MP (from 10 August)
Treasurer of the Household	Thomas, Viscount Savile
Treasurer of the Navy	Sir William Russell (to August)
	Sir Henry Vane, Jr., MP (from 8 August)
Vice Admiral	Robert Rich, Earl of Warwick (to 1 July)
	Sir William Batten (from March)

III. The Army

General for the King	Robert Bertie, Earl of Lindsey
General for the Parliament	Robert Devereux, Earl of Essex

IV. London

Lord Mayor	Sir Richard Gurney (to 12 August)
	Isaac Penington, MP (from 16 August)
Sheriffs	Sir George Clarke
	Sir George Garrett

V. Ireland

Lieutenant General of the Adventurers' Forces	Philip, Lord Wharton
Lieutenant General of the Army	James Butler, Earl of Ormonde
Lord Justices	Sir John Borlase
	Sir William Parsons
Lord Lieutenant	Robert Sidney, Earl of Leicester
Lord President of Connaught	Roger Jones, Viscount Ranelagh
Lord President of Munster	Sir William St. Leger (died 2 July)
Marshal	Edward, Viscount Conway
Master of the Rolls	Sir John Temple

Treasurer at Wars	Sir Adam Loftus
Deputy	Nicholas Loftus
Victualler	Walter Frost

VI. Scotland
General of the Army — Alexander Leslie, Earl of Leven

THE PRIVATE JOURNALS
OF THE
LONG PARLIAMENT

2 June to 17 September 1642

JOURNAL OF SIR SIMONDS D'EWES

[Harl. 163, f. 143a]   June 2, Thursday, 1642

The Speaker came about 8 of the clock. After prayers Mr. Scawen had leave to go into the country upon MR. NICOLL's motion. Vide M.[1]

MR. DENZIL HOLLES spake next and made report of the 12 ships which were to be set forth by th/[2]

I went out of the house between 8 and 9 and returned after 10.[3]

SIR JOHN EVELYN had made report of the names of such members as were absent and prepared an order for their forfeiture of an 100£ if they did not return by the 16 day of this month. After divers had spoken to it, at last it was put to the question and the order allowed, and the sum was to go to the use of the war of Ireland.[4]

MR. REYNOLDS made report of the new bill, being the 3d which had been drawn,[5] for the adventurers for Ireland from the committee, to which they had made some additions which were read and allowed; and then upon some new objections being made, the bill was recommitted to the said Mr. Reynolds, Mr. Grimston, and Mr. Pury to draw a new clause or two to add to it, who withdrew presently about it.[6]

MR. NATHANIEL FIENNES proceeded with the report of the treaty agreed upon with the Scottish commissioners for the sending of 10,000 Scots into

---

1. For John Moore's missing journal, see *PJ*, 1: xvi and 484, n. 15.

2. "An Ordinance of both Houses, concerning the additional Forces by Sea, this Day read; and committed." The new committee included Holles. *CJ*, II, 600. For earlier proceedings concerning this new ordinance for the sea adventure for Ireland, see *PJ*, 2: 286, 305.

3. For proceedings omitted by D'Ewes, see G, below, and *CJ*, II, 600–01. References to the three diarists included in this volume will be by the first initial of the last name, e.g., G for Gawdy. D'Ewes's entries which have been underlined by the editors represent renditions of his cipher.

4. For this order and the committee named on 1 June to formulate it, see *CJ*, II, 598, 601. Though it is often difficult to know whether the reference is to Evelyn of Surrey or of Wiltshire, it seems likely that it was the latter who dealt both with the attendance of members and subsequently with the propositions for defense. See below, 8 June, n. 9; and 16 June, n. 20.

5. I.e., the bill for enlarging the time of subscriptions. See *PJ*, 2: 309 and 366, n. 8. This was the third bill since the original act for reducing the rebels of Ireland. The others were (1) to explain certain clauses in the original act and (2) to enable corporations and bodies politic to participate in the act.

6. The bill was recommitted to the new committee for the ordinance for the sea adventure for Ireland, of which Grimston was a member. See above, n. 2. Reynolds, Wilde, and Pury were added. *CJ*, II, 601.

Ireland.[7] [f. 143b] And many particulars were allowed and some amended. These articles were most of them read before in the house long since.

The articles being finished, MR. LAWRENCE WHITAKER showed that two Scottishmen, papists, did refuse the Oath of Supremacy, saying that all of their nation were excused from taking it by the articles of the last treaty, which made the CHANCELLOR OF THE EXCHEQUER to stand up and move that a committee might be appointed to consider of the late treaty of pacification[8] whether or no all Scottishmen that should come into England were freed by that act from taking the Oath of Supremacy because he thought it to be a matter of dangerous consequence, and thereupon the said chancellor of the Exchequer and divers others by name and all the lawyers of the house were appointed a committee to consider of the same.

It was then moved that these articles we had passed might be compared with the original draft that so it might be seen whether they did agree or no, and thereupon a committee was appointed to compare them together, of which I was named one,[9] and they were ordered to meet at 5 of the clock this afternoon in the inward Court of Wards.

It being past 12 of the clock so as no new motion should have been made after that hour without leave of the house, SIR WILLIAM WIDDRINGTON delivered in a petition subscribed by about 700 inhabitants of the town of Newcastle, in which they desired that two of their preachers, who were questioned here before the committee for scandalous ministers,[10] might be dismissed and sent to them, which petition of theirs was very ill resented by the house because the matter was now in examination before the committee. And MR. CORBET that sat in the chair in that committee made report that for one of them he was proved to be a common drunkard and so was voted by the committee to be unfit to be restored to his place in Newcastle.[11] Whereupon the sense of the house was that the said committee should proceed speedily to the examination of the other minister.

7. For this treaty see *PJ*, 1: 57–58, and 2: 399 and passim. For the make-up of the two negotiating committees, see *PJ*, 1: 3, nn. 14, 17.

8. I.e., the treaty of Ripon, concluded in August 1641, following the second war with the Scots. See Samuel R. Gardiner, *History of England from the Accession of James I to the Outbreak of the Civil War, 1603–1642* (London, 1883–84), IX, 417.

9. D'Ewes's name appears as "Dr. Was" in *CJ*, II, 601. Roger Hill was also a member.

10. Identification information given concerning people, places, and committees in the first two volumes of *PJ* is not repeated in this volume if they can be easily traced through the Index.

In rough notes crossed out above because expanded upon here, D'Ewes has written: *Committee. I one.* On 9 May he had also referred to himself as a member of this committee, though his name does not appear in *CJ*. See *PJ*, 2: 297.

11. Doubtless George Wishart, lecturer at St. Nicholas Church. The other minister was Yeldard Alvey, the vicar. Both men had been summoned as delinquents, following a Newcastle petition, on 24 April 1641, though Alvey was released on bail on 20 May. See *CJ*, II, 127, 128, 151; and *Walker*, pp. 288, 291. *DNB* for Wishart.

And so we having appointed to meet at 8 of the clock tomorrow morning, the house rose between 12 and one.

JOURNAL OF FRAMLINGHAM GAWDY

[f. 123a]   Thursday, the 2 of June

An ordinance of parliament for providing men for the sea adventurers for Ireland.

Ordered, that the knights and burgesses of every county shall this day seven-night bring in the names of all the recusants in their several counties and their several estates.[12]

MR. SOLICITOR, that he yesternight received a command from his majesty to attend him at York for matters that concern his honor and person. He is his majesty's sworn servant. He desire leave to go.

Resolved by question, that Mr. Solicitor shall not have leave to go to York.

Resolved by question, that Mr. Solicitor shall be enjoined to stay.

MR. STRODE would have a bill to pass to confiscate the lands of those lords that are gone to York, to the benefit of the commonwealth, as promoters of the differences.[13]

[f. 123b] MR. MARTEN, that the king hath more relation to the parliament than the parliament hath to the king.

Ordered, that all members shall repair to this house for special service by the 16 of June upon the penalty of paying an 100£ and such other penalties as shall be imposed, and that all sheriffs in England and Wales shall respectively in their several counties give notice to those members excepting such employed in the service of Ireland. This order is resolved by question.

Resolved, this order shall be printed.

JOURNAL OF ROGER HILL

[p. 84]   [June 2, 1642][14]

Those members at York sent for.

All members required to be present 16 June, subpoena, 100£ and such punishment as the house, etc.

---

12. There is no record in the official or private journals that names were brought in.

13. For the departure of lords for York, see *PJ*, 2: xiv, 373.

14. Hill has combined the proceedings for 1–3 June; however, the editors have separated the entries under the appropriate dates.

Lord Brooke hath power to set out ships and to raise 1000 men to destroy towns.[15]

The names of recusants convict to be brought in by members of the house.

15. Hill appears to be citing one of the provisions of the ordinance for the sea adventure for Ireland. See above, n. 2, and *LJ,* V, 144.

D'EWES

June 3, Friday, 1642

The Speaker came a little after 8 of the clock. After prayers Mr. HAMPDEN made report from the Scottish commissioners of several demands made by them, which were allowed. Vide M.[1]

I withdrew out of the house between 8 and 9. I returned between 10 and eleven. Mr. PYM was speaking when I came in.[2]

Sir Edward Leech and Mr. Page, two masters of the Chancery, brought this message from the lords, that their lordships desired that the select committee of this house, which went into the City yesterday in the afternoon with a committee of their lordships to borrow money of the City, might meet this afternoon to draw a form of thanks to the City of London for their free offer yesterday (viz., to lend 100,000£) and for their care of the public, and then they withdrew, and we agreed that the committee should meet as was desired, which the SPEAKER related to them being again called in, and then they departed.

[f. 144a] The SPEAKER delivered in a letter sent to him bearing date at Lincoln June 1, 1642, from Sir William Armine, etc.[3]

The Lord Francis Willoughby.

All the high constables, near upon 80, appeared at Lincoln.

Earl of Lindsey, a commission from his majesty to be lord lieutenant.

Their presence revived all well-affected persons in the county.[4]

Then was read a copy of the king's letter bearing date at the court at York May 28, sent to Sir Edward Heron, Knight of the Bath, high sheriff of the county of

1. For these alterations in the Scots treaty, see *CJ*, II, 601.

2. Pym was reporting from the joint committee sent to the Common Hall in the City to borrow money. See *PJ*, 2: 400. During this period there were attempts to give Common Hall, traditionally an electoral body, some deliberative functions, in particular the right to consent to the raising of City loans, according to Valerie Pearl, *London and the Outbreak of the Puritan Revolution* (London, 1961), p. 53. For more details of Pym's report and other proceedings omitted by D'Ewes, see G, below, and *CJ*, II, 601–02.

3. In late April a committee for Hull and Lincolnshire had been named. See *PJ*, 2: esp. 234, 341. During the summer two separate, though occasionally overlapping, committees evolved with the following members: For Lincolnshire—Sir William Armine, Sir Edward Ayscough, John Broxholme, Thomas Hatcher, Sir Anthony Irby, Sir Christopher Wray, Sir John Wray. For Hull—John Alured, John Hotham, Peregrine Pelham, with Sir William Strickland and Michael Warton as sometime members. For this letter from the Lincolnshire committee, see *LJ*, V, 104.

4. Marginal note: *Ordered to be printed*. Wing, C 6148. On 26 March parliament had named Lord Willoughby of Parham as lord lieutenant for all of Lincolnshire. See *PJ*, 2: 89.

Lincoln, Sir Edward[5] Hussey, Knight and Baronet, and other deputy lieutenants (viz., such as the Earl of Lindsey had appointed),[6] in which the king gave them order not to permit any part of the magazine in the same county to [be] issued out or used by any person by virtue of any warrant, order, or ordinance of both houses, but it be kept safe by themselves or some of them or by such as they would answer for until it were otherwise disposed of by order from his majesty or from the Earl of Lindsey, lord lieutenant of that shire, his majesty's county, that so the peace thereof might be preserved. And this his majesty enjoined them upon their allegiance and as they would answer it at their peril.

Vide M.[7]

Sir Edward Leech and Mr. Page, two masters of the Chancery, brought down the bill for the assembling of divines from the lords with some amendments and so withdrew and departed.[8]

SIR EDWARD HUNGERFORD, being returned before these messengers came in, made his report that the lords would give a present meeting, etc., to both our conferences,[9] etc. (but in the issue upon our delaying to come up the lords rose, and so both these conferences were deferred till the afternoon).

SIR WALTER ERLE showed that Mr. Nathan Wright and Jacob Fortre[10] had received bills of exchange out of the Low Countries to pay 2000£ to Mr. Adrian May, which was conceived to be for the crown jewels sold there, whereupon it was desired that it might be ordered that a messenger of this house might be at the payment of this money and seal it up and bring it away. The house divided upon it. Ayes, 67, the Lord Ruthin and Sir Gilbert Pickering, tellers, went out. Noes, 32, Mr. Godolphin[11] and Mr. Killigrew, tellers, stayed in. I one. And it was thereupon ordered accordingly.

By this division of the house the lords rose, and so we missed our conference at the present.

MR. REYNOLDS delivered in an ordinance of parliament for allowance of the

5. MS: *Thomas*. Sir Edward Hussey had been MP for Lincolnshire in the Short Parliament. His son Thomas, MP for Grantham in the Long Parliament, had died in 1641. GEC, *Baronetage*, I, 60; Keeler, pp. 226–27.

6. For the text see *LJ*, V, 102. The Earl of Lindsey was subsequently sent for as a delinquent by the lords.

7. For proceedings omitted by D'Ewes, see *CJ*, II, 602.

8. For this bill see *PJ*, 2: esp. 296, 343, and 392, n. 1. The lords had passed the bill with several amendments. *CJ*, II, 602.

9. The house had requested a conference concerning the Hull magazine and the letters from Lincolnshire. *CJ*, II, 602.

10. Fawtree, in *CJ*, II, 602. Nathan or Nathaniel Wright, a merchant involved in the East Indies trade, was a member of the London Common Council. See Pearl, *London*, p. 331.

11. Probably Sidney Godolphin, a royalist, rather than his brother Francis, who was frequently absent after July 1641. Keeler, p. 188. For May's role in the sale of the crown jewels, see *PJ*, 2: 376. A biographical note on Adrian May appears in Margaret Toynbee and Peter Young, *Strangers in Oxford: A Sidelight on the First Civil War, 1642–1646* (London, 1973), pp. 168–69.

12 ships which were to go against the Irish rebels,[12] which the clerk read, and we allowed it, and Mr. Reynolds was appointed to carry it up and to desire the lords to join with us in it.

Upon MR. NATHANIEL FIENNES's motion SIR THOMAS WIDDRINGTON made report from the committee appointed yesterday to consider of the agreement with the articles of the Scottish treaty lately passed in the house with the old draft of them, and he showed that there were many differences, some more material and some less, and MR. NATHANIEL FIENNES and MR. HAMPDEN did in most of those differences give satisfaction to the house by showing the reason of them, so as we allowed every alteration almost.[13]

I went out of the house a little after one of the clock, and the house, having appointed to meet at 3 of the clock in the afternoon, did rise between one and two of the clock.

[f. 144b]   Post Meridiem

The Speaker came to the house about 3 of the clock in the afternoon but stayed awhile for company.[14]

An act for the draining of the great level extending itself into the counties of Northampton, Norfolk, Suffolk, Lincoln, Cambridge, and Huntingdon, and into the Isle of Ely.[15] Divers spake to it, and in the issue it was committed to the committee for the fens, and they were to meet on Monday come fortnight at 2 of the clock in the afternoon in the Chequer Chamber.

Sir Henry Vane was sent up to the lords to desire a conference touching the Scottish treaty and to desire their consent to the order we had made touching the seizing of the money come out of the Low Countries.[16]

An act for the further advancing of the effectual and speedy reduction of the rebels of Ireland to their due obedience to his majesty and the crown of England was brought in ready engrossed by MR. REYNOLDS[17] and was read *3ᵃ vice* and passed the house. Mr. Reynolds was sent up to the lords with the said bill and carried up the ordinance also touching the 12 ships which were to go to the coasts of Ireland against the rebels, which had been read and passed in the morning.

12. See 2 June, n. 2.

13. For details see *CJ,* II, 603.

14. A quorum of forty was required.

15. For this bill see *PJ,* 2: 394. It was given a second reading before commitment but apparently went no further. Henry Pelham was chairman of the committee. *CJ,* II, 603.

16. It was subsequently ordered that Wright and Fortre (Fawtree in *CJ*) should "forbear this Night to pay the Monies to Mr. Adrian May, or his Assignees . . . upon the Bills of Exchange they accepted from Holland." *CJ,* II, 604.

17. Earlier in the day the bill had been "re-committed to the same Committee: with the Addition of Mr. Hill." See 2 June, n. 6; and *CJ,* II, 602.

SIR ROBERT PYE preferred in a petition for one to transport above 300 dozen of calfskins which he had power to have transported by a former order, which after some debate was granted and ordered accordingly.[18]

MR. CROMWELL delivered in the petition of Peter Scott, a constable of St. Martin's, who had done several services for the house and was now several times arrested by the Cavaliers and others who go away to York and never declare against him. So it was referred to the committee of information, of which I was.[19]

SIR HENRY VANE, the younger, returned and made report that he received this answer from the Lord Wharton, that the lords would give us a meeting at this conference and at the two former conferences desired in the morning, and for the order they would send us an answer by messengers of their own.

Mr. Cromwell and Mr. Wingate were appointed to go and view the calfskins which were to be carried beyond the seas that no hides of leather might be transported with them.

The managers of the conferences and divers of the house went up to the Painted Chamber. Sir Thomas Widdrington began and first showed our exceptions against their lordships' amendment of our order touching the disposing of that part of the magazine which came from Hull.[20]

He then read the letter which the Speaker had delivered in to the house in the morning sent him from Sir William Armine and the rest of our committee in Lincolnshire and the copy of the king's letter enclosed in it.

Mr. Hampden and Mr. Nathaniel Fiennes managed the conference touching the Scottish treaty. Mr. Hampden read the articles, and Mr. Nathaniel Fiennes showed the reason of the alterations and additions of these articles from the first draft. I came in a little after the conference began and went out before it was ended.

The Speaker having again resumed his chair, MR. DENZIL HOLLES preferred in a petition for Sir George Hamilton, who remained under bail and desired to have liberty, being a papist, to go beyond seas to seek his fortune, and MR. HOLLES showed that he had lost his estate in Ireland and that Sir John Seton, an honest, gallant gentleman, would undertake for him that he should not return into Ireland.

18. For details see *CJ*, II, 603. For earlier orders concerning the transportation of calfskins, see *PJ*, 2: 205.

19. Though D'Ewes's name does not appear in *CJ* among the members of this committee, he may have attended its meetings.

20. On 1 June the commons had ordered that "the Officers of the Ordnance shall be required to . . . receive the Arms and Ammunition sent from Hull, into their Custody; and to deliver it out again . . . as shall be required, by Order of both Houses of Parliament." The lords' proposed amendment—"as shall be issued out by the King's Authority, signified by Order of both Houses of Parliament"—was subsequently overruled by the commons. See *CJ*, II, 597, 602; and *LJ*, V, 103.

I spake on his behalf[21] and showed that though he were a papist, yet he was no way active or dangerous but was at first stayed and questioned upon a mistake, being taken for another Sir George Hamilton, a papist now inhabiting in Ireland and a very dangerous man. It is true that he now remains under bail and is content to do so still if this house will take order for his maintenance, but his estate being all wasted and taken by the rebels in Ireland, he now desires to be wholly discharged, giving security that he will not return into Ireland, that so he may go into some parts of the world where he may find some means of subsistence. And it was thereupon ordered accordingly without any further opposition.

[f. 145b] Mr. Smith, vicar of Deeping in Lincolnshire, was brought in to the bar as a delinquent[22] for having said in the pulpit that it was treason to obey any order of parliament unless it had the king's hand and seal to it. He denied that ever he said so and withdrew. Then were 3 witnesses brought in with him who affirmed the same in substance, only two of them witnessed that he spake those words concerning the orders of this house. They all then withdrew, and the judgment of the house was that he should be sent to the Gatehouse for 6 months and pay an 100£ fine to the king. Then he was brought to the bar the 3 time, and kneeling all the time, the SPEAKER pronounced the judgment of the house upon him, showing him the greatness of his offense whilst he kneeled all the time, and then bade the sergeant take him away.

Upon SIR ROBERT COOKE's motion it was ordered that a warrant should issue out for a new writ to be sent for the election of a new burgess at Minehead in Somersetshire[23] in the place of Mr. Luttrell, lately deceased.

MR. KNIGHTLEY informed the house that he had received a letter and an examination from the mayor of Northampton, who had stayed a horse with a great saddle upon him which was going to York to one Captain Richard Neville and had also intercepted some letters, of which one sent to the said Captain Neville was read in the house, being of no moment save only that there was mention of his pistols to be sent to him. And yet the sense of the house was that the mayor of Northampton[24] should detain the horse and the great saddle till further order should be taken for the horse, which was ordered accordingly.

Upon MR. PRIDEAUX's motion it was ordered that the executors of Sir Ed-

---

21. See *PJ*, 2: 37, 132.

22. Smith had been summoned on 18 May. See *PJ*, 2: 337, 341.

23. MS: *Dorsetshire*. Alexander Luttrell had died in the spring. Keeler, p. 263. For his successor, Thomas Hanham, see Appendix A.

24. Lawrence Ball. *HMC, Portland MSS*, I, 42. The house subsequently reaffirmed this order depite the mayor's having received a "pretended Warrant" from the king. See *CJ*, II, 637, 663–64; and *LJ*, V, 198. For possible identification of Neville, see *Roy. Off.*, p. 271.

ward Coke have liberty to print his comment on Magna Charta and his other books and that none else have liberty to print them for a year next ensuing.[25]

MR. CORBET delivered in a petition from the inhabitants of Wymondham in the county of Norfolk, by which they desired that one Mr. Money[26] might be their lecturer for the Sundays in the afternoon and for one weekday, which was granted; and the Speaker going out of the house before the order was read, SIR THOMAS WODEHOUSE, a gentleman of Norfolk and a near neighbor to that town, did wish the clerk to put the other sermon in to be upon the Saturdays each week, which was the market day for that town.

We appointed to meet at 8 of the clock tomorrow morning and rose between 6 and 7 of the clock at night.

GAWDY

[f. 123b]   Friday, the III of June

MR. PYM, a report that the City with a great deal of cheerfulness condescend to lend this house an 100,000£ for the service of Ireland, no man denying it. One of them beginning but to make some exception was hissed down.[27]

Ordered, that some of our house be employed to the merchant strangers for the loan of an 50,000£, and that letters be sent to the College of Physicians [f. 124a] for lending of money and to some of the principal officers.

The money received from the 3 of November 1640 till the 1 of June 1642: 734,000£ by subsidy, poll money, and delinquents. We owe 500,000£ and above. There is to come in for the bill of land rate 400,000£. So we owe an 100,000£ and above, which will not be due to the Scots till Midsummer 1643.[28]

A message from the lords, they agree with us for the arms that came from Hull to be delivered to the officers of the army, only they would have it added: To be issued out by the king's command with the advice of both houses. We will send them an answer by messengers of our own.

25. Coke's commentary on Magna Charta, which appeared in *The Second Part of the Institutes of the Laws of England,* was first published in 1642; *The Third Part . . . Concerning High Treason, and Other Pleas of the Crown, and Criminal Causes* and *The Fourth Part . . . Concerning the Jurisdiction of Courts* were published in 1644, all by order of the House of Commons. See Catherine Drinker Bowen, *The Lion and the Throne* (Boston, 1957), pp. 552, 565. For more information concerning Coke's writings, see *PJ,* 2: 262.

26. For John Money see *Calamy,* pp. 351–52.

27. A committee was named to "prepare an Ordinance for Security to the City for the Monies they shall lend." *CJ,* II, 601.

28. This declaration of "Monies received and disbursed" was presented from the committee for accounts, of which John Trenchard was chairman. *CJ,* II, 602.

MR. GLYN, a report from the committee of both houses,[29] that many counties here about London are appointed presently to put the militia in execution. That there are 4 counties without deputy lieutenants—Dorset, Hertford, Shropshire, and Nottinghamshire—because the lord lieutenants[30] are gone to York. Warwickshire, Leicestershire, and Northamptonshire are likewise appointed to put the militia in execution.[31]

[f. 124b][32] A committee appointed to amend the order abovesaid.[33]

A message from the lords, they desire the committee sent to the City for loan of money may meet with theirs at 4 a clock to consider of giving them thanks. 'Tis assented to.

MR. MARTEN, that there may be new lord lieutenants chosen in the room of those lords gone to York for the 4 counties formerly named.[34]

A letter to the Speaker from our committee from Lincoln, June the 1. That my Lord Willoughby, our lord lieutenant, exercised the militia the last of May, which was performed with much cheerfulness, and that there are many volunteers. Though my Lord of Lindsey hath a commission under the great seal to be lord lieutenant of that shire, that the king sent a warrant to Sir Edward Heron, sheriff, and other old deputy lieutenants of that county that [f. 125a] they suffer not any of the magazine of that county to be employed or issued forth by any warrant or ordinance of parliament.

A message from the lords, they send us down the bill for the assembly of the divines with the amendments, which they have passed.

In the afternoon.

An act passed our house to give time till the 20 of July for the adventurers for Ireland to come in. They are to have 21 foot of land to the pole.[35]

I went this afternoon with the message to the lords house where there were but 14 lords, my Lord Wharton being Speaker.

---

29. I.e., the committee for defense of the kingdom. See *PJ*, 2: 376–77.

30. The Earl of Salisbury was lord lieutenant for Dorset and Hertfordshire, Lord Littleton for Shropshire, and the Earl of Clare for Nottinghamshire.

31. Cf. *CJ*, II, 602. For the militia ordinance of March 1642, see *PJ*, 1: 513, 514, and passim.

32. Crossed out in MS: *Ordered, that all deputy lieutenants not of this house shall attend the militia, and that all deputy lieutenants, members of this house and others, shall subscribe the warrants, and that such of them of this house as shall be commanded to attend in person shall.* This version of the order is also crossed out in the MS CJ.

33. The committee was to "prepare an Order concerning the Execution of the Militia in the several Counties, according to the Debate of the House." *CJ*, II, 602.

34. An order was to be formulated "to authorize the Deputy Lieutenants in such Counties where the Lord Lieutenants are absent, to put the Militia in Execution." *CJ*, II, 602.

35. Name of a lineal measure, especially for land, in statutory measure equal to 16½ feet but varying locally. *NED*. The act provided that instead of English measure (presumably 16½ feet to the pole) as prescribed in the first act, adventurers could now have lands "to the proportion of one and twenty foot to the Pole for every Acre," apparently a ploy to encourage additional adventure money. *SR*, V, 168, 177.

HILL

[p. 84]   [June 3, 1642]

New bill for adventure in Ireland.

That all such as will bring in all their adventures by such a day shall have 21 foot to the goad.[36]

We received a letter from Lincoln date 1 June from Sir Edward Ayscough, Sir Christopher Wray, etc., who have mustered the militia, who find more than they expected, besides the trainbands many volunteers, who cheerfully undertake it with protestations according to their Protestation for defense of the king;[37] notwithstanding letters sent by the king to the sheriff and other gentlemen requiring them not to suffer their magazine to be drawn away by any pretense of an ordinance or orders, he having appointed the Earl of Lindsey by his commission under great seal to be lord lieutenant for that county.

50 E. 3, $n°$ 10, an order devised by the commons that the king should have at least 10 or 12 councillors without whom no weighty matters should pass, and for smaller matters at the least 6 or 4 of them, whereto the king [p. 85] granted. Provided that the chancellor, treasurer, and keeper of the privy seal should by themselves end[38] all matters belonging to their offices and that these councillors should take no reward.

11 H. 4, the commons requests, etc., the king answers, $n°$ 14, and grants that certain of the most learned bishops, worthy lords, and others shall be assigned to be of his council; $n°$ 44, the last day of the parliament the Speaker required certain knowledge of the councillors' names, whereupon two were changed.[39]

Mr. Smith, vicar of Deeping in Lincolnshire, for saying in his pulpit when an order of this house came down for placing a lecturer there, he said that to obey any order of the houses without the hand and seal of the king to it was treason. He was brought to the bar with the witnesses viva voce and[40] he denied it, but it was testified by 3. He was committed to the Gatehouse for 6 months and 100£ fine to the king, there to remain till the fine paid.

36. A land measure. *NED*. The word is "pole" in *SR*, V, 177.

37. For the Protestation of 3 May 1641, see Rushworth, IV, 241.

38. The word is *esploiter* (to exploit) in *RP*, II, 322. This precedent and the following may have been cited by Hill with relation to certain of the Nineteen Propositions which dealt with privy councillors.

39. *RP*, III, 623–24, 634.

40. Hill's entries which have been underlined by the editors represent translations of his Law French.

D'EWES

June 4, Saturday, 1642

The Speaker came a little after 8 of the clock. Prayers being ended, MR. DENZIL HOLLES delivered in the petition of one John Copley, by which he promised to propound a course for defeating the rebels in Ireland far beyond any yet entered upon. So his petition was referred, though the house made but a jesting matter of it, to Sir John Conyers, lieutenant of the Tower, the controller of the ordnance,[1] and General Major Skippon, being none of them in the house, to see if there were any validity in it.

MR. PYM showed that Sir John Hotham and the soldiers in Hull were in great distress for want of money and thereupon desired that 2000£ of the contribution money for Ireland collected in the county of Lincoln might be paid to Sir Edward Ayscough to return it speedily to the said Sir John Hotham for the payment of the garrison there, which was to be repaid.[2]

MR. PYM then delivered in Sir Edward Ayscough's letter to him, in which [he] mistook his Christian [name] being John and called him William, which the clerk read, but he read no place or day of the date but only that it was out of Lincolnshire. In it he showed the readiness of the country to obey the parliament, seeing of near upon 100 high constables in that county but one failed to come, although the king's last proclamation was sent to each of their houses before they came, which high constables were summoned by the lord lieutenant appointed by the parliament to bring in a note of the several arms in their divisions. That other devices were also used to hinder them being met, the proclamation being fixed upon the [f. 146a] inn gate where they met and his majesty's answer likewise to our last votes touching his intention to levy war upon his parliament.[3] And that some others also had fixed under them the Lord Paget's letter to the Earl of Holland and our last declaration,[4] which declaration did give much satisfaction, and therefore he wished that more of them might be dispersed. That it was in every man's mouth that the Earl of Lindsey was

1. The petition was referred to Conyers and Sir John Heydon, lieutenant of the ordnance, but not Skippon, according to *CJ,* II, 604.

2. For the order see *CJ,* II, 604.

3. This letter to Pym is similar to the one sent to the Speaker. See 3 June, n. 3. For the king's message and proclamation, both dated 27 May, see *PJ,* 2: 386. For the latter, generally referred to hereafter as the king's proclamation against the militia, see Appendix D.

4. Probably the declaration concerning Hull. See *PJ,* 2: 361 and passim.

appointed lord lieutenant of that shire by commission from his majesty. That Sir John Hotham and the garrison in Hull were in great distress for money, and that himself had not yet received any order of the house to receive that which yet remained of the poll money.

Vide M.[5]

MR. CROMWELL delivered in a list of the names of the sea captains and other officers which were to go with the 12 ships to the seacoasts of Ireland against the rebels,[6] of which fleet Robert, Lord Brooke, was to be commander in chief, which names were all read and allowed.

SERJEANT WILDE brought in an ordinance of parliament to be passed for the securing of the 100,000£ to the City of London which they now were to lend. I went out of the house for a while, and the ordinance was recommitted, after it had been read, to the same committee to amend some particulars in it.[7]

When I returned, SIR ROBERT HARLEY was delivering in a note of the names of the Merchant Adventurers who refused to join with the rest of that company to lend money for the service of the commonwealth and desired that their names might be read in the house, but upon MR. PYM's motion it was referred to a committee to treat with them before their names should be publicly read.[8]

MR. GREEN made report from the committee for the navy touching the state of the fleet and the charge of it since we took upon us the care of it for about the space of two years, which held near upon an hour and consisted of many particular sums and showed that there was an 100,000£ lost this year in the tonnage and poundage, and that since May 25, 1641, there had been allowed 102,000£ to the maintenance of the king's household and that/[9]

Votes passed.

Bill, tonnage, poundage. Tuesday next.[10]

SERJEANT WILDE, ordinance again passed. To lords to join with us. Serjeant Wilde to carry.[11]

5. For proceedings omitted by D'Ewes, see G, below, and *CJ*, II, 604.

6. See D, 6–7.

7. See 3 June, nn. 2, 27.

8. This committee, which included Harley, had been named on 20 May to treat with the Merchant Adventurers and "with any others, as they shall think fit" for the borrowing of money. On 23 May it was ordered that the commons should be notified by the "Governor . . . of the said Fellowship [Sir Henry Roe] . . . to whom we are obliged, and to whom we are not." See *CJ*, II, 580, 583.

9. For details see H, below. The allowance for the maintenance of the king's household is the one figure cited by each of the diarists. For earlier expenditures for the king's household, see Frederick C. Dietz, *English Public Finance, 1558–1641* (London, 1964), II, 412–20; and G. E. Aylmer, *The King's Servants* (London, 1961), pp. 205–06.

10. It was ordered that on Tuesday the house should be "resolved into a Committee to take into Consideration the Bill of Tonage and Poundage," presumably a new bill. *CJ*, II, 605.

11. For the ordinance to secure the £100,000 lent by "several Companies and Citizens of the City of London," see *CJ*, II, 606.

CAPTAIN VENN, motion. 4 companies—Mercers, Grocers, Drapers, and Fishmongers—to meet Monday next, and the other 8 companies by 4 on each day next, viz., on next Tuesday and Wednesday.[12]

[f. 146b] Sir Robert Rich and Mr. Page, two masters of the Chancery, brought this message from the lords, that their lordships had consented to our order for the paying of 2000£ to Sir John Hotham, only they had added the words "with speed" for the repaying of it, and that they had assented to our order concerning the disposal of the magazine come from Hull.[13] And they having delivered in the said orders and departed, we agreed to the amendments which the lords had added to it.

MR. ARTHUR GOODWIN moved that we might send up to the lords to sit awhile, whereupon he was appointed to be the messenger.

The amendments in the bill for the assembling of divines, which had been added by the lords, were brought in ready engrossed by the clerk and read once and then were approved of by the house, and it was moved that Mr. Arthur Goodwin might be appointed also to carry it up to the lords and to desire the lords to send it away speedily to the king for his consent to be had to it.

Mr. Arthur Goodwin was thereupon sent up with this bill also, and upon my motion it was further ordered that he should acquaint the lords that we had agreed to their amendment in the order for the payment of the 2000£ to Sir John Hotham. It was added also that he should desire the lords to consent to the order for stopping the money which was to go to York[14] and that they would expedite the bills for innovations and pluralities.[15]

The LORD FALKLAND made relation that his majesty's agent at Paris in France had given intelligence that two regiments of Irish in France had been lately cashiered, and that though some of the officers were again taken into employment, yet the common soldiers had passports given them from the Prince of Condé to pass into Ireland.[16] This matter was laid aside for a time.

SIR WALTER ERLE moved that whereas the lords had appointed some of the king's learned council to look over the examinations touching Colonel Bell-

---

12. Venn, a warden of the Merchant Taylors' Company, may have proposed naming the committee to go to the companies "to advance the Loan of the said Monies by the best Means they can." Pearl, *London*, p. 188; *CJ*, II, 605. The days for the companies to meet differ in D'Ewes, *CJ*, and *LJ*, V, 106.

13. See 3 June, n. 20.

14. The money from the sale of the crown jewels. *LJ*, V, 104.

15. Innovations and scandalous ministers (not pluralities). *CJ*, II, 605; *LJ*, V, 104. For the bills see *PJ*, 2: esp. 75, 139, 158.

16. René Augier was the English agent in Paris. Aylmer, *King's Servants*, p. 358. Condé was a cousin-german to Louis XIII and a trusted servant of Richlieu. *Dictionnaire de Biographie Française* (Paris, 1933–). The officers had passes for Ireland, according to G, below, and *CJ*, II, 605.

ings[17] and that whereas some examinations concerning him which had been sent out of Ireland remained in his hands, he was ready if the house thought fit to deliver the same into the hands of those of his majesty's council whom the lords had appointed to consider of the other examinations, which was thereupon so ordered accordingly.[18]

SIR HUGH OWEN took occasion thereupon to declare to the house what care had been taken in the county of Pembroke in Wales and yet that they were so little regarded in respect of their safety as if they were no part of the kingdom, lying open to spoil and invasion from the west parts of Ireland, whereupon it was ordered that the said Sir Hugh Owen should repair to my lord admiral that one ship or more might lie upon those coasts for the defense of them.

MR. NATHANIEL FIENNES moved that the Lord Falkland might acquaint the Earl of Warwick with his information out of France, that so he might stop the said Irish at sea which should come out of France toward Ireland, whereupon the said Lord Falkland and Mr. Nathaniel Fiennes were appointed to repair to the Earl of Warwick to that end.

MR. ARTHUR GOODWIN returned and made report that he received this answer from the Lord Wharton, that the lords would sit again at 3 of the clock in the afternoon. That for the order touching the seizing of the money that come out of the Low Countries, the lords would send us an answer by messengers of their own. That they would with all speed expedite the bills against pluralities[19] and innovations.

MR. GRIMSTON brought in an order touching the deputy lieutenants being [required] to be present at the ensuing musters and that such as should neglect or refuse might have their names returned. Divers spake to it after the clerk had read it. I spake in effect following:

That when the ordinance for the militia was in debate in this house, it was moved by a member thereof that a clause might be added that none might be appointed a deputy lieutenant or any underofficer against his will, and you were pleased then to answer (viz., the Speaker, to whom we all direct what we say) that you would warrant none should be compelled against their will; and yet now in this order we appoint that their names should be returned that refuse [f.

17. Christopher Bellings and other Irishmen had been apprehended in Pembrokeshire en route to Ireland. See *PJ*, 2: 277, 333.

18. Subsequently the lords acceded to the commons' request that Bellings be "committed to a stricter Care and Charge" of the lieutenant of the Tower. On 9 September, however, the lords ordered that he be permitted to travel to France with Ferté-Imbaut, the French ambassador, on condition that he not return to Ireland during the rebellion. *CJ*, II, 605, 608; *LJ*, V, 345.

19. Again D'Ewes should have scandalous ministers. The lords appointed a committee on 23 June to amend the bill and on 30 January 1643 read it for a third time, passed it, and ordered that it be sent to the king. It did not, however, receive the royal assent. *LJ*, V, 156, 578. See also William A. Shaw, *A History of the English Church, 1640–1660* (London, 1900), II, 179n.

147a] to execute the same as if they were delinquents, when yet it is possible that divers in the country that are deputy lieutenants never heard thereof to this day and therefore still ought to have the liberty to accept or refuse it. But for those who have formerly accepted of the employment, I hold it just that their names upon their refusal might be returned. But notwithstanding the justice of my motion, the more violent spirits would admit no alteration but passed the order as it was.[20]

The LORD FALKLAND reported from the Earl of Warwick that he desired an order from this house for searching of all foreign ships as the house had desired him, whereupon some debate arose whether we should pass such an order or not, divers speaking against it in respect that by the very law of nations our fleet might search all such ships as we did suspect would carry any arms, victuals, or other supply to the rebels in Ireland or to any other enemy of this state, and therefore to make an order in this particular might perhaps draw the law itself into question.

During the debate Sir Gervase Clifton had liberty to go to the Bath for the recovery of his health.

The debate still continuing whether we should pass the former order or not touching the Earl of Warwick, I spake shortly in effect following:

That I did not conceive but that we might so frame an order of this house to be merely declaratory as that we might rather make the law in this particular evident and clear than any way[21] draw it into question, and therefore seeing that such an order is desired, I see no reason but that we should give satisfaction therein. Some two or three having spoken after me, Mr. Reynolds was appointed to draw such an order.[22]

Upon MR. GLYN's motion deputy lieutenants of Essex enjoined to go into the country to the training.[23]

Upon SIR JOHN EVELYN's motion Mr. Pym was appointed to write a letter to the committee in Lincolnshire.

SIR THOMAS BARRINGTON showed that he understood from divers places in Essex that they were much staggered with the late proclamation which his majesty had set forth against the putting in execution the ordinance touching the militia, and therefore desired that the declaration which was to be set forth in the name of both the houses[24] in answer to that proclamation might be brought into the house this afternoon that so it might be published [before] their going down

20. For the earlier debate and the text of the order, see 3 June, nn. 32, 33, and *CJ*, II, 605.

21. MS: *was*.

22. Also Nathaniel Fiennes. *CJ*, II, 605.

23. For the names of MPs ordered to execute the militia ordinance in Leicestershire, Essex, and Devonshire, see *CJ*, II, 604, 605.

24. For the appointment of a committee to draft this declaration, see *PJ*, 2: 387.

into Essex on Monday next. Divers called to rise whilst he was speaking, and nothing was ordered upon his motion.

We appointed to meet at 3 of the clock in the afternoon and rose a little before one.

Post Meridiem

The Speaker resumed his chair between 3 and 4 of the clock. I came a little while after he was set.

MR. REYNOLDS delivered in an order for Robert, Earl of Warwick, and Robert, Lord Brooke, and the officers under them to search all ships of any foreign nation bound for Ireland whether they brought any arms, ammunition, victuals, money, or men to the assistance of the rebels, which was read and passed.[25]

MR. PHELIPPS, Martock, lecturer.[26]

MR. ONSLOW, about priest searcher. BOSVILE, priests, Capuchins, I spake.[27]

MR. DOWSE, fellow of Pembroke Hall, Frank.[28]

MR. ONSLOW commended one to the house to be allowed by us for a searcher of priests, but MR. BOSVILE stood up and said that he desired that/

[f. 147b] CAPTAIN VENN moved that the 3 days appointed for the 12 chief companies to/

Serjeant Wilde was sent up to the lords with the two orders, the 1 concerning the deputy lieutenants brought in by Mr. Grimston in the morning and the other order touching the calling of the 12 chief companies together by 4 on a day next week, and to desire their lordships' concurrence.[29]

Sir Robert Rich and Mr. Page, two masters of the Chancery, brought this message from the lords, that they desired a free conference presently, etc., touching the ordinance sent up to them this day for the raising of land forces to be sent into Ireland.[30] Yielded to a present meeting. Mr. Reynolds and others appointed reporters and managers.

25. For the order, to which the lords agreed, see *CJ*, II, 607.

26. It was ordered that Hugh Gundery should be lecturer in the parish of Martock, Somerset. See *CJ*, II, 606; and *Calamy*, p. 238.

27. D'Ewes has repeated this information below. It was ordered that the committee for informations consider "in what Estate the Business concerning the Five Priests is" and "what public Resort is usually made unto them" or to the Capuchins at mass. *CJ*, II, 606. For the condemned priests see *PJ*, 2: 69–70, 180–81.

28. Mark Frank, who had been summoned in May for a sermon preached at Paul's Cross, was ordered to appear within seven days or be expelled from Pembroke College and Cambridge University. See *PJ*, 2: 328; and *CJ*, II, 606.

29. Wilde carried up the ordinance for security to the City as well as the order for summoning the livery companies, while Grimston carried up the order concerning the deputy lieutenants. *CJ*, II, 606.

30. I.e., the ordinance concerning the sea adventure for Ireland, actually sent to the lords on 3 June. See D, 7; and *LJ*, V, 102, 105.

Belfast, May 19, 1642, to the lord lieutenant from the Lord Viscount Conway and Killultagh.

King to come over to Dublin; the castle there provided for him.

Earl Antrim pretends himself to be a good subject and yet hath gone safe through all the rebels' countries.

Sir John Clotworthy's lieutenant colonel.

That such as pretend to raise horse troops there do but abuse the state.

Extreme want of money.

That if some course be not taken this summer, most of the poor English there will starve next winter if they do not starve before.

Belfast, May 23, 1642, from the same Lord Conway to the said lord lieutenant.

Mr. Hill[31] hath done great service in Ulster.

That the soldiers want clothes, shoes, and money for the/

Upon MR. STRODE's motion it was ordered that these two letters should be referred to the committee.[32]

Dublin Castle, May 20, 1642, from Sir John Borlase to the right/

Captain George Keyes, commission granted to raise an 100 foot. Wants moneys and arms.

[f. 148a] MR. ARTHUR GOODWIN preferred in a petition from divers inhabitants of the town of Bluntisham in Huntingdonshire. Mr. George Green, lecturer. No certain day appointed. Ordered.[33]

SERJEANT WILDE returned and made report that the lords had assented to both the orders.[34]

Mr. Reynolds and the other reporters and managers with divers of the house went up to the conference.

The Lord North, supplying the place of Speaker in the lords house, managed the conference and showed that the lords did conceive that this ordinance did run in the current or form of that commission sent unto his majesty.[35]

MR. REYNOLDS returned from the conference and made report of it, and after one or two had spoken to it, it was moved that the Lord Falkland, one of his majesty's principal secretaries, a member of the house, might be sent for to the

31. Doubtless Colonel Arthur Hill.

32. Both letters from Viscount Conway, marshal of the army in Ireland, to the Earl of Leicester, lord lieutenant, were referred to the commissioners for Irish affairs, as was the one below from Sir John Borlase, one of the lord justices of Ireland. See *CJ*, II, 606; and CIA, 9 June. For the role of the commissioners, see *PJ*, 2: xx, 48, 139.

33. For Green see *Calamy*, pp. 232–33. It was ordered that he should preach every Wednesday. *CJ*, II, 606.

34. For Grimston's report see G, below.

35. "And that they are not privy of any Answer that his Majesty has given to that Commission: And therefore they think it not fitting to pass this by Ordinance, until they have received his Majesty's Answer to that Commission." *CJ*, II, 606. For the commission see *PJ*, 2: 286, 305.

house to give an account of what he knew of it, which was instantly done accordingly, and one Mr. Humfries was sent for also who carried down the commission.

SIR WILLIAM BRERETON delivered in the petition of Thomas Measure[36] and others for Mr. Redman to preach in St. James Deeping each Sunday twice, being before appointed lecturer for once each Sunday. Their vicar, Mr. Smith, was lately imprisoned by this house. Ordered.

The relation preferred to the house by Lieutenant Colonel Audley Mervin touching what had passed in all or the greatest part of the province of Ulster since October last to the 27 day of this instant May was brought into the house by MR. NICHOLAS.

The LORD FALKLAND came into the house, and upon the SPEAKER's demanding of him if he knew anything of the commission sent to his majesty by Captain Humfries for raising of new land and sea forces for the adventurers to send into Ireland, he answered that he knew nothing more.

The clerk then read part of the said Lieutenant Colonel Mervin's relation toward the end of it, viz., from May 17 to May 27 last past, which being read it was ordered that he should be desired to print it.[37]

MR. PYM made report from the committee appointed to draw a declaration,[38] which was first read by himself in his place and then by the clerk, in which there was an endeavor to answer the king's late proclamation set out to inhibit the putting of the ordinance for the militia[39] into execution, and therein the committee did allow that for a statute which the king had cited to be made in $a°$ $7°$ E. 1,[40] which made me, after 3 or 4 had spoken to have some particular words amended, to speak in effect following:

That I should say nothing concerning the latter part of the declaration which consisted of strong lines but only concerning the former part of it, wherein we do allow that to be a statute of the 7th year of E. 1, which is so called in the proclamation and is at this day indeed so published amongst the printed statutes, whereas we have two particulars to answer to that proclamation: First,

36. Thomas Measure had been among the petitioners who requested on 19 March that Thomas Redman be their lecturer. *CJ*, II, 488.

37. Mervin was a lawyer, member of the Irish parliament, and military man who served against the Irish rebels. See John P. Prendergast, "Some Account of Sir Audley Mervyn," *Transactions of the Royal Historical Society*, 3 (1874): 421–22, 428–33. *DNB*. For Mervin's account see John T. Gilbert, *A Contemporary History of Affairs in Ireland from 1641 to 1652* (Dublin, 1879–80), I (Pt. 2), 464–75. Wing, M 1880.

38. See above, n. 24.

39. Crossed out in MS: *I spake. Glyn snarled. I answered him. Sir John Evelyn asked leave.*

40. See Appendix D, and *SL*, I, 71–72. Copies of many of the statutes from Magna Charta through the time of James I, as well as the first volume of *Statutes at Large*, were part of D'Ewes's library. See Andrew G. Watson, *The Library of Sir Simonds D'Ewes* (London, 1966), pp. 103, 108, 230, 233, and passim.

whether that which is there cited for a statute be one indeed or not, and secondly, admitting it be a statute, how far it extends to the inhibition of the militia. For mine own part I cannot deny but that the matter there cited may have been the substance of some statute, but I am sure, as it is now printed, it is the mere copy of the king's letters patent, and whereas the gentleman (viz., Mr. Rigby) behind your chair (viz., the Speaker's [f. 148b] chair, to whom we all direct our speech) did the other day wish that the Parliament Roll might be looked whether there were such a statute or no, it seems his better employments have not suffered him much to converse with those rolls, for there is no Parliament Roll remaining of that year of E. 1 nor ancienter than the 18th year of his reign.[41] Nay, in the old written book itself in the Tower of London containing divers parliaments of that king's time and of E. 2, his son, the first parliament of the said E. 1 remaining there is $a° 13°$ of his reign, only there is indeed an ancient roll in the Tower of London of some old statutes where this perhaps may be found, and for the printing of it amongst the statutes, whether it be so found in the old Magna Charta or in these new printed statutes, that doth not much sway with me to give it the repute or authority of a statute. For you shall find in the same book of printed statutes in the 15th year of E. 3 the king's letters patent printed for a statute,[42] whereas it appears evidently upon the Parliament Roll of that year remaining still upon record that there was no such thing then passed and so likewise in the/[43]

Instead of Mr. Humfries whom the house sent for, one Robert Bradshaw, servant to Sir Nicholas Crispe/[44]

MR. ARTHUR GOODWIN, one of the knights of the shire for the county of Buckingham, showed that he had received letters from the mayor of Chipping Wycombe,[45] by which it appeared that according to the order of this house he had searched and stayed a wagon which was going with arms through that town into Worcestershire, and that the same arms belonged to the Lord Coventry,

41. D'Ewes is correct. See *RP*, I, 15. For D'Ewes's collection of transcripts of the Parliament Rolls, some in his own hand, see Watson, *Library of D'Ewes,* pp. 104–06.

42. Ferdinando Pulton's *Kalender or table comprehending the effect of all the statutes* (London, 1606) was part of D'Ewes's library. See Watson, *Library of D'Ewes,* p. 104.

43. The declaration was agreed to by the commons and ordered to be sent to the lords. *CJ,* II, 607.

44. Crispe, a wealthy London merchant, customs farmer, and former MP, had been expelled as a monopolist on 2 February 1641. Keeler, p. 147; Notestein, p. 312. Bradshaw informed the house that Secretary of State Nicholas gave him this answer: "That unless his Majesty had Security given him, that these Forces should go only against the Rebels of Ireland, . . . he could not grant it." It was ordered that on Monday a conference should be requested with the lords, with Bradshaw and Humfries in attendance, concerning the sea adventure for Ireland and the king's answer to the commission. *CJ,* II, 607.

45. MS: *Wicken.* The mayor was William Guy, a linen draper. L. J. Ashford, *The History of the Borough of High Wycombe from Its Origins to 1880* (London, 1960), p. 146.

who was gone to York, and that there were divers little trunks in the said wagon locked being very heavy. Divers spake to it, and in the issue it was ordered that the wagon and arms should be stayed till we could acquaint the lords with it, and that the said Mr. Goodwin and Mr. Hampden, the other knight of the shire, should write to the said mayor to give him and one Mr. Collins of the same town thanks for their care.

We appointed to meet at 8 of the clock on Monday morning and rose between 6 and 7 of the clock at night.

GAWDY

[f. 125a]   Saturday, the IIII of June

Ordered, that 2000£[46] shall be sent to Sir John Hotham to Hull.

A letter from Sir Edward Ayscough, that of a 100 chief constables in that county all appeared but one, notwithstanding the king's proclamation forbidding the militia was set over the door w[h]ere the deputy lieutenants did meet. My Lord Paget's letter to my Lord of [f. 125b] Holland was placed by it. He doubteth not but that the county of Lincoln will faithfully serve the king and parliament. Sir John Hotham hath not yet the 2000£.

A committee appointed to take care that our orders and declarations and votes may be truly printed and dispersed into the kingdom according to the directions of the house.[47]

MR. PYM, that 2500 men under the command of my Lord of Ormonde hath beaten 7000[48] under the command of Phelim O'Neill. They have killed 3000 of them and taken 3000 cattle from them. This I had from Mr. Exton while I walked a little in the hall.

MR. GREEN, a report of the charge of the navy. The last year and this comes to 335,286£.

That we owe for the navy more than is received 198,306£.

That the officers of the king's household hath had for the maintenance of his house since May 1641 out of the customs 102,000£.

[f. 126a] An ordinance of parliament to give satisfaction to the City for the loan of an 100,000£ till an act of parliament may be passed.

A message from the lords, they agree to the 2000£ to be paid to Sir John

46. Crossed out in MS: *of the contribution of.*
47. This committee, which included Pury, was also to "consider of the best way of putting the publick Orders and Votes of the House in Execution." *CJ,* II, 604.
48. MS: *7000£.* The Earl of Ormonde was lieutenant general of the army in Ireland.

Hotham and likewise to the disposing of the magazine that's come from Hull as we appointed it.

The bill for the assembly of the ministers agreed to and sent to lords with desire to have it sent to the king.

My LORD FALKLAND hath information from the king's agent in France that 2 Irish regiments are disbanded in France. The men are taken into other companies. The officers have passes to go into Ireland. Our agent acquainted the Prince of Condé with it, who said that what was done by council should not be undone.

In the afternoon.

An order to enable the Earl of Warwick and my Lord Brooke to search all ships that shall carry any goods whatsoever to the rebels in Ireland and to be accountable for the same. 'Tis desired to desire the lords to join with us in this order.

[f. 126b] A message from the lords, they desire a present free conference concerning the levying of the land and sea forces for Ireland. 'Tis assented to.

A letter from Belfast from my Lord Conway, May the 16.[49] That there is suspicion of my Lord of Antrim because he passed through the rebels' country without interruption. They want money there extremely.

Another letter, the same time. If money be not presently sent, all the horse will disband.

The committee to take into consideration and to take order to supply the soldiers with shoes and clothes.

MR. GRIMSTON, a report that the lords hath agreed to the order for all deputy lieutenants to subscribe all warrants concerning the militia, and that such as doth refuse shall have their names certified to this house, and that the members of this house deputy lieutenants shall go down to their several counties at the times appointed, so many of them as shall be appointed by this house. My Lord North, Speaker.

HILL

[p. 85]   Saturday, June 4th, 1642

Sir Edward Ayscough writ that there are in Lincolnshire about 100 chief constable[s] and but one missed at our meeting. Every man had his declaration lie by him. It giveth great satisfaction. There hath been many wiles to distract us. Every chief constable had a proclamation sent to his house.

---

49. Conway's letters are dated 19 and 23 May in *CJ,* II, 606.

[p. 86] Statute of 17 *Car.* of 400,000£:[50]

That every person other than such as are excepted by the act shall be liable towards the payment thereof.

Enacted that every person, etc., for every pound that every of the same persons, etc., hath in fee s[imple], fee ta[il], for life term of years by execution, ward[shi]p, copy of court roll of and in any honors, castles, manors, etc., rents, services, etc., or other yearly profits or hereditaments of the yearly value of 20s. shall pay towards the sum of 400,000£ his proportionable part as are imposed, etc.

MR. PYM, that in the north of Ireland Sir Phelim O'Neill hath 3 bodies of 5 and 6000 apiece. The inhabitants of themselves have slayed 3000 and taken from [them] 3000 cattle.

MR. GREEN, report concerning the navy.[51]

That there are 52 ships of the best. 6300 mariners and every mariner presents office of 3 land men in service.

These ships furnished so well as never any had the like. 1200 pieces of ordnance.

The charge of this navy with perquisites and accidents, sc.,[52] payment of men in arrear, 335,280£ 19s. 8d.,[53] in which is included 20 ships set out the last summer.

The time begin 21 May 1641 when the first ships were set out to this day.

1. There is paid for 10 of king's ships and 10 merchants' for treasurer and victualler 57,592[£] 4[s.] 6[d.], which were set out 1641.

2. For the ord[ina]ry of his majesty's navy 1640 which is taken into charge, which is 26,610£ 3s. 9d.

[p. 87] The ordinary consists of all the stores for the king's ships provided this time of the year for another year. These were provided 1640 and made use of 1641. Besides it consists of payments.

Charge of navy 1641, 27,122[£] 3[s.] 4[d.]

For carrying ammunition to Hull 1641, 3200£ by 12 ships.

Carrying prince to Chatham, sc., the great ship, which cost 2160[£] (else she would be spoiled) to make her ready.

---

50. For the statute for the defense levy of £400,000, see *PJ,* 2: esp. 90, n. 9. For the two provisions cited by Hill, see *SR,* V, 145, 147.

51. These details do not appear in the other journals or in *CJ.* Perhaps Hill received a copy of the report from Green, father to Hill's first wife. *DNB.* For the complete report see *A declaration concerning the generall accompts* (1642). Wing, D 570. The editors are indebted to Professor Conrad Russell for calling this pamphlet to their attention.

52. MS: *s.* Hill apparently used this as an abbreviation for the word "scilicet." The editors have adopted the modern abbreviation.

53. Cf. G, above. This figure does not appear in the pamphlet. There are several other discrepancies between Hill's figures and those in print.

Repair of docks and wharves at Chatham, which comes to [1]620£.

Next the charge of the ordinary for this year 1642 now provided, 21,056£ 11s. 6d.

Victualler of navy for ordinary expense of this year, 7655£ [1]7s. 9d.

Charge for emptions[54] of office of ordnance, sc., provisions of stores to be brought in when we set out ships. A 4th part commonly is bought. The last year and this year, 5443£ 12s.

4 ships set out this spring to go for Ireland coast. The treasurer of navy hath 8979[£] 16[s.] 8[d.]

Victualler's charge, [5]364[£] 16[s.] 8[d.]

For 15 more of king's ships, 48,368[£] 10[s.], the treasurer's charge.

The victualler's charge for these ships, 27,359[£] 3[s.] 6[d.]

[p. 88] The charge of 23 merchants' ships come in the whole for victual and all, 74,372£ 8s.

Mr. Marten's ship, 7386£.[55]

Smaller ships for the coast of Ireland, 8 pinnaces provided, 7489£.

2 f[r]igates bought at Dover, 800 and 2500£.

Sum total, 335,280[£] 19[s.] 8[d.][56]

2. There is paid out of tonnage and poundage:[57] 52,000£, 10,800£, 27,123£ 3s. 4d., 1000£, 800£, 800£, 2058[£] 10[s.] 4[d.], 500£ (5000£ which we owe the Chamber of London), 6500£, 20,000£, 10,400£.

We have paid 136,988£ 19s. 8d.

We owe 198,300[£] 6s. 0d.[58]

From the customers we have received towards this payment:

Since bill of tonnage and poundage, which was 25 May 1641, they have received 315,670£, they confess.

It must be more, else will be a dead loss of 100,000£.

Of this they have paid into the Exchequer: 66,100[£], 82,423[£] 6[s.] 11[d.], 66,000£.

Paid in toto in Exchequer: 229,295[£] 13[s.] 6[d.]

They say there remain in debt 59,049£.

Here is 59,049[£] towards payment 198,300[£]. Out of this they demand 10,000£ forth.

[p. 89] Reasons of fall of customs besides decay of trade. This year is but 315,000£, and the last year was 432,000£.

---

54. Action of buying. *NED.*
55. Captain George Marten, brother to Henry Marten, MP.
56. The total in the printed version is £324,480 19s. 8d.
57. The remainder of Hill's report differs considerably from the printed version.
58. Cf. G, above.

They say they have not received receipts upon sea coal, which formerly came to 20,000£. Now Sir John Trevor receives it.

Sir Job Harby hath receipts of 4000£ per annum upon sea coal.

Sir Thomas Aston[59] hath receipts of 1500£ per annum at Chester notwithstanding bill of tonnage and poundage.

We have paid (during this necessity of ours) his household 102,000[£] since 25 May 1641.

59. Trevor, an MP, was part owner of the monopoly for farming sea coal at Newcastle. Keeler, p. 365. Harby was a customs farmer. See *PJ,* 1: 38. Aston, MP for Cheshire in the Short Parliament, was an importer of French wines. See *Roy. Off.,* pp. 10–11; and J. S. Morrill, *Cheshire 1630–1660* (London, 1974), p. 8. *DNB.*

D'EWES

June 6, Monday, 1642

The Speaker came about 8 of the clock. Some moved that Sir Henry Mildmay, being a deputy lieutenant of Essex, might be spared from going thither at the training, but it was ordered that he should go.[1]

Upon MR. HUNT's motion Mr. Exton had leave to go into the country to his wife, being dangerously sick.

York, June 4, 1642.[2]

Yesterday morning to the king.[3]

Urias Wright, ensign to Captain Overton.[4]

Postscript.

The king's message sent by the Earl of Newport to the committee and their answer was next read.[5]

The clerk next read the king's printed speech, which was read in several places upon Heworth Moor, where the multitude met near York being about 40,000.[6]

The clerk afterwards read the petition of Yorkshire offered to his majesty by Sir Thomas Fairfax (son and heir apparent of Ferdinando, Lord Fairfax), being pithy and home to the purpose.

Then was read by the clerk the petition of the county of York to us, complaining of the great affronts offered to them.[7]

1. Mildmay was one of several MPs named to execute the militia ordinance. See 4 June, n. 23.

2. This letter was from the committee appointed in early May to go to Yorkshire. See *PJ*, 2: 265. For this letter to the commons and a similar one to the lords, see G, below, and *LJ*, V, 107. Other accounts of the meeting on Heworth Moor on 3 June appear in *CSPD, 1641–43*, p. 336; and *CSP Ven., 1642–1643*, pp. 77–78.

3. "According to the Commands of the House, we presented your Petition and Propositions to the King, Yesterday Morning," i.e., the Nineteen Propositions. See *PJ*, 2: esp. 399–400; and *LJ*, V, 107.

4. Doubtless Robert Overton of Holderness, who subsequently served in the parliamentary army and in the mid-1640s was governor of Hull. *VCH, Yorkshire, East Riding*, I, 106–07. *DNB*.

5. The king's message commanded the Yorkshire committee not to attend the meeting at Heworth Moor on 3 June. The committee responded, "That we would obey His Commands herein at this Time; but that we protested it was a very high Breach of our Liberty." See *LJ*, V, 106–07.

6. MS: *40,000£*. This figure ranges from 40,000 to 80,000 in the various accounts. For the king's speech see Rushworth, IV, 624–25. Wing, C 2280.

7. For both petitions see *LJ*, V, 109–11. An account of Fairfax's attempt to present the petition to the king appears in Basil N. Reckitt, *Charles the First and Hull, 1639–1645* (London, 1952), p. 46.

York, June 4, 1642, from Sir John Bourchier to Sir Thomas Barrington.[8]

The Lord Savile took him by the belt.

The Lord Savile told him that he knew him well enough.

His company said they would cane him holding/[9]

[f. 150a] Captain Blague came to him, being talking with Sir Richard Darley and others.[10]

Some spake touching Captain Blague, that he had a company in the Low Countries and that we should send to the Dutch ambassador[11] that he might either return to his company in the Low Countries or be cashiered, but nothing for the present was ordered upon it.

I moved that Mr. Rushworth might make a particular relation of the passages at York, which for the present was not put in execution presently but awhile upon the revival of the business by another.

MR. PYM delivered in a copy of the petition of the malignant party in Yorkshire[12] intended to be preferred to the houses of parliament, which was read, in which they desired a compliance between the king and the parliament and showed the danger they were in in respect that the parliament commanded the exercise of the militia one way and the king another.

This being read, divers spake to several particulars in the letters and especially of the insolent and dangerous carriage of the Earl of Lindsey and the Lord Savile, but nothing was at the instant voted.

MR. CAGE moved what I had done formerly, that Mr. Rushworth might make relation of all the several passages which he could remember, which was seconded by MR. REYNOLDS. And after one or two others had spoken, Mr. Rushworth came up to his place where he usually sat on the left hand of the clerk and there first made relation how one King, a messenger of this house, had been abused, being sent to bring up Mr. Thomas Beckwith, a delinquent, being a papist who had sought to betray Hull.[13] For coming to York where Mr. Beckwith was, he found him alone in his chamber, and so having acquainted him with the command of the parliament and offering to show him all respect by

8. Marginal note: *Printed.* For the letter from Bourchier, a parliamentarian, concerning the Yorkshire petition to the king, see *LJ,* V, 111. Wing, B 3839. *DNB.*

9. The letter states: "Many that were with his Lordship [Viscount Savile] held up their Canes, in a terrifying Manner; and One of them said, Hold your prating, it were good to cane you [Bourchier]." Savile (incorrectly listed as comptroller in *PJ,* 2: xxxi) was treasurer of the king's household. *DNB.*

10. Marginal note: *Printed.* Darley, a justice of the peace in Yorkshire, was father to Henry Darley, MP. Keeler, p. 153. Blague is described in the letter as "One of my Lord Savill's Company." For Thomas Blague, see *Roy. Off.,* p. 31.

11. Albert Joachimi.

12. Wing, T 1685. The petition is not mentioned in *CJ.*

13. For Beckwith's role and William King's report, see *PJ,* 2: 375, 382, and *LJ,* V, 109.

going away privately with him, the said Mr. Beckwith seemed willing thereunto and told him that he would step up and take leave of some of his friends
above, to which he assented; and so a little while after the same Mr. Beckwith's
going, the said messenger was called up likewise, and upon his coming into the
chamber, he found there 9 or 10 Cavaliers who kicked him about the chamber
and then tumbled him down the stairs. Whereupon he sent to the committee of
the House of Commons at York to let them know how he had been abused, and
so Sir Philip Stapleton and Sir Henry Cholmley,[14] two of the said committee,
came presently to the house where the said Cavaliers were and expostulated
with them, they having offered such an affront to the parliament, and told them
that they must answer it, but they excused themselves as if they had not certainly known that he was employed by the parliament. And thereupon the said
Beckwith was delivered again to the said messenger and remained in his
custody about the space of an hour, till some of the said Cavaliers having been at
court and acquainted the king with it, his majesty did send for him and the said
Beckwith to come to him and, being come, [f. 150b] did cause him to read over
the warrant himself and then told him that the said warrant was against the
Petition of Right because it did not express the cause of the offense of the said
Mr. Beckwith for which he was to be taken into custody. 2dly, he said that if the
warrant were sent to apprehend the said Mr. Beckwith for his recusancy, that
should be proceeded upon within the county, or 3dly, if the said Mr. Beckwith
were sent for about the business concerning Hull, he said that he would then
suffer the parliament to do justice upon him when they should do him justice
upon Sir John Hotham.[15] And so the king did deliver the same Mr. Beckwith out
of the hands of the said messenger and discharged him, but before he was
admitted to his majesty's presence, the guard had restrained him from his
liberty for the space of about 8 hours, viz., from 12 of the clock at noon till
about 8 of the clock at night. All which the said Mr. Rushworth did affirm to
have been related unto him from the said messenger himself and then produced
a letter written from him to his wife bearing date June 2, 1642, which the house
caused him to open, wherein amongst other particulars he declared how he had
been kicked and abused but thanked God that he had no harm. (This King, the
messe/

Sir Ralph Whitfield and Sir John Glanville, two of the king's serjeants,
brought this message from the lords, that their lordships desired a present
conference, etc., touching a letter received from their committee at York with a
printed declaration or speech of his majesty's within it. They withdrew, etc. We
answered to send an answer by messengers of our own.

14. Lord Howard of Escrick came rather than Cholmley according to *LJ*.
15. For Hotham's refusal to admit the king into Hull on 23 April, see *PJ*, 2: 223–26 and passim.

Mr. Rushworth's relation being ended, there passed several votes, one against the Earl of Lindsey, one/[16]

Sir Thomas Barrington was sent up when it was near 12 of the clock to let/[17]

The Lord North managed conference on their part.

Mr. Pym managed the conference on our part and read all that came from York and the declaration against the proclamation.[18]

[f. 151a]   Post Meridiem

The Speaker came between 3 and 4. Divers particulars passed. Vide M.

I came in a little after the petition of the Scots to the council was read,[19] and Mr. Hampden was appointed to acquaint the Scottish commissioners with it to know whether they had received this news from Scotland.

Vide M. *diversa*.[20]

MR. HAMPDEN made report that the Scottish commissioners did acknowledge that they had received the said petition from a private hand out of Scotland but had not yet received it from the Scottish council.[21]

SIR WALTER ERLE showed that whereas there was a printed copy of a letter sent by the king to the council of Scotland, these words following were left out in that printed copy, viz.: "Ye our subjects of Scotland were the first causers of the rebellion in Ireland, but I think ye did it not expressly but your covenant was the occasion of it."[22]

Mr. Strode sent up to desire a conference touching the ordinance for levying of men and to show how the king had refused the commission.[23]

Sir Ralph Whitfield and Sir John Glanville/

Touching the 30 muskets belonging to the Lord Coventry.[24]

---

16. For the votes see G, below, and *CJ*, II, 607–08. See also Verney, *Notes*, pp. 178–80.

17. Barrington was to inform the lords that the commons were ready for the conference. *CJ*, II, 608.

18. I.e., the king's proclamation against the militia and parliament's declaration in response.

19. In addition to the petition "from divers Lords, Gentlemen, and Burgesses of Scotland," a letter from the king dated 20 May was read. Both were directed to the Scottish Privy Council. See *CJ*, II, 608; and *The Register of the Privy Council of Scotland*, 2d series (Edinburgh, 1899–1908), VII, 257–58, 260–63. Wing, T 2853A (S 2004 in the 1945–51 edition).

20. For proceedings omitted by D'Ewes, see *CJ*, II, 608.

21. It was ordered that the committee for Scottish negotiations should "draw a Declaration to be sent into Scotland, to express how well this Kingdom . . . accepts their Care and Affection to the Peace of this Kingdom." *CJ*, II, 609.

22. The king's letter, as it appears in *The Register of the Privy Council*, does not contain this sentence.

23. For the commission and the ordinance for the sea adventure for Ireland, see D, 18–22 passim, and below, n. 25.

24. The messengers (Leech and Page in *CJ*, II, 609; Whitfield and Glanville in *LJ*, V, 108) requested that the Lord Coventry's muskets be a subject of the next conference.

Mr. Reynolds managed the conference.[25]

The Lord North managed the conference and showed that the lords did agree with us to stop the 30 muskets of the Lord Coventry's stayed at Chipping Wycombe in Buckinghamshire.[26]

Sir Edward Leech and Mr. Page, two masters of the Chancery, brought this message from the lords, that their lordships, etc., a conference, etc., touching the matter of the conference in the morning, etc.[27] We agreed, etc. Myself and others named reporters. Went up and divers of the house.

The Lord North managed the conference and showed that the lords agreed in all particulars with us, only they had made a declaration to be printed before the two Yorkshire petitions and had made some additions also to our votes and the declaration touching the king's proclamation.

The Earl of Essex read the declaration of both houses to be prefixed before the two Yorkshire petitions to be printed.[28]

The Lord Robartes read the amendments or additions made by the lords to our votes and to our declaration[29] in answer of the king's proclamation against the militia.

[f. 151b] The Lord North then showed that their lordships had named a committee of 17 to meet presently in the Painted Chamber to consider further of the matters of the conference this morning and desired us to name a proportionable number and lastly showed that the lords had resolved to lay aside all other business but the business of Yorkshire, the safety of this kingdom, and the relieving of Ireland.

SIR HENRY VANE[30] after our return to the house made report of that which the Earl of Essex had read, and the clerk read it, and we agreed to it.

MR. WHITELOCKE made report of the additions which the lords had made to the votes and declaration; he reported also that the lords had named a committee of 17 to consider further of the matter of the conference in the morning and desired us to name a proportionable number to meet them presently in the

25. Reynolds managed that part concerning the king's denial of the commission for raising men and the consequent need to expedite the ordinance for the sea adventure for Ireland. The next day the lords ordered Viscount Falkland to write to Secretary Nicholas to "move the King . . . to pass the Commission" and to see that Sir Nicholas Crispe "be not delayed in receiving the King's Answer." Crispe was empowered to satisfy the king's demands "concerning the Names of the Officers, and employing the Forces only for . . . Ireland." See *CJ*, II, 608; and *LJ*, V, 113, 115.

26. For details see *LJ*, V, 108.

27. I.e., the conference concerning both the information from Yorkshire and the new militia declaration.

28. See *LJ*, V, 111. Wing, T 3507.

29. For the text of the declaration, see Appendix D. Wing, E 1371.

30. Doubtless Vane, Jr., since he was named to the joint committee on Yorkshire affairs. *CJ*, II, 609.

Painted Chamber, with other particular touching this kingdom and Ireland. The clerk having read the said amendments, we voted them. A committee of 34 was also named by the house to join with the lords, of which I was one.

We resolved also to lay aside all other business except that which/[31]

Sir Henry Vane sent up to let the lords know that we assented to all, that we had named a proportionable number who should meet presently, and that we had laid aside all other business.

MR. PURY gave an order for dispersing the declarations against the proclamation. Allowed.[32]

SIR THOMAS BARRINGTON delivered in an order to encourage the volunteers in Essex that would show arms, being over and above the number of the trained bands. Voted.

Sir Gilbert Gerard was appointed to carry up the said order to the lords tomorrow morning to desire them to concur with us in it.

We appointed to meet at 8 of the clock tomorrow morning and rose between 7 and 8 of the clock at night.

GAWDY

[f. 127a]   Monday, the VI of June

A letter from York, June the 4, from our committee to the Speaker.

They presented our articles. The king will give us answer. There was a great meeting on Friday, but nothing was said to them. They were 40,000. Sir Thomas Fairfax offered the king a petition in behalf of the country, but 'twas refused. My Lord of Newport delivered this message to the committee from the king, that they should not that day go into the field. Recusants' arms are commanded by the king. Few of the gentlemen met except such as were of the king's guard. There was a great noise in the field, but no man know what they said.

A printed declaration read which his majesty published to the people.

The petition read,[33] intended to be delivered. His majesty's drawing together of horse and foot illegal. Against the concourse of the Cavaliers. The decay of clothing. That he would advise with his parliament. That he would not put them

---

31. "The House shall meddle with no other Business, but what tends to the Preservation and Safety of this Kingdom, and the Kingdom of Ireland." *CJ,* II, 609.

32. Pury was apparently speaking for the new committee for printing and dispersing declarations. See 4 June, n. 47. For this order and future actions by the committee, see *CJ,* II, 609, 616, 628, 630.

33. I.e., the above-mentioned Yorkshire petition to the king.

upon the rock of taking part against the parliament. That he would send back the lords.

[f. 127b] A petition from Yorkshire to both houses of some violence offered to some people by my Lord of Lindsey and my Lord Savile. They desire the houses that they may have access to the king.

A letter from Sir John Bourchier to Sir Thomas Barrington, that he being at Heworth Moor reading of a petition, my Lord Savile laid hold on his belt and had liked to have pulled him off his horse and told him he came to sow sedition and said if he liked fighting, he should have enough. Divers other affronts were offered him. Captain Blague was a seconder of these affronts.

A letter to Mr. Pym, that the messenger[34] that apprehended Beckwith was thrown down the stairs and kicked. They were both carried to the king, who released Beckwith and committed the messenger, who by mediation of our committee was released.

A petition intended to be gotten but could not. To the parliament against the militia and many other things.[35]

[f. 128a] Mr. Rushworth, that the messenger apprehended Beckwith, that the Cavaliers kicked him down. A letter from the messenger to his wife, that the king commanded him to read the warrant, who said it was against the Petition of Right because the cause was not expressed but he imagined wherefore it was. When the house did him right about Sir John Hotham, then we should.[36] The messenger was committed, but at night the king released him and used him graciously.

There were at least 60,000 people at Heworth Moor, where Sir Thomas Fairfax pressed near the king's saddle to deliver this petition but it would not be received. 'Twas unanimously desired this petition should be delivered to the king.

Resolved, that Mr. Rushworth shall have an 100£ for his pains[37] and that the house will farther take him into consideration.

A message from the lords, they desire a present conference. That they have received a letter from their committee and a printed declaration set out by the king. They shall receive an answer by messengers of our own.

[f. 128b] Resolved by question, that the Earl of Lindsey be declared by this house to be a public enemy to the state and an incendiary between the king and his people.

34. Gawdy has interspersed his report of the 3 June meeting on Heworth Moor with Rushworth's account of the attempted apprehension of Beckwith by the messenger, William King.

35. The petition of the "malignant party" in Yorkshire. See above, n. 12.

36. See above, n. 15.

37. This was to be in addition to the £50 already agreed upon. On 16 August it was again ordered that Rushworth should be paid the £150 agreed to on 6 June. See *PJ*, 2: 401; *CJ*, II, 607; and *LJ*, V, 296.

Resolved, that my Lord Savile be declared by this house to be a public enemy to the state and an incendiary between the king and his people.

Resolved, these 2 votes to be a head of the conference.

Resolved, that this house doth approve of the Yorkshire petition.[38]

Resolved, that this petition shall be printed.[39]

Resolved, that the lords be moved how the recusants' arms may be hindered from coming to York according to the king's command.

Resolved, that we should desire the lords to join with us that the petition of Yorkshire may be delivered to his majesty.

SIR GILBERT GERARD, that there is 7 great horses and a wagon went this morning of the king's towards York, and that the [f. 129a] men said that our best days are past, that they will talk with us when they come back.

A warrant for stay of the great horses and the wagon.[40]

The declaration in answer to the king's proclamations and declarations concerning the militia sent up to the lords.

In the afternoon.

A letter from the king to the great council of Scotland from York, May the 20.

A letter from Edinburgh, the last of May, that the body of that kingdom is so bent of the preservation of the union of both kingdoms that there is no great fear that there should be any danger from thence.

A petition from lords, gentlemen, ministers, and burgesses of Scotland to the great council at Edinburgh to assay all means to beget a good understanding between his majesty and the parliament of England that they will not engage themselves against us.

MR. FIENNES, that there were 800 barons' hands to the petition.

38. I.e., the petition to the king. *CJ*, II, 608.

39. The Yorkshire petition to the parliament was also to be printed, along with an account of the attempt to present the petition to the king. *CJ*, II, 608.

40. It was reported that the horses and wagon were bound for York. Later "the House being informed, That the Waggon stayed at Watford, belongs to the Bishop of Norwich," it was ordered that it should be released. See *CJ*, II, 608, 609.

D'EWES

[f. 151b]   June 7, Tuesday, 1642

The Speaker came a little after 8 of the clock. After prayers the SPEAKER told us that he had received letters out of Ireland and from the mayor of St. Albans dated at St. Albans June 6, 1642, in which he showed that according to the order of this house he had stayed 6 great horses[1] which were carrying to York. The parties pretended that they belonged to the prince and were brought from Richmond but showed no testimony thereof. So we agreed to stay them and that Sir Gilbert Gerard would carry up the said letters to the lords to desire their concurrence with us as soon as they were set.

MR. ROLLE brought us the answer from Sir John Heydon[2] and other officers of the ordnance to our demand of June 4, 1642, whether they would issue out these arms by direction of the parliament which were brought from Hull if it were delivered to them. Their answer was in writing bearing date June 6, 1642. That they were ready in all things which lay in their power to obey the parliament, but that in this they could answer nothing without the consent of the Earl of Newport, the master of the ordnance.[3] Whereupon we voted that part of the said magazine which was brought up should be issued forth for the relief of Ireland according as there was need,[4] and the rest to be disposed of in some place in the City of London, and that so much of the said arms as should be used for the service of the commonwealth should be again made good out of the purse of the commonwealth; and Sir Gilbert Gerard was appointed to go up to the lords as soon as the lords should be set to desire their lordships' concurrence with us in the said votes.[5]

[f. 152a] The clerk then read the first of the letters which came out of Ireland bearing date at the castle of Dublin May 11, 1642, and was directed to the Speaker of the House of Commons, being sent to him from Sir William Parsons and Sir John Borlase, justices of Ireland.

1. Seven horses, in G, below, and *CJ*. It was subsequently ordered that the mayor, William Newe, allow the horses to proceed to York. *CJ*, II, 610–11, 696.

2. MS: *Mr. John Haines*. For the order see 4 June, n. 13.

3. For the message, which pointed out that Newport was now at York, see *CJ*, II, 610.

4. The commissioners for Irish affairs were to determine what part of the Hull magazine should go to Ireland. *CJ*, II, 610. For their subsequent action see CIA, 9 June.

5. Gerard was to request a conference concerning the votes. *CJ*, II, 610.

Received his letters of the 9th of April,[6] by which they found their services approved by the House of Commons above their desert, which gave them great comfort.

That they had great cares and troubles and run through great dangers, which have happened to them in their old age when they are least able to procure remedy for others or to repair their own fortunes.

That they therefore desired to have some recompense out of the rebels' estates.

That they conceived it was not through our default that succors have been so long kept off from being sent, which put them upon many extremities which might have been avoided. That they did not wonder that the rebels scandalized them as well as this honorable house, seeing they had done their uttermost to hinder them from the accomplishment of their wicked designs, and that they did think it very strange that the Lord Dillon should prefer such false accusations from the rebels to his majesty[7] against them, well hoping they should have reparation from him for the same.

The clerk did then read the letter sent to the Speaker also from Sir William St. Leger, lord president of Munster, bearing date at Cork May 9, 1642, in which he showed that he had received no supply of men or money since the arrival of Colonel Vavasour with his regiment and the troops of the Lord Inchiquin and Captain Jephson.

That he was joyed yet to hear that a large supply of men and some money was to be sent.

He desired a train of artillery of some 10 drakes and 2 cartows (or little drakes), being all fieldpieces, and one to govern them.

That he was supplied with French wheat by an English merchant, which would preserve the/

He then showed how great charge he had been at, that he had lost his estate and desired that the house would consider him in due time, with some other particulars of less moment.[8]

I went out when this letter was in reading and returned towards the house just as Sir Gilbert Gerard went up with a message,[9] and I accompanied him into the lords house where the Lord North supplied the Speaker's place.

6. Perhaps the reference is to the Speaker's letter of 19 April. See *PJ*, 2: 188.

7. Crossed out in MS: *Lord Dillon, reparation from him, not fit to be of council there*. Dillon had been sent as a prisoner to the parliament after carrying a message from the rebels to the king in December 1641. Several months later he escaped to York. See *PJ*, 1: 2; and Clarendon, *History*, II, 487–89.

8. The house referred both letters to the commissioners for Irish affairs and passed further orders concerning Ireland, including one for a loan of £10,000 for Munster. *CJ*, II, 610. For Sir Charles Vavasour see *Roy. Off.*, p. 387.

9. For Gerard's several messages, see above, and *CJ*, II, 610.

Vide M.[10]

SIR GILBERT GERARD returned and made report amongst other particulars that the lords would give a present meeting.

Some motions followed. Vide M. I was at the conference.

Mr. Pierrepont managed the conference and after a short introduction read the answers of the officers of the ordnance. Then Sir Gilbert Gerard read the votes we had made this morning upon it, and Mr. Pierrepont lastly desired their lordships' concurrence with us.

After our return from the conference SIR RICHARD BULLER and others complained of false news printed, as amongst the rest of a pamphlet intituled [blank], in which it was amongst other particulars declared that the king had 100,000 men who had declared themselves for him. It was thereupon referred to the committee for printing, where Mr. John White[11] was in the chair, and they were appointed to sit at two of the clock this afternoon.

SIR ROBERT HARLEY delivered in a warrant under the king's own hand directed to the sheriff of Montgomeryshire, commanding him to publish [f. 152b] a printed answer[12] to the declaration of the two houses touching the militia. Then others showed how the sheriffs did burden godly ministers with it in several places and forced them to read it in their churches, that it grew to be almost as great a snare as the *Book of Sports*[13] had been. It was then severally moved that some declaration might be made for prevention of this. The SPEAKER then showed that there had been a committee formerly appointed but they had not yet made any report, and then the SPEAKER further informed the house from the clerk that this business was long since referred to a select committee of lords and commons. I spake in effect following:

That I had been of this committee,[14] and that we had met several times about it but found the matter more difficult than at first we apprehended it to have been, and especially because we could not resolve how far such commands to the sheriffs might be lawful if sent under the broad seal which might perhaps be undoubtedly legal if sent otherwise, but there was then no mention of commanding them to be read by ministers on the Lord's Day, which would now much strengthen such a declaration being added to it.

10. For proceedings omitted by D'Ewes, see G, below, and *CJ*, II, 610–11.

11. MP for Southwark.

12. I.e., the king's proclamation against the militia, which he had also ordered to be read in all parish churches. See *PJ*, 2: 398, n. 2. On 30 August the house ordered that the sheriff, Thomas Nicholls, should be thanked for "performing his Duty in not publishing the Proclamations." *Sheriffs*, p. 263; *CJ*, II, 743.

13. In 1633 the king had republished, upon the advice of William Laud, Archbishop of Canterbury, his father's *Declaration of Sports*, which the clergy were required to read from their pulpits. See Gardiner, *History of England*, VII, 321–22.

14. The committee for defense of the kingdom. D'Ewes may have attended meetings of the committee, but his name is not among the members in *CJ*, II, 589.

Others spake after me, and in the issue a new committee of some 6 or 7 was nominated, of which I was one, and they were appointed to meet this afternoon at 2 of the clock in the inward Court of Wards, and power was given to any two of us to draw the said declaration.

Sir Robert Rich and Mr. Page, two masters of the Chancery, brought this message, etc., a present conference touching the votes presented at the last conference.[15] Agreed to meet, etc. The same named reporters, viz., Mr. Pierrepont, Sir Gilbert Gerard, and Sir Walter Erle, who were managers at the last conference. Divers went to it. I went not.

The Lord North did manage it and showed that the lords did consent to our votes, only they had added to the last of them that the place in the City of London should be the Tower and that Sir John Conyers, lieutenant of the Tower, should have the custody of them.[16]

As soon as the conference was ended, upon SIR ROBERT COOKE's motion Sir Samuel Luke had liberty to go into the country for recovery of his health.

MR. PIERREPONT made report of the lords' addition to our last vote, to which we assented, and he was sent up to the lords to let them know that we did assent to their amendment.

MR. ARTHUR GOODWIN delivered in an order for the repayment of the 6000£ lent by the Buckinghamshire men.[17]

MR. PIERREPONT returned and made report that he had done his message and craved pardon that he had forgot part of the report, which was that we should allow such as Sir John Conyers should appoint to look to the said arms some consideration for their pains.

SIR WILLIAM BRERETON informed the house that he had received a letter out of Cheshire which he delivered in, being sent from an honest constable there, and it was read, by which it appeared that one Captain Edward Gerard did strive to raise 30 horse in that county and offered them 2s. and 6d. a day as long as they lived if they would buy horses and mount themselves to serve the king, and that this offer was made by one Arrowsmith employed by the said Captain Gerard. SIR WILLIAM BRERETON showed that this Captain Gerard was a papist and brother to Sir William Gerard of Lancashire.[18]

Sir Robert Rich and Mr. Page, two masters of the Chancery/

15. The votes concerning the disposition of the arms from Hull. See above.
16. For this addition see *LJ*, V, 114.
17. For this loan and the order for repayment, see *PJ*, 2: 148, 236, and *CJ*, II, 611–12.
18. Sir William Gerard's name appears in John Moore's list of Lancashire recusants. See *PJ*, 1: 286, n. 22. Edward Gerard and William Arrowsmith were to be sent for by the sergeant at arms because of their efforts to raise a troop of horse out of Lancashire and Cheshire to go to York. See *CJ*, II, 611; and *LJ*, V, 121.

Select committee touching late doings at York to meet with the lords at 3 of the clock in the afternoon and that the house would sit at 5 of the clock.

The names of the committee read. I one of them.

Messengers called in. Agreed to all.

We resolved that the committee should meet at 3 and that the house should sit at 5.

Upon the motion of SIR HENRY VANE, Junior, some new men were appointed to go to the citizens to encourage them to lend, viz., Sir Thomas Dacres and others.[19]

We rose about one of the clock.

Post Meridiem

I was at the select committee in the Painted Chamber of lords and commons, being one of them. I came between 3 and 4 of the clock in the afternoon, but the lords came not till about 5 of the clock. We discoursed of the king's speech at York but voted nothing.

We parted between 6 and 7 at night, about which time our Speaker also did nothing else but resume his chair and adjourn the house to 8 of the clock tomorrow morning.

GAWDY

[f. 129b]   Tuesday, the VII of June

Mr. Speaker receive a letter from the mayor of St. Albans, that they have stayed 7 horses of the prince's that are going to York.

Resolved, that so many of the arms come from Hull that shall be employed in the service of the commonwealth shall be made good and shall be delivered to his majesty.[20]

Ordered, that the committee shall meet from day to day and appoint days for the putting the militia in execution in all the counties, and to appoint days.[21]

A letter to the Speaker from Dublin, the 11 of May, from the lord justices. They desire some proportion of the rebels' lands for their better maintenance.

A letter from Sir William St. Leger from Cork, the 9 of May. That though he

---

19. The reference is probably to the committee named to go to the livery companies; the new members replaced those who were also commissioners for Irish affairs. See 4 June, n. 12; and *CJ*, II, 611.

20. Gawdy's version of this vote is misleading. Cf. D, 35.

21. The joint committee for defense of the kingdom (militia). *CJ*, II, 610.

hears of supply of men, yet he hear nothing of the train of artillery without which he cannot go into the field. He desire a supply of victual because all the cattle unslaughtered are in the rebels' holds. [f. 130a] That all the towns in Munster are revolted except 4 or 5, of which Youghal and Kinsale are 2.

A petition from some of the citizens of London, that there may be a collection every Sunday and fast day for the supply of Ireland.

The citizens of London are called in and thanked. They were 12.

SIR GILBERT GERARD, a report of the message sent to the lords. That my Lord North said that if the horses stayed at St. Albans were the prince's, they think fit they should go.

The prince's horses are permitted to go to York.

A message from the lords, they desire a present conference concerning our votes about the magazine that's come from Hull. 'Tis assented to.

The house should have sat at 5 a clock, but they wanted company. But I was not there.

D'EWES

June 8, Wednesday, 1642

The Speaker came a little after 8 of the clock. As soon as prayers were ended, SIR WALTER ERLE moved that he had a packet of letters (which he held in his hands) out of which some further certainty might be known touching the pawning of the crown jewels, and that Mr. Lawrence Whitaker, being in the chair for the committee for informations, might open them, which was ordered accordingly.

Salop, May 3, 1642 (it should be June 3).

7000 pair of shoes and caps sent over to Dublin.

Upon MR. PYM's motion it was ordered that the commissioners should draw an order that this house would pay no officers but such as should be allowed by this house, and to draw a letter to the treasurer of the wars there to send an account to the house how the money already sent had been expended.[1]

The letter of the deputy lieutenants sent to the Speaker out of Essex dated at Brentwood June 7, 1642, in which they showed the alacrity of the Essex men to train. It was ordered to be printed.[2]

Upon MR. KNIGHTLEY's motion, to which others spake also, it was ordered that 4 of the deputy lieutenants of Northamptonshire, members of this house,[3] should only go down lest the house should be left too thin.

SIR GILBERT GERARD made report that the adventurers for Ireland were content to lend 10,000£ for Munster, so as it might be ordered that they might have 10,000£ out of the first money which should come in of the 100,000£ promised to be lent by the City of London.

Vide M.[4]

ALDERMAN PENINGTON delivered in an account from Mr. Hodgson, the chamberlain's clerk of London, that he had received 500,400£ and paid out so much and desired consideration for their pains. Some would have had 1000£ to

1. For this order see *CJ*, II, 612. The treasurer at wars for Ireland was Sir Adam Loftus.
2. Wing, B 4971.
3. Yelverton, Pickering, Crew, and Knightley were to go to Northamptonshire to execute the militia ordinance. *CJ*, II, 614.
4. The four City MPs (Penington, Soame, Vassall, Venn) plus Spurstow were added to the committee to go to the livery companies. See 7 June, n. 19; and *CJ*, II, 612. For the lukewarm response of most of the companies, see Pearl, *London*, pp. 208–09.

be allowed him, others ob.[5] per pound, others 2s. 6d. for each 100£, but I spake in effect following:

That there was a great sum of money now proposed to be allowed, so as I wished that/[6]

MR. DENZIL HOLLES moved about a printed letter touching some passages in Ireland which reflected with disgrace upon the Scots.[7]

SIR JOHN EVELYN of Surrey moved about a printed paper intituled *A True and Perfect Relation of the Particular Passages at York on Friday, the 3 of June 1642*,[8] which was likewise referred to the committee for printing to examine who was the author of it.

SIR JOHN EVELYN made report of the declaration.[9]

Serjeant Ayloff and Sir John Glanville, two of the king's serjeants, brought this message from the lords, that their lordships desired a present conference [f. 153b] by a committee, etc., touching a letter received from the Lord Willoughby of Parham, touching certain propositions received from the Scots, and touching a letter received from certain lords at York. They being withdrawn, we agreed after some debate to send an answer by messengers of our own, which the SPEAKER related to them being again called in, and so they withdrew and departed.

Upon MR. PYM's motion it was ordered that the Speaker should grant a warrant privately for a person whom the said Mr. Pym should nominate to him, the taking of whom, as Mr. Pym did affirm, did much concern the safety of the commonwealth, but if either his name or the matter were known, it might much prejudice the cause and give him the means of escape.[10]

We then proceeded with the declaration, which the clerk read once over without any man speaking to it and then began it again, and divers spake against several parts of the same declaration and others spake in maintenance of it,

5. Obolus—formerly used to denote a halfpenny. *NED.*

6. For the allowance granted to Edward Hodgson, clerk to Robert Bateman, for receiving, disbursing, and keeping an account of money paid into the Chamber of London, see G, below, and *CJ,* II, 612.

7. Wing, P 2224. Following a report from the committee for printing, the pamphlet was ordered to be burned and the publishers imprisoned. See *CJ,* II, 612, 613.

8. Wing, T 2564. For a letter from York see G, below.

9. On 6 June a new committee, with Evelyn as a member and doubtless chairman, had been named "to consider of the best Way of providing of Horse, Men, and Monies . . . for Defence of the King, Kingdom, and Parliament," and to formulate propositions to this end. Subsequently Evelyn was named to three ad hoc committees to promote the propositions in the City. See 12 September, n. 14; and *CJ,* II, 608, 617, 629, 632. It seems likely that this was Evelyn of Wiltshire, for he was a more ardent supporter of parliament than Evelyn of Surrey, according to Keeler, pp. 168–70. This assessment is confirmed by the fact that Evelyn of Wiltshire was excepted from the royal pardon in November 1642. Clarendon, *History,* II, 391.

10. Probably John Griffith, the younger, MP. See below.

during which time Sir [*blank*] and Mr. Page, two masters of the Chancery, brought this message from the lords.[11]

And a little after, as we still proceeded with the debate touching the preamble of the said declaration, Serjeant Ayloff and Serjeant Glanville, two of the king's serjeants, brought this message from the lords, that their lordships had adjourned.[12]

Mr. Griffith, Lady Elizabeth Sedley. I of committee.[13]

We proceeded with the declaration (which was afterwards printed),[14] of which the first part was to invite or persuade all men to bring in money or plate or to underwrite what horses they would maintain for the defense of the parliament. Divers spake for and against this clause,[15] and some alleged that there was need for us to prepare to defend ourselves because we had voted that the king intended war against the parliament[16] and that he had now made actual levies. I spake in effect following:

That I did conceive this expression might prove of dangerous consequence because it would fill men's hearts with the fear and expectation of a civil war, so as the very underwriting to find horses may disable men to do it; for most men's estates who are of rank and quality do arise out of the labors and sweat of other men's brows, and if they shall once perceive that all is like to come to confusion, will perhaps forbear paying in of those rents which must find and maintain these horses. And therefore I think the surest way for us to be prepared is not to talk of preparation. Neither do I know of such strength about the king which should thus suddenly draw us to this resolution. For if there were such garrison towns here as in France and the Low Countries out of which his majesty might draw forth in the space of a month or 3 weeks six or 7000 old soldiers, then it were indeed needful for us to be prepared with considerable preparations here. But as yet the greatest strength is held by us. The navy is in our power; Hull, the only fortress in the north, is held by our garrison; and the Scots have so declared themselves in their last petition to the Privy Council there[17] as we may rest

11. The request, brought by Leech and Page, was for consideration at the conference of how the magazine from Hull could be placed in the Tower. The lords' order was subsequently amended by the commons, omitting the phrase concerning "the King's Pleasure." *CJ*, II, 613, 615; *LJ*, V, 117, 118. For a similar change in an earlier order, see 3 June, n. 20.

12. In addition, they requested a conference concerning letters from Essex. *CJ*, II, 613.

Crossed out in MS: *Mr. Pleydell withdrew a little before 2 of the clock*. Exception had been taken to words spoken by Pleydell, apparently concerning the propositions for defense, "whereupon he explained himself," and the house resolved that it was satisfied with his explanation. *CJ*, II, 613.

13. For details see G, below; *CJ*, II, 613; and *HMC, Fifth Report*, p. 28. Lady Sedley was the widow of Sir John Sedley of Southfleet, Kent. GEC, *Baronetage*, I, 73.

14. D'Ewes's interlinear comment was doubtless added later.

15. I.e., the first clause of the declaration. See *CJ*, II, 613, and Appendix E.

16. This was one of three votes passed by both houses on 20 May. See *PJ*, 2: 349.

17. See 6 June, n. 19.

assured of them. Nay, we see his majesty cannot levy 30 horsemen in a county but we have notice of it before 15 of them can be gotten together. So as for us to stir up a general fear of civil war in the kingdom till there be an absolute necessity, I see no reason. I confess the only real index of such an intention was contained in that insolent speech of the Lord Savile to Sir John[18] Bourchier, that if he would fight, he should have fighting enough, but I conceive that lord to be of so shallow a judgment as there is no great heed to be taken to what he said. My humble desire therefore is that we forbear all underwriting and making preparations of men or horses until there be a real necessity, and for money that every man contribute what he shall be able, which may be collected for the supply of Ireland but be used for the defense of ourselves if occasion shall serve.

Others spake after me, and in the issue those hot earnest men, who either feared or knew more danger than I d[id and] had at first promoted this declaration with those who commonly followed their example as a rule, carried this part of the declaration affirmatively; and when we came to the second clause touching the repayment of such as should bring in money [f. 154b] or maintain and provide horses, MR. WALLER showed that this providing of arms and money would in the issue draw on a civil war which would destroy the law, which did put a difference between man and man, and so all in the issue must come to a parity and confusion. Divers spake after him, but especially MR. STRODE took great exception at what Mr. Waller had said, alleging that he had laid an aspersion upon the house in saying that we went about to destroy the law. Others spake after him. In the issue I spake in effect following about 3 of the clock in the afternoon:

That I did conceive the gentleman on the other side (viz., Mr. Strode) did mistake the gentleman below (viz., Mr. Waller) in understanding that his words or meaning tended to that scope as if this house went about to destroy the law. But he told you and told you truly that if by this preparation of ours civil wars should ensue, the law would be destroyed, and we have woeful examples of it before our eyes at this present both in Germany and Ireland, which is also verified in that common maxim, *Inter armorum strepitum silent leges.*[19] And in the elder times when this kingdom was a miserable spectacle to other nations during their civil wars, you have this entered upon record in the Communia Rolls, *Barones non sederunt in scaccario propter turbas regni.*[20] And there is

18. MS: *Henry.*

19. "The laws stand mute in war." For this maxim see Cicero, *Oratio pro Milone*, 4.11. For this and several other Latin translations, the editors are indebted to Professor Kenneth Pennington of Syracuse University.

20. "The barons did not sit in the Exchequer because of the tumult in the kingdom." D'Ewes seems to be referring to the civil wars which occurred during the reign of King Stephen (1135–54), when the Court of Exchequer did not sit. The Communia Rolls comprised the ordinary business of

no doubt but that all right and property, all *meum* and *tuum,* must cease in civil wars; and we know not what advantage the meaner sort also may take to divide the spoils of the rich and noble amongst them, who begin already to allege that all being of one mold, there is no reason that some should have so much and others so little. And we see what former effects these civil broils have produced amongst the Switzers and in Germany. Let us therefore defer the entering upon such a war till we shall be drawn to it by apparent necessity; not that I would have us defer it so long till the point of the sword were come to the button, but until such a necessity come upon us as may excuse us to all the world to have repelled force by force. And whereas we here promise to satisfy men their principal with interest for the money they shall lend and to repay them what they shall lay out upon their horses, I would first desire to know how we shall be able to make this good before we promise it, because I am afraid if there be use for these forces, every man will be disabled to support his own expenses and therefore much less able to satisfy others.

Some few having spoken after me, this also passed upon the question affirmatively, and so in the issue did all the rest[21] with some alteration.

All being passed, although it were near 4 of the clock, yet SIR JOHN NORTHCOTE rose up and made a new motion, that we should declare that all these preparations were only to be employed for our defense, but so hack[22] it and hew it in the uttering as the house had much ado to forbear laughter. I stood up and spake next in effect following:

That the gentleman who last spake had spoken his own sense and mine also, though it came very hardly from him (at which many of the house laughed outright). And therefore I desired that he might be appointed to draw the same clause and to bring it in.

It was near 4 of the clock in the afternoon when we appointed to meet at 8 of the clock tomorrow morning and so rose.[23]

---

the Exchequer Court. See William Stubbs, *The Constitutional History of England* (Oxford, 1903), I, 407–09, 487.

21. Crossed out in MS: *except one clause of calling up horses out of the several counties and excusing their service there against which we.* The declaration (hereafter generally referred to as the propositions for defense) was to be considered at the afternoon conference. See G, below, and *CJ,* II, 613–14.

22. To mangle or "make a hash of" words in utterance. *NED.*

23. William Montagu, brother to Edward, MP, wrote to their father, Edward, Lord Montagu, concerning this day's session:

My Lady Sydley presented her petition to the House of Commons against Mr. Griffing, one of their members, for uncivilly assaulting her. The Commons were locked in all day, and when they were let forth, their mouths were locked up by an order that none should reveal the passages of that day. But I screwed thus much out of one of them, that he thought now it would not be long ere we should have blows, for they are resolved to fetch my Lords Lin[dsey] and Savile by force, if denied, and they had

[f. 155a]   Post Meridiem

Vide M. The Speaker between 4 and 5 of the clock in the afternoon resumed his chair.

I came into the house a little before King, the messenger who had been at York, came into the house. The sergeant at first brought him in with his mace and turned down the bar, but then considering the order of the house better, he came up to the table and laid down his mace and then went back and turned up the bar and so went himself behind the said King also nearer the door, because this being an officer of the house, he was not to be examined or give his testimony in the house as others did with the bar down and the sergeant by. He had given in a paper into the house of all the abuses offered to him at York, and he only related to the house that after the guard had held him in custody 8 hours, the king called him before him and asked to see his warrant which he showed him and then spake as is before set down on Monday, the 6th day of this instant June, and so he withdrew, referring the house to the relation which he had given in in writing.

Some other particulars passed the house, which see in Mr. Moore's journal.[24]

The lords being set and Mr. Denzil Holles and others being named reporters, they with the greatest part of the house went up to those two several conferences which the lords had desired of us in the morning.

The Lord Wharton, supplying the place of Speaker in the lords house, managed the conference[25] and showed that their lordships, having received letters from the Lord Francis Willoughby out of Lincolnshire, thought fit to acquaint the house with it, whereupon he read it bearing date at Lincoln June 6, 1642, in which he expressed his readiness and resolution to obey the commands of the parliament and sent enclosed the copy of a letter sent unto him from his majesty with the answer he returned thereto. (See the letter in print.)

[f. 155b] The Lord Mandeville then read the copy of his majesty's letter to the Lord Willoughby, wherein he commanded him upon his allegiance to forbear any further proceeding with the training or mustering of any persons in that county, promising him pardon for what had been past and threatening, if he should proceed, he would call him to an account for it as a disturber of the peace of the kingdom. This letter was dated at the court at York June 4th, 1642.

---

many votes about raising of horse, and how acceptable it would be if any would bring in horse or arms; and how that they now see the King intends to levy war against the Parliament, [and] they must provide to defend themselves. God bless us all.

HMC, Buccleuch MSS, I, 305. Though the account is generally accurate, no order appears in *CJ* concerning locking either doors or mouths.

24. For proceedings omitted by D'Ewes, see *CJ*, II, 613–14.

25. D'Ewes has omitted that part of the conference concerning the propositions for defense. For Wharton's report to the lords, see *LJ*, V, 120.

The Lord Mandeville then read the copy of the said Lord Willoughby's answer sent to his majesty, in which he excused himself that he could not recede from what he had begun without perpetual dishonor and so humbly craved his majesty's pardon. (See the letter in print.)[26]

The Lord Wharton then showed that the lords had passed a vote for securing the said Lord Willoughby, by which they declared that they would interest themselves in his lordship's case.[27]

The Lord Mandeville then read the Earl of Warwick's letter to the lords bearing date at Brentwood June 7, 1642, being almost verbatim the same with that read this morning in the house from Sir Thomas Barrington and others[28] and is also imprinted, only in this letter was a petition from the captains and the lieutenants of the troops which assembled that day at Brentwood touching their resolution to defend [the] king's person and the parliament. (See it in print.)[29]

The next thing read by the Lord Mandeville was the letter sent by the 9 lords at York directed to the right honorable the Speaker of the lords house in parliament, being as followeth:

My lord. We whose names are here underwritten have received a summons dated the 30th of May to appear the 8th of June at the bar. We are come hither to York at this time to pay a willing obedience to his majesty's command signified by letters under his own hand, which command remains upon us still. And so we rest,
From York this 5 of May 1642. Your lordship's affectionate servants,

Hen. Dover	Northampton
Grey of Ruthin	W. Devonshire
C.[30] Howard	Monmouth
Tho. Coventry	R. Rich
Arthur Capel	

(The letter is dated May 5, but it should be June 5.)[31]

And lastly were the propositions from the Scottish commissioners read by the Lord Mandeville, by which they showed that they understood that there were 8000 of their army now landed in Ireland and in great want of money, victuals, and other provisions, having received but one month's pay, and that 20,000£

---

26. For the three letters see *LJ*, V, 115–16. Wing, W 2860.

27. See *LJ*, V, 117.

28. See above, n. 2.

29. For the letter from Warwick to his brother, the Earl of Holland, the petition from the Essex militia, and parliament's declaration in response, see *LJ*, V, 117–18, 119. Wing, W 2860.

30. MS: *W*. Charles Howard, Viscount Andover.

31. For the letter see also *LJ*, V, 115. Wing, L 1613. It had been prompted by an order of 30 May requiring several lords who were at York to return to the parliament on 8 June. The lords resolved to communicate the letter to the commons because it concerned "the Safety of the Kingdom, and the very Being of Parliament." See *LJ*, V, 92, 119.

was due to them for the brotherly [assistance][32] and 14,000£ for the pay of the soldiers.

And lastly the said Lord Mandeville read a paper sent to the said commissioners out of Scotland, in which they showed that some of their nation in Northumberland born postnati which were rated to the poll money as aliens, which they desired the parliament to consider of and to provide remedy according to their great wisdoms.[33]

The conference being ended, MR. DENZIL HOLLES made report of that part of it which concerned the Lord Francis Willoughby, and the clerk read his letter to the lords, the copy of the king's letters to him, and his answer to it. Then MR. HOLLES delivered in the vote which the lords had made for the securing of the Lord Willoughby, and we passed the same.

Upon the motion of SIR HENRY VANE, the younger (being son-in-law to Sir Christopher Wray, one of the deputy lieutenants of Lincolnshire), moved that we might pass the like vote for the security of the deputy lieutenants who were there with the said Lord Willoughby, which was done accordingly, and we further voted that the lords should be desired to join with us in the same vote.

We appointed to meet at 8 of the clock in the morning and rose about 7 of the clock at night.

GAWDY

[f. 130a]   Wednesday, the VIII of June

A letter from Brentwood from the deputy lieutenants, June the 7, that the companies that appeared there were very complete. That there appeared volunteers. 'Tis but a fourth part of the county. This is to be printed.

[f. 130b] Resolved, that the chamberlain[34] of London shall have 600£ for receiving and paying the million and 80,000£.

Resolved, that he shall have 2s. 6d. in the 100£ that he shall receive and pay hereafter.

A letter from Sir Matthew Boynton to Sir William Constable from York, June the 4. That the reason why there were not more hands to the Yorkshire petition[35]

---

32. See *PJ*, 2: 270.

33. For the two Scots papers, see *LJ*, V, 116. The postnati were those born in Scotland after the accession of James I to the English crown.

34. Actually the chamberlain's clerk, Edward Hodgson. *CJ*, II, 612.

35. For the petitions see 6 June, n. 7. Boynton's letter appears in *CSPD, 1641–43*, pp. 334–35. There are only ninety-three signatures to the petition to the king, which is preserved in HLRO, Main Papers.

was because there was a mistaking in the following the country to a wrong place, but it be necessary to have hands to it, there will be hands enough.

SIR JOHN EVELYN, a report, to make a declaration of the reasons of the propositions, which declaration he readeth. The houses doth declare that whosoever shall bring in either money, plate, or horses for the defense of the parliament shall do an acceptable service. That the measure of every man's proportion shall be accepted. That he shall have use for his money or plate that lendeth and shall have allowance for the charge of their horses and shall be discharged of finding horses in the country. Sir John Wollaston and others[36] to receive the subscriptions. Those that dwell within 80 miles of London shall bring in his money subscribed within a fortnight after notice and the rest within 3 weeks. That commissaries shall value the horses and arms so raised and the time they have been employed.

[f. 131a] A message from the lords, they desire a present conference about a letter received from Lincolnshire from my Lord Willoughby of Parham and some propositions that came to him from the Scots and likewise some propositions that came to him from some lords from York. We will answer them by messengers of our own.

MR. PYM, that an information hath been given him and some others that there is one now out of town that is able to inform you of a matter of great consequence. He desire the party may be sent for.[37] That he may not yet name the man nor the matter.

Resolved, that the Speaker shall send a private warrant for such a man as Mr. Pym shall name to him to be brought up in safe custody.

Ordered, that he shall speak with nobody but in presence of the messenger.

A message from the lords, they desire this committee may consider how the magazine that's come from Hull may be placed in the Tower. 'Tis assented to.

A message from the lords, they desire an addition to the conference concerning some letters they have received out of Essex. We will answer by messengers of our own.

The lords and commons doth declare that whosoever shall lend any money or plate or shall provide horses or arms for the peace of the kingdom shall [f. 131b] do an acceptable service to the parliament. This voted.[38]

A petition of the Lady Elizabeth Sedley, that she was drawn to a solitary

36. Thomas Andrewes, John Towse, and John Warner. See Appendix E. All four were aldermen. Towse, Warner, and Wollaston were members of the London militia committee; Andrewes, Towse, and Warner served as treasurers for the act for reducing Ireland. See *PJ,* 1: 362, 486, and 495, n. 8. These four men "became Parliament's leading financiers and financial administrators between 1643 and 1645," according to Pearl, *London,* p. 210.

37. Possibly John Griffith, the younger.

38. This is the first part of the first proposition for defense of the kingdom. See below.

house under color of seeing jewels at Madam Nurse's, which was the house of John Griffith, a member of this house, who offered violence to her person and honor. She desire he may not go out of the kingdom and that she may have liberty to take her course against him.

A committee to consider of the Lady Sedley's petition and to consider of the privilege of parliament.

Ordered, that Mr. Griffith shall appear here before Monday.

2 clause.[39] That no man shall be prejudiced by the smallness of the proportion, so he show his affection to the service.

3. That whosoever bringeth in money, plate, or horses shall be repaid with allowance of 8 percent, for which they shall have the public faith of the parliament.

4. That Sir John Wollaston and others to receive the money and plate and any 2 of them to give their acquittances for the same.

5. That commissaries be appointed to enroll the horses and what time [f. 132a] they came in and to have 2s. 6d. a day allowed them.

6. That whosoever bringeth in money, plate, or horses doth his duty therein, and the lords and commons engage themselves to bear them out in it.[40]

7. That all within 80 miles of London shall bring in their money, plate, or horses within a fortnight after notice and the rest within 3 weeks.

8. That because all men cannot have their money, plate, or horses presently, therefore those about London shall presently subscribe before those entrusted for the militia of London what they will provide.[41]

Lastly, that whatsoever is brought in shall not be employed to any other ends than aforesaid and that by the direction of the lords and commons. All this for the public peace of the king, kingdom, and parliament.

Resolved, that this shall be the declaration.

Resolved, that we shall desire the lords to join with us in this declaration.

[f. 132b] In the afternoon.

SIR HENRY VANE,[42] that he was with my lord admiral about stopping the ports that Mr. Griffith may not escape.

King, the messenger, when he came to his majesty, he bade him read it, who said 'twas illegal because the cause was not expressed. 'Twas against the Petition of Right.

---

39. This is the second part of the first proposition for defense. Gawdy's numbers 2 through 6 should be 1 through 5. For the text see Appendix E.

40. Gawdy has omitted proposition 6.

41. Gawdy has greatly condensed this proposition. Crossed out in MS: 8. *That whosoever shall bring up any horse hither shall be discharged of so many horses as they are charged with in the country.* See above, n. 21.

42. Probably Vane, Jr., former treasurer of the navy.

MR. HOLLES, a report from the conference. A letter from my Lord Willoughby to the lords of the readiness of that county of Lincoln about the militia. A letter from the king to my Lord Willoughby to forbid him to put it in execution. His answer to the king, that what he did was by virtue of the ordinance which was for his majesty's service. That my lord keeper and my Lord Banks[43] approved of it and made deputy lieutenants. A vote of approbation of my Lord Willoughby by both houses.

HILL

[p. 89]   Wednesday, June 8

A letter come from Essex sent by Sir Thomas Barrington and the rest of the deputy lieutenants.

At Brentwood the ordinance for militia put in execution. 5 companies of trainbands meet, numbers full, arms complete, one of the companies double. A 6 company appeared of 500 volunteers. There were but 4 companies of trainbands appointed to meet there. Those arms that were defective by the taking away of their arms for northern expedition were supplied by volunteers.[44]

SIR JOHN EVELYN made a report concerning finding horses, money for a defensive war, etc.

1. A declaration of the reasons of these propositions. Recite king's intention to levy wars against parliament and hath already begun it, etc. [p. 90] How the authority of parliament is vilified and scorned, etc.[45]

[1.] Lords and commons, whosoever shall bring in any money, plate, etc., or underwrite to maintain horse or foot shall be held an acceptable service, etc. 2. Whosoever shall do, etc., shall have their money repaid with interest at 8 percent and full recompense for charges. 3. Treasurers appointed. 4. Commissaries appointed to value horse and arms for this service. Account appointed from enrollment; 2s. 6d. per diem appointed to be paid. 5. Lords and commons engage themselves by parliament to secure them. 6. That money may be brought in with[in] fortnight after notice.[46]

43. Lord Littleton was lord keeper of the great seal; Sir John Banks, chief justice of the Common Pleas.

44. Crossed out in MS: *York, June 4, Sir Matthew Boynton's letter.*

45. This portion, which should not be numbered, is from the preamble to the propositions. See Appendix E.

46. This should be proposition 7.

D'EWES

June 9, Thursday, 1642

The Speaker came a little after 8 of the clock. MR. MOYLE delivered in a petition for one Mr. Huckmore, etc.[1] See Mr. Moore's journal. I was present at a great part of the service of the day.

Vide M. also till the very conference.[2]

Between 12 and 1 we went up to a conference to satisfy the lords touching those words in the declaration passed yesterday that the king had summoned other counties to assist him besides Yorkshire. Mr. Denzil Holles did manage it and acquainted the lords with such proofs and informations as had led us to put it in and so left it to their lordships' judgment whether they thought them sufficient or not.[3]

After the free conference ended and the Speaker's resuming his chair, Sir John Wollaston, one of the aldermen of London, and Captain William Gibbs were called into the house and commanded by the SPEAKER not to go to York whither the king had sent for them but to stay in the town and attend upon the militia. (It was done with their own good liking that they were enjoined to stay.)[4]

Upon the motion of SIR HENRY VANE, the younger, and my seconding him, it was ordered that the committee for the navy should take the accounts of those masters of the ships who brought the arms and ammunition from Hull and had now lain about 3 weeks upon the Thames without unlading them and that they might be paid what was due to them, and the said committee were appointed to meet this afternoon at 3 of the clock in the Court of Wards.

Upon MR. LOWRY's motion it was ordered that whereas the town of Cambridge had contributed above 230£ to the relief of Ireland, there might 30£ out

---

1. A master and servant, both named Gregory Huckmore, summoned on 21 May for cutting down woods despite an order of restraint, were committed to the Tower "for disobeying and contemning" the orders of the house. *CJ*, II, 582, 614.

2. For proceedings omitted by D'Ewes, see G and H, below; and *CJ*, II, 614–15.

3. The words in question appear in the first part of the preamble to the propositions for defense. See Appendix E. For a report of the conference, see *LJ*, V, 121.

4. Gibbs, a councilman, and Wollaston were members of the London militia committee and involved in the monopoly for the manufacture of gold and silver thread. Pearl, *London,* pp. 320, 329. For the king's letter of 6 June commanding their presence in York and parliament's order of 14 June that they remain in London, see *LJ*, V, 131.

of it be allowed to distribute amongst such poor as were come to that town out of Ireland.

One Robert White, a printer, being first called in to the bar and examined and after to receive his judgment, was sent to the King's Bench prison and was to be indicted at the bar of that court for printing a letter of news out of Ireland very scandalous to the Scots there sent against the rebels.[5]

Sir Robert Rich and Mr. Page, two masters of the Chancery, brought this message from the lords between one and two of the clock in the afternoon, that their lordships desired a present conference by a committee of both houses in the Painted Chamber if it might stand with the conveniency of this house touching some alterations and additions they had made to our declaration.[6] They being withdrawn, we agreed to meet presently, which the SPEAKER related to the said messengers being again called in. We then appointed Mr. Denzil Holles and the rest to be reporters, who were managers at the former conference. I went not up to the conference nor returned to the house after it was done.

The lords in that conference agreed with us in all particulars in the declaration.[7]

Post Meridiem

The house sat in the afternoon. Vide M. and the clerk's book.[8] The Portugal ambassadors were with me.[9]

GAWDY

[f. 132b]   Thursday, the IX of June

Mr. Huckmore and his man kneeling at the bar are sent to the Tower for disobeying an order of this house.

[f. 133a] MR. PYM, a report from the former conference.[10] A letter from my Lord of Warwick to my Lord of Holland, that a 4 part of the county of Essex

5. See 8 June, n. 7. For White see Henry R. Plomer, *A Dictionary of the Booksellers and Printers Who Were at Work in England, Scotland, and Ireland from 1641 to 1667* (London, 1907), p. 193. For White's role in printing this pamphlet, see *CJ*, II, 613, 615.

6. The propositions for defense. Whitfield and Glanville were the messengers, according to *LJ*, V, 121.

7. Following the conference Holles reported various amendments to the propositions, which were recommitted. A third conference was held in the afternoon. *CJ*, II, 616; *LJ*, V, 122.

8. See *CJ*, II, 616–17.

9. The ambassador, Antonio Dalmada, was about to return home. See *LJ*, V, 120.

10. The previous day's conference concerning Essex.

appeared very complete, and that there was a company of 500 men appeared under Sir Thomas Barrington's younger son being volunteers. A petition from some commanders of Essex to the lord lieutenant and deputies, that they will engage themselves to the king and parliament, whom they desire should know so much their proceedings in Essex is approved of by the lords and commons.[11]

MR. HOLLES, that he hath a note of brass pieces, pistols, muskets, and powder that is coming from Amsterdam into the north.[12]

MR. PYM produce a letter from Amsterdam, that ambassadors were coming from Holland but are suddenly stayed. That Tromp is commanded to lie before Dunkirk. That there are 20 ships newly come out of Spain that is feared are for Hull. That 2 of the States rid all night to the prince. That Tromp should have brought over the ambassadors.[13]

MR. FIENNES, that his father[14] had a letter from beyond sea, that there were 20 ships from Denmark put into Hull.

Resolved, that Mr. Wilmot, Mr. Ashburnham, Sir John Berkeley,[15] and Captain Legge, [f. 133b] and Sir Thomas Aston, all delinquents of this house, shall be sent for to York.

That the lord mayor of York and sheriffs shall be required to be assistant to our order that come for the persons above-named.[16]

MR. PYM, that my lord admiral was with the States ambassador, who know-

11. Captain Robert Barrington was one of the twelve signers of the Essex petition. *LJ*, V, 118. Warwick was lord lieutenant of the county.

12. For the king's need for arms, see Clarendon, *History*, II, 212.

13. On 6/16 June Zuanne Zon, Venetian secretary in the Netherlands, wrote to his government:

The government have once again directed the ambassadors for England to set out at the first opportunity. But the queen, seeing that affairs there have become somewhat favourable for her husband, is persuaded that their offices may prove of scant advantage to her house and does not urge their departure. She intimates that it is better to wait and see whether affairs there will straighten themselves of their own accord without the application of more vigorous remedies.

Zon added that Joachimi was to be

ambassador to the Parliament, and the other two to the king, so that the treatment of those most complicated differences may be conducted with more satisfaction to the parties . . . The queen cannot swallow this, considering it too prejudicial to the royal dignity, and as she wants this deleted from the instructions to the ambassadors she does not display much eagerness for their departure.

See *CSP Ven., 1642–1643*, pp. 76–77. Martin Harpertzoon Tromp was admiral of the Dutch fleet.

14. Viscount Say and Sele.

15. Sir John Berkeley, MP for Heytesbury, Wilts, in the Short Parliament, had like Wilmot, William Ashburnham, and Legge been involved in the army plots. See *Roy. Off.*, p. 25; and Gardiner, *History of England*, X, 28, 42. *DNB*. In 1641 Aston had been ordered to attend the committee for customers and then sent for as a delinquent for not appearing. See Coates, p. 257; and *CJ*, II, 179, 189–90, 337. Biographies for each of these men appear in *Roy. Off*.

16. Sir Edmund Cowper had been appointed mayor by the king upon his removing the court to York in March, thus supplanting Sir Christopher Croft. See Francis Drake, *Eboracum: or the History and Antiquities of the City of York* (London, 1736), p. 366; and Charles Brunton Knight, *A*

eth nothing of the information only Tromp was commanded to lie before Dunkirk. That the reason why the ambassadors came not over was because one of them fell sick, but by this time he believeth they are at York.

Resolved by question, that the house think it fit that the members of the house shall presently declare what money, plate, or horses they will provide;[17] and such as shall not declare themselves, a committee be appointed to receive their particular answers and report them to the house.

A message from the lords, that upon the last conference[18] they desire to know what proofs we have that the king summons other counties and that there should be rewards offered to such as will serve him. We will send an answer by messengers of our own.

A message from the lords, they desire a present conference concerning some additions and amendments in the paper we sent them last night. 'Tis the last clauses. 'Tis assented to.

[f. 134a] MR. HOLLES, a report from the conference. My Lord Wharton told us that in the 7th proposition a little alteration with an addition: That what is done is for maintenance of the Protestant religion,[19] the king's authority, person, and dignity, the laws of the land, and privilege of parliament. 'Tis committed.

The house sat at 4 a clock, but I was not there.

HILL

[p. 90]   Thursday, June 9th, 1642

At Mardyke near Dunkirk with provisions of munition and men, a design for Hull. Irishmen, Jesuits, etc., pretending for Ireland.[20]

House sent to the lord admiral to prevent it.

A declaration[21] of captains and lieutenants in Essex delivered at Brentwood at the putting the militia in execution. To the lord lieutenant and deputy lieuten-

---

History of the City of York (York, 1944), p. 465. Croft, not Cowper, should have been noted as mayor in *PJ,* 1: 42. The sheriffs were Thomas Caley and John Calvert. *Sheriffs,* p. 233.

17. Cf. *CJ,* II, 615: "Ordered, That the House be called To-morrow Morning, the first Business after Prayers: And that the Business concerning the Members declaring themselves, what Horse or Plate they will bring in, shall be then resumed."

18. I.e., the conference held the day before concerning the propositions for defense. The lords now requested a conference on this point. See above, n. 3.

19. This alteration was made in the ninth proposition. See *CJ,* II, 616; and Appendix E. This was the second conference of the day concerning the propositions. See above, n. 7.

20. "Information was this Day given of a Ship laden with Ammunition and Arms, riding before the Fort of Mardec near unto Duynkirke, bound for Ireland."*CJ,* II, 614.

21. The petition from Essex was part of Pym's report of the previous day's conference. See G, above.

ants confided in by the houses of parliament. We grieve[22] to see the heart and actions of the king, declining his own professions and protestations, following the counsels of wicked men, and declining the counsel of his parliament. We protest[23] to defend the high court [of] parliament and their members and therein his majesty's person. Subscribed by 6 captains and 6 lieutenants.

[p. 91] A ship of ammunition, of brass ordnance, muskets, pistols, match, powder, etc., bought at Amsterdam to be transported to the north of England.

Ordered, that we send to the lord admiral to prevent the coming of them and to the Dutch ambassador to see that nothing be done to the disturbance there by them. Letters come from Amsterdam date June 2 from some that are entrusted in the service.

Other letters, the Spaniards because of distraction in England have a design for England. Many ships now lie at Dunkirk.

Lord Say received letters from Flanders, in which writ 20 ships were coming from Denmark to Dunkirk for Hull.

Lords to be desired that a warrant may be sent from the lords to apprehend the Earl of Lindsey if he be present in Lincolnshire and exercise any power against our militia.[24]

22. The word is "bleed" in *LJ*, V, 118.
23. The word is "promise" in *LJ*.
24. Sir Edward Ayscough had notified the house "That the Earl of Lindsey will be in Lincolneshire To-morrow, at the Training and Mustering of the Train Bands, with his new Commission." The lords agreed that Lindsey should be brought up to the parliament. *CJ*, II, 615.

D'EWES

June 10, Friday, 1642

The Speaker came a little after 8 of the clock. Prayers being ended, after a motion or two of little moment, MR. PLEYDELL complained of a picture that was printed, in which the picture of Sir John Hotham was set out on horseback on the upper part of it and a little below the card[1] of the town of Hull and a horseman near the gate with his hat on and all the rest about him standing bareheaded, which was intended for the king, which he said was a scandalous picture and desired that it might be suppressed.[2]

Portugal ambassador's letter being in Latin read.[3]

I spake.

Mr. Denzil Holles, Sir Benjamin Rudyard, Mr. Lawrence Whitaker, and myself appointed to go to him and give him thanks.

SIR JOHN EVELYN of Wiltshire, 200£ and 4 horses.[4]

MR. WALTER LONG, 200£ in money or plate and 4 horses.

SIR PETER WENTWORTH, 100£ and 3 horses.

MR. TOMKINS.

MR. ARTHUR GOODWIN.

MR. STRODE, 50£ in money and some plate.

Vide M.[5]

During the offers of the members of the house, between the offer of MR. VASSALL and MR. VENN, Mr. Denzil Holles was sent up of a message to the

---

1. Map or plan. *NED*.

2. For the orders passed see G, below, and *CJ*, II, 617. For the incident depicted see *PJ*, 2: 223.

3. For the letter see *LJ*, V, 114–15.

4. The MPs' names and pledges, in response to the propositions for defense, were apparently recorded on a separate list, which was not incorporated in the *Commons Journal*. See Appendix F.

5. On 15 June Sir Edward Nicholas wrote to Sir Thomas Roe, MP and ambassador to Germany:

Of the Lords, 17 subscribed . . . Of the Commons, 70 subscribed . . . 33 craved time to consider . . . 50 absolutely refused, besides those that absented themselves upon dislike of the proceedings in the Houses. . . . The horse listed of both Houses are 400 and odd, the money about 18,000£.

See *CSPD, 1641–43*, p. 340. However, according to the list in Appendix F, 193 MPs subscribed. For the names of 18 lords who made pledges, see *LJ*, V, 123.

lords to let their lordships know that we had agreed to their lordships' amendments in the declaration and propositions.

Afterwards between the offers of SIR ROBERT HARLEY and MR. PURY, MR. STRODE moved that those propositions might be printed which concerned this matter, which was ordered accordingly, and then we likewise agreed that the lords should be moved that they might be printed, and Mr. Holles had notice given him of it to add it to his message.[6]

MR. THOMAS MOORE offered to find two horses. MR. PLEYDELL then stood up and showed that he could not give or lend any money or find any horses because he had given his No to all the propositions and so desired to be excused.[7]

ALDERMAN PENINGTON very rashly and against the order of the house stood up and wished that the gentleman who last spake had been gone out of the house before he had spoken.

Whereupon divers gentlemen called him[8] in question for it, showing that every man had liberty in this house to speak his conscience freely and ought not to be checked and therefore called upon him to explain what he had said. But others and many of them very honest men, conceiving that the rash speech of the said alder[man] had proceeded from a good intention, excused him, and so he was spared upon the question from explaining himself.

About eleven of the clock after about 80 had made their offers, we began to call the house, and divers as their names were called declared what they would give, in which the very liberty and freedom of the house suffered.[9]

Having proceeded as far as Derbyshire and entered into it, Sir Edward Leech and Dr. Aylett brought this message from the lords, that their lordships had appointed 6 members of their house to go into the City tomorrow in the afternoon to promote the service of the house there touching the propositions and desired that this house would name a proportionable number to join with them, and then they withdrew. We agreed to name a proportionable number to the end and purpose desired, which the SPEAKER related to them being again called in.

We then proceeded with calling the names.

When the clerk came to the borough of Sudbury in the county of Suffolk for which I served and read my name, I stood up and said: That according to the ancient orders of the house I stood up only to answer that I was here, and for the

6. Holles soon brought an affirmative answer from the lords. *CJ,* II, 617. For the text of the propositions, see Appendix E. Wing, E 1274.

7. See 8 June, n. 12.

8. I.e., Penington.

9. For the order that the house might be called for this purpose, see 9 June, n. 17. Actually about one hundred had subscribed before the calling of the house alphabetically by counties commenced, when Thomas Lane of Buckinghamshire was apparently the first to pledge. See Appendix F, n. 4. For comments concerning those who refused to pledge, see Clarendon, *History,* II, 180.

rest that I would declare my mind in due time.[10] And so the clerk proceeded till the names of all the knights, citizens, and burgesses with the barons of the Cinque Ports were read, of which many were absent. We finished them a little after one of the clock.

[f. 157b] The house named 12 members to go with the lords into London tomorrow in the afternoon.[11]

Sir George Garrett and Sir George Clarke, the sheriffs of London, were called into the house, who related at the bar that his majesty had sent his proclamation against the putting of the militia in execution with his writ to the lord mayor, who acquainted not them with it, who else would not have agreed to the publishing of it without the consent of the parliament. That the lord mayor caused it to be proclaimed yesterday without their knowledge,[12] and that they had imprisoned some of their officers for doing of it. That they were, notwithstanding the proclaiming of the same, ready still to obey the commands of the parliament and only desired our further direction. They were called in some three times, but this was the substance of what they delivered, and in the issue the SPEAKER by direction of the house told them that whereas divers former orders had been made both for their direction and indemnity, he wished them to proceed upon them, and that for their further security there should be a new order upon this new occasion.[13] That the house had commanded in their name to declare that they took notice of their great respect and service to this house and to the public and did for the same return them hearty thanks, and so they lastly withdrew and departed.

Sergeant Major General Skippon, Alderman Atkins, Alderman Wollaston, and divers common councilmen of the City of London, being all of them of the committee for the militia in the said City,[14] came into the house, and there the said Sergeant Major General Skippon showed us that the said committee thought themselves bound in duty to acquaint this honorable house with what had passed yesterday by reason of the publishing of a proclamation against the militia, the dangerous consequence of which they thought fit and worthy for the consideration of this house, although they themselves were resolved to go on constantly and cheerfully with the execution of the militia. Mr. Fowke, one of

10. On 11 October D'Ewes did indeed pledge £100, £50 to be paid "presently" and £50 more to be sent up "out of the Country." He was then given a month's leave. *CJ,* II, 803.

11. This joint committee for "Advancement of the Propositions," of which Sir John Evelyn (probably of Wiltshire) was a member, was also to "receive the Answers of such as have not declared themselves in the House." In addition, the MPs for London were to request the lord mayor, Sir Richard Gurney, to call a Common Hall the next day. *CJ,* II, 617, 618.

12. For the announcing of the king's proclamation in the City, see *LJ,* V, 122, 123–24.

13. "Ordered, That the Sheriffs of London and Middlesex do continue to give out their Warrants for the Bringing down of Guards to attend both Houses, as formerly they have done." *CJ,* II, 617.

14. For the makeup of the London militia committee, see *PJ,* 1: 361–62.

the Common Council, spake next him and showed that notwithstanding himself and all the said committee were fully persuaded that this militia was settled according to the fundamental laws of the realm, yet they could not tell what operation the publishing of the late proclamation yesterday might have in respect of others, and therefore they did desire this honorable house speedily to take into consideration some means and way for the prevention of any mischief or inconvenience that might arise thereby, and so they withdrew. Whereupon we resolved to give them thanks for their great care and fidelity and to let them know that we purposed tomorrow morning to take into consideration some means and course how to prevent all mischief that might arise thereby, which the SPEAKER related to them being again called in.

And then it drawing near upon two of the clock and I seeing that several persons were endeavoring to make new motions,[15] I withdrew, and the house rose a little after two of the clock.

GAWDY

[f. 134a]   Friday, the x of June

Resolved by question, that the scandalous picture of the king supposed and Sir John Hotham shall be burnt by the hand of the hangman. The party to be inquired out and punished that made it.

MR. PYM giveth an information that the Lord Cottington hath many arms in his house at Hanworth.[16]

A letter in Latin to this house congratulating the happy union between the King of Great Britain and the King of Portugal. He[17] is going away and send a compliment to the house. Four members sent to give him thanks for his respect.

The house called, and every man to declare what money, plate, or horse he will provide for the defense of the king, kingdom, and Protestant religion, which was a freewill offering.

[f. 134b] A message from the lords, they have appointed a committee of six of their house to go into London about the contribution of money, plate, or horse as aforesaid and desire that we would appoint a proportionable number to join with them. 'Tis assented to.

15. See *CJ*, II, 618.
16. Hanworth House in Middlesex was one of several properties owned by Lord Cottington, former chancellor of the Exchequer. This information concerning arms was confirmed after the outbreak of the civil war when his house was looted by parliamentarian soldiers. See Martin Havran, *Caroline Courtier: The Life of Lord Cottington* (London, 1973), pp. 154–55.
17. The ambassador, Antonio Dalmada.

D'EWES

[f. 157b]   June 11, Saturday, 1642

The Speaker came between 8 and 9 of the clock. MR. CROMWELL moved that the committee appointed to take the answer of such gentlemen of the house as would contribute to the propositions might have power to receive the said answers or any two of them, which was ordered accordingly.[1]

MR. DENZIL HOLLES moved that such members of the house as would contribute to this work for the defense of the king and parliament and desired to conceal their names might have them concealed, but this was opposed by divers men as very derogatory to the work, and in the issue it was rejected by the house.

MR. RIGBY delivered in certain instructions which were for the direction of himself and the other deputy lieutenants which were to go into Lancashire for the mustering a/[2]

[f. 158a] I went out of the house between 10 and 11 and returned again just about 11.[3]

MR. DENZIL HOLLES had a little before made report of that part of the conference had on Wednesday last, June 8, with the lords which concerned the letter received from the 9 lords at York, which bore date there May 5, 1642 (it should have been June 5), which was there read by the Lord Mandeville.[4] It was in debate when I came into the house what vote we should pass against the said lords, and at last after divers had spoken to it, a question was proposed by the SPEAKER to vote that the said 9 lords had offered an affront to the parliament by

---

1. "Ordered, that the Committee appointed to consider of Propositions for the Defence of the Kingdom . . . shall be the Standing Committee to receive the Answers of such Members of the House as did not declare themselves Yesterday." *CJ*, II, 619. Doubtless the committee for defense, which had formulated the propositions. See 8 June, n. 9.

2. On 9 June these MPs had been ordered to go as deputy lieutenants to Lancashire to execute the militia ordinance: Alexander Rigby, John Moore, Ralph Ashton of Middleton, MP for Lancashire, and Richard Shuttleworth, the elder, MP for Preston. The instructions were now submitted to a committee. See *CJ*, II, 598, 615, 619; and Ernest Broxap, *The Great Civil War in Lancashire (1642–1651)* (Manchester, 1973), pp. 31–34.

3. For proceedings omitted by D'Ewes, see G, below, and *CJ*, II, 619.

4. See 8 June, n. 31.

going to York and not returning back, being summoned, and that they might be justly suspected to further a civil war in the kingdom.[5]

Divers being against the putting of this question, the house was divided upon it. And the SPEAKER named Mr. Denzil Holles and Mr. Cromwell tellers for the Ayes, who sat still and were in number 109. I was one of them. The tellers for the Noes were Mr. Waller and Mr. White,[6] secretary to the Earl of Dorset, being in number 51. They went out of the house, and having lost it, the question itself was put and carried affirmatively also.

Some new questions were proposed and debated as to seize the arms of these 9 lords and to send for the other lords at York to appear, but they were in the issue laid aside.

Sir Robert Rich and Mr. Page, two masters of the Chancery, having stayed without about an hour, were called into the house between eleven and twelve of the clock and brought this message from the lords, that their lordships did consent with us that the members of their house being commissioners for the Irish affairs should sit every afternoon.[7]

Mr. Cromwell was sent up to the lords to desire them to sit awhile, who soon after returned and brought word that the lords would sit.

Sir Robert Harley was sent up to the lords to desire a conference, etc., touching the letter of the 9 lords sent from York, which was delivered in a conference from their lordships to us.

SERJEANT WILDE made report from the committee to whom the instructions for the deputy lieutenants of Lancashire had been recommitted, which the clerk having read passed the house.

SIR ROBERT HARLEY returned and brought word that their lordships would give us a meeting presently in the Painted Chamber. Mr. Glyn and others were appointed to manage the conference and to desire the lords to join with us in the vote we had passed this morning and to take order that no preparations of these lords either by arms or otherwise might be for the prejudice of the public. The said managers about one of the clock and divers of the house went away to the conference.[8]

---

5. For the resolution see Verney, *Notes,* p. 180, and *CJ,* II, 620.

6. John White, MP for Rye. Keeler, p. 390. It should be noted that in this division the Ayes, who generally were compelled to leave, retained their seats. Subsequently a committee, including Hill, was named to draw up an impeachment against the nine lords. *CJ,* II, 620.

7. Earlier Strode had gone to the lords to request that the commissioners should sit every afternoon, "notwithstanding that the House may chance to sit." *CJ,* II, 619. Cf. *PJ,* 2: 128, n. 15.

8. The lords subsequently issued an order "to stay all Arms, Horses, and Ammunition that are going to Yorke." *LJ,* V, 126. For the rest of the day, see G, below, and *CJ,* II, 620–21.

GAWDY

[f. 134b]   Saturday, the xi of June

That the committee for drawing the propositions shall meet in the inner Court of Wards, and that any 2 or more of them shall take the names of those that shall contribute. To meet this afternoon and so from time to time.

Instructions for Mr. Ashton, Mr. Moore, Mr. Rigby, and Mr. Shuttleworth, sent as committees into Lancashire for putting the militia in execution and quieting that county.

Sir Walter Erle, that there is good information that at Amsterdam the jewels are rejected. That there is ordnance and other ammunition there providing for England. Great expedition is used.[9]

Three of Marquess Hamilton's servants say they are going on Monday next in a ship to York for the king's service. That they have dangerous weapons.

[f. 135a] Resolved, that the 9 lords going from the parliament without leave, after such time as the parliament had declared that the king seduced by ill counsel intend to make war against the parliament, and do still continue at York notwithstanding the summons and commands, is a high breach of privilege and intend as much as in them lie to[10] desert the parliament.

The house divided whether this question shall be now put. The Ayes that sat were 109. The Noes that went out for deferring it, of which I was, was 51.

The letter of the 9 lords read. That they had received a command from the king to wait on him at York and that the same command lay still upon them, which was the cause why they did not obey the summons of the lords.

A message from the lords, they consent as is desired that the commissioners for Ireland shall sit daily.[11]

Mr. Pym offereth a letter to the house that was wrote from one Curson of Oxfordshire to my Lord Cherbury.[12] 'Twas left upon the threshold of his house

9. Erle reported that from the sale of the jewels £16,000 had been sent to England, the residue used for the purchase of arms and ammunition in Amsterdam, a list of which appears in *CJ.* Subsequently Erle and Ashe (probably Edward, a successful London merchant) were appointed to go into the City "to inquire after the Truth of this Information," and Dowse, secretary to the lord admiral, was to request that he send ships to guard the coast near Newcastle "to prevent the Coming in of any Arms." *CJ,* II, 619; Keeler, pp. 90, 158. See also *LJ,* V, 126–27, 130, 131.

10. Crossed out in MS: *promote a war in the kingdom.* The resolution in *CJ,* II, 620, concludes: "And that the said Lords therein did as much as in them lay, that the Service of Parliament might be deserted; and are justly suspected to promote a War against the Parliament."

11. Crossed out in MS: *Resolved, that a message be sent to the lords that the residue of the lords may be summoned to appear that are at York without leave.* Cf. D, above.

12. Lord Herbert of Cherbury, father to Richard Herbert, MP, had at various times served as MP, sheriff, and ambassador to France. See *Roy. Off.,* p. 187. *DNB.*

in the night. [f. 135b] The effect was to advise his lordship as a friend to provide for himself, for upon the 29 of June the king would come with horse and foot to the parliament. This I had from Mr. Noble.

A committee to go into Cheshire for the same reasons that the committee is sent into Lancashire.[13]

Sir Walter Erle at a conference deliver the informations that we have received from good hands from Amsterdam concerning the jewels and ammunition before recited.[14]

At a committee in the inner Court of Wards in the afternoon for subscriptions. I promised to lend fifty pounds freely for the defense of the king, kingdom, and Protestant religion conjunctively, not to be divided.[15]

HILL

[p. 91]   Saturday, June 11th, 1642

These 9 lords—Northampton, Devon, Dover, Monmouth, Rich, Coventry, Capel, Howard, Grey of Ruthin—voted to be suspected promoters of the civil war.

It appears upon examination that there are bought in Holland by one Webster employed for that service 4 pieces of battery at 18-pound bullet, 6 fieldpieces, 2 mortar pieces, 3000 saddles, 200 barrels of powder.[16]

13. On 9 June Sir William Brereton and Sir Thomas Smith had been named to go to Cheshire. However, on this day Smith was given leave to go "about a Fortnight hence, to the Bath." He apparently never returned to the house and in January 1644 was disabled for royalism. *CJ*, II, 615, 621; Keeler, p. 342.

14. For a report of the conference, including two letters from Amsterdam on which Erle's report was based, see *LJ*, V, 126. Wing, T 3475. It was ordered that the information should be communicated to the City.

15. Probably because Gawdy's pledge was made at the committee, it does not appear in the list of pledges until 13 June. On 10 June Hill had pledged £100. See Appendix F.

16. One hundred barrels, in *CJ*, II, 619. For John Webster's role in the sale of the crown jewels, see *PJ*, 2: 388.

At this point a portion of Hill's journal, not directly related to proceedings in the House of Commons, has been omitted. It includes material concerning honors created by parliament, Justice Heath and the imprisonment of Sir John Heveningham et al., the king's role in passing laws, the commission of array, and the coronation oath. Precedents are cited from such sources as Coke's Institutes and the Parliament Rolls. Hill's next entry appears on 23 June.

D'EWES

June 13, Monday, 1642

The Speaker came about 8 of the clock. After prayers several things passed. Vide M.[1]

About 9 of the clock MR. VASSALL made report from the committee appointed to that end how we might have our own corn transported for the relief of Ireland,[2] which held a long debate, and in the issue it was voted and ordered that the commissioners appointed for the affairs in Ireland should for the time to come contract only with English merchants to transport English corn into Ireland.

The SPEAKER showed that great quantity of arms were now sending down into Lincolnshire to one Mr. Charles Dymoke,[3] for which he desired a warrant from him for the transporting of them, which he would not grant in regard of the quantity of them till he had first acquainted this house therewith. So it was soon yielded to and ordered.

The LORD GREY moved that he might have license also to send down arms into the country,[4] and it was ordered that the Speaker should give him a warrant for transporting the same.

MR. PYM made report of the last part of the conference had with the lords on Wednesday last, being the 8th day of this instant June, touching the Scots propositions and the paper received out of Scotland touching the payment of poll money by the postnati of that kingdom within the county of Northumberland. And so it was ordered in the first place that some speedy course should be advised upon for the paying in of the said money, and for the latter point after a little debate it was resolved by the house that the postnati of the kingdom of Scotland were to pay as natural-born subjects and not as aliens.

MR. RIGBY moved for some addition to be made to the instructions of the deputy lieutenants for Lancashire, which was added accordingly.[5]

---

1. For proceedings omitted by D'Ewes, including a letter from the committee in Lincolnshire, see G, below, and *CJ*, II, 621.
2. For this committee see *PJ*, 2: 318; and *CJ*, II, 571, 600, 605.
3. A staunch royalist. *DNB* under Sir John Dymoke.
4. I.e., to Leicestershire, where the estate of his father, the Earl of Stamford, was located. *CJ*, II, 621. This request was doubtless prompted by the recent interference with the execution of the militia there. See G, below.
5. For the instructions see *LJ*, V, 128–29.

Sir Peter Wentworth was sent up to the lords to de/[6]

Serjeant Ayloff and Sir Nathaniel Finch, two of the king's serjeants, brought this message from the lords, viz., that their lordships desired a present conference touching letters they had received from the Lord Francis Willoughby out of Lincolnshire and touching the lord lieutenant of Ireland his going into that kingdom, and so they withdrew.

MR. ASHE[7] delivered in a copy of a letter sent from Mr. Alexander Popham to Sir Francis Popham, his father, being now at Littlecote in Wiltshire. It bore date at Dunster[8] (in Somersetshire) June 7, 1642, in which he gave notice to his father that next day after his departure that the said petition was sent to divers places to get hands to it.

That Sir Francis Doddington sent it to Bath to George Williams and Dick Chapman and desired them to further it by getting hands to it in that city.

That Sir Charles Berkeley's friends and Sir Ralph Hopton's labor for the advancement of it.

That the mayor of Bath,[9] having received the said petition, called a council of the town and sent to him (viz., the said Mr. Alexander Popham) to ask his advice what they should do therein.

That he told them that great aspersions were laid upon the parliament in it and so advised them not to have any hand in it.

(In a postscript.) That this petition was yet laid aside in Bath.

Within the letter was a copy of the said petition, being most dangerous against the proceedings of the parliament.

Mr. Strode was sent up to the lords to desire a conference about the said letter and petition when it might stand with their lordships' conveniency.[10]

The messengers from the lords called in, and the SPEAKER delivered unto them the sense of the house, which was that we would give them a present meeting as was desired.

6. Wentworth was to carry up the above-mentioned instructions and to request a conference concerning both the execution of the militia ordinance in Leicestershire and letters received from Lincolnshire. See G, below, and *CJ*, II, 621.

7. Doubtless John Ashe, deputy lieutenant for Somerset.

8. MS: *Hunster*. The date should be 11 June. For the letter and the Somerset petition, see *LJ*, V, 133–34. Wing, S 4652 (for the petition). The existence of this petition, which called for an accommodation with the king, had been rumored in the house on 5 May. See *PJ*, 2: 280.

9. For Doddington, a former sheriff, see *Roy. Off.*, p. 112. Doddington, Berkeley, and Hopton, MP, were leading members of the royalist gentry in Somerset. See David Underdown, *Somerset in the Civil War and Interregnum* (Newton Abbot, 1973), pp. 29, 32. The name George Williams appears as "Wilb." in *LJ*, V, 133, and has been lengthened to Wilb[erforce] in F. T. R. Edgar, *Sir Ralph Hopton* (Oxford, 1968), p. 29. The mayor of Bath was probably William Chapman. See C. W. Shickle, "A Copy of the Chamberlain's Accounts of the City of Bath" (bound typescript, BL, 1905), I, No. 85.

10. For proceedings omitted by D'Ewes, see G, below.

MR. STRODE made report from the lords that they would presently give a meeting in the Painted Chamber.

[f. 159a] The house appointed the Lord Grey to manage that part of the conference which concerned Leicestershire and Mr. Denzil Holles and Mr. Pym that part which concerned Lincolnshire and Mr. Ashe that part of it which concerned the information/[11]

MR. HAMPDEN moved that Sir Neville Poole might have liberty go to into the country in respect of his health, which was granted, and SIR NEVILLE POOLE himself expressed his resolution to stick to the parliament.[12]

SIR HARBOTTLE GRIMSTON showed that the high sheriff of Essex[13] had sent for him out to the door and had delivered to him a writ with a bundle of proclamations which came to him about the militia, which was laid aside till the conference were ended, at which conference I was not present.

The lords' conference began first, and that was managed by the Lord North, who after a few words spoken gave the Lord Mandeville the Lord Willoughby's letter sent to himself dated at Horncastle June 11th, 1642, which the said Lord Mandeville read, in which he showed that since his last letter to their lordships he had received another letter from his majesty of which he sent a copy enclosed, in which his majesty did inform him that he was mistaken in his last letter in what he had written concerning the Lord Littleton and the Lord Chief Justice Banks their consent to the ordinance of the militia;[14] therefore, he desired their lordships to inform him fully of the truth thereof whether he were mistaken or not. That Sir Philip Tyrwhitt and Sir William Pelham, two former deputy lieutenants, had written to him denying to deliver up the magazine, whose letters he had sent.

Then the Lord Brooke read the king's letter to the said Lord Willoughby bearing date at the court at York June 7, 1642,[15] in which his majesty still admonished him to desist from the unlawful execution of the ordinance of the militia, promising pardon for what was past. That he did err in saying that the lord keeper had voted for it for he was against it, and for the Lord Banks he never meddled in it, to which end the lord keeper had written to him to satisfy

11. Doubtless the information from Somerset.

12. Since no leave for Poole is noted in *CJ*, it is not clear whether he took his leave or remained in the house.

13. Robert Smith. *Sheriffs*, p. 46.

14. For Lord Willoughby's statement concerning their alleged approval of the militia ordinance, see G, 8 June, and *LJ*, V, 116. In May Sir John Banks had written from York to Giles Green, MP for Corfe Castle: "The king is extremely offended with me touching the militia; saith that I should have performed the part of an honest man in protesting against the illegality of the ordinance; commands me upon my allegiance yet to do it. I have told him it is not safe for me to deliver anie opinion in things which are voted in the housses [*sic*]." Quoted in *DNB* under Sir John Banks.

15. For the text see *LJ*, V, 127.

him. That the two houses misled by some factious spirits did in this arrogate supreme and boundless authority to themselves.

The Lord Littleton's letter to the Lord Willoughby bearing date at York June 7, 1642, was read next, in which he showed that he wrote to his lordship to rectify his error concerning the militia, for when the ordinance first passed, he was not in the House of Peers, and when it passed the 2d time, he voted against it.[16]

Then were read the two letters sent from the two deputy lieutenants, viz., the first dated at Stainfield 8 June 1642 from Sir Philip Tyrwhitt to the Lord Francis Willoughby, in which he desired to be excused from delivering up that part of the magazine which was in his custody, being commanded the contrary by his majesty's letters sent to the sheriff of that county himself and the other former deputy lieutenants. Then was read the other letter dated at Brocklesby 4 June 1642 being sent from Sir William Pelham to the same Lord Willoughby, in which he denied also to deliver up the said magazine without his majesty's consent, hoping that there would shortly be a better intelligence between his majesty and the parliament.[17]

The Lord North then showed that the lords thought it fit to refer the consideration of these letters to the select committee of lords and commons touching Mr. Beckwith and the breach of the privilege of parliament,[18] and that they had appointed their committee to sit this afternoon and desired that we would do the like with our committee.

The Lord North further showed that the lord lieutenant of Ireland was now very ready and willing, as he had been formerly, to go into Ireland and thereupon read certain propositions which he had made and delivered to the lords in writing, wherein he desired a considerable sum of money with other particulars fitting for his journey, knowing it was now a time of action in respect of the season of the year and that therefore he was loath to be absent any longer from his charge.[19]

16. For Lord Littleton's letter see *LJ*, V, 128. On 14 June Lord Robartes reported to the lords that perusal of the Journal book indicated that in March the lord keeper had acquiesced on several occasions concerning the militia ordinance. See *LJ*, V, 134; and HLRO, Main Papers. Wing, E 2837. The editors are indebted to Professor Conrad Russell for calling their attention to this pamphlet, a copy of which is preserved in BL, Loan MSS, Portland and Harley Papers, 29/46, Packet 12. Harley was a member of the committee for affairs in Yorkshire. See below, n. 18.

17. D'Ewes has interchanged the contents of these two letters, which appear in *LJ*, V, 128. For Tyrwhitt see GEC, *Baronetage*, I, 58. For Pelham, older brother to Henry Pelham, MP, see Keeler, p. 300, and *Roy. Off.*, p. 290.

18. The joint committee concerning affairs in Yorkshire. *CJ*, II, 608, 609. Before the conference the lords had ordered that Lord Willoughby should seize the Lincolnshire magazine and that Tyrwhitt and Pelham should be sent for as delinquents. *LJ*, V, 127.

19. On 10 June Leicester had reported to the lords that "divers Censures and hard Opinions are . . . abroad, because he is not gone into Ireland"; he then requested them to inform the

The conference being ended, upon MR. ARTHUR GOODWIN's motion it was ordered that the house should recommend Sir William Fenton,[20] that had lost his estate in Ireland, to the adventurers for that kingdom to be a reformado captain of horse (that is, to have a captain's place if any should fall).

ALDERMAN PENINGTON seconded a new motion made by MR. BLAKISTON about a report to be made concerning two scandalous ministers concerning Newcastle.[21]

[f. 159b] I thereupon stood up, scarce suffering Alderman Penington to speak to the end of his motion, and showed that it was according to the orders of the house that a business moved a little before the conference began by a worthy gentleman who sat by me (viz., Sir Harbottle Grimston) touching the high sheriff of Essex might be now taken into consideration as was then appointed in respect that the matter did very much concern the service of this house, he having brought to us the very writ in which the proclamations were sent unto him from his majesty to be published in that county against the militia,[22] and therefore I desire that that business might be taken next into consideration and some course settled in it.

Whereupon, two or three having spoken after me, the said sheriff being named Mr. Smith was called in; and the SPEAKER, having before his coming in received direction from the house, told him that he had very well discharged his duty in acquainting the house with such a writ as he had received from his majesty which concerned the parliament and that the house had commanded him to give him thanks for his care expressed therein and further showed him that the said proclamation had been declared by both houses to be against law and that he was not bound to publish anything against law though it came to him under the broad seal. And so the house dismissed the said high sheriff but still kept the said writ and proclamations.

Upon the motion of MR. PYM and others, order was taken for the payment of Sir John Hotham and the garrison of Hull.

MR. HAMPDEN made report from the committee appointed to that end that they had drawn a declaration of thankfulness to be sent to the Scots for their late petition preferred to the council there notwithstanding his majesty's letter of

---

commons that it was his desire to be "dispatched into Ireland." Following the conference the commons resolved to join with the lords "to desire his Majesty to expedite such Instructions he shall please to give the Lieutenant of Ireland, that his Journey may not stay upon those Instructions." See *LJ*, V, 123, 129–30; and *CJ*, II, 622.

20. The matter was referred to the committee for Irish adventurers, and on 6 July Fenton, who was the Earl of Cork's brother-in-law, was recommended for a post in Munster. *CJ*, II, 622, 656. *DNB* under Sir Geoffrey Fenton.

21. George Wishart and Yeldard Alvey.

22. For a similar case see D, 37.

accusation sent thither against the parliament here, which was ordered to be printed after it had been read.[23]

Upon MR. WALTER LONG's motion Mr. Denzil Holles was added to the committee nominated on Saturday last to prepare an impeachment against the 9 lords now at York whose letter had been read in this house upon Wednesday, the 8 day of this instant June, and the said committee was appointed to meet this afternoon at 2 of the clock[24] in the inner Court of Wards.

Upon the same MR. LONG's motion Mr. Arthur Goodwin was added to the committee which was appointed to take the answer of the members of the house concerning their bringing in of money or providing horse for the defense of the parliament.[25] SIR WALTER ERLE thereupon made report from the said committee of several men's answers, members of the house, some of which refused to do anything but by the joint consent of the king and parliament. Others promised to lend money or find horses, the whole number of horses which he made report of being 12. MR. LOWE, being present in the house, offered to lend 100£, which was accepted by the house.

MR. PYM made report of the conference had even now with the lords, and the clerk read all the several letters in such order as they are before set down, and then the house voted that our select committee formerly appointed to [f. 160a] consider of Mr. Beckwith's attempt to have surprised Hull, and they were appointed to meet this afternoon in the Painted Chamber with the select committee of the lords.

And in respect that the Lord Willoughby had expressed in his letters to the Lord North read at the said conference, amongst divers other particulars, that some gentlemen of the House of Commons had informed him that the Lord Banks had appointed his deputy lieutenants for the Isle of Purbeck, it was desired by MR. PYM that such gentlemen as knew anything in that particular would declare themselves. Whereupon SIR WALTER ERLE said that the Earl of Salisbury told him that the Lord Chief Justice Banks had appointed him[26] one of his deputy lieutenants, viz., for the Isle of Purbeck, of which place being a part of Dorsetshire he was appointed lord lieutenant by the ordinance of parliament.

MR. BLAKISTON moved again, as he had done a little before just upon the ending of the conference, to have had Mr. Corbet made report touching the two scandalous ministers of Newcastle, but it being very late, the house did order

23. See 6 June, nn. 19, 21. For the declaration of thanks, see *CJ*, II, 623–24. Wing, E 1340.

24. Three o'clock, in *CJ*, II, 622. For the committee see 11 June, n. 6.

25. See 11 June, n. 1.

26. I.e., Erle. Banks was lord lieutenant for the Isle of Purbeck, Salisbury for Dorset. Both had joined the king at York, though Salisbury returned to the House of Lords on 23 June. See *LJ*, V, 151, 156. For Banks's appointment see *PJ*, 1: 356, 361.

that the said report should be made tomorrow morning, at what time we appointed to meet at 8 of the clock and rose between one and two.

GAWDY

[f. 135b]   Monday, the XIII of June

My LORD GREY of Stamford, that Leicestershire men were obedient to the militia except one hundred,[27] which promised to come in.

Informations against Captain Wolseley and others that hindered the militia in Leicestershire. They are sent for as delinquents, and we are to desire the lords to join with us in sending for them.[28]

[f. 136a] A letter to Mr. Pym from the committee in Lincolnshire, June the 11. That the city of Lincoln and towns thereabout came in cheerfully except the mayor and dean and chapter.[29] So much of that county as hath appeared performed the service cheerfully. Sir William Pelham and Sir Philip Tyrwhitt refused to deliver up the magazine. A letter from the king to Captain Booth,[30] that he should not stir out of that county but come to him when he sent for him and that he should not march out of the county.

A message from the lords, they desire a present conference concerning a letter which they have received from my Lord Willoughby out of Lincolnshire and about my lord lieutenant going into Ireland.

MR. ASHE, that there is a petition getting out of Somersetshire to be preferred to the parliament, which is that the government of the church may be as it is till the synod by advice of parliament. To do our utmost power to allay these distempers. To take the king's message of the 20 of January[31] into consideration, with many other things.

27. "Six Hundreds were summoned, whereof Five appeared." *LJ*, V, 130.

28. For letters concerning the execution of the militia in Leicestershire on 8 June, see *LJ*, V, 132–33.

29. For the letter see *LJ*, V, 131–32. The mayor, John Becke, had at first complied with the request of the parliamentary committee not to publish the king's proclamation against the militia ordinance, but shortly thereafter he fled to York and submitted to the king. See J. W. F. Hill, *Tudor and Stuart Lincoln* (Cambridge, 1956), pp. 149–50. For the dean of the cathedral, Anthony Topham, see *Walker*, pp. 9, 106.

30. MS: *Moone*. According to this letter from the Lincolnshire committee, William Booth had been brought before them on 8 June for "Speeches to the Disgrace of our Service, and disheartening of the People." During their examination of him, they learned of the king's letter of 24 May, which appears in *LJ*, V, 128 and 132. For Booth see *Roy. Off.*, p. 37.

31. See *PJ*, 1: 113.

MR. HOLLES, that this petition is an arraignment of the parliament. That those that are the promoters may be sent for as delinquents.

[f. 136b] SIR SAMUEL ROLLE informeth of a seditious sermon preached yesterday at the Temple by Dr. Cressy, the lecturer.[32]

Resolved, that Mr. Cressy shall be sent for as a delinquent.

MR. LONG, that yesterday he heard something from the Archbishop of Armagh that was very offensive.

MR. SPEAKER, that yesterday he heard that in divers places in London there were divers strange sermons preached.

Resolved, that Sir Francis Doddington shall be summoned as a promoter of the Somersetshire petition.[33]

---

32. Hugh Cressy, formerly chaplain to the Earl of Strafford in Yorkshire and in Ireland, was son to Sir Hugh, justice of the King's Bench in Ireland. See *Walker*, p. 22. *DNB*.

33. Sir Charles Berkeley was also to be summoned. *CJ*, II, 622.

D'EWES

June 14, Tuesday, 1642

The Speaker came a little after 8 of the clock. I went out presently almost after prayers. I returned again about 10 of the clock.[1]

MR. PYM delivered in a petition from Captain Arthur Chichester and Mr. Hill which had been preferred to the commissioners for Irish affairs, which the clerk read, and therein they showed that they had at their own charge maintained in the north parts of Ireland since the rebellion began in that kingdom two regiments of foot and desired some consideration for the expenses for the time past and to be taken into pay for the time to come.[2] It was long debated, and the said debate was in agitation when I returned into the house, the sum of it being that all thought it reasonable that they should be considered of, and yet we were unwilling to engage ourselves further than in probability we might make good. So the whole matter was referred to a committee, with the former petitions of the Lord Clandeboye and others, to consider what was the best course to be taken therein, and a committee was named and they were appointed to sit tomorrow in the afternoon.[3]

SIR ROBERT PYE moved that we might proceed with the bill of tonnage and poundage as being a matter which most concerned, which MR. GREEN seconded and desired that MR. GLYN might make a report of certain new clauses to be added to that bill, which he did accordingly and delivered them to the clerk who began to read it; but MR. STRODE moved for the impeachment to be proceeded with against the 9 lords who had sent their letter from York, which was read on Wednesday last being the 8 day of this instant June, which MR. DENZIL HOLLES began to enter upon; but messengers having stayed without a

1. For proceedings omitted by D'Ewes, see *CJ*, II, 622.
2. Supporting letters from Lord Conway and Sir John Clotworthy were also read. On 13 June, in response to an order from the house that the commissioners "consider what Sum of Money is fit to be sent into Ulster, for the Payment of the Two Regiments there," the sum of £6000 was recommended. See CIA, 9 and 13 June; and *CJ*, II, 622.
3. For the petitions of Clandeboye et al., see CIA, 13 June. The members named to this committee, which was scheduled to meet "this Afternoon," appear several paragraphs after the information about the petitions. *CJ*, II, 622, 623. The MS CJ has a clarifying marginal note: *Committee for the petition, Chichester and Hill, etc.* The committee will generally be referred to hereafter as the committee for the Chichester petition.

good while some moved to have them called in and others opposed it, which made me speak in effect following:

That it was a constant rule in the house that if a message did attend without from the lords, they were to be called in before any new business was to be entered upon, and yet if I did conceive that the present business would admit a speedy dispatch, I should not move for calling in the said messengers, but because this may hold a long debate and I am sure we may speedily dispatch the messengers, for either they bring a message without desiring of a conference and then the performance of it end the business, or else they come to desire a conference and then it is in our power to answer them that we will send messengers of our own, and therefore I desire they may be called in, which was done accordingly without any further dispute.

Sir Robert Rich and Mr. Page, two masters of the Chancery, brought this message from the lords, that their lordships had appointed their select committee of 9 touching the propositions of raising of horse and money to sit this afternoon in the Painted Chamber and desired that the select committee of this house might meet with them,[4] and that their lordships did further desire a present conference by a committee of both houses if it might stand with the conveniency of this house touching a letter sent by the Earl of Warwick to the Earl of Holland [f. 160b] which concerned the fort of Landguard Point (in the county of Suffolk).[5] We answered that the committee should meet at the time appointed and that for the conference, etc., answer by messengers of our own.

The messengers being gone out, MR. HAMPDEN showed that the Lord Paget, lord lieutenant of Buckinghamshire, had withdrawn himself and that a general muster was to be there on Friday next and so desired that either some new lord lieutenant might be named or that the deputy lieutenants might have an order from both houses to proceed with it. Divers spake to it, and we all wondered at the Lord Paget's mean and unworthy spirit to go to York to the king, having already mustered the county, etc. Mr. Hampden and others were appointed to draw [this order].[6]

We then proceeded with the debate touching the impeachment of the 9 lords now at York with the king, in which besides the impeachment of them for their high misdemeanor of absenting themselves without license and not returning upon summons, we desired first that the lords would declare that they were causes of civil wars if any did ensue and that they would adjudge them to forfeit

---

4. I.e., the committee for defense (propositions). For the lords' committee, named on 10 June, to receive the answers of absent lords concerning the propositions, see *LJ*, V, 123.

5. The letter concerned "the great Decay and Want of repairing" of the fort. *LJ*, V, 126.

6. See *CJ*, II, 623. D'Ewes's words, written along the edge of the page, cannot be deciphered.

their estates to make satisfaction to the commonwealth. Divers spake to it. I moved in effect following:

That I might cite several precedents to be our direction at this time, but that I was loath to expose record to be vilified by any (this I meant by Mr. Strode), although this present impeachment being contrary to all former precedents, it will be sufficient only to show the errors of it. For I will not now dispute whether the punishment proposed here be proportionable to the offense or not, but this I say, it belongs only to us to carry up the impeachment and not to give the judgment also ourselves but to leave that wholly to the lords. Indeed sometimes when the House of Commons hath carried up an impeachment and the lords have been slow in proceeding upon it, they have sent up to them to quicken them and spur them forward but never directed them what judgment to give. Besides this offense chiefly concerns matter of custom and usage in the lords house which much differs from ours, for I have ever observed it in all their Journals[7] that any peer may be absent where his own consent and the king's concur together in it without asking leave of the other peers, but for the members of this house they cannot be absent without the license of this house. So as I desire that we may carry up this impeachment singly to the lords and not at all prescribe them what or how to judge in this particular, which is a direct breach of the privileges of their house.

Divers spake after me and seconded what I had said, so as in the issue we laid aside all the latter part of the impeachment upon the question according as I had moved.[8]

Sir Ralph Whitfield and Sir Nathaniel Finch, two of the king's serjeants, brought this message from the lords, that their lordships desired in the next conference by a committee, etc., that they might give us an account how far they had consented to the Scottish propositions.[9] They being withdrawn, we resolved to answer also that we would send an answer by messengers of our own, which the SPEAKER related to them being called in, and so they withdrew and departed.

Sir Robert Rich and Mr. Page, two masters of the Chancery, came immediately in after the two other messengers were gone forth and brought this message from the lords, that their lordships had appointed the select committee of their house touching the Yorkshire petition to sit this afternoon in the Painted Chamber at 4 of the clock and desired that our committee might do the like; and

7. For the treatment of proxies in each of the Elizabethan parliaments, see Sir Simonds D'Ewes, *A Compleat Journal of the Reign of Queen Elizabeth*, ed. Paul Bowes (London, 1693), Preface and passim.

8. It was resolved that "speedy and exemplary Justice be done upon these Lords" and that "this Declaration at the End of the Impeachment, shall be laid aside." *CJ*, II, 623.

9. I.e., the treaty with the Scots concerning their participation in the war in Ireland.

they also showed that the lords had appointed two of their house to speak with the merchant strangers this afternoon about money and desired us to name a proportionable number to accompany them. They withdrew. We named Captain Skinner and 3 others,[10] appointed our select committee to meet at the time desired, and the messengers being again called in, the SPEAKER told them that the committee would meet at the time and in the place appointed and that we had also named a proportionable number to go into London, and so the said messengers withdrew and departed.

Upon MR. PEARD's motion Mr. Denzil Holles was appointed to carry up the impeachment against the 9 lords tomorrow morning.

MR. HAMPDEN delivered in the order which himself and two or three other members had been appointed to draw, which was read and allowed,[11] and he was appointed to carry it up tomorrow morning to the lords; and it was further ordered that he should then carry up also the declaration of both houses touching their thankful acceptance of the respect of the Scottish nation [f. 161a] expressed in their late petition to the Privy Council there.[12]

SIR WILLIAM BRERETON moved that the deputy lieutenants of Cheshire might be enjoined to go down and attend the service of the house at the ensuing mustering there, and that the lord lieutenants and deputy lieutenants of Flintshire and the county of Denbigh,[13] being counties near adjoining, might be appointed to appoint their muster and training there at that time because it would much conduce to the advancement of the militia in Cheshire.

So it was ordered that the deputy lieutenants in Cheshire should be enjoined to go down,[14] and upon MR. GLYN's motion the deputy lieutenants of the two Welsh shires were appointed to attend that service.

Upon MR. ARTHUR GOODWIN's motion the deputy lieutenants of Buckinghamshire were likewise enjoined to go down to the general muster there on Friday next.

Upon MR. BODVEL's motion Sir Thomas Middleton, being a deputy lieutenant,[15] had liberty to continue in the country, and the said Mr. Bodvel was ordered to write to him to that effect.

10. The commons, who took the initiative in this matter by sending an earlier message to the lords, actually named six members to their committee. The merchant strangers, having been ordered to meet on this day by the lord mayor, subsequently subscribed £5000 for Ireland, according to a report in the lords house. See G, 3 June; *CJ*, II, 616–17, 618; and *LJ*, V, 135.

11. See above. For the order empowering the deputy lieutenants to execute the militia ordinance in Buckinghamshire, see *CJ*, II, 624.

12. See 13 June, n. 23.

13. Lord Feilding was lord lieutenant for both counties.

14. See G, 11 June. Brereton is the only deputy lieutenant actually named in the instructions, which appear in *LJ*, V, 134–35.

15. Middleton was MP and deputy lieutenant for Denbighshire. *CJ*, II, 623.

MR. HOLLES complained of a book containing a collection of sundry petitions of counties and other places on the behalf of episcopacy which seemed to be published in print by his majesty's authority,[16] but the publisher of it had prefixed an epistle before it full of scandal to the proceedings of parliament, and therefore he desired that the further examination of it might be referred to the committee for printing and that the printer might be sent for before them, which was ordered accordingly.

We appointed to meet at 8 of the clock tomorrow morning and rose between one and two of the clock in the afternoon.

GAWDY

[f. 136b]   Tuesday, the XIIII of June

One at the bar saith that yesterday the carrier of Doncaster carried 500 sword blades down to York.

Ordered, that a warrant issue forth for the staying these arms.

MR. HOLLES, a report of the impeachment of the 9 lords that went to York that wrote the letter to the Speaker of the House of Peers.

A message from the lords, they sent us word that they had appointed the committee of 9 concerning the raising of horse to meet in the afternoon and desire our committee may meet with them. They desire a present a [sic] conference about a letter sent from my Lord of Warwick to my Lord of Holland about Landguard Point.

[f. 137a] The first part is assented to. The 2 part we will send an answer by messengers of our own.

Resolved, that the declaration that is in the impeachment shall be laid aside but the impeachment is to go up.[17]

A message from the lords, that at the next conference they may tell us how far they have agreed to the Scots articles. 'Tis assented to.

A message from the lords, that the committee the lords appointed about the Yorkshire petition meet at 4 a clock. They desire ours may do so too. 'Tis assented to.

16. Wing, A 4072. The pamphlets were published under the name of Sir Thomas Aston.
17. See above, n. 8.

D'EWES

The Speaker came about 8 of the clock and after prayers complained of 2 pamphlets, the one intituled *New Orders of the Parliament of Roundheads*, etc., and the 2d *The Speech of a Warden to the Fellows of His Company Touching the Great Affairs of the Kingdom*, etc., both being extreme scandalous against the parliament.[1] Then were some stationers called in who had complained thereof to the Speaker and justified the printing of the one and selling of the other. And then they withdrew, and one Stephen Bulkley was sent for as a delinquent,[2] and some others were summoned to appear. It was then severally moved that some members of the house might withdraw presently and draw an order which might be confirmed by both houses for the inhibiting of the printing of such scandalous pamphlets, and Mr. John White of the Middle Temple and 2 or 3 more were named of the committee, and as they were called upon to go out of the house about drawing the said order, I moved in effect following:

That I did desire they might specify in the beginning of the said order what care the two houses had formerly taken to suppress such libels as these, and particularly that the fellow who had forged a scandalous letter to be sent by the queen's majesty out of the Low Countries had been set on the pillory and otherwise punished.[3]

Upon which motion of mine I was nominated to be one of the said committee that was to withdraw and awhile after went with them accordingly into the second inner Court of Wards commonly called the council chamber where we debated the matter awhile, and then wanting several former orders we could proceed no further at this time but adjourned ourselves to meet at the same place at 3 of the clock tomorrow in the afternoon.

I returned not presently into the house but first accompanied Mr. Hampden to the lords house where he delivered three several messages, etc., and I afterwards returned into the House of Commons about 10 of the clock.[4]

1. Wing, N 693, S 4862.

2. On 1 February Bulkley had been ordered to attend the committee for printing because of another pamphlet concerning the Roundheads. When summoned in June, he fled to York, taking his printing press with him. See *CJ*, II, 408, 624; and Plomer, *Booksellers and Printers*, pp. 38–39.

3. Probably William Umfreville. See *PJ*, 2: 97.

4. For Hampden's messages see D, 76; G, below; and *LJ*, V, 135–36. For other proceedings see *CJ*, II, 624–25.

Upon MR. STRODE's motion Mr. Denzil Holles was appointed to carry up the impeachment against 9 of the lords at York, and a word or two were added to it.

We proceeded with the clauses or articles which were to be added to the bill of tonnage and poundage, and in the issue we agreed to them all except 2 or 3, which were recommitted to the former committee to be considered of.

[f. 161b] Upon MR. SOLICITOR's motion the subcommittee for the bill of tonnage and poundage[5] was appointed to sit *de die in diem,* and upon the SPEAKER's motion it was further ordered that we should proceed with the bill itself upon Friday next in the morning.

Mr. Denzil Holles was sent up to impeach 9 of the lords at York (whose letter see before on Wednesday, the 8 day of this instant June), which he performed at the bar in the lords house, divers accompanying him thither.

MR. NATHANIEL FIENNES moved that the lords had sent to us yesterday for a conference touching the Scottish propositions, to which we had promised to send them an answer by messengers of our own, and therefore he desired the messenger might be sent up to them to let them know that we were ready for that conference. The SPEAKER then stood up and said that there was a conference or two more desired by the lords concerning other matters.[6] Whereupon I stood up and showed:

That there had been indeed two conferences desired by the lords and by several messengers, the first concerning a letter sent from the Earl of Warwick to the Earl of Holland touching the fort called Landguard Point and the other touching the Scots propositions.

Whereupon Mr. Strode, who had been appointed the messenger yesterday, was sent up to the lords to let them know that we were ready to give them a meeting presently touching both the said particulars.

MR. NATHANIEL FIENNES showed that a petition was lately printed by the king's printer in the name of the kingdom of Scotland, whereas it had been assented unto but by 4 noblemen and one of them had since disclaimed it and the other 3 had been punished, but that they were pardoned upon agreement and promised that it should be suppressed. Whereupon the said petition which he brought in ready printed was read, and then the said MR. FIENNES desired that the printer might be sent for and commanded not to disperse any of them, which was ordered accordingly.[7]

5. This committee had been named for the previous bill. See *PJ,* 2: 186.

6. At the bottom of f. 161a, D'Ewes has crossed out his brief rough notes which he has recorded in full. One line, however, is worth quoting: SPEAKER *showed another business but had forgot what. I showed it and afterwards more particularly.*

7. Wing, P 1824. The king's printer, Robert Barker, or his deputies were to attend the house. *CJ,* II, 625. Barker was confined to the King's Bench prison as a debtor from 1635 until his death in 1645 according to Plomer, *Booksellers and Printers,* p. 14, and *DNB.*

MR. OLIVER CROMWELL moved that an order might be made that the justices of peace in Yorkshire who had any of the arms of the papists of that county in their custody should not deliver them to any person whatsoever but by authority from his majesty signified unto them by both houses of parliament, and that no freeholder's arms who was not a papist ought to be taken from them without their consent,[8] all which was ordered accordingly.

Serjeant Ayloff and Sir John Glanville, two of the king's serjeants, brought this message from the lords,[9] that their lordships had appointed two members of their house to draw a letter presently for the recalling of the committee at York and desired that a proportionable number of this house should meet with them, and that their lordships had assented to the order for the deputy lieutenants to proceed with the mustering in Buckinghamshire with the addition of a few words only, and so they withdrew. We agreed to the addition, and then Mr. Pierrepont and 3 others were appointed to meet with the said 2 lords as was desired, and the messengers being again [called] in, the SPEAKER related to them that the house had nominated a proportionable number who should meet accordingly and that we had assented to their lordships' additions to the order.

[f. 162a] SIR JOHN NORTHCOTE moved that the petition of the greater part of the parishioners of the Savoy might be read, which was done accordingly, and therein it appeared that some 14 or 15 of them had before petitioned for one Mr. Gibbs to be a lecturer there and that now near upon sixscore of the same parish had petitioned for one Mr. Fuller to be the minister there,[10] which place had been formerly supplied by the said Mr. Gibbs under the name of a lecturer, and so desired that the said order touching the said Mr. Gibbs might be vacated, but upon SIR ROBERT HARLEY's justifying his delivering in the former petition upon which the said Mr. Gibbs was allowed, the house would at this time meddle no further with the business but proceeded to matter of more public concernment.

MR. STRODE made report that the lords would give us a meeting presently, and thereupon Mr. Nathaniel Fiennes and others were named reporters,[11] and so themselves and the greater part of the house went up to the conference, at which I was present.

8. Cf. *CJ,* II, 625: "And that the Train Bands be injoined to retain their Arms in their own Custody, according to Law." The recusants' arms had been seized "by virtue of the Ordinance for disarming of Recusants." *LJ,* IV, 384–87 (30 August 1641).

9. The lords were responding to the messages carried up by Hampden.

10. The request for Thomas Gibbs, a Puritan, to be lecturer at the Savoy chapel, situated within the precincts of the ancient Savoy Palace, had been made on 30 May. However, Thomas Fuller, the eminent church historian, received the appointment at the request of the majority of the parishioners and probably began his duties in midsummer. See *CJ,* II, 595; and William Addison, *Worthy Dr. Fuller* (London, 1951), pp. 99–100. *DNB.*

11. Fiennes is not named in *CJ,* II, 625.

The Earl of Holland began and managed that part of the conference which concerned the letter sent to himself from the Earl of Warwick and read the letter which the said earl had sent to him bearing date [blank], in which the said earl declared how much arrear was due to him for the said payment of the garrison of the fort of Landguard Point and that it was out of repair.[12]

That he understood the house had given order for the payment of the garrison of Portsmouth.[13]

The Earl of Holland spake somewhat before he read the said letter how the said fort had been committed to his charge and somewhat after of the great consequence of it, showing what great danger it would prove to let it come into the hand of an enemy.

The Lord Brooke managed that part of the conference which concerned the Scottish propositions and showed that in some three particulars their lordships dissented from us.[14]

SERJEANT WILDE moved that Mr. Denzil Holles might be desired to set down in writing the impeachment which he had this morning delivered at the bar in the lords house by word of mouth, which was ordered accordingly.[15]

SERJEANT WILDE made report of certain propositions prepared at the committee for the former propositions for the furnishing of horse and bringing in money, which were that the deputy lieutenants in every county should have power to take subscriptions of the gentry and others in each county for the defense of the kingdom.

Upon SIR JOHN EVELYN's motion it was ordered that we should desire the lords to join with us to move the lord admiral to send to Sir John Hotham to send away as many great saddles from Hull as he thought he might possibly spare.[16]

Upon the same SIR JOHN EVELYN's motion it was further ordered that such members of this house as had underwritten should bring in their horse[17] by Saturday come sennight next.

Upon MR. CROMWELL's motion it was ordered that the committee for the propositions should consider whether it were not fit to give the justices of peace power to take the subscription in those counties where there were no deputy lieutenants who had underwritten to the same propositions.

12. For more details concerning this issue, see John Louis Beatty, *Warwick and Holland* (Denver, 1965), pp. 169–70. The letter was dated 7 June. *CJ,* II, 634.

13. See *PJ,* 2: 78.

14. For the lords' proposed changes in the Scots treaty, see *LJ,* V, 125.

15. Holles was ordered to "digest in Writing the Impeachment of the Nine Lords." *CJ,* II, 626. Apparently what he had said in the lords house was not in proper form for the clerk to record it.

16. Horse arms and ammunition were also to be sent by ship to London. Evelyn carried this message to the lords the next day. *CJ,* II, 625; *LJ,* V, 140.

17. "Money or Horse," in *CJ,* II, 625.

Upon MR. PRIDEAUX's motion an additional article of instruction was passed for the deputy lieutenants of Lancashire to examine any parties that could inform them of such as should endeavor to hinder in the militia was allowed in the house, and it was ordered that we should desire the lords to assent to it.[18]

Upon MR. CROMWELL's motion that Mr. John Brograve (of Albury Lodge in the county of Hertford, Esquire) might be recommended from this house as a deputy lieutenant for Hertfordshire, it was after some debate ordered accordingly.

Upon SIR THOMAS BARRINGTON's motion it was ordered that Mr. Timothy Middleton should be recommended from this house as a deputy lieutenant for the county of Essex.

[f. 162b] MR. PYM made report from the commissioners for Ireland of some payments of money which they thought fit to have presently allowed, as 500£ for the payment of the Lord Cromwell's/[19]

MR. DENZIL HOLLES brought in the impeachment of 9 of the lords at York in writing as near as he could set it down, which he had delivered by word of mouth at the bar in the lords house this morning. And it was ordered that it should be entered in the Journal book here[20] and be carried up to the lords.

Sir Robert Rich and Dr. Aylett, two masters of the Chancery, brought this message from the lords, that the lord[s] sent down a copy of a letter to be sent to the committee at York to recall them and desired us to concur with them in it, and then they withdrew.

We read the letter, and whereas it was penned to have been sent singly from the Speaker of either house, we agreed to have it go jointly from both the Speakers. The substance of the letter was that in respect we understood that many affronts and indignities were offered to them at York, which did not only extend to the injury of themselves but to the dishonor also of both houses of parliament, we required them to return back to the parliament and yet willed them to acquaint the inhabitants of that county that we should be no less careful of their safety and well-being than when our said committee was there; and because we had made some alterations in the said draft, we thought fit to return an answer that we would send by messengers of our own, which the SPEAKER related to the same messengers being again called in, and then they withdrew and departed.

Sir Henry Vane, the younger, was sent up with the said letter to the lords to show them that we assented to their lordships and only desired that it might go

18. See *CJ*, II, 625.

19. For the payment of Lord Cromwell's troop, see CIA, 9 and 15 June, and *CJ*, II, 625.

20. D'Ewes seems to be in error here. As the impeachment charges would not be recorded in the Journal of the House of Commons, this part of the order does not appear in *CJ*, II, 626.

in the name of both houses and be signed by both the Speakers,[21] and he carried up also the additional instruction touching the deputy lieutenants of Lancashire, and the lords agreed with us in all as we desired.

Upon MR. HAMPDEN's motion it was ordered that 34,000£ should be paid to Mr. Nicholas Loftus out of 100,000£ to be lent[22] by the City of London and that he should pay it to the Scottish commissioners.

It was ordered also upon the same MR. PYM's motion[23] that 6000£ should be paid out of the said 100,000£ for the payment of the two regiments of the Lord Conway and Sir John Clotworthy (being in the province of Ulster in Ireland).

Upon MR. PYM's further report from the commissioners for the affairs of Ireland, it was ordered that Sir William St. Leger, etc., 3£ per diem from June 1 and 1£ former allowance included.[24]

Upon MR. HAMPDEN's motion it was ordered that the message of the two houses to his majesty touching the Yorkshire petition should be delivered to his majesty by our committee.[25]

Upon MR. NATHANIEL FIENNES's showing that the Scottish commissioners desired that the printers who had printed the said Scottish petition complained of this morning might be released, having submitted themselves, which was done accordingly.

MR. PYM showed that a letter was come from the Earl of Stamford to the Lord Thomas Grey, his son, which was without date.

To send up to lords tomorrow morning.

[f. 163a] Upon MR. WALTER LONG's motion the select committee for the propositions was appointed to sit this afternoon and three more added to it, of which Mr. Robert Goodwin was one.

MR. PYM, a little before the clock struck two, delivered in a letter bearing date May 13, Kinsale, 1642, being sent from Mr. Tristram Whitcomb to his brother Whitcomb, in which amongst other passages he showed that three castles in the province of Munster upon the River [*blank*][26] had been taken in by a few hundreds of our men with the loss of three men only, although the said castles were very strong, well manned, and abundantly provided with corn and other victuals. The lord president had since taken in two other strong castles near the city of Cork without the loss of a man.

---

21. For the text see *LJ*, V, 137.

22. MS: *left*. Nicholas Loftus, brother to Sir Adam, was deputy treasurer at wars for Ireland.

23. In the paragraph above D'Ewes has crossed out *Pym* and inserted *Hampden*.

24. St. Leger's daily allowance of £3 beginning on 1 June was to include his former allowance of £1. *CJ*, II, 626. For the origin of these orders, see CIA, 13 June.

25. I.e., the committee in Yorkshire. This message to the king had already been carried up to the lords by Hampden. See G, below, and *CJ*, II, 625.

26. The river Bandon. This letter, dated 30 May and 1 June, was from Tristram Whitcomb, mayor of Kinsale, to his brother Benjamin, a London merchant. Wing, W 1640.

I moved that it might be printed, and so the sense of the house was that Mr. Whitcomb, to whom it was sent, might print it.

The SPEAKER showed that the new Scottish petition complained of this day was printed by the king's own warrant, which the printer had brought unto him.

We rose between two and three of the clock in the afternoon.

GAWDY

[f. 137a]   Wednesday, the xv of June

MR. SPEAKER informeth of 2 pamphlets. One is *Orders from the Round-heads.*

MR. HAMPDEN, that our committees had not the liberty of free subjects when the great meeting was, for they were restrained. He desire they may be sent for home.[27]

Resolved by question, that our committees from York be sent for home and that the lords be desired to send for their[s].

A petition from both houses to his majesty to accept the petition of York-shire.[28]

Ordered, that the trained bands in Yorkshire shall not depart with their arms. That the lords be desired to join with us in this order.

[f. 137b] A message from the lords, they had appointed 2 lords of their house and desire us to appoint a proportionable number to join with them to draw a letter to call their committees from York. And they have agreed to give power to the deputy lieutenants of Buckinghamshire to exercise the militia in the absence of their lord lieutenant.

27. Hampden's reference is to the parliamentary committee in Yorkshire and the meeting on Heworth Moor.

28. This message urged the king's acceptance of the petition which Sir Thomas Fairfax had tried to present on 3 June. In addition, it included the main points of the petition itself. See *LJ,* V, 137–38. Wing, E 1574. Cf. the petition as it appears in *LJ,* V, 109–10.

D'EWES

[f. 163a]   June 16, Thursday, 1642

The Speaker came about 8 of the clock. CAPTAIN VENN delivered in 2 abstracts of two letters bearing date at Amsterdam June 9, 1642, in which it was showed that Mr. John Webster did still provide arms at Amsterdam and brass pieces for land service. That the said arms were put up in 36 cases and were to be transported in the bark of Robert Sheld. They further showed that the Lord Goring did provide the said arms and ammunition for the king by the order of the queen.[1] That the said Mr. Sheld's bark was to come for London, and so they desired that some course might be taken for the staying of the said arms.

SIR WALTER ERLE moved that there were certain letters sent from Mr. John Webster, who was to provide these arms at Amsterdam, which had been taken, which holding four in his hand sealed up desired that some course might be taken by the house for the opening and viewing of them, and so it was ordered that he himself should do it.[2]

The SPEAKER showed that he had received letters out of Northamptonshire and from York,[3] which he desired might be read. Whereupon the clerk read first the letters dated at Northampton June 14, 1642, being sent from Sir Christopher Yelverton, Sir Gilbert Pickering, Mr. John Crew, and Mr. Richard Knightley, 4 members of our house and 4 deputy lieutenants of that county appointed to put the militia there in execution according to the ordinance of parliament,[4] in which they showed:

That they had that day begun the mustering or training for that county at Northampton, where the trained bands of that division had appeared complete in their arms, and that there had besides a company of volunteers near upon 500 showed themselves with their arms, and another company conceived to be of a greater number of volunteers without arms did likewise show themselves, and that what was here written by their friends could not be contradicted by their

1. Having accompanied the queen to Holland in February 1642, Goring negotiated the sale of the crown jewels in order to buy arms. GEC, *Peerage*. One of these letters, from Henry Whitaker to Sir Nicholas Crispe, is preserved in the Bodleian Library, Oxford, Tanner MS 63, f. 49r.

2. Actually a committee of four, including Venn and Erle, was to peruse the letters. *CJ*, II, 626.

3. Neither the letters from Northamptonshire and York nor the report by Pelham which follows are noted in *CJ*.

4. See 8 June, n. 3.

enemies. That the lord lieutenant[5] and themselves did purpose to go tomorrow to Kettering, the next day to Oundle, to proceed with the training of the rest of the county in/

[f. 163b] York, June 13, 1642, from Sir Hugh Cholmley, Sir Philip Stapleton, and Sir Henry Cholmley.

That the said county was so inclinable to peace, and they had now so little to do.
That they had not now in 12 days heard any an/[6]
Their stay there very unpleasant.

MR. HENRY PELHAM[7] brought in a note of accounts from John Browne, founder of the ordnance and shot, showing what he had provided by order of the house, viz., mortar pieces 4, petards 59, great grenadoes 368, hand grenadoes 1600, whereof there is delivered to the right honorable the lord lieutenant of Ireland and his assigns:

Mortar pieces	4	Part of these are carried away, part are at
Petards	59	my house,[8] and part are at a warehouse at
Great grenadoes for		the Steelyard at the command of the said
mortar pieces	368	lord lieutenant and his assigns, to whom I
Hand grenadoes	993	did deliver them.

Delivered to Mr. Fryer for the use of the committee for Ireland which sits in London: Hand grenadoes 200.

More remaining, beside them above delivered at the warehouse in the Steelyard, at my house of hand grenadoes 407, which are bespoken for the use of the parliament, and I do not make or cast any of these commodities unless they be bespoken beforehand.

Then followed a long narration of what brass and iron ordnance he had cast and did intend to cast and what he had laid out and that 8000£ was already due to

5. Henry, Lord Spencer. For a similar letter from Lord Spencer, whose name incorrectly appears as William, see *LJ*, V, 139. William Montagu wrote to his father, Lord Montagu: "The King hath granted a commission of array in Northamptonshire . . . There is also a new commission of the peace for that county, wherein all the Deputy Lieutenants for the Ordinance are left out." Lord Montagu was among those named as commissioners. *HMC, Buccleuch MSS*, I, 306.

6. "It is now Twelve Days since we presented Him [the king] with your Propositions, but have not as yet heard of any Thing in Return." This statement concerning the Nineteen Propositions is from a similar letter to the lords from Lord Howard of Escrick, in which he requested that the committee be recalled to London. A letter from Secretary Nicholas to Sir Thomas Roe notes that they left York on 18 June. See *LJ*, V, 138; and *CSPD, 1641–43*, p. 344.

7. Crossed out in MS: *the lawyer*. D'Ewes has inserted the first name with a caret. The list that follows had been requested by the house on 13 June. See *CJ*, II, 621. For earlier action taken by the commissioners for Irish affairs to pay Browne for ordnance provided for Ireland, see *PJ*, 2: 449, 452.

8. I.e., Browne's house. The Steelyard, located on the bank of the Thames, had been occupied for centuries by merchants of the Hanseatic League. In 1598 Queen Elizabeth took possession of it for a navy office. Henry A. Harben, *A Dictionary of London* (London, 1918), pp. 549–51.

him, without the payment whereof he could not proceed with the intended works. So it was ordered that he should receive his money as soon as the timber in the forest of Dean should be sold.

The clerk read the order, which is printed, that such members as were absent this day should forfeit 100£ for the service of Ireland, and then he proceeded to the calling of the house.[9] Many members were excused upon the first calling who were absent in the service of the house or sick. I went out when the names of the members were almost all called. In my absence the defaults were called again, and when it came to Sir Christopher Hatton, although SIR ROBERT HATTON, his uncle, showed that he had received a letter from him showing that he was sick, yet the house was divided upon it, and 122 would have excused him and 142 carried it in the negative.[10]

After I came into the house, they were in debate about what further punishment should be laid upon such as were absent over and above the fine of 100£ which we had formerly voted should be laid upon them for that they should pay 100£. The vote passed without any great difficulty, and the question was whether before they were admitted they should make their excuse to a committee to be appointed by the house to that end and purpose, and divers spake for it and divers against it. MR. WALTER LONG moved it.

[f. 164a] Ayes went. Mr. Pierrepont and Sir John Evelyn, tellers.

Noes sat still. I one of them. Mr. Nicholas Weston and Sir John Strangways, tellers.[11]

I went out a little after one of the clock. The house sat till after 2 of the clock and rose between two and 3 and appointed to meet at 4[12] in the afternoon.

SIR JOHN EVELYN moved a proposition to get men to subscribe horses and money in the counties, which was passed, there being few above 40 in the house.[13]

Post Meridiem

The Speaker [came] a little after 4 of the clock. As soon as he had resumed his chair, SIR WALTER ERLE made report touching the letters of Mr. John Webster, which he was appointed to open, and show/[14]

SIR JOHN EVELYN moved that the proposition allowed in the morning to be

9. For this order see 2 June, n. 4. The list of absentees appears in Appendix G.
10. Sir Robert Hatton was one of the tellers for the Ayes. *CJ,* II, 626.
11. For this and a subsequent vote, see G, below.
12. Three o'clock, in *CJ,* II, 627.
13. For five propositions or instructions concerning taking subscriptions, see *CJ,* II, 627.
14. "That they find not much considerable in them," except bills of exchange to Adrian May for £3000, "in case the former Bills came not to his Hands." *CJ,* II, 627.

sent into the counties might be sent up to the lords, and he was appointed to carry it up.[15]

MR. NATHANIEL FIENNES made report of that part of the conference which was managed yesterday by the Lord Brooke touching some alterations which had been made by the lords in the Scottish propositions which came to them from us, and upon hearing those alterations, the house assented to the lesser but differed in the greater and resolved to continue in the former vote and resolution we had made.[16]

Mr. Denzil Holles was sent up with the impeachment in writing against 9 of the lords at York, which he had delivered yesterday by word of the mouth at bar [sic].[17]

Sir Samuel Rolle was sent up to desire a free conference touching the matter of the late conference concerning the Scottish proposition; this latter part of the message was added upon my motion, which had also been omitted.

MR. GREEN made report of those additional articles to be added to the bill of tonnage and poundage, which had been recommitted, and being read were allowed by us.

Sir Peter Temple, being one of those 51 members[18] who had been fined in the morning 100£ for his absence and being ordered/

[f. 164b] SIR HENRY VANE, the younger, delivered in the petition of the shipmasters who brought the ammunition from Berwick.[19]

Before this business was determined, Mr. Pym and the rest of the committee[20] came in who went out to receive Sir Peter Temple's excuse.

Sir Peter Temple admitted in and 100£ remitted.

It was then ordered that the petition should be referred to the committee for the navy.

MR. CORBET, petition of mayor of Arundel. Mr. Harman.[21]

15. In addition, he carried up the names of four commissaries "to inroll and value the Horse and Arms, to be raised according to the Propositions." *LJ*, V, 140.

16. See *CJ*, II, 627.

17. For a digest version of the impeachment, see *LJ*, V, 141. The unabridged version, along with Holles's speech in the lords house, appears in Rushworth, IV, 737–42. Wing, H 2476 (Holles's speech).

18. Fifty, according to G, below. Forty-five names appear in Appendix G. However, in addition to Temple, five more MPs were subsequently excused.

19. D'Ewes should have Hull. *CJ*, II, 627. See below.

20. The committee for defense, which had formulated the propositions, was to take the excuses of absent members. *CJ*, II, 626. This seems a further indication that Sir John Evelyn of Wiltshire was involved both with absentees and with the propositions for defense.

21. It was resolved that the committee for privileges should be revived concerning the election dispute between John Downes and one Harman, and that the lawsuit against the mayor, James Morris, should be stayed until the committee had reported. *CJ*, II, 628. For the Arundel election see *PJ*, 1: 76, 80, 349.

Sir Robert Rich and Mr. Page.

York, 13 June 1642.

To the order of parliament of the 7 of May.[22]

SIR JOHN EVELYN made report that the lords had given consent to the proposition for raising horse and contributing money and plate in the country, with some other answers, etc.

SIR SAMUEL ROLLE made report that the lords would give a meeting presently in the Painted Chamber.

MR. RICHARD WESTON[23] moved that a member of the house was without, being one of the 51 absent in the morning, and desired to satisfy the committee. So Mr. Pym and some others withdrew to speak with him. It was Sir Thomas Mauleverer.

SIR WILLIAM MASHAM moved that one Mr. Wollaston of Waltham Abbey, the elder, had said that such as had trained lately in Essex were rebels and that there were two witnesses without that would avow it; but when they came in, they spake only concerning volunteers that mustered, that the said Mr. Wollaston should speak so of them but not of the trained, and yet notwithstanding he was sent for as a delinquent.

Sir Nicholas Crispe, who had brought the paper above-read from York signed by Sir Edward Nicholas, one of his majesty's principal secretaries/

[f. 181b] Sir Nicholas Crispe was called in again the second time and related that the Prince Elector Palatine[24] did in the garden of that house at York where his majesty lies fall into discourse with him and told him that one of the committee of London had written to him to move him to accept of the command of these 12 ships that were to go against Ireland, and that for his part he should be ready if he were desired thereunto to accept of the same. Whereupon he, the said Sir Nicholas Crispe, told his highness amongst other discourse that his majesty had denied to pass the commission for the setting out of the said ships and that the Prince Elector answered him that he did not doubt but his majesty would pass the said commission if he might command the said fleet.[25]

22. The lords' messengers brought a letter dated 13 June from Sir Edward Nicholas expressing the king's refusal to sign the commission for setting forth additional forces by sea for Ireland. See 4 June, passim; 6 June, n. 25; G, below; and *CJ*, II, 628.

23. Crossed out in MS: *the lawyer*. D'Ewes has inserted the first name with a caret.

24. Queen Elizabeth of Bohemia, mother to Charles Lewis, Elector Palatine, had written to Sir Thomas Roe in late May: "My son . . . is still with the King. I am sure you have before this the whole relation of the exploit of Hull, where my son was sorely catched in." In mid–August his unexpected arrival at The Hague was reported by Zuanne Zon, Venetian secretary in the Netherlands. See *CSPD, 1641–43*, p. 330; and *CSP Ven., 1642–1643*, pp. 133, 138–39.

25. Lord Brooke had already been named as commander on 4 June. In the ordinance for the additional sea adventure for Ireland, formulated because of the king's refusal of the commission, Crispe was among those given authority to equip the twelve ships and six pinnaces, to place in them forces of horse and foot, and to appoint the officers. *LJ*, V, 144.

SIR JOHN EVELYN showed that the committee was satisfied with the excuse that Sir Thomas Mauleverer's excuse [*sic*], which was that his wife was not well and the notice he had of the order was late.[26]

Admitted in and fine remitted.

Mr. Nathaniel Fiennes was appointed to manage the conference and went up to it and divers of the house with him and did there manage it.

After the conference ended, upon MR. PURY's motion it was ordered that the additional propositions touching raising horses and contributing money and plate should be printed.[27]

We appointed to meet at 8 of the clock tomorrow morning and rose a little after 7 of the clock in the afternoon.

GAWDY

[f. 137b]   Thursday, the XVI of June

Information from Amsterdam, that there is much provision of arms making there to be sent to York by my Lord Goring and Mr. Webster, June the 9 dated.

Letters from the deputy lieutenants of Northamptonshire, the trained bands appeared full with divers volunteers.

A letter from York from our committee, June the 13. That that county is so inclinable to peace that they think there is no need of their longer stay. They delivered our propositions to the king 12 days since. Their stay there is tedious to them. They desire leave to come home.

This day the house was called, and I think there were about 240 in the house or 260.[28]

[f. 138a] The house divided whether Sir Christopher Hatton shall be excused (who is said to be sick). The Ayes that went out that would have him spared were 122. The Noes that sat, of which I was, was 142.

Resolved by question, that a committee shall consider how this 100£ shall be levied of the absent members towards the wars of Ireland.

There are 50 of our house that had no excuses made for them.[29]

Resolved, that these 50 men shall not come into the house till they have given reasons to a committee of their absence, and they to report it to the house.

The house divided whether this question shall be put. The Ayes that went

26. The house had given Mauleverer leave to go to the country on 18 March. *CJ*, II, 486.

27. See above, n. 13. Wing, E 2589B (I 242 in the 1945–51 edition).

28. The first division reveals that, in addition to the Speaker and tellers, 264 were present, the highest attendance recorded by means of a division since 27 January. See *PJ*, 1: 191.

29. See above, n. 18.

out, of which I was, was 147. The Noes that sat, which would not have it put, were 91.

The question that no member should go out of town without leave was waived, as I heard by divers.[30] I was not there.

In the afternoon.

Four commissaries for the enrolling and valuing the horse named in London.

[f. 138b] A message from the lords, that they have received a paper under Secretary Nicholas his hand which they thought fit to send to us. That the king is unsatisfied with the names of the commanders and commission concerning the forces that are going into Ireland. That because both houses stop such moneys as are coming to him under pretense that he meaneth to levy war against his parliament, which his majesty abhor to think of, for which cause and because the City is not able to give him caution,[31] he refuseth to give way to them. Dated from York the 13 of June.

Sir Nicholas Crispe at the bar saith that he spake with Secretary Nicholas, who told him he should have the commission sealed but showed him a letter which said those forces would do more harm than good in Ireland. The commission was denied. The Palsgrave told him he was desirous to go general of the fleet for the adventurers. Sir Nicholas liked it well but knew not how the king would like it, who was moved with it and told Sir Nicholas he liked it well and on that condition would sign the commission.

30. In the division for putting this question, the Noes were 100, the Ayes 79. *CJ,* II, 627.
31. "His Majesty conceives, no Caution in London can secure Him." *CJ,* II, 628.

D'EWES

[f. 182b]   June 17, Friday, 1642

The Speaker came a little after 8 of the clock. SIR BENJAMIN RUDYARD moved that Sir Percy Herbert (a papist, being son and heir of the Lord Powis), who had been sent for as a delinquent, might be bailed.[1]

Upon SIR GUY PALMES's motion Sir George Wentworth[2] had leave to go into Yorkshire.

Sir Oliver Luke and Sir Beauchamp St. John were enjoined to go into Bedfordshire to the mustering and training there, being deputy lieutenants.

Upon MR. DENZIL HOLLES's motion Sir Robert Hatton had leave to go into the country for a month.

Upon MR. PYM's motion Sir Thomas Cheeke had leave to go into the country.

Sir George Wentworth had liberty to stay 5 weeks and to take his own time to go out of town when he would.

SIR GILBERT GERARD delivered in an account from the county of Middlesex.[3]

Upon MR. GRIMSTON's motion it was ordered that an 100£ should be allowed to the town of Colchester for the Irish amongst them out of 2000£ subscribed and given by them.

The debate proceeded touching the collecting and paying in of contribution money, and in the issue the committee appointed to consider/[4]

SIR THOMAS BARRINGTON made report of the performance of the militia in Essex. That they went to Brentwood on Tuesday, the 7th day of this instant June.[5]

---

1. Herbert had been sent for on 29 January 1641 and again on 29 April 1642 for "the unfurnishing of the publike magazin [in Montgomeryshire] by night." It was now ordered that his impeachment be carried up to the lords, and on 6 July he was bailed. See Notestein, pp. 301–02; and *CJ*, II, 548, 628, 639, 656.

2. The MP who was cousin to the Earl of Strafford, not the latter's brother of the same name who had left for Ireland in February. See Keeler, pp. 383–85; and *Roy. Off.*, p. 402.

3. "A Certificate what Sums of Money have been collected . . . upon the Act of Contribution for Ireland, and are paid into the Chamber of London." *CJ*, II, 628. For the act see *PJ*, 1: 233, n. 28.

4. The committee for accounts was to "consider of the Certificate from Middlesex, concerning the Contribution, how it may be fitted for all the Counties of the Kingdom." *CJ*, II, 628.

5. "Barrington gave an Account of the Willingness of the whole County of Essex, in their Obedience to the Ordinance of the Militia; and presented the original Petition, presented by the Officers of the Train Bands and Volunteers." *CJ*, II, 629. For the petition see 8 June, n. 29, and H, 9 June.

MR. WALLER delivered in a petition for Sir William Boteler wherein he desired to be bailed. He was one of those who came up with the Kentish petition which Captain Lovelace delivered in.

After a long debate it was ordered that he should be bailed.[6] I went out of the house during the debate.

The Essex gentlemen were admitted in, and Mr. Smith, the sheriff, in the name of the rest delivered in the same petition which had been formerly subscribed by some of the military officers at Brentwood on Tuesday, the 7 day of this instant June last past.[7]

[f. 183b] MR. BAYNTUN delivered in the petition of Captain Lovelace in which he desired to be bailed, having formerly delivered in the dangerous Kentish petition, which said petition being full of submission, he was bailed accordingly without any debate.[8]

SIR JOHN EVELYN delivered in an order touching the enrolling of the horsemen's names who should subscribe,[9] which were to be brought to the lord admiral, to the Earl of Pembroke, the Earl of Essex, and the Earl of Holland or one of them, who as soon as 60 horsemen were listed should appoint officers for them. We agreed to this order and ordered further that we should send to the lords to desire their consent.

SIR THOMAS BARRINGTON showed that he would provide 4 horses and lend 500£ for defense of the true religion, the king, and the kingdom.

SIR WILLIAM MASHAM showed that he would provide 4 horses.[10]

MR. STRODE moved that there might a message be sent up to the lords to desire them that a day might be appointed to put the militia of Devonshire in execution, and upon SIR JOHN NORTHCOTE's motion the said Mr. Strode was appointed to go up with the said message.

We then upon the SPEAKER's motion took into consideration the king's answer sent by Sir Edward Nicholas, one of the principal secretaries, which was read yesternight, and so we proceeded with the debate of it; and seeing the king

6. Impeachment charges against Boteler, ordered for the following Monday, were apparently never brought in. *CJ*, II, 629; T. P. S. Woods, *Prelude to Civil War, 1642* (Salisbury, 1980), p. 85. For the Kentish petition see *PJ*, 2: 100–02, 249–50.

7. For the earlier petition see above, n. 5. The one delivered by the sheriff et al. was actually a new petition pledging support for parliament and calling for a restitution of arms taken out of the county. For the text see *LJ*, V, 143. Wing, T 1700. There are fifty-six sheets of signatures (a total of four to five thousand names) attached to the petition, which is preserved in HLRO, Main Papers. The number of signatures is reported as "not above Ten thousand" in *CJ*, II, 629.

8. Lovelace wished to be bailed so that he might serve against the rebels in Ireland; apparently he did not do so but eventually joined the king at Oxford. *HMC, Fifth Report*, p. 29, and *DNB*.

9. I.e., those horsemen who should come to be enrolled according to the new propositions. See 16 June, n. 13. For this additional order see *CJ*, II, 629.

10. These pledges appear under the date of 13 June in Appendix F.

had denied to pass the commission, MR. REYNOLDS moved that we should send up to the lords to agree to the ordinance for authorizing the said 12 ships in the performance of that service which had been expressed in the said commission.

Sir Edward Leech and Dr. Aylett, two masters of the Chancery, brought this message from the lords, that their lordships desired a present conference by a committee of both houses touching a printed book lately come forth intituled *His Majesty's Answer to a Printed Book Intituled "A Remonstrance or the Declaration of the Lords and Commons Now Assembled in Parliament 26 May 1642."* [11] They being withdrawn, we resolved to give a present meeting, which the SPEAKER related to the messengers being again called in, and so they withdrew and departed.

Mr. Pym and others were named reporters and went away with the greater part of the house to the conference, at which I was not present.

The Lord Wharton managed the conference and showed that there was a pamphlet newly come forth in print, being an answer to a declaration of both houses published May 26.

MR. PIERREPONT, to bail Mr. Cressy, lecturer of Temple, as soon as conference was ended.

MR. HOLLES made report of conference.

Sir Edward Hungerford and 3 others, first 4.

Mr. Pym and 7 others. [12]

Upon MR. LONG's motion it was ordered that the Lord Say added to the other 4 lords to appoint officers, etc. [13] Sir John Evelyn went up of his message.

MR. CROMWELL made report of message that take consideration of ordinance. Allowed Timothy Middleton; [14] and would appoint militia for Devonshire, should be July 1.

Upon SIR JOHN NORTHCOTE's motion order touching universities to read our declarations. [15]

11. For the text see Rushworth, IV, 588–99. Wing, C 2103. This was in response to parliament's declaration concerning Hull. See *PJ,* 2: 361. For comments concerning the king's message, see the letter of 17 June from Roger Hill to his wife Abigail in Appendix K.

12. Because the king's declaration prompted a concern for the safety of the kingdom, Hungerford, Evelyn (probably of Wiltshire), Barrington, and Pierrepont were named to a joint committee to advance subscriptions in the City. Pym and seven others were named to a joint committee to respond to the declaration and to consider how to disperse the declarations and orders of both houses. *CJ,* II, 629.

13. For the earlier order see above, n. 9.

14. The lords agreed to Middleton as deputy lieutenant for Essex and subsequently passed the ordinance concerning the sea adventure for Ireland, with the Earl of Leicester dissenting. *LJ,* V, 142, 143. For the text of the ordinance, see *LJ,* V, 144–45.

15. The burgesses for the two universities (Eden and Lucas for Cambridge; Roe and Selden for Oxford) were to send the declarations of parliament to each university so that they might be read "in a public Manner, in the several Colleges and Halls." *CJ,* II, 630.

MR. WALTER LONG gave in note of divers reformado officers new named in the places of them who had refused, which were read and allowed by us.

[f. 184b] Sir Edward Leech and Dr. Aylett, two masters of the Chancery, brought this message from the lords, that their lordships had appointed 5 members of their house to meet with a proportionable number of this house in the Painted Chamber at 3 of the clock in the afternoon to consider of the validity of commissions of array which were now sending out into all parts of England, and that they had been informed by the Earl of Stamford of such a commission ready to issue out for Leicestershire.[16] So we named a proportionable number of 10 to join with them, of which I was one.

MR. PYM moved that we might send up to the lords to desire them to appoint a time for the commissioners of Ireland to sit this after- [f. 185b] noon, and Sir Robert Harley was sent up with the same message, and divers accompanied him.

The lords' messengers were again called in, and the SPEAKER informed them that the house had appointed a proportionable number to meet at the time and place desired, and so they withdrew and departed.

SIR THOMAS BARRINGTON moved that the order made on Monday last for the security of the high sheriff of Essex/[17]

We then proceeded upon the rest of the names of the reformado officers, which we allowed of.[18]

And then we allowed them half pay from the time of their listing till they should come into actual service. But for allowing them any horse the house would not assent to it, but it was carried negatively upon the question.

SIR JOHN EVELYN made report from the lords that he had carried up the message to the lords as he had been commanded and that the lords had assented to the order he had carried it up.

Upon MR. WALTER LONG's motion it was assented unto by the house that the officers of the adventurers' regiments for Ireland might receive pay from Tuesday next and then receive a month's pay beforehand.

SIR ROBERT HARLEY returned from the lords and made report that the commissioners for Ireland should sit this afternoon.

Upon MR. PIERREPONT's motion that Mr. Cressy, the lecturer of the Temple,

---

16. See *LJ*, V, 139, 142.

17. Barrington and others were to prepare an order requiring Robert Smith, the sheriff, "not to publish the Proclamations, or other Declarations," against the militia ordinance. *CJ*, II, 630.

18. Long, as chairman, was reporting from the committee for Irish adventurers. See above and below, and *CJ*, II, 630. The list of reformados is cataloged in Wing, L 2465. For the view that few if any of these unemployed officers ever went to Ireland but were actually intended for the service of the parliamentary army at home, see Peter Young, *Edgehill 1642* (Kineton, 1967), pp. 5–6.

might be called in, MR. PYM desired it might be tomorrow morning, which was ordered accordingly.

MR. STRODE moved that the order touching the sitting of the committee about the election of Arundel might be reversed. Divers spake in it and said it was a private committee, which made me speak in effect following:

That this was the first time that I ever heard this doctrine that the privilege of the house was a private business, for in former parliaments when they appointed public committees in the beginning of them, that of privileges was one of the first, and we have as great cause as ever that this committee should sit, for there is a public scandal upon us, how just I know not, that there are between 30 and 40 members of this house who sit here amongst us that have no right at all to sit here.[19] Neither do I think it fit that we should hinder any man from taking his just remedy against the mayor or other officer of any borough town who shall make an unjust or illegal return, for hence comes much of the mischief which we suffer at this time. Neither do I [f. 186b] believe that there were ever in any former parliaments so many double and treble indentures returned from one and the same place. My desire therefore is that this committee may sit as it hath been appointed and that they may proceed with the election of Arundel.

Some few spake after me, and in the issue (though all men were convinced upon what I had said that it was a public committee and not a private) it was overruled by some few voices that the committee should not sit this afternoon.[20]

[f. 187b] Sir Edward Leech and Dr. Aylett brought this message from the lords, that their lordships desired that the committee that was to go into London this afternoon[21] might have power to dispose of that part of the magazine which came from Hull, and then they withdrew, and the house resolved to give the same power to their members as the lords had done concerning the disposing of the said magazine, which the SPEAKER related to the said messengers being again called in.

Upon MR. DENZIL HOLLES's motion it was ordered that Mr. Thomas Bolton[22] should be recommended to the lords as a deputy lieutenant for Warwickshire.

Upon SIR THOMAS BARRINGTON's motion it was ordered that the Speaker should bring in the form of the thanks in writing, as near as he could remember,

---

19. A number of unresolved election disputes had been referred to the committee for privileges in the early days of the Long Parliament. See Keeler, pp. 33–80.

20. "And that That Election shall take its Turn at the Committee where it is depending." *CJ*, II, 630. At some point the Arundel election must have been settled in favor of Downes, for nothing further is heard of Harman.

21. See above, n. 12. The messengers were Rich and Aylett in *CJ*, II, 630, Leech and Aylett in *LJ*, V, 143.

22. Boughton, in *CJ*, II, 630.

which he gave the Essex gentlemen this day upon delivery of their petition that it might be printed.

MR. BAYNTUN delivered in the names of the bail offered by Captain Lovelace, of which the first was allowed, and one Sir Denner Strutt,[23] the latter being lately created a baronet, was disallowed because none in the house knew him.

We appoint to meet at 8 of the clock tomorrow morning and rose between 1 and 2 of the clock in the afternoon.

GAWDY

[f. 139a]   Friday, the XVII of June

Sir William Boteler is bailed.

A petition from Essex to the lords and commons with 10,000 hands. That they are ready to serve the parliament against the disturbers of their peace. They are thanked at the bar. This petition was delivered by the sheriff.

Mr. Lovelace is bailed.

That the horsemen that shall come in shall give tickets of the places where they lie to the commissaries at Guildhall, and that when there is 60 horsemen come in, the commissaries shall give notice to the lord admiral, the Lord of Pembroke, the Lord of Essex, and the Lord of Holland, or to any one of them, that so there may be captains and officers appointed over them. 'Tis resolved by question.

A message from the lords, they desire a present conference about an answer to the king's declaration to both houses of parliament. 'Tis assented to.

MR. HOLLES, a report from the conference, that they except against many parts of his majesty's declaration by way of answer to both houses but especially to one part. They have appointed 2 of their house to go into London to see the subscriptions what they are, and they have appointed 4 of their house likewise to answer his majesty's declaration. Desire us to appoint proportionable numbers to both.

23. MS: *Demster Stout*. Sir Denner Strutt of Essex had been created a baronet on 5 March. GEC, *Baronetage*, II, 161.

D'EWES

June 18, Saturday, 1642

The Speaker came a little after 8 of the clock. Prayers being ended, MR. GRIMSTON brought in an order to be allowed by both houses for the justification and indemnity of Mr. Smith, the high sheriff of Essex, for refusing to publish the king's proclamations against the ordinance of the militia, which was read and allowed by the house, and then it was likewise ordered that we should desire the lords to consent with us in it.[1] I went out of the house while the said order was in reading.

Upon MR. SOLICITOR's motion Mr. Cressy, the lecturer of the Temple, was called in and, kneeling at the bar as a delinquent, was bid to stand up and, having in some measure excused himself, delivered in the notes of his sermon and so withdrew out of the house. I came into the house a little after, and the further examination of the business was referred to the committee for scandalous ministers, and they were appointed to sit on Monday next in the afternoon.

SIR WALTER ERLE delivered in the king's printed letter to the lord mayor and sheriffs, by which he did command them to signify his pleasure to the wardens of each company that they should not assist in the raising of horse nor lending of money to that end, which was read in the house but no order settled what should be done with it for the present.[2]

The SPEAKER showed that he had received a letter from the Lord Ruthin and Sir Arthur Hesilrige out of Leicestershire,[3] in which were divers papers enclosed worth our consideration, and thereupon delivered them all in to the clerk to read, who read them accordingly.

The letter bore date at Leicester June 16, 1642, in which they showed that Mr. Henry Hastings, younger son to the Earl of Huntingdon, had come to the town of Leicester the day before that they had appointed to muster and train

1. For the order, which included "other Sheriffs of other Counties," see *LJ*, V, 149–50.

2. The lord mayor was instructed "to publish this Our Letter to the . . . several Companies . . . that such Money as they shall lend . . . may be only employed for Ireland or Scotland, and not towards such Guards, which (in Truth) are intended . . . to be employed against Us." For the text see *LJ*, V, 148. Wing, C 2832. It was referred to the committee for defense (propositions) to prepare an answer and to order the letter's suppression. *CJ*, II, 630.

3. As deputy lieutenants Hesilrige and Lord Ruthin had been ordered on 4 June to go to Leicestershire to execute the militia ordinance. *CJ*, II, 604. For the letter see *LJ*, V, 147–48.

there and had delivered a proclamation to the mayor of the town[4] against the training by virtue of the ordinance of the militia, by which the said town was much disheartened from their former readiness and alacrity, and other means was used to dishearten the country also so as some failed to come, many left their arms behind them, and yet there was a reasonable appearance and [f. 188b] volunteers also. That they had sent enclosed a copy of the king's letter, of the commission of array, and of two warrants. The clerk then read the copy of the king's letter bearing date at his court at York June 12 in the 18 year of his reign and directed to divers of the commissioners in the commission of array:[5]

That whereas it was voted by both houses of parliament upon the 13 day of May[6] last past that the kingdom was in danger of invasion from abroad and from a popish party at home, and whereas in cases of danger it belonged to his majesty to give command for the training and mustering of the kingdom, and whereas there had been an ordinance of parliament made against law without his consent for the training and mustering of his good subjects, and whereas he had by his proclamation of the 27 of May last past[7] he had forbidden the execution of the same ordinance, he did now intend for the safety of his people to send out such commissions of array as were legal and warranted by the statute *de a° 5° H. 4*, being upon record, to which he required obedience and commanded them to do their uttermost for execution thereof, with other particulars of less moment.

The clerk then read the commission itself, being in Latin, which was drawn much according to the form of the commission upon the Parliament Roll *de a° 5° H. 4, n° 25°*.[8] The commissioners were Henry, Earl of Huntingdon, William, Earl of Devonshire, Henry Hastings, Esquire, son of the Earl of Huntingdon, and divers others, and the last of them was the sheriff, etc. It bore date at York [*blank*].[9]

Then was next read the warrant of Mr. Gregory, the undersheriff of the county of Leicester,[10] to the high constable of the hundred of Framland to give order to the petty constables to warn all of the trained bands to appear in arms on Wednesday, the 22 day of this instant June next ensuing. Dated 16 June 1642.

Next was read the warrant of Mr. Henry Hastings, younger son of the Earl of

---

4. Thomas Rudyard. *LJ*, V, 147. For Henry Hastings of Ashby de la Zouch, see *Roy. Off.*, pp. 179–80. *DNB*.

5. For the text see *LJ*, V, 148–49.

6. D'Ewes should have 15 March. For the votes see *PJ*, 2: 40–41, 43.

7. The proclamation against the militia.

8. See Appendix H. For the Leicestershire commission see *LJ*, V, 147.

9. The date was 11 June. *CJ*, II, 631. The sheriff was Archdale Palmer. *Sheriffs*, p. 75.

10. This warrant from the sheriff was sent out in his absence by the undersheriff, William Gregory. *CJ*, II, 631. For the text see *LJ*, V, 148.

Huntingdon, Sir Richard Halford, Sir John Bale, Mr. John Pate, bearing date at Leicester June 16, 1642, in which they showed that being commissioners of array, they thought good to give him[11] notice that they intended to have an array of the trained bands with their supplies of that county in the Raw[12] Dykes without the town of Leicester near it on Wednesday, the 22 day of this instant June, and therefore required him to cause them the trained bands within a certain circuit then to appear with their arms.[13]

I went out of the house about 10.[14]

Return from committee circa 1. SERJEANT WILDE made report of vote.[15] MR. GLYN of reason of vote. Then we voted the same vote. And a vote for a declaration to be drawn (and reasons of vote was proposed), which upon my motion was omitted.[16]

MR. VENN, lord mayor's message to wardens with printed letters.[17]

MR. WALTER LONG, names of commanders and to raise volunteers allowed.[18] To meet at 3 afternoon. Rose between 1 and 2 p.m.

[f. 189b]   Post Meridiem

The Speaker resumed his chair about 4 of the clock in the afternoon. MR. CORBET made report of the two scandalous lecturers at Newcastle, viz., Dr. Wishart, a Scottishman, who had been driven from thence as an incendiary,[19]

---

11. I.e., the sheriff. For the text see *LJ*, V, 148. Bale, Halford, and Pate were justices of the peace and former deputy lieutenants; Pate had been sheriff in 1640–41. See *LJ*, V, 147, 191; GEC, *Baronetage*, II, 150, 214–15; and for Pate *Roy. Off.*, p. 287.

12. MS: *Rough*. One of the open fields outside the walled town. *VCH, Leicestershire*, IV, 100.

13. "Resolved, That the Commission be referred to the Committee Yesterday appointed to consider of the Preventing the Going forth of the Commissions of Array into the several Counties." *CJ*, II, 631. For the joint committee see D, 95. For additional actions see G, below.

14. For proceedings omitted by D'Ewes, see G, below, and *CJ*, II, 631–32.

15. This committee (see above, n. 13) was "of Opinion, that this Commission of Array is against the Law, and against the Liberty and Property of the Subject." *CJ*, II, 632.

16. The parentheses apparently enclose the omitted clause. A drafting committee, composed of six members of the above-mentioned joint committee (including Selden and D'Ewes), was named to draw up a declaration concerning the illegality of the commission of array. *CJ*, II, 630, 632.

17. The lord mayor, aldermen, and sheriffs were not to publish the king's letter among the London livery companies without further order from parliament. See above, n. 2, and *CJ*, II, 632.

18. Long was doubtless reporting, as on 17 June, from the committee for Irish adventurers. For resolutions concerning pay for the forces going to Ireland and the appointment of Lord Wharton as colonel general, see *CJ*, II, 631. A discussion of the choice of Wharton to command the adventurers' army, which never left England, appears in G. F. Trevallyn Jones, *Saw-Pit Wharton* (Sydney, 1967), pp. 45–47.

19. Crossed out in MS: *and Mr. Mo/* In Wishart's place William Morton, a nominee to the Westminster Assembly, was recommended to be lecturer at the church of St. Nicholas. *CJ*, II, 632. For more details concerning Wishart and Alvey, see Roger Howell, Jr., *Newcastle upon Tyne and the Puritan Revolution* (Oxford, 1967), passim. For Morton see *PJ*, 1: 411, and 2: 491.

who was voted in the house to be a common drunkard and incapable to be a lecturer there. I came into the house before this vote passed.

Upon the LORD GREY's motion Sir Thomas Barrington was sent up to the lords with the votes we had passed in the morning touching the illegality of the commission of array for Leicestershire read this morning also in the house.[20]

[Committee of the Whole House]

About 5 of the clock in the afternoon the Speaker left his chair, and Mr. Solicitor came into the clerk's chair, and we proceeded with the debate of the bill of tonnage and poundage in the grand committee and amended some particulars in it.

[f. 193b] Sir Robert Rich and Mr. Page, two masters of the Chancery, brought this message from the lords, that their lordships desired a present conference by a committee of both houses touching the votes we had sent up to them and touching the king's printed letter sent to the lord mayor and the sheriffs of London. They being withdrawn, we agreed to give a meeting presently, which the SPEAKER related to them being again called in, and so they withdrew and departed. We appointed Mr. Prideaux and others reporters, who [went] up to the conference.

The Lord Mandeville managed the conference and showed that the lords agreed to our votes sent up to them this afternoon and showed that they had made an order for the sending for Sir Richard Halford and the rest concerning whom we had sent to them.[21]

The lords also had passed a declaration[22] (which was appointed by us at the select committee of lords and commons this morning) which was delivered in to our reporters, being an answer to his majesty's printed letter, which will be printed.

The conference being ended and the Speaker having resumed his chair, MR. PRIDEAUX made report of the conference. And after the vote had been again voted by us, upon MR. GLYN's motion we voted a new vote against all those who should put this commission of array in execution.[23]

Then MR. PRIDEAUX[24] delivered in the declaration which had been delivered

20. Barrington also carried up the order that the king's letter should not be published by the lord mayor; however, the lords had already formulated a similar order. See *CJ*, II, 632; and *LJ*, V, 146, 150.

21. For the order see *LJ*, V, 150.

22. I.e., "the Declaration concerning the King's Letter to the City." *LJ*, V, 150.

23. For the earlier vote see above, n. 15. The new resolution stated that all who executed the commission of array were "Disturbers of the Peace of the Kingdom, and Betrayers of the Liberty of the Subject." *CJ*, II, 632.

24. Actually Evelyn reported. *CJ*, II, 632.

and read at the conference against the king's letter sent to the lord mayor and sheriffs.

The said declaration was first read by the clerk,[25] and MR. CHARLES PRICE moved that in respect it was of great weight and the house thin and the season late, that we might defer the passing of it until Monday morning next, but divers hot spirits called to have it put to the question, whereupon the Speaker stood up and was ready to have done it until I had spoken in effect following:

That I was very sorry to see a matter of this great weight to be brought to us at this time of the night and to be accompanied with such an urgent necessity that it must be passed by us at the instant. It was referred in the morning to one lord and two commoners to draw by the select committee of lords and commons, and I thought that it should have come thither again to have been considered of by them and then to have been presented to the house. There are in it several passages that need a review. His majesty too often mentioned with the terms only of "he" and "his" besides other expressions which need which may well admit [sic] alteration. Whereupon the house thought fit to have it read again and spoken unto by parts before it were put to the question, which was done accordingly by the clerk, and myself and others took divers exceptions to it, whereupon many indiscreet passages in it were left out or altered, and so it passed.

We appointed a committee of 12 to meet in London tonight with the lords,[26] but when we thought to send them up the declaration with the amendments, we understood that they were risen.

Upon SIR DUDLEY NORTH's motion Mr. John Cotton, son of Sir John Cotton, had license to travel into France.

We appointed to meet at 8 of the clock on Monday morning and rose between 7 and 8 at night.

GAWDY

[f. 139b]   Saturday, the XVIII of June

The letter from the king to my lord mayor against the lending of money and raising of horse for a guard. 'Tis referred to the committee of propositions.

---

25. Crossed out in MS: *2dly read. I spake often to it as some others spake seldomer, and divers indiscreet passages in it were amended.* This sentence is expanded upon in the text below.

26. This committee, of which Sir John Evelyn (probably of Wiltshire) was a member, was to go into the City "about the Propositions and Declaration." Meanwhile the lords had asked the lord mayor to call a Common Hall on Monday to be attended by committees from both houses. *CJ,* II, 632; *LJ,* V, 150.

A letter from Leicester to the Speaker from my Lord Ruthin and the rest of the deputies. That Mr. Hastings divulged the proclamations against the militia. There was good appearance of men, but many left their arms by the way, meeting with some that told them 'twas dangerous to show their arms.

They send us a commission of array, the copy of it, sent from the king to my Lord of Huntingdon and my Lord of Devonshire and other deputy lieutenants.

A letter from the king to the Lord Huntingdon, Lord of Devonshire, and others, that he intend to proceed with commissions of array in all counties.

The sheriff's warrants to the constables by virtue of the king's commission. A warrant from some deputy lieutenants to the constables for to warn the trained bands to appear by virtue of the king's commission the 22 of June.

Resolved, that Mr. Hastings shall be sent for as a delinquent.[27]

A message to the lords to acquaint them with this vote and the letters abovesaid, with other things.

[f. 140a] Resolved, that my Lord Wharton shall be colonel general of the Irish adventurers.

SIR GILBERT GERARD, a report from the lords, that they agree with us in all.[28]

A message from the lords, they agree with us for bringing the rest of the horse arms from Hull except 300 and some powder.[29] They agree with us for the order concerning the freeing the sheriff of Essex for not publishing the king's proclamation about the militia, with some exceptions.

The commission for array sent by the king into Leicestershire is adjudged by both houses to be illegal, as I hear by many after I came away.

The house sat a little in the afternoon, but I came away.

27. Halford, Bale, Pate, and Gregory were also to be sent for by the sergeant at arms. *CJ*, II, 632.

28. Gerard had carried up the papers concerning Leicestershire and the king's message to the lord mayor. *LJ*, V, 145.

29. See 15 June, n. 16.

D'EWES

[f. 194b]   June 20, Monday, 1642

The Speaker came between 8 and 9 of the clock. After prayers upon MR. WALTER LONG's motion, it was ordered that the ordinance for raising of soldiers[1] and the warrant for repayment of 10,000£ to the adventurers for Ireland[2] should be sent up to the lords as soon as they were set.

MR. PYM moved that we might consider of the lord lieutenant's propositions presented to us from the commissioners for the affairs of Ireland,[3] that so he might hasten into Ireland because some did ill offices therein for the army.

Thereupon the propositions were read.

The first was that he desired to be allowed 3000£ for buying of tents for the field, great saddles and pistols for his servants, hangings and household stuff for himself, with other particulars. Divers spake to it. I moved in effect following:

I spake/

The 2d proposition was that he desired an increase of his entertainment of 10£ per diem and showed that/

I spake/

In the issue we ordered 3000£ to be given him.[4]

[f. 195b] When I returned into the house between eleven and 12, the house was debating of the paper in French sent hither long since.[5]

Upon MR. STRODE's motion Sir John Northcote had liberty to go into Devonshire, being a deputy lieutenant there.

1. The next day Long reported to the lords "that the Adventurers for Ireland have made Choice of the Officers for Five Thousand Men and Five Hundred Horse, to be sent into Ireland; and . . . of the Lord Wharton to be Colonel General of that Army." The lords immediately approved of Wharton and on 5 July of the ordinance for raising these forces. See *LJ*, V, 153, 181, 182. The complete list of officers is preserved in HLRO, Main Papers. For the order of 30 July diverting these men to serve the Earl of Essex "in this Kingdom, for the Defence of the King and Parliament," see *CJ*, II, 698. See also Young, *Edgehill*, pp. 248–49.

2. This sum was to be repaid out of the £100,000 which the City had promised to lend. For the order, passed by the commons on 18 June, see *CJ*, II, 631.

3. These propositions had been presented to the commissioners on 21 May. See *PJ*, 2: 458–59; 13 June, n. 19; and CIA, 17 June.

4. In addition, £5000 was to be "issued out for incident Charges." See *CJ*, II, 633; and CIA, 27 June. For proceedings omitted by D'Ewes, see G, below.

5. For the proposal attributed to Sir Thomas Roe for the restitution of the Palatinate, see *PJ*, 2: 304–05. The matter was now referred to a committee. *CJ*, II, 633.

Upon MR. PIERREPONT's motion Sir Robert Cooke had liberty to go into the country.

SIR GILBERT PICKERING made report/[6]

MR. WALLER made report that the lords would give us a present meeting about the Prince of Anhalt's letters and that for the other particular[7] they would send an answer by messengers of their own.

SIR JOHN EVELYN made report from the lords also that they consented to the declaration with our amendments which had passed here on Saturday night last.[8]

[f. 196b] The conference being ended and the Speaker having resumed his chair, the SPEAKER showed that the Trinity House would lend money if they were sent unto. So some were appointed to go unto them concerning it.[9]

Sir Edward Leech and Dr. Aylett brought this message from the lords, that their lordships desired a present conference by a committee of both houses in the Painted Chamber if it stand with the conveniency of this house about certain prisoners brought out of Ireland.

MR. PYM made report of that part of the conference had on [blank] last past with the lords which was managed by the Earl of Holland, and the clerk read it being dated June 7, 1642, and sent from the Earl of Holland to the Earl of Warwick.[10] That he had laid out much for the fort near Harwich (called Landguard Point). Arrear of 4000£ due in the Earl of Portland's time[11] besides other payments since. That if he had not so paid them, the garrison there must ere this have disbanded. That the fort also was now out of repair. That the said fort was a great safeguard for our own ships and would be of great danger to the kingdom if it should come into the hands of an enemy.

That we had paid the garrison at Portsmouth, and therefore he hoped we would take some course to pay this garrison. That there were not 3 pieces mounted of 40.

6. See G, below.

7. The repayment of the £10,000 to the treasurers for the Irish adventure. *CJ,* II, 633. For the Prince of Anhalt, see G, below.

8. For the declaration in response to the king's letter to the lord mayor, see *LJ,* V, 152–53. Wing, E 1439. When the joint committee presented the declaration to the lord mayor and Common Hall in the afternoon, "the City shewed much Forwardness to observe their Lordships Commands; and the Lord Mayor desired the said Declaration might be . . . published to the several Wards." *LJ,* V, 154.

9. On 16 August it was ordered that an ordinance be prepared for securing the loan from Trinity House, the mariners' fraternity established in 1514. *CJ,* II, 722; *PJ,* 1: 232, n. 21.

10. This letter, read at a conference on 15 June, was actually from Warwick to Holland.

11. In June 1635 the Earl of Holland had sent a declaration to the lords of the Treasury concerning the defenseless state of the fort, stating that "there is in arrear . . . 5600£, for which the late Lord Treasurer [the Earl of Portland] has been from time to time solicited, but it could not be obtained." *CSPD, 1635,* p. 121.

MR. PYM then showed that my Lord of Holland did further inform us of the great necessity of taking care of this fort. And after some few had spoken to it, it was referred to committee for navy.

Upon MR. CROMWELL's motion MR. DARLEY, who had promised 200£, did offer instead thereof to maintain 4 horses, which was allowed.

The messengers called again in and told that we would meet presently.

Upon MR. VENN's motion it was ordered that the Speaker should give a warrant for 12 muskets and 12 bandoliers to be sent to an inhabitant of Leicester. [12]

Mr. Pym and others were appointed managers of the conference and went up to the Painted Chamber and divers with them. I went not up.

The Earl of Leicester, lord lieutenant of Ireland, showed that the Earl of Maguire, MacMahon, and Colonel Reade were sent prisoners hither out of Ireland and that they had sent them prisoners with a guard to the Tower, intending to proceed to a speedy trial against them this term. [13]

The conference being ended, MR. JOHN BLAKISTON delivered in a letter sent to him from Newcastle bearing date there June 16, 1642 (the date being on the top of the letter), in which it was written unto him that the king had appointed the Earl of Newcastle to be governor of that town, [14] and that Sir William Carnaby and Captain Legge were gone post thither, and that there was an intention to put a garrison of 1000 men upon the town, that his majesty had sent also to Carlisle and Berwick, with some other particulars of less moment.

Some spake concerning this letter and how great a danger it might prove for his majesty to seize upon Newcastle, and it was also much disliked that Sir William Carnaby, being a member of the house, should undertake such an employment.

[f. 197b) A little after the said letter was read and a debate begun upon it, SIR JOHN EVELYN moved that some might be ordered to search in the Chequer records concerning the king's oath, whereupon I myself and 3 others were named and appointed a committee for the doing of it. [15]

---

12. Cf. *CJ*, II, 634.

13. The prisoners had been sent for on 21 March. See *PJ*, 2: 67. For a letter concerning them dated 10 June from Borlase and Parsons to Leicester, see *LJ*, V, 152; and *HMC, Ormonde MSS*, n.s., II, 151–53. For Reade see Toynbee and Young, *Strangers in Oxford*, pp. 132–33.

14. See Margaret, Duchess of Newcastle, *The Life of William Cavendish, Duke of Newcastle*, ed. C. H. Firth (London, [n.d.]), pp. 10–11. The control of the city of Newcastle gave the king a much-needed port in the north. J. R. Powell, *The Navy in the English Civil War* (Hamden, Conn., 1962), p. 18.

15. The committee, which also included Hill, Prideaux, and Constantine, was "to see what Oath his Majesty took at his Coronation." *CJ*, II, 634. The oath had been discussed at length in connection with the declaration concerning Hull. See *PJ*, 2: 340, 344, 360–61, 493.

We then proceeded with the debate touching the said letter sent to Mr. Blakiston, and it was ordered that Sir William Widdrington should write to Sir William Carnaby to return speedily to the house, and for the letter itself it was referred to the committee for the navy to consider what course to take concerning Newcastle.[16]

Sir Edward Leech and Dr. Aylett brought this message from the lords, that they had sent us down a letter sent to the Earl of Bedford from the mayor and sheriff of Exeter, and that their lordships did desire us to return thanks unto them for the same, and that the like order might be made for the said mayor and sheriff of Exeter as had been lately made for the sheriff of Essex,[17] and that we would recommend the said sheriff of Exeter to be a deputy lieutenant for the county of the city of Exeter. And so the messengers withdrew, and the clerk read the said letter bearing date at Exeter June 18, 1642, being sent from Mr. Richard Saunders, mayor of that city, and Mr. Walter White, sheriff of the county of the same city, to William, Earl of Bedford, appointed lord lieutenant of the county of Devon by the ordinance of parliament.

The whole letter was written from the mayor, and there only followed a postscript written from the sheriff. In the said letter the mayor showed that a writ with proclamations against the militia was come to his hands, in which writ he was commanded to publish the said proclamations, but that he had suspended the publishing of the same till he heard from the parliament, being ready in all particulars to obey them and conceiving that the said proclamations did tend to the disservice of the king and the parliament, with some other particulars of less moment.

We then agreed that the same declaration should be made for the mayor and sheriff of Exeter[18] as had been made for Mr. Smith, the sheriff of Essex. We agreed also that a letter of thanks should be drawn to be sent by the Speaker to the said mayor and sheriff, and Mr. Strode and some others were appointed to draw it. We voted also that Mr. Walter White, now sheriff of Exeter, should be recommended to be a deputy lieutenant for the county of the city of Exeter.

The messengers were again called in, and the SPEAKER gave them notice that we had considered of their message and had agreed with the lords in all particulars.

We appointed to meet at 8 of the clock tomorrow morning. We rose a little before two of the clock in the afternoon.

16. Actually a committee concerning the port of Newcastle was named. *CJ,* II, 634.

17. See 18 June, n. 1.

18. MS: *York.* The message to the mayor and sheriff was approved the next day. *CJ,*II, 635. For a response sent by the lords, see *LJ,* V, 154.

Post Meridiem

Divers of the committee for the Lady Sedley's petition sat in the inner Court of Wards, of which I was one and there present. The horrible practice of Mr. John Griffith, the younger, a member of the House of Commons, to have violated her chastity was there laid open by herself, in having drawn her by false pretenses to an obscure house standing between Westminster and Chelsea on Ascension Day last past, being the 19 day of May, between 5 and 6 of the clock in the afternoon. The story was full of wonder in respect of her resisting his villainous attempt till he had wearied himself and then of her estrange[19] escape out of a backyard whilst he retired from her. Many concurrent circumstances were proved by such as either came thither with her or did help her to escape or to whom she repaired soon after her escape, amongst whom the Archbishop of Armagh was one.[20]

GAWDY

[f. 140a]   Monday, the xx of June

Propositions of my lord lieutenant to both houses before his going into Ireland:

1. He desire 3000£ to buy him pistols, field beds, tents, wagons, and other things.

2. That during the war there may be an increase of his pay of 10£ a day.

3. Because the perquisites of that country is abated.

4. [blank]

[f. 140b] My Lord Paget's letter read, which is said to be a fiction. 'Tis referred to the committee. The printer is sent for.[21]

All those that put the commission of array in execution are enemies to the state and disturbers of the peace. This vote sent up to the lords.[22]

The messenger of the Prince of Anhalt within the bar tells us by his interpreter that he hath a letter from the prince to the parliament of England, another

19. Strange, unusual, wonderful. *NED*.

20. Upon leaving Ireland the Archbishop of Armagh took up residence in London in November of 1640. *DNB*.

21. The letter, which was referred to the committee for informations, gave Paget's reasons for joining the king. The lords subsequently ordered that it be burned by the hangman. See *CJ*, II, 633; and *LJ*, V, 152. Wing, P 170.

22. The lords agreed to this new vote. See 18 June, n. 23; and *LJ*, V, 151.

to the parliaments of England and Scotland,[23] and a third to the king. He showed his letter of credence. He is answered that we will acquaint the lords with it and give him answer tomorrow morning.

SIR GILBERT PICKERING, that in Northamptonshire there was a full appearance about the militia with 900 volunteers.

Mr. Wollaston at the bar as a delinquent for speaking against the militia, which he denieth. He saith he found 4 volunteers. He is discharged.

The effect of the Prince of Anhalt's letter was to desire the parliament to mediate with the king to answer for his third son because he is of the same religion and because his mother was Queen Anne's sister.[24]

23. For details of this letter, see *HMC, Fifth Report*, p. 18. Christian II, Prince of Anhalt-Bernburg, was the son of Christian I (d. 1630), a strong Calvinist who had been chancellor to Frederick V, Elector Palatine. C. V. Wedgwood, *The Thirty Years War* (Harmondsworth, Middx, 1961), p. 53.

24. Gawdy is incorrect about the relationships. The Prince of Anhalt's mother was Anne of Bentheim. Queen Anne's sister was Elizabeth, Duchess of Brunswick, mother to Christian, administrator of Halberstadt. *The Cambridge Modern History* (Cambridge, 1904–12), III, 717; Wedgwood, *Thirty Years War*, pp. 133, 464.

D'EWES

June 21, Tuesday, 1642

The Speaker came about 8 of the clock. After prayers upon MR. NICHOLAS moved [*sic*] that the votes against the commissions of array might be printed, but others opposed it and desired that the declaration might be first made ready to print with them, in which it was to [be] demonstrated why the said commissions were void.[1]

This was done before I came into the house. A little after I came in, MR. TRENCHARD made report from the committee appointed to that end of the account which they had drawn and made up of what money had been given and paid in in subsidies and poll money and how it had been laid out for the defense of the public, which was to be printed. After it had been read by the clerk and divers had spoken to it, it was ordered to be recommitted that some things might be made more clear and evident in it.

SIR EDMUND MOUNDEFORD moved that Sir Roger North might have liberty to go into the country for a short time, which drew on another debate, though he had leave given him,[2] whether or no the house should not be appointed to be called some day next week, and some moved to have had it ordered that it might have been called every week at a day uncertain, which made me stand up and speak in effect following:

That I had formerly showed them how the ancient course had been to call the house often[3] and that I wished it might again be put in practice, but I conceived it to be contrary to all former order to surprise the house by calling it upon a day uncertain, and therefore I desired that if they would call it weekly, we might call it upon each Friday or some other day when the house should think fit.

Others spake after me, and in the issue all those motions touching the calling of the house were laid aside.[4]

Upon the SPEAKER's motion according to the order made yesterday, we

---

1. For the votes and proposed declaration, see D, 100, 101, 108. They were subsequently printed together in a pamphlet. See 28 June, n. 10.

2. Two other leaves had been approved earlier. See Appendix B.

3. See Coates, p. 287.

4. During June attendance ranged from 264 on the 16th, the day the house was called, to 69 on the 27th, according to the figures from divisions. Some MPs were departing because of loyalty to the king, others because of responsibilities as deputy lieutenants.

agreed to take the bill of tonnage and poundage into consideration in a grand committee of the house.

[*Committee of the Whole House*]

And thereupon the Speaker left his chair, and Mr. St. John, the king's solicitor, came to the clerk's chair, and so the committee proceeded with the bill of tonnage and poundage where it had last left, during which debate I went out of the house.[5]

And staying about half an hour out, before my return again the Speaker had resumed his chair, and the clerk of the house was reading the king's answer to the propositions sent unto him lately by this house which are in print, which was very long and penned with great judgment.[6]

Sir Robert Rich, Mr. Page, declaration printed.[7] Committee 13, 3 of the clock in the afternoon. Read names, 26. I one. Messengers answer. Sir Gilbert Gerard, paper.[8]

3 horses, Enfield. Upon SIR JOHN EVELYN's motion, reward.[9]

Mr. Denzil Holles, judges from Dorchester to Sherborne, etc. Mr. Holles and others sent to judges to know why they altered. Sir Thomas Barrington to consider of Justice Malet.[10]

5. For proceedings omitted by D'Ewes, see G, below, and *CJ*, II, 635.

6. For the king's message, dated 18 June, and his answer to the Nineteen Propositions, see *LJ*, V, 153, and Rushworth, IV, 725–35. Wing, C 2122.

Edward Hyde, who had left London before the Nineteen Propositions were approved, gave this account of the framing of the king's answer: "Because he [Hyde] had so much work then upon his hands . . . the lord Falkland and sir John Colepepper undertook to prepare an answer . . . themselves; and . . . sent it to the king, and desired that Mr. Hyde might peruse it, and then cause it to be published and printed." Falkland and Colepeper arrived in York soon after the draft message had been sent to the king and before it was printed. See [Edward Hyde, Earl of Clarendon], *The Life of Edward Earl of Clarendon* (Oxford, 1857), I, 130–31. For an analysis of Hyde's role, see Michael Mendle, *Dangerous Positions* (University, Ala., 1985), pp. 5–20.

7. This book, *His Majestie's declaration to all his loving subjects,* contained a declaration, dated 15 June and subscribed by forty lords and others at York, stating that the king did not intend to make war on the parliament. In the lords' view, however, it signaled "a Preparation of a War, and an Opposition to the Parliament." See *LJ*, V, 154; Gardiner, *History of England*, X, 204–05; and Clarendon, *History*, II, 185–90. Wing, C 2237. Among the signers were the nine impeached lords.

8. A joint committee of thirteen lords and twenty-six commoners, including Gerard, was to consider the declaration. *CJ*, II, 635.

9. "Those Persons that made Stay of the Horses in Colman-streete and Endfield Chace, that were going for Yorke," were to be paid 20s. See *CJ*, II, 635, 637, 694, 698, 700.

10. Members of the house were to go to the judges of the western and Sussex circuits (Sir Robert Foster and Sir Thomas Malet respectively) to know why they had altered the locations for the assizes. In addition, the house was to consider the advisability of "Judge Mallett his going Circuits; being complained of . . . for Misdemeanors committed by him the last Circuit he went" (the Lent assizes at Maidstone, where the Kentish petition was framed). See *CJ*, II, 635; and Woods, *Prelude*, pp. 96, 107. For Malet's role at Maidstone, see *PJ*, 2: 100–01, 111, n. 5, 114, 253–54.

The grand committee for tonnage and poundage to sit this afternoon.

Upon MR. BAYNTUN's motion Captain Lovelace['s] bail accepted.[11]

MR. BOSVILE's motion, his own suit stopped with Sir Francis Wortley at the ensuing assizes at York.[12]

We appointed to meet at 8 of the clock tomorrow morning. We rose between 2 and 3 of the clock in the afternoon.

GAWDY

[f. 141a]   Tuesday, the XXI of June

MR. STRODE, that the house is thin. That we may appoint a day to call it.

No day is appointed to call it, but 'twas moved that it might be called when 'twas most empty.

[Committee of the Whole House]

The house in a committee about the bill of tonnage and poundage.

The Speaker to the chair.

A message from the lords, they take notice of a ship of Mr. Courteen's that's come in ballasted with saltpeter because it is a necessary commodity for the kingdom at this time. They desire it may be bought.[13]

Instructions for the deputy lieutenants of Warwickshire. 'Tis recommitted.[14]

MR. PYM, that he hath received information from the deputy lieutenants that they expect the commission of array in that county within 10 days. They desire therefore they may tarry a fortnight longer.[15] They desire about 2000£ for the supply of Sir John Hotham. That Hull is very quiet and content with their garrison.

11. See *CJ,* II, 635.

12. On 19 March the Speaker had been ordered to write to the judges of assize for Yorkshire that Godfrey Bosvile, MP, "hath the Privilege of Parliament, in a Suit wherein he is interested, between Jo. Rudston, and Sir Fra. Wortley . . . to be tried at the next Assizes at Yorke; and that the Suit be stayed." *CJ,* II, 488.

13. Several MPs plus Samuel Cordwell, the gunpowder maker, had already been appointed "to try the Salt-petre in Mr. Courten's Ship; and to bargain with him for it." However, on 11 August he was given license to dispose of it anyplace in England or Wales. William Courteen was son to the late Sir William, wealthy merchant and trader. See *CJ,* II, 621, 633, 714; and *PJ,* 1: 209, n. 21.

14. The following MPs, who were deputy lieutenants for Warwickshire, were ordered to execute the militia ordinance there: Sir Peter Wentworth, Godfrey Bosvile, William Purefoy, and John Barker. Their instructions were similar to those for Lancashire. *CJ,* II, 635.

15. This message was apparently from the committee in Lincolnshire.

A message from the lords, they have received a letter from the king with an answer to our 19 propositions, which he desire may be communicated to us. York, the 18 of June. [f. 141b] The beginning of the message was in high language, but when he came to answer the articles, he used moderate language, concluded with the having of Hull and the magazine restored to him. The answer from the king to us concerning the 19 propositions was an hour in reading.

Resolved by question, that the king's message shall be taken into consideration on Thursday.

A message from the lords, a book intituled *A Declaration to All His Loving Subjects* is come to their hands. There is something in it deserve consideration. They have appointed a committee to consider of it and desire us to join with them.

D'EWES

[f. 201b]   June 22, Wednesday, 1642

[Committee of the Whole House]

The grand committee for the bill of tonnage and poundage met in the house about 8 of the clock, Mr. Solicitor taking the clerk's chair, and the Speaker came awhile after, but the committee sat till about ten of the clock and went through the remainder of the bill of tonnage and poundage and settled all particulars but only the fees which should be allowed to the officers of the custom house or some other particulars of as little moment.

I was [not] present during that debate but came into the house just as prayers were beginning about ten of the clock.

After prayers upon MR. PURY his motion, Mr. Brett had liberty to go into the country.

MR. SOLICITOR made report of the additions, alterations, and amendments which passe[d]. SOLICITOR, what prisage, what butlerage.[1]

I spake to prisage.

Mr. James Maxwell/[2]

After return to the house upon Sir Thomas/

Sir Edward Leech and Dr. Aylett, two masters of the Chancery, brought this message from the lords, that their lordships desired a conference by a committee of both houses, etc.: 1. touching the Scottish treaty, 2. touching the disposing of the magazine at Hull, 3. touching letters received from the Lord Willoughby, lord lieutenant of Lincolnshire. They then withdrew.

The SPEAKER delivered in a letter dated at Lincoln 19 June[3] from Sir John Wray, Sir William Armine, and divers other deputy lieutenants there to himself.

Rather an account of the whole service than in parts.

Made show in 9 several places.

19 several foot companies, many well armed and some defective in respect their arms at Hull.

That where some high constables did forbear to send out their/

1. Prisage and butlerage were ancient customs levied on imported wine.
2. For the message brought by Maxwell, gentleman usher of the black rod, see G, below.
3. Though the date is 11 June in *CJ*, II, 636, it appears to be *19th* in the MS CJ. This letter from the committee for Lincolnshire is similar to Lord Willoughby's letter to the lords. See below.

114

In Boston 100 volunteers.

[f. 203b] That the horse made a thin appearance, many being in soil, but that they supplied divers themselves to attend the lord lieutenant.

The greatest want of officers, having put out most who were entrusted by the Earl of Lindsey. That they were at/

The SPEAKER then delivered in/[4]

Hull, June 20, 1642, from Sir William Strickland, Mr. Alured, Mr. Peregrine Pelham, and Mr. John Hotham, wherein amongst other particulars it was showed:

That one Mr. Thornton, comptroller of the customhouse and collector of the impositions, and one Mr. Corney, a minister there, were dangerous men and did ill offices in the town, so as Sir John Hotham, the governor/[5]

Mr. Alured put in Mr. Corney's[6] place.

Some examinations were then read by the clerk of words spoken by Mr. Thornton, the minister,[7] and Mr. Corney of no great moment.

MR. PYM delivered in a letter bearing date at Hull Tuesday, June 21, 1642, sent to himself from Sir John Hotham, in which he showed:

That he had received his letter of the 16 of June and had since written but he feared his letters were miscarried.

That 300£ would suffice to make some new outworks and secure the town thereby.

That he had 1000 men complete in the town, which would suffice for the present defense of it.

Suspected the townsmen, but keep this to yourself.

That he desired that money might be sent in time.

The Lincolnshire men could send no force.

If need were, there might be 500 men be sent from London to Hull. MR. HAMPDEN and others thereupon called out to have the letters read no further. Others called to have them read, which made me speak in effect following:

That I did as little desire to hear news as any man; yet in respect that [he] read no more, I spake to it. This letter had been thus/

The letter was delivered back to Mr. Pym.

The messengers being called in and their answer given them that we would meet presently, they departed, and Mr. Pym and others were appointed to be reporters and went away with divers of the house to the said conference. I went not.

4. This letter was from the committee for Hull.
5. Maurice Corney, minister of the Church of St. Mary the Virgin, was ejected by Sir John Hotham in 1642. *VCH, Yorkshire, East Riding*, I, 295.
6. D'Ewes should have Thornton. Alured was a collector of the customs at Hull. *CJ*, II, 636.
7. Thornton was the comptroller.

The Lord Wharton began and read the letter of the Lord Francis Willoughby.[8]

[f. 204b] The conference being ended and the Speaker having resumed his chair, upon SIR EDWARD BOYS's motion Sir Edward Master had leave to go into the country.

Upon MR. HAMPDEN's motion Captain Skinner had leave to go into the country.

Upon MR. CROMWELL's motion it was ordered that no private committee should sit in the afternoon.[9]

Upon MR. PYM's motion seconded by others, it was ordered that 2000£ should be taken out of the contribution money in London and paid to Mr. Durand Hotham, Sir John Hotham's son,[10] for his use (viz., the father's use) and that it should be repaid out of the bill of 400,000£.

We then after some debate ordered upon the question that the bill for tonnage and poundage should be engrossed.[11]

The messenger who came from Hull and brought the committee's letter there from thence to the Speaker was brought into the house and witnessed what he knew of the offense of Mr. Thornton and Mr. Corney and so withdrew.

We then ordered that Mr. Thornton should be sent for as a delinquent and that Mr. Corney, the minister, should be summoned to be brought up under safe custody.[12]

MR. PYM then moved that we might allow Sir John Hotham 300£ to make up some new fortifications at Hull, being only some outworks. Some few spake to it.

I showed: That no man was against the fortifications if there were need, but Sir John Hotham in his own letter relates that there was likelihood of the king's going further off and then there would need no new fortifications, and therefore I desired that the said money might not be laid out till there were a true and real necessity. So it was only ordered that he might make such outworks if he saw it fit, so as the sum should not exceed 300£.

Upon MR. GREEN's motion it was ordered that 200£ should be paid to those who had transported the magazine of Hull.

SERJEANT WILDE made report of the amendments of the instructions which should be delivered to the deputy lieutenants of Warwickshire, where the amendments being read upon my motion, we passed the articles or instructions.

8. For the letter dated 19 June and an enclosed declaration from Lincolnshire, "attested by many Thousand Hands," see *LJ*, V, 155. Wing, D 542 (for the declaration).

9. Cf. *CJ*, II, 636: "Ordered, That no Committees shall sit this Afternoon."

10. Hotham's fifth son, who was admitted to the Middle Temple in November 1640. Charles Henry Hopwood, *Middle Temple Records* (London, 1904), II, 902; Joseph Foster, comp., *Pedigrees of the County Families of Yorkshire* (London, 1874), II, n.p.

11. There is no indication in *CJ* as to when the bill received its first two readings.

12. Corney was to be sent for as a delinquent, Thornton to be brought up in safe custody. *CJ*, II, 636.

[f. 207a] SIR ROBERT COOKE moved that whereas there had been a petition preferred from the gentlemen of Gray's Inn (which was against the election of one Dr. Jackson for their minister) and that the original petition was in Sir John Hotham's hands and that he had there a copy of the said petition in his hand (which he delivered into the house), that the committee to whom the original petition itself had been referred might proceed upon the said copy, being agreed on all sides to be a true one, as if they had the original petition itself and that some might be added to the committee, all which was ordered accordingly and those who were to be added were particularly named.[13]

MR. PYM moved that some course might be taken for the examination and trial of the Lord Maguire, Captain MacMahon, and Colonel Reade, who had been sent over from Dublin to be tried here, and thereupon Mr. Constantine and some other members of the house[14] were appointed to be present at their examination before the judges of the King's Bench, in which court they were to be tried as traitors, having been main actors in the rebellion in Ireland.

SIR JOHN CURZON had liberty upon his own motion to go into Derbyshire, being one of the deputy lieutenants there.[15]

We appointed to meet at 8 of the clock tomorrow morning and rose about 2 of the clock in the afternoon.

GAWDY

[f. 141b]   Wednesday, the XXII of June

The black rod came for us to see the bill pass for the reducing the rebels in Ireland.[16]

Resolved, that the bill of tonnage and poundage shall be passed till the 1 of March next.[17]

A message from the lords, they desire a conference: 1. about the Scots commissioners, 2. about the magazine that's come from Hull, 3. about a letter received from my Lord Willoughby, lord lieutenant of Lincoln.

[f. 142a] A letter from the deputy lieutenants of Lincolnshire, June the 19.

13. For John Jackson and the committee for Gray's Inn, see *PJ*, 1: 411, 429, 456. In his rough notes concerning this petition, crossed out at the bottom of f. 204b, D'Ewes has written: *I spake*.

14. Hill, Prideaux, and Pury. *CJ*, II, 636. For details see Gilbert, *History of Ireland*, I (Pt. 2), 497–512.

15. This military leave is not noted in *CJ*.

16. See *LJ*, V, 154. *SR*, V, 176–77: 16 Car. I, c. 37. This was the last bill to which King Charles gave his assent.

17. The bill was to be in effect from 1 July 1642 to 1 March 1643. *CJ*, II, 636.

That the country about the militia came in cheerfully with many volunteers. They say there is a rumor of the king's visiting those parts. Therefore, they will attend in that county for their better security.

A letter from Hull, June the 18,[18] that a minister there and the customer hath carried themselves very tumultuously in that town. 'Tis desired we would take some order with them.

A letter from Sir John Hotham to Mr. Pym, June the 21. That 300£ will sufficiently fortify the town. That he hath 1000 men complete. That we should send 400 men[19] from London down to him to Hull. That he was fearful of the townsmen if there were any trouble. That while he was employing his men in the outworks, there might be danger in the town. That 'twas not safe to have men out of Lincolnshire, the king being so near. He desired to have this kept secret.

18. The date should be 20 June. See D, above, and *CJ*, II, 636.
19. Cf. D, above.

D'EWES

June 23, Thursday, 1642

The Speaker came about 8 of the clock.[1] After prayers a debate was entered upon touching the allowance of Captain Chichester and Captain Hill for the horse and foot maintained by them and that we should take them into pay for the time to come, and in the issue it was voted that we should so do and the proportion was limited to a certain number.[2]

MR. PYM delivered in a copy of a letter bearing date at Portumna May 18, 1642, and sent from the Earl of Clanricarde to the lord justices of Ireland,[3] in which he showed amongst many other particulars:

That he had received their lordships' letters of the 18 of the last month and the 3 of this month.

That he had taken the town and fort of Galway before the succors came to him.

That he had taken the mayor of Galway[4] into his majesty's protection and the young men of the town who had laid down their arms. That he especially used the help of Captain Willoughby.[5]

That he was much joyed with the succors which were come to him.

That his friends in several of his castles had served faithfully in joining with him against the rebels.

Sir Valentine Blake, Francis Blake, and others with two friars named Valentine Browne and Francis Fleming were the chief instigators of the rebellion.[6]

1. For a letter from Yarmouth omitted by D'Ewes, see G, below.

2. The commissioners for Irish affairs were now to draw up an appropriate order. See *CJ*, II, 637; and CIA, 22 and 27 June.

3. This letter is calendared in *HMC, Fifth Report*, p. 33. The commissioners for Irish affairs had referred the matter of Galway to the house. See CIA, 21 June.

4. Walter Lynch. See Sir Richard Bellings, *History of the Irish Confederation and the War in Ireland, 1641–1649*, ed. John T. Gilbert (Dublin, 1882–91), II, 34.

5. Captain Anthony Willoughby was commanding the fort at Galway in the absence of his father, Sir Francis Willoughby, governor of the fort. See *PJ*, 2: 426, n. 3. For events in Galway from mid-February to mid-April, see *HMC, Fifth Report*, pp. 32–33; and Richard Bagwell, *Ireland under the Stuarts* (1909–16; reprint, Frome, 1963), II, 6–8.

6. Browne, a Franciscan friar, served as an emissary from Galway to County Meath in the early months of 1642. Sir Valentine Blake, a member of the Catholic confederacy, was expelled from the Irish House of Commons on 22 June. Francis Blake was one of the signers of the submission of Galway. See Bellings, *Irish Confederation*, I, 274–77, and II, 34; and Bagwell, *Ireland*, II, 11, 19.

That he would endeavor to get in the king's composition rent as he [*sic*] soon as he could receive instructions from the former collector.

The letters were very long, and he concluded with a desire to have all his errors pardoned.

Then were read the copy of the articles passed between the said Earl of Clanricarde and Captain Willoughby on the one part and mayor and town of Galway on the other part,[7] in which amongst other things the exercise of the Romish religion was to be permitted.

Then was read the copy of the instrument of the submission of the mayor, sheriffs, and free burgesses of the town of Galway.[8]

MR. PYM moved that we might not allow of this agreement made by the Earl of Clanricarde with the town of Galway which was seconded by others,[9] and in the issue it was put off, and it was ordered that we should take up the debate of it again tomorrow morning at 9 of the clock.

The order of the day was then read which had been made on Tuesday last, by which it had been appointed that we should take into consideration his majesty's answer sent to the 19 propositions of both houses.[10] The order being read, MR. TOMKINS and SIR BENJAMIN RUDYARD moved in general that we should embrace an accommodation of peace, which made me stand up and move in effect following:

That I did not conceive that general motions of an accommodation would expedite the work of this day, but that we were to enter into particulars and see how far his majesty had answered our desires, and that I conceive that there are two parts in this answer of his majesty's: the first part in which there are many asperities and corrosives in the expressions, and the latter part beginning at page 23 (viz., of the printed copy which I had in my hand) wherein his majesty doth [f. 210b] satisfy or at least endeavor to satisfy divers of our demands. And I could wish that we might first begin there. Divers spake after me, and at last we agreed to read over the whole answer, which the clerk began accordingly, and after he had finished the preamble or preface, which contained many vehement and virulent expressions against those members of both houses that had been the contrivers and framers of these propositions and of some former messages sent to his majesty and some declarations or remonstrances to the kingdom which had been formerly published, divers spake concerning the bitterness of expressions there[11] and would have it referred to a committee which few did

---

7. These articles are calendared in *HMC, Fifth Report,* p. 32.

8. For the text of the submission, dated 6 May, see Bellings, *Irish Confederation,* II, 33–34.

9. For the action of the commissioners for Irish affairs, see CIA, 21 June.

10. See 21 June, n. 6. For the text of the Nineteen Propositions, see *PJ,* 2: 494–97.

11. For the preamble see Rushworth, IV, 725–27. These additional comments appear in Verney, *Notes,* p. 181:

oppose, only they conceived that it was not yet fit to be referred to a committee. But in the issue after a long debate, it was at last referred to a committee to consider of and to prepare an answer to it. I went out of the house for a while just as the committee was naming, of which Mr. Selden and Mr. Waller were two. Before I returned again, the clerk had begun to read his majesty's answers to our 19 propositions.[12]

GAWDY

[f. 142a]   Thursday, the XXIII of June

A letter from Yarmouth to Mr. Corbet, June the 20. That they have an information that there is ships coming from Dunkirk for Yarmouth. That there is 500 men billeted in Newcastle on Saturday last.[13]

[f. 142b] Resolved by question, that the preamble of the king's message in answer to the 19 propositions shall be referred to a committee.

Resolved, that the answer of the king's to our 19 propositions shall be referred to a committee of the whole house.

In the afternoon.

[Committee of the Whole House]

The committee of the whole house sit about the propositions.[14]

There were about 260 in the house at the committee.

Resolved, that a subcommittee shall draw up a declaration to vindicate the house of those aspersions laid upon them in the answer to the 1 proposition.

Resolved, that this house will not insist any further in the first proposition as now it is.[15]

Waler. Let us first look to our saifty, and then to our honour.

Pierpoint. Either wee have, or have not, deserved these imputations. If wee have, let us confesse them, if not, let us cleare ourselves.

Sir Jo. Cooke. Princes are jealous of there honour, and consider it as other princes value it abroad. The honour of parliament is to settle the peace and welfaire of the publique.

12. For the rest of the day, see G and H, below.

13. The information was referred to the committee for Newcastle, to which the knights and burgesses for Norfolk (including Gawdy) were added. CJ, II, 637.

14. Bulstrode Whitelocke was in the chair. CJ, II, 637.

15. For the king's answer to the first proposition concerning the removal of all privy councillors and other officers of state except those approved by parliament, see Rushworth, IV, 727–28. For the comments of Giovanni Giustinian, the Venetian ambassador, see CSP Ven., 1642–43, p. 92. William Montagu wrote to his father, Lord Montagu, concerning the first proposition: "Mr. Pimm, Mr. Hampden, Mr. Hollis, Mr. Stroud, and most of their part opposed the vote, and would have had the proposition stood (sic)." HMC, Buccleuch MSS, I, 306.

The Speaker to the chair.

Resolved, that this house will not insist further in the first proposition as now it is.

The house rose not till nine a clock.

HILL

[p. 102]   Thursday, June 23, 1642

The king's answer to the 19 propositions of both houses of parliament were taken into consideration by the whole house.[16]

The preface referred to a committee to consider and prepare an answer to it.

[Committee of the Whole House]

The houses [sic] began with the propositions.

Selden, no question of ancient time officers have been chosen in parliament. Not granted therefore that they must be chosen in parliament.

And some acts made that they shall be chosen [in] parliament, but those acts repealed.

Question: If we shall acquiesce with the king's answer to the first proposition.

Demand is that all great officers shall be chosen by both houses.

Glyn, not acquiesce with the king's answer. If we should, we agree that the houses' demand that present parliaments, neither others;[17] but this hath been done in good kings' times.

[p. 103] It is reason why these things were demanded.

We demand it not as a right but as a security for time to come.

The king saying 'tis unreasonable.

[Er]go, necessary we should cite precedents of officers named by king and approved by parliament. 5 H. 4, vident folio 25.[18]

Reason of this proposition: Neither could think that they conceive their councillors do evil, nor could think that they perceive that the ills were from them that made secret and null their acts. When they do, this was the way to meet with ill councillors.

16. Cf. Verney, Notes, pp. 181–82.
17. Glyn's point is not clear.
18. The commission of array. See Appendix H.

Solicitor, precedents frequent. 5 E. 2 desire of removal.[19] 15 E. 3 both repealed and desired a new law in the case.[20]

If we insist upon this proposition, it must be because it is an act of law, not of grace.

It hath be[en] done for removal in case of nonage or great excess of ministers. 17 E. 2 was repealed and enabled this bill 15 E. 3, but 17 E. 3 was repealed.[21] He know no law in point of right.

2. Parliament in case of necessity says require not only things in Petition of Right but a conscience to demand things in point of necessity.

Here, videlicet, is oath of execution[22] put in to observe not only Magna Charta, execution general, but here Petition of Right made particular, and theirs is oath of public admon[ition]. It calls not only God to witness but makes himself and estate liable to punishment.

He wishes [to] decline that will insist here that approbation should be here.

Mr. Pierrepont, 'tis not denied as unreasonable but 'tis said we ask it as a mockery.

Question: If as unreasonable or out of fear, we should leave it.

[p. 104] Committee declare that in reason and justice we demand it. We leave it, if we do leave it, because we would avoid all inducements of bringing of civil war.

Reasons not to insist upon it: 1. Because the king saith he will use best caution for time to come. 2. That he will remove any as shall be charged. See other reasons urged by him. Look upon king's answer how it may be reconciling to our propositions, not look upon the propositions as just and legal.

Mr. Fiennes, to it declare reasons of our demand, precedent by former times, yet not to decline it but to leave as a *non liquet*[23] for better calms.

Lenthall, if we insist and resolve to have it and king resolves not to grant it, what inconvenience is of both sides.[24]

If we decline it, we fall into scorn and worthy to be taken no good advisers.

[Er]go, take this course in giving reasons and precedents.

19. See *SR*, I, 160: 5 E. II, c. 13 ("Of removing evil Counsellors from the King").

20. See *SR*, I, 296: 15 E. III, St. 1, c. 4 ("How such Officers shall be appointed, and answerable in Parliament"). Because this statute had been made without the king's consent, it was repealed by *SR*, I, 297: 15 E. III, St. 2.

21. See *RP*, II, 139: 17 E. III, n. 23 (*De l'estatut fait a Westm' l'an xv, q'est repellez*).

22. The first proposition stated that the privy councillors should take an oath "for the due Execution of their Places."

23. "No decision."

24. Verney, *Notes*, p. 182, has: "Mr. Lenthall. To insist uppon our trust, and shew the reasons, but then leave it to the king."

2. Insist upon inconvenience of evil counsels. 3. Conclude we hold it necessary but leave it to his majesty to consider it, that it be no cause of breach betwixt us and his majesty.

Pym, 'tis clear by the common law of the kingdom till H. 3 time who assumed choice of officers of state when prerogative increased upon us.

He at first gave his consent to this proposition, considering who were the causers of all our miseries. 2. He saw no alteration but from worse to worse till king incline to the parliament. [Er]go, council chosen as they have been, we shall soon return to the same mischiefs and break through all laws made or to be made.

It is said king promise there shall be an oath. Answer: A great obligation to tender conscience, but men without conscience will break over that. Ill counsel come not within our aegis to prevent. They that are called in council are bound by an oath of se- [p. 105] crecy. We should propound it by way of approbation whereby we give king great advantage of honor.[25]

Objection: It may be a cause of great breach and another time more fit. Answer: This is the fittest time. We do it not by way of compulsion, he abhors all such thoughts, but to lay it home[26] to the king and let it lie upon his conscience.

Subcommittee to draw declaration for vindicat[ing] aspersions laid upon this house in answer to the first proposition and to show reason and precedents whereupon parliament had just grounds to make that proposition to his majesty.

Glyn, one wishes [to] insist upon this proposition as it now went to the king and res[olve] to put out all officers. Yet 5 E. 2 it was so, all put out by parliament when ordinance against law. 15 E. 2 then repealed,[27] and time H. 6 divers Privy Council remove[d] from the king by desire of the parliament, unless 2 that he desired might remain for a year.

4 precedents time E. 2, 2 in time R. 2, E. 3, but the commons because of inconvenience brought it back again.

Whistler, he not satisfie[d] with this answer. 2. Clear not wish [to] recede. 3.

25. Verney, *Notes*, p. 182, has:

Pim. Henry 3. the first king that did chuse the great officers without the consent of parliament, and that it was, and is, the common law of the kingdom.

An oath bindes honest men but not knaves. Parliment holds but 50 [*blank*]. Councellors take an oath of secresy. The king will not reveall ill councellours. Petition still, and leave it to the kings consideration.

26. MS: *whom*.

27. Hill probably intended to write *15 E. 3*. See above, n. 20. 13 E. 2 is cited in Verney, *Notes*, p. 182.

If we insist upon this on[e] only, he conceive nothing except it were of right. If it were, then a Petition of Right might be demanded.[28]

Ordered, that the first of the 19 propositions tendered to his majesty as now it is shall not be insisted upon. Resolved upon the question in the grand committee and after in the house.

28. Hill's notes for 23 and 28 June and 6 July are particularly difficult to decipher. The editors are deeply grateful to Maija Jansson of the Yale Center for Parliamentary History for her help with the paleography, the Law French, and the legal citations.

D'EWES

June 24, Friday, 1642

The Speaker came about 8 of the clock. We went to prayers awhile after, and I then went out of the house.

Before I returned, divers motions were made and some ordered.[1]

MR. PYM also made report of that part of the conference which was desired by the lords on Wednesday last touching the magazine come from Hull, which was that it should be disposed into several halls of London and other places convenient and that the committee for the militia of London should appoint officers to look to it and to pay them, to which the house assented.[2]

I returned into the house [as] they were in debate about the Earl of Clanricarde's agreement made with the townsmen of Galway in Ireland, which had been read yesterday, in which he being a papist had agreed with them being papists that they should amongst other particulars have the free exercise of the Romish religion. Divers spake against this agreement as being against the direct act of parliament lately passed[3] and that the Earl of Clanricarde had no authority to make it and therefore that we should speedily send to his majesty to have it made void, and in the issue upon MR. CROMWELL's motion that the whole matter of the debate might be referred to a committee, it was upon the motion of SIR HENRY VANE, the elder, referred to the commissioners for the affairs of Ireland, who were appointed the committee to whom this should be referred.[4]

Mr. Walter Long was sent up with several messages to the lords.[5]

MR. ARTHUR GOODWIN delivered in a petition from the officers of the trained bands and of the volunteers of the county of Buckingham who met last Friday at Aylesbury in the same county, which was directed to both houses, which was read; and it agreed in many particulars with that of the officers of the trained bands of Essex, only they desired a new lord lieutenant in lieu of the Lord Paget, who

1. See *CJ*, II, 637.

2. For the order see G, below, and *CJ*, II, 637.

3. Possibly a reference to the first of the four acts for reducing the rebels of Ireland, which required practicing Roman Catholics to forfeit their lands and tenements. See *PJ*, 2: 62; and *SR*, V, 170–71.

4. The committee was composed of the MPs who were commissioners plus Vane, Sr., and Mildmay. *CJ*, II, 638. For a letter from Parsons and Borlase concerning Galway, see G and H, below.

5. For his messages see below, n. 8, and *LJ*, V, 157.

had withdrawn himself to York. The petition being read, the said MR. GOODWIN showed that besides the trained bands there came near upon a 1000 volunteers and that all sorts expressed much cheerfulness.

We voted that the said Mr. Goodwin should carry it up to the lords, that the Lord Paget should be discharged, the Lord Wharton appointed in his room, and that the petition should be printed,[6] and that he should desire the lords to join with us in all.

MR. NATHANIEL FIENNES reported of that part of the conference which [we] had with lords on Wednesday last touching Scottish treaty. We assented. And MR. HAMPDEN then made report of more of that treaty from Scottish commissioners. We assented. And Mr. Hampden sent up to the lords to desire the[ir] consent.[7]

Rose a little after 12. To meet at 2 afternoon.

[f. 217b]   Post Meridiem

The Speaker resumed his chair, and a motion or two of little moment having passed, he left the chair.

[Committee of the Whole House]

And Mr. Whitelocke came into the clerk's chair, and the committee proceeded with the matter touching the king's answer to our propositions. But some raised an unnecessary dispute about taking up a new debate touching the vote which we passed yesternight both at the committee and in the house, so as the said vote might have been in some possibility to have been hazarded but that, by the coming of Mr. Justice Foster and Dr. Aylett from the lords, the Speaker was desired to resume his chair and Mr. Whitelocke left the clerk's chair.

They brought several messages from the lords touching their agreement to the articles of the Scottish treaty and other particulars carried up to them in the morning with some small alterations and amendments in some of them, and so they withdrew and departed. The house agreed to the same alterations and amendments.[8]

MR. STRODE moved to have the proclamation read which had been sent down

6. For the text see LJ, V, 159. Wing, H 3488. For the Essex petitions, see 8 June, n. 29, and 17 June, n. 7.

7. For details see CJ, II, 638.

8. The lords also agreed to the orders for disposing of the magazine from Hull, for securing the loan of £100,000 from the City, and for paying £2000 to Sir John Hotham, as well as to the instructions for the deputy lieutenants of Warwickshire and the list of ordnance for Ireland. For details see LJ, V, 158, 159–60.

to the house in the morning from the lords, which was done accordingly, in which the king forbade all raising of men and horses and contributing of plate and money under color of defense of the parliament, which proclamation is in print. I came into the house about 3 of the clock a little after it had been read, having not been there this afternoon before. The house was then in debate concerning the said proclamation, and in the issue it was ordered to be referred to a committee to prepare an answer to it, of which committee Mr. Selden and others were named.[9]

[Committee of the Whole House]

This being done, the Speaker left his chair, and Mr. Whitelocke took the clerk's chair and then proceeded with the reading of the king's answer to our second proposition and read the proposition itself being as follows (transcribe it out of the printed book).[10] We then fell in debate upon the first part of it, to wit, that his majesty should not advise with private men or unknown or unsworn counselors touching the great affairs of the kingdom, and that those matters which were proper for parliament should be transacted and concluded there and nowhere else. We all agreed to insist upon the latter part of this clause so as it might be reduced to some certainty what were the matters proper to parliament, but for the first part of it Mr. Selden, myself, and others did speak against it. Mr. Selden and others showed how necessary it was for the king upon several occasions to advise with others than such as were his sworn councillors, and Mr. Selden did particularly instance in the calling of this parliament that the king was advised to it by the petition of divers of the nobility and others who were not his sworn councillors.[11] I spake in effect following:

No man can deny but that the happiness of the king and kingdom doth consist in the choice and use of good and faithful councillors, and such was the advice of the parliament *13° H. 4, n° 3°,*[12] but I much doubt whether by this that we here desire we shall attain that end that we aim at; for I do conceive that there are cases in which there is a necessity for the king to advise with private counsel or matters of great weight may be lost and perished, for we know there are certain

9. On 22 June the proclamation had been "proclaimed in London, and pasted upon the Door where the Committee of London sit" (i.e., the militia committee). See G, below, and *LJ,* V, 157, 160. For the text see Edward Husbands, *An Exact Collection* (London, 1643), pp. 367–72. Wing, C 2651. Hill was a member of the new committee. *CJ,* II, 638.

10. D'Ewes did not transcribe the proposition; however, see *PJ,* 2: 494–95. For the king's answer see Rushworth, IV, 728–30.

11. On 28 August 1640 twelve peers, most of whom were not sworn councillors, petitioned the king to summon a parliament "within some short and convenient time." See Samuel Rawson Gardiner, ed., *The Constitutional Documents of the Puritan Revolution 1625–1660* (1906; reprint, Oxford, 1968), pp. 134–36.

12. *RP,* III, 647.

great affairs proper for the kings of England to do of themselves, as money mint, leagues, fortifications, peace and war, and the like, wherein there may sometimes be great necessity and use of private counsel. For the greatest action that ever [f. 218b] was undertaken by any king of England and which brought the most glory to this nation were those conquests of E. 3 in France, and those were at first undertaken merely by the advice of Monsieur d'Artois.[13] We know also that Queen Elizabeth took the advice of a private man touching the farming of her customs notwithstanding that the said advice was opposed by some of her council who received great yearly gratuities from the farmers of the customs.[14] And there may be such business of weight and require so much speed and secrecy as the whole will be lost. And that uncertainty which drew me to dissent from this clause when it first passed persuades me to be of the same mind still. Neither is there here any distinction made between the sitting and not sitting of a parliament which notwithstanding will breed a great diversity or difference, for I think no man will doubt but if a peer of the realm shall raise arms against the king and a parliament be not sitting before his trial, [he] shall be tried or adjudged by the ordinary course with the advice of the judges; but we find in the Parliament Roll *de a° 5° H. 4, n° 12°,*[15] that whereas the Earl of Northumberland raised power against the king, that the king had referred the consideration thereof to his justices, whereupon the lords in parliament protested against it and took the judgment thereof to themselves and did adjudge it neither treason nor felony but a trespass only finable at the will of the king. And it may sometimes also happen that a great favorite may be so potent, as we know there was one of late (viz., George Villiers, Duke of Buckingham), who may so overawe the king's council as that he shall obtain any unreasonable demand by their vote, and so the sovereign may be left naked of counsel unless he may have liberty to advise in secret with private men; and though the kings of England have often advised with their parliament concerning those great affairs of the kingdom that were in their own power to have disposed of, yet sometimes the House of Commons have excused themselves from intermeddling in such affairs and desired the king to transact the same by the advice of his council. And therefore my desire is that we may lay aside this first part of the second proposition and insist no further upon it.

Divers spake after me, and in the issue in respect that the Speaker did put all

13. Probably Jean d'Artois, constable of France. *Dictionnaire de Biographie Française.*

14. Probably a reference to Thomas Smyth, a prominent London merchant who served as collector of tonnage and poundage during the first half of Queen Elizabeth's reign. The councillors who benefited were the Earl of Leicester, Lord Burghley, and Sir Christopher Hatton. See Dietz, *English Public Finance,* pp. 307–23.

15. *RP,* III, 524. For Northumberland's revolt against the king, see E. F. Jacob, *The Fifteenth Century 1399–1485* (Oxford, 1978), pp. 46–54.

the clause together to the question (which should rather have been put severally), it was carried in the affirmative that we should still insist upon it.

We then fell upon the debate of several other clauses of the said second
proposition, and some particulars were altered and amended in it. That whereas
the assent should be by one half of the council, we altered that the same assent
should suffice to be by any six or more of them.[16] The greatest matter which
caused the longest debate amongst us was concerning their subscription to
every warrant or order that should be made, against which divers spake and
others answered that else it could not be known who did assent to such warrants
or orders. I spake in effect following:

That I saw the main objection was that unless they should subscribe, it could
not be known who were the authors of evil counsels, but for that I conceived
that it might well enough be known what privy councillors were present though
they did not subscribe, for at every meeting of the council when any acts were
passed by them, the presence of them is set down, so as by that means we may
easily come to know who were the advisers of any evil counsels; but I think we
shall do well to permit this to pass because it will be a means to make all men
afraid to be of the Privy Council, seeing they are to be questioned in parliament
if they shall intermeddle with any particulars which are proper to be discussed
in parliament. Others spake after me, and in the issue the question passed.[17]

The house rose about 8 of the clock at night.

GAWDY

[f. 142b]   Friday, the xxiiii of June

[f. 143a] Ordered, that the magazine that is come from Hull shall be put int[o]
Leadenhall, Apothecaries' Hall, and Leathersellers' Hall, and other places.
That those that are for the militia in London to have the government of it.[18]

My Lord Willoughby send us a declaration of the Lincolnshire men, that they
will spend their lives and fortunes in defense of king and parliament according
to their Protestation.[19]

---

16. According to the second proposition there should be at least fifteen but not more than
twenty-five privy councillors. *PJ*, 2: 495.

17. After the Speaker had resumed the chair, Whitelocke reported concerning the resolutions
passed by the committee. See *CJ*, II, 638–39.

18. This paragraph and the next are part of Pym's report of the conference of 22 June. The
London militia committee was to have jurisdiction over the arms and ammunition. *CJ*, II, 637.

19. See 22 June, n. 8.

A letter from the lord justices to my lord lieutenant, June the 9,[20] about the submission of the rebels of Galway to my Lord of Clanricarde, which they mislike that rebels after the committing of great outrages should be taken into protection when they please. They desired to be taken into protection till the king's pleasure be further known.

A message to the lords to desire that my Lord Paget may be displaced of being lord lieutenant of Buckinghamshire and my Lord [Wharton] may be nominated in his room.

The letters of the lord justices and other informations concerning the protecting the rebels of Galway referred to a committee.

A message from the lords, they send us down the king's proclamation against the levying of horse and money. I had this from many, but I was not there.

[f. 143b] In the afternoon.

A message from the lords, they agree with us about the instructions for Warwickshire, for 2000£ for Sir John Hotham, and other things.

The proclamation against levying of horse and money read and referred to a committee.

[Committee of the Whole House]

The house turned into a committee about the answer to the 19 propositions.

HILL

[p. 106]   Friday, June 24th, 1642

Earl of Clanricarde, his taking of Galway, upon terms which will pluck up by the roots all that we have done this parliament for suppression of the rebellion there.

June 9, Dublin, chief justices writ rebels lay siege to Galway for 6 weeks. The earl sent provisions to them and wrote for forces to quench that flame. Finding trouble upon treaties of submission, we gave caution though they submitted, yet he should admit no terms. The messenger was surprised, who burnt the letter.[21] Since mayor of Galway submitted and yielded with submission till his majesty's pleasure were further known, yet to have and enjoy all they have by which he invites all others to come in. It is until his majesty's

---

20. For the text see *HMC, Ormonde MSS*, n.s., II, 148–51.

21. The lord justices' letters cautioning Clanricarde against promising anything to the rebels "came not to his hands, but were by the messenger burnt, when his person was intercepted by the rebels." *HMC, Ormonde MSS*, n.s., II, 148.

arrival here, so drawn, but yet they conceive it their intention was till his majesty's pleasure were further known. All their arms are left in their own hands, not put into the fort. Had we consulted herein, we had never yielded unto it, the rather seeing the fort is so strengthened by us as all the rebels cannot fetch it from us.

Their opinions:[22] The taking them into protection for their lives and upon those terms is destructive to all his majesty's designs. Town of Galway is the main conduit to the province of Connaught, which is a harbor lying open to France and Spain.

[Committee of the Whole House]

This day a house put into a grand committee concerning the king's propositions.

Wilde, there is no direct answer but returns [p. 107] with a recrimination. Here this is Petition of Right.[23]

Resolved, that the same subcommittee[24] to consider of the vindication of this house in the aspersions in the answer to the 2d proposition. And also of the answers to the rest of the propositions.

22. I.e., the lord justices of Ireland.
23. This reference to the king's evasive response to the Petition of Right may have been made by Wilde, for he was a member of the 1628 parliament. See *PJ*, 2: 356.
24. See G, 23 June.

D'EWES

June 25, Saturday, 1642

The Speaker came about 8 of the clock. MR. HAMPDEN after prayers delivered in a petition from the town of Berkhamstead in the county of Hertford to set up a lecture there, which was after a little dispute yielded unto by the house and ordered accordingly.

I then withdrew out of the house for a while, and when I returned in again, the bill of tonnage and poundage had been newly read the 3d time. MR. SOLICITOR brought in a clause ready engrossed for the settling of the customers' fees, which after some debate was allowed with a little amendment.

Then MR. WHISTLER delivered in another proviso for a freedom for all persons to transport over white cloths and undressed. This cost a long and a vehement dispute, some showing that the Duke of Lenox had only a monopoly now to license all white cloths to be carried over the sea paying to him 2s. 8d.[1]

Post Meridiem

The Speaker came about 4 of the clock. SIR WALTER ERLE moved that some course might be taken to pay the warders of the Tower. And upon Sir Henry Mildmay's/[2]

MR. REYNOLDS made report from the committee to whom the business of Galway was referred,[3] that they/

That the Earl of St. Albans do show by what warrant he granted this protection to the town of Galway.

That his majesty be desired that the protection do cease.

That the lord lieutenant and lord justices may summon the town to yield upon discretion to his majesty's pleasure.

Agreed upon MR. PYM's motion that/[4]

---

1. The bill passed and was sent to the lords along with the printed book of rates. *CJ,* II, 639. For the rest of the morning's proceedings, see G, below, and *CJ,* II, 639–40.

2. The warders of the Tower, perhaps on the motion of Mildmay, master of the Jewel House, were to be recommended to the commissioners for the Treasury. *CJ,* II, 640.

3. See 24 June, n. 4. Reynolds reported that although Galway, "the most important Town of all Ireland, in respect of the Strength, Wealth, and Situation . . . was in actual and open Rebellion, . . . the Earl of St. Albanes [i.e., Clanricarde] did entertain a Treaty with the Town." *CJ,* II, 640.

4. "Resolved, That these Votes be carried up to the Lords at a Conference." *CJ,* II, 640.

[f. 231b] Upon MR. CROMWELL's motion it was ordered that the commissioners for Ireland should consider what course might be taken with the papists in Dublin,[5] there being above 10,000 of them there, for he showed that by that means they are not only enforced to keep a constant garrison of 10,000 men in the said city but also all their designs and counsels are revealed by the said papists to the enemy, so as the other day when some forces should have gone into the province of Connaught for the assistance of the lord president there, the very draft horses that should have drawn the carriages, being near upon the number of 300, were taken away from the walls of Dublin the very night preceding that day on which the said forces should have gone in the same expedition.

The SPEAKER delivered in a letter bearing date at Mallow[6] 14 June 1642, being sent unto him from the Lord Inchiquin, Sir Charles Vavasour, and others of the council of war in the province of Munster, in which they showed that during the lord president's sickness (viz., Sir William St. Leger, whose daughter the said Lord Inchiquin had married) matters had been referred to him, the Lord Inchiquin, the vice president, and them, the council of war.[7]

That they could not proceed in their former victories without speedy supply but must quit the castles they had gotten. That they wanted money, artillery, victuals, and clothing for their soldiers and supply of men because many were sick and some dead.[8]

Upon MR. PYM's motion and delivery in/

Divers of the officers/[9]

GAWDY

[f. 143b]   Saturday, the xxv of June

The bill of tonnage and poundage with the book of rates passed our house till the 1 of March next.

A message from the lords, they desire a conference concerning a paper that is

---

5. Cf. *PJ*, 2: 268.

6. MS: *Mayalle*. For the letter see James Hogan, ed., *Letters and Papers Relating to the Irish Rebellion between 1642–46* (Dublin, 1936), pp. 42–43.

7. When St. Leger died in early July, the command in Munster devolved upon Inchiquin. See Hogan, *Irish Rebellion*, pp. 61, 62–64.

8. "And the House was informed, That the Commissioners had taken Order in all these Particulars." *CJ*, II, 640. For various orders concerning provisions for Munster, see CIA, passim.

9. Fifteen officers, whose pay was in arrears from the Scots wars, were to be paid out of the money received from the defense levy of £400,000. For their names see *CJ*, II, 640.

enclosed in a letter from the king,[10] which is of the highest concernment that ever came to both houses of parliament.[11]

The paper was long and sharp.

A committee appointed to take this message into consideration and to vindicate the house of the aspersions laid upon them,[12] and though this sharp message cometh to us when we are answering the propositions and though there be a garrison now put into Newcastle, yet we intend to go on with the propositions [f. 144a] and to let the people know how necessary it is to go on with the subscriptions about the horse. That we intend to proceed so with the propositions as shall most conduce to the peace of the kingdom.[13]

In the afternoon.

MR. REYNOLDS, a report that Galway was in actual rebellion. That the Earl of St. Albans hath taken them into his protection upon their submission.

Resolved, that the Earl of St. Albans be required by the lord justices by what authority he took them into his protection.

Resolved, that the king be moved that my Lord of St. Albans may revoke his protection to them.

Resolved, that the town of Galway be forthwith summoned by the lord justices to submit themselves to the king's mercy.

Resolved, that these be heads for the conference with the lords.

10. The king was responding to parliament's message concerning the Yorkshire petition. See 15 June, n. 28. In his message the king lamented that he had not been sent the petition itself so that he "might have discerned the Number and Quality of the Petitioners," which he had "great Reason to believe was not in Truth so considerable as is pretended." See *LJ*, V, 160, 161–63. Wing, C 2137. With regard to the number of signatures, see 8 June, n. 35.

11. The lords further observed: "That divers scandalous and false Informations are come to His Majesty's Ears, even of Things . . . within their own Walls." *LJ*, V, 160. For Pym's report of the conference, see *CJ*, II, 639.

12. It was ordered that the message be referred "to the Committee formerly appointed to clear the House from the Imputations laid on them in his Majesty's Messages, to peruse and consider this Message, and all other; and to collect the Falsities and Scandals contained in [them] . . . and to set them forth together in One Declaration." *CJ*, II, 639.

13. William Montagu wrote to his father, Lord Montagu, that the messenger who brought the king's message from York reported that "the Lords subscribe there to the raising of 2,000 horse" for the king. This information is followed by an incomplete list of the names and subscriptions. See *HMC, Buccleuch MSS*, I, 306. Cf. a more complete list in *CSPD, 1641–43*, p. 344.

D'EWES

[f. 231b]   June 26 [*sic*], Monday, 1642

The Speaker came about 8 of the clock.

I returned in about 10 of the clock. The house/[1]

Mr. Archdale Palmer, the high sheriff of Leicestershire, was named a deputy lieutenant of the same shire upon the LORD RUTHIN's motion and approved by the house.

Some other motions being made which came to nothing, Sir Francis Knollys, the elder, being a very/[2]

[f. 235a] MR. PYM delivered in certain letters which were sent to himself from Sir John Wray and other deputy lieutenants of the county of Lincoln, members of this house, bearing date at Lincoln June 22, 1642,[3] in which they showed that one William Clarke of Grantham had preferred a petition to the Lord Willoughby, lord lieutenant of that county, which they thought fit, having received the said accusations taken upon examination which the mayor of Grantham sent them, to send up the said party in safe custody and the said examinations with him, the substance of which examinations was as followeth:

That the said William Clarke, being an apothecary of Grantham, had said when the king went to York that if the prince had stayed behind him, he should have been crowned king, and now that the prince was gone with the king, the Duke of York should be crowned king. That he had also asked one of his neighbors whether he would be for the king or for the parliament, and he answering that he was both for king and parliament, he further pressed him to know whether if they two should differ which he would be for, and the other answering that he would be then for the king with all his heart, the said William Clarke said to him, "Thou hast a rotten, stinking heart within thee, for if thou wilt be for the king, thou must be for the papists," with some other dangerous words.

Whereupon there grew a debate in the house whether or no the said William Clarke should be examined in the house or transmitted over to the King's Bench

---

1. For proceedings omitted by D'Ewes, see G and H, below, and *CJ*, II, 640–41.

2. Knollys was ninety when elected to the Long Parliament. Keeler, p. 243. There is nothing in *CJ* to complete D'Ewes's comment; however, there are several gaps in *CJ* on this day.

3. The letter from the Lincolnshire committee concerning Clarke is calendared in *HMC*, *Portland MSS*, I, 40.

in respect that these examinations had been taken before George Floyd, mayor of the town of Grantham, and other justices of the peace.

Divers pressed to have him called in and heard which drew me to speak in effect following:

That there were two parts to be considered in this man's speech. The first without all question concerning the parliament, wherein he said that the prince or in his absence the Duke of York should be crowned in the king's absence. Another is those dangerous speeches spoken concerning the king himself. Wherefore I see no reason to call him in at all unless we will call him in as a delinquent for the first speeches, and therefore I desire that he may be transmitted over to the King's Bench there to be tried.

Others spake after me, and in the issue it was ordered as I had moved that he should be transmitted over to the King's Bench.

MR. CROMWELL returned and showed that the lords had agreed to our instructions for Warwickshire and had resolved to send for the Earl of Northampton in the same means by which they had sent for the Earl of Lindsey.[4]

Sir Walter Erle was sent up to desire a conference concerning the business of Galway and concerning the Scottish treaty and to let the lords know that we understood that there was an intention for the judges to adjourn next Michaelmas term the last day of this term to York and therefore to desire the lords to send to the judges about it.[5]

MR. DENZIL HOLLES moved that Sir John Bramston, lord chief justice of the King's Bench/[6]

SIR WALTER ERLE returned, lords' conference presently. Mr. Reynolds, Mr. Nathaniel Fiennes, and Mr. Hampden managers.

Mr. Reynolds managed that of Galway. Mr. Nathaniel Fiennes that of Scots. I not present. Conference ended.[7]

Sir Edward Leech, Dr. Aylett, lords' conference about bill of tonnage and poundage. We went.[8]

Lord Say managed it. Fees to *1° Jac.* when no fees taken,[9] and clause

4. The Warwickshire instructions appear in *LJ*, V, 165–66. For the decision to summon the Earl of Lindsey and the letter concerning the Earl of Northampton, see H, 9 June, and G, below.

5. "All the Judges did aver, 'That they have not heard any Thing concerning the Adjournment of the next Term to Yorke.'" The peers thereupon ordered that should such a command come, the judges were to inform the upper house "and forbear to do any Thing therein." *LJ*, V, 166. For the king's attempt to remove the law courts to York for Trinity term, see *PJ*, 2: 335, 367, 381.

6. William Clarke was to be sent to Bramston. *CJ*, II, 641.

7. At the conference it was ordered that Clanricarde's protection of Galway should cease, and the Scots treaty was further amended. See *LJ*, V, 166, 167.

8. D'Ewes was one of the four reporters. *CJ*, II, 641.

9. "That *1° Jac.* there is no certain Settlement of Fees for Officers of the Custom-house; and therefore desire you to fix upon some Year, when Fees were certain." The year was therefore changed to 4 *Jac*. *CJ*, II, 641.

touching white cloths which repeals a statute in H. 8 time and may hinder bill and hurt commonwealth. [10] Lord Wharton then delivered a writing touching the Scottish exceptions. It was [*illegible*] put in. [11] When it ended, I withdrew.

[f. 235b] The conference being ended, MR. PEARD made report thereof to the house in my absence. And the house agreed to the amendment of the 4 year of King James in that proviso for the customers' fees. The house agreed also to the paper of the Scots exceptions in which they desired an alteration of the book of rates.

The house rose between 2 and 3. I was returned again when the house had newly ordered to send for the sheriff of Lancashire [12] as a delinquent.

Post Meridiem

Propositions. Debate 3 proposition. I spake to it.

[Harl. 164, f. 269a] The house proceeded with the debate of the 3d proposition of the 19 propositions sent to our committee at York to present to his majesty, being in print, in which we desired that we might have the approbation of divers great officers as of the high steward, high constable, earl marshal, and divers others, even to the two chief justices of either bench and the chief baron of the Exchequer, but the master of the rolls was not named. After the proposition was read and the king's answer in print, the house remained a pretty whiles silent, which made me stand up and speak in effect following:

That in respect all men were silent, I thought fit to begin and to lose no further time, hoping that I was fully satisfied myself that there was no reason for us to insist any further upon some of these great offices here named, so I should satisfy others that we should leave them wholly to the king's disposing; only I was glad that the master of the rolls his place was so sufficiently supplied as that there was no mention of him here amongst the rest (at which divers smiled because Sir Charles Caesar, now master of the rolls, was the next step to a natural fool and no way fit for that place of judicature, which he had bought for some fifteen or 16,000£). [13] I shall therefore first begin with the three great

10. "Next, they desire, That the Clause concerning White Cloth might be omitted." In a division to determine whether to put the question concerning white cloth, the Ayes were 27, the Noes 42. *CJ,* II, 641. For a subsequent action see below. For the cloth trade during the reign of Henry VIII, see George Unwin, *Industrial Organization in the Sixteenth and Seventeenth Centuries* (1904; reprint, London, 1957), pp. 88–90.

11. The "exceptions" presented by the Scots commissioners were customs imposed upon "native Commodities" of Scotland which they desired might be abated in the book of rates. *CJ,* II, 641. Because the MS is frayed, one word is illegible. However, for the decision concerning the exceptions, see below.

12. Sir John Gerlington. See *Roy. Off.*, pp. 153–54; and *Sheriffs,* p. 73. For proceedings omitted by D'Ewes, see G, below, and *CJ,* II, 641–42.

13. For Caesar's purchase of his office, see Brian P. Levack, *The Civil Lawyers in England 1603–1641* (Oxford, 1973), p. 57, and *DNB.*

officers here mentioned, which although they have for a long time in respect of the two first discontinued except revived only upon some particular and emergent occasions, yet if we consider the original and use of them, there will be no color for us to insist any further upon this third proposition, against the voting of which I spake when it was at first proposed.[14] For these offices are mere tenures in grand serjeanty and were originally attendants upon the court, for howsoever we now call them high steward and high constable of England, yet they were anciently styled *magnus seneschalus* and *magnus conestabilis in aula regis*. I might in the evidencing of this truth vouch many records, but I shall only give you the narrative and historical part as briefly as may be.[15]

Hugh Grantmesnil held the barony of Hinckley in grand serjeanty by being hereditary high steward of England. This came to the families of Bellomont,[16] earls of Leicester, by the marriage of Petronell, his daughter and heir, from whom that office and barony descended by an heir general to the family of Montfort, all which came by forfeiture to H. 3 who bestowed them on Edmund surnamed Crouchback, his younger son.

William 1 created William Fitzosbern Earl of Hereford and constable of England in fee, from whom it descended to Roger de Breteuil, his son. King Stephen restored this office and earldom to Robert de Bellomont, Earl of Leicester, who held it till the loss of the battle of Lincoln by that king and his imprisonment at Bristol. When Maud, the empress, seized both as forfeited and granted them to Milo Fitzwalter, they both were devolved by the heir general to the great family of Bohun, in which they continued till they were swallowed up by the crown upon the match of H. 4 with a coheir general of Bohun.

The family of Marshal also held the place of earl marshal of England in grand serjeanty, and upon division of the lands of that family amongst the coheirs, this office was assigned to Maud, the eldest daughter, married to Hugh Bigod, Earl of Norfolk, who as appears in the Communia Roll *de a° 31° H. 3, Rot.° 2do*,[17] on the side of the lord treasurer's remembrancer did assign over the office of earl marshal to Roger Bigod, her son and heir, then Earl of Norfolk, and for this office it is now vested also by inheritance in that noble family which enjoys it

14. There is no record of D'Ewes's speech.

15. For a discussion of grand serjeanty and these offices, see J. Horace Round, *The King's Serjeants and Officers of State with Their Coronation Services* (1911; reprint, New York, 1970), pp. 21–98. For the specific holders of the office cited by D'Ewes, see *DNB*.

16. See Beaumont in *DNB*. D'Ewes's account of this office is compressed and garbled; yet all of the persons mentioned except Grantmesnil were in fact high stewards, and the office descended along hereditary lines. See Round, *King's Serjeants*, pp. 68–76.

17. For this assignment see Matthew Paris, *English History*, ed. J. A. Giles (London, 1853), II, 165. D'Ewes possessed the 1640 edition of this volume. Watson, *Library of D'Ewes*, p. 103. For another reference to the Communia Rolls, see 8 June, n. 20.

only by letters patent during life, but the truth is that it is hereditary to them as the great chamberlainship was and still is to the family of Vere, earls of Oxford.

For the other offices of lord chancellor, lord treasurer, and the rest, as I was against the instancing in them at the first, so for the same reason I am against the desiring of them now because when in *a° 15° E. 3* there had a law passed by which their nomination was given to the parliament, about two years after as appears in *Rotuli Parliamentorum de a° 17° E. 3, n° 23°*,[18] that law was repealed, and it is alleged that it was not only against the king's rights and prerogatives but against the ancient laws and usages of the realm.

[f. 269b] Some two or three spake after me, and in the issue the house agreed not to insist upon those great officers.[19]

[Harl. 163, f. 235b] We went over 4 and 5 and modified them, rested with the answer to the 6.[20]

Then upon MR. STRODE's motion agreed to bill of tonnage and poundage to take out clause concerning white cloths.

MR. PYM, a paper to French ambassador, etc.[21]

MR. BLAKISTON, information from Newcastle and new danger of fort on the south side.[22]

Upon MR. CROMWELL's motion the quartermasters who were to be sent into Ireland by the adventurers with the army were to have a month's pay.

Upon SIR HUGH OWEN's motion letter to mayor of Plymouth to dismiss an arrested man who had stayed, etc. John Poyer's letter dated at Plymouth June 14, 1642.[23]

MR. DENZIL HOLLES, arms permit to Lord Cottington, etc.[24]

Upon MR. WHEELER's motion 3 of committee for recusants' arrears to consider recusants' arrears, etc.

18. *RP*, II, 139. See 23 June, n. 21. D'Ewes's speech is mentioned in Verney, *Notes*, p. 182. Verney's journal concludes with this day.

19. For the resolutions on these and other great officers, see H, below, and *CJ*, II, 642.

20. For the king's answer to these propositions and the response of the commons, see Rushworth, IV, 733, and *CJ*, II, 642.

21. It was ordered that the following message should be delivered to the ambassador:

That this House doth not know of any Instructions given to Sir Tho. Roe, whereby he might be authorized to engage this Kingdom to the Assistance of any of the Princes of the House of Austria, in such manner as is mentioned in the . . . Letter presented to them, or in any other Manner prejudicial to the Alliance and Amity betwixt the Two Crowns of England and France."

CJ, II, 642. For comments by the Venetian ambassador, see *CSP Ven., 1642–1643*, pp. 85–86.

22. See H, below.

23. John Poyer, mayor of Pembroke, had been unjustifiably arrested for staying, by order of the House of Commons, ships bound for Galway, "a Town in open Rebellion." Thomas Ceely, mayor of Plymouth, was to investigate and to release Poyer. *CJ*, II, 642–43.

24. For Cottington's store of arms, see G, 10 June. Whatever action Holles was recommending is not mentioned in *CJ*.

Upon MR. PLEYDELL's motion Mris. Winter had leave to go into the Low Countries.[25]

[*Illegible*] 7 of the clock.[26]

GAWDY

[f. 144a]   Monday, the XXVII of June

A letter from Coventry to my Lord Brooke from Mr. Barker, June [*blank*].[27] That my Lord of Northampton was come thither with a commission of array. The bailiffs of that town will obey the militia. My Lord of Northampton [f. 144b] is gone from that town. He said he had not yet his commission, for 'twas not finished when he came from York.

SIR ARTHUR HESILRIGE, a report of Leicestershire, that they obeyed the militia readily. That on Wednesday last Mr. Hastings, Sir Richard Halford, and Sir John Bale made out their warrants to congregate the people at [*blank*].[28] That Mr. Hastings levied 120 muskets charged with bullet and 80 pikes out of Derbyshire, with whom Mr. Hastings marched towards Leicester, set up the king's proclamation of array, and sware they would have my Lord of Stamford's blood and that he would fire his house.

The sergeant[29] saith that the inhabitants of Leicester (except the mayor) assisted the sergeant's man and armed themselves with halberds and went and disarmed the Derbyshire men many of them. That Mr. Hastings got away.

MR. DARLEY,[30] that on that day there was 200 horse marching out of York towards Leicester but they were countermanded.

MR. PYM hath letter from our committee from Lincoln, June the [*blank*].[31] [f. 145a] They have sent up certain informations. That James Kelham heard William Clarke say that now the king and prince is gone to York, you shall see the crown set upon the Duke of York's head.

There were divers other informations.[32]

25. Minor Winter and her son, brother, and servant were to go to friends in Holland, having lost their estate to the Irish rebels. *CJ,* II, 643.

26. Because the MS is frayed, several words, doubtless reading *We rose at,* are illegible.

27. For the letter dated 25 June, see *LJ,* V, 164–65. John Barker was a member of the committee for Warwickshire; Lord Brooke was lord lieutenant.

28. The Raw Dykes. For events in Leicestershire see also Rushworth, IV, 669–70; and *VCH, Leicestershire,* II, 110–12.

29. MS: *sergeants.* See 18 June, n. 27.

30. MS: *Darnell.*

31. The date is 22 June.

32. Crossed out in MS: *Ordered, that William Clarke shall be referred to his trial in the King's Bench.* An earlier version of the order has also been crossed out in the MS CJ.

Resolved, that Mr. William Clarke shall be sent to my lord chief justice with the several examinations against him.

MR. PURY, that there is a rumor amongst the clerks in the courts that the judges have order to adjourn Michaelmas term to York.

A message to the lords to acquaint them that we hear that the judges have order to adjourn the next term to York. To desire them to send to the judges not to adjourn Michaelmas term.

A letter to Mr. Speaker from our committee from Lancashire,[33] that the sheriff hath seized on some of the magazine there. That my Lord Strange hath done the same. That 3 of them went to my Lord Strange about [how] to compose the business without blood. My lord hath withdrawn his forces. So hath they.

[f. 145b] A letter intercepted from Sir Edward Fitton to Sir Thomas Aston, that he would have stopped the subsidy in Lancashire but that 'twas to be paid to my lord mayor of York, where the king may see it may go in the right way for which it was intended. He hope that hundred[34] will go for the king. He for his part will be ready to serve him. He hear Sir William Brereton is putting the militia for the parliament in execution with a company of Roundheads. You know of what spirit he is.

A letter from Mr. Rigby to the Speaker, that there was a party a making for the king. That about 400 cried out for the king. That the malignant could think they got not anything at Preston Moor but rather lost, and hopeth that that county will prove faithful to the king and parliament.[35]

A letter from Sir William Brereton to the Speaker,[36] that there is a commission of array granted to my Lord Strange. That the king is expected in those parts.

[f. 146a] Resolved, that Sir John Gerlington and Sir Edward Fitton shall be sent for as delinquents.

Resolved, that the lords be made acquainted with this.

Resolved, that the lords be moved to require my Lord Strange to deliver up the magazine of the county.

In the afternoon.

33. For this letter of 25 June, see George Ormerod, ed., *Tracts Relating to Military Proceedings in Lancashire during the Great Civil War* [Chetham Society] (London, 1844), pp. 16–18.

34. I.e., Manchester. For this letter of 22 June, see Ormerod, *Tracts,* pp. 18–20. Fitton, like Aston, was a prominent Cheshire royalist. See *Roy. Off.*, p. 131; and Morrill, *Cheshire,* pp. 16, 46–47, 55.

35. For this letter of 24 June, see Ormerod, *Tracts,* pp. 325–30. On 20 June about five thousand people had gathered on Preston Moor at the summons of Sheriff Gerlington, who was accompanied by Lord Strange. Following the reading of the commission of array, all but about seven hundred departed.

36. For an abstract of this letter of 24 June, see *HMC, Fifth Report,* p. 31. All of these letters from Lancashire are preserved in HLRO, Main Papers. See also Wing, S 2775.

The house take the propositions into consideration. 'Tis in the house.[37]

The house pass the bill of tonnage and poundage as it was amended by the lords without the proviso which we added.

HILL

[p. 107]   June 26 [*sic*]

Sergeant's man informed that Mr. Hastings came to Leicester with 120[38] Derbyshire men. Colliers and others in arms. Captain Wolseley gave the word, "Make ready," and leveled his musket to the sheriff. One took away his match. 23 ministers came in with Hastings.[39] Colliers double charge with bullets. Reported they intended to have the blood of the Earl of Stamford. Derbyshire men were disarmed by the town except the mayor, who came with his mace under his arm. Hastings got away out of the town presently.

MR. DARLEY, at York last week it was reported that the Lord Stamford['s] house was besieged and 200 horse were provided to go to assist Mr. Hastings.

Hastings at Loughborough, Leicestershire, read a proclamation and the commission of array and said if any wanted arms, he should repair to the town's end for arms. Hastings rode, but when he came to towns, he unhorsed and marched before them. Sir Richard Halford and Sir John Bale was with Mr. Hastings. That before they came into Leicester towns, they were commanded to charge and light their [p. 108] match. That he marched through a town, Coleborne, in the head of a great army frighting everyone where he came. Examination of Edward Coleman.[40] That Hastings said that he would have the blood of the Lord Stamford.

The house assumed the debate of the propositions tendered to the king, and to debate it because of the delay in the committee.

Resolved, that the last words of the 3 proposition, "in the intervals of parliament by assent of major part of the council in such manner," etc., not to be insisted upon.[41]

Resolved, that the high steward and high constable shall be left out.

37. The Nineteen Propositions were to be debated in the full house rather than in the committee of the whole. *CJ,* II, 642.

38. MS: *120£*.

39. "That as well the Trained-Soldiers, as private Men, and the Clergy, should come thither on the Wednesday following [22 June], to be mustered according to his [Hastings's] Commission." Rushworth, IV, 669.

40. One of several informants concerning affairs in Leicestershire. *CJ,* II, 641.

41. See below, n. 44.

Resolved, to insist upon chancellor [or] keeper, and treasurer.

Resolved, we shall not insist upon the lord privy seal.

Resolved, earl marshal not insisted upon. He that now is[42] hath a freehold, and the grievances are remedied already.

Resolved, that we shall insist upon lord admiral.

Resolved, not insist upon the warden of Cinque Port.

Resolved, insist upon governor of Ireland.

Resolved, not insist upon chancellor of Exchequer.

Resolved, insist upon master of wards.

Resolved, secretaries of state[43] not insisted upon.

Resolved, that we shall insist upon the 2 chief justices and chief baron.

The house would not put it to a question now whether we should insist to have the approbation of the other judges because we would not seem to make new demands being upon terms of reconciliation.

And such of them as shall be chosen by his majesty in the intervals of parliament shall not continue except they are approved of within 40 days[44] the next [p. 109] parliament.

June 23, 1642, from Newcastle.[45] The Earl of Newcastle is governor, came thither Friday before. The town is now guarded. Captain Legge is there with many debauched commanders. Drums beat up for soldiers. They say to serve for king and parliament. 300 soldiers sent to guard Tynemouth Castle. They are casting [up] trenches as fast as may be for a new blockhouse. 6 pieces of great guns sent down to them.

At haven mouth[46] is a fort making to command the ships. Earl of Newcastle hath forced all his ten[an]ts to take up arms, and many of Sir William Widdrington's ten[an]ts are in arms.[47] His steward brought them in. They have taken a list of such as have arms in the town. Engineers out of Germany and gunners for great guns are come.

Resolved, that 4th proposition/[48]

42. The Earl of Arundel. See Mary F. S. Hervey, *The Life, Correspondence, and Collections of Thomas Howard, Earl of Arundel* (1921; reprint, New York, 1969), esp. p. 235.

43. MS: *estate*.

44. Thirty days, in *CJ*, II, 642. This new wording was to be substituted at the end of the third proposition.

45. For this letter, read at a conference with the lords on 30 June, see *LJ*, V, 170. Another committee for Newcastle, which included Hill, was named. *CJ*, II, 642.

46. I.e., at the mouth of the Tyne River.

47. Two months later Widdrington was disabled "for neglecting the Service of the House, and for raising Arms against the Parliament." See *CJ*, II, 738, and Appendix A.

48. At this point a section of Hill's journal pertaining to the coronation oath has been omitted.

D'EWES

June 28, Tuesday, 1642

The Speaker came a little before 9 of the clock.

MR. PYM moved, just as we were about to go on with the propositions, that a letter of great moment was come out of Leicestershire dated June 27, 1642, being sent from Mr. Archdale Palmer, high sheriff of that county, to Sir Arthur Hesilrige, in which he showed that Edmund Woodhouse, one of his majesty's messengers, had brought him a writ with several proclamations which he was commanded by that writ to publish.[1] That he had told/

Bradgate House,[2] Monday, 5 of the clock, June 27, 1642, from Geffrie Bodin, servant to the Earl of Stamford, to the said earl.

Then arose several debates how to prevent the calamities of war, and SIR JOHN STRANGWAYS moved to have/

SIR HUGH CHOLMLEY moved to move the king to suspend commissions of array and we to suspend the execution of our militia.

MR. PIERREPONT moved that we might consider of the report for the illegalities of the commission of array when the reporter (viz., Mr. Glyn) came in and in the meantime to proceed with the propositions.

[f. 239b] The clerk then proceeded with the propositions and read the 7, which concerned the taking away the votes of the popish lords.

I spake to that of lords' votes and nipped Strode. Yet to insist upon it. Content with later part touching papists' children.

Then to 8th proposition touching religion. MR. PLEYDELL spake. *Ego respondi.*

[Harl. 164, f. 257a] Upon reading the 8th proposition in print and the king's answer touching religion,[3] MR. PLEYDELL spake pretty long and showed that the king had fully satisfied us in this proposition and so handled the 4 particulars

---

1. The three proclamations, which were referred to the committee for the commission of array, were as follows: (1) "Concerning the free Passage of the Subjects, and their Goods, etc. from Place to Place." Wing, C 2857. (2) "Forbidding all Levies of Forces, without his Majesty's express Pleasure signified under his Great Seal." See D, 127–28. Wing, C 2651. (3) "To inform the Subjects of the Lawfulness of the Commissions of Array." See Rushworth, IV, 659–61. Wing, C 2857. *CJ,* II, 643.

2. The ancestral home of the Earl of Stamford, situated northwest of Leicester.

3. For the king's answer to the seventh and eighth propositions and the commons' response, see Rushworth, IV, 733–34, and *CJ,* II, 643.

here expressed: 1. Offense taken not given. 2. An injury to them who first framed this church government. 3. Want[4] reformation, not an extirpation. 4. He would know what consultation.

I answered him in effect following: That I did not conceive that his majesty had fully satisfied us in this particular, for whether the offense were taken or given, in respect of tender consciences it would be needful to relieve them. And seeing those ceremonies which do give offense are no ways necessary, they are to be utterly abolished and taken away, and so we shall have no further trouble how to satisfy weak consciences in the use of them, which can scarcely stand without the abuse of them. For the second objection made by the same gentleman (viz., Mr. Pleydell), that if we should now alter the church government amongst us, we should do an injury to the memory of those learned men who had first framed the Book of Common Prayer and settled the frame of our church government in the days of E. 6 and afterwards suffered martyrdom,[5] I answer that if those men had but lived to our days and had but seen what great advantage the wicked prelates and their instruments have to ruin all godliness and conscientious preaching by the overpressing the observation of that church government which they had framed, they would have blamed themselves for framing of it. Besides they did much, considering that they were newly come out of darkness themselves, and 'tis more than probable also that at that time they durst not reform some particulars so far as they thought it needful because they desired to accomplish it in a peaceable way and to bring the common people from their old customs by degrees, and 'tis very likely also that [had] they lived longer, they would in the issue have reformed that reformation themselves which they at first made. And this I know that when the same church government had been again taken up in the beginning of Queen Elizabeth's reign with little or no alteration and though the prelates had most of them some piety at that time and all of them executed their power with great moderation, yet there were nine several bills prepared in the session of parliament held in the 5th year of her reign[6] for the better settling of the church government and discipline amongst. And for the gentleman's 3 objection I wonder at it more than at any of the two former in that he saith that we ought not to make our reformation an extirpation, for we are not now in debate about altering any fundamental or essential part of our religion established but only to alter some things in the outward frame or government of the church, so as if we should alter that frame wholly according to the example of some other Protestant

---

4. MS: *What*. Marginal note: *Mr. Pleydell*. Pleydell was a staunch supporter of the established church. Keeler, p. 307.

5. See W. K. Jordan, *Edward VI: The Young King* (Cambridge, Mass., 1968), pp. 310–23.

6. For proceedings during 5 Elizabeth, see D'Ewes, *Compleat Journal,* pp. 57–77.

churches in Europe, yet I hope no honest man will say that we go about to extirpate religion. For the 4th objection that hath been made (by the said Mr. Pleydell), that he would know what consultation we desire to have with divines for the effecting of this reformation, it is intended to be had with an assembly of able and godly divines, and therefore I desire that we may humbly press his majesty to give a more full, clear, and gracious answer in this particular.

[Harl. 163, f. 239b] *Post longam agitationem* a committee appointed to draw an answer to it upon SIR HENRY VANE, Junior, his motion seconded by others, and himself named with some 5 or 6 more withdrew.

Between eleven and 12 Sir Robert Rich and Mr. Page, etc., brought this message, etc. The lords had consented to our proposition touching the business of Galway and to the propositions concerning the Scottish treaty and had appointed two of their members to draw a petition touching Galway to be presen/[7]

Appointed to meet at 2 in the afternoon. Rose about 12. I newly before gone out of the house.[8]

[f. 241a]   Post Meridiem

The Speaker resumed his chair a little after three of the clock in the afternoon.

Upon MR. HOLLAND's motion it was ordered that a writ which had been brought against the mayor of Windsor upon the late election there should be stayed in respect that the matter depended undetermined in this house whether the return were rightly made or not.[9]

MR. GLYN made report from the committee appointed to draw up a declaration against the commission of array sent into Leicestershire (of which committee I was one),[10] and then the clerk read the said declaration with the copy of the statute and the commission of array upon the Parliament Roll *de a° 5° H. 4, n° 24°* and *n° 25°*,[11] with a copy of which record I had acquainted the select committee of lords and commons on Friday, the 17 day of this instant June, in the afternoon.[12] After MR. SOLICITOR had spoken shortly and MR. SELDEN

7. A petition concerning Galway was to be drawn up by a joint committee and presented to the king. *CJ*, II, 643.

8. For proceedings omitted by D'Ewes, see *CJ*, II, 643.

9. William Taylor, MP for New Windsor, had been expelled from the house in May 1641. The subsequent election dispute involving Richard Braham and Richard Winwood was finally resolved in favor of Winwood. See Keeler, pp. 34–35, 397. The mayor who had returned Winwood, though he had the smaller number of votes, was a Mr. Hall, according to D'Ewes's account of 6 July 1641. Harl. MS 163, ff. 380b–381a.

10. For the committee see 18 June, n. 16. The declaration appears in Rushworth, IV, 661–69. Wing, E 1475.

11. See Appendix H.

12. See D, 95.

very largely to it[13] and some three others to no great purpose, it passed upon the vote, and then it was likewise ordered that we should send up to the lords to desire a conference about it, and Sir Philip Stapleton was named for the messenger, and upon MR. SELDEN's motion he was appointed to desire a free conference with the lords.[14]

Upon COLONEL GORING's motion an order was read for the allowing of 5200£[15] to the garrison of Portsmouth for a year's pay, and Sir Philip Stapleton was likewise desired to carry that up also to the lords to desire their concurrence with us therein, but whilst we were debating these particulars, the lords rose.

Upon SIR PHILIP STAPLETON's motion Sir John Fenwick and his son, being both members of the house, had both leave to go into the county of Northumberland.

Upon SIR ARTHUR HESILRIGE's motion seconded by the Lord Grey, it was ordered that we should take up the informations out of Leicestershire read this day in the house upon Thursday morning next at 8 of the clock, and upon MR. BLAKISTON's motion it was then ordered that we should take into consideration the business of Newcastle which he had informed the house of yesterday.

Upon MR. ARTHUR GOODWIN's motion it was ordered that we should sit tomorrow though it were the day of the public fast, at 4 of the clock in the afternoon after the second sermon should be ended, and so we rose between 6 and 7 of the clock at night.

GAWDY

[f. 146a]   Tuesday, the XXVIII of June

A letter from the sheriff of Leicestershire to Sir Arthur Hesilrige, that he hath received 2 proclamations from the king, the one for the opening the ways, the other forbidding to raise arms without his consent.

The house goeth on with the propositions.

A message from the lords, that those propositions concerning the Scots they

13. See H, below. In a letter to Lord Falkland written the day after this speech, Selden confirmed that in his opinion the commission of array was "against law." See *Biographie Britannica* (1747–66; reprint, Hildesheim, Germany, 1969), VI (Pt. 1), 3617. For the view that Selden believed that both the militia ordinance and the commission of array were illegal and should be rejected, see Clarendon, *History*, II, 205–06.

14. It was also ordered that the committee should "take into Consideration the Pains and Expences of Sir Jo. Burroughs, and of his and other Clerks," who had supplied information concerning the commission of array from records in the Tower. Borough was Garter king of arms and keeper of the Tower records. See *CJ*, II, 643, 657. *DNB*.

15. £5030, according to *CJ*, II, 643–44.

assented to and to the propositions concerning Galway, and to that purpose they had appointed 2 lords to draw a petition to the king and desire we will name a proportionable number to join with them.

[f. 146b] In the afternoon.

The declaration against the king's commission of array was read, argued, and passed our house by vote.

Resolved, that we shall desire the lords to join with us in this declaration.

A message to the lords to desire a free conference about the declaration.

HILL

[p. 114]   June 28, Tuesday[16]

MR. GLYN brought in his declaration concerning the commission of array.

SELDEN, this commission of 5 H. 4 was made upon the matter upon the statute then in force. Statute 13 E. 1 of Winchester[17] appointed how every man shall be cessed to arms. The commission, in the first cause, that every man shall be assessed *iuxta facultates suas*,[18] etc., in the general. Whatever was enacted before 21 *Jac.* of repeal was law.[19]

2. Clause that lead them *ad costeram maris*,[20] that is direct[ed] against statute 1 E. 3 if it is pressed indefinitely; but [if] it is *ad debel[l]andum et expellendum inimicos*,[21] then the sense is that enemies [of] the king have come, and then it is within 1 E. 3.[22]

3. Clause of commitment, until king declares pleasure that was by him, and it is against law. And saving that last clause, not vital within commission of array of 5 H. 4 that was not with[in] the law before.

The words that say no commission hereafter shall issue out in other words.[23]

16. Hill's account is of the afternoon proceedings only.

17. *SL*, I, 114: 13 E. I, stat. 2, c. 6. "For the Statute of Winchester, made the 13 E. I then in force, did declare the certain Proportion of Arms every Man was to have according to his Estate, in Land or Goods; and the times, and how often their Arms were to be viewed, and by whom, and in what manner their Defaults were to be punished." Rushworth, IV, 662.

18. "According to his ability."

19. *SL*, III, 117: 21 *Jac.* I, c. 28. "In the Parliament 21 Jac. cap. 28 the Statute of 13 E. I cap. 6 . . . [was] repealed, . . . yet when the Statute of 13 Ed. I is repealed, then that Commission [of array] is likewise repealed and become unwarrantable." Rushworth, IV, 664.

20. "To the seacoast."

21. "In order to defeat and expel enemies."

22. *SL*, I, 193: 1 E. III, stat. 2, c. 5. The statute declared: "That no Man be compelled to go out of his Shire but where Necessity requireth, and sudden coming of strange Enemies into the Realm, and that it shall be done as heretofore for Defence of the Realm." Rushworth, IV, 663.

23. See the second paragraph of Appendix H, and Rushworth, IV, 664.

Question: How will it be taken? If literally, then it will be parts absurdities because then any commission of array must issue in those very names of those commissioners. Then [it] will be taken second in subiectum materii.

6 H. 4, Welsh in rebellion.[24] Commission of array issued, and commission in Kent able [to] resist invasion of the French, and no compulsory clause in that.

5 H. 4 was not act of parliament made by bill, but entry of the story by clerk of the parliament.

Thus he is satisfie[d] that at that time was not any intention to enact anything but that which was law before.

Statute 4 et 5 P. et M. Statute says every man shall be mustered and serve in his arms which he hath for his own person, and upon that statute a commission may issue to array.[25]

Objection: Every subject bound to serve the king in his wars. Answer: There was search made that ser- [p. 115] vice was against Scots. So [there] was indictment of any that had refused, and none can have been [illegible]. [Er]go, no obligation by which one will be punish[ed]. It is no obligation because no compulsion by fine and imprisonment or otherwise. In law some legal bond seen in [illegible] that was punishment. [Er]go, are left as bounds to affection with allegiance.

I do homage to the king and swear that I do make these services for land held. I am bound to do it by my oath, yet no punishment for violation of fealty because it is remedy for the revenue.[26]

24. See Jacob, Fifteenth Century, pp. 30–66.

25. SL, II, 500–03: 4 and 5 P. and M., c. 2, 3. This statute "repeals all former Statutes concerning the finding of Arms, and all Penalties and Forfeitures touching the same; and by that Act settled the Proportions of Men, Horses and Arms that every Man was to find, according to the Value of their respective Estates, and sets down the Penalties and Forfeitures of such as should disobey." Rushworth, IV, 664.

26. Hill again breaks off his parliamentary journal and includes a brief report of a case involving one Heber as well as precedents concerning sheriffs chosen in the county court.

D'EWES

[f. 251b]   June 29, Wednesday, [1642]

Was the public fast.[1]

[f. 252a] The public fast was celebrated by divers of the House of Commons and many others in St. Margaret's Church in Westminster, Dr. Gouge, minister of Blackfriars, preaching in the morning and Mr. William Sedgwick preaching in the afternoon.[2]

The house after the two sermons were ended met about 4 of the clock. I was not present, and it was first ordered that thanks should be returned to the said preachers and to desire them to print their sermons,[3] and it was then also ordered that Mr. Reynolds and Mr. Hill should preach the two sermons at the next fast day.[4]

Mr. Ashe was ordered to desire Dr. Burges and Mr. Ashe, who preached at the fast held the 30 day of March, to print their sermons.[5]

There was lastly one order made for a lecturer to be settled (which see in the clerk's book).[6]

GAWDY

[f. 146b]   Wednesday, the xxix of June

Was the fast at St. Margaret's. Dr. Gouge and Mr. William Sedgwick preached. I was at Lincoln's Inn.

The house met at 4 a clock, where I was not, but nothing was done but the appointing Mr. Hill and Mr. Reynolds to preach.

---

1. The public fast was held the last Wednesday of each month. See *PJ,* 1: 447, n. 1.

2. They had been selected to preach following the fast on 25 May. See *PJ,* 2: 370.

3. For the sermons see John F. Wilson, *Pulpit in Parliament* (Princeton, 1969), pp. 65, 257. Wing, G 1397, S 2392.

4. Both Thomas Hill, a strong Puritan, and Edward Reynolds, a moderate Anglican, served parishes in Northamptonshire and were subsequently members of the Westminster Assembly. See Wilson, *Pulpit in Parliament,* pp. 116, 126; and Robert S. Paul, *The Assembly of the Lord* (Edinburgh, 1985), pp. 549, 551. *DNB.*

5. The sermon by Ashe was printed sometime in 1642; the one by Burges did not appear until 1645. Wing, A 3949, B 5688.

6. James Eliott was to be lecturer at St. Vedast Church in Foster Lane, London. See *CJ,* II, 644; and *Walker,* p. 42, under James Batty.

D'EWES

[f. 251b]   June 30, Thursday, 1642

MR. MILLINGTON delivered in a petition from the mayor and certain inhabitants of the county of the town [of] Nottingham,[1] which was read, and therein they desired that they might have liberty to muster and train within their own town in respect that they did not know when the ordinance of the militia would be put in execution in that town and county or in the county itself and withal that such volunteers who would come out of the county and train with them might have like liberty of exercising themselves. Divers spake to it. I moved in effect following:

That though the lord lieutenant[2] had occasions to absent himself, yet we might do as in the case of Buckingham and appoint the deputy lieutenants by an ordinance of parliament to proceed with the militia, that so the town of Nottingham and the rest of the county might be proceeded withal together, or if that could not be done speedily, that then we might only order that the town of Nottingham might exercise the said militia within itself; for I did not see but that if any of the county of Nottingham should come and join themselves to them, it would be all one as if some out of another county should do the same, and those volunteers must be commanded by somebody, and so in the issue it must come to pass that they shall be commanded by the deputy lieutenants of the same town. And therefore I desired that our order might only extend to the said townsmen of Nottingham to train and muster within the said town, but MR. MILLINGTON showed that one of those whose names were to the petition was a deputy lieutenant of the county of Nottingham[3] and might command those volunteers of the county, and so the order was passed according as it was desired in the petition.

1. For the petition see *LJ*, V, 173.
2. The Earl of Clare, brother to Denzil Holles, had been at York at least since early June and was one of the signers of the declaration of 15 June from the king and others at York. However, by 11 August Clare had returned to London and was thanked by the lords for his conduct at York. See 3 June, n. 30; 21 June, n. 7; and *LJ*, V, 282. For his vacillations see also Alfred C. Wood, *Nottinghamshire in the Civil War* (Oxford, 1947), p. 15.
3. John James, mayor, was both a signer of the petition and a deputy lieutenant. Another signer, Henry Ireton, subsequently also a deputy lieutenant, was named captain of a horse troop for Nottingham. Ireton and Francis Thornhagh (Thorneley) had endorsed an earlier Nottinghamshire petition. See *LJ*, V, 173–74, 275; *PJ*, 1: 482; and Robert W. Ramsey, *Henry Ireton* (London, 1949), pp. 5, 9. *DNB*.

SIR WILLIAM LYTTON showed that the town of Watford in Hertfordshire had sent in 1200£ to lend upon the propositions and offered 150 foot volunteers and 50 horse and intended to make them up 60 horse, and it was referred to the committee for the propositions.[4]

Upon SIR JOHN EVELYN's report from the committee appointed the 16 day of this instant June,[5] Mr. Erisey, Mr. Godolphin, and Mr. Manaton, who were then absent and appointed to pay 100£ apiece, were freed and discharged from the payment thereof and admitted into the house, their excuses for their absence being allowed by the house.

SIR DUDLEY NORTH delivered in a letter which was sent him out of Cambridgeshire by one who had been a collector of the subsidies who was sued for distraining for the same, and it was referred to a committee to consider of it and to report to the house.[6]

MR. TRENCHARD made report from the committee appointed to make up the account to be printed touching the sums which we had received and laid out. It was not now all read but the preamble only, and divers orders were made upon it. I went out of the house for a while.[7]

Sir Philip Stapleton was sent up to desire a free conference with the lords concerning the commission of array, the garrison and fort at Newcastle, and the English ship not suffered to have fresh water, of which the house had been informed this morning, and he returned not long after and brought word that the lords would give a present meeting.

I was returned to the house when a debate was in agitation touching the best means to get in the moneys arrear in several counties, which was in the issue referred to a committee.[8]

The managers went away to the conference. Mr. Lawrence Whitaker read the declaration against the commission of array and read the copies of some records

4. The petition and propositions from Watford, presented by Cornelius Burges, were approved the next day. *CJ*, II, 646; *LJ*, V, 172. For the text see *LJ*, V, 173. Wing, T 1443.

5. The above-mentioned committee for defense (propositions), which was also to receive the excuses of absent members. See 16 June, n. 20; and Appendix G.

6. John Manby, minister of Cottenham, Cambs, had been distrained by the collector for nonpayment of his assessment. The house now ordered that Trenchard, as chairman of the committee for accounts, should summon Manby to appear. See *PJ*, 2: 275; and *CJ*, II, 644.

7. *CJ*, II, 644, states:

Mr. Trenchard likewise presented the general State of the Accounts: And ordered to be printed; and not to be published, but upon Mr. Trenchard's Warrant and Allowance: And Mr. Green's Account to be likewise printed and published upon Mr. Green's Allowance. And they are to take Order, that Nine thousand of them be printed for the Service of the House.

Trenchard had previously reported on 21 June. For proceedings omitted by D'Ewes, see G, below, and *CJ*, II, 644–45.

8. The committee for accounts. *CJ*, II, 645.

concerning it.[9] Mr. Glyn managed it. Mr. Reynolds managed that part which concerned Newcastle and Mr. Lawrence Whitaker aforesaid that which concerned the ship.[10]

I returned into the house about one of the clock in the afternoon. Awhile after my coming in MR. DENZIL HOLLES moved concerning the election of Cockermouth in the county of Cumberland,[11] for which place Sir Thomas Sandford was returned a burgess and now present in the house, and one Mr. Allen pretended some right to it but had preferred no petition into the house. Divers spake to it, and MR. STRODE, speaking the 2d time, pretended to speak to the orders of the/

Ayes 34,[12] went out. Mr. Denzil Holles and Mr. Strode, tellers. Noes 49, sat still. I one. Sir Patrick Curwen and Sir George Dalston, tellers. It was ordered that it should not be referred to a committee.

Upon MR. PYM's motion Sir Guy Palmes had leave to go into the country.[13]

Upon MR. WHISTLER's motion Sir James Thynne had license to go into the country.[14]

Upon MR. ROBERT GOODWIN's motion it was ordered that we should proceed with the debate of the 19 propositions tomorrow morning. Another motion or two of little moment.[15]

We appointed to meet at 8 of the clock tomorrow morning. We rose a little after two of the clock in the afternoon.

GAWDY

[f. 146b]   Thursday, the xxx of June

Ordered, that the town of Nottingham shall muster and train when they please, and that they shall have power to suffer any volunteers of the county to muster amongst them.

Ordered, that every Wednesday the house shall take into consideration matter of money.

9. See 28 June, n. 10.

10. For a report of this part of the conference and the papers read there, see *LJ*, V, 170–71. For proceedings omitted by D'Ewes, see G, below, and *CJ*, II, 645.

11. MS: *Northumberland*. For information concerning this disputed election, see *PJ*, 2: 475–76. Allen apparently was not present in the house.

12. Thirty-five, in *CJ*, II, 645. The question was whether the committee for privileges should examine witnesses concerning this election. Dalston was Sandford's father-in-law.

13. Palmes as a deputy lieutenant was to assist in executing the militia ordinance in Rutland. *CJ*, II, 645. The instructions for Rutland appear in *LJ*, V, 183–84.

14. Thynne's leave is noted on 2 July by the clerk. *CJ*, II, 648.

15. See *CJ*, II, 645–46.

MR. WHITAKER, a report that my Lord of Newcastle hath a warrant to put 500[16] foot and 100 horse into Newcastle. That there is 200 put in already. That 300 men are making a fort upon the mouth of the river Tyne and have planted [f. 147a] six pieces of ordnance there.

MR. MARTEN, that we should send for my Lord of Newcastle. That we have raised horse. If he will not come, we should send the horse for him. 'Tis not consented to.

SIR ARTHUR HESILRIGE maketh relation of the business of Mr. Hastings his coming with 200 men out of Derbyshire to Leicester. That he fled to York. That the said Mr. Hastings is returned from York thither again and 'tis said he is high sheriff.[17]

The house divided whether the witnesses for Cockermouth shall be examined at a committee. Not in his course.[18] The Ayes that would have them examined that went out were 34.[19] The Noes that sat, of which I was, was 49. This concerned Mr. Allen.

16. Six hundred foot, in *CJ*, II, 644. Whitaker, who was reporting from the committee for Newcastle, stated that Newcastle was "the Magazine for Fuel, and the Nursery for Shipping." For additional details of the royalist occupation there, see Howell, *Newcastle*, pp. 144–46.

17. A committee, which included Hesilrige and Wilde, was named to draw up an impeachment against Hastings and others involved in the Leicestershire affair, and "to consider of the Business concerning the High Sheriff." *CJ*, II, 645. The king had made Hastings sheriff in Palmer's place on 25 June, with an order to the peers in Leicestershire to aid him in the discharge of the office. PRO, Lists and Indexes, Special Series, XXII, *Henry E. Huntington Library, Hastings Manuscripts* (Kew, 1987), p. 215.

18. This phrase appears to mean "not in his turn." *NED*. Again it appears that election disputes were to be resolved in the order determined by the committee. See 17 June, n. 20.

19. See above, n. 12.

D'EWES

[f. 252b]   July 1, Friday, 1642

The Speaker came between 8 and 9.[1]

Divers moved that we might proceed with the order of the day, which was to take into further consideration the 19 propositions sent to his majesty with his answer, that so some means might be thought upon for an accommodation; but MR. PYM diverted the business and said we must look to our present safeties and thereupon delivered in a letter newly come out of Leicestershire bearing date at Bradgate June last 1642 and was sent to the Earl of Stamford from William Danvers,[2] a gentleman of Leicestershire, being then at Bradgate aforesaid, the said Earl of Stamford's house, wherein he showed the great danger that himself and others were in who were there in respect that since his lordship's departure thence the face of things were changed, the sheriff (viz., Mr. Archdale Palmer) not daring to appear in public but being fled to London and Mr. Henry Hastings, younger son to the Earl of Huntingdon, being proclaimed sheriff of that county.[3]

That the said Mr. Henry Hastings arrived at Ashby de la Zouch having divers muskets and pikes with him with some captains and officers and had also three fieldpieces. That it was reported that he intended to use force against his lordship's said house, and therefore that they needed some speedy supply to be sent, for such of the trained bands as lived thereabout were unskillful and raw men and wanted also a leader. That scarce any durst appear for them. That the mayor and aldermen of Leicester were false brethren,[4] with divers other particulars of lesser moment.

There ensued some debate upon the reading of this letter, and the sense of the house did incline very strongly to send down some horsemen speedily for the suppressing of the forces gathered by Mr. Henry Hastings, but we agreed first to

1. For proceedings omitted by D'Ewes, see *CJ*, II, 646.
2. Crossed out in MS: *by his servant.*
3. Ellis, Lane, and Pury were consequently sent "to the Exchequer, and to the Petty Bag Office, to see if Mr. Hen. Hastings be returned Sheriff." *CJ*, II, 646.
4. A newsletter from York dated 17 June noted: "It seems the mayor of Leicester and divers gentlemen of the county opposed Lord Stamford's proceedings at Leicester. The King has sent a letter of particular thanks to the mayor for that service, and desires to know the rest of the gentlemen's names, that he may do the like to them." *CSPD, 1641–43*, p. 342.

have a conference with the lords about the same. This was a sad morning's work as will further appear also by the abstracts of the ensuing letters.

Dunham, June 28, 1642, from Sir William Brereton to the Speaker.[5]

MR. JOHN MOORE made relation of the condition of affairs in Lancashire.[6]

MR. HAMPDEN delivered in a letter sent him from Sir William Brereton bearing date at Dunham June 22, 1642, in which he showed the condition/[7]

[f. 253a] MR. MOORE spake again after letter read.

One Mr. Newton called in, who brought the letter.

I returned towards the house between eleven and 12 of the clock,[8] and understanding that there was a conference to be in the Painted Chamber, I went in thither where myself with some others sat expecting it above half an hour. At last the members of our house came first and then the lords, who having sat awhile did most of them again return into their house to order somewhat which they had forgotten and then returned very soon after back to us.

The Lord North managed the conference and first showed that/[9]

Pym spake, like informations. Mr. Corbet, two letters dated at Rotterdam, one July 1, the other July 4 *stylo novo,* etc.[10] In first names Prince Rupert, etc. Then Mr. Pym, said letters out of Leicestershire. Mr. Lawrence Whitaker, letter to Earl of Stamford read in the house, etc. Then Mr. Pym himself read Sir William Brereton's two letters, etc., read in the house and the two warrants[11] in the first. Then Mr. Pym showed that an ordinance made to settle the fleet, and that Mr. Lawrence Whitaker read.[12]

[f. 253b] The conference ended about one of the clock. I returned not afterwards into the house whilst it sat.[13]

The house appointed to meet at three of the clock in the afternoon and rose between one and two.

5. Brereton's letter from Cheshire reported "the State of the Proceedings upon the Commission of Array, and the Ordinance touching the Militia." *CJ,* II, 646.

6. For conditions in Lancashire at this time, see Broxap, *Lancashire,* pp. 11–16.

7. This letter concerning the magazine at Manchester, directed to both Hampden and Arthur Goodwin, appears in *LJ,* V, 174. It is dated 18 June in *LJ* and 28 June in *CJ.*

8. For proceedings omitted by D'Ewes, see G, below, and *CJ,* II, 646–47.

9. One subject of the conference was the king's "sudden Removal of the Lord Admiral." *CJ,* II, 646.

10. The committee for informations had reported to the house concerning these letters. See *CJ,* II, 646; and *HMC, Fifth Report,* pp. 34–35. Wing, T 3462.

11. Brereton's letter contained "the Sheriff of Cheshire's Precept to the Head Constables; and the Copy of the Constables Warrant." *CJ,* II, 646. The sheriff was either Hugh Calveley or Thomas Legh.

12. This ordinance, drafted by the committee for informations, authorized "the Earl of Warwick's commanding the Fleet in Chief, upon the sudden Discharge of the Lord Admiral by his Majesty." *CJ,* II, 646, 647.

13. For proceedings omitted by D'Ewes, see *CJ,* II, 647.

Post Meridiem

See Mr. Bodvel's journal.
The house met between 3 and 4 of the clock in the afternoon. I seeing all matters tending to speedy destruction and confusion had no heart to take notes this afternoon.[14]

Amongst other passages MR. WHITEHEAD made report that himself and the other deputy lieutenants of Hampshire under the Earl of Pembroke, lord lieutenant of that county, had put the ordinance of the militia in execution there by training and mustering in several places.[15] That he never saw the trained bands appear so full nor so cheerfully, and that there appeared likewise divers volunteers, and that the officers had sent a petition to the house which had been read in the hearing of the soldiers and approved by them, which he delivered in, and then the clerk's assistant read it, being inscribed both to the lords house and us, and then upon several motions it was ordered that Mr. Whitehead should carry it up to the lords and that he should return thanks to the officers and that the said petition should be printed.[16]

MR. GREEN made report from the committee for the navy, how the time for which 6 or 7 merchants' ships were hired was within a month of expiring, and so it was agreed to hire them for 2 months longer.[17]

Sir Edward Leech and Dr. Aylett brought down the ordinance of parliament for the continuance of the Earl of Warwick in the command of the navy a little before 7 of the clock with some amendments which we assented unto, and then they being called in again, the SPEAKER related as much to them and so delivered them back the said ordinance, being engrossed in parchment.[18]

We appointed to meet at 8 of the [clock] tomorrow morning. We rose a little after 7 in the evening.

14. D'Ewes's last reference to the journal of John Bodvel, which is missing, was on 29 December 1641. See Coates, p. 363, n. 18; and *PJ*, 2: xii. For proceedings omitted by D'Ewes, see *CJ*, II, 647–48.

15. On 31 May a committee had been ordered to go to Hampshire to execute the militia ordinance. A letter of 21 June from the deputy lieutenants to the Earl of Pembroke tells of proceedings there. See *PJ*, 2: 394; and *LJ*, V, 156.

16. For the text see *LJ*, V, 172. Wing, T 1670.

17. "Ordered, That the Merchants of Bristoll and London, that first set forth the Eight Ships to Sea, for the Service of Ireland, be desired to victual their Ships for Two Months longer." *CJ*, II, 647.

18. For the ordinance see *LJ*, V, 174. In the spring the parliament had appointed Warwick vice admiral in charge of the summer fleet in place of the king's appointee, Sir John Penington. See *PJ*, 2: esp. 122–23. Now upon his dismissal of Northumberland, the king named Penington, who was at York, to the chief command of the fleet while at the same time the parliament named Warwick. See Clarendon, *History,* II, 216–20.

GAWDY

Friday, the 1 of July

MR. PYM, that there is post come that Mr. Hastings is come into Leicestershire. That he is proclaimed sheriff. That Captain Lunsford, Captain Digby,[19] an[d] others are come with a cartload of muskets and other munition to assault my Lord of Stamford's house.

[f. 147b] A letter to my Lord of Stamford from his servant in Leicestershire, June the 29. That his tenants will make good his house, but they want somebody to conduct them. That Mr. Hastings and others are come with munition to beat down your house. Mr. Hastings is proclaimed sheriff. The mayor and others of Leicester will be assistant to Mr. Hastings.

Mr. [Newton], a letter to the Speaker from Sir William Brereton, that some of the deputy lieutenants refuseth to join in the service. That he is afraid it will hinder the service. That the commission of array is come into Cheshire granted to 6 lords and some 20 others deputy lieutenants.[20]

MR. MOORE, that he demanded of my Lord Strange the magazine, who said that if 4 deputy lieutenants were put out named by the house, he would deliver it. That my lord said he would not yet put the array in execution. He was loath to do anything to offend the parliament. That my Lord Rivers put the array in execution, and there appeared 12 pikes and a half.[21] When my Lord Strange appeared in it, the people did much adhere to him.

[f. 148a] A letter from Sir William Brereton to Mr. Hampden, that he did forbear to put the militia in execution because he thinketh it would much have disadvantaged the service. He desire my Lord Wharton[22] may be sent down.

MR. PYM, that the case of Leicestershire and Lancashire is to be considered. That the navy is to be considered in regard my lord admiral's patent is countermanded. That our religion and liberty is aimed at. That we should declare to the kingdom in what state we stand. That we should provide for our safety. That we should acquaint the king with it.[23]

---

19. Doubtless John Digby, MP.

20. Sir Thomas Aston and Earl Rivers had gone from Cheshire to York, returning shortly thereafter with the commission of array containing seventeen names. Morrill, *Cheshire,* p. 56. For Rivers see *Roy. Off.,* p. 331.

21. I.e., a half pike, about half the length of a full-sized one. *NED.*

22. Lord lieutenant for Lancashire.

23. These issues became heads of a conference with the lords. *CJ,* II, 646.

MR. LANE, that it doth not appear that there is any new sheriff made for Leicestershire by anything he and others can find in the Exchequer.[24]

SIR ARTHUR HESILRIGE, that what should be done in the Exchequer is done at York.

A message from the lords, they desire a present free conference about the admiralty and the peace of the kingdom. We will send an answer by messengers of our own.

MR. CORBET deliver 2 letters sent him from Rotterdam. That some desperate men are going from thence into the north of England in 2 of the king's ships. He heareth not of any more pawning of the jewels. That Mr. Percy, [f. 148b] Mr. Walter Montagu, Mr. Jermyn, and Mr. D'Avenant[25] came to The Hague on Wednesday in the queen's coach with her footmen. The letter dated the 1 of July *stylo novo*.

The other letter, that Prince Rupert, the Prince of Orange,[26] the Earl of Denbigh, the Lord Digby, Daniel O'Neill, with divers Cavaliers are coming for England. They are very jovial and drink healths. They divide the parliament's lands amongst them. That they will fight it out to the last man. Daniel O'Neill is amongst them.

ALDERMAN PENINGTON, that he hath letters to that purpose.

A message to the lords to desire a free conference about the peace of the kingdom and my lord admiral's being put out of his place.

A letter intercepted from Mr. Wilmot writ from York to Mr. Crofts in Holland, that the king that was dejected was now the favorite of the kingdom and that the parliament had lost, so that he hoped that they should share the parliament men's lands. This I had from Mr. Pury while I was at dinner. 'Tis ordered this letter shall be printed.[27]

[f. 149a] In the afternoon.

MR. WHITEHEAD, that there was a very full appearance in Hampshire when the execution of the militia was. That there were many volunteers. They sent a declaration and protestation to the house that they would be ready to maintain the militia.

24. See above, n. 3. *CJ*, II, adds: "Mr. Lane brings Answer, That all Sheriffs, before they sue out their Patent, they enter Recognizance; and that there is no Recognizance entered, and that there is no Discharge entered."

25. Montagu, a Roman Catholic convert, was younger brother to Viscount Mandeville and a confidant of the queen. *DNB*. William D'Avenant, poet and dramatist, was accused of involvement in the first army plot, in which Henry Jermyn and Henry Percy were deeply implicated. See *Roy. Off.*, pp. 104–05, 211, 293. *DNB*.

26. Gawdy should have Prince Maurice, younger brother to Prince Rupert. *CJ*, II, 646.

27. In this letter, also presented at the conference, Wilmot wrote that the messenger from the house, who had come to York to summon him and Ashburnham, was given "a short Cudgel; so he is returned to London . . . with his Arm in a Scarf." See G, 9 June; and for the letter, *LJ*, V, 169. Wing, W 2885. For William Crofts see *Roy. Off.*, p. 93.

D'EWES

July 2, Saturday, 1642

The Speaker came a little before 9 of the clock, and a little after he was settled in his chair, he did put the house in mind of the order made yesterday that we should proceed with the 9th proposition of those 19 which had been sent to the king (and answered by him). Whereupon the clerk read it, and therein we desired his majesty that he would rest satisfied with the late ordinance of the militia and the putting it in execution until a law might be prepared to that end and purpose. One or two having spoken shortly to it and calling to the Speaker to put the question, Mr. Selden stood up and showed that *nolumus leges Angliae immutari*[1] was the answer to the statute of Merton, it being then conceived that some clauses in the statute of Merton would alter or destroy some part of the ancient common law, and he showed that the king had no further meaning in using that answer now.

That the king's resting satisfied with this ordinance of the militia will not make it a law or add any further force to it, no though he should give his consent to it at York, but that which must make it a law must be allowing of it in person or by authority of the great seal in the presence of the two houses of lords and commons. That he[2] conceived we ought no further to insist upon it, seeing the king had so solemnly expressed his dislike of it and may justly so do in respect that we have desired in the said proposition that the ordinance of the militia may continue till a bill be preparing, which may never be done for aught the king knows. And the people may justly dislike it, for here is a power given by an ordinance to dispose of their goods and persons because they are to muster and train as often as they shall be required. And they may dislike it also for a greater reason in respect that a punishment unknown which may terrify them is here ordered against such as shall disobey it, for they are left to be punished according as the two houses of parliament shall think fit, which no man can guess or imagine how great and vast it may be, whereas in all other offenses men can probably tell and have a rule in law to direct them what the punishment shall be.

---

1. "We do not wish that the laws of England be changed." The word is *mutari* in the king's answer to the Nineteen Propositions. Rushworth, IV, 732. In the statute of Merton, passed in a great council called in 1236, the barons declared that they would not have the laws of England changed. Stubbs, *Constitutional History,* II, 53.

2. I.e., Selden.

But whereas necessity is pretended to be a ground of this ordinance, that can be no true ground of it, for in that case where there is a true and apparent necessity, every man hath as great a liberty to provide for his own safety as the two houses of parliament; neither can any civil court pretend to do anything out of necessity which they cannot do by the ordinary rules of law and justice, for when such a real necessity comes, there must be a stop of the course of justice. And therefore he desired in conclusion that we would think of some way of accommod[at]ing all matters of difference with his majesty by naming a committee that may prepare some heads to this purpose. This gentleman as his lear/

No end of his resting satisfied for 'tis endless; 'tis till a law be prepared.

Think of some way to accommodate things. A committee to be named.

MR. STRODE moved answ/

I spake:

Scripture ill applied.

Rex, etc. Inconveniences. Ill effects.

Errors ought to be receded from. St. Austin's *Retractations.*[3]

Et numquam stabilis, etc.[4]

Sir Robert Rich, Mr. Page, about eleven of the clock, a conference touching a new printed declaration concerning his majesty's levying of horse and raising force. Divers spake. Order to resume, etc.[5] We went.

Wharton managed it. Read printed declaration.[6] The [?][7] delivered a note in writing in which the House of Commons were desired to provide for the common safety of ourselves and others.

The conference being ended, etc., MR. WASTELL first moved for the brothers of the Beckwiths[8] to go into France, which was granted.

MR. DENZIL HOLLES made report of the conference. The clerk read the book

3. In his Prologue St. Augustine states: "With a kind of judicial severity, I am reviewing my works—books, letters, and sermons—and, as it were, with the pen of a censor, I am indicating what dissatisfies me." See Saint Augustine, *The Retractions,* trans. Sister Mary Inez Bogan (Washington, D. C., 1968), p. 3.

4. "And never stable."

5. Following the conference the house was to resume consideration of the ninth proposition. *CJ,* II, 648.

6. For this declaration concerning levies, entitled *His Majesty's Answer to a printed Paper, Intituled, A new Declaration of the Lords and Commons in Parliament, of the 21st of June 1642, in Answer to his Majesty's Letter, dated the 14th of June, and sent to the Lord Mayor, Aldermen and Sheriffs of the City of London,* see Rushworth, IV, 748–51. Wing, C 2190. For the earlier message from the king and the declaration in response, see 18 June, n. 2, and 20 June, n. 8.

7. The omitted word should probably be either "Speaker" (Lord Wharton) or "Lord Kimbolton," who had reported to the lords from a committee concerning what should be presented at this conference. *LJ,* V, 175, 176. For this request from the lords, see H, below, and *CJ,* II, 648.

8. Mathew and William Beckwith. *CJ,* II, 648.

and then the note, and we then proceeded to the debate of the 9 propositions touching the militia. MR. COKE spake to it not to have it insisted on.[9]

Sir Robert Rich and Mr. Page, etc., brought down the ordinance of parliament for constituting the Lord Wharton lord lieutenant of Buckinghamshire. (Paget gone.) They being withdrawn, we proceeded with the debate till at last the SPEAKER informed us that the messengers stayed still without, and then we proceeded with the matter of their message and allowed the Lord Wharton's name to be put into the said ordinance, and then the SPEAKER related the same to them being again called in and delivered them the ordinance.

[f. 255b] Between 2 and 3 of the clock in the afternoon, Sir Robert Rich and Mr. Page, two masters of the Chancery, brought this message from the lords, that their lordships had sent down a paper to us concerning the Scottish propositions, which because it concerned matter of money they sent to us. They being gone, the clerk read the paper which they had brought. It concerned the 12 article of the treaty and was as followeth: It is agreed that the Scottish army shall receive their discharge from the king and parliament of England or from such persons as shall be appointed and authorized by both houses of parliament. So it was referred to the commissioners of this house appointed to treat with the Scottish commissioners.[10]

We appointed to meet at 8 of the clock on Monday morning and rose a little after 3 of the clock in the afternoon.

GAWDY

[f. 149a]   Saturday, the 2 of July

The house goeth on with the propositions for the militia.

A message from the lords, they desire a conference about a book set out by the king against the raising of horse and money.

There is about 250 in the house.

Resolved by question, that we shall insist upon the proposition for the militia, after a long debate.

A message from the lords, they have received a paper from the commissioners. That the Scots army shall receive their discharge from the king and both houses of parliament.

---

9. However, it was resolved "That this House shall insist upon this Ninth Proposition concerning the Militia." *CJ,* II, 649. It is not clear whether the speaker was Henry or Thomas Coke.

10. Further debate was postponed until Monday morning. *CJ,* II, 649.

HILL

[p. 117]   July 2, 1642, Saturday

MR. SELDEN, we see by laws and force. The courts declare law and see that it be executed where is resistance by compulsion.

We desire in 9th proposition that the king will rest satisfie[d] with the ordinance (according to the authority by which it is now made). What the king said at York is not obligatory until both states[11] and king in parliament settle it.

'Tis [not][12] fit we insist upon it in this form as it is asked, sc., till a bill be preferred.

1. In the ordinance the persons trusted have a power of imposing and charging.

2. If any disobey, shall be subject to such punishment as parliament shall think fit.

The mischief is much; none can say what punishment he shall bear if refractory.

He know not how there is a mixture of anything civil in matter of necessity.

Here it is grounded upon necessity.

3. Till upon necessity, till a bill be asked, what time is that.

Commissions of array are against law.

The king's declaration to be published in all churches in answer to the declaration of 21 June 1642 of lords and commons.[13]

Have usurped supreme power, etc. Persuade London to take up arms against us. Horse, men, and money.

Protestant religion opposed and like to be destroyed by Brownists and Separatists,[14] maintained by persons in both houses.

[p. 118] Laws trampled under foot, new laws made, peace shaken, declare war against us. Under privilege of parliament make any order, and[15] he is an enemy to commonwealth. All they do is lawful because they do it. That we intend [blank]. Declare against ordinance as against law, sovereignty, and bound by our oath and our subjects by their[s] of allegiance to oppose to that ordinance. Sir John Hotham's act treason and taking our munition an act of

---

11. I.e., lords and commons.

12. Without the word "not," Hill's version of Selden's speech is directly opposite to that of D'Ewes. For Selden's opposition to both the militia ordinance and the commission of array, see 28 June, n. 13.

13. For the declaration see above, n. 6.

14. "Brownists, Anabaptists, and other Sectaries," in Rushworth, IV, 749.

15. The words "whosoever breaks their Privileges" should be inserted here. Rushworth, IV, 749.

mistrust. For both, by help [of] God and the law we will adventure our lives. The kingdom were brought to confusion and destruction by those few men.

He will proceed against such as execute the ordinance of militia and Hull as if done against our person. Shows that wealth of city not like to be destroyed another way, but by providing[16] against us and the wives and children violated.

Proceed against all persons that assist levy of money, horse, etc., as disturbers of public peace.

Lords desire that we consider what condition they are brought into that maintain peace.[17] That our house take speedy course to consider for safe sitting the parliament, preserving the lives of the members and such as execute their commands.

16. The word is "rebelling" in Rushworth, IV, 751.
17. *CJ*, II, 648, reads: "who have obeyed the Orders and Commands of the Parliament."

D'EWES

July 4, Monday, 1642

The Speaker came between 8 and 9 of the clock, and some motions of little moment were made and ordered, which see in the clerk's book.[1]

About a quarter of an hour after the house was set, the Lord Ruthin (son and heir of the Earl of Kent, being a minister or preacher in the western parts of England)[2] delivered in the copy of a letter sent to Henry, Earl of Stamford, bearing date at Leicester on Sunday morning, 3 of the clock, July 3, 1642, which was subscribed by William Warde, Daniel Decon, Richard Ludlam, and William Franke, which letter was read, the therein they showed that Mr. Henry Hastings (younger son to the Earl of Huntingdon) did now style himself *Vice-comes*[3] *Leicestriae* and that he came to Leicester the night foregoing. That one Dr. Lake was sent from the said Mr. Hastings to William Reynar (an inhabitant of the town of Leicester) for that part of the magazine which was in his custody, and that the said William Reynar returned this answer to him, that Henry, Earl of Stamford, had left the said magazine with him and to him he would deliver it. Whereupon the said Mr. Henry Hastings did at 12 of the clock the same night in the marketplace at Leicester proclaim the said William Reynar, Mr. Sherman, Mr. Stanley, and Mr. Norrice traitors,[4] and the mayor of Leicester did affirm also that he had received a letter from the king to proclaim the Earl of Stamford traitor because he had levied war against the king in taking away the magazine of the county and keeping of it with a guard.

Hereupon there followed several debates, and one vote or question was passed, that the said Earl of Stamford should be sent down into the said county of Leicester and some deputy lieutenants with him to preserve the peace thereof. It was then further proposed that we should likewise give him power by a vote to call in aid from the adjoining counties, and MR. ARTHUR GOODWIN moved that he, the said Earl of Stamford, or any of the deputy lieutenants might

1. See G, below, and *CJ*, II, 649.

2. Anthony Grey, who became Earl of Kent in 1639, was rector of Aston Flamville, Leics, from 1590 to 1643. GEC, *Peerage*.

3. The medieval title bestowed on a sheriff of a county when he was regarded as the deputy of an earl.

4. William Sherman, William Stanley, and John Norris, according to *CJ*, II, 658. Subsequently both Lake and Rudyard, the mayor, were summoned to attend the house. *CJ*, II, 651. For another letter from Leicestershire, see G, below.

require the like aid from the lord lieutenants of the county of Lincoln and Northampton, which made me stand up and move in effect following:

That though I were not altogether well satisfied with the matter of this vote, because whereas the first vote tended to preserve the peace of that county, this threatens war, being one of those resolutions of which a man may justly say, *Morte spirantia vota*,[5] yet I did more dislike the manner of it because it is so full of uncertainty and especially in respect of that which the gentleman moved who spake last (viz., Mr. Goodwin); [f. 256a] for he would have it to lie in the power of any deputy lieutenant in the county of Leicester to command or require, for so much the word in law imports, the lord lieutenants of the two neighboring shires to send in such aid as either their fear or other consideration shall persuade them to think necessary. And we know that there are two noble young lords full of courage who are lord lieutenants of these two shires (viz., the Lord Willoughby of Parham of Lincolnshire and the Lord Spencer of Northamptonshire), who perhaps will be loath to be under the command and direction of a deputy lieutenant of another shire; neither is the number proportioned for how many they shall send, nor is there any provision made for these two counties, one of them especially lying near Yorkshire, in case they should need help themselves. And therefore my humble motion is that this vote may be referred to a committee to draw up and to prevent those inconveniences that are now in it.

Divers spake after me, and in the issue the vote was very much altered and no power left in the deputy lieutenants of Leicestershire to require but only to desire the aid of the said two former specified counties and of some others near adjoining counties if need should require.[6]

[f. 256b] Divers other particulars ensued touching this business of Leicestershire, and afterwards there followed a conference with the lords upon it, all which see in the clerk's Journal[7] or in Mr. Bodvel's notes, if the kingdom continue, for I saw all things in so desperate a condition and so near to ruin and confusion as it even discouraged me in my very begun course of annotations.

Post Meridiem

The Speaker resumed his chair between 3 and 4. A number of particulars passed.

The chief was a report from MR. NICHOLAS how the Earl of Warwick,[8] how

---

5. "Vows inspired by death."

6. For the resolutions see G, below, and *CJ*, II, 649.

7. There is no evidence in *CJ* or *LJ* that a conference was held.

8. Nicholas reported that he had delivered the ordinance to Warwick giving him command of the fleet; meanwhile Warwick had received a letter from the king "commanding him to deliver up the Ships, otherwise he would proceed against him as guilty of High Treason." See 1 July, n. 18; and

the king's fleet had all submitted to him except 4 ships, to which end divers letters were read[9] and a conference was desired upon it and upon other particulars which happened this afternoon.[10] See the clerk's book.[11]

The house appointed to meet at 8 of the clock tomorrow morning and rose between 7 and 8.

GAWDY

[f. 149a]   Monday, the 4 of July

A warrant to the sergeant to search all places for arms or money going to York. All officers to be assistants to him.[12]

[f. 149b] A letter to my Lord of Stamford from his man[13] from Bradgate, July the 2. That Mr. Hastings marched with drums and colors before 30 horse and 30 foot. The foot increased 30 more. The horse increased 40 more. Mr. Hastings proclaimed my Lord of Stamford traitor and said he raised those forces by the king's command to apprehend my Lord of Stamford and to take the magazine from Bradgate, my lord's house. There was a warrant read for the gathering these forces subscribed Henry Hastings, *Vicecomes*. A letter from Leicester, that Mr. Hastings, *Vicecomes*, demanded the magazine there. Dated July the 3.

Resolved,[14] that officers be sent into Leicestershire for the assistance of the lord lieutenant and deputies in putting the ordinance for the militia in execution and for preserving the peace of that county and for the defense of the magazine.

Resolved, that if force be brought out of other counties, then it shall be lawful for the lord lieutenant and deputies to desire the assistance of the adjacent counties.

CJ, II, 650. For the king's letter and Warwick's response, see *LJ*, V, 178; and *HMC, Portland MSS*, I, 42.

9. When Warwick called a council of war of the captains of the ships then upon the Downs, five "refused to come to the Earl, or to deliver up their Ships." *CJ*, II, 650. They were Sir John Mennes, Robert Slingsby (cousin to Sir Henry Slingsby, MP), John Burley, Richard Fogg, and Baldwin Wake. For the first three see *DNB*. For their letters to Warwick, see *LJ*, V, 179–80; and *HMC, Fifth Report*, p. 34.

10. For the conference and a declaration of both houses thanking Warwick for his service and sending for the five captains as delinquents, see *LJ*, V, 178, and *CJ*, II, 650.

11. For the rest of the day, see G, below, and *CJ*, II, 650–51.

12. For details and the text of the warrant, see *CJ*, II, 649–50. The warrant ordered the sergeant at arms and his deputies, assisted by mayors, sheriffs, constables, and other officers, to search for money and "Instruments of War" that might "be sent to Yorke, and other Places . . . of this Kingdom."

13. The servant's name was Salisbury. *CJ*, II, 649.

14. Crossed out in MS: *that if the force of Leicestershire be not sufficient to preserve the peace of that county and the magazine and.*

[f. 150a] In the afternoon, after I came away.

An information against Mr. Thomas Elliott, that if the king had been as good as his word, he had been together by the ears[15] with the parliament before this time. That he[16] was uncertain. That the parliament men were a company of [*blank*]. That they had no more religion than a company of dogs. 'Twas informed that he had given the prince some pernicious counsels.[17] This I had from Sir Richard Buller.

15. At variance. *NED*.
16. I.e., the king.
17. Elliott was groom of the bedchamber to the prince. See Clarendon, *History*, II, 116; and Toynbee and Young, *Strangers in Oxford*, pp. 147–49. For Elliott's remarks and the subsequent conference with the lords, see *LJ*, V, 180–81, and *CJ*, II, 651.

D'EWES

July 5, Tuesday, 1642

The Speaker came between 8 and 9 of the clock. After prayers he showed that a letter was come to him from the committee at Hull, which he delivered in to the clerk who read it. There was no date, but the same was sent from Hull upon Sunday or [yesterday][1] and subscribed by Sir John Hotham, Sir Edward Ayscough, Mr. John Hotham, Mr. John Alured, and Mr. Peregrine Pelham, in which they showed that having lately notice that some persons of quality came in disguised habits to the riverside of Humber and discovered that they did expect some ship shortly to come thither, which made them to desire Captain Pigot to put to sea with his ship,[2] which he did accordingly and within 2 or 3 days met with a small ship coming from Holland called the *Providence,* which after some parley with him did promise to go along with him to Hull. But after they had gone awhile together, the master of the said ship did run himself into a creek called the Paull[3] some 4 miles from Hull so as Captain Pigot's ship could not draw water to come near it, and although they sent down some pinnaces, yet the birds were flown before they could get thither, and that they had already landed 4 brass pieces and began to entrench themselves and to raise the trained bands of Holderness, and that the king was expected there this day at 10 of the clock. That the said Captain Pigot had taken a small pinnace, in which were Colonel Ashburnham, Sir Edward Stradling, and/[4]

Sir William Lewis sent up to desire the conference.[5]

Post Meridiem

The Speaker resumed his chair between 5 and 6 of the clock.

Upon MR. PURY's motion it was ordered that the lord mayor, aldermen, and

---

1. The bracketed word has been crossed out in the MS. For the letter see *LJ,* V, 182–83. See also Rushworth, IV, 601; and Reckitt, *Hull,* pp. 47–48.

2. John Pigot was captain of the *Mayflower.*

3. Paull is actually the name of a village with a small creek nearby. *LJ,* V, 182.

4. Stradling, elder brother to Sir Henry, was MP for Glamorganshire in the Short Parliament and a soap monopolist. See *Roy. Off.,* pp. 359–60. *DNB.* Henry Wilmot, Sir John Berkeley, Sir Hugh Pollard, and a Frenchman were also aboard. Pollard had been expelled from the House of Commons on 9 December 1641 for his part in the first army plot. See Keeler, p. 308; and *Roy. Off.,* pp. 299–300.

5. For the conference see *LJ,* V, 181. For the rest of the morning, see G and H, below, and *CJ,* II, 651–53.

Common Council should continue the loan of the money due to him for powder for 9 months longer.[6]

The SPEAKER delivered in a letter bearing date June 28, 1642, sent from Sir William Carnaby to himself, in which he/[7]

Then was read another letter sent to the Speaker also from Sir George Booth, Sir William Brereton, and Mr. George Booth bearing date at Dunham (Sir George Booth's house) July 2, 1642.[8]

This day 3 weeks was appointed to put the militia in execution in Suffolk upon MR. GURDON's motion.[9]

Sir George Gresley, Baronet, and Sir Samuel Sly were appointed to be commended/

From aboard the *James,* his majesty's ship, on the Downs, July 4, 1642, the Earl of Warwick's letter to Mr. Pym which the said MR. PYM delivered in himself, in which he showed how these 4 ships who stood out in his majesty's fleet were come in.[10]

Sir Robert Harley was sent up to the lords with the said letter, etc.

MR. DENZIL HOLLES made report from the committee of 3 votes.[11]

I spake against the 1 concerning levying forces in Lincolnshire. Checked Mr. Long.[12]

[f. 258a] SIR PHILIP STAPLETON delivered in a letter bearing date July 4, 1642, sent to himself from Hull, subscribed by Sir John Hotham, Mr. John Hotham (his son), Mr. John Alured, and Mr. Peregrine Pelham.[13]

6. The loan was for powder made and delivered by Samuel Cordwell. *CJ,* II, 653.

7. This letter, though not noted in *CJ,* may well have been in response to the summons of 20 June by the house. On 26 August Carnaby was disabled and subsequently served as treasurer at wars to the Earl of Newcastle. See Appendix A; and *Roy. Off.,* p. 60, under Francis Carnaby.

8. This letter expressed the willingness of Cheshire to execute the militia ordinance. *CJ,* II, 653. Sir George Booth, father to Brereton's first wife and grandfather to George Booth, was a prominent supporter of parliament in Cheshire as well as deputy lieutenant for Lancashire. Morrill, *Cheshire,* p. 24; *CJ,* II, 495. *DNB.*

9. Crossed out in MS: *and the same day was appointed.* Actually various days were appointed for several other counties, with Sir Robert Crane named as deputy lieutenant for Suffolk, Gresley and Sly (Sleigh in *CJ*) for Derbyshire. *CJ,* II, 654. For Gresley, a former MP, see GEC, *Baronetage,* I, 40.

10. There were actually five ships' captains who ultimately submitted. See 4 July, n. 9. For Warwick's letter see *LJ,* V, 185. Wing, W 1004.

11. For the votes concerning Hull reported from the joint committee for defense of the kingdom, see G, below, and *CJ,* II, 654. This new committee (also referred to as the committee of safety) had been named the previous day. *CJ,* II, 651; *LJ,* V, 178. The commons' members were Holles, Stapleton, Marten, Meyrick, Fiennes, Hampden, Pierrepont, Glyn, Pym, and Sir William Waller. For the role of this committee until the end of 1643, see Glow, "Committee of Safety," *English Historical Review,* 80: 289–313.

12. This proposition, when considered in the House of Lords the next day, was "suspended." *LJ,* V, 186.

13. For the letter see *HMC, Portland MSS,* I, 41.

The king had about 2000 foot and 300 horse ready and meant instantly to besiege Hull.

That divers brass pieces were brought over in the *Providence,* which lately put in in a creek in the low countries.[14]

SIR ROBERT HARLEY brought answer that the lords would give a meeting.[15]

SIR PHILIP STAPLETON's report for money to be issued to buy 500 horse. All voted.

Sir John Evelyn sent up to desire a conference about these several votes.[16]

We appointed to meet at 8 of the clock tomorrow morning when there were not 40 in the house.[17] The house rose a little after 8 of the clock at night.

GAWDY

[f. 150a]   Tuesday, the 5 of July

A letter from Hull from the committee, that the *Providence,* the king's ship, put into Humber. That Pigot went to take her but the *Providence* ran on ground. Pigot was not able to follow her. 'Tis supposed there are persons in her of good quality and much munition that came out of Holland. They are fortifying there and planting ordnance. That the trained bands of Holderness are to be brought thither, and 'tis said the king will be there by 10 a clock. They desire 500 men should be sent to Hull and that the sea should be kept open. They have taken Mr. Ashburnham and Sir Edward Stradling who are in Hull to be disposed by the parliament.

[f. 150b] MR. SPURSTOW, that there are 3 or 4 citizens, nameless, that will set out an 100 horse to send into Leicestershire and so forth into Lancashire where there is occasion to use them. 'Tis consented to.

A message to the lords to desire a conference about the letter sent from Hull, which is to be read, and to acquaint them that we have received divers other

---

14. I.e., the creek in Holderness. The letter contained this request:

You have oft had it reiterated from hence the necessity of a good Committee here, you have appointed some, but we are no better. We are not at this instant four. We desire you will be pleased to send down Sir William Strickland, Sir Hugh Cholmeley, Sir Philip Stapilton, Sir Henry Cholmeley. They are gentlemen that in these times may do good with their credit in the country.

15. Actually the lords had sent messengers to request a conference concerning Warwick's letters, for the Earl of Northumberland had received one similar to that sent to Pym. See above, n. 10; and *LJ,* V, 184. Wing, W 999.

16. For the votes concerning the disposition of money "come in upon the Propositions" as well as the raising of ten thousand foot soldiers, see G, below, and *CJ,* II, 654. This part of the conference was reported in the lords house the next day. To most of these votes three lords registered their dissents—Leicester, Portland, and Spencer. See *LJ,* V, 186.

17. For proceedings omitted by D'Ewes, see *CJ,* II, 654.

letters which were intercepted, not read, which we desire should be referred to the close committee for the defense of the kingdom.[18]

Ordered, that the 100 horse that is found by some well-affected citizens, moved by Mr. Spurstow, shall be referred to the committee for the defense of the kingdom how they shall be disposed.

Mr. Clement Spelman[19] at the bar on his knees for coming to the benchers' table in Gray's Inn and desired that the king's declaration might be read in the chapel.

MR. PEARD, that Mr. Spelman may be committed to the Tower and there lie till Michaelmas term that so he may lose his circuit.

[f. 151a] Ordered, that Mr. Spelman shall remain in the sergeant's hands and that there shall be an impeachment drawn up against him.

In the afternoon the house sat at 5 a clock. I was not there.

A letter from Sir John Hotham, that there is 2000 foot and 300 foot[20] to besiege Hull with pieces of battery. That the king is expected.

That 5000 men to be raised in the City and 5000 in the adjacent counties for the defense of the parliament. That there should 10,000£ be employed to furnish horse and things necessary for them.[21] This I had from Mr. Catelyn.

That committees are to go into Lincolnshire to provide force to put into Hull,[22] and that there shall 500 men be sent from hence thither. This I had likewise from Mr. Catelyn.

HILL

[p. 119]   Tuesday, July 5

Impeachment of lord mayor:[23] 1 June 1642 seditiously causing in several places the proclamation for execution of the commission of array to be published in the City of London.

---

18. For the new joint committee, see above, n. 11. Four letters, "stiled, Mr. Ashburneham's Pacquet" and supposed to have come from the king, were enclosed in the letter from Hull. *CJ*, II, 651.

19. Spelman had been summoned as a delinquent concerning "the King's last Declaration against the Parliament"—doubtless the declaration concerning levies. See 2 July, n. 6; and *CJ*, II, 650, 653. Spelman, though a lawyer, devoted himself largely to literary and antiquarian pursuits, as did his father Sir Henry and his brother Sir John. See Edward Foss, *The Judges of England* (London, 1848–64), VII, 171–73. *DNB*.

20. Gawdy should have written *horse*. For this letter see above, n. 13.

21. Cf. *CJ*, II, 654.

22. See above, n. 14. It was also resolved that two ships should be sent from the Downs to Hull. *CJ*, II, 654.

23. A committee, including D'Ewes and Wilde, was named both to prepare a declaration concerning Leicestershire and "to consider of the Impeachment of the Lord Mayor," which subse-

Papists and clergy advance 80,000£ to the king.

A ship of ammunition of 1300-pound barrels of powder, ammunition, and minions,[24] which the country conveyed to the king, being run aground.

---

quently took place at the lords' bar. (On 1 July the committee to impeach Henry Hastings et al. had been charged with the impeachment of Gurney also. See 30 June, n. 17; and *CJ*, II, 647.) According to the impeachment it was "on or about the last Day of June 1642" (not 1 June) that the king's proclamation for executing the commission of array was issued. See 28 June, n. 1; *CJ*, II, 652; and *LJ*, V, 182.

24. Small kind of ordnance (cannon). *NED*. The ship was doubtless the *Providence*.

D'EWES

July 6, Wednesday, 1642

The Speaker came a little before 9 of the clock. Several motions of no great moment during my absence, for I went out a little after prayers.[1]

When I returned into the house, they were in dispute concerning the offense of Mr. Henry Hastings in Leicestershire in putting the commission of array in execution there, whether it did not amount to levying of war within the statute of 25 E. 3[2] and so was treason or whether it were only a misdemeanor. So after it had been a long time debated, it was laid aside and nothing determined in it.

MR. HENRY MARTEN made report from the committee of lords and commons appointed to provide for the safety of the kingdom.[3] That they conceived that there was now no longer doubt whether the king intended to levy war against the parliament or not, for the king had now besieged the town of Kingston upon Hull with a considerable army of horse and foot and that he had also cut away the river of fresh water so as they had only well water left and had forbidden all men upon pain of death to carry in any provisions. That Sir John Hotham had let in the water about Hull and drowned the ground near it so as no approaches could be made near it. That the Earl of Lindsey and the Lord Willoughby (of Eresby, his son) were passed over into Lincolnshire with 200 horse. That therefore the committee had agreed upon two votes: The first, that the Earl of Warwick should be sent unto to send two of his majesty's ships, or three if he could spare them, to Hull for the defense thereof to observe the directions of Sir John Hotham. They had further voted that 2000 men should be sent down to Hull as soon as they could be raised for the further defense of the said town, both which with reference to the votes passed yesterday, so as we voted one ship more having before voted 2 and 1500 men more having before voted 500 to be sent.[4]

1. For two resolutions concerning the sitting of the house, see G, below.
2. *SR*, I, 319–20: 25 E. III, Stat. 5, c. 2. For Wilde's report concerning Hastings, see H, below, and *CJ*, II, 654–55. He was doubtless reporting from one of the committees recently named for Leicestershire affairs. See 30 June, n. 17, or 5 July, n. 23.
3. For Marten's report see also *CJ*, II, 655.
4. For the earlier votes see G, 5 July. In the afternoon Marten reported both the ordinance and the warrant for raising men for Hull. *CJ*, II, 656. For the texts see *CJ*, II, 659.

[f. 259a][5] These votes being passed, I spake in effect following:

That I did well hope we should now begin to think of framing a petition to his majesty, having provided for all particulars for the security of Hull, which if we do not, but that his majesty go on with his preparations on the one side and tell us not what he expects from us and we go on with our preparations on the other side and show not to his majesty what we desire from him, we may kill one another to the world's end; for certainly I think no man is of so mean a capacity as to think Hull is the main thing we contend for but that both his majesty and we do aim at somewhat else in our desiring to keep and his endeavoring to get Hull, so as this is but the *medium ad fine*, the means to some other end, we all aim at. If we look upon ourselves in respect of civil affairs, I dare be bold to say that the liberty and propriety of the subject were never so clearly asserted to them as the[y] are at this present since the foundation of this monarchy, whether we consider it under the Britons or under the English Saxons or since it was founded by the Norman, so as we have little or nothing more to desire in that respect. The main matter then which yet remains to be secured to us is the reformation of religion, and I desire that we may come to particulars in that, for if it shall be objected that we have no certainty of all that is promised us but that it is like a spider's web easily blown away, then to what end should we desire more; nay if a monarchy continue amongst us, there must of necessity remain a confidence from the subjects towards the prince. For the town of Hull itself I desire not that it should be delivered up to his majesty but that[6] we might humbly supplicate his majesty to appoint Sir John Hotham governor there till other things were peaceably composed between his majesty and us, and that he should not deliver it up but by his majesty's command signified to him by both houses of parliament. My humble request therefore is that a committee may be nominated to draw up such a petition to his majesty as may set forth our desires to him and prepare a way to an accommodation.

No man answered or confuted my motion, but some violent spirits diverted the house from the consideration of it by other motions, though many gave a public allowance of the proposition I had made by crying out, "Well moved."[7]

[f. 258b] MR. NICHOLAS delivered in a letter sent to him from Mr. Robert

5. Crossed out in MS: *I spake touching a petition to his majesty. Kill to world's end. Know wha[t] we or king would have.*

6. Crossed out in MS: *some third person in whom we both, his majesty and the two houses, might.*

7. Actually it was ordered that the committee of safety should prepare a declaration "concerning warlike Preparations . . . which necessitates the Parliament to raise Forces for their Defence." *CJ*, II, 655.

Cotmore bearing date from aboard the *James* July 5 from the Earl of Warwick's secretary, which letter is in print.[8]

Captain Burley, master of the *Antelope*.

Captain Slingsby and Captain Wake now prisoners.

That Sir John Penington was come down to Deal in Kent with some 40 men, and that Mr. Edwin Sandys being named a deputy lieutenant.[9]

Sir Henry Heyman and Sir Edward Boys were appointed to return thanks to Mr. Sandys and the other gentlemen there, and then it was moved that we might send up to the lords that the lord lieutenant of Kent, viz., the Earl of Leicester, to grant out deputations.

Kent to muster this day fortnight.[10]

MR. DENZIL HOLLES made report of the conference had yesternight with the lords about 8 of the clock at night managed by the Lord Mandeville, where the Earl of Warwick's letter to the Speaker/[11]

His majesty's w/

To Captain Wheeler, captain of the *Greyhound*, to/

At the court of York, June 29, 1642.

MR. HOLLES then delivered in the copy of a letter which was del/[12]

MR. HENRY MARTEN made report from the lords that they assented to our vote concerning Youghal[13] and to the two votes concerning the relief of Hull.

The house rose between 12 and 1 of the clock. We appointed to meet again at 4 of the clock in the afternoon.

[f. 259a]   Post Meridiem

The Speaker resumed the chair between 4 and 5 of the clock. Several motions were made and ordered. See Mr. Bodvel's journal.[14] I was present all the afternoon except a little at the beginning.

8. Wing, W 999. Of the five captains who "stood out" against Warwick, Burley was the first to submit. *LJ*, V, 185.

9. A member of a Puritan family, Sandys played a decisive part in securing Kent for the parliament in 1642. Alan Everitt, *The Community of Kent and the Great Rebellion, 1640–60* (Leicester, 1966), pp. 63, 111. *DNB* under Sir Edwin Sandys.

10. The lords, however, ordered the execution of the militia in Kent for 1 August, after the conclusion of the Maidstone assizes. *LJ*, V, 186; Woods, *Prelude,* p. 99. For proceedings omitted by D'Ewes, see G and H, below.

11. This letter, actually sent to the Earl of Northumberland, mentioned "a Warrant from his Majesty to Captain [Abraham] Wheeler . . . to come to Newcastle" to receive directions from the newly appointed governor, the Earl of Newcastle. See 5 July, n. 15; *CJ*, II, 655; and *CSPD, 1641–43*, p. 347.

12. This letter from the lords to Warwick acknowledged "his good Service, and the Service of the Officers and Mariners." *CJ*, II, 655. For the text see *LJ*, V, 184–85.

13. For the order to send £100 to Youghal for relief of distressed Protestants, see *LJ*, V, 187.

14. For proceedings omitted by D'Ewes, see *CJ*, II, 655–56.

The LORD RUTHIN moved that we might proceed with the business of Leicestershire; then it was debated whether we should accuse Mr. Henry Hastings and some others of treason or of high crimes and misdemeanors. Divers spake to it. MR. WALTER LONG moved that we should impeach them of treason, for he did think that it was treason because of that which he heard today in the morning.

I answered him: That if the gentleman who last moved to have us call Mr. Hastings's offense treason had given us some reason for it, I might perhaps have been drawn by his reason to have been of his opinion, but now he tells us only that he thinks 'tis treason because he heard somebody else say that it was so in the morning. Truly I have read somewhat of treason as well as he, and yet I cannot conceive the present offense to be treason by anything which was said in the morning. This I am sure, that if we impeach this gentleman of treason and then be not able to make it good, we shall bring much dishonor upon this house, but if we call it an high misdemeanor at the first, we may call it treason afterwards, as the House of Commons proceeded in $a°\ 27°$ H. 6 against de la Pole, Duke of Suffolk,[15] as appears upon the Parliament Roll of that year, for they first preferred articles of misdemeanor against him and afterwards of high treason. And besides also which I hope will fully satisfy this gentleman (viz., Mr. Long), I can assure him if the lords shall upon examination find this offense to be treason, they may adjudge it to be so, and therefore I desire that we may only call it an high misdemeanor.

Divers spake after me, and at last the house moved the name or title of high treason,[16] as I had moved. See the clerk's book.

We appointed to meet at 9 tomorrow. Rose about 7.

GAWDY

[f. 151a]   Wednesday, the VI of July

Resolved by question, that the house shall not sit till one a clock.[17]

The reason of this is MR. STRODE's motion that the committee for the defense and for the peace of the kingdom may sit in the morning and acquaint the house with it in the afternoon.

[f. 151b] MR. MARTEN, a report from the committee for the defense of the

15. D'Ewes should have 28 H. VI. See *RP*, V, 176–83. *DNB*.

16. D'Ewes surely intended to write *misdemeanor*. Cf. H, below. In August, however, Hastings was accused of high treason by the commons.

17. I.e., the house was to sit "every Day, at One of the Clock." *CJ*, II, 654. However, see below and *CJ*, II, 655.

kingdom. That Wilmot, Berkeley, and others have landed 14 pieces of brass ordnance. That my Lord of Lindsey raise forces to lie before Hull. That the king lay at Beverley. That Sir Thomas Glemham and others are to command horse.[18]

'Tis desired by the committee that there should be 2000 foot sent to Hull. That my Lord of Warwick may send 3 ships into the river of Humber.

Resolved, that my Lord of Warwick be desired to send one ship more be sent into Humber to be directed by Sir John Hotham.

MR. MARTEN told us further that the king had turned a fresh river from Hull. That Hotham had drowned the country about Hull.

Resolved, that 2000 men be raised and sent by sea to Hull.

Ordered, that the committee for the defense of the kingdom prepare a declaration that the war is begun, which is the cause that forces are levied by the parliament.

Resolved, that the house shall sit at 8 a clock notwithstanding the former order, which is reversed.

[f. 152a] A letter from my Lord of Warwick's secretary to Mr. Nicholas. That he had been with some in the fleet that stood out who used him courteously, but Captain Slingsby said he made a difference between Charles Rex and John Browne. That Captain Burley was threatened by his mariners that if he submitted not to my Lord of Warwick, they would deliver him to my lord. That my lord summoned the 4 ships that opposed him and in-ironed them and told them he would turn the glass.[19] The mariners boarded Wake and Slingsby and took them and delivered them to my lord without bloodshed.

Mr. Crosse tells us at the bar that the county of Warwick hath submitted themselves to the militia totally with many volunteers. That the commissioners of array that was my Lord of Northampton and my Lord Dunsmore did not put their commission in execution.[20]

---

18. The king had arrived at Beverley on 4 July. *CJ*, II, 655. During the summer of 1642 Glemham was made governor of York. *Roy. Off.*, p. 158. *DNB*. For accounts of the siege of Hull during July, see Rushworth, IV, 610–11; and Reckitt, *Hull*, pp. 54–61.

19. These actions are described in Warwick's letter to Pym, which appears in *LJ*, V, 185:

I weighed my Anchors, and caused the rest of my Ships so to do, and came to an Anchor round about them, and besieged them; and when I had made all Things ready, I summoned them. Sir John Mennes and Captain Fogg came in to me; but Captain Slingsby and Captain Wake stood out: Whereupon I let fly a Gun over them, and sent them Word that I had turned up the Glass upon them; if in that Space they came not in, they must look for me aboard them.

In nautical usage *glass* generally referred to the half-hour glass, and thus the time taken by the sand of such a glass to run out. A square–rigged vessel was said to be *in irons* when, the yards being so braced that some sails were laid aback in coming up into the wind, she would not turn either way. *NED*.

20. Crosse was a servant to Lord Brooke. *CJ*, II, 655. For the king's instructions to the commissioners of array, see Rushworth, IV, 674–75.

SIR JOHN HOLLAND offereth a bill for settling the militia.[21]

The house sat at 4 a clock, but I was not there.

An impeachment against Mr. Henry Hastings and the rest of high crime. This I had from old Mr. More.[22]

HILL

[p. 119]   July 6, 1642, Wednesday

Mr. Hastings came into Leicestershire with men in arms marching in a warlike manner, which he brought out of Derbyshire and other counties with arms, muskets, etc., charged with bullet, and with intention to take away the magazine of the Earl of Stamford by ordinance of both houses, who was in execution there of the ordinance of both houses for the militia, and with intention to take away the earl's life and burn his house as appeared by their threats, there being now a design to raise forces in the whole kingdom against the parliament as both houses have declared, and did rescue himself and company from the sheriff that came in the king's name and required peace, etc. Question: Upon the whole matter whether it were a levying of war and so treason within the statute of 25 E. 3, ca. 2.

SERJEANT WILDE cites the cases in Mr. Solicitor's argument which in conceit matches this in point of treason.[23]

Nota, before this Hastings was accused of misdemeanors and an order of parliament a- [p. 120] gainst him. When the messenger and high sheriff required his obedience, he acknowledged that he knew of it. Then Hastings gets into Derbyshire and raiseth forces without any pretense of commission of array.

If he did, yet he hath no power by the commission of array to call them out of another county. He tells them he would arm them, and he came with 300 in their march, etc., and the messenger did actually attach him; and he promised obedience, but afterward this company which marched 8 miles with himself did rescue him and abused the messenger.

Question: If it is treason within 25 E. 3, within words.

Answer: GLYN. 1. Here was warlike forces gathered without legal authority in intention to resist authority of parliament. Are 2 treasons in statute: 1. Against person of the king. 2. Levying war against king. You must have 2

21. This was a new bill, not to be confused with the militia ordinance or the earlier militia bill rejected by the king. For the content see H, below.

22. Richard More.

23. Hill's reference is apparently to St. John's speech of 29 April 1641 at Strafford's trial. See John Rushworth, *The Tryal of Thomas Earl of Strafford* (London, 1680), pp. 675–705.

expositions if talk levying war against person of the king. Was absurd, for that is in the first clause.

If company levy war with intent to do some public act, as with intent to destroy the Privy Council, it is levying war within 25 E. 3. Was those prentices in Spenser's time, that was mayor of London.[24]

Inhabitants consult how to revenge themselves against lords of manors. They resolve (claiming interest) to pull down enclosures. Indict of high treason, and all judges resolve that was high treason within 25 E. 3, for was [p. 121] public intent.

The case, one [*illegible*] enter[ed] with intention, without weapon, to pull down archbishop's house, and fellow hang for treason.[25] There was no public intention, but they conceived archbishop ill instrument of commonwealth. Resolved, upon this distinction, that [it] can have been possible to levy war against authority of the king. Here was authority of the king to be put in execution. He confessed notice, and by this levying war he rescued himself.

Some of the committee differ. Ergo, their[26] intention was particular and nothing universal.

Wilmot, Pollard, etc., hath 14 pieces of ordnance within 4 miles of Hull and entrenched. Hull[27] hath drowned the country round about. 3 ships to be sent into Humber to assist Hull to be directed by Sir John Hotham.

2000 men to be sent to Hull by water forthwith to be levied in Middlesex, London, and Essex by ordinance of parliament.

The king hath cut the passage of the fresh river which runs into Hull and turned it another way.

King hath commanded that no provisions be carried into Hull upon pain of death.

[p. 122] Captains Slingsby and Wake are prisoners with the Earl of Warwick, etc. Surrounded.

Mr. Crosse inform concerning Warwickshire for the militia. It is divided into 4 hundreds. 200 horse at Stratford upon Avon. 300 volunteers completely armed. Trained band came in fully. 3 months at own charges offered to wait upon. At Warwick 200 volunteers. 1 troop of horse. 3 place, 300 volunteers. 4 place, 150 horse. 50 to be a guard to the castle. 600 horse went with him to

---

24. Sir John Spencer, a wealthy merchant and member of the Clothworkers' Company, was lord mayor in 1594–95. *DNB*.

25. During the Peasants' Revolt of 1381, the manor at Lambeth of Simon of Sudbury, Archbishop of Canterbury and chancellor, was attacked and pillaged. The archbishop fled to the Tower and was beheaded shortly thereafter by the rioters. John Ball, a militant priest, was subsequently hanged for his part in the uprising. See L. C. Hector and Barbara F. Harvey, eds., *The Westminster Chronicle, 1381–1394* (Oxford, 1982), pp. 3–7, 15. *DNB*.

26. MS: *ils* (*they*).

27. Hill should have Sir John Hotham.

Coleshill. 7000 volunteers out of Birmingham. 1 man brought out 300 completely arme[d]. All men showed themselves very forward and wept for joy. Lord Brooke is lord lieutenant there.

The bill concerning the militia by SIR JOHN HOLLAND:

1. To have power to charge all men after their abilities and faculties. To find men, horse, arms, weapons, and ammunition for wars. Such as are between 18 and 60 to call together, and them to array, train, exercise, and put in readiness, and to take the muster of them in places most convenient, etc.

2. To nominate persons of quality to be their deputies, to be approved by both houses.

3. That any two of the deputies in the absence or by the command of the lord lieutenant shall have the like power and authority.

[p. 123] 4. The lord lieutenant have power to make colonels, captains, and other officers.

5. The lord lieutenant and his deputies in his absence or by his command to lead, conduct, or employ the persons so arrayed and weaponed for suppression of all rebellions, [in]surrections, and invasions which may happen within their limits according as they shall rec[eive] directions from his majesty under his great seal, privy seal, or signet, warranted under his majesty's sign manual by advice and consent of the lords and commons signified by order of both houses.

Provided that all now extraordinary guards shall be forthwith discharged, and in case his majesty shall raise or retain the same or any other extraordinary guard or shall have or allow any soldiers without advice and consent of the lords and commons, then it shall be lawful for any one of[28] the said lieutenants or their deputies to suppress the same.

And any county where such guard or force shall be raised, the lord lieutenant or his deputies shall suppress the same, and all other lords and their deputies shall assist him or them as he shall require.

[p. 124] Such persons as shall not obey in any of the provisos, not having a lawful excuse and convict thereof by confession or 2 witnesses before any lord or 2 deputies, shall suffer such fine not exceeding 8£ or imprisonment not exceeding 6 months as they shall think meet, the fines to be employed for provision of arms and ammunition and in case of refusal distress.

To continue till Lady Day 1644.

Mr. Hastings and others impeached of high crimes and misdemeanors concerning the opposing the Lord Stamford, lord lieutenant of Leicestershire by ordinance of both houses. Serjeant Wilde carried it up to the lords and delivered it at their bar.[29]

---

28. MS: *or.*

29. The others to be impeached were Halford, Bale, and Pate. The articles of impeachment were to be engrossed and carried to the lords the next day. *CJ,* II, 656.

D'EWES

July 7, Thursday, 1642

The Speaker came about 9 of the clock. After prayers MR. MOYLE delivered in a petition for Mr. Huckmore, who had lain in the Tower about 6 weeks because he had disobeyed the order of the house concerning timber.[1]

SIR THOMAS BARRINGTON also delivered in a letter from the mayor of Colchester[2] directed to Mr. Harbottle Grimston, recorder of that town (they two being burgesses for it), in which he showed that he had received divers proclamations from his majesty which he did forbear to publish till he had heard from this house. So the said Sir Thomas Barrington and Mr. Grimston were directed to write to the said mayor and to give him thanks for his care and to send him the printed order in which all sheriffs of counties and magistrates of towns and corporations were forbidden to publish proclamations of that nature which opposed the proceedings of both houses of parliament.[3]

I withdrew awhile out of the house. When I returned, the debate continued touching Mr. Huckmore, and it was ordered that his petition should be referred to that committee to whom the business had formerly been referred[4] and that they should speedily make their report. Some other matters of little moment passed.

Between 10 and 11 of the clock the SPEAKER delivered in a letter which he had received from Sir Edward Nicholas (one of his majesty's principal secretaries) bearing date at York July 4, 1642, in which he showed that whereas he had received a letter from him desiring that he should procure his majesty to sign a warrant for certain pieces of artillery and other arms to be delivered out of the Tower for the use of Ireland,[5] he had acquainted his majesty therewith,

1. It was reported that Huckmore's servants were "still cutting down and carrying of Timber away." *CJ,* II, 656.

2. The mayor was Thomas Wade, not Robert Taylcot as erroneously stated in *PJ,* 1: 123. Philip Morant, *The History and Antiquities of the Most Ancient Town and Borough of Colchester* (London, 1748), p. 55.

3. A new "Ordinance to restrain the Publishing of Proclamations, Declarations, etc.," had been approved by both houses on 5 July. See *CJ,* II, 652, 653. Wing E 1398.

4. The committee for Sir Francis Popham's bill, of which Hill was a member. On 11 July the commons ordered that Huckmore should be released, "giving good Security that no more Wood or Timber be cut." His servant, also named Huckmore, had been freed on 5 July. *CJ,* II, 228, 652, 656, 664, 666.

5. For the message from the House of Commons which prompted this response, see CIA, 21 June, n. 2.

whose answer was that he did conceive that the houses of parliament did write this to put a scorn upon him, having already taken them away by force, and if he should now grant a warrant/[6]

It was observed by divers that these arms were to be taken out of the Tower where they were under the custody/

The Scottish treaty engrossed in parchment.[7]

The house rose between 12 and one of the clock and appointed to sit at 4 in the afternoon.

Post Meridiem

The house met about 4 in the afternoon and rose about 7 of the clock in the evening.[8]

GAWDY

[f. 152b]   Thursday, the VII of July

A letter from Mr. Secretary Nicholas to Mr. Speaker, July the 4, from York. That his majesty taketh it for a scorn to be desired to issue out arms by his warrant for Ireland, we having taken his arms violently from him. He desire the restitution of his arms. Then he shall be ready, otherwise not.

Ordered, that all ships now in service of the state shall obey my Lord of Warwick in such manner as they did before my Lord of Northumberland.

Ordered, that this order be sent to every captain, that the committee for the defense of the kingdom see these orders sent.

Ordered, the lords be desired to join with us in these orders.[9]

Articles of treaty between the commissioners of England and commissioners of Scotland concerning the 10,000 men sent by the Scots for his majesty's service in Ireland.

Resolved, that these articles are consented to by this house.

The articles of treaty are sent to the lords.

---

6. For the letter from Nicholas, which was referred to the commissioners for Irish affairs, see *CJ,* II, 656–57. On 8 July the lords ordered that the commissioners "take Care that the Ammunition and Ordnance be sent into Ireland, according to a List sent to the Lord Lieutenant from the King, and approved of by both Houses." *LJ,* V, 191. See, however, CIA, 28 July, n. 4.

7. The lords agreed to the completed treaty. *LJ,* V, 188.

8. For the rest of the day, see G, below, and *CJ,* II, 657–59.

9. In addition, both houses agreed to release Captain Mennes, who had "submitted himself" to the Earl of Warwick. *CJ,* II, 657, 658. For letters of 2 and 4 July from Warwick to Mennes, see *CSPD, 1641–43,* pp. 349, 350.

The bill against Sir Henry Compton and others about the soap recommitted.[10]

[f. 153a] A message from the lords, they agree to the order for one deputy lieutenant to give assistance to another.[11] They agree to that concerning Tristram Whitcomb with some alterations. 'Tis about the hindering of an indictment preferred against Tristram Whitcomb of high treason at Kinsale for some information given this house.[12]

MR. MARTEN, that the committee for the defense of the kingdom desire this house would give them leave to issue out any arms or munition out of the Tower or any other of his majesty's magazines at such time as they shall think fit for the service wherewith they are entrusted. This is resolved by question.

Resolved, the lords be desired to join with us in this.[13]

In the afternoon the [house] sat at 4 a clock.

The impeachment against Mr. Henry Hastings, second son to the Earl of Huntingdon, Sir Richard Halford, Baronet, Sir John Bale, and Mr. Pate reading.[14] Then I came away.

10. Compton had been MP for East Grinstead, Sussex, in the Short Parliament. See Judith D. Maltby, ed., *The Short Parliament (1640) Diary of Sir Thomas Aston* (London, 1988), pp. 46–47. For his involvement in the soap monopoly in 1641, see *CJ*, II, 260, 273, 299; and Coates, p. 52, n. 11. For the bill concerning the soap boilers, which apparently went no further, see *PJ*, 2: 137, 157.

11. For the genesis of this order, see D and G, 4 July.

12. "Some ill-affected Persons in the City of Corke . . . conspired to indict" Whitcomb of treason because of information given to the parliament in his letter of 13 May from Kinsale. As a result on 6 July the commons ordered that all proceedings against Whitcomb should be forborne. Subsequently, because the lords failed to take action, the order went from the commons alone. See 15 June, n. 26; and *CJ*, II, 652, 655, 657, 674.

13. The lords, however, did not concur. *LJ*, V, 190.

14. Subsequently the articles of impeachment were carried up to the lords, along with a declaration concerning the indemnity of the Earl of Stamford and his supporters, and a conference was held. The following week the orders of impeachment were delivered to the four men at their homes. See *CJ*, II, 658; and *LJ*, V, 190, 191–92, 218. The articles of impeachment are preserved in HLRO, Parchment Collection, Box 179.

D'EWES

July 8, Friday, 1642

The Speaker came a little after 8.

The declaration concerning his majesty's having begun a war was in reading when I came into the house.[1] I took exceptions to 2 or 3 particulars in it, as whereas it was said we are credibly informed that the Lord Digby (viz., the eldest son of the Earl of Bristol) was come out of Holland into England and that others were in the ship called the *Providence,* which lately put in at the place called Paull near Hull. I moved in effect following:

That for matters which passed beyond the seas I did conceive we might well use that expression of our being credibly informed, but for matters which passed here at home I rather wish we may mention nothing but what we are assured to be true lest it should prove in the issue as other informations have done incredible, that is, false, and then his majesty will have/[2]

Serjeant Ayloff, the king's serjeant, and Sir Edward Leech, a master of the Chancery, brought this message from the lords, that they desired a present conference, etc., touching a letter received from Sir Thomas Roe, his majesty's ambassador with the Emperor of Germany,[3] and so they withdrew.

MR. EDMUND WALLER delivered in a letter sent unto him from the said Sir Thomas Roe bearing date at Vienna June 3, 1642, which after some debate whether it should be read or no before we went up to the conference, it was at last agreed to be read, which was done accordingly by the clerk.[4] And the said Sir Thomas Roe did therein show that he understood that the French ambassador had delivered in a complaint against him to the parliament, as if he had offered the King of Hungary in his majesty's name a league offensive and defensive against all other states of Christendom, by which the said French ambassador had done him a great injury, that scandalous report being false in the first contriver of it, for neither had his majesty ever given him authority for

---

1. See 6 July, n. 7. After some alteration the declaration of warlike preparations was recommitted. *CJ,* II, 659.

2. The declaration was not, however, amended in accordance with D'Ewes's suggestion. See *LJ,* V, 202.

3. For this letter of 3 June to the Earl of Holland, see *CJ,* II, 659–60.

4. Wing, R 1778. On 6 July Secretary Nicholas wrote to Sir Thomas Roe: "The King likes exceedingly well of your defence to the French Ambassador's complaint and your manner of address." *CSPD, 1641–43,* p. 351.

the making of such a proposition and much less was it consistent with the integrity of his former life to make it of himself; and therefore he desired him to make known his innocency to the House of Commons of which he was a member, with some other particulars of less moment.

This being read, we agreed to give a present meeting to the lords, and the messengers being again called in, the SPEAKER returned them that answer, and so they withdrew and departed.[5]

I went out about one of the clock. See Mr. Bodvel's journal.[6]

The house appointed to sit at 5 of the clock and rose about two in the afternoon.

Post Meridiem

The house met about 5 of the clock.

The business against Mr. Barton, parson of Aylesbury[7] in the county of Buckingham, for preaching dangerously against the parliament was in examining between 5 and 6 of the clock when I came into the house, and in the issue it was ordered to send for him as a delinquent.

MR. PURY showed that Sir William Boteler had drawn his sword upon Mr. Madison in justification of a printed libel touching the declaration and resolution of Herefordshire.[8]

Sir Ralph Whitfield and Sir John Glanville, the king's serjeants, brought a letter and certain examinations from the lords. They being departed, the clerk read the letter bearing date at Leicester July 7, 1642.

William Reynar/[9]

The 8 of July at midnight, the examination of William Cally, that he was disarmed at midnight.

[f. 261b] Mr. Justice Foster and Mr. Justice Malet brought this message from the lords, that they desired a present conference, etc., touching a printed paper styled *A Declaration or a Resolution of the County of Hereford*. They being withdrawn, we agreed to meet, which the SPEAKER related to them being again called in. Sir William Lewis and others were appointed reporters and went to the conference.[10]

5. For Waller's report of the conference, see G, below.

6. For proceedings omitted by D'Ewes, see *CJ*, II, 660–61.

7. For John Barton see *Walker*, p. 72.

8. MS: *Leicestershire*. Following Madison's report to the house of his encounter with Boteler over the Herefordshire pamphlet, it was ordered that Boteler's bail should bring him to the house the next day. The pamphlet was referred to the committee for printing. See *CJ*, II, 661.

9. In addition to the letter from Reynar, one of the Earl of Stamford's supporters, concerning disposing of the magazine of Leicester, an accompanying paper contained information about events there. *CJ*, II, 662.

10. For Harley's report of the conference concerning the above-noted "scandalous and infamous Libel" and the resolutions passed, see *CJ*, II, 662. Wing, D 786.

I then withdrew out of the house, (and went to the Lady Win's, but my cousin, Katherine Willoughby,[11] was not there).

I went out about 7 of the clock.

GAWDY

[f. 153a]   Friday, the VIII of July

Ordered, that the order be renewed for paying 12d. for not being present at prayers,[12] and that the sergeant return the names of such as he hath taken which hath not paid.

[f. 153b] MR. PYM, a report from the committee for the defense of the kingdom. That they think it fit there should be a declaration of the cause of our proceedings, which he readeth.

One part of the declaration is that the war is begun. The parliament think it to make a timely preparation for defense of the parliament, the good people of this kingdom, and such as both houses have employed.

A message from the lords, they desire a present conference concerning a letter which they have received from Sir Thomas Roe. 'Tis assented to.

A letter from Vienna, June the 3, from Sir Thomas Roe to Mr. Waller, who denieth the charge that the French ambassador layeth to him in saying that he offered to the King of Hungary from the King of England an offensive and defensive league so the Palatinate might be delivered.

MR. WALLER maketh a report from the conference, that Sir Thomas Roe wrote a letter to my Lord of Holland dated June the 3 from Vienna the same in substance with the former. That he never offered any offensive or defensive league so the [f. 154a] Palatinate might be delivered, neither had he any such thing in charge from his majesty.

Resolved, that this letter shall be shown to the French ambassador which was wrote to Mr. Waller. That the lords be desired to show him my Lord of Holland's. That Sir Thomas Roe his letter be entered in our book.

---

11. On 20 September 1642 D'Ewes married Elizabeth Willoughby, younger sister to Katherine. His first wife, Anne Clopton, had died in July 1641. In two letters, dated 9 July and 1 August 1642, to Elizabeth's father, Sir Henry Willoughby of Risley, Derbyshire, D'Ewes asked for her hand in marriage and mentioned her aunt, the honorable Lady Win. See John Bruce, "The Long Parliament and Sir Simonds D'Ewes," *The Edinburgh Review,* 84 (1846): 52; Halliwell, *D'Ewes,* II, 293–99; and GEC, *Baronetage,* I, 56.

12. See *PJ,* 2: 185.

A message from the lords, that my lord mayor was ready to put in his answer. That they desire we should come up. 'Tis assented to.[13]

The house sat at 5 a clock, but I was not there.

HILL

[p. 124]   Friday, July 8

From Leicester, William Cally examined.

13. The members sent up to the lords included Hill. Following Gurney's answer of "not guilty" to the impeachment charges, it was ordered that his cause should be heard on 11 July. See H, 5 July; *CJ*, II, 660; and *LJ*, V, 191, 192.

D'EWES

[f. 261b]   July 9, Saturday, 1642

The Speaker came about 8 of the clock. After prayers upon MR. STRODE's motion Sir William Dalston had license to go into the country.

Upon MR. GRIMSTON's motion an order was made for the payment of 1000£ to the Earl of Warwick[1] for the payment of the soldiers in the fort called Landguard Point.

Upon MR. VENN's motion an order was read for the more speedy collection of the subsidies and other moneys in the City of London,[2] which being read by the clerk was spoken unto by two or three, and then it was committed to two or three to withdraw and amend.

The SPEAKER delivered in a letter and a copy of a petition which had been sent him out of Warwickshire. I went out of the house before they were read. But the letter was directed to him from Sir Peter Wentworth, Mr. Bosvile, and other deputy lieutenants of the same county, bearing date at Coventry July 5 (last past, but the year of the Lord was not added).[3]

[f. 262a] When I returned into the house, there were matters in debate touching Ireland.[4]

Upon SIR ROBERT CRANE's motion the petition of Dame Magdalen Tyringham, widow and relict of Sir Arthur Tyringham, was read.[5]

MR. ROBERT GOODWIN moved that in respect the castle of Limerick was taken, that the commissioners for the affairs of Ireland/[6]

1. The name appears mistakenly as Norwich in *CJ*, II, 662.
2. The order included expediting the City's loan of £100,000. *CJ*, II, 662.
3. For the committee sent to Warwickshire, see 21 June, n. 14. These documents concerning the execution of the militia ordinance appear in *LJ*, V, 195–96. Wing, H 3447. For an order to apprehend those attempting to execute the commission of array in Warwickshire and several other counties, see *CJ*, II, 662.
4. For several resolutions from the committee for the Chichester petition, see *CJ*, II, 662–63. One concerned pay for the troops of Chichester, Arthur Hill, and others.
5. It was recommended that the Chichester committee "consider of the Arrears, and Engagement, and Merits of her Husband, in the Service of Ulster." Tyringham's death had occurred sometime before 18 March. On 13 January 1643 the house ordered that Lady Tyringham be paid £138. See *CJ*, II, 663, 926; and *HMC, Ormonde MSS*, II, 5.
6. It was ordered that the commissioners should meet to consider how forces might be drawn from other provinces to regain Limerick, which had surrendered to the rebels on 21 June. See *CJ*, II, 663; and CIA, 11 July. For an account of the surrender of the castle, commanded by Captain George Courtenay, see Maurice Lenihan, *Limerick; Its History and Antiquities* (Dublin, 1866), p. 150.

MR. PEARD made report of the additional articles against the lord mayor, which were read, and after some had spoken and some particulars were amended, and so they were allowed.

MR. HENRY MARTEN made report of 6 votes which the committee of lords and commons appointed for the safety of the kingdom.[7] The clerk read all the votes first and then began to read them particularly. The first was that we should forthwith raise an army of 10,000 men.

Ayes 125, went out. Mr. Denzil Holles and Sir John Evelyn, tellers. Noes 45, stayed within. I one. Sir John Strangways and Mr. Selden, tellers.

2. That officers shall be appointed to muster and train these men.

3. That the said forces may be ready to go by order of both houses whithersoever they shall be directed.[8]

[f. 261b] That the committee had proceeded with a great deal of care and prudence, and yet that we might not verify that of Seneca, *Morbi genus est perire per sapientiam*,[9] I did desire that we might thoroughly weigh these votes before we passed them, for I did conceive that being considered together they might be an occasion of more evil than good and would in the consequence of them be very pleasing and acceptable to the Cavaliers and the rest of the malignant party at York. For here we do not only take order for the raising of 10,000 men which is a complete army, but we do declare to all the world also that we will employ them in other parts of the kingdom as well as in and about this City for the defense of it and the parliament, so as we may perhaps give not only just occasion to the king's suspicion that his own person is in danger but put a sword also into his hands to raise another army of the like or a greater number for the defense of himself, and so we shall in a short time kindle such a fire of civil war on either side as perhaps will neither be in his majesty's power nor ours suddenly to quench. And I have observed that his majesty hath of late followed us step by step: our raising of a guard here gave him color for raising one at York also; our voting that he intended to levy war against the parliament hath given him occasion to declare that under that color we intend to levy war against him; the propositions which we have made and published for bringing in of money and plate and providing horses for the defense of the king, kingdom, and parliament hath given his majesty occasion to obtain the same subscriptions at York. And therefore my humble advice is that we may for a while lay aside the voting of all these particulars now reported to us from the committee except the last of them touching the magazine brought from Hull.

7. For the six propositions see also G and H, below, and *CJ*, II, 663. Eight additional propositions appear in *LJ*, V, 196–97.

8. For this radical departure in military policy, see also 4 July.

9. "It is a type of sickness to perish on account of wisdom." It is not certain whether D'Ewes is correct in attributing this quotation to Seneca.

[f. 262a] 4. That such of the City of London as will may lend arms to these men.

5. That the/

6. That the arms which came from Hull may be disposed of in the City.

[f. 262b] Mr. Henry Marten was sent away with the said propositions.[10]

SIR HUGH CHOLMLEY moved that we might read the bill for the militia that so we might go on with the peace of the kingdom as well with providing force, which drew on much debate pro and con, and at last it was ordered that it should be read presently, and it was further ordered that a declaration should be drawn to show that we would not desert the ordinance of the militia in the meantime.[11]

Sir Robert Rich and Mr. Page, two masters of the Chancery, brought this message from the lords, that their lordships desired a present conference, etc., and touching certain letters received from the Earl of Warwick.[12] These messengers had stayed without about an hour's space and were called in after one of the clock, so as the lords being risen before they were admitted, we had no other answer to return but that we would send an answer by messengers of our own, which the house having agreed upon after the messengers were withdrawn, the SPEAKER related it unto them, and so they departed.

MR. HENRY MARTEN made report of his message, that the lords had agreed with us in all our propositions and had named two members of their house to go into the City of London. He showed further that they thought it fit to send to Sir John Hotham to send up Colonel Ashburnham to the parliament by sea, but because this was no answer to any part of his message and it was contrary to the order and custom of both houses that the lords should send down any message to us by our own messenger, the house would take no notice of it but were ready to reprove Mr. Marten because he had called it a part of his report. We then named Sir John Potts and three others[13] who were to accompany the said two lords into London.

An act for the ordering of the militia of the kingdom of England and the dominion of Wales was read *1ª vice* after divers had spoken against the reading of it. It was then also after some further debate read *2da vice*. And then a debate followed whether it should be referred to a committee of some few or to a

10. Marten was sent to the lords with the propositions, which were then to be presented to the Common Council by members of both houses. *CJ,* II, 663.

11. A committee was named for this purpose. *CJ,* II, 663.

12. For the letters see *LJ,* V, 194, 195. Another subject of the conference was to be the payment of £80,000, part of the brotherly assistance due on 24 June, for which the Scots commissioners were pressing. See *PJ,* 2: 270; *CJ,* II, 663; and *LJ,* V, 194. Apparently the conference was not held until 11 July, with no mention of Scots assistance.

13. Lytton, Barrington, and Lumley. *CJ,* II, 663.

committee of the whole house, during which debate, it being past 3 of the clock in the afternoon, I withdrew out of the house.[14]

GAWDY

Saturday, the IX of July

A lett[er] from Coventry from the deputy lieutenants, that the trained bands consisted of 650,[15] of [which] appeared 550. There appeared in that county of Warwickshire 2850 volunteers.

A petition from Warwickshire. They desire that the militia may be confirmed. That they will be ready to spend their blood for the king and parliament. They desire the malignant spirits may be removed from the king.

A further impeach[ment] against my lord mayor.

[f. 154b] MR. MARTEN, a report from the committee for defense.

Propositions to be made to the Common Council of London by both houses:

1. That 10,000 men volunteers be speedily levied in London and liberties.

2. That they be put into regiments. They to have 8d. a day.[16]

The house divided whether 10,000 men shall be raised. The Ayes that went out that would have them raised were 125. The Noes that sat, of which I was, was 45.

2. That they be put into regiments and be exercised and have officers and shall have 8d. a day.

3. That this body shall march into any part of the kingdom as both houses of parliament shall direct.

4. 'Tis desired that such of the City as are willing may lend as many arms as they can well spare, which shall be restored to them again.

5. That considering the preparations in the north, that this may be done speedily, within 3 or 4 days if it be possible.

6. That the City will take into consideration the safe laying up of the magazine from Hull.

Resolved, that the lords be desired to join with us, and that they [f. 155a] will appoint some of their house to go to the Common Council along with our members about these propositions for raising 10,000 men.

Resolved, that the bill for settling the militia shall be read.

14. For the select committee and other proceedings, see *CJ*, II, 663–64.

15. Six hundred, in *LJ*, V, 195.

16. Gawdy has repeated the second proposition below.

Resolved, that a declaration be drawn that we mean to proceed with the militia.

A message from the lords, they desire a present conference about money for the Scots and about a letter from my Lord of Warwick.

MR. MARTEN, a report from the message, that the lords agree with us in all our propositions, and that they have appointed 2 lords and desire us to nominate a proportionable number.

An act for the ordering of the militia of the kingdom of England and Wales. That the king is to signify his pleasure under his great seal to the lord lieutenant. That all guards to be laid aside. That if the king raise or keep any extraordinary guards, then the lord lieutenant or any 2 of his deputies are to suppress them. To continue till Our Lady 1644. Read once.

A committee appointed to draw a declaration that we mean to proceed with the militia, notwithstanding the bill for settling the militia, in case it doth not pass.

[f. 155b] The act for settling the militia read the second time.

MR. MARTEN speaketh for the rejection of the bill. So he did at the first reading.[17]

The bill is committed to a select committee.

HILL

[p. 124]   Saturday, July 9

Report from committee for preparations:[18]

1. For 10,000 men volunteers to be raised in and about London speedily. 2. That these are to be formed into companies and regiments. Soldiers, 8d. per diem. 3. That they be ready to march into any part of the kingdom as both house[s] shall direct. 4. City to lend arms such as they can spare, which shall be restored. 5. Considering preparation in the north that in 3 or 4 days [p. 125] these be dispatched. 6. City provide place to dispose the magazine in that came from Hull.

A bill read for the militia. Sir John Banks for Purbeck.[19]

17. For Marten's opposition to the first militia bill, see *PJ*, 2: 191–92.

18. I.e., the committee for defense (safety).

19. Presumably Banks was named lord lieutenant for Purbeck in this bill, as he had been in the militia ordinance.

D'EWES

July 11, Monday, 1642

The Speaker came a little before 9 of the clock. After prayers SIR JOHN POTTS moved for one to be bailed. (I then withdrew out of the house.) He moved it on the behalf of Mr. Clement Spelman of Gray's Inn, but the house denied it.[1]

MR. PYM made report from the committee appointed to draw a declaration to satisfy the world concerning our preparations to defend the parliament and kingdom, which was read, amended, and allowed.[2]

MR. PEARD made report from the last conference,[3] that the Lord Mandeville showed that the lords had received a letter from the Earl of Warwick, being dated from aboard the *James,* his majesty's ship, July 9, 1642, in which he showed that he had taken the *Lion* coming out of Holland. That Prince Rupert and Prince Maurice, brothers to the Prince Elector Palatine, had put to sea in her, but a storm happening they became sick. That Prince Rupert had continued vomiting almost 3 days, which made them put to land again in Holland, with divers other particulars.[4]

Upon MR. HAMPDEN's motion Mr. Venables, Baron of Kinderton, a member of the house, was sent for.[5]

Sir Edward Leech and Dr. Aylett brought this message from the lords, that their lordships intended to sit at 4 of the clock this afternoon and desired that this house would sit accordingly if it might stand with their conveniency. The messengers being withdrawn, divers motions were made and one ordered, viz.: Upon MR. REYNOLDS's motion it was ordered that the commissioners for Ireland should sit at two of the clock in the afternoon, and the house agreed to

---

1. Instead a committee was named to prepare an impeachment against Spelman. *CJ,* II, 664. For proceedings omitted by D'Ewes, see G, below, and *CJ,* II, 664–65.

2. The declaration of warlike preparations. See 8 July, n. 1.

3. D'Ewes has omitted one part of the conference concerning a further impeachment of the lord mayor, who was subsequently ordered by the lords to answer by 19 July. Meanwhile he was sent to the Tower because of his refusal, at a Common Council meeting on 9 July, to put the question concerning storing the arms and ammunition from Hull in the City. See *CJ,* II, 664; and *LJ,* V, 197, 198.

4. However, they subsequently returned to Newcastle and were with the king when he raised his standard at Nottingham. Clarendon, *History,* II, 289n. For Warwick's letter see *LJ,* V, 199.

5. Venables was to be examined by the committee of safety concerning the paper from Herefordshire. See 8 July, n. 10; and *CJ,* II, 665.

sit. The messengers being called in, the SPEAKER made report thereof to them that the house would sit in the afternoon as was desired.

The SPEAKER delivered in a letter bearing date at Hull July 8, 1642, which was sent him from Mr. John Hotham, Mr. John Alured, and Mr. Peregrine Pelham, all members of our house and now with Sir John Hotham at Hull, in which they showed what preparations was making against them and that there were proclamations for pardon of all but some few. That by the opening the sluices they had done little good save only the filling up of the ditches and overflowing of some of the highways. That though some of the trained bands of Yorkshire were called in to the king's assistance against them, yet if consider-able forces were in time sent from the parliament, they were very confident that most of the said soldiers would leave their captains and join with them, with some other particulars of less moment.

[f. 263b] The SPEAKER delivered in another letter bearing date at Hull July 9, 1642, sent from Sir John Hotham to him, in which he showed that by the unfortunate escape of the ship called the *Providence,* the king had proceeded with some hostility against them. That unless speedy supply of men and money were sent, they should soon be in great danger, for his son of the Temple[6] could find means to return but little of that 2000£ which had been paid to him. He further showed that no respect to his own estate, respect, or family should make him fail in performing the trust the parliament had reposed in him, no though it cost him his life. That he conceived if considerable forces were sent down in time, many of those which now seemed to stand for the king would join with them.

MR. STRODE and others took great exceptions that the said letters were read in the house and said that it had been better that the said letters had been referred to the committee of lords and commons entrusted for the safety of the kingdom and desired that it might be ordered that if any such letters should hereafter come to the Speaker, they should be referred to that committee, which was ordered accordingly.[7]

We rose a little before one.

Post Meridiem

The Speaker resumed his chair a little before 5 of the clock.

MR. ROUS moved that a bark stayed by the Earl of Warwick belonging to some western merchants might be set free.

Upon ALDERMAN PENINGTON's report of his message done to the lord

---

6. Durand Hotham.

7. This order both gave the committee significant additional power and deprived the members of the house of confidential tactical information. *CJ,* II, 665.

mayor, being in the Tower of London, about calling a Common Council, and it was ordered the 3 aldermen should be summoned to appear.[8]

I seconded Mr. Rous's motion that an order might be made for discharging the said bark.

The two men called in who, one who was Mr. Ford,[9] had interest in the said ship for the powder and gave satisfaction to the house what he intended to do with it, and then they withdrew and it was ordered accordingly, and it was added to the said order that we should desire the lords to join with us.

Sir Edward Leech and Dr. Aylett, two masters of the Chancery, brought this message from the lords to desire a conference, etc.:

1. Touching the French ambassador's answer touching Sir Thomas Roe.
2. Touching what they had done with the lord mayor.

Agreed to meet.

Sir William Lewis was sent up with 3 messages:

1. The order for bark.
2. Touching lord mayor.
3. Touching Earl Rivers.[10]

SIR ARTHUR HESILRIGE delivered in instructions for the Lord Ruthin and the said Sir Arthur Hesilrige, which were read, allowed, and amended.[11]

SIR WILLIAM LEWIS returned and showed that the lords would give a meeting presently, and Mr. Rous and others were appointed reporters and managers, who went accordingly. I was not present at the conference.

The Earl of Holland managed that part of it which concerned the French ambassador, and the Lord Robartes that which concerned the lord mayor's being sent to the Tower.

I was not present in the house at the report of the conference[12] after the Speaker had resumed his chair but came in a little after that MR. HENRY MARTEN had made report touching a vote passed at the committee of lords and commons for the defense of the kingdom, which was that 10,000£ should be

8. Penington and Vassall had been sent to the lord mayor following the morning's conference. See G, below. After being informed of the commons' order to appoint a locum tenens, Gurney "desired Time to consider of an Answer, till To-morrow." Penington therefore went to the three senior aldermen, Sir Henry Garway, Sir Nicholas Rainton, and Sir George Whitmore, to require them to call a Common Council. "But they excused it; alleging, that they were aged and infirm." As a result they were summoned to attend the house. *CJ*, II, 665. For the aldermen, see Pearl, *London*, pp. 299–301, 304–07. *DNB*.

9. Thomas Ford was a merchant of Exeter and "a very honest Man." For information sent to the lords by Warwick concerning the bark, see *LJ*, V, 198–99, 200.

10. The commons wished to inform the lords of the execution of the commission of array in Cheshire by Earl Rivers, who was subsequently sent for as a delinquent. *LJ*, V, 199, 200.

11. They were to go to Leicestershire to assist the Earl of Stamford in executing the militia ordinance. *CJ*, II, 664, 665. For their instructions see *LJ*, V, 202–03.

12. For the report see G, below, and *CJ*, II, 665–66.

delivered to the said committee to dispose of it, which we allowed. The said Mr. Marten was sent up with the said vote to desire the lords' concurrence and with two other messages.[13]

MR. RICHARD MORE delivered in a petition for Mr. Clement Spelman to be bailed, but it was overruled negatively upon the question.

[f. 264b] I made report concerning the message or thanks which myself and some others were appointed to carry to the Lord Antonio Dalmada, the Portugal ambassador, on Friday, the 10th day of June last past (which was performed by Mr. Lawrence Whitaker and myself on Monday, the 13th day of the said month of June), which report I made in effect following:

That I had a report to make to the house concerning a service which I had with some other gentlemen been employed in and had been so long hindered from making the report by reason of the great affairs of the public as it was almost slipped out of my memory. Some of us who were appointed by this house have attended the Portugal ambassador and did make relation to him of the fair acceptance of his letters by this house. His answer was that the lords and we had done him so great an honor in sending to him as he should make report of it to the king, his master, upon his return. And he further added as an expression of his great thankfulness (which I hold myself bound to make report of) that it was an occasion of great grief to him to understand of the unhappy differences that had fallen out between his majesty and his parliament. That he did request this house by their great wisdom to endeavor to make up those differences, for it were better for us to have a war with all the world than to have a civil war amongst ourselves.

Sir John Glanville, the king's serjeant, and Dr. Aylett brought this message from the lords, that their lordships had agreed with us in some particulars sent up to them. (See the clerk's book.)[14]

MR. JOHN MOORE delivered in a letter sent to him out of Lancashire bearing date at Middleton 9 July 1642, in which being read he showed what great benefit might ensue for the peace and quiet of that county if the Lord Strange might be regained to our part and made and [sic] lord lieutenant of that county.[15] That he desired him to acquaint the House of Commons therewith and to give

13. The declaration of warlike preparations and a declaration "for the Reparation of Losses . . . by Sir Jo. Hotham's letting forth the Water about Hull." *CJ*, II, 665. For the texts see *LJ*, V, 200–02.

14. "That the Lords have assented to all the Propositions brought up at the last Conference: And . . . that the Barque stayed with Powder in the Downes, shall be forthwith discharged." *CJ*, II, 666.

15. Crossed out in MS at the bottom of f. 263b: *Middleton, 9 July 1642, from Mr. Ralph Ashton.* Clearly Ashton had written the letter as a member of the committee for executing the militia ordinance in Lancashire. See 11 June, n. 2. The naming of Lord Wharton rather than Lord Strange as lord lieutenant of Lancashire had occasioned considerable controversy. See *PJ*, 1: 338–39, 342.

him speedy notice what was to be done and to return himself to them for the further execution of the ordinance touching the militia and desired him to hasten back to them. After the letter was read, some moved that Mr. Moore might speedily go down into Lancashire, others that he might stay still here and only write to Mr. Ashton to proceed with the militia, which later opinion prevailed, but we resolved nothing concerning the Lord Strange.

We appointed to meet at 8 of the clock tomorrow morning and rose between 6 and 7 this evening.

GAWDY

[f. 155b]   Monday, the XI of July

A letter from Sir William Brereton, July the 5, that the generality of people is well affected to king and parliament. That Sir Thomas Aston threaten those that obey the militia. That the militia is far better obeyed than the commission of array, they having more appearance in one hundred than the commission of array had in 4, and they had more volunteers 3 to 1 than the commission of array had. This came from Cheshire.[16]

A message from the lords, that at the conference which we have desired with them, they desire to communicate a letter to us which they have received from my Lord of Warwick. 'Tis assented to.

Resolved, that this shall be the declaration.[17]

Resolved, that the lords be desired to join with us.

[f. 156a] MR. PEARD, a report from the conference. A letter from my Lord of Warwick to the Speaker of the lords, July the 9, from the Downs. That Prince Rupert and young Prince of Orange[18] were put into the *Lion* to come for England, but Prince Rupert fell so sick and casting of blood that they were landed again in Holland. That my Lord of Warwick hath the *Lion,* to whose captain[19] he showed the ordinance of parliament, who making scruple my lord hath him prisoner. My Lord of Warwick hath taken another bark with her wherein he hath found some powder.

MR. PEARD telleth us that the lords intimated to him that they took much offense that Sir William Boteler, that was a notorious delinquent, should come to the conference and there, as it were, outface both houses.[20]

16. Doubtless as a result of this letter, which is not noted in *CJ,* Aston was again sent for as a delinquent, as he had been on 9 June and 5 July. *CJ,* II, 614, 653, 664.

17. The declaration concerning warlike preparations.

18. Gawdy should have Prince Maurice. Cf. *LJ,* V, 199.

19. Captain Fox.

20. Apparently the conference concerning the Herefordshire declaration. See 8 July, nn. 8, 10.

That my Lord of Warwick desired to have some members of our house with him as a committee.

A message from the lords, they resolve to sit at 4 a clock. They desire us to do the like. 'Tis assented to.

[f. 156b] Ordered, that Alderman Penington and Mr. Vassall be sent to my lord mayor (who is committed to the Tower by the lords) to require him from this house to appoint a locum tenens to call a Common Council tomorrow morning, and in case he shall not, then the ancientest alderman to do it. I heard my lord was committed for refusing to call a Common Council as he promised.

A letter from Sir John Hotham and Pelham to the Speaker from Hull, July the 8. That there are divers pieces of ordnance landed near Hull. They have blocked up the town. They have enemies without and within.

Another letter from them, July the 9. That the king is expected at Hull. That some of the trained [bands] are compelled to come to Hull. That if we had men there, he think they would take our parts. He desire 500 men.

The house sit this afternoon at 4 a clock, but I was not there.

At the conference the lords told they had committed my lord mayor to the Tower for refusing according to promise to call a Common Council to lay up the magazine that came from Hull. They told us they had acquainted the French ambassador with Sir Thomas Roe's letter, with which he was satisfied. This I had from Mr. Nash.

D'EWES

July 12, Tuesday, 1642

The Speaker came between 8 and 9 of the clock. After prayers SIR SAMUEL
ROLLE made report from the committee appointed to take an account of such
members as were absent the 16 day of June last past when the house was
called.[1] That Sir Thomas Hele had liberty to go into the country the 7 day of
March last past. That he had since stayed at home and did not know of the last
order by which the members of the house were appointed to appear upon the
said 16 day, living about 200 miles off, and so desired that the 100£ fine then set
upon him might be taken off and that he might be again admitted into the house.
MR. STRODE spake against it and showed that if we did pass by this business, it
would be a leading case to others. MR. WALTER LONG said that if we did pass
this gentleman over and admit him into the house without paying his fine/[2]

I spake touching Mr. Weston's report also.[3]

Vide M. where a number of motions and orders followed.[4]

Sir Robert Rich and Mr. Page brought down the declaration touching the
propositions for raising horse and bringing in plate and money[5] and the instructions for the deputy lieutenants of Leicestershire and showed that the lords had
assented to them with some amendments, and so they withdrew. We then read
the said amendments and allowed them. I withdrew awhile out of the house.

Before I returned back again into the house, MR. GRIMSTON made report
from the committee to whom the bill touching the militia had been referred, that
they had added divers amendments to it which were read twice, and then as/

1. See 16 June, n. 20; and Appendix G.
2. It was resolved, however, that Hele, who was from Devonshire, should be admitted without
paying his fine. *CJ*, II, 666.
3. It is not clear which of the three MPs named Weston (Benjamin, Nicholas, or Richard) was a
member of the committee for postmasters. His report "concerning the Patent touching the Letter
Office" was postponed until 19 July, at which time Prideaux was to report "such Matters as shall be
passed at the Committee." The reports, however, continued to be postponed until 16 August. It
appears that either Prideaux or Weston was chairman of the committee. See *CJ*, II, 500, 561, 666,
681, and passim.
4. See *CJ*, II, 666–67.
5. Actually it was the declaration of warlike preparations, referred to incorrectly as "the
Declaration concerning Religion" in *CJ*, II, 667. Cf. G, below. Later an order "for advancing the
Propositions of Bringing in of Plate, Money, and Horse" in the counties was approved and carried to
the lords. See *CJ*, II, 667–68. For detailed instructions concerning the propositions, approved by
both houses on 1 July, see *LJ*, V, 175.

MR. DENZIL HOLLES delivered in an order about the Earl of Warwick's coming into the river of Humber to relieve Hull, which was voted and allowed, and the said Mr. Holles was sent to the lords to join with us in it and with divers other messages.[6]

MR. WALTER LONG moved that the officers might be paid who were to go into Ireland, might be paid this day, which was allowed and voted.

Sir Robert Rich and Mr. Page, two masters of the Chancery/[7]

[f. 267b] MR. DENZIL HOLLES brought in 3 votes from the committee appointed to consider of the safety of the kingdom: 1. To name a general. 2. To raise an army. 3. To petition to prevent a civil war. I spake to prevent the two first questions:

[f. 268a] I conceive that there is no man in this house can expect that a matter of this weight which had only passed at a committee of a few, though I confess they be persons of great ability, should be voted here without being first discussed, for we are all equally trusted here with the public and should bring with us competent understandings to discern of such matters as are to be debated here. The first exception that I take is at the order of these votes, for here we speak of naming a general and raising an army, and then in the last place we come to vote that a petition should be preferred to the king to prevent a civil war; whereas I am confident if we proceeded with the last vote, we might spare the two former, but I fear if we proceed with the two former, it will be destructive to the latter. The end I believe that we all aim at is one and the same to preserve the true religion and the liberty and propriety[8] of the subject and with these the royal dignity and just rights of his majesty, but the question only is which is the best and surest means, whether we should come to a safe end by a safe and quiet way or by a means full of destruction and violence in itself, which will hazard the ruin of that very thing for which we strive; for certainly if there be no way left for us to obtain peace but by wading through an ocean of blood or to procure our safety but by hewing it out of the rocks of danger, we are in a sad and deplorable condition, much like the case of an aged man that is sick of a pleurisy, who if he be let blood must hazard his life that way and if he be not let blood must certainly die. And this I will be bold to say, that when we have exposed the lives of innocent men to mutual slaughter and destruction, we must then perhaps come to accept of a worse end than I do verily believe we may now have without the expense of one drop of blood. Let us but remember that wise action of the nobility of England when they met King John at Runnymede and had an army far more potent than his; yet considering that they came but to

---

6. For details see G, below, and *CJ*, II, 667.
7. See G and n. 16, below.
8. Property. *NED*.

demand their just liberties and that to have them granted by a kind of enforcement would be disadvantageous to themselves, they fell in treaty with the king,[9] were embraced by him and dismissed their army, and had the most advantageous charter and liberties granted to them that ever the subjects of England obtained, which continued in force till by the evil counsel of Hubert de Burgh it was afterwards infringed. For that great charter which we have now in print and stand so much upon, calling it the statute of Magna Charta,[10] doth want some ells and yards [f. 268b] of that which was granted at Runnymede. And we might learn also prudence of our wise brethren of Scotland, who when they had a strong army on foot and might have done the work as we all agree for we have printed it, yet they rather chose to proceed in a peaceable way of petitioning than to go by force.[11] And though I were sure that we should gain more by force than by treaty, yet we shall in that but imitate a man who, having his house a little on fire and water in his yard sufficient to quench it, yet sends away all his servants to call in the neighboring dwellers with their cart and vessels to fetch water from a river so to quench the fire after it hath grown to a great height and perhaps burnt down the better half of his house. My humble advice therefore is that we proceed with the last of those three votes in preferring a petition to his majesty, and if that shall not prevail, then to proceed with the two former.

Many allowed of what I had moved, but the greater number being carried along by an implicit faith to assent to whatsoever some hot spirits should propose, the two first propositions were put to the question and voted affirmatively, and then was the third voted also and a committee appointed to draw the said petition.[12]

[f. 267b] MR. PYM delivered in a note touching money and plate to be sent down to the king from Oxford.

SIR ROBERT HARLEY delivered in a letter bearing date July 11th, 1642, by which the news was related touching what had been done in the same university by some of the/[13]

We rose between one and two of the clock, having formerly appointed/[14]

9. Crossed out in MS: *soon agreed upon the form.*

10. Hubert de Burgh was chief justiciar during the reigns of King John and Henry III. *DNB.* D'Ewes owned a sixteenth-century copy of Magna Charta which he had purchased in 1623. Watson, *Library of D'Ewes,* p. 118.

11. This appears to be a reference to the declaration promulgated by the Covenanters in February 1639 to prevent the resumption of hostilities with the English. See Gardiner, *History of England,* VIII, 389; and Rushworth, II, 797–802.

12. Apparently the committee of safety. It was ordered that the debate be resumed in the afternoon. See *CJ,* II, 667, 668.

13. The letter revealed "the intention of the Masters of Colleges to lend the King all the Colleges Plate." In consequence, both houses agreed to an order to prevent the sending of money and plate from Oxford to York. See *CJ,* II, 667, 669.

14. For the afternoon proceedings see G, below, and *CJ,* II, 668.

GAWDY

[f. 157a]   Tuesday, the XII of July

A message from the lords, they send us the instructions for Leicestershire, which they have assented to with some alterations. The other, the assenting to our declaration of our reasons of raising arms.

Certain gentlemen of Buckinghamshire appointed to take the subscriptions of gentlemen of that county for levying of horse, plate, or money. This resolved by question.

This is resolved for many other counties near London, and that the lord lieutenants shall have power to nominate captains of the troops and to stay in the several counties till they shall receive a command. 'Tis desired that the lords should join with us.

MR. GRIMSTON maketh report of the bill for the militia.

Resolved, that my Lord of Warwick be desired to go with his ships into Humber to the assistance of Sir John Hotham. That my Lord of Warwick should bring from Hull all such horse arms as are at Hull. The lords to be desired to join with us. That Mr. William Ashburnham be brought from thence and Sir Edward Stradling and the Frenchman and such others as were in the ship.[15]

Resolved, that the officers shall be paid from this day, that the lords be desired to join with us.

[f. 157b] A message from the lords, they send us a declaration that none shall be compelled to go to the king when he send for them.[16] That they will sit at 4 a clock. 'Tis assented to.

MR. HOLLES, a report from the committee for the defense of the kingdom:

1. That a general be forthwith named.

2. That an army be forthwith raised for defense of the king and kingdom and those that the parliament have employed.

3. That a petition be preferred to the king for the hindering of a civil war.

MR. PYM, a report that the committee[17] hath information that it is passed in the convocation at Oxford that all the university plate and the plate of the colleges there is presently to be sent to York to the king.

15. The Frenchman was Lord Digby in disguise, according to Clarendon, *History*, II, 251–57. See 5 July, n. 4.

16. This brief declaration, sent to the lords on 7 July, stated that no subject "should be compelled by the King to attend Him at His Pleasure, but such as are bound thereto by special Service." See *CJ*, II, 658, 667; and *LJ*, V, 189, 205. Wing, E 1330. On 26 July an enlarged declaration concerning the indemnity of those in the service of parliament was approved. See *CJ*, II, 691, 692, 693. BL, Thomason Tracts, 669 f. 5 (61).

17. Possibly the committee for the universities, of which Harley was chairman.

In the afternoon.

Resolved by question, that my Lord of Essex shall be general.

Resolved, that there shall be an army raised forthwith for the defense of the king, parliament, the Protestant religion, those that the parliament employ, the laws and liberty and peace[18] of the kingdom.

Resolved, that a petition be preferred to the king to desire him to accord with his parliament.

[f. 158a] Resolved, we should desire the lords to join with us in these votes.

Resolved, that we shall live and die with this general for the defense of the king, both houses of parliament, the Protestant religion, those that the parliament employ, the laws, liberty, and peace of the kingdom.

Resolved, the lords be desired to join with us in this vote.[19]

A declaration read. That though we go on with a bill for the militia, yet we intend to proceed with the ordinance for the militia in case the bill pass not. 'Tis laid by till we see what will become of the bill.[20]

Ordered, that the bill for the militia shall be proceeded withal tomorrow morning.

MR. PYM read the petition to be sent to his majesty for a pacification.

Resolved by question, that this petition shall be sent to his majesty.

Resolved, that we shall desire the lords to join with us in this petition.

Resolved, that this petition be presently sent to the lords.[21]

18. Crossed out in MS: *of the people.*

19. For these votes, which Holles carried up to the lords, see also *CJ,* II, 668. Wing, E 2149.

20. For the genesis of this declaration, see D, 192.

21. For the petition (hereafter generally referred to as the petition of peace), see Appendix I. Wing, E 1585A.

D'EWES

[f. 269a]   July 13, Wednesday, 1642

The Speaker came a little after 9 of the clock. I came in between 9 and 10. Before I came in, upon SIR GILBERT GERARD's motion that Mr. Clement Spelman had been long in the sergeant's custody and that some order might be taken, and thereupon he was after a little debate permitted to go upon bail.

Just as I came in, upon MR. PEARD's motion that divers clergymen were without who had long attended this house and were in the sergeant's custody, and desired that they might be called in and heard.[1]

First there came in Dr. Dukeson,[2] who was minister of St. Clement Danes, and kneeled, and then the SPEAKER asked him divers questions about reading the king's last declaration of his majesty which he commands the ministers and curates to read in the title page to read it in the churches.[3]

Dr. Fuller, Mr. Hutton, Mr. Hall, curate of Covent Garden, called in next.[4]

MR. DENZIL HOLLES made report of the message which he delivered yesterday in the evening to the lords and that they agreed with us in all.[5]

Sir Ralph Whitfield and Sir John Glanville, two of the king's serjeants, brought this message from the lords, that their lordships had appointed the Earl of Holland to carry/[6]

[f. 269b] The master of the rolls and Dr. Aylett, a master of the Chancery, brought this message from the lords, that their lordships had sent us a letter enclosed sent from the Earl of Warwick, in which was enclosed a copy of a letter sent to Captain William Batten,[7] vice admiral of the fleet. That their lordships

1. These ministers had been summoned on 4 and 5 July for publishing the king's declaration concerning levies in their churches. See 2 July, n. 6; and *CJ,* II, 650, 652.

2. For Richard Dukeson see *Walker,* p. 46. Because Dukeson "did most insolently prevaricate with the House; and gave nothing but shuffling Answers," he was committed to the Gatehouse. *CJ,* II, 669.

3. The title page of the declaration does indeed indicate that it should be "Published in all Churches and Chappells" in England and Wales. Wing, C 2190.

4. Timothy Hutton was William Fuller's curate at St. Giles, Cripplegate. For Fuller, Hall, and Hutton, see *Walker,* pp. 48, 49, 51.

5. I.e., the orders concerning Warwick and Hull, the votes from the committee of safety, and the petition of peace to the king. *CJ,* II, 669.

6. Holland was to carry the petition of peace to the king. See 12 July, n. 21; and G, below.

7. MS: *Watton.* When in March Warwick had been made vice admiral (literally deputy lord admiral for Northumberland), Batten, the surveyor of the navy, was named second in command under Warwick. See Clarendon, *History,* II, 22–23; and Powell, *Navy,* pp. xv, 14. *DNB.*

also desired a conference, etc., touching a letter and a message newly come unto them from his majesty, and so they withdrew.

And then the letter from the Earl of Warwick directed to the Speaker of the lords house was read bearing date from aboard the *James* in the Downs July 11, 1642,[8] in which he showed the great want of money and victuals in the navy. That his majesty had given command to his officers of the storehouse at Chatham to deliver out no more materials necessary for the navy, and that some speedy course was to be taken therein. That he had new victualed a ship which carried over the Portugal ambassador.

There was next read a copy of a letter sent from Sir William Russell, Mr. George Carteret, Mr. W. Barlow, officers of the navy,[9] dated July 8, 1642, to Captain William Batten, vice admiral of his majesty's fleet, by which they showed amongst other particulars the great want of money to furnish the fleet or to pay the officers and workmen belonging to it so as they feared some sudden violence. Some thought fit to have taken this business into debate presently, but others that we should first go up to the conference.

We then called in the messengers and appointed to give the lords a meeting presently. Mr. Denzil Holles and others were appointed reporters and went up to the conference.

I was awhile at it where it was managed by the Lord Mandeville, where he first showed that their lordships, having received a letter, message, and proclamation from his majesty, desired to communicate them to the House of Commons as soon as they had perused them, and so he read them all three. (Ask me, and see them in the next folio b ensuing.)[10]

Upon MR. HILL's motion, as soon as the conference was ended and that the Speaker had resumed his chair, there was a lecturer allowed for Bridport in Dorsetshire.[11]

Upon MR. REYNOLDS's motion it was ordered that 3000£ should be allowed to some merchants as an adventure upon the proposition for Ireland.[12]

8. For the text see *LJ*, V, 206.

9. Russell, longtime treasurer of the navy, was soon to be replaced by Sir Henry Vane, Jr. *DNB*. For the near-appointment of Carteret, who was comptroller of the navy, rather than Batten as vice admiral, see Clarendon, *History*, II, 224–25. *DNB*. Perhaps D'Ewes should have Thomas Barlow. See *CSPD, 1641–43*, p. 562. The letters were referred to the committee for the navy. *CJ*, II, 670.

10. Probably an instruction to James Hornigold, D'Ewes's secretary. For the conference see below.

11. The lecturer's name was Robert Tuchin. See *CJ*, II, 670; and *HMC, Fifth Report*, p. 37. Hill was both recorder and MP for Bridport. Keeler, p. 215.

12. The act for reducing the rebels of Ireland was based upon the propositions formulated in February 1642. See *PJ*, 1: esp. 349–50, 395, and 2: 62. The £3000 was part of £7000 due to Maurice Thomson and other merchants. *CJ*, II, 670. For a biographical note on Thomson, see Richard L. Greaves and Robert Zaller, eds., *Biographical Dictionary of British Radicals in the Seventeenth Century* (Brighton, 1982–84), III, 233–35.

The LORD GREY delivered in a letter which had been sent to Sir Arthur Hesilrige from his servant, which showed what hostile preparations Mr. Henry Hastings made in Leicestershire and how he was made high sheriff and intended to proclaim the assizes to be shortly at Leicester.

SIR ROBERT HARLEY moved that we might send up to the lords [f. 270b] to desire them to hasten messengers to seize the doctors as delinquents in the University of Oxford which were so voted yesterday and to send also some order to stay their plate and money from going to York,[13] and Sir Robert Harley himself was appointed the messenger.

Upon MR. PRIDEAUX's motion he was further ordered to desire them to send down their examinations of the Irish rebels taken in the Tower of London by the judges, to whom the said Mr. Prideaux and Mr. Hill having been sent for the said examinations understood from them that they had delivered in the said examinations to the lords.[14]

Upon MR. ARTHUR GOODWIN's motion it was further ordered that he should desire a conference with the lords touching the brotherly assistance due to the Scots.

MR. DENZIL HOLLES made report of the conference and showed that the Lord Mandeville managed the same, and having declared unto them what they had received from his majesty, he read the particulars which the said Mr. Holles delivered in to be read by the clerk.

Sir Robert Harley went away, but the lords were risen before he came up to their house, it being between 12 and one.

The clerk then proceeded first with the reading of his majesty's letter, being dated or given under our sign manual at Beverley July 11, 1642, directed to the Speaker of the House of Peers, in which his majesty required him that he should communicate the enclosed message to his House of Peers and afterwards to his House of Commons and that the said letter should be his sufficient warrant.

Next was read the king's message (which is printed), in which he did propose to have the town of Hull rendered to him and did then promise to give full satisfaction to his houses of parliament in that they should desire for the public peace and good of the kingdom (which message see in print).

Then was lastly read the king's printed proclamation, by which it did amongst other particulars set forth the many calamities that have happened to

13. Those named as delinquents were Dr. John Prideaux, Bishop of Worcester and vice chancellor of the university; Dr. Samuel Fell, dean of Christ Church; Dr. Christopher Potter, provost of Queen's College; and Dr. Accepted Frewen, president of Magdalen College. See Charles Edward Mallet, *A History of the University of Oxford* (London, 1924–27), II, 351. *DNB*.

14. The lords had named a committee on 5 July to peruse the examinations of Maguire, MacMahon, and Reade. *LJ*, V, 182.

the town of Hull and the country thereabouts by Sir John Hotham's being put into it with a garrison.[15]

These being read, MR. HENRY MARTEN stood up and moved that whereas his majesty had desired in his message a speedy answer because the business admitted no delay, he conceived his majesty was therein mistaken, supposing that the town of Hull could not long hold out, which he hoped it would and therefore wished us to lay aside his majesty's message and to proceed with the consideration what to do with the letter sent from the Earl of Warwick, which made me stand up and to answer with some indignation in effect following after two or three others had first spoken:

That I conceived the gentleman who spake behind (viz., Mr. Marten) was himself mistaken in conceiving that his majesty was mistaken, which I believe he was not. For whereas the gentleman thinks that his majesty's meaning is that Hull cannot long hold out and that therefore he saith the matter will admit no delay, I do not conceive the same to be any part of his meaning. But that what he proposeth is done like a wise and Christian prince, for in saying that this matter will admit no delay, his meaning doubtless is that unless some speedy course be taken for an accommodation and settling of things in a peaceable way, the fire will grow to that height that it will not be easily quenched, and truly for mine own part I do agree with his majesty therein and think we are all bound in conscience immediately to consider of some speedy course whereby all arms and preparations for the present may be laid aside and some speedy trial made whether things may be composed or not. For the town of Hull itself I will not advise that it shall be delivered up to the king with any peril [f. 271b] to Sir John Hotham, who hath done the part of a faithful and honest man in preserving what the parliament had committed to him, so as for his security I had rather lose one of mine own hands than Sir John Hotham should lose one of his fingers. And therefore I should rather advise that the town might for the present be committed into the hands of a third person by the authority of the king and the parliament until other things may be composed, and that we may express both a due respect to his majesty's message and to our own propositions for peace. In the meantime it is my humble motion that a committee be named to draw up an answer to his majesty's message.

Divers spake after me, and in the issue a committee was appointed to prepare an answer to the same.[16]

15. For the king's message and proclamation, see *LJ*, V, 209, and Rushworth, IV, 601–03. Wing, C 2456.

16. The committee of safety. For the rest of the day, see *CJ*, II, 670–71.

GAWDY

[f. 158b]   Wednesday, the XIII of July

The curate of St. Giles, Cripplegate, sent to the King's Bench for reading the king's declaration in the church.[17]

MR. HOLLES, a report from the lords, that they agree with us in many votes and in particular in appointing my Lord of Essex general.[18]

A message from the lords, that they have appointed my Lord of Holland to carry the petition[19] to the king. They desire us to appoint a proportionable number.

We have appointed Sir John Holland and Sir Philip Stapleton to go with the petition.

A message from the lords, they send us a letter which they have received from my Lord of Warwick. They desire a present conference about a letter and a message which they have lately received from his majesty.

MR. HOLLES, a report from the conference. That my Lord Mandeville told us they had received a letter from his majesty directed to the Speaker of the lords house requiring him to read the message enclosed to both houses the first sitting at a conference, and likewise a proclamation. The letter dated July the 11 from Beverley.

[f. 159a] The letter: Before we shall use force to Hull, we thought fit once more to require Hull, which if it be delivered, we shall be ready to receive from you and propose to you such propositions as may tend to the peace of the kingdom, which he promise in the word of a king, and if it be not, then he shall be innocent of the distractions of the kingdom. He requires our answer on Friday, the 15 of July.

The title of the proclamation was "Of His Majesty's Royal Intention to Go before Hull in His Own Person," from Beverley, July the 8.

HILL

[p. 125]   Wednesday, July 13

Dr. Dukeson[20] committed to the Gatehouse for refusing to answer questions concerning the publishing the king's last declaration.

17. Hutton was released on 4 August. *CJ*, II, 703.
18. Following this appointment the Venetian ambassador described Essex as "the commander who enjoys most credit among the malcontents, who with open obstinacy has consistently opposed the royal interests, regardless of his duty." *CSP Ven., 1642–1643*, p. 106.
19. The petition of peace.
20. MS: *Juxon*.

Mr. Hutton, curate to Dr. Fuller of St. Giles, Cripplegate, sent to the King's Bench for reading the declaration.

Dr. Fuller discharged without paying fees because he knew not of the reading.

Mr. Hall of Covent[21] Garden discharged.

Earl of Holland, Sir John Holland, Sir Philip Stapleton sent to the king with a petition to return to his parliament.

A letter from Earl of Warwick, July 11, from the Downs:

For money and indemnity and to provide for supplies because at Chatham is a command from his majesty not to furnish us. 3 ships provided for Humber, but the *Lion* coming hither, I sent but 2 to Hull.

Hastings keeps his house with 120 horse. At the ferry are 100 horse more to assist Hastings, who inquired for the Earl Stamford. King will be at Newark July 12.

[p. 126] A letter from the king to the lords, Beverley, 11 July 1642:

A declaration [to] show the cause of his journey to Hull, requiring it be delivered up to us. If you conform, we shall admit redresses[22] and to send propositions to you befitting, etc. Do your duty. Requires answer at Beverley, 15 July.

With a proclamation declaring our purpose to go to Hull in person:

Shows the affront by Sir John Hotham. His denial of admitt[ance]. [Hull] detained[23] against us by the malignant practice of many in both houses. Justified as legal by several votes.

The manner of Sir John Hotham's carriage. He hath made outworks to defend the town, cut the banks, set out a pinnace to intercept a pinnace of ours, permitted his soldiers to pillage the country, disarmed the town, put many out of the town, destroyed 1000ds of acres of great value. Continued in pay many 100ds of soldiers at public's charge out of moneys provided for Ireland and Scots. Our port kept by Earl of Warwick, though discharged. Earl of Northumberland paid dutiful obedience. [Warwick] hath imprisoned divers captains for dutiful obedience. Chased our ships.

Upon all which to right our court[24] and subjects and Hull, which we expected from 2 houses of parliament but failed through the malice of some few ill persons there, etc. To force Sir John Hotham, etc., to their[25] obedi- [p. 127] ence. And we require all assistance of our subjects and declare and[26] whoso

21. MS: *Common.* Hall confessed that he read the declaration because the messenger who brought it threatened that otherwise he would inform the king. *CJ,* II, 669.

22. The word is "addresses" in *LJ,* V, 209.

23. The word is "maintained" in Rushworth. All corrections to Hill's version of the proclamation are from Rushworth, IV, 601–03.

24. The word is "crown."

25. The word is "that."

26. The word is "that."

shall assist us by horse, men, and money, we shall look upon it as a service never to be forgotten. A protestation to make good his former promises. Beverley, 8th July.[27]

27. Again a portion of Hill's journal, not directly related to proceedings in the House of Commons, has been omitted. It includes material concerning sheriffs and cites precedents from Coke's Institutes, the Statute of Winchester, Bracton, Fleta, and Fortescue. Hill's next (and final) entry in his journal occurs on 28 July.

D'EWES

July 14, Thursday, 1642

The Speaker came between 8 and 9 of the clock. After prayers MR. GREEN delivered in an order to be passed by both houses, that we owing them[1] 7000£ lent by them out of purse to this house, they might be allowed 3000£ of it to be accounted as a part of their adventure for Ireland, which after some debate I settled by moving that it might be deferred till tomorrow morning that so the adventurers might be fully satisfied with the said order, that we might preserve union amongst ourselves, for/

Robert Hill [and] undersheriff of Hereford, sum[moned]. MR. PYM delivered in the petition.[2]

SIR OLIVER LUKE delivered in a letter bearing date at Luton 12 July 1642 (in Bedfordshire) sent unto him from one Edward Watford, constable of that town, which was read, and therein he showed that he had seized two great horses of Sir John Byron's and 3 great saddles which were going towards/

Upon SIR WILLIAM LYTTON's motion it was ordered that the knights for the county of Hertford,[3] the Lord Cranborne, and others that served for places in that county might go down thither to the assizes tomorrow to be held at Hertford to advance the propositions for horse, money, and plate.

[f. 272b] MR. WALTER LONG made report from the committee for adventurers for Ireland of divers votes passed by them touching the payment of reformados and other particulars,[4] which after some debate we had voted in the house, during which report MR. STRODE moved that whereas we had given leave to divers members of this house to go down into Hertfordshire to the assizes, that we would give them order in respect Justice Malet went judge in

1. Maurice Thomson and other merchants. The matter was referred to the committee for Irish adventurers; it was subsequently ordered that £4000 to be paid to Thomson. See 13 July, n. 12; and *CJ*, II, 671, 685.

2. Crossed out in MS: *One Watkins, the Speaker's man, against them.* According to *HMC, Fifth Report*, p. 37: "Petition of William Gwatkin, to H. C. Prays that William Hill and others may be sent for to answer for their contempt in seizing his goods under colour of a pretended writ notwithstanding his protection as servant to Mr. Speaker Lenthall." The undersheriff was Humphrey Dicary. *CJ*, II, 671.

3. Lytton and Sir Thomas Dacres. On 8 July Lord Cranborne had replaced his father, the Earl of Salisbury, as lord lieutenant for both Hertfordshire and Dorset. *CJ*, II, 660. For the recent order for advancing the propositions in the counties, see 12 July, n. 5.

4. For details see *CJ*, II, 671.

that circuit, who had misbehaved himself in his last circuit and might possibly speak somewhat now in derogation of the proceedings of parliament, that therefore the said gentlemen might interrupt him if he should do it and defend the honor of the parliament. Others spake to it. I moved in effect following:

That I conceived that the gentleman who first begun this motion below (viz., Mr. Strode) was a little mistaken for the matter of time, for I hold it not fit that the judge should be interrupted in his charge but that if anything shall slip from him which shall be derogatory to this parliament, they may desire liberty afterwards to speak and justify our proceedings, for to interrupt a judge when he is speaking is such an offense as I believe the judge hath power to commit him for it.

Others spake after me, and SIR HARBOTTLE GRIMSTON moved that a like order might be made for their Essex assizes shortly to be held at Chelmsford because Judge Malet went that circuit also.[5]

I thereupon moved that the order might be made generally for England and that a committee might be appointed to prepare and draw it. Some one or two spake after me, and thereupon a committee of some six or seven, of which I was one, were presently nominated and required to go about the same. I went with them out of the house but went not presently to them and afterwards, looking for them in several places and not finding them, returned into the house where divers particulars were agitated.[6]

And amongst others the answer to be sent to his majesty's message was read, which MR. DENZIL HOLLES made report of from the committee appointed for the defense of the kingdom, etc.[7]

See Mr. B. and clerk's book.

Post Meridiem

The house met about 5, appointed to meet at 10 of the clock tomorrow morning, and rose about 6. See the clerk's book.[8] Matter of little moment passed. I was absent.

5. For an account of the summer assizes in Hertfordshire and Essex, see Woods, *Prelude*, pp. 95–99.

6. Strode later reported that "the Committee was of Opinion to make no Order herein; but to leave it to those that shall be on the Bench at the Assizes, to discharge their Duties herein, if any such Occasion be offered by any." *CJ*, II, 672.

7. The committee ordered that the messengers who were to present the petition of peace to the king should inform him that it was a sufficient answer to his new message concerning Hull. See 13 July, n. 15; and *CJ*, II, 672.

8. See G, below, and *CJ*, II, 672–73.

GAWDY

[f. 159a]   Thursday, the XIIII of July

Resolved by question, that a committee be named to draw an order that any members of this house may at any assizes vindicate the honor of this house if any aspersions shall be laid upon it.

A message from the lords, they send us a letter from my Lord of Warwick from the *James* in the Downs, July the 13. That he hath received orders for his going to Hull to fetch the horse arms and Colonel Ashburnham and Sir Edward Stradling.[9] That Humber run swift. He hath sent some of his small skiffs to perform that service.

[f. 159b] This was done by the advice of the council of war because that the channel of Humber is narrow. The house approved of that my Lord of Warwick hath done.

MR. STRODE, that the committee think not fit to make any order for the judges of the assize to observe our orders, for if they shall not, they shall be liable to the censure of this house.

Whereas 'tis informed that there is an intention to billet soldiers in Lynn and Yarmouth, both houses of parliament do order that they shall not receive them nor any other town whatsoever.[10]

Resolved, the lords be desired to join with us in this order.

Ordered by the lords [and] commons, that they think the petition which they have sent his majesty (which they were preparing before they received his message) is a full answer to his message. This to be sent after our messengers which are sent to the king, which they are to deliver to him in answer to his message.

MR. ERLE,[11] that his father send him word that Captain John Digby is raising of a troop of horse in Dorsetshire, which on Monday next is going toward York.

[f. 160a] Ordered, that Captain Digby shall be summoned to do his service here, and that the committee for the defense of the kingdom shall consider how these horse shall be stayed.

MR. STRODE, that Mr. Hyde that is at York that was summoned to appear here and do not, that he may be expelled this house.[12]

9. For the order see G, 12 July.
10. For the order see *LJ,* V, 210.
11. Thomas Erle, son to Sir Walter. The latter had been given leave on 1 July "to go into the Country," presumably to his home in Charborough, Dorset. *CJ,* II, 648; Keeler, p. 165.
12. Hyde had been summoned twice in March and was among those absent without leave when the house was called on 16 June, having joined the king in late May or early June. On 11 August he

That the messengers that are gone to his majesty move him to know his pleasure concerning the bill of tonnage and poundage and to desire him to pass the bill for the pluralities and the bill for the assembly of the divines.[13]

Resolved by question, that the Earl of Bedford shall be general of the horse.

Resolved, that the lords be made acquainted with this vote.[14]

MR. PLEYDELL, that all those that are listed may take the Oath of Allegiance and Supremacy.[15] This I had from Sir John Potts and that 'twas voted as I take it.

The house sit at 5 a clock, but I was not there.

---

was disabled. See *PJ*, 2: 75, 108; [Clarendon], *Life*, I, 123; and Appendixes A and G. See also Richard Ollard, *Clarendon and His Friends* (New York, 1988), pp. 72–74.

13. For this order of 13 July, see *CJ*, II, 670. In addition, a committee, including Hill, was named to "peruse the Bill for calling the Assembly of Divines" because the date for convening the assembly (1 July) was past. The committee reported that the king should be moved to pass the bill, which he failed to do, but that at the same time a new bill should be prepared. See *CJ*, II, 672; and *LJ*, V, 211, 234.

During the months that followed four new bills were prepared, none of which received the royal assent. Finally in June 1643 an ordinance, including a new list of members of the assembly, was agreed to by both houses; and the assembly convened on 1 July 1643. See Shaw, *English Church*, I, 124, n. 5, 145; and *LJ*, VI, 92–94.

14. Both the House of Lords and the Earl of Essex approved of Bedford. *LJ*, V, 211.

15. The committee of safety was to consider how the parliamentary army might take the Oaths of Supremacy and Allegiance and the Protestation "before their Names be entered." *CJ*, II, 672.

D'EWES

[f.272b]   July 15, Friday, 1642

The Speaker/[1]

I spake. Not time yet to put it. *Libera gens, etc. Rex est qui posuit* [*illegible*] *pectoris.* [*Illegible.*][2] In all parleys a cessation, 6 months of this charge undo kingdom. I hope not like sick man in fable. I will not say this larger than any was ever granted but larger than ever any was legally granted. Precedents of R. 2.[3] King's person only secured. Whether to force men to serve and only volunteers, except members of parliament. King's person, royal posterity.[4]

MR. WALLER, artificial thing. Otho, Vitellius, father and son. George, schechelus in Hungary.[5]

Objection: MR. MARTEN, parliament an artificial thing, so a king. A general at Beverley, Earl of Lindsey. There is no need of necessity but of conveniency. If both be artificial, yet some qualifications.[6]

Objection: A court may appoint a guard, MR. HOLLES.

To recommit it and to amend it.

---

1. "The Draught of a Commission whereby to constitute . . . the Earl of Essex Captain General, by virtue of an Ordinance of Parliament, of all the Forces, Train Bands, Forts, and Castles . . . within the Kingdom of England, and Dominion of Wales, etc. was this Day read Twice." *CJ,* II, 673.

2. "Free people, etc. The king is he who placed . . . of the heart." The editors have been unable to decipher a portion of D'Ewes's Latin as well as a marginal and interlinear insertion.

3. In November 1386 Richard II was compelled to agree to a commission of several prelates, lords, and others with extensive powers for reform, but only for one year. See *SR,* II, 39–43: 10 R. II. Marginal note: *H. n° 4°.* Because the note is partially covered by tape, it is not possible to determine to which King Henry it refers.

4. The commission gave Essex broad military powers, which D'Ewes wanted to limit in both scope and duration, hence his allusion to Richard II.

5. Waller was referring to the theoretical distinction between the king as a person (natural body) and the king as the corporate symbol of society (artificial body). The allusion to Otho and Vitellius, two military usurpers who succeeded Nero and Galba as Roman emperors, demonstrated the artificiality of authority, for upon becoming emperor, Otho invited Vitellius to be his father-in-law and share the imperial powers. See Suetonius, *The Twelve Caesars* (Harmondsworth, 1965), pp. 255–72. Waller also alluded to George of Poděbrady, ruler of Bohemia in the fifteenth century. See Frederick G. Heymann, *George of Bohemia: King of Heretics* (Princeton, 1965), passim.

6. Marten countered by saying that parliament, like kingship, was artificial, thus limitable by human artifice. The Earl of Lindsey had been named general of the king's army in early July. See Clarendon, *History,* II, 214, 266. Crossed out in MS: *Objection. A natural body useth not phlebotomy nor destructives.* MR. PYM.

Divers seconded my motion. Question first put for recommitment and ruled negatively. Then question put for passing and ruled affirmatively.[7]

MR. DENZIL HOLLES delivered in an order which the lords had passed touching the calling of a Court of Aldermen in London[8] and desired that an amendment might be added to it. MR. STRODE moved that we might [f. 273a] amend it and then send up to the lords to join with us in it, which made me stand up and speak in effect following:

That I conceived the gentleman who last moved (viz., Mr. Strode), though he be well skilled in the orders of the house, now moved quite out of all order, for the order now before us was made by the lords and they never sent it down to us to desire our consent to it but it comes unto us merely by intimation from a member of our own, and therefore we can neither amend it nor add to it but must only send it up to the lords by some private intimation and let them know what we desire to have added to it and that so they may pass it anew and send it down to us to desire our consent.

The SPEAKER stood up and moved as had been before moved that we might only add the amendments and send it up to the lords, which made me stand up and speak again to the orders of the house in effect following:

That if we would send it up to the lords, there was but one way according to the orders of the house to do it, and that was that we should make this as a new order of our own and then add to it what amendments we thought fit and so send it up to the lords and desire their concurrence with us in it, which motion of mine being allowed by the house as the only fit way, we proceeded with it accordingly.[9]

Sir Robert Harley was sent up to the lords to desire them to sit awhile.[10]

MR. DENZIL HOLLES delivered in a letter bearing date Exeter, July 10, 1642, sent from Mr. Richard Saunders, mayor, and Walter White, sheriff of the city of Exeter and the county of the same city, to himself or in his absence to Mr. John Pym, in which they showed:

That whereas they had formerly deferred the publishing of the king's procla-

7. The lords subsequently agreed to the commission, with only the Earl of Portland dissenting. *LJ*, V, 212. For the text see Appendix J.

8. Because of the lord mayor's refusal to appoint a locum tenens, the lords had ordered Sir George Whitmore to call a Court of Aldermen to do so or to consider some other way "for the Safety and good Government" of the City. See *LJ*, V, 210.

9. The new order required the aldermen to meet the next morning and "to make Choice amongst themselves of One Alderman, to be a Locum Tenens, to execute the Office of the Lord Mayor." See *LJ*, V, 213.

10. Subsequently Harley carried up the above order as well as one for provisions for the navy, to both of which the lords agreed. The latter order apparently resulted from the reports in the house on 13 July of the navy's need for supplies. See D, 207; *CJ*, II, 673; and *LJ*, V, 212. For proceedings omitted by D'Ewes, see *CJ*, II, 673–74.

mation against the ordinance of the militia and the execution of it,[11] which was done by the general consent of that city, they had since received a letter from his majesty which they had sent enclosed commanding them again to publish the same. That a letter had been sent from divers of the Common Council there to the Lord Falkland, which was secretly plotted and hands gotten in private houses and many men drawn to subscribe who did not well understand what they did. That this letter was sent up to London either to Mr. Ball,[12] the recorder of the town, or to one of their two burgesses who had sent it to York, in which letter they excused themselves as if they had not consented to the same but laid all the blame upon them, the said mayor and sheriff. That they had also sent with the said letter to the Lord Falkland a petition to his majesty to the same effect, from which they feared much inconvenience might proceed. The clerk next read his majesty's letter, which they had sent enclosed, bearing date or being given at the court at York July 2, 1642, sent to the mayor, sheriff, aldermen, and Common Council of the city of Exeter, in which he showed that he understood that whereas he had lately sent them a proclamation against the militia with a legal writ commanding them to publish the same, he understood that they had forborne to do it till they could color their disobedience by procuring an order from both houses of parliament, which seemed the more strange to him in respect that the liberties and privileges of their city had been so enlarged by the charters of so many kings and that they had in former times showed so much loyalty to the crown, and therefore he expected speedy obedience.

MR. DENZIL HOLLES delivered in another letter bearing date at Exeter July 13, 1642, directed to himself in the first place and to Mr. Pym in the 2d place, being sent as the former letter was from the said mayor and sheriff of Exeter, in which they showed that since their letter of the 10th of this month, they had received from his majesty three other proclamations which they did likewise forbear to publish till they had further direction from this house, with some other particulars of less moment.

Divers spake to it, and in the issue a committee[13] was appointed to examine Mr. Ball of the Middle Temple, recorder of the said town, and the two burgesses of this house serving for the said town, viz., Mr. Snow and Mr. Walker, whether they had not sent such a letter to York to the Lord Falkland which they had received from York.

MR. CROMWELL moved that we might make an order to allow the townsmen of Cambridge to raise two companies of volunteers of 100 men apiece and to

11. See D, 107.
12. Peter Ball was also the queen's attorney general. See *PJ*, 1: 216.
13. The committee of safety. *CJ*, II, 674.

appoint captains over them, which was just upon ordering, but I stood up and moved/[14]

The house appointed to meet at 8 of the clock tomorrow morning and rose about 4 of the clock.

GAWDY

[f. 160a]   Friday, the xv of July

[f. 160b] A commission read which is granted to my Lord of Essex to be lord general by both houses of parliament. This reported by MR. PYM from the committee for the defense of the kingdom.

MR. TOMKINS desire that this commission may not pass the question till our messengers return from the king.

MR. PYM, that if we receive a gracious message from the king, as I hope we shall, then we shall easily and quickly undo that which we have done. If not, then we are in a forwardness.

Resolved, that this commission shall pass.

Resolved, that the lords be desired to join with us.

A message from the lords, they had sent us the articles between us and the Scots concerning Ireland. They sent it to the king, which they have received from him with some amendments, which he made with his own hands.[15]

14. Cromwell had also sent arms into Cambridgeshire. For the rest of the day, see *CJ*, II, 674.
15. For a covering letter from Secretary Nicholas concerning the Scots treaty, see *LJ*, V, 211.

D'EWES

July 16, Saturday, 1642

The Speaker came between 8 and 9 of [the clock]. Vide clerk's book.[1] I came in about 8 of the clock.

SIR THOMAS BARRINGTON delivered in a writing from the Scottish commissioners bearing date July 15, 1642, in which they desired that some speedy course might be take/[2]

Upon SIR ROBERT PYE's motion Sir Thomas[3] Whitmore had license to go into the country.

MR. SPURSTOW delivered in a petition from Mr. Thomas Hunt, the mayor, and aldermen of Shrewsbury.[4]

SIR WALTER ERLE came out of Dorsetshire and said he came 30 miles this morning and informed that Captain Digby was at Sherborne and was raising a troop of horse, of which he had raised some 30 horse already and mounted them and was preparing the rest.

MR. REYNOLDS made report from the commissioners.[5]

44,800 now in Ireland under pay, horse and foot. Out of these 10,000 out of the forces in the provinces of Leinster and Ulster.[6]

Dr. Aylett and Dr. Heath,[7] two masters of the Chancery, brought down from the lords a letter sent from the Earl of Warwick and directed to the right

1. See G, below, and *CJ*, II, 675.
2. A paper from the Scots commissioners again requested £80,000 of the brotherly assistance. Consequently, it was ordered that the house should meet as a committee about this payment. See *LJ*, V, 214; and *CJ*, II, 675, 680.
3. MS: *William*.
4. John Weld, sheriff of Shropshire, had persuaded Hunt, an alderman, to desist from further military training of Shrewsbury volunteers. As a result this petition requested that the mayor, Richard Gibbons, "be enjoined to encourage such exercises." A committee, which included Hill, was named to draft an order "for the Indemnity of the Volunteers of Shrewsbury; and to make the Order general." *HMC, Fifth Report*, p. 38; *CJ*, II, 675; *Sheriffs*, p. 120; H[ugh] Owen and J. B. Blakeway, *A History of Shrewsbury* (London, 1825), I, 407n, 534. The petition with fifty-two signatures, including thirteen aldermen, is preserved in HLRO, Main Papers.
5. Reynolds was reporting from a committee named on 14 July "to treat with such Gentlemen of Ireland, as they shall think fit," concerning the affairs of Munster. See *CJ*, II, 672, 673, 675.
6. I.e., ten thousand foot from Leinster and Ulster plus several troops of horse were to go to Munster to regain the castle at Limerick and subdue the rebels. For details see *CJ*, II, 677. Apparently Pym had previously presented proposals concerning Limerick to the commissioners for Irish affairs. See CIA, 11 July.
7. For Thomas Heath see Levack, *Civil Lawyers*, p. 238.

honorable his very good lord, the Speaker of the House of Peers. It bore date from aboard the *James* in the Downs July 14, 1642, in which he showed that his majesty had/

[f. 274a] A long debate ensued upon this letter touching the putting of the militia in execution in the county of Kent, and that we should send to the lords to desire them/[8]

Sir Henry Vane, Junior, was sent up with that message and two others. I withdrew for a while out of the house a little before 12 of the clock.[9]

When I returned to the house, it was in debate about Mr. Reynolds's report to pass it in the house and not to refer it to the commissioners for the affairs of Ireland, and so at length it was voted accordingly that the troops proposed by him should be sent out of the other provinces into Munster. And we voted further to desire the lords to join with us in it, and Mr. Cromwell was sent up to the lords to desire a conference about the same, and Mr. Reynolds was appointed to manage it.

SIR THOMAS BARRINGTON made report from the lords.[10]

MR. CROMWELL made report from the lords that they would give us a meeting at 3 of the clock in the afternoon in the Painted Chamber.

Dr. Aylett and Dr. Heath, two masters of the Chancery, brought down two orders from the lords which they delivered in, desiring our consent unto them, and then withdrew. The first order concerned the sending for up of Captain John Digby and hindering of the troop of horse which he had raised at Sherborne, where was the house of the Earl of Bristol, his father; and the other order was for to authorize the mayor and townsmen of Dorchester to exercise themselves.[11] The clerk read both. We agreed to the first order with some amendment, to the other without any amendment, and the SPEAKER made report to the said messengers, being again called in, that we had agreed to the said orders and we had agreed to both orders.

We appointed to meet at 3 of the clock in the afternoon, and we rose a little before two of the clock.[12]

Post Meridiem

The Speaker came between 4 and 5 of the clock in the afternoon.

SIR HENRY MILDMAY delivered in an original letter of Sir Phelim O'Neill

8. For Warwick's letter and for resolutions passed concerning the Earl of Leicester, lord lieutenant of Kent, and Sir Henry Palmer, former comptroller of the navy, see G, below; *LJ*, V, 213; and *CJ*, II, 675.

9. For a message from the lords concerning the bill opposing innovations, see G, below.

10. The lords approved of Warwick's action concerning Palmer. *CJ*, II, 676.

11. I.e., to execute the militia ordinance. For both orders see *LJ*, V, 215. The mayor of Dorchester was Henry Maber. See A. R. Bayley, *The Great Civil War in Dorset, 1642–1660* (Taunton, 1910), p. 46.

12. For proceedings omitted by D'Ewes, see *CJ*, II, 676.

bearing date November 23, 1641, and sent from him to Sir William Hamilton, in which he desired him to assist for the Catholic cause, to which all the papists in England and Ireland had assented.[13]

The SPEAKER delivered in a letter sent him out of Worcestershire from Serjeant Wilde and Mr. Salway bearing date July 13, 1642, and a petition, both which were ordered to be printed.[14]

CAPTAIN VENN moved for an order to be passed touching the landing of the magazine which came from Hull.[15]

We went up to the conference touching the sending of 10,000[16] men out of the armies in the provinces of Leinster and Ulster into Munster, which was managed by Mr. Reynolds just in the same manner as he had made report of it in the morning.

After the conference ended, MR. HAMPDEN delivered in divers propositions and requests of the Scottish commissioners that money, arms, and other provisions might be sent to them, to most of which we either agreed or gave satisfaction by other answer.[17]

During this debate, upon CAPTAIN VENN's motion that an order might be sent up to the lords, Sir William Lewis was sent up with it.

We proceeded with the Scottish propositions and concluded them.

CAPTAIN VENN moved that the committee[18] appointed to meet about the hire of the house for the Scottish commissioners might meet on Monday next because there was 600£ to be paid for it, which was ordered accordingly.

Upon MR. LISLE's motion it was ordered that a parson in Hampshire[19] should be summoned to appear because he had discouraged divers from paying the money due upon the bill for 400,000£, saying that it was treason to pay [f. 274b] it because his majesty had set out his proclamation against it.

Upon SIR HENRY LUDLOW's motion it was ordered that the mayor of Salisbury should be summoned to appear before this house because he endeavored to hinder the militia.[20]

13. Hamilton, however, deserted the rebel cause, and O'Neill soon relieved him of his post as commander of the castle of Dunnamanagh near Strabane in Ulster. See Gilbert, *History of Ireland,* I (Pt. 1), 372, 373.

14. Wilde and Salway had been given leave on 8 July to go to Worcestershire to oppose the commission of array, which according to their letter "was this day quite deserted by the whole Countie." *CJ,* II, 662. Wing, W 2163.

15. The materiel from Hull was to be dispersed to various locations in the City. For the order see *CJ,* II, 676.

16. MS: *10,000£.* On 23 July the lords agreed to the propositions concerning Munster. *LJ,* V, 234.

17. For the propositions see *CJ,* II, 676–77.

18. The committee for accounts, of which Trenchard was chairman. *CJ,* II, 677.

19. Mr. Baker, minister of Pittleworth. *CJ,* II, 677.

20. The mayor, Thomas Lawes, appeared before the commons on 29 July, was committed to the Gatehouse, then released on 8 August. *CJ,* II, 696, 709.

The SPEAKER delivered in a petition from certain poor men in Yorkshire.[21]

Upon MR. TRENCHARD's motion the report touching the paymasters of Berwick and Carlisle was appointed to be heard on Wednesday morning next.

Upon MR. PYM's motion one William Sargent, who had caused the Speaker's servant to be arrested, was sent for as a delinquent.[22]

MR. PYM showed that he had a letter delivered even now directed to the Speaker, which he delivered in, and the Speaker having opened it, the clerk read it. It was dated at Oakham July 14, 1642, from Sir Edward Harington and other deputy lieutenants of that county, in which they showed that in respect that their lord lieutenant[23] was disabled by sickness to be present, that the commission of array was come into the county and divers men of power appointed in it, that there were no members of the House of Commons there to countenance the business, that they themselves were put out of the commission of peace which abated that power they had in the county, and that the innovating clergy did publish such books as came from the king and not such as came from the parliament, they thought it not safe to proceed with the militia but desired further direction from this house what course to take.

Upon MR. CAWLEY's information it was ordered that the mayor of Chichester[24] should be summoned to appear before this house for hindering the militia and other practices.

We appointed to meet at 8 of the clock on Monday morning and rose a little before seven of the clock in the evening.

GAWDY

[f. 160b]   Saturday, the XVI of July

A warrant from the king to his officers of the navy, that they issue out no provision for the navy out of his stores upon [f. 161a] an order of one or both houses of parliament.[25]

21. The petitioners requested stopping the actions of Sir William Savile, MP, of Thornhill, Yorks, concerning "certain Moors, Wastes, and Commons," so that the inhabitants might be "settled in the Possession of the Premises." *CJ*, II, 677.

22. Sargent had made "disgraceful and opprobrious Speeches" against the parliament and the Speaker. *CJ*, II, 677. Cf. 14 July, n. 2.

23. The Earl of Exeter was lord lieutenant for Rutland. Part of the letter appears in *HMC, Portland MSS*, I, 43. For Harington see GEC, *Baronetage*, I, 53.

24. Robert Exton, the mayor, did not appear until 21 September, having meanwhile gone to York. However, "upon his humble Submission" the house discharged him. See *CJ*, II, 677, 768, 775.

25. Parliament's order empowered Warwick, in place of Northumberland, to issue warrants for naval supplies. The house was to meet as a committee on Monday to discuss the king's "Warrants of

Resolved by question, that the arms be stayed that are going down to Cambridge.

Resolved, that the 500 horses that are to go into Ireland shall be supply with 500 horse arms that came from Hull.[26]

Resolved, that the lords be desired to join with us in this.

SIR WALTER ERLE, that there is a troop of horse providing at Sherborne by Captain Digby. There is 50 provided to go to the north or else to surprise a magazine of consequence in the west country.

MR. REYNOLDS, that there is now in our pay in Ireland 44,800 men besides these 5500 men that are going thither.

A message from the lords, they send us a letter which came from my Lord of Warwick to the Speaker of the lords house. That Sir Henry Palmer came to him, who said he had received a command from his majesty to demand certain goods of his that were in the *Lion* and that he should suffer that ship to fall down to Scarborough for his service. My lord said that there was no goods [f. 161b] in the ship and that it was one of the fleet committed to him by the parliament. That he would not suffer it to go. That he had displaced the captain, that was Captain Fox. From the *James* in the Downs, the 14 of July.

My Lord of Warwick likewise sendeth us word that the commission of array is putting in execution in Kent.

Resolved, a message be sent to the lords to know of Lord of Leicester whether he will execute the militia in Kent or not, and that he should grant his deputations to his deputy lieutenants.

Resolved by question, that this house doth approve of my Lord of Warwick's resolution to Sir Henry Palmer concerning his demands from his majesty.

A message from the lords, they send us the bill for the suppressing of innovations and for the better preaching of God's word with some amendments.[27]

In the afternoon.

A letter from Worcester, July the 13, from Serjeant Wilde and Mr. Salway, that by their coming the commission of array was deserted. That Mr. Sherrington Talbot [f. 162a] appeared there with much boldness, who is gone to York.[28]

Restraint" and other naval matters. The meeting was, however, postponed. See 15 July, n. 10; and *CJ,* II, 673, 675, 680.

26. For details of this order for 560 horse arms, see CIA, 14 July, and *CJ,* II, 675.

27. The lords had passed the amended bill on this day. Though further amended, it never received the royal assent but in August 1643 was replaced by an ordinance. See *LJ,* V, 214, and VI, 200–01; and Shaw, *English Church,* I, 108–10.

28. On 6 June and 8 July the house had summoned Talbot of Salwarpe, Worcs, as a delinquent for furthering the commission of array. See *CJ,* II, 608, 661; J. W. Willis Bund, *The Civil War in Worcestershire, 1642–1646* (Birmingham, 1905), p. 23; and *VCH, Worcestershire,* II, 219.

A petition from the great inquest at the sessions to the justices, who much desire the militia may be put in execution in that county for the safety of king and kingdom.

Resolved, that the magazine that came from Hull shall be laid up in certain warehouses in Leadenhall and other warehouses in London.

D'EWES

[f. 275a] July 18, Monday, 1642

The Speaker came a little after 9 of the clock. See M. and clerk's journal. I withdrew out of the house and returned again about 10 of the clock. The sheriff's man of Lincolnshire had then newly delivered in a petition in the name of divers gentlemen and others of the county of Lincoln, which had divers particulars in it against the ordinance of the militia and other proceedings of the two houses.[1] SIR EDWARD AYSCOUGH, one of the knights of the shire of that county, looking upon the hands that had subscribed to the said petition, showed that the greater part of them were men of very mean condition and esteem and known to bear ill will to the parliament, which was seconded also by SIR ANTHONY IRBY; and a committee was appointed, of which I was named one, to draw an answer to the said petition. They were to meet this afternoon at 2 of the clock in the Chequer Chamber.

MR. WALTER LONG moved that a month's pay might be paid to the officers which were to be sent by the adventurers into Ireland but that no levy money might yet be paid them, which was ordered accordingly.

MR. HAMPDEN made report from the committee appointed for the safety of the kingdom. That they had lately received some letters from Hull which they had thought fit to communicate to the house, the first of which he told the Speaker was directed to himself bearing date at Hull July 12, 1642, being sent from Mr. John Hotham, Mr. Peregrine Pelham, and Mr. John Alured, in which they showed that they were in a good condition and that the king's forces without were of no considerable strength, being about some 2400.[2] That Captain Pigot and Captain Moyer[3] had done very good service upon the river of Humber, being captains of two of the king's ships sent thither by the Earl of Warwick. That one ketch (a little vessel) had been taken with 4 pieces of ordnance in it and some Cavaliers. That some of the mills had been burnt near Hull. That the Earl of Newport had like to have perished in a ditch. That Mr. Warton, who was appointed to be their 4th

1. For this petition, prompted by the king's recent visit to Lincoln, see Hill, *Lincoln,* pp. 150–51. Wing, H 3453. For the Venetian ambassador's comments, see *CSP Ven., 1642–1643,* pp. 105, 112. A message of 16 July from the king to Sheriff Heron concerning searching for arms appears in *CSPD, 1641–43,* p. 355.

2. The letter, dated 13 July, stated that "the King's Forces that block us up from Victuals are small and inconsiderable," not above twenty–five hundred horse and foot. See *LJ,* V, 217.

3. Lawrence Moyer was captain of the *Hercules.* Reckitt, *Hull,* p. 59n.

committee, could not find the way thither all this while to them though he were but 5 miles distant from them, and therefore they thought that they were better to miss him than to have his society,[4] and that they thought some had been killed by their cannon for two or three nights last past, with some other matters of less moment.

Some particulars in this letter are more fully explained in that of Sir John Hotham which ensueth.

[f. 275b] MR. HAMPDEN then delivered in another letter sent from Sir John Hotham bearing date at Hull July 12, 1642, directed to Sir Philip Stapleton or in his absence/[5]

Great want of money. His son of the Temple[6] could find no means to return the money paid to him.

Mills burning, and houses to be burnt. Townsmen now took pay above 500£ per week.[7] That the Earl of Newport's horse at the burning of the mills threw him into a ditch where he hardly escaped drowning.

Captain Pigot and Captain Moyer had done great service with the two ships they commanded.

The letter being read, MR. HAMPDEN made report what course the committee had taken for the defense of the town of Hull, viz., that 10,000£ should be sent unto them out of the contribution money that came in upon the propositions.[8] That Mr. John Hotham, Mr. Peregrine Pelham, and Mr. John Alured might have the full power of a committee as well as if there were four. That there should be thanks given to Captain Pigot and Captain Moyer.

All these particulars voted by us.[9]

Upon MR. POPHAM's motion it was ordered that Mr. Edward Horner, who was come out of Somersetshire and taken by a ketch as he was crossing the Humber in a pass boat and was now detained there, should be set at liberty.[10]

Debate whether a message or a conference were the most proper way to

4. For Michael Warton's subsequent career as a royalist, see Keeler, p. 380.

5. For the text see *LJ*, V, 217–18. Stapleton, Sir John Holland, and the Earl of Holland were delivering the petition of peace to the king. See G, 13 July.

6. Durand Hotham.

7. "Our Charge is now more than Five hundred Pounds a Week, having much increased our Numbers by entertaining most of the Town into Pay, who, for the Generality, we conceive, are now very firm to us." *LJ*, V, 217.

8. I.e., the propositions for raising money, horse, and plate.

9. For more details see *CJ*, II, 678.

10. Horner, who was Popham's cousin, had protested that "his Business in this Country was to a Lady that he is to marry" and not "any Business that concerned the Parliament." His father, Sir John Horner, was a former MP and a parliamentary leader in Somerset. See *LJ*, V, 217; and S. W. Bates Harbin, "Members of Parliament for the County of Somerset," in *Proceedings of the Somersetshire Archaeological and Natural History Society*, 83 (1937): 145–46.

communicate these two letters to the lords with the votes we had made upon them, and it was agreed that a conference was the most proper way.

The Lord Grey sent to desire a conference touching the safety of the kingdom.

Upon MR. PYM's motion it was ordered/

Lord Brooke, magazine.[11]

Sir Charles Caesar, the master of the rolls, and Dr. Heath, a master of the Chancery, brought down a letter from the lords which was sent from the Earl of Warwick to the Speaker of the lords house bearing date from aboard the *James* in the Downs July 17, 1642,[12] in which he showed that he had received an answer from his majesty.

That he had intercepted a letter from Lieutenant Waters.

Mr. Waters's letter to Captain Slingsby read.[13]

Then was read the Earl of Warwick's letter to his majesty bearing date from aboard the *James* in the Downs July 5, 1642.[14]

Newark, July 13, 1642, from Sir Edward Nicholas to the Earl of Warwick. His majesty unsatisfied with his letter and thought that no commands should have induced him to commit treason.

[f. 276b] Then was [read] another letter of the Earl of Warwick sent to Mr. Pym bearing date from aboard the *James* in the Downs July 17, 1642, in which he showed:

That there was great want of victuals.

That he had sent enclosed certain letters concerning the proceedings in the north about Hull.[15]

The LORD GREY returned and made report that he received this message from the Lord Mandeville, that the lords would give a present meeting in the Painted Chamber.

We agreed to give the lords a meeting presently.

The master of the rolls and Dr. Heath were again called in, and the SPEAKER made report that we would give them[16] a meeting presently as was desired.

Mr. Hampden and others were appointed reporters and managers between 12

---

11. For Pym's report and the resulting order, see G, below, and *CJ*, II, 678.

12. For the text see *LJ*, V, 216. The letter to Pym noted below was doubtless similar. The messengers also requested a conference concerning Lincolnshire. *CJ*, II, 678.

13. In a letter of 12 July to Slingsby, Lieutenant Waters wrote: "Yesterday walking in Westminster I heard people . . . say how much Parliament was incensed against you. . . . I exhort you to adhere to the course you have taken." *HMC, Portland MSS*, I, 43.

14. For this letter and the response from Nicholas, see *HMC, Fifth Report*, p. 38.

15. It was ordered that hereafter Warwick and Sir John Hotham should direct their letters to the committee of safety, who should "take Care to answer them." *CJ*, II, 678.

16. MS: *us*.

and one of the clock and went up with the greatest part of the house to the said double conference.

Mr. Pym and Mr. Hampden first managed our conference, and the letters were read which had been read here this morning which came from Hull.

The Lord Mandeville managed the conference on the lords' part and after a short preface read a warrant of his majesty's directed to one Thomas Smith, a messenger, by which he was commanded to seize upon the persons of one Watson, an alderman of Lincoln, and one Emis,[17] the sheriff of the city of Lincoln, and to bring them before his council at York for putting the ordinance for the militia in execution. At our court at Beverley July 9, 1642.

The Lord Mandeville then read the declaration and protestation of above 10,000 of the gentry and others in Lincolnshire. (It is ordered to be printed.)[18]

Then was a vote of the lords read that they would defend and protect all such as had obeyed or executed the orders and ordinances of parliament.

After the conference ended, upon SIR ROGER BURGOYNE's motion it was ordered that the horses which were stayed in Bedfordshire as Sir John Byron's, proving to [be] the Lady d'Aubigny's,[19] should be returned to her, paying the charges due for their keeping.

MR. PYM made report of that part of the conference which was managed on the lords' part.

The copy of the warrant and the declaration and protestation of the Lincolnshire men were read, and the declaration was ordered to be printed. We agreed also to the vote.[20]

And upon several motions Mr. Pym and 3 other members of the house were appointed to go to the Lord Willoughby of Parham[21] and to let him know what special approbation this house gave to the service he had done in Lincolnshire, having put the ordinance for the militia in execution there.

The master of the rolls and Dr. Heath brought down the order from the lords

17. MS: *Ames. Sheriffs,* p. 196. For the warrant for the arrest of William Watson and Edward Emis, see *LJ,* V, 216. The king had issued the commission of array for Lincolnshire on 4 July. See Hill, *Lincoln,* p. 150.

18. This brief petition in support of parliament is apparently the one delivered to the lords by Lord Willoughby on 4 July. See *LJ,* V, 177; and *HMC, Fifth Report,* p. 34. Wing, T 1607. The number of signatures to the petition, which is preserved in HLRO, Main Papers, appears to be nearer 2500.

19. Sister to the Earl of Suffolk and wife to George Stuart, Seigneur d'Aubigny. GEC, *Peerage.* The house had been informed about the horses on 14 July.

20. I.e., the above-mentioned vote defending all who executed the orders of parliament. See *CJ,* II, 678–79.

21. Willoughby and others of the Lincolnshire committee had recently returned to London to avoid a direct clash during the king's visit to Lincoln. Hill, *Lincoln,* p. 150. Cf. G, 21 June.

for Yarmouth and Lynn to defend themselves against force[22] that should be put upon them, which we had sent up to the [f. 277b] lords, and showed that they had assented with us and had added some amendments to it. And so they withdrew and departed.

We then assented to the said amendments and passed it.

Two poor men of Buckinghamshire were committed to the Gatehouse for discouraging such as trained in Buckinghamshire and arresting one of them upon a false action.[23]

MR. HAMPDEN made report from the committee for the safety of the kingdom touching an examination taken upon oath July 11, 1642, of one [blank] Page, servant to Mr. Venables, Baron of Kinderton, and one Carter, examined upon oath, [who] did both prove that the said Mr. Venables, being a member of this house, had seen the declaration and resolution of Herefordshire before it was printed and had endeavored with the said Carter to get it printed, which was a most scandalous declaration and of dangerous consequence.

So the house discharged Page and resolved to hear Carter further before they discharged him. And it was ordered that Mr. Venables should attend the house within 4 days.[24]

Upon MR. CROMWELL's motion Mr. Frend,[25] the undersheriff of Middlesex, was called in and questioned for publishing the king's proclamation against the militia, who confessed that he kept it by him 4 days before he read it and was at last so terrified that he read it. So he withdrew, and then we agreed that he should only be reprehended, which the SPEAKER did accordingly upon his second calling in.

Mr. Barton, a minister of Aylesbury in Buckinghamshire, was brought in to the bar as a delinquent, and several accusations which had been laid against him were opened by the Speaker.[26]

22. MS: *horse.* For this order concerning the billeting of soldiers by force, see G, 14 July. In addition, the deputy lieutenants for Norfolk were to execute the militia ordinance in both towns. *CJ,* II, 679.

23. The two men, having been sent for on 14 July, were soon released. *CJ,* II, 672, 679, 683, 698.

24. The informants were Humphrey Page and Humphrey Carter. Venables, who had been summoned on 11 July, was among those suspended from the house for nonattendance on 2 September. On 25 July the house ordered that the declaration should be read at the next assizes in Herefordshire to see whether anyone there would avow it. *CJ,* II, 679, 690, 750.

25. Prinne, in *CJ,* II, 679. For an earlier dispute with Frend, see Coates, pp. 263–69 passim.

26. Barton, having been sent for on 8 July for reading the king's declaration and using language "opprobrious to the . . . Parliament," was committed to the Gatehouse, then released on 26 July. *CJ,* II, 679, 692.

I withdrew out of the house a little after two of the clock in the afternoon.[27] The house rose about 3 of the clock within an hour after.

GAWDY

[f. 162a]   Monday, the XVIII of July

A petition from Lincolnshire send by the sheriff's man with many baronets', knights', and gentlemen's hands to it:

1. That his majesty may have Hull.
2. That all guards be discharged, the militia laid aside.
3. [*blank*]
4. That there be a forgetting.
5. That there be no votes but with his majesty's consent.
6. For settling religion.
7. For suppressing the press.
8. For suppressing tumults, and to adjourn the parliament to some other place according to his majesty's desire.

This petition was sent by the sheriff's man. 'Twas subscribed by the sheriff, baronets, knights, and gentlemen.

[f. 162b] The petition for Lincolnshire referred to a committee to take into consideration.

MR. HAMPDEN, a report from the committee from lords and commons. A letter from Hull, July the 13, that they are in a good condition. That the king's forces are not above 2500 horse and foot. Mr. Warton, one of the committee, come not to them. They desire he may be discharged, that they may have a fourth man. John Hotham, Mr. Pelham, and Mr. Alured, subscribers.

A letter to Mr. Hampden[28] from Hull, that some of the town of their part should have fired the town last night in several places when there should have been an attempt upon the town. My Lord Newport escaped drowning narrowly, his horse falling with him into a ditch. We shot ordnance at the mills where he fear he hath some hurt. Subscribed John Hotham.

That the townsmen are all come in, that the charge is 500£ a week, and if we send more men, 'twill increase the charge.

Resolved, that there shall be 10,000£ [f. 163a] issued out from Guildhall by the commissioners for the subscription money for the maintaining the garrison at Hull.

---

27. For the rest of the day, see G, below, and *CJ*, II, 679–80.
28. For this letter, directed primarily to Stapleton, see above, n. 5.

Ordered, that those that be of the committee now in Hull shall be sufficient.

Ordered, that there be six pieces of ordnance sent back to Sir John Hotham as he desire.

MR. PYM, a report from the same committee. That they desire my Lord Brooke should take men into Warwick Castle for the defense of the magazine there, and that they shall be paid out of the subscription money in that county of Warwick. This to be ordered by both houses.

A message from the lords, they send us letters from my Lord of Warwick, and they desire a conference about a warrant sent by his majesty into Lincolnshire.

The letter was that he had received a letter from Secretary Nicholas, by which he perceive his majesty account it treason in him to serve the parliament, which he shall most faithfully do to the utmost drop of his blood. He desire the ship may be victualed.

[f. 163b] A letter from my Lord of Warwick to the king, that he hath received your majesty's discharge from commanding the navy. That he hath received an ordinance of parliament to command it. He is in a great strait, but he hopeth his majesty will think him as fit to do him service as Sir John Penington. That he will make it appear how faithfully he will serve the king and parliament.

While I was at dinner, there was a petition delivered from Lincolnshire to a contrary sense to the former petition. This I had from Mr. Salway.

Resolved, that Mr. Venables, the Baron of Kinderton, shall be summoned to appear here within 4 days (he being a member of this house), for that he is suspected to be a means to procure the scandalous remonstrance from Herefordshire to be printed. After dinner.

The undersheriff of Middlesex is reprehended at the bar for proclaiming the proclamation against the militia.

[f. 164a] Mr. Barton,[29] a minister, committed to the Gatehouse for reading the king's declaration and for some other passages against the parliament.

A letter read wrote from York to Sir William Allanson, that certain pioneers appointed to work near Hull were withdrawn. That the lords were discontented because their counsels were rejected and the counsel of the Cavaliers followed.[30] This I had from old Mr. More and Mr. Blakiston after I was gone.

29. MS: *Martyn*.
30. This may be a reference to the newly appointed lifeguard which went with the king from York to Beverley on 7 July. See H., P., *Terrible and true newes from Beverley* (1642). Wing, H 104. For the lifeguard, commanded by Lord Willoughby of Eresby, see also Toynbee and Young, *Strangers in Oxford*, p. 37.

D'EWES

July 19, Tuesday, 1642

The Speaker came a little before 9 of the clock. After prayers the matter touching the repair of Dover was awhile agitated, and in the issue it was referred to the committee appointed to that end, and they were appointed to meet tomorrow in the afternoon.[1]

MR. GREEN made report touching the state of the navy, and it was awhile debated whether we should discharge six or seven of the king's ships or the merchants' ships, and in the issue it was first referred to the committee for the defense of the kingdom to consider of.[2]

The Speaker left the chair, and we intended to have proceeded with the brotherly assistance due to the Scots, being 80,000£, what course we should take to pay it. Mr. Reynolds was called to the clerk's chair, but upon Mr. Hampden's desire the Speaker did again resume the chair, and then we proceeded with the Scottish treaty which the lords had sent us down.[3] The clerk read a letter dated 13 July 1642 sent from Secretary Nicholas to the Earl of Leicester and other commissioners appointed to treat with the Scots about their army sent into Ireland,[4] in which he showed that he had presented the Scottish treaty to his majesty engrossed in two parts, which his[5] majesty had altered and amended with his own hand.

The alteration in the 3d article agreed unto touching/

Ayes 69. Sir Gilbert Gerard and Sir Walter Erle, tellers. Went out. I one of them. Noes 51. Sir William Lewis and Sir Anthony Irby, tellers. Sat still.[6]

The alteration in the 6 article where "parliament" was struck out we agreed not.

---

1. For a committee concerning Dover, see *PJ*, 2: 159, n. 18. For proceedings omitted by D'Ewes, see *CJ*, II, 680.

2. Green, Pye, and Vane (doubtless Jr.) were ordered to write to the Earl of Warwick, in response to his letters reported on 18 July, about calling in some ships and revictualing the rest. *CJ*, II, 680.

3. It was ordered that the arms, which according to the treaty were to be delivered to the Scots, should come out of the store of arms from Hull. *CJ*, II, 680.

4. The other lords named on 3 December 1641 to treat with the Scots, along with the commons' committee for Scottish negotiations, were the Earl of Bedford and Lord Howard of Escrick. *LJ*, IV, 461.

5. MS: *had*. For the letter see 15 July, n. 15.

6. Lewis was teller for the Ayes, Erle for the Noes, according to *CJ*, II, 680.

The alteration in the 10th article of "parliament" with the addition of "both houses of" in two several places was allowed of.

To the last alteration where the word "parliament" was struck out for discharge of the Scottish army we agreed not.

[f. 278b] Sir Robert Rich and Mr. Page, two masters of the Chancery, brought this message from the lords, that their lordships had assented unto 2 orders sent to them by us, the one touching Sir John Clotworthy's subscription of 1000£ and other touching 10,000£ of contribution money to be delivered to Mr. Nicholas Loftus with one word alteration in both, and then they withdrew and departed. We agreed to the amendments.[7]

MR. CROMWELL made report of the lords' answer to his message.[8]

MR. HAMPDEN moved that some members of this house and others might be nominated and appointed to go into Somersetshire and Dorsetshire to advance the subscription of money, plate, and horse. So divers spake after him, and several persons were named for both counties.[9]

Upon SIR THOMAS BARRINGTON's motion that an order might be made to authorize the deputy lieutenants of each county to disperse themselves as it should seem fit to them, after some had spoken to it, the said Sir Thomas Barrington and Mr. Grimston were appointed to draw up the same order.[10]

Sir Robert Rich and Mr. Page, two masters of the Chancery, brought this message from the lords, that their lordships had appointed this day for the lord mayor to make answer to his impeachment, and that if this house [sees] fit to send up some of their members to be present at the same, they might. They being withdrawn, we agreed to send up some members, which the SPEAKER related to them being again called in, and so they withdrew and departed. Mr. Solicitor, Serjeant Wilde, and others were appointed to go up to the lords house, which they did accordingly.[11]

SIR GILBERT GERARD delivered in a petition to have a lecture at Hitchin each Tuesday in the week, which was granted.[12]

Upon MR. REYNOLDS's motion a committee was appointed, of which I was

7. As "Part of his Entertainment in Ireland," Clotworthy was to be paid £1000, which he was in turn subscribing "as an Adventure for Ireland." Both orders had been carried up to the lords by Cromwell. See *CJ*, II, 649, 680; and *LJ*, V, 221.

8. Cromwell had also carried up orders for the indemnity of volunteers in Shrewsbury and in Hertford, to which the lords agreed. See 16 July, n. 4; and *CJ*, II, 680, 681. For both orders see *LJ*, V, 221–22.

9. For the orders with the names of those who were to execute them, including Roger Hill for Somerset, see *LJ*, V, 225–26.

10. Reynolds was also named. *CJ*, II, 681.

11. For Gurney's answer of "not guilty" to the additional impeachment charges of 9 July, see *LJ*, V, 219, 221.

12. Fifteen "orthodox Divines" were named to rotate as lecturers at the parish church of Hitchin, Herts. *CJ*, II, 681.

one, to search into the commission by which the lord justices were to summon the present parliament now sitting in Ireland.[13]

MR. DENZIL HOLLES brought in a letter to be sent by the Speaker with a jewel to the Earl of Ormonde in the name of the house. The letter was to thank him for his great services and to let him know that the House of Commons had sent him that jewel as a testimony of their thankfulness to him. The clerk having read the letter, the Speaker holding both the letter and the jewel/[14]

Sir Robert Rich and Mr. Page, two masters of the Chancery, brought this message from the lords, that the lords had appointed Friday next for the trial of the lord mayor and that then we might produce our proofs to make good our said charge. They being withdrawn, we appointed certain of our members to attend that trial, which the SPEAKER reported to the said messengers being again called in.[15]

Upon MR. SOLICITOR's motion it was ordered that the committee appointed to draw the commission for the treaty of the Scots should meet this afternoon.[16]

The house appointed to meet at 8 of the clock tomorrow morning; we rose about one of the clock.[17]

[f. 279b] In the afternoon I was first present at the committee of privileges, though I was not of it, where the case of Sir Thomas Sandford was in agitation, being returned a burgess for the town of Cockermouth in the county of Cumberland by Sir Henry Fletcher, Baronet, sheriff of that county.[18] The writ was first read, in which mention was made that William Lenthall, Esquire, Speaker, had certified that whereas Sir John Fenwick, Baronet, had been elected, etc., one of the knights of Northumberland and one of the burgesses of the said town, etc., therefore to cause a new burgess to be elected. The said sheriff sent his answer to one [blank] Stephens, bailiff of that town, to summon the townsmen there before himself at a day to come to make an election of a new burgess. He then made the return himself also, and one Mr. Allen was returned by the said Stephens.[19]

13. The committee, which also included Hill, was "to consider of the best Way for the Continuance of the Parliament there." *CJ*, II, 681.

14. Proceedings concerning the jewel had begun on 4 May. It was now ordered that Holles should send both the letter and the jewel (valued at £620). See *PJ*, 2: 276; and *CJ*, II, 681, 685. For another account of sending the jewel, see Thomas Carte, *An History of the Life of James Duke of Ormonde*, I (London, 1736), 312–13.

15. Hill and Wilde were among those named to manage the evidence. *CJ*, II, 681.

16. "To-morrow, at Two," in *CJ*, II, 681. The reference is to the treaty of pacification, not the treaty for sending Scots forces to Ireland, according to *CJ*.

17. For proceedings omitted by D'Ewes, see *CJ*, II, 681.

18. In addition to their mothers being sisters, both Fletcher and Sandford had married daughters of Sir George Dalston, MP. See *Roy. Off.*, pp. 134–35, 327.

19. This election dispute was finally settled in Francis Allen's favor in 1645. Meanwhile in 1644 Sandford was disabled. See *PJ*, 2: 475–76.

GAWDY

[f. 164a]   Tuesday, the xix of July

SIR ROBERT PYE, that we have at sea 17 of the king's ships and as many more as make up in all 50 and odd ships, all at the charge of the commonwealth.

The house divided whether the words of amendment by the king in the Scots articles shall stand. The Ayes that went out that would have them stand, of which I was, was 69. The Noes that sat were 51.

A message from the lords, they send us two orders which they received, from which they have assented to one the alteration of a word.

MR. HAMPDEN, a report from the committee for defense, that some gentlemen may be sent into Somersetshire and Dorsetshire to look to the subscriptions and militia.

[f. 164b] A message from the lords, my lord mayor of London was now at the bar ready to put in his answer. They desire that some members of our house may be present. 'Tis assented to.

D'EWES

[f. 280a]   July 20, Wednesday, 1642

The Speaker [came] between 8 and 9 of the clock. Prayers being ended after 9/[1]

[Committee of the Whole House]

I returned a little after 10 of the clock. Mr. Reynolds was then in the clerk's chair, and the committee of the house debated how to provide the 80,000£ which was due at Midsummer last for part of the 300,000£ for the brotherly assistance, and in the issue we voted that a subcommittee should go and see what moneys were come in upon the bill of 400,000£, and Sir Robert Pye and others were appointed to take care in it.

The Speaker resumed his chair, and Mr. Reynolds left the clerk's chair.

Sir Robert Rich and Mr. Page brought down a letter from the lords which had been sent from the Earl of Holland bearing date at Beverley July 18, 1642,[2] and directed to the right honorable his very good lord, the Speaker of the House of Peers, and showed that their lordships desired after that we had perused it that it might be returned to them again because they had kept no copy, and then they withdrew and departed. The clerk read the said letter, and the Earl of Holland showed that they came on Saturday night last to Beverley. That the king came late that night from Lincoln and yet after supper admitted them to his presence and heard their petition and spake sharply to some particulars of it. That they found divers officers but few lords there, they being gone into several counties to put the commission of array in execution. That upon Wednesday his majesty intended to go to Nottingham and Leicester[3] to assure those counties to himself as he conceives he hath done others. That his forces seem not so great as they are because it is said that he is sure of very many whom he may call together

---

1. For proceedings omitted by D'Ewes, see *CJ*, II, 682.

2. Holland, as a member of the committee to deliver the petition of peace to the king, reported that "His Majesty told us it was a Business of great Importance, and required Time for to advise of His Answer." For the letter see *LJ*, V, 224. In a letter of 20 July to Sir Thomas Roe, Secretary Nicholas described the petition of peace as "carrying more show of accommodation than all the former." *CSPD, 1641–43*, p. 359.

3. John James, the mayor of Nottingham, though a supporter of parliament, received the king, who shortly thereafter went to Leicester. Failing to secure possession of the magazine there, he returned to Nottingham, then proceeded to Yorkshire. See Wood, *Nottinghamshire*, pp. 16–17.

when he pleaseth upon summons. But that yet for 2 reasons they are not drawn together, first because he expects to have a direct answer concerning Hull and 2dly to avoid charge. That divers noblemen and gentlemen have raised troops of horse for the king's service, with some other particulars of less moment.

MR. DENZIL HOLLES delivered in another letter sent from Sir John Holland and Sir Philip Stapleton to the Speaker bearing date at Beverley July 18, 1642, being almost verbatim the same with that of the Earl of Holland.

After some few had spoken to them, we agreed to refer these two letters to the committee of lords and commons appointed for the safety of the kingdom.

MR. PYM delivered in two letters sent to him from Sir John Clotworthy out of the province of Ulster in Ireland, the one bearing date June 28, 1642, and the other June 30, 1642, in which he showed that they had cleared all places in that province which the rebels possessed except Charlemont, which he hoped to clear as soon as the Lord Conway's forces should join with them. That they were in great want of victuals and money, and that if some speedy course were not taken to relieve them, they must perish in the end, with many other particulars.[4]

MR. GREEN delivered in a draft of a letter which was to be sent by the Speaker to the Earl of Warwick to know the state of the navy and that 500£ had been sent to him for the sick men.[5] We allowed of it.

MR. PYM delivered in a letter dated at Bunratty June 25, 1642, from the Earl of Thomond to the lord commissioners and others for the affairs of Ireland, in which he showed in what a sad condition himself and the English near him were in great danger and the more in respect of the loss of Limerick Castle, with other [f. 280b] particulars, in conclusion of which he showed that unless some speedy succor were sent within a month, he must be enforced to quit the place.[6]

Divers spake to it, and at last upon MR. REYNOLDS's motion we resolved that one regiment of/[7]

Between 12 and 1 of the clock the master of the rolls and Dr. Heath, a master

4. Charlemont Castle in Co. Armagh had been captured by the Irish under the leadership of Sir Phelim O'Neill at the outbreak of the rebellion. *CSP Ire., 1633–1647*, p. 342. For Clotworthy's activities in Co. Tyrone and Co. Antrim between 25 June and 8 July, see Gilbert, *History of Ireland*, I (Pt. 2), 512–15. Wing, T 3050.

5. The order for £500 was in response to Warwick's letter of 11 July which mentioned, among other needs, the "extreme Want, for the discharging of sick Men." See 13 July, n. 8, and 19 July, n. 2.

6. This letter is referred to in another letter from Thomond dated 31 August. See Hogan, *Irish Rebellion*, p. 117; and CIA, 19 July.

7. For orders that a regiment commanded by Lord Kerry, one of five to be raised for Munster by the adventurers for Ireland, should be sent to the relief of the Earl of Thomond, see *CJ*, II, 682. See also CIA, 26 July. In addition, it was ordered that a ship and a pinnace be sent by the Earl of Warwick "for the Defence of Duncannon Fort." For the request for this aid, see CIA, 19 July. Warwick's response, detailing various difficulties, appears in *LJ*, V, 240.

of the Chancery, brought this message from the lords, that their lordships were ready to give judgment upon the 9 lords impeached by us if our Speaker would come up and demand judgment.[8] So they withdrew. The SPEAKER then demanded in what manner he should impeach them, whether he should enumerate up all the offenses that we had impeached them of and name them particularly.

I stood up and showed that he should not need make an enumeration of the offenses but must name the men in particular.

The SPEAKER then further demanded whether he should demand judgment against them all jointly or severally, and divers cried out, "All, all." So the messengers were again called in, and the SPEAKER related to them that the house was resolved to send up the Speaker and to demand judgment, and so they withdrew and departed.

I stood up and moved that whereas he had even now propounded a question whether he should demand judgment against these impeached lords jointly or severally, that many had cried, "All, all," I did not know whether they meant against them all, which [f. 281b] we all agree of, or whether they intended that judgment should be demanded against them all in a confused and joint demand, which if they did I conceive that that is not according to the ancient course and form, for judgment ought to be demanded against every particular man, to which opinion of mine others and amongst them the Speaker himself assented, though he did not afterwards expressly pursue it at his demanding of judgment in the lords house.

I was present there, coming a little after the Speaker had begun. The judgment was pronounced by the Lord Mandeville, etc.[9] There were 15 peers only present in their robes and the Earl of Bedford and the Lord Spencer without their robes.

Divers matters of little moment passed after our return to the house, which see in the clerk's book.[10]

The master of the rolls and Dr. Heath brought down an order from the lords, by which they gave authority to the committee appointed for the safety of the kingdom to dispose of the arms which came from Hull for the defense of the kingdom,[11] but the master of the rolls (being a very silly man and of weak parts) forgot part of his message and did not desire us to join with the lords, and so they withdrew.

We fell into debate whether we should agree to this order or not. I spake in effect following:

8. Though the nine lords had been scheduled to answer the impeachment on 27 June, it had not been proceeded with until 15 and 19 July. See *LJ*, V, 141, 212, 219.

9. See G, below, and *LJ*, V, 222–23.

10. See *CJ*, II, 683.

11. For the order see *CJ*, II, 683.

That I was not altogether against our agreeing to this order but only against the doing of it at this time, because we may remember that the gentleman who then sat here above behind me (viz., Mr. Henry Marten) did bring in several votes upon the 9th day of this month,[12] one of which being the 4 or 5 in number was that such citizens as had spare arms by them might lend them to such volunteers and that satisfaction should be made them. And therefore I desire we may first know what further arms shall be needful before we pass this vote, and the rather because we have already disposed of a great part of them for the service of Ireland and to make good our promise to the Scots.[13]

Others spake after me, and in the issue the question was carried affirmatively that we should concur with the lords.

We appointed to meet at 9 of the clock tomorrow. The house rose about two of the clock in the afternoon.

GAWDY

[f. 164b]   Wednesday, the xx of July

Resolved by question, that all judges in their charges in their circuits shall declare the illegality of the commission of array.[14]

[Committee of the Whole House]

The house turned into a grand committee to take into consideration how money shall be provided to pay the Scots their brotherly assistance, being 80,000£.

The Speaker to the chair.

A message from the lords, they have received a letter from my Lord of Holland from Beverley, the 18 of July. Their admittance to his majesty was quick. There were not many lords there, being as is said gone to put the commission of array in execution. There were many officers. When the petition was read, his majesty said it was of great consequence. He observed some passages in the petition with sharpness. The king is not so strong as is reported in appearance. The reason they say there is [f. 165a] two, one because he expecteth our answer about Hull, the other because he would save charges, for they say he can be much stronger when he please, which I believe. The king

---

12. See D, 191–92.
13. See 19 July, n. 3.
14. For this order, which the house had ordered Wilde to formulate, see *CJ*, II, 681, 682.

gave them admittance so soon as he had supped, though it were late ere he came from Lincoln. The king is going to Leicester and Nottingham. I hope to set forward to you presently.

Another letter from Sir John Holland and Sir Philip Stapleton to us, the very same word for word that came to the lords from my Lord of Holland.

Resolved, that this letter shall be referred to the consideration of the committee for the defense of the kingdom.

The lords sent us word that they were ready to give sentence against the nine lords if we were ready to demand it, whereupon Mr. Speaker went up and demanded it.

My Lord Mandeville, being Speaker, called them and pronounced against them severally that they were excluded from having any votes in parliament during this parliament, to lose the privilege of parliament, and that they were ipso facto to be committed to the Tower. This I had from Mr. Noble, I being at dinner. The 9 lords were all absent.[15]

[f. 165b] A letter from my Lord of Thomond in Ireland, that they are there in great distress that are with him. That they eat horseflesh. Another from Sir John Clotworthy, that his men hath little but bread and water. They desire timely assistance. These letters were read before the impeachment of the lords.

15. Despite the ambiguity above, the lords indeed had "refused to appear." *LJ,* V, 223.

D'EWES

July 21, Thursday, 1642

Upon SIR THOMAS HELE's motion the petition of Dr. Dukeson, which he delivered in, was read, and in it he showed that he had stood committed about a fortnight since for offending this house, which he did unwillingly and ignorantly and was sorry for it, and was dismissed.

SIR SAMUEL ROLLE moved that some speedy course might be taken to secure the western coasts, for the Turkish pirates were very rife there. He then delivered in a letter dated at Plymouth July 18, 1642, sent to him from the mayor there, and MR. WADDON, one of the burgesses for the same town, delivered in another letter of the like date sent to him also from the same mayor, being named Thomas Ceely.

The said letter sent to Sir Samuel Rolle was first read, and in it was set forth in short the danger those western coasts were now in by reason of Turkish pirates, which appeared more fully by an enclosed examination which was read, being an examination of Ambrose Chappell, mariner of Redriffe,[1] who had been examined July 18, 1642, before Thomas Ceely, mayor of Plymouth, touching 3 Turkish pirates who had pursued a ship he was in twice or thrice and had taken another ship and that divers other Turkish pirates were coming to this coast.

The letter Mr. Waddon had delivered in, being sent to him from Mr. Thomas Ceely aforesaid, was dated at Plymouth also July 18, 1642, and in it he showed that he had received certain proclamations from his majesty which he did yet forbear to publish, though one Mr. Trelawney[2] advised him to proclaim them, with other particulars.

SIR HUGH OWEN showed that some Turkish pirates appeared about Milford Haven and had taken some ships lately there and so desired some course to be taken to secure those coasts. Mr. Waddon and others appointed to be a committee to consider of these informations.

MR. WADDON said 1500£ sent into the Chamber of London upon the propositions, that he hoped for 1500£ more, that 500£ was gathered for the contribution of Ireland, and that they had a godly minister, one Mr. Mark Paget, amongst them for whom they desired that a petition of his might be read in the house.

---

1. Possibly Redruth, Cornwall.
2. Perhaps Robert Trelawney, formerly MP for Plymouth, who had been disabled in March. See *PJ*, 2: 17–18.

[f. 284b] The petition of Mr. Mark Paget was read, in which he showed his great loss in Ireland and his numerous family now here and so desired some relief. After it was read, the SPEAKER asked what should be allowed him, and I proposed the sum of an 100£, which was allowed upon the question though some one or two besides proposed 50£, and Mr. Waddon was appointed to write to the mayor of Plymouth to pay the said 100£ to him out of the 500£ contribution there gathered.[3]

MR. NATHANIEL FIENNES made report from the committee appointed for the safety of the kingdom, that a National Assembly of the Church of Scotland was to meet on Tuesday next, and that therefore they thought fit to set out some declaration to satisfy that nation and all the world how desirous we were to have the effusion of Christian blood saved.

So the clerk read the said declaration,[4] which especially showed how much the parliament desired to have religion reformed but that the malignant party resisted it, consisting of papists and corrupt clergymen backed by the avarice and ambition of the bishops.

MR. ROUS moved to have "dissoluteness" added to "the avarice and ambition" of the bishops. Others spake to it. I moved in effect following:

That we might do well to bestow this other adjective upon the clergy, and I would have it come in after the word "corrupt" but not in the place where mention is made of the bishops. And then the sense will be very perfect when we call them "corrupt and dissolute clergy," for the first will relate [to] the errors of their judgments and the later to the wickedness of their lives, and we all see by common experience that those clergymen who have brought in those wicked tenants amongst (viz., the Arminians) are for the most part men of most scandalous lives. So the said word was added as I had moved, and the declaration passed upon the question.

The said Mr. Fiennes was sent up with the same declaration to desire the lords' concurrence with us in it and with another message or two.

MR. GREEN made report from the committee to which the bill concerning Sir Abraham Dawes's creditors [was referred][5] but was interrupted a little after he had begun by MR. DENZIL HOLLES, upon whose motion it was ordered that the inhabitants of Poole in Dorsetshire might have liberty to train their volunteers and to defend the magazine there under the command of one Captain Harwood.[6]

3. For Paget, rector of Marlestowne and dean of Ross in Co. Cork, see *PJ*, 2: 3. An order for paying him £100 appears in *LJ*, V, 233.
4. For the text see *LJ*, V, 229. A copy of the petition of peace was to be sent also. *CJ*, II, 684.
5. This much delayed bill, which had been referred to the committee for the customers, concerned the creditors of Sir Thomas Dawes, not his father Sir Abraham. See *PJ*, 2: 151.
6. Captain John Howard, in *CJ*, II, 684. For the order see *LJ*, V, 229.

MR. GREEN proceeded with the report and showed that the committee had made divers amendments in the said bill, which were twice read.

MR. GRIMSTON brought in a clause ready drawn in paper for 800£ to be paid to one Mr. Harvey,[7] a member of this house, which was also twice read and allowed, and then the bill with the several amendments was ordered to be engrossed.

Upon the motion of MR. ROUS Sir Samuel Rolle had liberty to go into the country by reason of his indisposition in health.

MR. CROMWELL brought in a copy of [a] letter to be sent by the Speaker to the lord justices of Ireland touching the assistance of the Lord Esmonde, who commanded the fort of Duncannon, which was allowed by the house.[8]

MR. ELLIS made report from the committee whom the house had appointed to consider of Captain William Booth's petition to his majesty, which is in print,[9] that the said committee had framed a declaration in answer to it, which was read and allowed. And then upon my motion it was ordered to be printed;[10] yet I only spake to the Speaker to put the question as I sat near him in my usual place.

[f. 285b] MR. NATHANIEL FIENNES made report from the lords that they concurred with us.[11]

MR. ELLIS moved that we might send up to the lords to desire them to command an habeas corpus to be sent for the two aldermen of Lincoln[12] who were [in] custody at York for the putting of the militia in execution. So Mr. Ellis was sent up to desire the same of them and with two other messages.

SIR NATHANIEL BARNARDISTON delivered in the information of Mr. Edward Colman and one Griggs against Mr. Frederick Gibb, parson of Hartest and Boxted in the county of Suffolk, which was that on Sunday was sevennight when he began to read the king's late declaration, he the said Mr. Colman told him publicly in the church that it was forbidden by the parliament. Yet the said Gibb proceeded with the reading of it and when he had done said he would maintain it with his life and blood. The said Colman and Griggs were called in

7. John Harvey was one of Dawes's creditors. *CJ*, II, 684.

8. Cromwell and Strode had been directed on 20 July to prepare this letter, requiring the lord justices to send a regiment of Leinster forces to Lord Esmonde. *CJ*, II, 683.

9. This committee had been named on 12 July to examine the truth of Booth's petition concerning his interrogation by the Lincolnshire committee on 8 June. See G, 13 June, and *CJ*, II, 667. For the petition and the king's response of 30 June, see Husbands, *Exact Collection*, pp. 384–86. Wing, B 3741.

10. For this declaration "in vindication of divers Members of their House from a false & scandalous Pamphlet," see Husbands, *Exact Collection*, pp. 479–81. Wing, E 2567.

11. In consequence, the declaration and the petition of peace were to be delivered to the Scots commissioners and thence to the General Assembly in Scotland. *LJ*, V, 228, 231.

12. I.e., Alderman William Watson and Sheriff Edward Emis (John Anys in *CJ*, II, 684). Cf. 18 July, n. 17. The lords subsequently ordered the clerk of the crown, Thomas Willis, to issue a habeas corpus. *LJ*, V, 227.

and witnessed the same, and after some debate it was ordered that the said Gibb should be sent for as a delinquent.[13]

Sir Robert Rich and Mr. Page, two masters of the Chancery, brought this message from the lords, that their lordships had received a declaration or certificate/

Sir Thomas Barrington and others were nominated a committee to consider of this certificate, and they were appointed to meet tomorrow in the afternoon.[14]

The high sheriff of Worcestershire,[15] who had been summoned upon Serjeant Wilde's information to appear before the house, came in and showed that he had sent forth warrants for the execution of the militia, and that when the copy of the commission of array came to him, he deferred it nine days before he did send out warrants to the high constables concerning it, with some other particulars with which the house received good satisfaction.

He being withdrawn, the Speaker had order to admonish him to be careful for the time to come but no way to reprehend him for anything that was past. The SPEAKER then told him that the house did further require of him to deliver in the copy of the instructions and the warrant which came to him from some of the commissioners for the said array, and then the SPEAKER did further require of him in the name of the house to take and safe convey up Mr. Sherrington Talbot, for whom a warrant was sent. The sheriff then delivered in the said copy of the instructions and the said warrant sent to him from the said commissioners, in which he was required to send out warrants to the high constables for divers trained bands to meet at Worcester on the 13 day of this instant July.

Then the clerk read the instructions sent to the commissioners for Worcestershire, of which Prince Charles was the first, and they were much milder than the commission of array itself and did mitigate several particulars in it.

MR. SERJEANT WILDE desired an addition to the committee for the Lady Sedley and brought in a note of divers names in paper which he desired might be added, but MR. CAGE (an old parliament man) stood up and spake to the orders of the house and showed that no man ought to bring in the names of a committee or an addition to a committee written in paper but that they ought to be named by the house, whereupon the paper of names was rejected by the house and an additional committee named by the house.

13. For reading the king's declaration concerning levies, Gibb was subsequently placed in the sergeant's custody and bailed on 5 October. See *Walker*, p. 335; and *CJ*, II, 789, 794.

14. D'Ewes was a member. The certificate from fifteen London aldermen indicated that there was no precedent for them to choose a locum tenens, as parliament had ordered, during the lord mayor's imprisonment. See 15 July, n. 9; and *CJ*, II, 684.

15. Edward Vernon. *Sheriffs*, p. 159.

MR. LISLE made report of certain votes which were passed by the committee appointed [f. 286b] to consider of the late scandalous Lincolnshire petition[16] which were three in number: The first, that the said petition was false, scandalous, and seditious, intending to set division between the king and the parliament. The second, that the contrivers of the said petition deserved exemplary punishment. The third, that Sir Edward Heron, now high sheriff of Lincolnshire, should be sent for as a delinquent. The first of these three particulars being put to the vote, divers spake to the second. The SPEAKER had put the affirmative when I stood up and spake in effect following:

That in respect the first vote had sufficiently branded this offense and that the third vote did particularly fix it upon the high sheriff of the county, I desired we might spare this second vote till he were sent for and examined. For he would either confess his fault or else he would impeach others to have been the contrivers of it, and then we might have a just ground to proceed against them. Whereas if this question should be now put, I did much fear it might receive a negative voice, and therefore I desire that we may either lay it aside or put the question whether the question shall be now put.

So this 2d vote was laid aside upon the question as I had moved, and the 3d vote for the sending for Sir Edward Heron, the sheriff, was allowed by the house.[17]

Upon the motion of MR. WALTER LLOYD the petition of Sergeant Major Vaughan was referred to Captain Chichester's committee. Another motion or two were ordered.

We appointed to meet at 9 of the clock tomorrow morning. We rose between 12 and 1 of the clock in the morning.

GAWDY

[f. 165b]   Thursday, the XXI of July

MR. FIENNES, a report from the committee for defense of the kingdom, that on Tuesday next there is an assembly in Scotland. 'Tis thought fit we should send thither the petition which we sent his majesty to Beverley for a pacification and a declaration to them to set forth the state of our condition.

SIR EDWARD AYSCOUGH, that one told him that came to town the last night

---

16. See 18 July, n. 1.

17. Impeachment proceedings against him were begun on 14 September, and on 8 October he was committed to the Tower. See *CJ,* II, 766, 801; and Hill, *Lincoln,* p. 152.

that there was on Saturday night last a fierce assault given to Hull, and though there were no dead bodies found, yet there was much blood seen.

Resolved, that this declaration is agreed unto to be sent to the Scots.

Resolved by question, that the lords be desired to join with [us] in this declaration to the Scots.

[f. 166a] Ordered, that the proclamations now in the post's hands going into Norfolk and Suffolk[18] be stayed.

MR. FIENNES, that the lords do agree with us in the declaration and a copy of the petition to be sent to the Scots assembly.

Resolved, that Mr. Gibb, a parson in Suffolk, shall be sent for as a delinquent for reading the king's declaration and for some speeches. The information preferred by Sir Nathaniel Barnardiston.

A message from the lords, that the aldermen of the City of London whose names are subscribed, that the aldermen hath never appointed a locum tenens in the absence of my lord mayor, but they have some precedents that my lord mayor in case of his sickness hath appointed a locum tenens, the sword still remaining with him.

Mr. Vernon, the sheriff of Worcestershire, at the bar for sending forth his warrant for the commission of array, for that he was slow in putting the militia in execution, saying the militia should be tears [sic].

He is called in and advised to execute the orders of both houses and so dismissed.

18. Also Essex. *CJ,* II, 684.

D'EWES

July 22, Friday, 1642

The Speaker came about nine of the clock.

MR. CROMWELL moved whilst the declaration was in reading[1] that the committee which was this day to manage the evidence against the lord mayor might withdraw and prepare themselves for it, which Serjeant Wilde and the rest of them did accordingly.[2]

The clerk then proceeded with reading the said declaration till a message came to the door.

Sir Robert Rich and Dr. Heath, two masters of the Chancery, brought this message from the lords, that the lord mayor was ready attending there, and that they intended to proceed with the trial against him and so desired that some of our members might attend. They being withdrawn, we agreed that they should go.

MR. ROUS moved that a scandalous pamphlet was come out this morning against certain observations which had been before printed.[3] So it was referred to the committee for printing to consider.

The messengers were again called in, and the SPEAKER made report to them that the house would send up some of their members to attend the said/[4]

The clerk then proceeded with the reading of the declaration till he was interrupted by MR. HENRY MARTEN, who made report from the committee for the defense of the kingdom, that they had understood of certain practices in hatching at the next assizes in Kent and had therefore thought fit to send down divers of the members of this house for that county to be present at the said assizes, which were to begin there tomorrow morning. Sir Edward Hales and the rest of them were particularly named. So the clerk having read the order or resolution of the committee voted it here.[5]

1. This was apparently a new declaration in response to the king's message and proclamation concerning Hull, even though it had been decided that the petition of peace was an adequate answer. See 14 July, n. 7.

2. See 19 July, n. 15.

3. The pamphlet, entitled *Animadversions upon those notes which the late Observator hath published,* was in response to a pamphlet by Henry Parker (the Observator) entitled *Observations upon some of his Majesties late answers and expresses. CJ,* II, 685. Wing, A 3209, P 412. *DNB* for Parker.

4. For proceedings at the lord mayor's trial, see *LJ,* V, 230–31.

5. For the order see *CJ,* II, 686. Those named to attend the assizes were MPs for either Kent or the Cinque Ports plus both Sir Henry Vanes. Sir Peter Wroth of Bexley, Kent, should be added to the sixteen names in *CJ,* according to Woods, *Prelude,* p. 192.

MR. CROMWELL made report that he had carried up the message yesterday touching the letter to be sent to the justices touching the sending of forces to the aid of the Lord Esmonde, that he had delivered the said letter, and that the lords' answer was that they would send an answer by messengers of their own.

Then upon SIR WALTER ERLE's motion and others seconding it, Sir Gerard Napier and divers other western gentlemen were sent for out of the country to attend the house and Mr. Kirkby out of Lancashire.[6] Some moved to have the lawyers of the house sent for up also, but I desired that we might give them liberty till the circuits were ended, for it was great reason that they should have some good means to furnish their purses as we had formerly their help here. SIR ROBERT PYE seconded me, and so the matter went no further.

Sir Robert Rich and Dr. Heath brought down the copy of the letter we had sent up to them touching forces to be sent to the aid of the Lord Esmonde, to which they had assented with some alteration, and so they withdrew and departed. We after one or two had spoken to the same amendment assented to it.[7]

The Kentish gentlemen withdrew to draw instructions for their going into Kent.

Upon SIR ROBERT HARLEY's motion Mr. Robert Goodwin had leave to go down to Sussex assizes to a trial which he was to have there.

[f. 289a] MR. TRENCHARD showed/[8]

The declaration was proceeded withal, and some spake to it.[9]

SIR HENRY VANE brought in instructions to be given to the committee to go into Kent.[10]

SIR WILLIAM LEWIS desired that an order might pass to hinder the execution of the commission of array in Hampshire, and so he tendered/[11]

Upon SERJEANT WILDE's motion Sir Thomas Widdrington had leave to go into the country.

[f. 289b] MR. PYM delivered in a letter sent unto him out of Somersetshire from Mr. John Pyne, a member of the house, bearing date July 18, 1642, but the name of the place the clerk could not well read,[12] in which he showed that there

---

6. For the names of the absent MPs, see G, below, and *CJ*, II, 685.

7. For the letter to the lord justices concerning Esmonde, see *LJ*, V, 245.

8. Trenchard, Harley, and Bedingfield were to "treat with the Merchant Adventurers, about the Forbearance" of £40,000, part of the £70,000 which they were to receive out of money coming in from the bill for £400,000. *CJ*, II, 685.

9. The reading of the declaration was to be continued the next day. *CJ*, II, 685.

10. Augustine Skinner, one of the committee, was ordered to have all the instructions "in a readiness." See *CJ*, II, 685, 686–87. For proceedings omitted by D'Ewes, see G, below, and *CJ*, II, 685–86.

11. For the order see *CJ*, II, 686.

12. Pyne, one of the committee named to go to Somerset, was from Curry Mallet. See 19 July, n. 9; *LJ*, V, 226; and Keeler, p. 319.

was great endeavoring in that county to gain it for the king against the parliament and that there were 700 horse promised the king out of the same, which he thought was more than the county could yield or afford. Neither did he doubt but that divers of the gentry and generally all the yeomanry stood well affected to the parliament. That he was informed that [there] were some intentions for the seizing upon himself and the keeping of him in safe custody, but he knew no offense that he was guilty of. That he was further informed of a new oath which was framed and was to be sent into that county and imposed upon all men to take to assist the king against the parliament, which would reduce this kingdom to a miserable condition. That he had received two informations from two very honest neighbors of his which he had sent enclosed, and there were contained in the said letter some other particulars of lesser moment.

The clerk then read the first of the said informations, in which he showed that the Lord Poulett and Sir Francis Hawley were providing horse to be sent to the king out of that county and that the Lord Digby's horses were in readiness to be sent away (viz., from Sherborne in Dorsetshire).[13] Then the clerk read the second information, in which there was a discovery that generally the yeomanry of the county of Somerset were well affected to the parliament, and that if there were but a standing committee sent down to be there, it would be a great comfort and an encouragement to the country. These particulars being read, the further consideration of them was referred to the committee of lords and commons that was appointed for the defense of the kingdom.[14]

MR. GREEN delivered in a letter drawn by the committee to whom the informations touching the Turkish pirates that had appeared upon the western coasts in England and near Milford Haven in Wales, which letter was to be sent to the Earl of Warwick that he might send some ships for the relief of the said coasts.

We appointed to meet at 9 of the clock tomorrow morning. We rose about two of the clock in the afternoon.

Post Meridiem

Towards the evening I went into the first inner Court of Wards, where the committee touching the Lady Sedley, of which I was one, sat. The debate was by what means we might give her reparations from Mr. John Griffith, the younger, who had in a most barbarous manner attempted her chastity. We all

13. Three troops of horse under Sir Ralph Hopton, John Digby, and Sir Francis Hawley were hastily assembled. Underdown, *Somerset,* p. 32. For Hawley see *Roy. Off.,* p. 182. Lord Poulett was father to Sir John Poulett, MP, who was among those summoned on this day.

14. On 19 July Alexander Popham had been given leave to execute the militia ordinance in Somerset. It was now ordered that ammunition, expert commanders, and commissions to raise volunteers should be sent into the county. *CJ,* II, 680, 686.

conceived that by the law now in force we could not sufficiently give her reparations, his father being alive and he himself being fled. So it was proposed that there should be a bill drawn either for his perpetual banishment or to question his life or otherwise, but the committee adjourned itself between 6 and 7 of the clock in the evening to the same place Tuesday next in the afternoon and concluded nothing thereupon at this time.

GAWDY

[f. 166b]   Friday, the XXII of July

An answer to a declaration of his majesty's, which he set forth concerning Hull, read.

A message from the lords, that my lord mayor is attending above, this being the day appointed for his trial. They desire us to send up some members of our house to manage the evidence. 'Tis assented to.

MR. MARTEN, a report from the committee for defense, that some ill affected in the county of Kent intend to divulge something of this house that is scandalous at the assizes. It is therefore ordered that many of the knights and burgesses of Kent shall go down to the assizes and prevent all such scandals and to secure the peace of that county.

Ordered, that Sir John Poulett, Sir John Stawell, Mr. Smith,[15] Sir Nicholas Slanning,[16] Sir Bevil Grenville, Sir Edward Rodney, Sir John Strangways, Mr. Rogers,[17] Sir Gerard Napier, Mr. Kirkby, Mr. Coventry, Mr. Strangways, [f. 167a] and Serjeant Hyde shall be sent for to do their service in this house.[18]

A message from the lords, they have sent us down the letter which is to be sent to the Earl of Esmonde, with some little amendments which they have consented to.

SIR GILBERT GERARD, a report that of 416 horses that should be listed by members of the House of Commons, but 61 of them are listed.

Ordered, that the members of this house that have subscribed for any horses shall list them on Tuesday or before in Moorfields.

15. Doubtless Thomas Smith, MP for Bridgwater, Somerset, who had previously been summoned on 5 May. See *PJ*, 2: 280.

16. Stoury, in *CJ*, II, 685.

17. Doubtless Richard Rogers, MP for Dorset. "Mr. Rose" is also included in the *CJ* list. Richard Rose, in contrast to the others, was a parliamentarian and had been granted leave on 1 June to go to the country. *CJ*, II, 597. Cf. Appendix G, n. 2.

18. Each of these men was eventually disabled. See Appendix A; and Brunton and Pennington, *Members,* pp. 218, 221–22.

Ordered, that of Mr. Thomas Moore an 100£ shall be accepted of instead of his two horses because one of them is fallen lame.

Ordered, that Mr. Phelipps be sent for to do his service here.

Ordered, that the committee for defense take order that some volunteers may be armed to keep the county of Somerset may be preserved in peace.

[f. 167b] Ordered, that those members that are sent for that went without leave shall pay the sergeant for his pains.

D'EWES

July 23, Saturday, 1642

The Speaker came about 9 of the clock. Prayers being ended between 9 and 10, MR. GREEN delivered in a letter sent to himself and the rest of the committee for the navy bearing date at Scarborough July 16, 1642,[1] being sent from one Mr. John Stevens, master of one of the London ships now under the command of the Earl of Warwick, in which he showed that he stayed a ship going towards York with divers stamps and other materials for coining, and that he had stayed it. So the house voted that the said Mr. Stevens had done well in that particular in staying the said particulars, and the committee was appointed to examine some of the officers in the mint[2] and the customers about it.

The clerk proceeded with the reading of the long and tedious declaration (which Mr. Nathaniel Fiennes had brought in yesterday)[3] where he then left until he was interrupted by MR. REYNOLDS, who made report from the committee appointed to consider how the matter for the present parliament in Ireland stood[4] and showed that they had perused divers commissions granted to the Earl of Strafford, formerly lieutenant of Ireland, and since. That by one commission granted since to Sir William[5] Parsons and Sir John[6] Borlase, the two lord justices of Ireland were authorized to adjourn or continue the parliament there as they should think fit. That since there was a commission granted to Robert, Earl of Leicester, lord lieutenant of Ireland, without any direction concerning the parliament. That the committee doubted by his coming into Ireland whether or no the justices' power would not be determined, and therefore they had drawn the form of a new commission to be sent speedily to York after the said lord lieutenant who was going thither,[7] by which the power of continuing or adjourning the said parliament might be granted to him before his going thither, which commission was read. Divers spake to it. I moved in effect following:

---

1. The date is 15 July in *CJ*, II, 687.

2. Particularly Nicolas Briot, the king's engraver, who had been ordered on 21 June "to repair at once to York, bringing with him all his instruments for coining money." He apparently followed the king to both York and Oxford. *CSPD, 1641–43*, pp. 344, 347. *DNB*.

3. See 22 July, nn. 1, 9.

4. See 19 July, n. 13.

5. MS: *John*.

6. MS: *William*.

7. On 21 July the lords had granted Leicester leave to go to his charge in Ireland. *LJ*, V, 227.

That I was very confident that the granting of the commission to the Earl of Leicester, now lord lieutenant of Ireland, did not determine the former authority given to the lord justices there of adjourning or continuing this parliament as they should think fit, because that is a royal power vested in the crown and cannot be transferred to the lord lieutenant but by special words. If I forget not, about the 5 year of H. 5 there was a *custos regni*[8] appointed here, and yet there was a commission granted to several persons to adjourn, continue, and dissolve the parliament. And therefore though I am not against the passing of this new commission for the greater surety, yet I am confident that there is no necessity of it.

Others spake after me, and in the issue it was recommitted that some clauses might be amended in it.[9]

Mr. Nicholas made report that he had yesterday performed the several messages upon which he was sent up to the lords and that the lords concurred with us in all.[10]

Mr. Henry Marten moved that we might send up to the lords to know of them whether the Earl of Leicester had granted out his commission for deputy lieutenants for the county of Kent as we had desired or not.[11] Divers spake to it, and at last the house was divided upon it whether we should put the question for sending up or not. Ayes 43, stayed within. Sir William Lewis and Mr. Henry Marten. Noes 89. Mr. Nathaniel Fiennes and Mr. Carew.[12] I one. We went out. Thereupon it was ordered that no question should be put.

Sir Robert Rich and Mr. Page, etc., brought this message from the lords, that their lordships sent us word that Captain Slingsby and Captain Wake were sent up in safe custody, and that if we intended to prefer any impeachment against them, they desired that we would do it speedily,[13] and that their lordships intended to sit at three of the clock in the afternoon and desired this house to sit then also if it might stand with our conveniency. So they withdrew, and we agreed to send an answer to the first part of their message by messengers of our

---

8. "Guardian of the kingdom." Probably a reference to Henry V's appointment of the Duke of Bedford in 1417 as the king's lieutenant while he was in France. See Stubbs, *Constitutional History,* III, 91–93.

9. Subsequently the commission was amended and approved by both houses. *CJ,* II, 687, 689. For the text see *LJ,* V, 234–35.

10. For his various messages see *LJ,* V, 231.

11. See G, 16 July. On 21 July Leicester had informed the lords that he had not yet appointed his deputy lieutenants and threatened that if commanded to, he might deliver up his commission as lord lieutenant of Kent. *LJ,* V, 227.

12. Carew was teller for the Ayes, Lewis for the Noes, according to *CJ,* II, 687.

13. On 19 July the lords had received a letter from the Earl of Warwick concerning Slingsby and Wake. Their examination was now referred to the committee for the navy, and on 30 July the lords committed both men to the Gatehouse. See *CJ,* II, 687; and *LJ,* V, 218–19, 249.

own and to sit again at 3 of the clock as they had desired, which the SPEAKER reported to them being again called in.

[f. 291b] I withdrew out of the house about 12 of the clock and returned a little while after. This long, impertinent, and dangerous declaration was then read through, and one was speaking unto it as I came into the house. Divers fiery spirits then called to the question and the Speaker was standing up to put it, which made me ask him sitting near him what question he meant to put. He answered me whether it should pass or[14] not.

Whereupon I stood up and spake in effect following, being extremely provoked at their unjust and violent proceeding: That I conceived it to be against the constant order and use of the house to put this declaration, being of so great length, to the question before we had given it a second reading and spoken to it by parcels, for the use hath been, as we have often seen it observed by the worthy gentleman at the bar (viz., Mr. Pym), that the reporter should first read what the committee hath drawn and then the clerk to read it twice. But the gentleman who brought in this declaration (viz., Mr. Nathaniel Fiennes), though he hath amongst his other good parts an able voice, yet hath omitted that performance, and therefore there is the greater reason that the house should give it a second reading. Besides I am very much afraid that a great part of this declaration is already printed in a pamphlet of observations[15] and that part of it also is confuted in print by him that hath answered that observator,[16] and therefore that also may be well examined and weighed before we pass it, for it would be much to the dishonor of this house to put out that for their declaration which is already to be had in a published pamphlet and so be taken out of a budget or a pocket. And though I will not speak to any particular passage in it, yet this much I must add, that in one place it doth lay a scandal upon Queen Elizabeth's reign.[17]

I have entered this speech at large so far as I could call it to memory that so posterity to come may see that when those furious spirits of the House of

14. MS: *it*.

15. D'Ewes's reference is to Henry Parker's *Observations*. See 22 July, n. 3. The fact that Nathaniel Fiennes, who was Parker's cousin, and other "fiery spirits" reacted with much sensitivity to D'Ewes's charge seems to confirm the connection between the pamphlet and the committee's declaration. Parker subsequently became secretary to the committee of safety. See Greaves and Zaller, *Dictionary of British Radicals*, III, 7–9.

16. The pamphlet entitled *Animadversions upon . . . the late Observator.*

17. The pamphlet states: "Without question Queene Elizabeth might do that which a Prince lesse beloved could never have done. . . . without doubt had her goodnesse and Grace been fained, shee might have usurped an uncontroleable arbitrary lawlesse Empire over us." Parker, *Observations*, p. 7. D'Ewes, who had written favorably of Queen Elizabeth in his *Compleat Journal*, was offended by this aspersion.

Commons were irritated with my freedom of expression that had for about four months' space last past resisted (and often also alone without being seconded by any who were most of them overawed, as the king hath well set out in some of his late declarations and answers) their bitter and irreverential language towards his majesty and their fierce and hot preparations for a civil war, they took this frivolous and unjust occasion to call in question what I said at this time.

The first fiery tongue that fell upon me was one MR. WILLIAM STRODE, a notable profaner of the Scriptures and a man doubtless void of all truth of piety (whose vanity I had several times of late reproved publicly), and he said that I had offered wrong to the committee[18] whom the house had entrusted in laying an aspersion upon them, as if they had transcribed this declaration out of a pamphlet in print, and therefore desired that I might explain myself.

Whereupon I stood up and said: That if the gentleman who last spake had but observed as well the whole as that part of that which I had said, he would have spared this exception, for I did not charge the committee to have taken it out of the said printed pamphlet but only that I feared much of it was already there in print, which I did desire and still do desire that it may be well examined before we pass this declaration.

But notwithstanding the just apology I had made, divers of the violent and fiery spirits called upon me to withdraw, and one MR. CAREW, my formerly seeming friend, and MR. NATHANIEL FIENNES and MR. DENZIL HOLLES, a proud, ambitious man, took other frivolous exceptions at what I had said, which I thought not worth the answering but rather chose to withdraw into the committee chamber, although MR. WALLER stood up and offered to speak against my withdrawing. Divers cried that I should not withdraw, and some catched at my cloak to stay me as I went along towards the committee chamber.[19]

[f. 292b] After I was withdrawn, these fiery spirits (though I had always concurred with them, hoping that their profession of religion, at least of some of them, was unfeigned, and oftentimes held up their cause ever since the beginning of the parliament except in the matter of the triennial bill[20] and their last

18. The committee of safety, of which Fiennes, Holles, and Marten were all members, had been ordered to prepare an answer to the king's message and proclamation concerning Hull. See 13 July, n. 16; and *CJ*, II, 651, 659.

19. The following account appears in *CJ*, II, 687–88:

Exceptions were taken at some Words spoken by Sir Simonds D'Ewes, before the passing of this Declaration: Which laid Aspersions and Imputations upon the Committee that brought in this Declaration; viz. "That there were many Things in this Declaration, that were taken out of other Mens Pockets and Budgets, and before printed," and he was thereby commanded to withdraw.

20. See Notestein, pp. 264–65.

four months' violent preparations for a civil war) grew ashamed to execute their malice against me to the full, which at first I verily believe they had intended; for I expected nothing less than that, having caused most unjustly to withdraw, they would either have sent me prisoner to the Tower or discomposed me out of the house. But God who restrained the devil in the case of Job did so far overawe them as, though the said Strode and Holles and one Mr. Henry Marten (whom I had once or twice brought off in the house, being questioned),[21] for indiscreet words which deserved a reproof far better than mine, did vent their scurrilous and windy wit upon me, yet the house agreed to have me speedily called down again and to express an acknowledgment in my place for what I had said and that the Speaker should admonish me for it.

Being thereupon called down to my place and standing up, the SPEAKER told me that the house took offense at what I had said and therefore expected from me that I should acknowledge my fault and my sorrow for it, but I, knowing the integrity and uprightness of mine own heart and how unjustly I had been questioned, spake in effect following:

Sir, I did in that which I spake this morning touching this declaration speak my conscience freely as at other times for the service of the house, so as from the matter of what I spake I hope that no offense could arise, having no intention to cast any blemish upon the committee. But if in the manner of the delivery of it I have erred and the house have taken offense thereat and require me to express my sorrow for it, I think it very fit that I should do so, being sorry for it.[22]

Having thus spoken, I sat down in my place and did put on my hat. Whereupon that firebrand STRODE, who had first taken exception at what I had spoken, stood up and said that he was altogether unsatisfied with what I had done, for I had rather justified myself in what I had delivered than acknowledged any fault, in which his malicious heart did dictate rightly indeed to his tongue; but MR. NATHANIEL FIENNES stood up and did very nobly express himself, saying that I had spoken enough to satisfy the house in saying that I was sorry, and so the said Strode's malicious motion came to nothing.

The SPEAKER then spake to me again, and I stood up, and told that the house

---

21. Crossed out in MS: *like a monster.*
22. The *CJ* account continues:

Resolved, upon the Question, That Sir Simonds D'Ewes shall ask the Committee Pardon, for the Imputation he has laid upon the Committee by these Words; and the Offence that he has done to the House thereby: And that he should acknowledge his Offence.

Resolved, upon the Question, That Sir Simonds D'Ewes shall, in his Place, receive a Reprehension for it.

Sir Simonds D'Ewes was then called down; and did, in his Place, acknowledge his said Offence; and expressed his Sorrow for it.

took it worse from me in respect of my great learning and knowledge (such were the words he used) that I should speak anything which might trench upon the actions of a committee than they would have done from another man because the actions of the committee were derived from the authority of the house, with some other words to the like effect, and so I sat down again in my place and continued there till the house rose.[23]

Then the house proceeded with the debate of the said declaration, and MR. PLEYDELL said that there were many curses in this declaration against many persons but never an one against the king's enemies. Whereupon MR. DENZIL HOLLES stood up and would have had him questioned for it, saying that he had spoken it with a malicious intention, but some of the more sober men of the house declined any further questionings at this time, and so in the issue the declaration passed upon the question,[24] and we further voted that we should desire the lords to join with us in it and so rose between 12 and one of the clock.[25]

(This horrible ingratitude for all my services and injustice towards me proceeding from divers who professed religion made me resolve to leave off further writing and speaking in the house and to come as seldom amongst them as I could, seeing liberty of speech was taken away, hoping to spend my time much better upon my invaluable studies. Nay divers of these men, forgetting the solemn Protestation they had made before God to preserve the privileges of parliament, would have excused this vast injury done unto me by affirming that they did it only to be merry with me. Others who abhorred this action of theirs observed that by my vindicating and justifying myself after my return from the committee chamber, they received more dishonor by questioning me than if they had been silent when the king, etc., as in *fratris codicillis*.[26] What I wrote after this day I never took any note of it in the house but wrote it out of my memory after my coming home to my lodging.)[27]

---

23. The *CJ* account concludes:

Then Mr. Speaker did reprehend him in his Place; and admonished him to be more careful of his Expressions hereafter; and to be careful hereafter not to lay any Imputations upon any particular Member; much less upon any Committee, that, being employed in the Service of the House, shall bring any thing into the House.

24. Actually it was ordered that the declaration should be recommitted "as to that Part concerning the Accursings, and the People saying Amen," and that it should be brought in again in the afternoon. *CJ*, II, 688.

25. For the rest of the day, see G, below, and *CJ*, II, 688–89.

26. "From the codicil of a brother."

27. The last sentence, which must have been added later, is written upside down at the top of the folio. Though D'Ewes continued to attend the house briefly on most days, he did not speak again until 27 August.

GAWDY

[f. 167b]   Saturday, the xxiii of July

An information from Scarborough, that they have taken some minting tools going to York.

Resolved, that the master of the ship hath done well in staying these tools.

The declaration to the kingdom in answer to his majesty's declaration concerning Hull reading the second time.

A commission sent up to the lords concerning my Lord of Leicester his lieutenancy in Ireland, who goeth towards Ireland this day.

The house divided whether my Lord of Leicester shall grant his deputations in Kent before his going into Ireland. The Noes that went out that would not have him grant them, of which I was, was 89. The Ayes that stayed in were 43.

A message from the lords, that if we intend to have any impeachment against Captain Slingsby and Captain Wake, to do [f. 168a] it speedily. They desire we would sit at 3 a clock.

For the first part of the message we will send an answer by messengers of our own. For the 2 we will sit at 3 a clock.

Sir Simonds D'Ewes is commanded to withdraw for laying an aspersion upon the committee for the declaration in saying they had part of it out of other men's pockets.

Resolved, that Sir Simonds D'Ewes shall acknowledge his fault, committed to the committee.

Resolved, that he shall have a reprehension in his place.

Sir Simonds D'Ewes acknowledgeth his offense to the committee.

Mr. Speaker giveth Sir Simonds D'Ewes a reprehension.

The declaration is recommitted.

In the afternoon.

A letter from my Lord of Warwick, the 21 of July,[28] that the ships of the king's are in good case except 3. That care be taken if they be called home, they may not be employed against us, as likewise for the merchants' ships. He referreth all to this house that sitteth at the helm. He heareth there be 3 Turkish pirates[29] in the west country coasts.

[f. 168b] Resolved, that the merchants' ships shall be victualed for 2 months longer, as likewise so many of the king's ships as shall not be called in.

Resolved, that the committee for the defense of the kingdom shall consider how many of the king's ships shall be called in.

---

28. For this letter, in response to the Speaker's letter of 20 July, see *HMC, Fifth Report*, p. 39.
29. I.e., "three Turks men-of-war . . . each of 30 or 40 pieces of ordnance."

Resolved, that this shall be the declaration.

Resolved, that the lords be desired to join with us in this declaration.[30]

SIR JOHN HOLLAND, a report of the king's message.[31] That on Saturday my Lord of Holland found my Lord of Newport to help him to prefer the petition.[32] My Lord of Holland told the king that he was come to offer him a petition of peace. The petition was read. He said it was of consequence. He said he had been robbed, he sought his own. He said 'twas like a pill well gilded. They came not to court till Tuesday night, when his majesty sent for them and delivered the message which was read by Mr. Walker.[33] He demand an answer by Wednesday. In the meantime nothing shall be done against Hull if they of Hull be quiet.

[f. 169a] The message: Complaineth of the commitment of my lord mayor and the making my Lord of Essex general and the voting to live and die with him in defense of those the parliament have employed. That he was driven from Whitehall for safety of his life. Then he mention the militia and the taking of Hull. He will remove his force from Hull when that is done for which they were brought thither. He justifieth the commission of array. That there is a declaration coming forth to that end. He complaineth of the tumults. He professeth to protect those that have lent him money and such like. He requireth Hull, and he will give a general pardon to all there. That the magazine be delivered to whom he shall appoint. That the navy be delivered up. That arms be laid down. That the parliament be adjourned to some other place. These being granted, he protests before God to lay down all arms. He expecteth an answer on Wednesday next.

SIR PHILIP STAPLETON, that they had no answer for the bill of tonnage and poundage nor for the bill of pluralities.[34] [f. 169b] That the king's horse he taketh to be near 2000, his foot not above 400.[35] They perform their duties unwillingly.

A message from the lords, they concur with us concerning the declaration of

30. There is, however, no further mention of this declaration in either *CJ* or *LJ*. It may have been incorporated in the new declaration initiated on 25 July in response to the king's latest message.

31. For the earlier report of the king's response to the petition of peace, see 20 July, n. 2. The new message, to which the king expected an answer by 27 July, appears in *LJ*, V, 235–37.

32. The Earl of Holland and the Earl of Newport were half brothers. *DNB*.

33. Perhaps Edward Walker, who held various posts in the College of Arms, accompanied the king to York and in September became the king's secretary at war. *DNB*. The king's answer was "read aloud in the king's presence, and a full room, by the clerk of the council," according to [Clarendon], *Life*, I, 134.

34. Neither bill received the royal assent. See *LJ*, V, 211, 234. For the complete history of the bill against pluralities, see Shaw, *English Church*, I, 110–12.

35. The Earl of Holland reported that the king had 3000 foot and 300 horse at his command. *LJ*, V, 234.

my Lord of Stamford.[36] They send us a warrant which the king granted to apprehend my Lord of Stamford and to seize on the magazine in Leicestershire.[37]

MR. MORLEY, that we se[e] what preparations are made against us. That the committee for defense may take care for our security.

MR. MARTEN, that we have the strength at sea. That we have the City and we have the hearts of the people, who are ready whensoever we shall hold up our finger.

Ordered, that the king's message shall be taken into consideration on Monday morning.

[f. 170a] Resolved by question, that my Lord of Essex shall be desired to levy forces with all speed and vigor for the defense of the king and parliament and the Protestant religion. The lords voted the same at the same time, as it appeared when they came to the conference about it, which caused some laughing. This I had from Mr. Rushworth and others, for I came away a little before but after the king's message was read.[38]

36. The declaration concerning his indemnity. See 7 July, n. 14.

37. The king's warrant of 25 June, directed to Henry Hastings as high sheriff of Leicestershire, appears in *LJ*, V, 232. For an account by Secretary Nicholas of the king's being "gladsomly received by above 10,000 of the gentry" in Leicestershire, see *CSPD, 1641–43*, p. 362. Cf. 20 July, n. 3.

38. This resolution and the subsequent conference, which was reported by Holles, were prompted by the king's message. *CJ*, II, 689.

D'EWES

July 25, Monday, 1642

The Speaker came about 9 of the clock. Prayers being ended between 9 and 10, MR. RIGBY delivered in a letter sent to himself from one Mr. Newton in Lancashire, which was dated at Manchester July 18, 1642,[1] in which he showed at large that the late tumult at Manchester proceeded from the Lord Strange his coming thither with a guard of horse with pistols and other weapons, who first began the assault upon them that stood for the ordinance of parliament touching the militia, and that divers were wounded by them, of which one was since dead and another like to die. That a coroner's inquest had since found one of the said horsemen to have killed him that died, and divers other particulars. MR. RIGBY then made a long discourse touching the same matters and showed that one Mr. Kirkby, a member of this house, being one of the knights of the shire for Lancashire, was one of the commissioners for the said commission of array and did join in the execution of the same, which he said Mr. John Moore could justify. The said MR. JOHN MOORE then stood up and said that he had indeed heard that the said Mr. Kirkby was put into the commission of array but did not know that he did at all execute it.[2]

Mr. Reynolds was sent up to the lords of a message about eleven of the clock in the forenoon, with whom I went out of the house but went not up with him with the said message, which was to desire the lords that arms might be sent after the Earl of Leicester, lord lieutenant of Ireland, having now begun to take his journey towards that kingdom.[3]

At this time that I stayed in the house, I neither spake to any business nor

1. The letter described "Passages at Manchester on Saturday last." *CJ,* II, 689. However, the disturbances actually occurred on Friday, 15 July. For details see Broxap, *Lancashire,* pp. 16–20.

2. A committee was named "to examine the Proceedings of the . . . Commissions of Array, and of their Adherents." *CJ,* II, 689.

3. In mid-August both houses agreed to request Leicester, who was still at York, to proceed toward Ireland by 25 August. Yet on 9 September Leicester wrote from Nottingham to the Earl of Northumberland that he had continually beseeched the king to dispatch him, but to no avail. Two letters from Sir John Temple, master of the rolls in Ireland, reveal that in late December Leicester was still in England, ostensibly because of the weather, and that in mid-January 1643 he was summoned to attend the king at Oxford. In fact, he never did go to Ireland. See *CJ,* II, 721; *LJ,* V, 294, 358–59; and *HMC, De L'Isle and Dudley MSS,* VI, 413, 416–17. Wing, L 967.

wrote anything in respect of the breach of freedom of parliament which I suffered in for speaking on Saturday last.[4]

After my going out of the house divers things were agitated, but the chief was the taking into consideration his majesty's answer (which is in print)[5] to the late petition of both houses presented to him by the Earl of Holland and two members of our house, upon which followed a long debate.[6] MR. WALLER,[7] SIR JOHN POTTS, and others speaking for an accommodation to be had with his majesty and that a civil war might be avoided, but MR. DENZIL HOLLES, MR. STRODE, and other fiery spirits would not hear of it, so as in the issue a debate being taken up the second time, it was voted that they could not yield to his majesty at this time in what he required saving their trust to the kingdom. It was further voted that a declaration should be drawn up to satisfy the kingdom.[8]

The house appointed to meet at 9 of the clock tomorrow morning and rose about 2 of the clock in the afternoon.

GAWDY

[f. 170a]   Monday, the xxv of July

MR. RIGBY, that at Manchester there is a man killed and another sore hurt by the side that put the commission of array in execution.

One at the bar averreth that 3 men were committed by Justice Stampe of Hackney for offering to serve my lord general for defense of the king and parliament.

Resolved, that the vicar of Stepney[9] [and] Walmsley, the constable, shall be sent for as delinquents for attacking the 3 men.

4. For proceedings omitted by D'Ewes, see G, below, and *CJ*, II, 689–90.

5. See 23 July, n. 31. Wing, C 2091. The printed version is merely a summary of the king's answer to the petition of peace.

6. On 27 July Secretary Nicholas wrote from Beverley to Sir Thomas Roe: "We understand [the king's answer] is not at all relished, as we hoped it might have been, and that thereupon the preparations there for war are eagerly pursued." *CSPD, 1641–43*, p. 362.

7. Waller, one of the Cavalier poets, remained in the house in order to further the king's cause until imprisoned and disabled following his unsuccessful plot of June 1643. See Samuel R. Gardiner, *History of the Great Civil War, 1642–1649* (London, 1893), I, 7, 89, 146, 158.

8. For the votes see also *CJ*, II, 690. An answer to the king and "a Declaration to the People" were to be prepared by the committee of safety. See 23 July, n. 30.

9. William Stampe, the vicar, aided by William Walmsley, had interfered with the enlisting of volunteers in the Stepney churchyard. On 28 July the house referred the affair to the committee for scandalous ministers. Stampe was subsequently imprisoned in the Gatehouse, and Walmsley was bailed. See *CJ*, II, 690, 695, 703; and Walker, p. 58. *DNB* for William Stampe.

Resolved, that Justice Stampe and Gray,[10] the constable, shall be summoned.

[f. 170b] Resolved, that Justice Swallow shall call the 3 fellows before him committed by Justice Stampe and bail them.

A message from the lords, that they are ready to proceed against my lord mayor if we be ready. 'Tis assented to.[11]

The king's message was read.

MR. GODOLPHIN[12] moveth to take the king's message into consideration. He is for an accommodation.

MR. PYM, that the same jealousies still remain. That the king is still ruled by the same counsels. That we should go on with the levies we agreed on on Saturday.[13]

MR. MARTEN, that there be a declaration made to the people that we have petitioned for peace but 'tis denied us but upon such conditions as is worse than war. That though the king be king of the people of England, yet he is not master of the people of England.

[f. 171a] MR. LONG will as soon come with a halter about his neck as yield to those things that are propounded. He desire the committee for defense may provide for our safety.

SIR JOHN HOLLAND, that there is no security but in the actual going on with your preparation. He thinketh it fit we should give the world satisfaction that we desire peace. He would go on with the bill of the militia, which will make an end of all differences.[14]

Resolved by question, that in respect of the trust the country hath reposed in us, we cannot consent to his majesty's propositions. This I had from Mr. Cage and Mr. Rushworth while I was at dinner.

10. Cray in *CJ*. For Timothy Stampe, justice of the peace, see *Middlesex County Records,* III (London, 1888), 174.

11. For the proceedings see *LJ,* V, 239–40.

12. Probably Sidney Godolphin.

13. For the resolution to levy forces, see G, 23 July.

14. However, the bill apparently went no further.

D'EWES

July 26, Tuesday, 1642

The Speaker came about 9 of the clock in the morning. After prayers and some motions of little moment, a messenger[1] that was come out of Lancashire, who had been with the lords, came into the house and made a long narration concerning the late tumult or affray that had happened at the town of Manchester in the said county between the Lord Strange, who came to execute the commission of array, and some of the deputy lieutenants appointed by the Lord Wharton for the execution of the militia according to the ordinance of parliament, and that the occasion of that tumult did arise from some horsemen that came with the Lord Strange by whom divers persons of the other side were wounded, one of which was since dead and another very likely to die. (I conceive the said relation will be in print.)[2]

After some other motions of lesser moment were passed, MR. REYNOLDS related how that on[e] Gibbons, a debtor of his who was laid in the Fleet upon an execution of 200£, did daily walk freely abroad in Westminster Hall and elsewhere under color of a writ sent by Justice Crawley[3] to him to appear before him as if he meant to examine him, which writ lasted but for a day and this was commonly granted him every day whereas he never came near the said Justice Crawley. That the said Gibbons meeting him (viz., the said Mr. Reynolds, in Westminster Hall the other day) gave him ill language when he asked him for his money and offered to draw his sword upon him, and that one Roe who came with him as his keeper did likewise give him, the said Mr. Reynolds, ill language and forbade him to meddle with the said Gibbons. MR. BULLER[4] of the Middle Temple did witness all these latter passages to be true, being a member of the house. Whereupon it was ordered that the said Roe[5] should be sent for as a delinquent, and a committee was appointed to examine the abuse of the said writs.

---

1. Thomas Birch, a captain in the Manchester militia. *CJ*, II, 690; Broxap, *Lancashire*, p. 18.

2. See Ormerod, *Tracts*, pp. 31–35. Wing, V 280.

3. Sir Francis Crawley, justice of the Common Pleas.

4. Both Francis and George Buller were affiliated with the Middle Temple. Keeler, pp. 120–21.

5. MS: *Rose*. Thomas Roe, servant to the warden of the Fleet prison, was committed to the Gatehouse on 12 September and released on 15 November. *CJ*, II, 691, 762, 851.

I withdrew out of the house about 11 of the clock this morning and returned not thither [f. 294b] again this day. See the rest of this forenoon's passages in Mr. Bodvel's journal.[6]

The house appointed to sit at 3 of the clock in the afternoon and rose/

Post Meridiem

The house sat between 3 and 4 of the clock[7] and proceeded with a new reply (to the king's answer to the late petition of both houses) full of asperity and violence; yet the hot fiery spirits prevailing, it passed the house in the issue, there being a very thin house.[8]

GAWDY

[f. 171a]   Tuesday, the XXVI of July

A letter from my Lord of Warwick, July the 25, from the Downs aboard the *James*. That the Hollanders hath taken some of merchants' ships, whereupon he hath taken some of the Holland ships. He desire to know the pleasure of the house.[9]

'Tis referred to the committee for defense of the kingdom.

[f. 171b] Birch at the bar informeth that at Manchester my Lord Strange with a troop of horse offered to take away the arms of the town by virtue of the commission of array. There was one of the townsmen killed and another hurt. The townsmen would not shoot.

Between 10 and 11 a clock I told the house, and there was not above sevenscore or thereabout.[10]

Some sent for out of Buckinghamshire for disturbing those that exercised in their arms.[11]

6. See G, below, and *CJ*, II, 690–91.

7. For proceedings omitted by D'Ewes, see *CJ*, II, 691–93.

8. This new message to the king, initiated the day before, was reported by Pym and approved by the lords, who subsequently ordered that it should be "published in all the Chapels and Churches of the Kingdom." See 25 July, n. 8; *CJ*, II, 692; and *LJ*, V, 242, 244. For the text see *CJ*, II, 693. Wing, E 2230.

9. For a similar letter to the lords, dated 23 July, as well as one from Warwick to Admiral Tromp concerning this incident, see *LJ*, V, 238.

10. Attendance was much smaller in the afternoon, when a division revealed only 83 members present. *CJ*, II, 691.

11. Volunteers from Aylesbury had been harassed for "peaceably training." In the afternoon a general order for the indemnity of "all such Volunteers, and Trained Bands, that exercise themselves, according to the Ordinance of Parliament," was approved by both houses. *CJ*, II, 690, 692. For the text see *CJ*, II, 693.

A message from the lords, a letter from my Lord of Warwick. A note from my Lord Warwick how all our ships are employed. They send an information of Captain Blythe. [12] That my lord mayor is at the bar and desire to send up some members to manage the evidence. 'Tis assented to. [13]

The house sat at 2 a clock, but I was not there.

12. Captain Blythe of the *Mary Rose* had sent a report to Warwick concerning the seizing of the English and Dutch merchant ships. Warwick's letter of 24 July and the lords' order that he should release the Dutch ships appear in *LJ*, V, 240. For further information concerning this controversy, see *LJ*, V, 243–44, 253–54; and *CSP Ven., 1642–1643*, p. 120.

13. For the proceedings, including a summary of the charges, see *LJ*, V, 240–41. The trial continued until 12 August, when Gurney was judged guilty, removed from office, and committed to the Tower, where he died in 1647. See *LJ*, V, 284–85; and Pearl, *London*, pp. 154–58. The draft of the judgment against Gurney is preserved in HLRO, Main Papers.

D'EWES

[f. 294b]   July 27, Wednesday, 1642

The greater part of the house kept the public fast in St. Margaret's Church in Westminster. Mr. Reynolds preached in the forenoon and Mr. Hill in the afternoon.[1] I was there present.

After the sermons ended between 4 and 5 of the clock in the afternoon, the House of Commons met.[2] I was not there at the beginning, but when I came in, they were debating of some course to be taken to restrain people from working on these fasting days.[3]

We appointed to meet at 9 of the clock tomorrow morning and rose between 5 and 6 in the afternoon.

GAWDY

[f. 171b]   Wednesday, the xxvii of July

I was at the fast at Lincoln's Inn.[4]

1. For the sermons see Wilson, *Pulpit in Parliament,* pp. 66, 258. Wing, H 2031, R 1256.

2. William Carter of London and Calybute Downing of Hackney were chosen to preach at the fast on 31 August. Both were nominees to the Westminster Assembly, though Downing did not attend. See *CJ,* II, 694; Wilson, *Pulpit in Parliament,* pp. 117, 119, 130n; Paul, *Assembly,* pp. 547, 548. *DNB* for Downing.

3. It was ordered that both a bill and a declaration should be prepared "for the more solemn Observation of the Days of publick Fast and Humiliation." The bill was read twice and committed on 4 August but apparently went no further. The ordinance was approved by both houses on 22 and 24 August. *CJ,* II, 694, 702, 732; *LJ,* V, 319. For the text see *LJ,* V, 320. Wing, E 1943. Hill was a member of the committee for the bill and along with Prideaux was named to draft the ordinance.

4. Apparently Gawdy fulfilled his fast day obligations at Lincoln's Inn rather than at St. Margaret's, Westminster. In Caroline England the Inns of Court in general and Lincoln's Inn in particular provided pulpits for Puritan preachers. See John Dykstra Eusden, *Puritans, Lawyers, and Politics in Early Seventeenth-Century England* (New Haven, 1958), pp. 10–11, 24, 61.

D'EWES

[f. 294b]   July 28, Thursday, 1642

I was not present in the house this day,[1] but amongst other particulars two declarations passed, the one brought in by MR. GREEN touching tonnage and poundage[2] and the other by MR. DENZIL HOLLES touching satisfaction to be given to the whole kingdom. This latter was full of virulent expressions against the king; yet the injustice I had suffered on Saturday last past discouraged all men to speak their consciences freely, so as this declaration passed the house without much debate.[3]

The house rose about 2 of the clock in the afternoon.

GAWDY

[f. 171b]   Thursday, the xxviii of July

I came out of town with Sir Edmund Moundeford.[4]

1. For the day's proceedings, see *CJ*, II, 694–95.

2. This ordinance, formulated because the latest bill had not received the royal assent, was agreed to by the lords on 1 August. See G, 23 July; *CJ*, II, 694, 695; and *LJ*, V, 250. For the text see *LJ*, V, 254–56. A division concerning the ordinance indicated an attendance of 114 on this day.

3. This declaration, "expressing the Reasons and Grounds that force the Parliament to raise Arms," was agreed to by the lords on 2 August. See 25 July, n. 8; *CJ*, II, 694; and *LJ*, V, 256. For the text see *LJ*, V, 257–59. Wing, E 1450.

4. Moundeford had been given leave on 25 July to go to the country for his health. On 26 July the Norfolk MPs who were deputy lieutenants, including Gawdy, were ordered to execute the militia ordinance. *CJ*, II, 689, 691–92. An ordinance and instructions for this committee appear in *LJ*, V, 251–53. Gawdy's journal concludes at this point with four brief entries for 1643–45.

HILL

[p. 138]   [July 28, 1642][5]

Our petition to the king and his answer and our reply.[6]

MR. FIENNES, declaration.[7]

Our declaration why we take up arms reported July 28 by MR. HOLLES.[8]

5. This undated entry occurs on the next-to-last page of Hill's notebook. Though his journal concludes with this day, Hill continued as an active member of the house and was named to numerous committees.

6. The petition of peace, the king's answer reported on 23 July, and parliament's response of 26 July.

7. The declaration discussed on 22 and 23 July.

8. The newest declaration. See above, n. 3.

D'EWES

[f. 294b]   July 29, Friday, 1642

The Speaker came about 9 of the clock. Amongst other particulars agitated this morning, MR. WILLIAM STRODE delivered in a petition for some Southwark men, who suggested that they were falsely accused by some persons because they had shown their good affections to the proceedings of parliament[1] and that they were bound to answer at the now ensuing assizes and so desired that this house would take some course to free them. Divers spake to it, and in the issue, because they were to be tried according to the law of England, it was agreed that we should not at all interpose in it, and so it was laid aside.

After two or three motions of little moment,[2] MR. HAMPDEN delivered in a letter which had been sent to him from Sir John Hotham bearing date at Hull July 19, 1642, which the clerk read, and therein he showed that the charge of the garrison come now weekly to 600£, for he was compelled to take most of the poorest of the inhabitants of the town into pay. That he could not maintain them in order and discipline without a supply of money. That he had now left but 400£ for their next week's allowance. That he had sent up by this ketch or small pinnace some hundreds of great saddles (I think it was 600) with bridles and would shortly send up the rest if he could spare them with some horse arms. That for his own rents he was like to receive none, his house being rifled and spoiled, his cattle being taken away, and his officers abused. That if a good peace might be concluded, it were the happiest course, but if the wars should continue, he did desire the parliament that himself and those who were with him might not only be spoiled without remedy but that they might have liberty to make up their losses by the spoil of their enemies, with some other particulars of less moment.

The letter being read, MR. HAMPDEN made report from the committee appointed for the safety of the kingdom what course had been taken for the sending of money to the said Sir John Hotham, with divers other particulars.[3]

I withdrew out of the house between 11 and 12 of the clock.[4]

---

1. The petitioners allegedly did "good Service . . . to this House, in pulling down from off the Maypole a Proclamation concerning the Commission of Array." *CJ*, II, 695.

2. See *CJ*, II, 695.

3. For several orders concerning Sir John Hotham and Hull, see *CJ*, II, 695–96.

4. For the rest of the day, see *CJ*, II, 696.

D'EWES

July 30, Saturday, 1642

I was absent all this day. Vide Mr. Bodvel's book.[1]
The house rose about 2 of the clock in the afternoon.

1. For the day's proceedings see *CJ*, II, 696–98.

D'EWES

[f. 257b]   August 1, Monday, 1642

The Speaker came about 9 of the clock; after prayers between 9 and 10 Mr. Harman, one of the citizens for the city of Norwich, delivered in a letter which had been sent to himself and Mr. Catelyn elected with him from the mayor of Norwich,[1] which the clerk read, and therein it was related how one Captain [*blank*][2] was come to the city of Norwich with a warrant from the Earl of Lindsey[3] directed to him to raise a company of foot of volunteers. That himself and the aldermen had denied to give license to him to beat up a drum, which notwithstanding he did of himself and raised several tumults, whereupon in the evening they had taken him and his two servants and imprisoned them, and so desired to know of the parliament what should further be done with them. The letter being read, the said Mr. Harman stood up and showed that he was very glad to see the respect of the city of Norwich to the parliament and desired that they might receive encouragement for the same and direction what to do with the said persons whom they had committed to prison.

Sir John Potts, one of the knights of the shire for Norfolk, desired that whereas himself was shortly to go into the country by the appointment of the house,[4] that the said Mr. Harman might likewise go down to give thanks to the city of Norwich in the name of the house; he further showed also that there was great need of all the assistance that may be there, for some deputy lieutenants which had been formerly appointed did refuse to meddle with the militia, and that some captains also who had received commission were likely to fail. He further showed that divers gentlemen of the country had been lately with his majesty and were returned back and that it was likely that they would be ready

---

1. William Gostlyn, a royalist, had succeeded Adrian Parmenter, a parliamentarian, as mayor in May. John T. Evans, *Seventeenth-Century Norwich* (Oxford, 1979), pp. 99, 120. The following comment appears in R. W. Ketton-Cremer, *Norfolk in the Civil War* (Hamden, Conn., 1970), p. 174: "He [Gostlyn] must have assented reluctantly to many of the measures passed by his colleagues during his tenure of the mayoral chair."

2. Moses Treswell. Following a report to the house on 30 July of the warrant granted to Treswell, it was ordered that he be "forthwith summoned in safe Custody" and that the affair be referred to the committee of safety. See *CJ,* II, 697, 698; and Evans, *Norwich,* pp. 122–23.

3. As general of the king's army.

4. Potts was one of the committee going to Norfolk. See 28 July, n. 4.

to assist my Lord Maltravers,[5] who was shortly expected in that county with the commission of array, and that the papists there also who lately expressed much fear began now again to grow confident, especially Sir John Hobart and others who stood well affected to the parliament being put out of the commission of peace; and therefore he desired that he,[6] living in the city of Norwich, might be nominated a deputy lieutenant for the county of that city, which was agreed unto.

The house then desired Mr. Harman to go into the country, but he excused himself by indisposition of health.

Awhile after Sir John Potts had spoken, I went out of the house and returned not again.[7] The house appointed to meet at 2 of the clock in the afternoon and rose about eleven.

[f. 258a]   Post Meridiem

The house met between 2 and 3 of the clock in the afternoon. A new oath was amongst other passed to be taken by all that should serve under the Earl of Essex[8] without one man speaking against it, all men were so discouraged by the injustice which I had suffered on Saturday was sennight. For this oath was utterly against the law and the liberty of the subject and could not be new framed but by an act of parliament.

The house rose about 6 of the clock.

5. In 1633 Maltravers (also known as Lord Mowbray) had been appointed lord lieutenant for Norfolk jointly with his father, the Earl of Arundel. For the royalist faction there, see Ketton-Cremer, *Norfolk in the Civil War,* pp. 33, 135–49.

6. I.e., Hobart, who was already a deputy lieutenant for the county. *CJ,* II, 698; *PJ,* 2: 54. For further orders and instructions concerning Norwich, see *LJ,* V, 265–67.

7. For the rest of the day, see *CJ,* II, 698–700.

8. The oath is as follows in *CJ,* II, 699:

A. B. chosen to be an Officer in the Troops now raised by Ordinance of Parliament, under the Command of the Earl of Essex, do here vow, promise, and protest, in the Presence of Almighty God, that in this Employment and Service I will defend, maintain, and obey, the Two Houses of Parliament; and, in pursuance of their Direction and Command, the Right Honourable Robert Earl of Essex, as Captain General of all the Forces raised, and to be raised, for the Defence of the Protestant Religion, the King's Person, Honour, and State, the Power and Privileges of Parliament, and the just Rights and Liberties of the Subject, and the Security and Peace of the Kingdom; and will, to the utmost of my Power, oppose, resist, and subdue, all Force raised against them, by Pretence or Colour of any Commission or Warrant whatsoever.

D'EWES

August 2, Tuesday, 1642

The Speaker came between 9 and 10 of the clock. I came into the house between 10 and eleven, and divers congratulated my coming in as if I had come from a far journey, although I had only been absent all Saturday and the greatest part of yesterday.[1] MR. PYM was upon a report of divers particulars concerning Ireland upon which divers resolutions passed, which see in the clerk's book.[2]

SIR HENRY MILDMAY showed that some of the Scottish commissioners had newly sent for him out of the house and desired to know whether the 80,000£, part of the brotherly assistance which was to have been paid to them at Midsummer last, were ready,[3] for they had received command from Scotland to return home without fail the 10th day of this month.[4] That the best affected people of Scotland to the parliament in England were those to whom this money was due and that they were in great want of it, and that if half of it only were paid in, all could not receive satisfaction, and that the same would breed more discontent and division than if no part at all were received. The SPEAKER thereupon showed that 40,000£ of this money was to be received of the Merchant Adventurers and the other 40,000£ of the merchant strangers. Whereupon SIR HENRY MILDMAY only desired that some course might be taken for the speedy paying of it in to the Scots.

SIR HENRY HEYMAN, being one of the committee that were sent to the late assizes held for the county of Kent,[5] begun at Maidstone on Saturday was

1. D'Ewes had also been absent on Thursday, 28 July.
2. For these orders see *CJ*, II, 700; and CIA, 26 July, and 28 July, nn. 7, 8.
3. For discussion of the payment at a committee of the whole house, see D, 20 July.
4. On 4 August the commissioners urged the expediting of the Scots treaty because they were to return home by 22 August. Subsequently the Scots Privy Council resolved that, despite the king's objections, two commissioners should remain in London to see that the Scots army in Ireland was provided for and that the remainder of the brotherly assistance was paid. See *CJ*, II, 702; *LJ*, V, 262; and *Register of the Privy Council of Scotland*, 2d ser., VII, 318–19.

Though the treaty, which had been much amended, was never ratified by the king, this fact did not prevent its implementation. See *CJ*, II, 707–08; *CSPD, 1641–43*, p. 449; and Stevenson, *Scottish Revolution*, pp. 244–45. For a summary of the provisions, see *HMC, Fifth Report*, pp. 41–42.

5. For the committee sent to the assizes at Maidstone and their instructions, see D, 22 July. A full account of the proceedings and the part played by the commons' committee appear in Woods, *Prelude*, pp. 100–08. Before Heyman's report "Instructions for the County of Kent to Mr. Augustyn Skinner, whereby the Desires of this County may be presented by him to the Honourable House of

sennight, made report that on the same morning Sir Thomas Malet, one of the judges of the King's Bench who went that circuit, was gotten to the bench before they could come early enough to attend him on the said Saturday morning, and that scarce any of the justices would vouchsafe them room to sit or stand conveniently nor the said Mr. Justice Malet permit them to perform the instructions given them by the House of Commons.

SIR HENRY VANE, the younger, did proceed with the said report and showed at large how the said committee had on Monday morning was sennight[6] sent Sir Edward Hales and Sir Humphrey Tufton, two of their committee, to the said Mr. Justice Malet to desire access to him to speak with him, which he granted accordingly. That thereupon they repaired to him to his lodging and could not for a long time prevail with him to hear them at all in his private chamber but that what they said to him should be spoken publicly in another room where the justices of the peace were. This being at last obtained, he, the said Sir Henry Vane, did propose to him in the name of the committee that he would be pleased to give them his best assistance for the communication of such instructions as they had for the preservation of the peace of that county. Mr. Justice Malet took time to deliberate thereupon and returned his answer by Sir Edward Hales and Sir Humphrey Tufton, that he would be ready to assist the said committee so far as might stand with his commission and should be agreeable to the law of the kingdom. The committee further desired that the said Justice Malet might appoint them a convenient room where they might come and sit upon the bench, to which after a little deliberation he answered that if they would have come upon the bench without demanding it, he should have been willing to have connived at it, but that now they had demanded a place to be assigned to them, he thought it a matter of so great moment as that he could not answer it without consideration. And after further debate both with him and with[7] divers justices of the peace of that county being there present at his lodging, they could in the issue get nothing from him but dilatory and unsatisfactory answers, which in effect were that the said places of the bench were appointed only for such as were authorized to sit there by his majesty's commission under the broad seal and those were only the judges of assize and the justices of peace of the same county. Whereupon after some other discourses the committee resolved to forbear coming upon the bench for that day and did against the next day prepare a declaration to be read unto the county, by which they were to show to them how they had been hindered from the execution of those instructions which they

---

Commons," were read. *CJ*, II, 700. For these instructions (misdated April in *CSPD*), which were to settle "the distractions of these times . . . [and] to give the King full satisfaction in his just desires," see *CSPD, 1641–43*, p. 314.

6. I.e., 25 July.

7. MS: *of*.

had from the House of Commons which tended [f. 258b] only to the settling of the peace of that county and to bring a right intelligence between them and the parliament. And accordingly the day following in the afternoon the said committee came to the bench and some of them got convenient rooms, but others stood with much inconvenience and crowding. The said Mr. Justice Malet was then upon the trial of the jails, so as they were fain to stay three hours before they could have opportunity at all to move him or speak to him, which after they had gotten, Sir Henry Vane, the younger, did move the judge in the name of the committee that they might deliver some commands they had received from the House of Commons to the county and therefore desired that the grand jury might be sent for to come into the court, to which Justice Malet replied that he would permit nothing to be said or done there but that which he was authorized to do by the commission which he had received from his master but would rather lose his life, after which there followed many answers and replies between the said Mr. Justice Malet and young Sir Henry Vane, who spake in the name of the committee, and one part of the company present hummed when Mr. Justice Malet spake and the other when Sir Henry Vane spake. And in the issue the judge resolving rather to adjourn the court than they should speak, Sir Henry Vane showed that seeing they could not be heard, rather than they would hinder the business of the assizes, they would withdraw, which they did accordingly.[8]

8. The proceedings at the assizes were referred to the committee of safety, who were to send for Judge Malet. On 4 August at the Surrey assizes Sir Richard Onslow presented a parliamentary warrant to Malet, who was thereupon brought to London and imprisoned in the Tower for two years. See *CJ*, II, 700; *LJ*, V, 264, 268; and Woods, *Prelude*, pp. 109–12, 117–18. For the rest of the day, see *CJ*, II, 700–01.

D'EWES

August 3, Wednesday, 1642

The Speaker came between 9 and 10 of the clock. I came into the house about 10. Soon after upon MR. CORBET's motion one of the sheriffs of Norwich[1] was called in, who had brought up with him one Captain Moses Treswell that had caused a drum to be beaten up in Norwich for volunteers upon a warrant which he had under the hand and seal of the Earl of Lindsey. The sheriff related the manner of it in effect as had been formerly set forth in a letter sent from the mayor of the said city and read in this house. The sheriff then withdrew and the said Captain Treswell was called in, who acknowledged what he had done in respect of the matter of fact and only desired that seeing the Earl of Lindsey had a commission under the broad seal of England and he had a warrant from the earl derived from the authority of that commission, that he might be excused for what he had done. And thereupon he withdrew.[2]

Divers spake to this matter, and in the issue it was voted that he should be [sent] prisoner to the Gatehouse,[3] and some said that his offense did amount to high treason, wherein their zeal or ignorance did exceedingly mislead them.

Divers other particulars during my continuing in the house, which was till between eleven and twelve of the clock.[4]

1. Matthew Lindsey or Robert Baron. *Sheriffs*, p. 114.

2. For more details see Ketton-Cremer, *Norfolk in the Civil War*, pp. 145, 147. Captain Treswell's "Beating of Drums" was referred to the committee of safety, and on 5 August both houses passed an order for the indemnity of the mayor and sheriffs of Norwich in this affair. In September disposition was made of Treswell's money and horses, which the mayor and sheriff had seized. See *CJ*, II, 701, 704, 758, 766; and *LJ*, V, 266.

3. On 13 March 1643 a committee was ordered to investigate his escape from prison. *CJ*, II, 1001.

4. For the rest of the day, see *CJ*, II, 701–02.

D'EWES

[f. 259a]   August 4, Thursday, 1642

I was not in the house this day,[1] but the chief thing that was agitated was what course to take [concerning] Portsmouth, which had been given up to the king by Colonel George Goring, eldest son to the Lord Goring, who had originally been made governor there by his majesty and about February was 12 month had revealed Mr. Jermyn's conspiracy with the knowledge of which the king had entrusted him,[2] and from that time some of the hotter spirits of both houses had put a great confidence in him and had taken care to supply him with money both for the payment of himself his yearly stipend as governor there and for the paying of the garrison also.[3] But now the king had used such means with the said Colonel Goring, being a loose profane man, as that he took in several papists and others into the town and so made it wholly for the king. This news so staggered the hot spirits in both houses as they scarce knew what counsel to take; yet were many things debated and divers resolutions passed for the reducing back of the town to the service of the parliament, as may appear by the clerk's book.[4]

Mr. Serjeant Hyde, recorder of the city of Salisbury, being a member of the house, was this day also questioned[5] for bailing a fellow at Salisbury who had been questioned and imprisoned for saying that the House of Commons were all traitors, as also for that when the mayor of Salisbury came to him and asked his advice what to do with certain proclamations which were sent to him from his majesty against the proceedings of the two houses of parliament, he answered him that he should do according to his oath, which was to obey and perform the king's command. The said SERJEANT HYDE having made what excuse he

1. For proceedings omitted by D'Ewes, see *CJ*, II, 702.
2. Goring actually revealed the first army plot, which involved Henry Jermyn, in early April 1641. See Gardiner, *History of England*, IX, 317. Following Goring's betrayal of Portsmouth, parliament sent Sir William Waller to reclaim it. See Clarendon, *History*, II, 268–83.
3. On 12 July Stapleton had been ordered to write to Goring "to satisfy him with the clear Opinion this House has of him, and of his Worth." *CJ*, II, 667.
4. It was resolved "That the Lords be moved, That the Person of the Earl of Portland be . . . secured. . . . in regard of the Condition of Portsmouth" and that he be replaced as governor of the nearby Isle of Wight by the Earl of Pembroke, lord lieutenant of Hampshire. Despite professions to the House of Lords of "Faithfulness to the Parliament," Portland was placed in the custody of Sheriff Garrett and subsequently sent to the Tower. *CJ*, II, 702; *LJ*, V, 261–62, 270, 284. For the order making Pembroke governor, see *CJ*, II, 708.
5. Hyde had been summoned by the house on 22 and 29 July. *CJ*, II, 635, 696.

thought fit in those particulars, he was commanded to withdraw into the committee chamber, and after a short debate it was agreed and voted by the major part of the house that he should be sent to the Tower and be declared incapable of being a member of the house during this parliament. Whereupon the sergeant called him down out of the committee chamber, and he kneeling at the bar, the SPEAKER pronounced the said judgment against him, and so he withdrew out of the house.[6]

6. Hyde was released from the Tower on 18 August. *CJ*, II, 725. During the next five weeks forty-three MPs were disabled, in contrast to four during the previous seven months. Not all were noted by D'Ewes; however, the complete list appears in Appendix A. For the rest of the day, see *CJ*, II, 703.

D'EWES

[f. 259a]   August 5, Friday, 1642

The Speaker came between 9 and 10. I came into the house about 10 of the clock.[1] The clerk was then reading a letter bearing date August 4, 1642, at Shepton Mallet in Somersetshire sent to the Speaker from Mr. Alexander Popham, Mr. Pyne, and divers other deputy lieutenants of that county appointed for the militia,[2] in which they showed how Sir Ralph Hopton and Mr. Thomas Smith, two members of the House of Commons, had offered violence to one Mr. William Strode,[3] one of the deputy lieutenants allowed by the two houses of parliament for that end.

The clerk having read the letter, divers spake to it, and several votes passed upon it against the said Sir Ralph Hopton and Mr. Smith, by which they were disabled to sit in the house during this parliament, and others who were sent for as delinquents. The said letter and votes were ordered to be printed.[4]

We then resolved also to desire a conference with the lords about these particulars, and Mr. Lawrence Whitaker moved that before the said message went up, that he might communicate to the house some matters of importance beyond the seas, which was read by the clerk, the substance of it being that one lately come from the Brill in Holland[5] did testify that there were two captains there who were lately come from the Prince of Orange his army and said they were to come into the north parts of England to serve the king, and that the queen had sent to the Prince of Orange for divers other commanders and officers to be sent out of the said army into England. That Mr. Henry Jermyn

---

1. For proceedings omitted by D'Ewes, see *CJ,* II, 703.

2. For a summary of the letter from the committee in Somerset, actually dated 1 August, see *LJ,* V, 265. Wing, S 4649. For the Marquess of Hertford's account of the same affray, see *HMC, Fifth Report,* pp. 44–45. The events of 28 July to 1 August are also recounted in Underdown, *Somerset,* pp. 32–34.

3. Not the MP. However, this William Strode, a clothier of Barrington, Somerset, was elected to parliament for Ilchester, Somerset, in 1646. See Underdown, *Somerset,* pp. 21, 130–32; and Edgar, *Hopton,* pp. 34–35.

4. Hopton and Smith were also sent for. Among the other votes was one for the committee of safety to "speed away such Forces, and other Necessaries, as shall be fit for the Safety of that County." An ordinance to that effect was reported by Pym and approved by the lords on 8 August. See *CJ,* II, 703–04, 710. For Hopton's role in Somerset in early August, see Edgar, *Hopton,* pp. 34–40.

5. For the text see *LJ,* V, 265. Wing, S 4649.

had hired a ship of Scarborough to be freighted by him into England, and that when the master of the ship understood that he was to bring arms into the north parts thereof, he refused to carry the same, with some other matters which in my opinion as well as these I have named were very slight and frivolous; yet the house concluded to make them one head of their conference with the lords. Mr. Strode was sent up to desire the said conference.[6]

I went out of the house awhile after, it being about 12 of the clock.[7]

6. For the report of the conference, see *LJ*, V, 264.
7. For the rest of the day, see *CJ*, II, 704–06.

D'EWES

[f. 259b]   August 6, Saturday, 1642

The Speaker came between 9 and 10 of the clock. I came into the house about 10 of the clock.[1] The clerk was then reading a letter which came from Sir John Corbet and others, the deputy lieutenants appointed by both houses for Shropshire,[2] in which they showed amongst other things that Sir Richard Leveson and Mr. Newport, two members of this house, had been very active in putting the king's commission of array in execution in that county, so in the issue it was voted that they should be summoned to appear that so they might answer the same to this house.[3] See more concerning this letter[4] and the whole proceedings of this day in Mr. Moore's journal.

Mr. Pym and divers others came into the house, being of the committee for the defense of the kingdom. MR. PYM made report of certain instructions which the said committee of lords and commons had prepared for Sir Henry Wallop and others in Hampshire, being of a very high and strong nature: That they should instantly raise the trained bands of that county, horse and foot, and to besiege or seize upon the town of Portsmouth, into which Colonel Goring had admitted many papists and betrayed the trust the two houses of parliament had reposed in him by joining with those wicked counselors and malignant party about his majesty in the great design for the destroying of the Protestant religion and the parliament. That they should arrest the said Colonel Goring as a traitor and bring him up to the parliament, with divers other instructions for the obeying of the Earl of Essex, chosen lord general of the army by both houses of parliament. All which instructions tended to no other end but to the kindling and promoting of a desperate and dangerous civil war. And yet notwithstanding when the clerk had read them, as if all freedom of speech had been lost upon

---

1. For proceedings omitted by D'Ewes, see *CJ,* II, 706.

2. On 22 July Corbet, Pierrepont, and Richard More had been named as a committee for Shropshire to inform the county of the illegality of the commission of array and to promote the propositions for money, horse, and plate. See *CJ,* II, 686.

3. Sir Richard Lee and Sir Robert Howard, both MPs from Shropshire, were also summoned. On 6 September they were disabled, as was Leveson on 24 November. See *CJ,* II, 706, 862; and Appendix A.

4. For the letter, which was referred to the committee of safety, see *LJ,* V, 269–70. The committee named several delinquents to be summoned, including Sheriff John Weld and Richard Gibbons, mayor of Shrewsbury. See *CJ,* II, 706.

Saturday, July 23, in my unjust suffering, there was scarce one man spake for the alteration of one word in them; but the SPEAKER put them to the question, and so they passed between 11 and 12 of the clock. And MR. PYM desired that the clerk might instantly take order to have them fair written out and that a message might be sent up to the lords to desire them to sit about an hour in respect of matters of great importance which was of necessity to be communicated to their lordships before they rose. And the SPEAKER nominated Sir Christopher Yelverton for the messenger, who went accordingly, and I at the same time withdrew out of the house.[5]

5. The instructions were subsequently carried up by Anthony Nicoll, nephew to John Pym, who had been added to the committee of safety on 16 July. Keeler, p. 285; *CJ*, II, 675. For the rest of the day, see *CJ*, II, 707–08.

D'EWES

August 8, Monday, 1642

The Speaker came about 9 of the clock. After prayers between 9 and 10 of the clock MR. JOHN PYNE, a member of this house, being newly come out of Somersetshire in his doublet and hose without coat or cloak, made a relation that he, understanding that the Lord Marquess Hertford and others were gathering force together in the same county and intended to put the commission of array in execution, did on Friday last[1] get together about five hundred of the trained bands and was going with them from Somer[ton] to Glastonbury (and after he had proceeded thus far, I came into the house). That one Captain Preston[2] commanded them. That though they had their muskets charged, yet they gave them order to shoot at no man unless they should be first assaulted. That at a hill in the way Sir John Poulett (son and heir of the Lord Poulett), Sir John Stawell (which two served as knights for that shire in the parliament), Captain John Digby (younger son of the Earl of Bristol and a member of the House of Commons also),[3] and some others were gathered together with several horse and foot, but the certain number of them he could not descry because the greater part lay in ambuscade. The said Sir John Poulett and the rest sent earnestly to him to speak with him, which he assented unto. And when they met, they spake very courteously unto him and told him how much they desired and should endeavor to preserve the peace of that county and so demanded whither he intended to go with those trained bands which he discovered; and then soon after, they parting, one of their company gave notice to those with Captain Preston that they should not march forward, for if they did that he would give fire, and [f. 260a] when they did so he gave fire accordingly and so did divers others, and he believed that divers of his company were hurt and he had heard that some 9 or 10 of them were slain. For himself he said that riding

---

1. Crossed out in MS: *Saturday / Thursday.* On Thursday there were "Endeavours to put the Commission of Array in Execution," according to *CJ*, II, 708. The king had named the Marquess of Hertford lieutenant general of the western counties and ordered him to execute the commission of array. Bayley, *Dorset*, p. 41. For the text of his commission, dated 2 August, see Rushworth, IV, 672–74.

2. John Preston was among those captured by Hertford's men. For more details of the events of 4 August, see Underdown, *Somerset*, pp. 35–36.

3. He had, however, been disabled on 5 August. See Appendix A.

amongst of his company and understanding that some of the horse on the other side were hastening up towards him threatening to cut him in pieces, he set spurs to his horse and so escaped them, coming away directly for London without cloak or coat. He came into town this morning, and speaking several times afterwards, he declared amongst other particulars that when Sir John Poulett and the rest met with him at the bottom of the hill, that they came in a warlike manner with their pistols and great saddles. After this business had been awhile debated, it was at last resolved upon the question that the said Sir John Poulett and Sir John Stawell should be uncapable of serving during this parliament in the house, and then it was resolved upon a second question that a warrant should go out for a new writ for the election of two knights of the shire for the county of Somerset and that we should make declaration of this relation to the lords in a conference.[4]

MR. HENRY[5] HERBERT delivered in a letter sent to him from Mr. Herbert, his father, out of Monmouthshire bearing date at Coldbrook his house there July 31, 1642, in which he showed that Sir Edward Henden, Knight, one of the barons of the Exchequer, judge of the assize there, had neglected to publish the order of the House of Commons against the commission of array. That himself and divers other justices of peace were put out of the commission of peace and others popishly affected and of mean condition put in, of whose names he had sent a note.[6] That there was order come thither to disarm separatists, under color whereof they may disarm the best Protestants and then leave them naked to the papists, who were not yet disarmed, to cut their throats. That the Earl of Pembroke was put [out] of the commission of peace in all shires where he was formerly in and the Lord Philip Herbert, his son, put in his stead,[7] with divers other particulars of lesser moment, and in the issue desired that some assistance might be sent into the said county to join with them that stand for the king and parliament. This letter being read, upon some debate it was ordered that we should desire a conference with the lords about it and that they would join with

4. On 9 and 12 August the house received further letters from Somerset dated 7 and 8 August from John Ashe, a member of the county committee. *CJ*, II, 711, 716. An imperfect version of the earlier letter appears in *LJ*, V, 278–79. Wing, A 3945, A 3946.

5. MS: *Edward*. For Henry Herbert, MP, and his father William, see *PJ*, 2: 474–75.

6. "Mere Creatures of the Earl of Worcester and his Allies, put in; and . . . neither the Earl of Worcester, nor his son [Lord Herbert], are yet disarmed." In addition, it had been reported in the lords house that the earl was executing the commission of array. On 20 August it was voted, as had been urged in May, that the recusants in Monmouthshire should be disarmed. See *PJ*, 2: 295; *CJ*, II, 708; and *LJ*, V, 248, 307.

7. On the other hand, the Earl of Pembroke had recently been named by parliament to replace his son Philip, Lord Herbert, as lord lieutenant for the counties of Monmouth, Brecon, and Glamorgan. *LJ*, V, 248.

us for the disarming of recusants in the said county,[8] and Sir John Evelyn[9] was appointed to be the messenger and to carry up to the lords certain instructions touching the city of Salisbury for their fortifying and defending themselves.

MR. GREEN made report also of an order drawn by the committee for the navy by which Sir Henry Vane, the younger, was made treasurer of the navy,[10] and the clerk read it. We voted it without any debate, only two or three words were added to it upon the said Sir Henry Vane's motion, and we voted also that we should desire the lords to join with us in it, and Sir John Evelyn was appointed to carry it up with the other particulars; but as he was upon going, MR. CAGE informed the house that the lords did not sit till the afternoon, and so he stayed.

MR. NICOLL delivered in a letter sent to Mr. Gilbert Millington, a member of this house, bearing date at Nottingham the 2 day of August 1642, in which it was declared and showed that the Lord Newark[11] (son and heir to Robert Pierrepont, Earl of Kingston upon Hull) did lately come to Nottingham with about a hundred horse in his company and demanded of the mayor there one half of the powder which belonged to the magazine of that county remaining in that town and one barrel of the magazine that belonged to that town, both which he pretended he would only borrow but for 10 days. The mayor overnight having for fear given him a promise of it, divers gentlemen and others were sent unto the same night into the country, who came in so great number the next morning into Nottingham to the assistance of the mayor and aldermen there as the Lord Newark could not obtain one corn[12] of powder. He was one of the commissioners named in the commission of array but did carry himself there very moderately, with some other particulars of less moment.

The clerk having read the said letter, the house directed Mr. Millington to write a letter to the mayor of Nottingham and to return thanks in the name of this house to him and the aldermen of that town and to the gentlemen of the county who came in to their assistance.[13]

8. It was ordered that Henry Herbert should go to Monmouthshire to execute the militia ordinance. See *CJ*, II, 708; and *LJ*, V, 280. For the instructions for the deputy lieutenants, see *LJ*, V, 285–86.

9. Doubtless Evelyn of Wiltshire.

10. For the ordinance see *LJ*, V, 272–73. Vane's earlier tenure (1639–41) as joint treasurer of the navy with Sir William Russell had ended with Vane's dismissal by the king in December 1641. A move to reinstate him in March 1642 had not succeeded. See Coates, p. 268, n. 5; *PJ*, 2: 55 and 60, n. 4; and *DNB*.

11. Brother to William Pierrepont, MP, and the king's appointee as lord lieutenant of Nottinghamshire. *DNB*. For another description of the encounter between Lord Newark and Mayor John James, see Lucy Hutchinson, *Memoirs of the Life of Colonel Hutchinson*, ed. James Sutherland (London, 1973), pp. 54–56.

12. A round particle of gunpowder formed by the granulating process. *NED*.

13. Instructions for the deputy lieutenants of Nottinghamshire, one of whom was Millington, appear in *LJ*, V, 275–76. For an account of events there, see also Wood, *Nottinghamshire*, pp. 17–18.

MR. ALDERMAN PENINGTON delivered in a letter sent to him from Sir William Brereton bearing date at Chester August 6, 1642, in which he showed that the gentry and others of Cheshire did yet refuse to subscribe what money or plate they would contribute or provide any horses till they might be assured that they should be employed for the defense of their own country where there will be great need of them, with divers other particulars of lesser moment.

I withdrew out of the house between 11 and 12 of the clock. The house, having appointed to meet at 2 of the clock in the afternoon, rose about 12.

[f. 260b]   Post Meridiem

The house met between 2 and 3 of the clock in the afternoon. I was not there. See the clerk's Journal and Mr. Bodvel's journal.[14]

14. For the rest of the day, see *CJ*, II, 709–10.

D'EWES

            August 9, Tuesday, 1642

The Speaker came about 9 of the clock. After prayers between 9 and 10 some motions of small moment were made and ordered. MR. SALWAY, one of the knights of the shire for the county of Worcester, delivered in a letter sent to him from one Mr. Steele[1] bearing date at [*blank*] August 7, 1642, in which he showed that he had formerly been an high constable but now was put out of his place. That at the late assizes held for Worcester August 3 last past, there was a packed grand jury and a declaration agreed upon by them and divers others of the gentry against the proceedings of parliament.[2] That there was a commission of array come into the country which was shortly to be executed. That he had sent the names of many of the grand jury and of some of the commissioners of array. That divers freeholders had preferred a petition to Sir Edward Henden, Knight, judge of the said assizes, for the justification of the proceedings of parliament which he had refused to accept of it, with some other particulars.

The clerk having read the letter, the said MR. SALWAY delivered in the other particulars which were read.[3]

See Mr. Moore's journal for the rest of this morning's passages.[4] I went out of the house between 10 and eleven. The house rose about one of the clock.

1. William Stephens, according to *CJ,* II, 710.
2. For the declaration see J. W. Willis Bund, ed., *Diary of Henry Townshend* [Worcestershire Historical Society] (London, 1915–16), II, 68. Wing, D 540.
3. Salway and Wilde were ordered to return to Worcestershire "with the Instructions for the Counties; and to use their best Endeavours for the Preservation of the Peace." See 16 July, n. 14; and *CJ,* II, 711. For a declaration of 5 August concerning the indemnity of Worcestershire residents who opposed the commission of array, see *CJ,* II, 705.
4. For the rest of the day, see *CJ,* II, 711–12.

D'EWES

August 10, Wednesday, 1642

The Speaker came about 9 of the clock but stayed as he had usually done for divers days past about half an hour that some considerable company might draw together. For the hot fiery spirits, having begun a civil war, carried all things now as they listed so as men made no great haste to the house, neither did many at all assemble.

After prayers SERJEANT WILDE made report from the committee (of which I was one) appointed to consider of the barbarous violence offered by Mr. John Griffith, the younger, a member of the house, to the Lady Sedley, and then there were 4 votes he read and delivered in to the house against the said John Griffith.

The clerk then read a great part of the narrative which the Lady Sedley had delivered in to the committee under her own hand. I withdrew out of the house between 10 and 11 of the clock just as he began to read it.

All the votes passed except the third, which was for the reading of a bill newly drawn against the said Mr. Griffith.[1]

See the rest of this day's passages in Mr. Bodvel's journal and in the clerk's Journal.[2]

1. The three votes declared that Griffith was guilty of the crimes and misdemeanors set forth in Lady Sedley's petition, that he should be disabled as a member of the House of Commons, and that the proceedings against him in the King's Bench were by permission of the house. *CJ*, II, 712.
2. For the rest of the day, see *CJ*, II, 712–13.

D'EWES

August 11, Thursday, 1642

The Speaker came about 9 of the clock, and prayers were ended between 9 and 10. I came into the house between 10 and eleven.[1] Just as I came into the house, some provisos that had been added to the bill touching the creditors of Sir Thomas Dawes were amending, so as there continued a long silence in the house. The bill had been read *3ᵃ vice* before my coming in, and then the provisos, being brought in ready engrossed in parchment, were thrice read, and so both the bill and the provisos passed upon the question.[2]

Dr. Aylett and Dr. Heath brought down 3 bills from the lords,[3] which having first passed by them and then brought down to us, we had added some amendments to them, to which said amendments the lords having assented did send them down to us with notice thereof, and then the said messengers withdrew and departed.

There was one passage this morning which because it doth not often happen I shall set down at large, and that was one of the senators or lords of the city of Hamburg did desire to [f. 261a] be admitted into the house with letters that he had from the magistrates of that city to the parliament, so divers called to have him admitted in, and the sergeant was ready without any more ado to bring him in as he did other ordinary men, which made me sitting in my usual place near the table to tell him privately just as he was taking up his mace that he ought not to bring him in to the bar as he did other persons. For I yet held my resolution not to speak publicly by reason of the injustice I had suffered on Saturday, July 23 last past. The sergeant upon my speaking to him retired from his mace, and the SPEAKER, as I gathered, overhearing what I said to him, stood up and desired the house to consider before he were called in in what manner he must be called in. Thereupon divers spake to it, some that he might have a chair or

---

1. For proceedings omitted by D'Ewes, see *CJ*, II, 714.

2. The bill had actually received its third reading on 6 August, but because of "some urgent Business," further debate and passage were delayed until this day. On 13 August it was sent to the lords, where it did not go beyond the second reading. Nevertheless, Dawes's creditors were given satisfaction on 15 April 1645 by an order formulated by the commons on 6 August 1641 in case the bill should not pass. See *CJ*, II, 706, 714, 718; and *LJ*, V, 365, 563, and VII, 321.

3. One was the bill for the indemnity of the Earl of Pembroke and his wife. See *PJ*, 2: 136; and *CJ*, II, 714.

stool brought, others that he might have his interpreter come in with him, but all agreed upon that which I had informed the sergeant, that he was not to stand without the bar but to come within it, and in the issue also it was agreed that he should have his interpreter come in with him. But in respect that the messenger whom the Prince of Anhalt sent lately to the house had no chair set for him, therefore it was thought fit to spare that ceremony at this time.

The sergeant then went out with his mace and brought in the said senator of Hamburg with his interpreter. He, coming in some two yards' space within the bar after two or three lowly reverences made first to the Speaker and then to either side of the house, spake a pretty whiles in his own tongue, and then the clerk's assistant went down to him and took his letters of him being two, the first of which was directed to the lords and us and contained the business about which he was sent; the other was directed also jointly to them and us and was only a letter of credence, in which they showed that they had appointed him, being one of their senators, to attend the parliament of England about the business that was expressed in the other letter. The clerk's assistant then brought up the said letters and delivered them to the Speaker, and presently after the interpreter who came in with him related the substance of what the said senator had spoken in his own language, which was not much more in effect than was contained in his letter of credence, and so he withdrew out of the house with his interpreter.

The SPEAKER, then looking upon the superscription of the said letters, found that they were directed to both houses and so desired to know the pleasure of the house whether we should open them till we first had a conference with the lords, but after a short debate we agreed to open them because they were first brought to us, not doubting but that if they had been first brought to them, they would in like manner have perused them before they had communicated them to us, and thereupon the Speaker opened the first letter which contained their business, being written in Latin as the other was also. The clerk read it, and the substance of it was, whereas a Scottish ship had been taken by some of their city, the king had granted letters of marque or reprisal to take the Hamburg ships by force to make satisfaction to those that had lost the other ship, and they desired that the parliament would be a means that this course of hostility might be avoided, and they promised to give satisfaction and justice to the party that was wronged or damnified. The clerk next read the letter of credence, which contained no more in effect than is above set down.

The said letters being read, we agreed after a little debate to return this answer to the senator of Hamburg, that the house had heard his letters, but because they did concern the lords as well as ourselves, we would with all convenient speed communicate them with their lordships and then return a further answer,[4] which the SPEAKER reported to the said senator being again called in, and then his interpreter having informed him of it in his own tongue, they both withdrew and departed.[5]

Dr. Aylett and Dr. Heath brought this message from the lords, that their lordships desired a present conference in the Painted Chamber touching a proclamation which they lately received from his majesty, and so they withdrew. The SPEAKER in his reporting of the message according to the usual form observed Dr. Aylett's mistake in that he had omitted the words "by a committee of both houses," but we, conceiving it to be but his mistake, resolved to give a meeting presently, which the SPEAKER related to the same messengers being again called in between 12 and 1 of the clock, and then they withdrew and departed.

[f. 261b] They being withdrawn and reporters named, the greatest part of the house went up to the conference. I was not present at it nor went again into the house after they returned from it.

The conference was managed by the Lord Mandeville, who showed that the lords had received a letter from his majesty directed to the Speaker of his House of Peers with a proclamation enclosed in it that was to be communicated to the House of Commons, so he read the letter bearing date at [blank] August [blank], 1642,[6] containing no more in substance than is before set down. He then read the proclamation,[7] in which the Earl of Essex and all that did adhere to him were declared traitors unless they should lay down arms and come in and submit themselves to his majesty within 6 days, with other particulars that declared his majesty's resolution to proceed with the war.[8] The Lord Mandeville, having read the proclamation, made report from the lords that they, having perused the said proclamation, had resolved notwithstanding the same to maintain the Earl of Essex with their lives and fortunes in the execution of the place of lord general, to which he had been elected and chosen by both houses of parliament, and desired the concurrence of the House of Commons with them therein.

The Earl of Essex stood up and showed that it was not out of any ambition that he had taken upon him the said place of general but to preserve his country from ruin, and that therefore he was so far from being disheartened from that resolution by this proclamation as that he would proceed with a greater courage

4. On 16 August a joint committee was named to consider the letters. *CJ,* II, 722.
5. For proceedings omitted by D'Ewes, see *CJ,* II, 714–15.
6. For this letter from York dated 9 August, see *LJ,* V, 282.
7. For the proclamation see Rushworth, IV, 769–71. Wing, C 2637.
8. The proclamation commanded that "Our good and loving Subjects within this Realm, shall . . . repair to Us at such place where We shall pitch and set up Our Royal Standard; and where We purpose, in Our own Person, to be present." Rushworth, IV, 771.

and alacrity therein and be ready to hazard his life and fortune in the cause; neither should he be afraid to meet a great man that was to be opposed against him, by which he meant the Marquess of Hertford, who was named in the said proclamation[9] (which shows the calamity of civil war, for this Marquess Hertford had married the said Earl of Essex his sister, had divers children by her, and was like to be heir to the Earl of Essex himself who had no children).

Divers of the members of the House of Commons being returned from the conference, notwithstanding it was so late, yet caused the door to be presently shut so as those that would come in might but none could go out; and then the report being made,[10] divers of the hotter spirits were not content to pass the vote which the lords had passed in a fair, ordinary, and parliamentary war by one general question to which every man might have freely given his Aye or his No without fear but, contrary to the Protestation and contrary to all precedent, forced every man to answer particularly whether they would venture and hazard their lives and fortunes with the Earl of Essex, lord general.[11] And whereas one MR. JESSON, one of the burgesses for Coventry, being an ancient man, did only desire a little time to consider of it before he gave his answer, they would not permit that but compelled him to answer presently, whereupon he not being satisfied in his conscience gave his No, at which those hot spirits taking great distaste, the SPEAKER, unworthy of himself and contrary to the duty of his place, fell upon him with very sharp language for giving his No; and when the poor man, terrified with the displeasure he saw was taken against him, would have given his Aye, they would not permit him to do that neither. SIR GUY PALMES, MR. FETTIPLACE, and others were so overawed by Mr. Jesson's misfortune as they answered Aye without any further debate, and so did many others who came dropping in from dinner not knowing what had been done and was in doing in the house. Nay, they were not satisfied with this vote but agreed to have a covenant drawn which every man should be engaged in, and so a

---

9. Hertford was designated as "Our Lieutenant-General of all Our Forces" for Wales and the western counties of England. Rushworth, IV, 770.

10. For the report, made by Sir Robert Harley and Sir John Holland, see *CJ*, II, 715.

11. The resolution was as follows:

That, whereas the Lords and Commons in Parliament did formerly chuse the Earl of Essex to be Captain General of such Forces as are or shall be raised for the Maintenance and Preservation of the true Protestant Religion, the King's Person, the Laws of the Land, the Peace of the Kingdom, the Liberty and Property of the Subject, and the Rights and Privileges of Parliament; this House doth now Declare, That they will maintain and assist him, and adhere unto him the said Earl, with their Lives and Estates, in the same Cause.

This memorandum follows: "When this Question was put, every Man, in his Place, rose up, and gave his Answer unto it distinctly, one after another." Furthermore, it was resolved that those members who had not yet declared themselves should do so "from time to time, at their coming into the House." *CJ*, II, 715.

committee was named to that end who were also appointed to prepare a declaration against this new proclamation and to sit this afternoon.[12] And so the house rose about 2 of the clock.[13]

12. The committee was to prepare both "a Covenant to be taken in Pursuance of this Resolution" and "a Declaration concerning the Advisers, Contrivers, Abettors, and Publishers" of the king's proclamation. *CJ*, II, 715.

13. For several orders, presented earlier in the day by Giles Green, concerning tonnage and poundage and customs, see *CJ*, II, 715–16.

D'EWES

August 12, Friday, 1642

The Speaker came about 9 of the clock and went to prayers between 9 and 10. In respect of the dangerous and violent proceedings yesterday, I abstained from the house, supposing that the new covenant would have been brought in by the committee this morning, but they had not prepared it; whereupon Mr. Strode and some other violent spirits were added to the same committee to hasten on the work, and they were appointed to sit in the inner Court of Wards[1] at two of the clock this afternoon.

There was no other matter of moment passed in the house,[2] for I viewed the clerk's Journal out of which supply this day's passages.

1. Star Chamber, according to *CJ*. For the members named to the committee on 11, 12, and 15 August, see *CJ*, II, 715, 717, 722. Strode's name appears twice.

2. Actually much took place on this day, including the disabling of four more MPs and the approval of detailed instructions pertaining to county committees. See *CJ*, II, 716–18.

D'EWES

August 13, Saturday, 1642

I abstained from the house also this day,[1] supposing that the new covenant would have been brought in, but the committee had not prepared it; only the declaration against the king's proclamation was reported and allowed by the house,[2] which rose about two of the clock.

1. For the day's proceedings see *CJ*, II, 718–20.
2. The declaration, presented by Reynolds from the committee, was agreed to by the lords and ordered to be printed. It included the resolution to adhere to the Earl of Essex, to which members of the house had been asked to subscribe. The committee was to meet in the afternoon to prepare the covenant; it seems, however, never to have been completed. See 11 August, n. 11; and *CJ*, II, 718, 719. For the declaration see *LJ*, V, 288. Wing, E 1313.

D'EWES

August 15, Monday, 1642

The Speaker came about 9 of the clock. Prayers being ended about half an hour after, some persons who had taken one Newport[1] at Ware in Hertfordshire were brought into the house, and one of them related that he, the said Newport, having set up one of these new proclamations by which the Earl of Essex and all that adhere to him are proclaimed traitors and hidden a cloak bag which he had in a haymow, they first took him and after found his cloak bag, in which were divers of the said proclamations and several letters. They being withdrawn, the said Newport was called in and confessed that he had received the said proclamations from the lord keeper,[2] and for the letters he said that he received them from several hands but knew not the parties. He being withdrawn, we agreed to dismiss the said Ware men with thanks and referred the consideration of the said letters to the committee of information.

SIR PHILIP STAPLETON made report from the committee of the lords and commons appointed for the defense of the kingdom, that the said committee and the Earl of Essex, lord general, desired to acquaint the house how the forces had been disposed of which had been sent from hence, being eleven troops of horse and 4800 foot, viz., that 3 troops of horse had been sent to Portsmouth, 6 troops into Somersetshire with the Earl of Bedford or elsewhere to find out Marquess Hertford, and that the remaining but 2 troops and the 4800 foot with the train of artillery were sent to Warwick.[3] That the master of Captain Marten's ship had surprised a pinnace near Portsmouth which was going into that town with corn. That Mr. Cromwell, one of the burgesses [for] the town of Cambridge, had gotten together divers of the trained bands of that county, had seized upon the magazine of powder in the castle there, and had stopped the plate from going to York which the colleges were sending thither.[4] Sir Philip Stapleton having ended his report, MR. PYM delivered in a letter by which the taking of the

---

1. Newbolton, in *CJ*, II, 720.

2. "With a Command to disperse them; and that he left some of them at Lincolne, Boston, and Cambridge, as he came along." In consequence he was committed to the sergeant's custody. *CJ*, II, 720. For the proclamation see 11 August, n. 7.

3. Cf. *CJ*, II, 720.

4. For details see Abbott, *Cromwell*, I, 187–89. An order for the indemnity of Cromwell and Valentine Walton for preventing the Cambridge plate, valued at about £20,000, from going to York was subsequently formulated. *CJ*, II, 720, 726. For the order see *LJ*, V, 307.

said pinnace and some other particulars were set forth, which was read by the clerk's assistant.[5]

Whilst this letter was in reading, I came out of the house between ten and eleven of the clock, having stayed there about half an hour's space.[6]

5. MS: *assistance*. For a letter of 12 August from the Hampshire parliamentary committee describing, among other things, the capture of the pinnace and the situation in Portsmouth, see *HMC, Portland MSS*, I, 50–51.

6. For the rest of the day, including a division which indicated an attendance of seventy-five, see *CJ*, II, 720–22.

D'EWES

August 16, Tuesday, 1642

The Speaker came about 9 of the clock and went not to prayers till half an hour after. Before my coming into the house there was amongst other passages a letter read sent from his majesty to the Speaker, by which he did require to receive satisfaction why we had diverted a hundred thousand pound of the adventurers' money from the service of Ireland.[1] (This hundred thousand pound had been voted at a thin committee of the adventurers, packed on purpose without the knowledge and to the great discontent of the rest and of many other in the house, to be employed for the maintenance of the civil wars here in England,[2] there being only a color pretended that it should be paid again out of the plate which had been brought in upon the propositions as soon as it could be coined.)[3] The letter bore date at York August 13, 1642, and was directed to the Speaker, and therein he calls this act impious and unjust.[4]

I came into the house a little after ten of the clock, and then MR. PRIDEAUX was making report from the committee to whom it had been referred touching the illegality of the letter office, being a mere project or monopoly which the Earl of Warwick desired to have confirmed to him. Divers spake against it. I went out of the house whilst it was in debate some half an hour after I came in. It

---

1. For the text see Rushworth, IV, 775. Wing, C 2476.

2. On 28 July a letter from the committee of safety to the committee for Irish adventurers indicated that "the distresses of the kingdom are so pressing and the disbursements . . . so great that greater sums are now necessary for the defence of the kingdom than the Lords and Commons can for the present raise." Therefore, a loan of £100,000 was requested. *HMC, Fifth Report*, p. 40. The letter was signed by Holles, Sir William Waller, Stapleton, and Hampden plus five members of the House of Lords. HLRO, Main Papers.

On 30 July the house authorized the loan, which was "to be repaid . . . within so short a Time, that it shall not be diverted from that Purpose for which it was intended; . . . the Consent of the Committee of Adventurers being first thereunto had." *CJ*, II, 698. The Venetian ambassador commented concerning this diversion of money originally intended for Ireland: "The defence of that country is no longer pressing and apparently it is completely abandoned." *CSP Ven., 1642–1643*, p. 130. It was also on 30 July that troops intended for Ireland were ordered to serve the Earl of Essex instead. See 20 June, n. 1.

3. This order, that plate valued at £100,000 should be carried to the Tower to be coined, had also passed on 30 July. *CJ*, II, 697. For D'Ewes's earlier suggestion that money for Ireland might be diverted, see D, 44.

4. The king's letter was referred to the committee named to respond to his recent proclamation. See 11 August, n. 12; and *CJ*, II, 722.

was voted illegal,[5] and many particulars passed after my coming away, which see in the clerk's book.[6]

5. For the earlier history of the letter office dispute and the many postponements of this report, see *PJ,* 2: 72, 95–96; and 12 July, n. 3. It was resolved that the sequestration of the inland letter office to Philip Burlamachi was illegal and should be taken off. The votes concerning him were agreed to by the lords on 8 September. In addition, Sir John Coke and Sir Francis Windebank, former secretaries of state, and Thomas Witherings were declared delinquents, all having been involved with the letter office. See *CJ,* II, 722; *LJ,* V, 343–44; and *HMC, Fifth Report,* p. 47.

6. For the rest of the day, see *CJ,* II, 722–23.

D'EWES

August 17, Wednesday, 1642

The Speaker came between 9 and 10. After prayers where I was present and a motion or two, a letter was read touching the passages at Portsmouth without name bearing date August 15, 1642, in which was showed how cruelly Colonel Goring[1] had spoiled the inhabitants of the island of Portsea near Portsmouth by taking their goods violently and forcibly from them and by committing divers other oppressions upon the inhabitants of the town of Portsmouth themselves, which letter was ordered to be printed.[2]

MR. STRODE showed that he had received two letters out of Somersetshire, one from Mr. Alexander Popham which contained little more than the former letter which he had received from him,[3] and so he thought it not necessary to prefer that into the house to have it read, but that if the house were at leisure, he had another letter which he had received from Mr. William Strode that he desired might be read because it contained a narrative of the passages in Somersetshire.[4] The clerk's assistant thereupon read it bearing date August 11th, 1642, in which he made a long historical narration of most of that which had happened between Marquess Hertford and other commissioners for the commission of array and himself and Mr. Alexander Popham and the rest of the deputy lieutenants for the putting of the ordinance of the militia in execution. How Marquess Hertford and the rest had misbehaved themselves in oppressing the city of Wells and in the violent taking away of the arms of the inhabitants of the town Shepton Mallet, by which the whole country were so provoked as there came in near upon 20,000 of them armed to their assistance against the said commissioners of array. Whereupon the said Marquess Hertford was forced to leave Somersetshire and retired to Sherborne Castle in Dorsetshire where he had fortified himself. He therefore desired that if the Earl of Bedford, lord

---

1. Goring had been disabled to sit in the House of Commons on 16 August. See Appendix A.

2. Wing, C 6132. Portsmouth surrendered to the parliament in early September, Goring departed for the Continent, and Sir William Lewis was appointed governor in his place. See *CJ*, II, 758; Rushworth, IV, 683–84; and Clarendon, *History*, II, 314–15.

3. Popham was among the signers of the letter received on 5 August. For subsequent letters see 8 August, n. 4.

4. For a brief letter from Strode of Somerset to the Earl of Bedford, in which this letter was apparently enclosed, see *LJ*, V, 286. See also Underdown, *Somerset*, pp. 37–38.

lieutenant, were not yet come out of London[5] with those troops of horse with which he was to be sent to their assistance, that he might come away, and then he did not doubt but that his lordship should soon provide for the safety and peace of that county, with divers other particulars too long to be set down here.

The said Mr. Strode had also before delivered in a letter sent to one Mr. Taylor,[6] a citizen of Bristol, a member of the house, but no name was subscribed to it, which the clerk's assistant did likewise read, in which it was showed that they heard that in Wales Sir Edward Stradling and Baronet Kemys[7] were very active for raising men for the king against the parliament. That it was reported that 15,000 men were to be sent from thence to the king, that some of them were to be sent to the said city, but that the citizens were generally resolved not to admit them, with some other particulars of less moment.

MR. HILL delivered in a letter sent to Mr. Dennis Bond, a member of this house, one of the burgesses for the town of Dorchester, without either name or date sent to him from Bristol, in which he desired him to hasten Mr. Denzil Holles his coming to Bristol, being their lord lieutenant, because he conceived that there was never a fitter opportunity offered him for the putting of the ordinance touching the militia in execution[8] because they were extremely irritated with the wrongs and injuries which the Marquess of Hertford and the other commissioners of array had offered to the citizens of Wells.

MR. PYM made report from the committee of lords and commons appointed for the safety of the kingdom, that they had drawn some additional instructions for the Earl of Bedford, lord lieutenant of Devonshire and Somersetshire, for the Earl of Montgomery,[9] lord lieutenant of Wiltshire and Hampshire, and for the Lord Cranborne, lord lieutenant of Dorsetshire, which were read and al-

5. On 12 August the lords had ordered Bedford to depart for Somerset the next day. *LJ,* V, 284. For affairs in Somerset and Dorset, see also a letter to Lenthall from Sir Walter Erle, cited in *HMC, Fifth Report,* pp. 42–43; and Rushworth, IV, 685. Sherborne Castle was the ancestral home of the Digby family.

6. MS: *Flower.* For John Taylor and Sir John Glanville, who had succeeded Humphrey Hooke and Richard Long as MPs for Bristol, see Appendix A.

7. Sir Nicholas Kemys was a former sheriff for Glamorganshire and Monmouthshire and former MP for the latter county. See *Roy. Off.,* pp. 213–14. The letter also related "some suspicious Passages" of Captain Thomas Kettleby, governor of the fort of Kinsale until replaced in late May, and Sir Henry Stradling, Sir Edward's brother. Having been "appointed to guard the Coasts of Ireland" and having "lately deserted that Charge," they were ordered to submit to the commands of the Earl of Warwick. See *CJ,* II, 723, 724, 735; and Hogan, *Irish Rebellion,* pp. 38–39.

8. It was so ordered by the house. *CJ,* II, 723. Bond was among those named to go to Dorset to collect subscriptions of money, horse, and plate. See 19 July, n. 9; and *LJ,* V, 225.

9. I.e., the Earl of Pembroke and Montgomery. Bedford had replaced the Marquess of Hertford on 24 March as parliament's lord lieutenant for Somerset. *CJ,* II, 495. For Cranborne as lord lieutenant, see 14 July, n. 3.

lowed by the house.[10] I went out whilst they were in reading about eleven of the clock.

After my departure besides other particulars which were agitated, SIR PHILIP STAPLETON delivered in a letter bearing date August 13 which was sent to himself and was read, showing the distractions in Yorkshire and that [the] king intended to set up his royal standard at Nottingham on Monday next. (It is printed.)[11] SIR PHILIP STAPLETON showed that such were now the divisions in Yorkshire amongst the gentry and other inhabitants there that unless some troops of horse were speedily sent thither, he gave up that county for lost. It was also informed that Sir Henry Cholmley's house in that county had been rifled by the Cavaliers.[12]

10. These instructions, first submitted to the commons on 12 August, were subsequently agreed to by the lords. They were directed particularly to those appointed "for the Suppression of the Rebellion and Commotion" raised by the Marquess of Hertford in Somerset and other western counties and by the Earl of Northampton in Leicestershire, Northamptonshire, and Warwickshire. See *CJ*, II, 717–18; and *LJ*, V, 297. On 13 August Hertford and Northampton, along with Henry Hastings, had been accused of high treason by the commons and ordered to appear in the lords house on 29 August. *CJ*, II, 718; *LJ*, V, 286.

11. For the letter from Yorkshire and the king's proclamation concerning setting up his standard, see *LJ*, V, 301–03, and Rushworth, IV, 774–75. Wing, F 2358, C 2698. Following a conference with the lords to consider responses to the letter and proclamation, both were referred to the joint committee of safety. See *CJ*, II, 724, 726; and *LJ*, V, 301.

12. In response to the letter to Stapleton, a declaration, directed to Yorkshire and other northern counties, was agreed to by both houses on 20 August. *CJ*, II, 729. For the text see *LJ*, V, 309–10. Wing, E 1477. For the rest of the day, including a division indicating an attendance of fifty-nine, see *CJ*, II, 724–25.

D'EWES

[Harl. 163, f. 295b]   August 18, Thursday, 1642

I was not in the house this day. There was a letter read amongst other things touching the firmness of the inhabitants of the Isle of Wight to the parliament, and that all the castles in the said isle but one, of which Captain Brett[1] was captain, were in the power of the parliament, and that the inhabitants of the said isle were so incensed against him as that, having gotten him out of the castle, they would have torn him in pieces had it not been for the intercession and mediation of two gentlemen in the isle.

See the clerk's book for the rest of this day's passages.[2]

1. Doubtless Jerome Brett, governor of Carisbrooke Castle and member of the commission of array in Hampshire. See *Roy. Off.*, p. 42. The letter is not noted in *CJ*.
2. See *CJ*, II, 725–27.

D'EWES

August 19, Friday, 1642

The Speaker came to the house between 9 and 10 of the clock. I came in a little after prayers were begun. After some trivial motions MR. GREEN preferred in an order to be passed for 600£ of the Lady Benion's, which had been[1] seized upon as if it were to go to York where her husband was (after he had been knighted there, after he had been questioned and fined in parliament),[2] to [be] delivered to the present lord mayor[3] and to be kept and disposed of for her use, upon which ensued some debate; but in the issue it was ordered that Sir Thomas Soame, an alderman of London and member of the house, should have 200£ of it to pay and discharge a past debt due from her husband, and that the other 400£ should be put into the lord mayor's hand to be issued out weekly for the maintenance of her family.[4]

Upon this the SPEAKER stood up and after leave of the house acquainted them that the stopping of this money was occasioned by a general warrant granted by him for the stopping of all arms and money going towards York[5] and that he had by order of the house granted out near upon an hundred such general warrants, wherein although the intention of the house were at first only to search for such things to be carried out of town by or unto persons justly suspected, yet now these warrants were so abused as no man almost could be in safety, for they searched what houses they listed under color to search for arms or money. They came sometimes at midnight and other unseasonable times and often broke open the doors by violence and, when they came into the house, broke open

---

1. Crossed out in MS: *stayed from her as.*

2. Following George Benion's impeachment for his role in framing the London petition of February 1642, he had been sentenced to two years in Colchester Castle. However, he was still in the Tower on 2 July when the king's warrant for his release was presented to the lords; on 28 July he was knighted at Beverley. See *PJ*, 1 and 2: passim; *LJ*, V, 175; and Toynbee and Young, *Strangers in Oxford*, p. 152. On 12 August a petition from Lady Alice Benion was referred to a committee, with Hill as a member, named to look after Benion's money recently diverted to Guildhall. Reportedly £4000 or £5000 in gold belonging to Benion had been found "on a porter's back" ready to be carried to York. See *CJ*, II, 711, 713, 717; and *CSPD, 1641–43*, p. 368.

3. On 16 August Isaac Penington, alderman and MP for the City of London, was elected lord mayor in place of Sir Richard Gurney, who had been removed from office four days earlier. See *CJ*, II, 723; *LJ*, V, 284–85, 297–98, 301; and Pearl, *London*, pp. 157–58.

4. Despite these orders the house subsequently decided that the money should remain at Guildhall. See *CJ*, II, 727, 729, 747.

5. See 4 July, n. 12.

trunks, chests, and other places; and afterwards if they saw a house well furnished, though it were of never so honest a Protestant and a well-wisher to the parliament, they would say he was a malignant person and so get his house to be rifled. Whereupon after some debate the house agreed that these general warrants should be called in and no more granted but in special cases only or searching of carts or wagons or horses which were to carry things out of town, and that if any house were suspected and thought fit to be searched, they should in particular name it and so have a particular warrant for it. (And thus did every day discover to us into how much injustice and inconvenience these violent proceedings that we were now fallen upon did enforce us to run and though we were now at above fifteen thousand pounds' weekly charge for the payment of the new-levied army; and that contrary to what we had published and protested in print, these fiery spirits had employed the supplies of horse and foot which were prepared for the relief of distressed Ireland for the maintenance of the civil war here;[6] yet the insolencies of these new-levied soldiers were almost everywhere intolerable, as may in part appear by the complaints of two members of our own this day being as followeth.)[7]

MR. BELL, one of the burgesses for the borough of Westminster, made complaint that having taken a house of his own in Hackney[8] into his hands wherein was much of his own household stuff, some of these new-levied soldiers had violently broken the doors and taken away all his household stuff and sold it and sold that for 2s. which had cost him twenty. That they had threatened to pull [down] his house the next day, which he verily believed they had done unless he had sent to [f. 296b] prevent it. He desired therefore that some of the principal[s] in that riot might be punished and that he might have authority from the house to search for his goods in Hackney, which had been so unlawfully sold, and to seize them in whose hands soever he found them. Some few spake to it, and in the issue the house thought fit to refer it to some neighboring justices of peace to examine, to punish the offenders, and to see restitution made of the said goods.

MR. WINWOOD, another member of the house, showed that he bringing up divers goods to the town and being himself with the wagon in which they were, yet some of those new-levied foot forces, which are taken into pay by the two houses of parliament, did violently take away some of his said goods in his own presence and threatened himself also when he told them that he was a member

6. For this diversion of money and men to the Earl of Essex, passed on 30 July, see 20 June, n. 1; 16 August, n. 2; and *CJ*, II, 698.

7. On 18 August an order had been formulated concerning "Disorders committed by the Soldiers," requiring that they be "kept from straggling up and down the Countries" and that their officers should be "in Person amongst the Soldiers." *CJ*, II, 727.

8. Hampton town, in *CJ*, II, 727.

of the House of Commons, telling him that he was of the malignant party. After two or three had spoken to this particular, I withdrew out of the house about eleven of the clock.

See Mr. Moore's journal.[9]

9. For the rest of the day, see *CJ*, II, 727–29.

D'EWES

[f. 296b]   August 20, Saturday, 1642

The Speaker came between 9 and 10. I came in awhile after.[1] I had not been long in the house before MR. SALWAY, one of the knights of the shire for the county of Worcester, being returned up from thence with Serjeant Wilde, his fellow knight, in great haste for fear of some violence that should have been offered unto them by the commission of array, delivered in the warrant which was sent to the said Mr. Serjeant Wilde[2] from Thomas, Lord Coventry, Sir Thomas Littleton,[3] and others to command him to make show of his horse before them. The hand of Sir Henry Herbert and of two other members of the house, viz., Mr. Samuel Sandys and Sir John Pakington,[4] were also to the same warrant. The said MR. SALWAY then delivered in a letter which had been sent to him from one who was present at Worcester the same day that the said commission of array was put in execution,[5] wherein he showed that the greater of those who appeared that day were of mean condition. That it was well for himself and the said Serjeant Wilde that they were not then present, for there was an intention to have seized upon them and to have sent them to York, with other particulars of less moment.

These particulars being read, some were of opinion that Sir Henry Herbert and the other two members of the house who had subscribed their names to the said warrant sent to Mr. Serjeant Wilde should be summoned to appear at a certain day and to answer the same, but MR. HENRY MARTEN and some other violent spirits being the major number (for we were not above 60 in the house) cried to have the question put for expelling them out of the house. The SPEAKER

1. For proceedings omitted by D'Ewes, see *CJ*, II, 728–29.
2. The warrant, dated 5 August, commanded Wilde "on the 12th to bring those horses, arms and array he stands charged with to the Pitchcroft [a great meadow], near Worcester." Furthermore, "it was commonly affirmed that they [the commissioners of array] intended to surprise Serjeant Wylde and Mr. Salwey and carry them to York." See *HMC, Portland MSS*, I, 47, 53; and Bund, *Diary of Townshend*, II, 67.
3. MP for Worcestershire in the Short Parliament, Littleton had been defeated by Wilde and Salway in the Long Parliament election. Keeler, p. 72.
4. In the instructions to Worcestershire of 21 June, the king named Sandys to command the horse of the county. Pakington was brother-in-law to Sandys and son-in-law to Lord Coventry. See Bund, *Diary of Townshend*, II, 63; and *Roy. Off.*, pp. 283, 328.
5. For another letter describing the implementation of the commission of array, see Bund, *Diary of Townshend*, II, 73–74. For an order of 16 August for the disarming of all "Countenancers of the Commissions of Array, in all Counties," see *LJ*, V, 297.

then stood up and asked whether any proof could be made that it was their own handwriting which was subscribed to the said warrant, and SERJEANT WILDE stood up and said that he knew it to be their handwriting, which was certainly a bold and rash information. But thereupon the question was put and carried affirmatively that the said Sir Henry Herbert and the other two should be disabled from being members of the house during this parliament, and then was a second vote passed which followed of course that warrants should be sent to the clerk of the crown for new writs to be issued forth for the election of others in their places.[6]

It was then showed that Sir John Strangways, Mr. Giles Strangways, [f. 297b] his son, and Mr. Rogers did ill services in the county of Dorset and had neglected to return to the house being summoned. The SPEAKER stood up and showed that he had received a letter from Sir John Strangways, wherein he did excuse his absence from the house by reason of the tumultuary proceedings and troubles raised in the county of Dorset where he lives not far from his house. That he desired the favor of the house to continue a little while there and look to his own, but some of the hotter spirits were so far from admitting this excuse as they would presently have expelled him and his son and the said Mr. Rogers out of the house; but they were at length persuaded by some wiser judgments to set them a day by which, if they did not come to the house, we might proceed against them, and so we appointed Monday come sevennight to be the day by order of the house upon the question.[7]

MR. KNIGHTLEY[8] showed that there were some of the members of this house in Northamptonshire that were providing of horses to send to the king and wished that they might likewise be summoned to return to the house, and so being required to name them, he showed that they were Sir Christopher Hatton, Sir Robert Hatton, Mr. Geoffrey Palmer, and Sir Robert Napier. And so the same Monday come sevennight was likewise ordered upon the question to be the day for them to come up and attend the house.[9]

I went out about eleven of the clock.[10]

6. A new committee had been named on 17 August "to consider of such Members of the House as are absent." It was now instructed "to prepare a Declaration concerning the Disabling of divers Members of this House, and . . . to consider of some convenient Way for the House to be filled," a move doubtless precipitated by low attendance. Hill was a member and possibly chairman of the committee. *CJ*, II, 725, 729.

7. Though no action was taken on 29 August, the three men, along with several others, were suspended because of absence on 2 September. Subsequently they were disabled. See *CJ*, II, 750; Appendix A; and Brunton and Pennington, *Members*, p. 221.

8. Knightley was a member of the committee sent to Northamptonshire in June and again in August to execute the militia ordinance. For their names and instructions, see 8 June, n. 3; *CJ*, II, 711; and *LJ*, V, 276–78.

9. For their summons see *CJ*, II, 729.

10. For the rest of the day, see *CJ*, II, 729–30.

D'EWES

August 22, Monday

I came into the house about 10 of the clock.

MR. ERLE delivered in a letter sent to him from Mr. Dennis Bond from Dorchester, where it bore date August 18, 1642,[1] which said Mr. Bond was one of the burgesses for that town, in which he showed how the Marquess of Hertford did fortify himself in Sherborne Castle, and that they did not doubt if the troops which were sent for from the parliament did come, they should prevail against him, which if they had come last week, they might have done much more easily. He therein sent a copy of a warrant which the said Marquess of Hertford had sent to the mayor of Poole[2] and a copy of his commission which he had received from his majesty by which he, the said marquess, was appointed captain general of his majesty's forces. The warrant was first read bearing date August the 13, 1642, the substance of which was that the said mayor should preserve the town for the king's use and suffer no forces to be levied or raised therein but by the king's authority. Then was the commission read, which was ordered to be printed, and that especially because of one clause in it whereby the said marquess had authority given him to make laws.[3]

I came a little after out of the house about eleven of the clock and was not there present again this day.[4]

1. The date is 20 August in *CJ,* II, 730.
2. Henry Harbin. For events in Poole and Dorchester in August, see Bayley, *Dorset,* pp. 44–46.
3. Hertford's commission stated: "We give you full Power and Authority to make, constitute and ordain Laws and Proclamations . . . for the good Government and Order of all the Forces that shall be under your Command." Rushworth, IV, 673. Wing, C 2168. See also 8 August, n. 1.
4. For the rest of the day, see *CJ,* II, 730–32.

D'EWES

August 23, Tuesday, 1642

I was not at the house this day. But there came an information from Colchester in the county of Essex[1] that whereas Sir John Lucas,[2] who dwelt near the said town, had an intent to go away to his majesty with certain horse against the parliament, the said town set a guard about his house, and he intending to have slipped away about midnight at a back garden gate, some of the horses were espied and laid hold upon, and the report of it being carried into the town, there were great numbers flocked thence to the said Sir John Lucas his house and rifled it, taking away his plate and household stuff and not sparing his very evidences,[3] so as his own person and his lady's were in very great danger.[4] The mayor of the town was forced to take him into his own custody to secure him, but the multitude not satisfied therewith required to have him committed to prison, threatening else to pull down the said mayor's house, whereupon he was compelled to commit him to a house in the town which was formerly used for a jail where he now remained, but that such multitudes of the country still came in as they desired speedy direction from the parliament what to do. So the whole matter being made known to the house, it was ordered that Mr. Harbottle Grimston, recorder of the said town, and Sir Thomas Barrington should speedily be sent down to disperse the said multitude and to let them know that this matter should be fully discussed in parliament and to cause the said Sir John Lucas to be sent up to the parliament.[5]

There were a great many other particulars passed this day, which see in the clerk's book.[6]

---

1. For this letter of 22 August from Mayor Thomas Wade to Harbottle Grimston, see *HMC, Abergavenny and Braye MSS,* pp. 146–47.

2. Lucas, who had been previously summoned by the house on 9 June, "had made great Provisions of Horse, Arms, and Ammunition, to be secretly conveyed to the King." See *CJ,* II, 615, 705, 732, 734. Lucas and his brothers, Sir Charles and Sir Thomas, subsequently became prominent royalist officers. See *Roy. Off.,* pp. 240–41. *DNB.*

3. Documents, especially title deeds. *NED.*

4. In addition, a petition from his mother, Elizabeth Lucas, concerning her losses is noted in *HMC, Fifth Report,* p. 46.

5. Lucas's horses, arms, ammunition, and plate were also to be seized. A declaration to be sent to Colchester was prepared and along with the mayor's letter was one subject of a conference with the lords. See *CJ,* II, 732, 734; and *LJ,* V, 318.

6. See *CJ,* II, 732–34.

D'EWES

[f. 298b]   August 24, Wednesday, 1642

I came into the house a little before 10 of the clock and was present at prayers. After prayers upon MR. HEVENINGHAM his motion, it was ordered that the Speaker should give a license for Sir John Hobart dwelling in the city of Norwich to send down arms to his house.[1]

SIR HENRY MILDMAY delivered in an order drawn by the committee for printing (of which I was one) for suppressing such scandalous pamphlets as were printed to the scandal of the state and parliament, which he said should have been delivered in by Mr. White, who sat in the chair in that committee.[2] The said order was thereupon read and contained in it, besides those passages against scandalous pamphlets, a clause or two by which the wardens of the Company of Stationers were authorized to exercise all that illegal and tyrannical power which they did put in practice before the beginning of this parliament by virtue of the king's letters patent and by color of certain orders made at the council table and in the Star Chamber, which made me (having as yet never spoken publicly in the house since the injustice I received there on Saturday, July 23 last past) to speak privately to Mr. Miles Corbet, one of the burgesses of Yarmouth in the county of Norfolk, who sat next me on my right hand, to move that the said order might be recommitted because it was of dangerous consequence in divers passages of it. And so upon his motion it was recommitted to the same committee,[3] and myself and others who were of the committee were appointed to withdraw presently and amend it, which we did accordingly after we had withdrawn into the inner Court of Wards, for upon the speaking of myself and others all those dangerous passages which had been before in were left out and deducted,[4] which being done we departed thence, and awhile after I returned into the house.

1. Hobart was to be allowed to travel to Norfolk with his arms "without any Lett or Molestation." *CJ*, II, 734.

2. The ordinance had been reported to the house on 1 July by Serjeant Wilde, then recommitted. The names of Wilde and Mildmay do not appear among the members of this ad hoc committee. See D, 78; and *CJ*, II, 624, 647.

3. Except for White and D'Ewes, the membership of this committee was not the same as the one named on 15 June. Cf. *CJ*, II, 624 and 734.

4. The ordinance was approved by both houses. *CJ*, II, 736; *LJ*, V, 321. For the text see *CJ*, II, 739. Wing, E 1467.

There were divers trivial things moved and ordered,[5] and there was great expectation that the Scottish commissioners should have come into the house to have communicated to us certain instructions which they had received from the assembly lately congregated in Scotland sent hither to them by the Lord John Maitland.[6] But MR. PYM stood up and showed that he had spoken with the Scottish commissioners, and whereas the house had determined to have given them an honorable admittance, they were very thankful for it, but that their instructions were such which they had received out of Scotland that they were to communicate the matter to both houses either together or as a committee or to the commissioners of both houses, and that they having communicated the same to the lords, their lordships had thought it fit to have the business dispatched in a committee of both houses;[7] and so Mr. Pym went out to acquaint the Scottish commissioners therewith, having first showed us that the lords did resolve to sit there bareheaded, that so we might not seem to appear with any disadvantage.

I withdrew out of the house about eleven of the clock.[8]

5. See *CJ*, II, 734–35.

6. The General Assembly of the Church of Scotland had convened in St. Andrews on 26 July. For the declaration sent by parliament to the assembly, see 21 July, n. 4. Maitland's role was to forge a new link between the Covenanters and the parliament, according to C. V. Wedgwood, *The King's War 1641–1647* (New York, 1959), pp. 109–10. The following year he was one of the Scottish commissioners to the Westminster Assembly. *DNB*.

7. The lords and commons agreed to meet together as committees of the whole the next afternoon. *CJ*, II, 735.

8. For the rest of the day, see *CJ*, II, 735–36.

D'EWES

[f. 298b]   August 25, Thursday, 1642

The Speaker came about 10 of the clock. I came into the house a little whiles after prayers were past, before which time SIR WILLIAM MASHAM had delivered in to the house such information as he had received out of Essex from Sir Thomas Barrington and Mr. Harbottle Grimston, who had been sent down to Colchester on Tuesday last to disperse those riotous tumults of people which had been assembled there and had pillaged [f. 300a] the house of Sir John Lucas near Colchester. In which information they showed that after the pillaging of the said Sir John Lucas his house and before their coming down to Colchester, the multitude had gone to St. Osyth, the house of the Countess Rivers,[1] and had rifled that also, taking away her money, plate, and goods to the value of divers thousands pounds; that they had used their uttermost endeavors to disperse the said multitudes, some of them promising to bring in and restore such goods as they[2] had taken. A little after my coming into the house, Sir William Masham and some other Essex gentlemen had order to carry the same information to the committee of lords and commons for the defense of the kingdom.[3]

Besides other trivial things which were agitated during my being in the house, information was given that the Earl of Northampton had at Coventry lately taken away many suits of clothes which were carrying to West Chester to be sent into Ireland to the army there. The commissary who bought the said clothes and the carrier who conveyed them were both brought into the house, and the first witnessed that the clothes cost near upon 600£, and the other showed that the Earl of Northampton took also from him his wagon and horses

1. A Roman Catholic, mother to Earl Rivers, and widow of Thomas, Viscount Savage. GEC, *Peerage*. The letter from Mayor Wade reporting the pillaging of Lucas's house had concluded: "We fear they will not stay here, for they say they will go to Lady Savage's at St. Osith, and to some other places about the town." As a result the lords had ordered Barrington and Grimston to search the house of Countess Rivers (Viscountess Savage) and "to give Direction that the House and Inhabitants shall be freed from any Tumults." See 23 August, n. 1; and *LJ*, V, 318.

2. MS: *I*. An account of the pillaging also appeared in print. Wing, E 2624A (M 1911 in the 1945–51 edition).

3. It was subsequently ordered that the Earl of Warwick should go to Essex for a few days "for the better Preservation of the Peace of that County." In addition, the MPs for Essex, who were also deputy lieutenants, were to write to the rest of the deputy lieutenants there "to use their Endeavour for the Quieting of the People." *CJ*, II, 737. For additional details concerning the pillaging in Essex, see William Hunt, *The Puritan Movement* (Cambridge, Mass., 1983), pp. 301–05.

which he valued at some 70 pounds. He related amongst other particulars that the said earl took the said clothes away the said goods from him [*sic*] at Coventry, and when he told him that they were to be sent into Ireland, the said earl answered that they should serve for the king. They then withdrew, and we voted that the said Earl of Northampton should make satisfaction for the said clothes out of his goods here at his house in Bishopsgate Street in London, and that the carrier should likewise receive an 100£ for satisfaction of his wagon, horses, and his damage since sustained by the interruption of his trade.[4]

Divers other particulars passed this day. I went out of the house about eleven of the clock.[5]

Post Meridiem

See the manner of the Scottish commissioners' meeting this afternoon with the committee of lords and commons in the Painted Chamber in Mr. Moore's journal.[6]

4. A committee, which included Hill, was named to make reparations. *CJ*, II, 736.

5. For the rest of the day, see *CJ*, II, 736–37.

6. Despite the previous day's decision to meet as committees of the whole with the Scots commissioners, the commons named six members and the lords four as a joint committee. *CJ*, II, 737; *LJ*, V, 321.

D'EWES

August 26, Friday, 1642

The Speaker came about 10 of the clock. There were divers trivial things moved and ordered during my being in the house, which was not above three quarters of an hour.[1] The main thing in agitation while I continued in the house was touching a letter sent up from the aldermen and Common Council of the city of Shrewsbury to one or both of their burgesses here, which was delivered in by MR. SPURSTOW[2] bearing date at Shrewsbury August 22, 1642, in which they showed that the mayor of the said town and the recorder had tendered a kind of declaration or protestation for them to subscribe unto, to which the said mayor and recorder had before subscribed. And the grand jury held for that county at the last assizes,[3] they not knowing how far the said declaration might trench upon the privilege of parliament, had refused to subscribe the same till they might first receive advice and so desired them to acquaint the House of Commons therewith and to show them the enclosed new declaration or protestation, being the same which had been agreed upon by the grand jury at the last assizes for Worcester[4] where Baron Henden sat as judge as well as at the assizes at Shropshire. Then the copy of the said declaration or protestation was read, the substance of which was that they did acknowledge that all the good laws that had passed this parliament did solely proceed from his majesty's goodness. They did allow of the commissions of array and the present church government and liturgy and did promise to adhere to his majesty against all persons whatsoever for the defense of his person, of the laws, and of the just privileges of parliament. I went out of the house between 10 and eleven of the clock much about the time that this was in reading, so as I cannot tell what was determined upon it.[5]

1. For proceedings omitted by D'Ewes, see *CJ*, II, 737.
2. The other burgess, Francis Newport, was sympathetic to the royalist cause. See *Roy. Off.*, p. 273. For the situation in Shrewsbury in July and August, see Owen and Blakeway, *Shrewsbury*, I, 417–18.
3. The assizes had been held on 8 August. *CJ*, II, 737.
4. See 9 August, n. 2. The Shropshire declaration was also printed. Wing, D 539.
5. A committee, including Hill, was named "to examine the Proceedings . . . of all the Justices of Assize, and Sheriffs . . . in Packing of Grand Juries," as well as the "Protestation agreed upon by the Grand Jury of Salop," and to consider how to prevent grand juries from "meddling with Matters they are not concerned in." *CJ*, II, 737. In addition, the indictment of Thomas Hunt and others for military training was removed. See 16 July, n. 4.

Upon report made of what had been delivered yesterday in the afternoon in the Painted Chamber by the commissioners of Scotland to the select committee of both houses and the reading of the said papers which had been read there, it was ordered that the said business should be taken into debate tomorrow morning.[6]

6. For the approbation from the Scots Privy Council (18 August) and the declaration from the General Assembly of Scotland (3 August), see *LJ*, V, 323–35. Wing, H 1438 (declaration). The latter, a response to parliament's declaration of 21 July, set forth the following objective: "Unity of Religion; that, in all His Majesty's Dominions, there might be One Confession of Faith, One Directory of Worship, One Public Catechism, and One Form of Kirke Government." The debate was subsequently postponed until 1 September. *CJ*, II, 740, 742. For the rest of the day, see *CJ*, II, 738–39.

D'EWES

August 27, Saturday, 1642

The Speaker came about 10 of the clock.

I came into the house a little after prayers were ended and found them very hot in dispute whether they should not presently expel Sir John Colepeper (being a member of the house and chancellor of the Exchequer)[1] and being newly come to town this morning bringing a gracious message to this house from the king, which was sent from Nottingham by himself and Sir William Uvedale,[2] another member of the house, as was also the same message sent to the lords house by the Earls of Southampton and Dorset. The ground of the debate arose from hence, that the said Sir John Colepeper had been summoned with other members of the house then at York with his majesty to return to the house, which he had neglected to do and had also underwritten to furnish horses for his majesty, which they interpreted to be against the parliament and thought that they might justly expel him upon these grounds. Not any man spake against his expelling in due time but only against the doing of it at this time when he had brought a message from his majesty.[3] Yet some fiery spirits were so hot upon it as they would scarce permit Mr. Pym himself to speak for Sir John Colepeper.

The SPEAKER informed the house that the reason why Sir John Colepeper did forbear to come into the house, though he were a member of it, was in respect of an order made here the 16 day of July[4] last past, that none of the members then absent, whom the house had fined 100£ apiece for their said absence, should come into the house till they had either paid the said money or satisfied a committee that was then nominated to take the excuse for their absence[5] and so to present it to the house, that then the house might judge of it whether they would allow it or not. And therefore he desired to know whether the said committee should go forth to take his excuse, and thereupon a letter sent to him yesterday from the said Sir John Colepeper, being then in his journey, was

---

1. Colepeper was among those absent without leave when the house was called on 16 June. Apparently he and Falkland had by then joined the king at York. See Appendix G; and 21 June, n. 6.

2. Uvedale, having joined the king by early August, was soon thereafter replaced as treasurer of the army by Sir Gilbert Gerard. See *CSPD, 1641–43*, pp. 368, 369; and *LJ*, V, 281–82. For Uvedale's political vacillations see Keeler, pp. 369–70, and Aylmer, *King's Servants*, pp. 391–92.

3. Colepeper was not disabled until January 1644. Brunton and Pennington, *Members*, p. 215.

4. The date should be 16 June.

5. For the committee see 16 June, n. 20.

produced by him and read, in which he showed that he desired the favor of the house to be admitted into it and that he would forbear coming in until he had satisfied the house with the reasons of his absence, bringing a very gracious message from his majesty as he hoped.

But notwithstanding this letter and all that the Speaker or any other could say, Mr. HENRY MARTEN, Mr. STRODE, and the other fiery spirits in the house (fearing, I think, lest this gracious message might beget some right understanding between his majesty and the house) would have had the question put for expelling him out of the house presently; but then others desiring that the question according to our ordinary custom might be first put whether that question should be now put or not, it was so done accordingly, and the house was divided upon it, and the Ayes who sat still were 29, and the Noes which went out (myself being one of them) were 67.[6] So as I well hoped we should have carried it in other particulars also so as Sir John Colepeper would have been brought into the house and delivered his message in his place, but it was[7] strongly moved by those fiery spirits that he should either deliver it [at] the bar or send it into the house by the sergeant. Whereupon Mr. SOLICITOR stood up and showed that Sir John Colepeper had a little before spoken to him as he came into the house and desired him to acquaint the house that his command was such from his majesty that he could not deliver the said message but as a member of the house in his place, which notwithstanding it was in the issue overruled by the major part of the house that he should either come in to the bar and deliver his message or else send it into the house if it were in writing.[8]

[f. 304a] Nay, Mr. HENRY MARTEN, disliking as it seems that there was any way pitched upon by which we might receive the said message, to divert us from this business moved to the orders of the house that whereas upon the receipt of the late proclamation by which the Earl of Essex and others were declared traitors, that there had been a declaration made to adhere to him for the maintenance of the true religion, the king's person, the laws of the land, and the privileges of parliament,[9] and that it was also ordered at the same time that all such members of the house as were then absent should give their Ayes or their Noes to the said declaration from time to time as they came into the house, and that there were some Sussex men that were lately come up now present in the house and he desired that they might give their Aye or their No to the same declaration, meaning Sir Thomas Bowyer, Sir William Morley,[10] and others. I

---

6. The vote was 26 to 69 according to *CJ*, II, 739.

7. Crossed out in MS: *soon agreed upon by the major.*

8. There was a comparable dispute in the House of Lords as to whether the Earl of Southampton might personally deliver the king's message. He finally reluctantly sent it in by the black rod. See *LJ*, V, 326.

9. See 11 August, nn. 7, 11; and 13 August, n. 2.

10. They had been summoned on 9 August. *CJ*, II, 711.

had come into the house divers days since the said declaration [was] made and was never called upon either to give my Aye or my No to it, but now these fiery spirits upon his majesty's sending in this manner grew to the very height of insolency.

The clerk then read the said declaration, and the SPEAKER declared that every man must say Aye or No and no more, whereupon MR. GLYN (a lawyer of Lincoln's Inn and recorder of Westminster, a swearing, profane fellow yet now temporizing with the fiery spirits, began first and) showed that he was absent from the house when this declaration was passed yet did very readily give [f. 304b] his assent now to it. SIR HENRY VANE, the younger, SIR WILLIAM ARMINE, SIR WILLIAM MORLEY, and others having given their single Ayes to it,[11] some called up SIR THOMAS BOWYER who sat next me on my right hand, who thereupon stood up and said that he did agree to the same declaration so far as it might stand with the Oaths of Supremacy and Allegiance, at which divers violent spirits called out to him to withdraw as if he had committed some great offense, and he rose up being ready to do it, but I sitting next him wished him to stay which he did accordingly, and then the SPEAKER told him that if he were not satisfied to give his single Aye, he might give his No which he did.

I sitting next him and seeing many in expectation that I should declare myself and one or two that sat near me desiring me privately to rise, I stood up, being the first time I had done so since the unjust proceedings against me on Saturday, the 23th of July last past. And I said that I saw the particulars for the defense of which I was to declare myself were all conjoined, and therefore I might very well give my Aye to it which I did in the *toto composito,* at which some snarling spirits began to take exception; but the SPEAKER, conscious to himself how he had overdone his work on the said 23th day of July, stood up and said that I had answered as fairly and fully as possibly could be desired and that he himself had given his Aye in the same notion, and thereupon the house slighted those begun cavils and I sat still.

SIR THOMAS BOWYER, hearing what I had said, stood up again desiring the favor of the house that he might not be surprised upon the sudden, this question being new to him, and that now understanding from what had been last spoken, by which he meant what I had answered, that all these particulars were taken in a conjoined sense, he was ready to give his Aye to it and so he did, which was accepted though MR. STRODE and one or two more opposed it, and some afterwards gave their single Aye without any further addition.

This being past, the house returned again to the business touching Sir John

11. For the names of sixteen MPs, including D'Ewes, who subscribed to the declaration on this day, see *CJ*, II, 740. Armine's name, however, does not appear. For additional names through 17 September, see *CJ*, II, 741, 743, 755–56, 765, 769.

Colepeper, and having agreed that he should come in to the bar, some little debate arose whether the sergeant should go call him in with his mace or without it, and in conclusion it was agreed he should carry the mace, which he did accordingly. And I verily thought that Sir John Colepeper in respect of the message he sent in by Mr. Solicitor would never have come in to the bar with him, but whether he were surprised with fear or astonishment or the unexpectedness of his calling in I know not, he followed the sergeant in almost as soon as he could possibly return back again; and being come to the bar and there standing bareheaded, he looked so dejectedly as if he had been a delinquent rather than a member of the house, a privy councillor, or a messenger from his majesty. The SPEAKER then, sitting in his chair and keeping his hat on, spake in effect following: Sir John Colepeper (without styling him Mr. Chancellor of the Exchequer), the house understands that you have a message to deliver to them from his majesty which they give you liberty to perform. Whereupon he said only that his majesty had sent a message by him in writing which he had ready to deliver to them and so delivered it in, and then the SPEAKER wished him to withdraw, which he did accordingly; and then his majesty's message was read in the house by the clerk, having the words "Charles Rex" in the top of it, which made one move that the Speaker himself should read it, but the SPEAKER answered that if his majesty had sent it to him, he was indeed to have read it, but now being sent to the house by another hand, he was not to do it.

[f. 307b] The clerk read the said message being directed only to the House of Commons (and another of the same nature sent by the Earls of Southampton and Dorset being directed to the House of Peers).[12] It appeared that his majesty had sent the same by Sir John Colepeper and Sir William Uvedale and that he descended lower in desiring peace of the two houses than ever any prince had done before, offering to appoint some to meet and treat with a like number to be appointed by both houses, promising security to such as we should send and requiring the same from us, and then giving liberty to us to appoint the place of meeting that so all matters in difference might be composed and civil war be avoided.[13]

I did not believe that the fiery spirits in the house would have so slighted this message as they did, though they had undervalued the messenger, but they found a way utterly to make void all the good this message might have produced by alleging that they could not receive it till his majesty had laid down his standard[14]

12. For the message, dated 25 August, see *LJ*, V, 327–28. Wing, C 2333.

13. At the end of the message, however, the king declared: "If this Proposition shall be rejected by you, We have done Our Duty so amply, that God will absolve Us from the Guilt of any of that Blood which must be spilt."

14. The king had raised his standard at Nottingham on 22 August. See Rushworth, IV, 783–84; and Gardiner, *History of England*, X, 218–20.

set up against them and recalled his proclamation by which he declared the Earl of Essex and all that did adhere to him to be traitors (which indeed his majesty would and must have done of necessity with all speed if we had but embraced his message). But MR. STRODE not content with this exercised his profane and scurrilous wit to scoff and vilify the king himself, as though the running away of the Earls of Newport and Northampton and some 1200 horse more of Cavaliers and others near Coventry had been a full defeat of all the king's forces.[15] And therefore he said that his majesty had done well in proclaiming us traitors that so we might be the fitter to treat with those about him being all traitors; and therefore he did not well see, if the proclamation were recalled, how the king could name any about him with whom we could admit a treaty. And for putting down his royal standard, that, said he, 'tis very likely he will easily yield unto because he can keep up no longer; just as it was done in the Spanish match[16] when they could continue it no longer, then they came to the houses to dissolve it, with some other such like irreverential expressions. The house then resolved to have a conference with the lords about it[17] and so sent up Sir Christopher Yelverton between 12 and one of the clock to them to desire them to sit awhile, and so I took the opportunity thereupon to withdraw out of the house and returned back no more this day. But after my departure a declaration or answer was agreed on by both houses to send to his majesty to let him know that unless he called in that proclamation and took down his standard, they were not in a condition capable to enter into further treaty touching his message, and Sir John Colepeper was appointed to be the messenger to carry it.[18]

15. The king had found the gates of Coventry shut against him on 20 August. For the situation there see *CJ*, II, 731; *LJ*, V, 321; Rushworth, IV, 783; and Clarendon, *History*, II, 288–90.

16. Strode was a member of the 1624 parliament when James I capitulated concerning the Spanish match. See Robert E. Ruigh, *The Parliament of 1624* (Cambridge, Mass., 1971), pp. 102, 348–51.

17. Another head of the conference was "to desire the Lords to join with this House in a Direction to the Lord General, that he advance his Forces, with all possible Speed, for the Defence and Safety of the Kingdom." *CJ*, II, 740.

18. The message originated in the House of Lords. For the text see *LJ*, V, 328. Wing, C 2333. For the rest of the day, see *CJ*, II, 740.

D'EWES

August 29, Monday, 1642

The Speaker came about ten of the clock. Besides other trivial business passed this morning during my being in the house, SIR THOMAS BARRINGTON made a report what Mr. Harbottle Grimston and himself had done, being lately sent into Essex to appease the multitudes there, and showed that if the house had but dismissed them (as they desired) four hours sooner than they did, they might have saved forty thousand pounds' worth of goods. And yet he said that though they went out of town at four of the clock in the afternoon,[1] yet they went eight and twenty miles that night (viz., to Chelmsford). That the first place they came at where they saw any pillaging was called Yeldham, where there being divers houses in pillaging, upon their letting the people know that the parliament did dislike such their proceedings, they presently gave over, alleging that what they had done they did with an intent to serve the parliament and would obey their commands, and thereupon many of them instantly brought in such goods as they had taken and made restitution of them. Coming to Colchester, they there found a body of 5 or 6 thousand men, who upon their telling of them how displeasing the rifling and pillaging of Sir John Lucas his house was to the parliament, they all expressed much sorrow for what they had done and said that they would be willing to obey the parliament, conceiving that what they had done had been [f. 308a] grounded upon an order of parliament,[2] and therefore if the parliament were safe, it was as much as they desired, and that they did thereupon disperse themselves and made restitution of divers of those goods that they had taken. That Mr. Grimston went to the Countess of Rivers her house to St. Osyth, where the mariners and others had pillaged goods and spoiled the house to the value of forty thousand pounds,[3] and that there also had been near upon 4 thousand pounds' worth of goods brought in and restored since the said Mr. Grimston's going thither. That himself came away bringing up Sir John Lucas with him and 8 of the 12 horses which had been taken from

1. They had departed on 23 August.

2. Probably the order concerning arms going to York and other places. See 4 July, n. 12. For Barrington's report on pillaging, see also *CJ*, II, 741. Two recent orders to restrain the pillaging and searching of houses by soldiers and others appear in *LJ*, V, 327, 328.

3. Her house at Long Melford, Suffolk, had also been pillaged. See *HMC, Fifth Report*, pp. 45, 47; and Mary Anne Everett Green, ed., *Diary of John Rous* [Camden Society] (London, 1856), pp. 121–22.

him, being very good ones with pistols and saddles to them; and that fearing the people would have stoned Mr. Newcomen, the minister,[4] who should have accompanied Sir John Lucas, he was fain to take him into his own coach to free the town of Colchester from innocent blood, and then showed that some advised and desired him to have raised the trained bands, which might have set the whole country into a combustion, and therefore he declined it. That this miscarriage of the people proceeding from their zeal to the parliament had yet wrought this good effect, that divers persons who were esteemed malignant before and refused to contribute money, horse, or plate to the parliament did now bring in some money or plate and others horses. That the multitude generally declared their affections to be so great to the parliament as they only desired to hear that they were in safety, and that he durst affirm that if we had need of them, they would 40,000 of them come to our assistance. He could not say all armed but all with pitchforks or some weapons. He then showed that he had brought up 8 of those 12 horses which Sir John Lucas had provided to carry to York and desired to know whether he should deliver them in to the lord general, and said that Mr. Grimston, who was gone to St. Osyth to appease the multitude there, would bring up the other four horses. And then he fell to a vain boasting of the good service which he had done by giving God thanks for it and saying how much he had spoken and labored and yet confessed that Mr. Grimston had done very well also.[5] And then he desired that a committee might instantly be appointed to draw some declaration to send particularly into Essex for the appeasing of the present tumults and the prevention of them for the future. So it was agreed by the house that the 8 horses brought up should be delivered to the lord general, the Earl of Essex, with all their furniture, and Sir Thomas Barrington and some others were named a committee to draw up the said declaration.[6]

I withdrew out of the house about eleven of the clock and came in no more this day.[7]

4. Thomas Newcomen, royalist minister of Holy Trinity Church, Colchester, was brother to Matthew, Puritan lecturer in Essex. Lucas was sent to the Gatehouse and a committee named to draw up an impeachment; however, on 30 September it was ordered that he should be bailed. Newcomen, who was sent to the Fleet, was released on 24 December. See *Walker*, p. 159; *CJ*, II, 743, 788–89, 900. *DNB*.

5. On 8 September Grimston reported to the house concerning his "Proceedings in . . . Essex, in what Distemper he found it, and how he left it in a Calm." See *CJ*, II, 758.

6. For the committee and the subsequent approval of the declaration by both houses, see *CJ*, II, 741, 749, and *LJ*, V, 335. The declaration was to be published throughout England and Wales as well as in Essex. For the text see *LJ*, V, 337. Wing, E 1411.

7. For proceedings omitted by D'Ewes, see *CJ*, II, 741–43.

D'EWES

            August 30, Tuesday, 1642

I was this day about an hour in the house, and trivial things only were in agitation, of which Mr. Moore took notes.[1]

I withdrew out of the house about eleven of the clock, and then the Lord Strange[2] and divers others[3] were awhile after voted guilty of high treason.

1. For the day's proceedings, see *CJ,* II, 743–46.

2. On 29 August a committee, including Hill, had been named to prepare the impeachment of Lord Strange. On 16 September the commons ordered that it should be published in Lancashire and Chesire and that Lord Strange should be brought to the parliament to "receive condign Punishment." See *CJ,* II, 742, 745, 757, 768. For the text of the impeachment, see *LJ,* V, 354. Wing, E 2587B (I 96 in the 1945–51 edition).

3. Among the "Lords and Gentlemen" accused of high treason were seven MPs, all of whom had already been disabled, as well as Lord Poulett, the Marquis of Hertford, the Earl of Northampton, and Henry Hastings. All were "to appear at a Day certain, or . . . stand attainted of High Treason." The new committee named to prepare the impeachments also included Hill. See *CJ,* II, 745.

D'EWES

August 31, Wednesday, 1642

The public fast was celebrated by the House of Commons in St. Margaret's Church in Westminster. Dr. Downing preached in the morning and made a dangerous, seditious prayer and sermon tending only to civil war and bloodshed. Mr. Carter preached in the afternoon and made a good, honest sermon.[1]

We met at the house after the second sermon ended about 4 of the clock in the afternoon, and upon SIR ROBERT HARLEY's motion one Mr. Hodges was [f. 308b] appointed to preach at the next fast day, and upon the motion of SIR HENRY HEYMAN one Mr. Wilson was appointed to be [the] other preacher.[2]

Upon the SPEAKER's motion it was ordered that thanks should be given to the two preachers who had preached before us this day.[3]

MR. GLYN moved that an order had been formerly obtained in this house, by whose motion he knew not, that 30£ should be given to a French gentleman out of the collection gathered for the poor in the church of St. Margaret's on these fasting days, 10£ of which he had received, and he desired that the order might be recalled and annulled as to the residue.[4] It appeared that the order had been gotten upon Mr. Denzil Holles's motion, and after divers had spoken to it, we resolved to lay aside the said order for the time to come and that the poor of the said parish should have the contribution gathered on these fasting days, and all of us who were in the house gave 2s. 6d. apiece for the said Frenchman, there being near upon 100 present. I went out of the house about 5 of the clock, and the house rose soon after.

1. For Carter's sermon see Wilson, *Pulpit in Parliament*, pp. 66, 258. Wing, C 679A. Downing's sermon was apparently not published.

2. Thomas Hodges was vicar of Kensington, Middx; Thomas Wilson was rector of Otham, Kent, and lecturer at Maidstone. Both were subsequently members of the Westminster Assembly. See *AC*, II, 383; *PJ*, 1: 355; and Paul, *Assembly*, pp. 549, 553.

3. Following the fast sermons it was ordered that "all Stage Plays may be put down, during this Time of Distractions, and of Fasting." The lords agreed to the order. *CJ*, II, 747; *LJ*, V, 335. For the text see *LJ*, V, 336. Wing, E 1411. On 26 January there had been an unsuccessful attempt to suppress "all interludes and plays." See *PJ*, 1: 182.

4. Francis De Nevile, a Frenchman "of good Descent," had left a considerable fortune in France and had come "into this Kingdom . . . to embrace the true Protestant Religion." For the order of 22 July, see *CJ*, II, 686.

D'EWES

September 1, Thursday, 1642

The Speaker came about 10 of the clock. I was at prayers and stayed in the house till between one and 2 of the clock. After several businesses of less moment had been agitated, about eleven of the clock the clerk read over the answer of the assembly of Scotland to the declaration which we had sent thither and then the declaration of the lords of the secret council thereupon,[1] in all which both houses were advised to abolish the bishops root and branch as having been the great incendiaries and mischief workers in all his majesty's dominions.[2]

There followed many speeches thereupon, I cannot say any debate, for all men argued for the abolishing of bishops after MR. ROUS had first made the motion, and scarce a man spake for them. About two of the clock MR. SOLICITOR and others desired that we might put off the debate till Saturday morning next ensuing because, it being a matter of great weight, we might argue it upon the greater premeditation; and I thought the house so strongly inclined this way as I went out much about that time, but after my departure the house sat till about three of the clock and then voted the abolishing of them.[3]

See the rest of this day's passages in the clerk's book.[4]

1. See 26 August, n. 6.
2. The fourth provision of the declaration from the General Assembly, which appears in *LJ*, V, 325, stated:

What Hope can the Kingdom and Kirke of Scotland have of a firm and durable Peace, till Prelacy, which hath been the main Cause of their Miseries and Trouble first and last, be plucked up Root and Branch, as a Plant which God hath not planted, and from which no better Fruits can be expected than such sour Grapes as this Day set on Edge the Kingdom of England.

3. The vote abolished archbishops, bishops, and "Other Ecclesiastical Officers . . . found . . . to be a great Impediment to the perfect Reformation and Growth of Religion, and very prejudicial to the State and Government of this Kingdom." A committee, which included Hill, was named to prepare a declaration, with this vote as one head, in answer to that from the General Assembly. See *CJ*, II, 747–48. For subsequent proceedings, including a bill for the abolition of episcopacy, see Shaw, *English Church*, I, 120–21.
4. For proceedings omitted by D'Ewes, see *CJ*, II, 747–49.

D'EWES

[f. 312b]   September 2, Friday, 1642

The Speaker came about 10 of the clock. I came into the house awhile after. Besides some motions and orders of little moment during my being in the house, MR. HILL, an utter barrister, made report from the committee appointed to inquire touching the absent members,[1] that they had collected together a note of their names and had digested them into two classes or divisions: the first being such as either had been formerly summoned or were justly suspected, and those the committee desired that they might be specially summoned; and for another number of names they thought that a general summons would suffice. The names in the first catalog were about 60, among which were Sir Thomas Jermyn and [f. 313a] Mr. Henry Coke, two of our Suffolk burgesses.[2] That fiery boutefeu, MR. HENRY MARTEN, would have had them all expelled without further trouble, others would have had it ordered that none of them should be admitted to sit again in the house for 6 months, and others desired that we might have the names read over again and expel such as were fit to be expelled for some ill offices which they had done.[3]

Whilst this was in debate, I went out of the house about eleven of the clock.[4]

1. For this committee see 20 August, n. 6. On 1 September the house ordered that members who appeared upon summons, then departed without leave, and continued to be absent should be disabled. *CJ*, II, 747.

2. The clerk's list breaks off after twenty-three names. *CJ*, II, 750.

3. It was ordered that members who had been summoned should be suspended until the committee could examine "the Cause and Time of their Absence . . . and the House give further Order therein." The next day Hill was given leave to go to the country, and Sir William Strickland was ordered to report in his place. On 7 September the committee, with several new members added, was requested "to consider of a Declaration for the Satisfying of the Kingdom, concerning the Putting out of those Members that are put out; and to consider which way the House may be replenished." On 16 September the house ordered that absent members should attend by 29 September. *CJ*, II, 750, 751, 756, 769.

4. For the rest of the day's proceedings, including a division indicating an attendance of sixty-nine, see *CJ*, II, 749–50.

D'EWES

September 3, Saturday, 1642

The Speaker came between 9 and 10. I came into the house about 10 of the clock. Amongst other particulars agitated there, MR. ROBERT GOODWIN made report from the committee for adventurers for Ireland that things in that kingdom began to grow into a very bad condition for want of money and that therefore the committee had made this vote, that the 100,000£ which had been borrowed from them by the committee appointed for the defense of the kingdom should speedily be repaid.[1] Then he further showed that another cause of the bad proceedings in Ireland was the not sitting of the commissioners appointed for the Irish affairs[2] and that therefore the said committee had made another vote, which was that a special committee should be appointed to take the affairs of Ireland into their speedy care.

MR. PYM thereupon stood up and, sitting in the chair amongst the said commissioners for the affairs of Ireland and taking himself to be somewhat touched by this report, desired that if the house thought fit to appoint such a new committee, that then they would discharge the said commissioners from any further intermeddling with the said Irish affairs. And he further showed that though it were true that divers of the said commissioners were now out of town upon the service of the house so as they could not meet so frequently as he desired, yet the sole and only cause of miscarriage of affairs was the want of money, which happened by reason of the taking away of the said 100,000£ from the stock of the adventurers for Ireland and employing of it otherwise by the committee appointed for the safety of the kingdom. And therefore he conceived it very fit that not only the said sum but that another sum also formerly borrowed of the said adventurers at several times, being in the whole 28,000£, should be repaid back also although the same had been borrowed for the use of Ireland.[3]

1. See 16 August, nn. 2, 4. Goodwin's report is not noted in *CJ,* but the response to the king's message concerning the loan, having been twice recommitted, was approved by the house. The message recounted the many differences between king and parliament regarding Ireland and concluded with an assurance that the loan would be repaid "with all possible speed." On 7 September the house ordered that the message be sent to the king. See *CJ,* II, 744, 745, 750, 756. The text appears in Rushworth, IV, 775–78.

2. In August the commissioners had met only three times. See the attendance list which follows the CIA minute book. For the temporary measure whereby the commissioners were to meet as a joint committee, see CIA, 18 August, n. 2.

3. See CIA, 26 July, n. 3.

He further showed that they had taken a course to have provided clothes and victuals for the army there for divers months to come but that for want of money they could not accomplish it. He further confessed that they had failed of payment of near upon 20,000£ for clothes and victuals which was due at days already past to such as had provided them upon credit or promise given them to be paid at the said day. He informed the house also that unless some ready money were speedily sent into Ireland, both the Scotch army in Ulster and the English forces elsewhere would fall into great disorder.

SIR ROBERT HARLEY also, being another of the commissioners for the Irish affairs, desired as Mr. Pym had done that if another committee were named, they might be discharged from any further trust or care in the business of Ireland. And divers spake to it after him and showed that the said commissioners for the affairs of Ireland were appointed under the broad seal and that we could not discharge them,[4] and that therefore the said commissioners should be nominated to be of this committee and that the said Mr. Pym should be appointed to sit in the chair at the said committee, that so all things which were done there might be consistent with and in order unto what the said [f. 313a] commissioners had formerly agreed upon. And when the said commissioners could sit, then they should sit, and when they could not, then the said committee should sit. And so a new committee was named, and the said Mr. Pym and others of the said commissioners were nominated to be of it.[5] And then a vote was likewise passed for the repayment into the said committee for adventurers of the money that had been borrowed of them. The said MR. GOODWIN presented other votes also which I did not stay to hear but withdrew out of the house about 11 of the clock.[6]

4. For the commission establishing them, see *PJ*, 2: 403–04.

5. Twenty-three members were named to this new committee for Irish affairs, including Pym and Marten who were already members of the commission. In addition, it was resolved that "any Adventurer of the House shall be admitted to have a Voice." See *CJ*, II, 750. In essence this committee superseded the commission even as the commission had replaced the joint committee for Irish affairs named in November 1641. The recently constituted joint committee, which acted on behalf of the commission, apparently met only two more times. See above, n. 2; and CIA, 16 September and 12 October.

The final section of the CIA minute book, entitled "Orders of parliament transferred to the select committee appointed to take care of the affairs of Ireland," contains such orders from 3 September 1642 through 20 September 1644. There are, however, no minutes of committee proceedings.

6. For additional proceedings on this day, see *CJ*, II, 750–51.

D'EWES

September 5, Monday, 1642

I was not in the house this day, but perusing the clerk's Journal the next morning, I found amongst other particulars the sad and fatal contempt of the king's submissive and peaceable message sent to both houses, offering to recall his proclamation and to lay down his standard if we would call in our declarations by which we had pronounced divers persons guilty of high treason who had assisted him. 'Tis in print.[1]

The Lord Falkland (a viscount of Scotland), one of his majesty's principal secretaries and a member of the house, brought it to the House of Commons, but they caused him to come in and to deliver it at the bar in such an unworthy manner as Sir John Colepeper had done upon Saturday, the 27 day of August last past. And after the message was read, instead of having pity upon the king's calamity (who in sending this and the former message had gone lower than ever any king of England had formerly done), they triumphed over it,[2] and some of those wicked fiery spirits in the house made this sinister and uncharitable construction of it, that by this message his majesty had put an affront upon his parliament by proposing a condition to clear them whom he had unjustly accused to be traitors if they would clear those [who] were traitors indeed by assisting him against the kingdom and parliament, with other most insolent inferences as may easily be collected out of the clerk's book.[3] And which was worst of all, instead of expressing some pity towards his majesty in respect of the calamity into which he was fallen and instead of giving him or any that serve with him any hope to have comfort from them, both houses declared (which furious declaration came first from the lords) that they would not lay down the arms they had taken up till his majesty had given up or left to the justice of the parliament all such as the two houses of parliament had declared delinquents or

---

1. For the king's message, which was also delivered to the lords, see *CJ*, II, 753. Wing, C 2489. It was in response to the exchange of treaty messages. See 27 August, nn. 12, 18.

2. Following Falkland's delivery of this message, the king's instructions to the commissioners of array for England and Wales, dated 29 August at Nottingham, were read. The house was quick to note that the date of the instructions was later than the king's treaty message received on 27 August. See *CJ*, II, 752. Wing, C 2350.

3. There is no evidence of such "inferences" in *CJ*. A conference was subsequently held with the lords concerning the king's message and the instructions to the commissioners of array. Three votes presented by the commons were agreed to by the lords. See *CJ*, II, 752, 753. For the votes see *LJ*, V, 339.

should declare to be delinquents. By which they expressed too haughty a confidence in their own forces and made not only many particular persons of the nobility and others but some whole counties also quite desperate, declaring also that they meant to repair the charges which the commonwealth had been at to maintain this war out of their estates,[4] by which means, without a special providence of God, they were likely to help the king in his distressed condition with those considerable forces which he was never else like to obtain. See the clerk's Journal for the residue of the passages of this day.[5] This declaration of the two houses is likewise in print.[6]

4. The declaration stated:

That those great Charges and Damages wherewith all the Commonwealth has been burthened . . . may be borne by the Delinquents, and other . . . disaffected Persons; and that all his Majesty's . . . well–affected Subjects, [who] have by Loan of Monies . . . assisted the Commonwealth . . . may be repaid . . . out of the Estates of the said Delinquents.

For the text see *CJ*, II, 753. Wing, C 2489. For an assessment of this policy of confiscation, see Gardiner, *Civil War*, I, 18, and III, 196–97.

5. For the rest of the day, see *CJ*, II, 752–53.

6. In addition to the declaration, both houses agreed on a message to be sent to the king concerning laying down his standard. *LJ*, V, 338; *CJ*, II, 754. For the text see *LJ*, V, 342. Wing, E 2370+ (T 1518 in the 1945–51 edition). The new Wing number has been provided by John J. Morrison, editor, from the as yet unpublished revision of the first volume of Wing.

D'EWES

September 6, Tuesday, 1642

The Speaker [came] between 9 and 10 of the clock. I came into the house after prayers a little before 10 of the clock. MR. PYM was then making report from the committee appointed to draw up a reply to the answer which had been sent from the National Assembly of Scotland (read in the house on Thursday last) to our declaration sent to them.[1] He had read part of the said reply before my coming into the house, and having finished it, the clerk read it over again by parcels, and divers spake to it, and some particulars were amended in it. It contained a short declaration of our thankfulness to them for desiring an uniformity in church government and that we were resolved to that end and purpose to alter and extirpate the government by archbishops, bishops, deans, etc., and to settle a new one by the advice of learned and godly divines. This passed upon the question and will be printed.[2]

[f. 319a] The said MR. PYM did then further make report from the same committee of an answer which they had framed to that message which we had received from the lords of the secret council in Scotland for the abolishing of episcopacy, wherein we expressed our thanks to them for their care and our resolution to make a change of the church government. MR. PYM first read it, and then the clerk read it by parcels, and after some few had spoken to it and some particulars had been amended in it, it passed the house, out of which I withdrew about eleven of the clock.[3]

1. See 1 September, n. 3.
2. Subsequently a conference was requested with the lords concerning the reply to the General Assembly. *CJ*, II, 754.
3. For additional proceedings see *CJ*, II, 754–55. Among other things twelve MPs were disabled, the largest number since this procedure was begun in earnest on 4 August. See Appendix A.

D'EWES

September 7, Wednesday, 1642

The Speaker came to the house between 9 and 10 of the clock. I was there myself a little after prayers before 10 of the clock. Just as I came into the house, the question was in putting for disabling Sir Christopher Hatton to be any longer a member of the house during this parliament. He had been formerly at York with the king, and the house had been lately informed that himself, Sir Robert Hatton (his uncle), Sir Robert Napier, and Mr. Geoffrey Palmer were providing horse in Northhamptonshire to send to the king against the parliament; and thereupon they had been summoned to appear at a day certain,[1] of which they failed. The question passed for his putting out, as did also another question for the putting out of the said Sir Robert Hatton. But upon Mr. Geoffrey Palmer there followed much dispute, MR. REYNOLDS, MR. JOHN WHITE, and other lawyers speaking for him, so as it was for the present laid aside, and I thought it would have been no more spoken unto this morning. For we proceeded to the expelling of Mr. Henry Coke out of the house (being a younger son of Sir Edward Coke, deceased), which said Mr. Coke was one of the burgesses for Dunwich in the county of Suffolk; and this happened upon the motion of MR. JOHN GURDON,[2] a hot, violent, ignorant man, being seconded by SIR HENRY MILDMAY. I withdrew out of the house about eleven of the clock, and after my departure some of the fiery [spirits] called for the question to be put concerning the expelling of Mr. Geoffrey Palmer and carried it affirmatively.[3]

See the rest in the clerk's journal.[4]

1. See 20 August, n. 9.
2. Gurdon was also a Suffolk man.
3. Napier, however, continued as a member of the house until Pride's Purge in December 1648. Brunton and Pennington, *Members,* p. 208.
4. For additional proceedings see *CJ,* II, 755–57.

D'EWES

[f. 320b]   September 8, Thursday, 1642

The Speaker came about 10 of the clock. I came into the house about a quarter of an hour after ten. Sir Hugh Cholmley was speaking just as I came into the house for the bailing of Roger Twysden, his wife's brother, which was granted.[1]

Upon Mr. Solicitor's motion the bill touching the Earls of Pembroke and Cumberland touching the sale of certain lands, which passed the lords house and from them been sent down to us ready engrossed, was read the 3d time. Mr. Solicitor showed that upon his knowledge the bill had been drawn by consent of all parties, and so it passed the house upon the question, and it was ordered that Mr. Solicitor should carry it up as soon as the lords were set.[2]

Mr. Darley delivered in a petition for the Lady Audley, in which she showed that her husband was formerly gone beyond the seas[3] and that she and her children, residing near Colchester, had been lately there plundered by the tumultuous and riotous assemblies who met in and about that town and herself and her children affrighted, having lost in money, plate, goods, and household stuff above the value of 800£, and therefore desired license that she might travel beyond the seas with her children, two menservants, and two maidservants to her husband, which was granted and ordered accordingly.

After the said Lady Audley's petition above-mentioned had been granted, there was nothing to do in the house nor our numbers there very many, and therefore the Speaker desired to go up into the committee chamber, which was granted, and then it being between eleven and 12 of the clock, I withdrew out of the house.[4]

1. Sir Roger Twysden, one of the promoters of the Kentish petition, had originally been bailed on 9 April. In August, because of his role at the summer assizes in Kent, he was returned to custody, first of the sergeant, then of Cholmley, whose wife was Twysden's sister Elizabeth. See *PJ*, 2: 100–01, 114, 305, n. 5; *CJ*, II, 520, 704, 735; and Frank W. Jessup, *Sir Roger Twysden, 1597–1672* (New York, 1967), pp. 14, 53–61.
2. The bill, however, never received the royal assent. There had been litigation over family estates since the death in 1605 of the 3d Earl of Cumberland, father to the Countess of Pembroke and Montgomery. Upon the deaths of the 4th and 5th earls in 1641 and 1643, the matter was finally settled in favor of the countess. See *HMC, Fourth Report*, p. 108; and *PJ*, 1: 1. *DNB*.
3. Sir Henry Audley, a recusant, had been suspected of raising a popish army at Berechurch, Essex, in the summer of 1640. On 1 July 1641 a pass had been granted to both him and Lady Audley "to travel into foreign parts for three years." Hunt, *Puritan Movement*, p. 302; *CSPD, 1641–43*, p. 36.
4. For additional proceedings see *CJ*, II, 758–59.

D'EWES

September 9, Friday, 1642

The Speaker came about ten of the clock. I came into the house about half an hour after ten. Sir William Boteler of Kent was then standing at the bar and making a relation concerning the plundering of his house in Kent, wherein he said that what was done was done by the command of Colonel Sandys himself. That they took one of his servants and set matches to all his fingers and burned them to the bone to make him confess where the money and plate of him, the said Sir William Boteler, was, of which he neither did nor could confess because he knew it not. That they had violently beaten and robbed all his other both menservants and maidservants and defaced his house and taken away his goods and torn the very evidences of his estate and inquired for him, the said Sir William, saying they would either have him alive or dead, and lastly took away two horses out of his stable, whereupon he wrote to such parliament men as were near him that being under bail by the order of parliament, he expected to have been protected by them. And having notice of the violent threats of the said Colonel Sandys's soldiers against him, although he had an intention to come up presently to the parliament being then from his house in another place in Kent, yet by the earnest persuasions of his wife he first purposed to go to his majesty, whose sworn servant he is, and was in his journey to his majesty taken and stayed in Northamptonshire and brought before Mr. Crew and others of the committee at Northampton,[1] to whom he related the whole discourse that he now made to the house, having only fled from the said Colonel Sandys and his soldiers as from so many robbers and murderers, and that the said committee desired him to set it down in writing which he did, they promising him to send it up to the House of Commons. And thereupon the said Sir William was desired to withdraw, which he did accordingly, and then CAPTAIN LEE, a member of the house who was present at the same time with Colonel Sandys,[2] made declaration to the house that most of this that Sir William had related he had received from his own servants and that it was untrue, Colonel Sandys having done his uttermost to preserve both his house and goods.

MR. PYM then showed that the same relation which Sir William had made, having been brought to the committee of lords and commons for defense of the

---

1. See 20 August, n. 8.
2. Both Richard Lee and Edwin Sandys were deputy lieutenants for Kent. *CJ*, II, 724.

kingdom, [f. 322a] they were at first much moved with it, abhoring that such a cruelty should be committed in England, but upon examination of the matter they found the truth to be otherwise than had been suggested. And therefore he desired that in respect that this report was now far spread and that some believed it, that a special committee might be appointed to examine the particulars thoroughly, and that if Sir William Boteler had spoken truth, some exemplary punishment might be done upon the malefactors, and if not, that reparation might be had from him for the crime that he had laid to their charge. And then upon the motion of SIR HENRY VANE, the younger, and seconded by others, it was agreed that so much of the relation of this late service done in Kent by Colonel Sandys and some others as concerned the entering into and searching of the said Sir William Boteler's house might be openly read in the house in his presence. And the said Sir William Boteler was thereupon again called into the house, and the SPEAKER told him that the house had considered of the relation which he had made and were well assured that in much of it it was very untrue, he having received it from the report of others, and yet that for his satisfaction the house was willing that he should hear a relation made of the same business under the hands of gentlemen of quality and had also in further favor of him resolved to appoint a select committee to take a full examination of the said business. And then the clerk read the relation of the said business, being under the hands of Sir John Seton, a Scottish knight and a great soldier, and four other persons of good quality,[3] which was in effect following:

That Colonel Sandys with divers of his horsemen went towards the evening to the house of Sir William Boteler at [blank][4] (in the county of Kent), being informed that they should there find some resistance, but when they came thither, they only found the door kept fast against them, which they forced open with two or three musket shot spent against the lock thereof. And then the said Colonel Sandys with some others entered the house and inquired of one who called himself the steward what arms his master had in the house and where they were, who told them he would go show them and thereupon carried them into the house of office and bid them search there, at which foul abuse and indignity, though the said Colonel Sandys had great cause to be moved, yet he did so far moderate himself as he offered no manner of violence to the said fellow but went himself to search in other rooms of the house. But some of the soldiers in his absence without his knowledge or consent, hearing of the foul affront the said steward had done him, did tie fiery matches to his fingers, which burning

3. For the names see *CJ*, II, 760. A letter to the Earl of Essex from Seton et al., dated 20 August at Rochester, reported their other activities in Kent and concluded: "We intend, with the advice of the Deputy Lieutenants, to visit some of the gentry of the country, of whom we hear no good report, and where it is imagined there are arms." See *CSPD, 1641–43*, pp. 374–75. For proceedings in Kent see also *HMC, Fifth Report*, pp. 46–47; and Everitt, *Kent*, pp. 111–16, 123.

him and he crying out with the pain was overheard by the said Colonel Sandys, who came presently came [*sic*] and caused him to be released. That they found upon search in the said house 24 muskets filled with powder and bullets which they heard had been prepared but that day and 3 bags of money in obscure places which they brought away with them, and that the said Colonel Sandys was very careful to preserve the writings and evidences of the said Sir William Boteler from spoiling and defacing, which relation being thus read, the SPEAKER desired the said Sir William Boteler to withdraw, which he did accordingly. He being withdrawn, after some few had spoken, we resolved upon the question to desire the lords to name a committee of their house to join with a committee of this house for the speedy examination of [f. 323b] the said business touching Sir William Boteler. Then it was debated what should be done with the said Sir William Boteler[5] in the meantime, the SPEAKER showing that he was at this time in the custody of the undersheriff of Hertfordshire,[6] who had to his great expense brought him up hither. And so in the issue it was resolved upon the question that the said undersheriff should be discharged and that the said Sir William Boteler should be sent prisoner to the Gatehouse during the pleasure of the house.[7]

Dr. Aylett and Dr. Heath, two masters of the Chancery, brought this message from the lords, that the Earl of Essex, the lord general, did purpose to set out of town this afternoon[8] and did desire to take his leave of both houses together before his departure, and therefore the lords desired a present meeting by both houses in the Painted Chamber if it might stand with the conveniency of this house.

The messengers being withdrawn, the SPEAKER made report of the message according to the usual manner and then told us that he believed that it was mistaken by the messenger (viz., Dr. Aylett who delivered it being a great tall, dull fellow) and that the intention of the lords was to have a meeting by a committee of both houses, which MR. PYM affirmed to be so, saying that he knew so much by intimation from the lords; and yet for the greater certainty Mr. John Rushworth, the clerk's assistant, was sent out to the said Dr. Aylett to know the truth of it, who confessed his error and that the meeting was to be by a committee of both houses.

[f. 324a] The house agreed presently to give the lords a meeting but stayed

---

4. Barham Court, Teston. GEC, *Baronetage*, II, 96.

5. The resolutions concerning a joint committee appear in *CJ*, II, 760.

6. Henry Marston. *CJ*, II, 761.

7. On 14 March 1643 Boteler's escape from the Gatehouse is noted in *CJ*, II, 1004.

8. On 8–10 September four MPs were given leave to attend the Earl of Essex: Sir Philip Stapleton, Charles Pym (son to John Pym), William Strode, and Sir Peter Wentworth. *CJ*, II, 759, 760, 761.

awhile before they called in the messengers, MR. PYM making a relation of a ship which had brought money into the kingdom, but the further debate of that business was put off till tomorrow morning.

SIR ROBERT HARLEY moved that before the messengers were called in, we might send up a message to the lords to know of them whether they had yet assented to our reply to the answer of the National Synod of Scotland, and then the said Sir Robert was appointed to be the messenger, who went out of the house.[9]

I withdrew from thence also and retired home to my lodging, having no joy to go up to the Painted Chamber and to see the Earl of Essex take his leave in triumph of the two houses to go against his distressed sovereign, being now reduced to the greatest calamity of any person living, for he had sent twice to the two houses within this fortnight several submissive messages to crave peace, which were rejected with infinite scorn and contempt. His majesty in person (having nothing but the name and shadow of majesty left) was now at Nottingham or near thereabouts and had wanted money for about a week's space to pay any of his soldiers, horse or foot, who daily slipped from him as did also many of his servants. And those who yet stuck to him (amongst which my dear and only brother, Richard D'Ewes,[10] was one) were merely left to slaughter and destruction if they fought it out, to punishment if they were taken, or to an ignoble flight if they would save themselves. And for such noblemen and gentlemen as had been drawn to him by his own letters and to whom he had given his promise to protect and defend them from violence, they were everywhere pursued, taken, and made captives and like to be utterly ruined in their fortunes because the two houses of parliament had already declared that the commonwealth should be satisfied all the charges of this war out of their estates,[11] and that was like to grow to an immense sum, for we were now at above 30,000£ charge weekly for the maintenance of the forces under the command of the said Earl of Essex and his officers. And great also was the calamity everywhere of those counties in which his majesty's forces or ours came, neither side abstaining from rapine and pillage, and besides the rude multitude in divers counties took advantage by these civil and intestine broils to

9. See 6 September, n. 2. On 10 September the lords agreed to amended replies to be delivered by Lord Maitland to the Scots Privy Council and the General Assembly. The latter reply included a request that the Scots send "some Godly and Learned Divines" to the forthcoming Westminster Assembly. *CJ,* II, 761. For the texts see *LJ,* V, 348–50. Wing, E 1320.

10. Richard D'Ewes, a lieutenant colonel in the royalist army, was wounded at the battle of Reading in April 1643 and died a few days thereafter. D'Ewes's account of the death of his brother, who was thirteen years his junior, is preserved in BL, Harl. MS 164, ff. 377a–b, 401b.

11. See 5 September, n. 4.

plunder and pillage the houses of the nobility, gentry, and others who were either known papists or being Protestants had sent or provided horses, money, or plate to send to the king, or such as being rich they would make malignant that so they might have some color to rob and spoil them. Thus were Sir John Lucas and other Protestants, the Countess Rivers, the Lady Audley and other papists plundered in Essex and not only their goods and household stuff taken away and spoiled but their very houses defaced and made unhabitable, of which see more upon Monday, the 29 day of August last past. And for that which was done in Kent, it appeareth in part in the pillaging of Sir William Boteler's house, and for their outrages in Suffolk see what is set down on the next ensuing day, being Saturday. These tumults also gave a stop to all trading almost everywhere and to the payment of rents. Nay, the king's forces grew into that distress for want of pay as Prince Rupert (second son to the Princess Palatine and Queen of Bohemia, unfortunately come hither of late to ruin himself and to make his mother and his family odious to this kingdom), who commanded some 1200 horse in Leicestershire,[12] was enforced to send his warrant to the town of Leicester to furnish him with 2000£ or else he threatened to fire the town about their ears, so as it seemed that the miseries and calamities of some parts of this kingdom were grown to as great an height as those of Germany itself. And this want of money at court grew from hence because the whole power of the shipping, as well his majesty's own fleet now commanded by the Earl of Warwick as all the mer- [f. 324b] chants' ships being in the power of the two houses and their horsemen and other forces dispersed in many places of this kingdom, there could no supply of horse, arms, money, or plate come to his majesty either from beyond the seas or from any part of this kingdom but it was intercepted and taken and turned against these forces which were with him, who the truth is were most of them very wicked and debauched in their lives and conversations. But above all his majesty's infelicity was that he did too vehemently and obstinately stick to the wicked prelates and other the looser and corrupter sort of the clergy of this kingdom, who doubtless had a design by the assistance of the Jesuits and the papists of this kingdom here at home and into foreign parts to have extirpated all the power and purity of religion and to have overwhelmed us all in ignorance, superstition, and idolatry, which was doubtless the main cause that put the two houses, with the help of the City of London and other parts of the kingdom, to enter upon this great, high, and dangerous design, that so they might the more easily compass and bring about a full and perfect reformation in the church, which they evidently foresaw that it could not possibly be otherwise effected.

12. Shortly after Rupert's arrival in England, the king had made him general of the horse. See Gardiner, *Civil War,* I, 2–3.

Awhile after my departure out of the house between 11 and 12 of the clock, the messengers were called in, and the SPEAKER made report to them that the house would meet as was desired, and then they withdrew and departed.

The greater part of the house went up to the Painted Chamber, conceiving (I believe) as I myself did that the Earl of Essex would have made some set or solemn speech at his departure or leave-taking; but the lords coming out with the said Earl of Essex a little after the committee of the House of Commons had placed themselves, the said earl stood up and spake only these or the like words ensuing, "My lords, you have employed me about a service which I am very willing to undertake, and therefore I desire to know what you will please to command me," and so putting on his hat made an end of speaking.[13] And the company soon after departed, thinking this passage somewhat ridiculous that the lords should send a solemn message for the committee of the House of Commons to meet them in the Painted Chamber because the said earl might take his leave of them and then in that which he did speak he did only apply himself to the lords and not so much as take notice of the House of Commons or name them, which it seems was the reason that as soon as the House of Commons was set, the lords sent down a message to them by Dr. Aylett and Dr. Heath that if the Speaker or any of the members of the House of Commons would be pleased to come and take their leaves of the said Earl of Essex at Essex House in the afternoon, he would be very ready to give them entertainment, or to that effect as appears in the clerk's journal.[14] And the house rising soon after, the Speaker and divers of the members of the House of Commons went into the Court of Wards to the said earl, who being then taking of tobacco did salute them with his hat in one hand and the pipe in the other.

He went through London between 2 and 3 of the clock, going from Essex House with about 300 horse, the trainbands of London standing in the streets, the pikemen on one side and the musketeers on the other to guard him as he went along and to make the solemnity the greater. He passed through Fleet Street and so up of Ludgate Hill and into Cheapside and so to Bishopsgate and so crossed over Moorfields up to Islington, and there a little after he was past the Artillery

13. The following account (including the ellipsis) appears in *CJ,* II, 760:

Mr. Pym reports from the Conference, That the Earl of Essex, my Lord General, only spake at the Conference, to this Effect: That as he had undertaken this Service upon the Commands of both Houses, so he was . . . ever would be, ready, from time to time, to obey such Orders and Directions as he should receive from both Houses.

14. "Ordered, That Mr. Speaker is desired to go to take Leave of the Lord General at Essex House, and so many of the Members as shall please to go with him." The next day both houses ordered that the committee for defense (safety) should have power "to issue Money, and to do all other Things incident to the Army, or the Safety of the Kingdom, in the Absence of the Lord General." See *CJ,* II, 760, 761; and *LJ,* V, 346.

Garden lighted off his horse and went into his coach with six horses, and having coaches lay by the way for him went this night to Dunstable, 30 miles from London, in his way to Northampton whither he got the next day, a great part of his army attending him there, and among other particulars he caused to be carried along with him his coffin and winding sheet and funeral scutcheons ready drawn.[15]

15. For another account of Essex's departure, see Vernon F. Snow, *Essex the Rebel* (Lincoln, Neb., 1970), pp. 324–25. For additional proceedings on this day, see *CJ*, II, 760.

D'EWES

September 10, Saturday, 1642

The Speaker came between 9 and 10. I came into the house awhile after ten, and then the house was about ordering that a book written by a Jesuit, in which he showed that the papists of this kingdom might safely come to church here, should be printed.[1] The book was delivered in by MR. ROUS a little before my coming into the house, and it was further ordered that the said Mr. Rous should call to his assistance Dr. Featley[2] or such other learned divine as he should think to add a preface to the same book and such marginal notes as they should think fit. The clerk had entered the said order with the word "Catholics" only in it, but I sitting near the table spake out aloud to him to add the word "Roman" before the word "Catholics," which he did accordingly.

The SPEAKER then showed that he had received a letter out of the county of Suffolk which he delivered the clerk to read, which he did accordingly. It bore date at Bury St. Edmunds September 6, 1642, and was subscribed by Sir William Castleton, high sheriff of the said county, and ten of the justices of the peace of the same county, of which Sir Robert Crane, a member of the House of Commons, was one:

In which they showed that there had lately assembled in that county a great number of rude and disorderly people who had pillaged the houses as well of the Protestants as papists, whereby they, the said justices of peace, with the assistance of the sheriff have been enforced to raise the power of the county for the suppressing of them and had taken the principal offenders amongst them and committed them to the jail in the said town and had sent forth their warrants into several suspected houses for the searching of such goods as had been so violently taken away, whereupon many had voluntarily brought in the said goods to the constables of several towns, which goods remain still with the said constables, and they desired to be directed by the house what should be done with them. That since the suppression of the said first tumult, divers other persons have refused to deliver such goods as they had taken and had not only threatened to take those goods away again violently which remained in the possession of

---

1. The book by a priest named Green was entitled "A Safeguard from Shipwreck to a prudent Catholick." *CJ,* II, 760.

2. Daniel Featley (or Fairclough) of Lambeth and Acton, Middx, was subsequently a member of the Westminster Assembly. Paul, *Assembly,* p. 548. *DNB.*

several constables as aforesaid but had also menaced them, the said justices of the peace, and had assembled themselves together and were likely to have effected their wicked purposes if they had not been timely suppressed, and therefore they humbly besought the house that exemplary punishment might be inflicted on them that were in hold according to law and to secure them from further violence, or that else they should be enforced to leave their several habitations and to retire to other places of better security, and so the country would be exposed to the rage and rapine of that unruly multitude. The letter being read and some few having spoken to it, and the house being informed that there was a meeting of the gentry of the county to be on Wednesday next at Stowmarket and that Sir Nathaniel Barnardiston, one of the knights for the shire, was going down [f. 325b] with the general order of the house against those riotous assemblies[3] and with the instructions sent into other counties fitted for this, there was no further matter taken concerning this letter, but the whole contents of it were left to the consideration of that meeting. Only the house thought it fit at one time to have sent down two or three other members of the house with Sir Nathaniel Barnardiston, being present in the house with him, but that was in the issue declined because there were four or five of our members there already.[4]

MR. ROBERT GOODWIN made report from the committee of adventurers for Ireland that the said committee had agreed to send over Sir Henry Mildmay and Mr. Reynolds thither about the settling of their affairs there.[5] So the house resolved that they should go accordingly, and upon MR. REYNOLDS's own motion they had till Thursday come sennight given them to be gone, and it was further resolved upon the question that the committee of London[6] should be moved to appoint two amongst themselves to go along into Ireland and to assist the said Sir Henry Mildmay and Mr. Reynolds.

The SPEAKER then moved that the undersheriff of Hertfordshire, who had brought up Sir William Boteler, Sir George Devereux, and others who had been taken in Northamptonshire, might be discharged, having not only brought them up but kept them here at his great charge, which motion was seconded by some others, and so the [under]sheriff was called in and discharged. Then Sir George Devereux was called in and first kneeled at the bar as a delinquent and then, being bidden to stand up by the SPEAKER, did so and drew much pity from me in respect of the nobleness of his family and his old age. The SPEAKER then asked him whether he had not been with the king and sent him in horses in War-

3. Possibly the order of 18 August to "suppress all Riots [and] Tumults." See *CJ*, II, 727.

4. For the names of the deputy lieutenants for Suffolk, see *LJ*, V, 342.

5. For the resolutions of 7 September concerning sending a committee to Ireland, see *CJ*, II, 756.

6. The "Committee for Adventurers of London, for Ireland." *CJ*, II, 760.

wickshire, to which he answered very ingenuously (being indeed a plain, downright man) that he was one night in Warwickshire with his majesty, and that when the commission of array was there put in execution by the Earl of Northampton, he sent in two horses to show which stayed about one night. Then being asked by the SPEAKER whether he had not gone into Wales to raise men for his majesty, he protested that his going into Wales was only with an intent to go to his wife, that he had neither commission to levy men nor order to treat with any, but that traveling upon the way and being in discourse with one he met, he told him that he was informed that his majesty would give 6s. a week pay to all such Welshmen though they were 2000 as would come and serve him as footmen. And then upon the SPEAKER's bidding him to withdraw, he went out of the house, and awhile after, notwithstanding all that he had alleged, it/[7]

7. Devereux was committed to the King's Bench prison. *CJ,* II, 760. For the rest of the day, see *CJ,* II, 761–62.

D'EWES

[f. 342a]   September 12, Monday, 1642

The Speaker came between 9 and 10 of the clock, and I came into the house between 11 and 12.[1] The relation of the defeat of the Lord Poulett and the Cavaliers at Sherborne Castle by our forces under the command of the Earl of Bedford was read before I came into the house, where some 30 of them were slain. The letter is much of it in print;[2] and an order was then entering to question some persons that had lately printed a book touching the deposing and killing of tyrants or to that effect.[3]

SIR WILLIAM ARMINE made report from the commissioners of Scotland touching an order that had lately been sent to their forces in Ireland from the commissioners here for the Irish affairs to send over hither into England the Earl of Antrim in safe custody, whom Sergeant Major Monro had lately taken prisoner.[4] He showed also that the justices of Ireland had written a letter to General Leslie[5] to send the said Earl of Antrim unto Dublin, the copy of which letter together with the copy of the said order he delivered in to the clerk's assistant who read them both. The order was the same in effect which Sir William Armine related to be. The letter was dated at Dublin Castle the 20th of August 1642 and was sent from Sir William Parsons and Sir John Borlase, the lord justices of Ireland, to General Leslie, in which they showed that they understood that the Earl of Antrim had been taken by Sergeant Major Monro and therefore desired that, being a peer of that kingdom, might speedily be sent to them to Dublin with a safe convoy there to be tried according to the law that he might either be acquitted or condemned, unless they had order to the contrary by the parliament of England, and then they expected also that notice should be given them thereof, being entrusted at this time with the supreme command of that kingdom under his majesty, with some other particulars of less moment.

1. For proceedings omitted by D'Ewes, see *CJ,* II, 762.
2. Bedford and his troops had reached Sherborne on 2 September. For the encounter there and at Yeovil, see Underdown, *Somerset,* pp. 41–42. Wing, R 811.
3. The house ordered that the book, entitled *King James his judgement of a king and of a tyrant,* should be both referred to the committee for printing and burned. *CJ,* II, 762. Wing, J 137.
4. See CIA, 19 July. Armine was doubtless representing the commons' committee for Scottish negotiations.
5. Alexander Leslie, Earl of Leven, was general of the Scots forces in Ireland.

The letter being read, SIR WILLIAM ARMINE showed that the Scottish commissioners had desired him to acquaint the house that General Leslie was [f. 342b] ready either to deliver up the said Earl of Antrim to any person the house should appoint to receive him that so he might be sent into England or would send him to the lord justices if we should appoint it, only he had no means himself to undertake the secure sending of him into England. Divers spake to this matter, and in the issue it was resolved that the said earl should be brought into England and that we should take care for the safe bringing of him hither.[6]

MR. NICOLL (a black, tall, ignorant fellow, nephew to Mr. Pym), who had lately been added to the committee of lords and commons for the defense of the kingdom,[7] made report from that committee that they had drawn divers instructions for the Lord Say, Colonel Arthur Goodwin, Sir John Seton, and others who were to go to the city and University of Oxford to settle it in peace and to chase away, take, or slay Sir John Byron[8] and other Cavaliers there who had lately committed many outrages upon the citizens and fortified the town and university in an hostile manner; and one instruction amongst others was that they shall call together the trained bands of that county and of the adjoining counties of Berks and Buckingham and dismiss them after that service done to return again home to their own dwellings.

MR. HENRY MARTEN moved that they might not return to their own dwellings but that the work begun at Oxford might pass into Cheshire to free that city from the Welshmen which were entered into it.[9]

And thereupon MR. RIGBY stood up and showed that it was not only needful for forces to be sent into Cheshire but into Lancashire also in respect that the Lord Strange had there raised 3000 men to go to the king and was in raising 4000 more to keep in the said county to overawe it, so as that Protestant party which stood well affected to the parliament in that county is in daily danger to be ruined and plundered. He showed that some citizens in the City of London had offered to send about 1000 soldiers thither at their own charge and required only the public faith that they might be repaid again. Upon this some interrupted him

6. Actually it was ordered on this day that Antrim should temporarily continue in custody in Ulster, then in early October that he should be brought to London. However, he escaped to York. See *CJ*, II, 763, 793, 797. *DNB*.

7. See 6 August, n. 5.

8. Byron, former lieutenant of the Tower and now a colonel in the royalist army, had been sent by the king to Oxford in late August. See *Roy. Off.*, p. 54. *DNB*. On 2 September the lords and commons had agreed on an order for the safety of Oxford, both city and county. For the text see *LJ*, V, 336–37.

9. Crossed out in MS: *1400 Welshmen come into Cheshire, and 300 raised in Lancashire*. This information appears at the bottom of f. 342a as part of D'Ewes's rough notes. For an order of 8 September concerning persons unjustly imprisoned at Chester for refusing to obey the commission of array, see *LJ*, V, 344.

and said that this ought to be considered of by the committee for the defense of the kingdom, to which MR. RIGBY, being permitted to speak again, answered that he had acquainted the said committee with it and that they had taken no course therein and therefore he was enforced to address himself to the house for remedy.

The said MR. NICOLL thereupon stood up and showed that it was very true that the said committee had been acquainted therewith and had thought it fit to lay aside all further care therein in respect that they did conceive there could not any force be so soon made ready to send from hence as from the lord general, who was himself now marching that way with his army. This Mr. Rigby was the true and only cause of all these calamities in Lancashire and Cheshire, for when we were to name the deputy lieutenants divers months since, out of a private grudge and malice against the Lord Strange had railed[10] us many things done by him during the exorbitant proceedings of the lord lieutenants and deputy lieutenants before the assembling of this parliament, by which means the said Lord Strange was only nominated lord lieutenant of Cheshire by the House of Commons and the Lord Wharton, a man of small estate, [f. 354a] was made lieutenant of Lancashire, where he was not at all known nor had a foot of land, by which means the Lord Strange, being a man of a great spirit, did with much indignation refuse to accept the lieutenantship of Cheshire;[11] and whereas he had before during all this parliament gone most constantly in his vote with those that were commonly called the good lords, this affront (after the said Lord Wharton had once been confirmed in this lieutenantship of Lancashire in the House of Peers) caused the said Lord Strange to leave the said House of Peers and to adhere to the king against the two houses of parliament[12] and at this time had brought him more considerable force than any other six noblemen in England.

After the said Mr. Nicoll had spoken, the motion made by Mr. Rigby was laid aside, and the said instructions for the Lord Say and the rest before named were allowed upon the question.

MR. ROBERT GOODWIN made report from the committee for the adventurers for Ireland concerning certain instructions which they had drawn for Sir Henry Mildmay and Mr. Reynolds, two members of the house who were to be sent into Ireland, which instructions being delivered in by them were not ready for the present but were laid up by the clerk till the ensuing morning, when they were read and passed by the house.

---

10. Bragged or boasted. *NED*. For a letter to Rigby concerning Lord Strange, see *HMC, Fifth Report*, p. 47.

11. Following his refusal to serve, Lord Strange was replaced by Viscount Say and Sele. For this controversy see *PJ*, 1: 338–39, 341, 342; and 2: 86, 88.

12. For the current impeachment proceedings, see 30 August, n. 2.

There was then read a copy of a letter which had been sent from Dr. Prideaux, vice chancellor of Oxford, to the Earl of Pembroke, chancellor of that university, in which he requested him to use some means with the parliament that the forces which were intended to be sent from here to Oxford might be stayed, with the copy of the Earl of Pembroke's answer, both which after they had been read were ordered to be printed.[13]

MR. GURDON, one of Ipswich burgesses in Suffolk, being in himself of no learning and little experience, affected of late a violent way of moving things, being therein only Mr. Henry Marten's Aye, and therefore he made this unseasonable and idle motion: That whereas divers members of the House of Commons had promised to bring in plate and money or to send in horses and neglected to do it, the same did discourage divers citizens in their readiness to contribute, and therefore he desired that a committee might be appointed to bring in a note or list of their names and the reasons of their neglect and that the same committee might have power to receive the answer also of all the other members of the house who had not yet declared themselves whether they would do anything or not. I call this an unseasonable and idle motion because there had been a committee appointed near upon three months since to this very end and purpose, where Sir John Evelyn sat in the chair,[14] and was long since ready to have made a report. And yet notwithstanding the same, the house being but thin, MR. HENRY MARTEN (whose Aye, as I said before, this Gurdon was) seconding this motion, it [was] upon the question voted and ordered, and then a committee was nominated.[15] The house, having appointed to meet at 9 of the clock tomorrow morning, rose between one and 2 of the clock in the afternoon.

13. Wing, P 2267.

14. For the committee see 11 June, n. 1. D'Ewes's comment confirms Evelyn's chairmanship of this committee.

15. For the new committee and its duties, see *CJ*, II, 763, 764, 765, 767. For additional pledges of money, horse, and plate, which continued to be made throughout the rest of the year, see Appendix F.

D'EWES

September 13, Tuesday, 1642

The Speaker came between 9 and 10 of the clock. I was present at prayers about 10.

MR. REYNOLDS delivered in a letter bearing date at Youghal (in the province of Munster in Ireland) August 31, 1642, sent to him from the Lord Dungarvan, in which he showed that he had taken in the castle of Ardmore near Dungarvan with a matter of 300 foot and horse, had during their lying there beaten away above 500 of the enemy who came to relieve it, and forced them afterwards to yield upon discretion, putting to death the next day all the men, which were above one hundred,[1] and saving all the women, being about 400, and so he desired that speedy supply might be sent of men and money or else that all which they had done would be lost.

I did much abhor this cruelty of butchering so many men who yielded upon discretion and might have sold their lives at a dear rate before they yielded.

After the letter was read, MR. ROBERT GOODWIN stood up and moved that the instructions that had yesterday been delivered in by him for the direction of Sir Henry Mildmay and Mr. Reynolds might be read, which was done accordingly, which instructions were in effect following: to advance the conquering of the rebels, to see the laws put in execution against the papists there, with some other particulars to that effect.

It was then also voted to desire the lords to consent with us that these instructions might be sent to the king to desire his consent to them, with a note of their names who were to be employed in this service in Ireland.[2]

SERJEANT WILDE made report of an order which had been drawn by the committee appointed to that end to authorize the citizens and other inhabitants of the city of Worcester to train and arm themselves and to make their defense against all such as should offer violence unto them, which order, though it had

---

1. One contemporary pamphlet, giving a full account of the capture of Ardmore Castle, confirms this number; another puts it at seventy to eighty. Wing, J 852, J 1100. See also Bagwell, *Ireland under the Stuarts,* II, 22.

2. The lords agreed to the amended instructions on 20 September, and a letter was sent to Sir Edward Nicholas requesting the royal assent. See *LJ,* V, 364, 365.

some dangerous clauses in it, yet easily passed the house, and it was then also ordered without any dispute that we should desire the lords to join with us in it.[3]

[f. 363b] The SPEAKER delivered in a letter sent unto him from the city of Gloucester subscribed by William Capel and Thomas Pury (a member of the house), two aldermen of that city,[4] bearing date there September 9, 1642, in which they showed that there were two servants of the Lord Herbert's, son to the Earl of Worcester, lately passing through that town with 7 geldings which they had stayed and had sent the examinations of the said servants. That there was great raising of men for the king against the parliament in Herefordshire, Monmouthshire, and other counties in Wales, and that they conceived that they would omit no practices to make themselves masters of that city, and therefore they desired to receive some directions from the parliament for the defense of themselves. The examinations of the Lord Herbert's two servants were then read, in which amongst other particulars they confessed that they were carrying the said geldings to Raglan Castle in Monmouthshire to their lords.[5]

The SPEAKER then showed that he had likewise received a letter from the town clerk of the said city, in which he informed him that militia had been there readily raised and put in execution and that if the parliament would be pleased to bestow those 7 geldings upon the said town, they would provide 40 horses more and so maintain a troop of horse for the defense of the said town at their own charge. Whereupon the house presently voted that they should retain the said horses and make use of them,[6] which to me seemed a strange piece of justice to take the goods [of] any man away merely because he was an active papist, but I had just cause given me on Saturday, July 23 last past, still to hold my peace.

MR. HENRY[7] HERBERT of Monmouthshire then showed that there were many in that county well affected to the parliament but that they wanted some assistance to help them against the other party who were wholly supported by the Earl of Worcester and the Lord Herbert his son, [f. 366b] though they did not show themselves openly in it; but when the commission of array was put in execution, the said commissioners did constantly repair to the said Raglan Castle and there consulted what to do and received their instructions and direc-

3. Wilde and Salway had been named on 10 September to prepare this order. *CJ*, II, 761. For the text see *CJ*, II, 764. The order gave the same authority to the city of Worcester to oppose the commissioners of array as had been given "to other Cities and Towns within this Kingdom."

4. For Capel see *VCH, Gloucestershire*, IV, 377. Pury had been given leave to go to Gloucestershire on 20 August. *CJ*, II, 729.

5. Both Lord Herbert, second in command to the Marquess of Hertford in 1642, and the Earl of Worcester, commander of the garrison of Raglan Castle, played significant roles in the royalist war effort. See *Roy. Off.*, pp. 350–52.

6. For the order to this effect, see *CJ*, II, 766–67.

7. MS: *Edward*.

tions from thence. But the house ordered nothing in this particular during my being there,[8] which was until about eleven of the clock in the forenoon.

There came this day another gracious message from his majesty to desire peace, being the third he had sent from Nottingham to the two houses within the space of about 3 weeks, in which he gave general promises to grant our desires if we petitioned him.[9] It was sent to the lords house by Mr. Adrian May and communicated from them to us.

See the clerk's book.[10]

8. It was ordered that Lord Herbert and the Earl of Worcester should be summoned to attend the parliament, and that Henry Herbert, MP, should report to the committee of safety concerning the state of affairs in Monmouthshire. *CJ*, II, 763.

9. For this message of 11 September, see *LJ*, V, 350. Wing, C 2370. The house ordered that the committee of safety should consider the message; subsequently a new committee was named to draft a response. *CJ*, II, 764, 766.

10. For the rest of the day, see *CJ*, II, 764.

D'EWES

September 14, Wednesday, 1642

The Speaker came between 9 and 10 of the clock. I came into the house about 10 of the clock a little before prayers were ended. The first done after prayers was the reading of an ordinance of parliament to be passed by both houses for the securing of such moneys to the merchant strangers of London (that is, such as were free of no company) as they should lend to the parliament for the good and safety of both the kingdoms of England and Ireland, which having been twice read passed the lords.[1]

Upon MR. CORBET's motion a committee was revived.[2]

There was delivered in a petition from the Turkey merchants trading into the Levant Sea which was read, being subscribed by Sir Henry Garway, the governor,[3] and therein they complained of some oppression offered to them by Sir Peter Wyche, formerly ambassador at Constantinople, and by Sir Sackville Crowe, now ambassador there,[4] which they desired that it might be heard before a committee. That their liberties might be settled and confirmed by act of parliament. That they might have power to appoint the person who should be resident at Constantinople as ambassador because they allowed him his maintenance there, with some other particulars. The petition being read, divers spake to it, and in the issue it was referred to the committee for trade, and a day was appointed upon which Sir Peter Wyche or his solicitor might attend the said committee and Sir Sackville Crowe's agent here might attend the said committee.

I came out of the house about 11 of the clock in the forenoon. The house rose about one of the clock in the afternoon.[5]

---

1. The ordinance actually gave security to those Londoners willing to contribute "to the Support of that great Charge [of] the Kingdom" who were "neither Members of those Companies in London, which formerly did advance great Sums, nor Merchant Strangers; who have now also declared themselves to do the like." See *CJ*, II, 765, 766. For orders concerning repayment of the merchant strangers' loans, see *CJ*, II, 755, 771.

2. Apparently the committee for trade, chaired by Sir Henry Vane, Sr. *CJ*, II, 765.

3. Alderman Garway, one of the wealthiest London merchants, was also governor of the East India, Greenland, and Russia Companies. Pearl, *London*, p. 299.

4. Crowe succeeded Wyche as ambassador to Turkey in 1638 or 1639. Subsequently Wyche was made comptroller of the king's household. Aylmer, *King's Servants*, pp. 92, 367. *DNB* for Wyche.

5. For the rest of the day, see *CJ*, II, 765–67.

D'EWES

September 15, Thursday, 1642

The Speaker came between 9 and 10 but was fain to stay a great while for company before he went to prayers. I came in before they were ended, and there was scarce twenty of us present at them, which made [me] as soon as they were ended to withdraw out of the house because I knew they could not sit without the number of 40. Before I returned in again, which was about 10 of the clock, the house was entered into business and were debating about some prisoners that were at Gloucester which were presently to be sent up hither, but upon MR. PYM's motion it was ordered that they should be kept there awhile before they were sent up.

The SPEAKER then showed that he had received a letter from the mayor of Norwich, by which he gave him information of certain persons who were now in prison in that city and had spoken scandalous words against some lords of the peers house and against some members of the House of Commons, and that the mayor had informed him that if this house would give order, they would proceed against them themselves and that they should not want justice; and thereupon MR. TOLL, one of the burgesses for Lynn, showed that neither of the two citizens for the city [of] Norwich[1] were now in town but that he had likewise received letters from thence that the sessions would be held there on Monday next and that they might this night send away by the post that they might have due punishment. And so it was ordered that the said Mr. Toll should write to the said mayor of Norwich and to give him thanks for his care and to desire him that the said offenders might receive due punishment from himself and the other justices of that city.

[f. 369a] Then was another information given the house of Mr. Windebank (son to Sir Francis Windebank, late secretary of state,[2] who fled into France about the beginning of the parliament) was taken near Reading by the means of Sir Robert Pye, the younger, and so the house took order for the keeping of him in safe custody.[3]

1. Richard Catelyn and Richard Harman.
2. It is not certain whether this was Thomas, the eldest son, who had been MP for Wootton Bassett, Wilts, in the Short Parliament, or John, the youngest son. See Toynbee and Young, *Strangers in Oxford,* pp. 55–57. *DNB* under Sir Francis Windebank.
3. On 12 September Pye, son to the MP, had written to Tanfield Vachell, sheriff of Berkshire, requesting that Windebank be conveyed to London because he had "taken up arms in Oxford

MR. PYM then made report from the committee appointed to draw an answer to the king's last message[4] that they had prepared the same and so read it in the house, and afterwards the clerk read it. It contained in substance this insolent resolution, that we would enter into no treaty with his majesty for peace, promise pardon to none of those that had assisted his majesty or were now with him, but that we would prosecute the war unless he would immediately return to us without condition or limitation, letting him also know that his person or life was in danger in the condition he was in, only there was an expression of moderation that we would distinguish of the offenses of men. After the clerk had read it, divers spake to particular passage in it, and to such a height or crisis was the spirit of violence grown amongst us that whosoever moved to have anything mitigated in it spake to no purpose, but such as pressed to have it made more bitter and unpleasing easily prevailed, excepting old Sir Henry Vane, which I confess gave me some content amidst my sorrow to see how things were carried, that his hypocrisy had no better success. For whereas he had been one of the most dangerous instruments of state before this parliament began (whilst he was treasurer of his majesty's household and afterwards principal secretary also) that ever this kingdom had since the reformation of religion and was therefore beholding to us for our mercy in passing him by when we had questioned so many lesser offenders, yet he to ancillate[5] to those hot spirits moved that we might not so much as promise any moderation or mitigation to any about the king. And whereas we had promised the king that if he would return to us, we would supply him with support or money, he would have had that put out also; but the house rejected both these motions in respect of the person that made them and in respect of his late Machiavellian carriage also, for he had absented himself from amongst us for about the space of three months last past because he did not know whether the king's party or ours would prove strongest, and now as soon as he heard that the king's forces failed him, he returned to us again to this end, to blow the flame to a greater height than it was before. The said answer, in the issue being made worse than it was when MR. PYM had brought it in, passed the house, and Mr. Henry Marten was nominated a messenger to go up to the lords to desire a conference with their lordships by a committee of both houses touching an answer to be sent to his majesty's last message.[6]

---

against the parliament." The house now ordered that Windebank be committed to the Gatehouse. See *CSPD, 1641–43*, p. 387; and *CJ*, II, 767, 779. For Pye and Vachell, see Greaves and Zaller, *Dictionary of Radicals*, III, 69–70, 259. *DNB* for Pye.

4. See 13 September, n. 9.

5. To be subservient. *NED*.

6. The following day the amended message to the king, including an addition proposed by the lords for "bringing of Delinquents to a Trial," was agreed to by both houses. *LJ*, V, 355; *CJ*, II, 770. For the text see *LJ*, V, 358. Wing, C 2370.

MR. ERLE moved for 3 deputy lieutenants to be allowed for Dorsetshire, whose names he gave in, and they were allowed accordingly.[7]

I withdrew out of the house just as the first of the three was allowed upon the question and as Mr. Marten was going of his message between eleven and 12 of the clock in the forenoon.[8]

7. For the names see *CJ*, II, 767.
8. For the rest of the day, see *CJ*, II, 767–68.

D'EWES

September 16, Friday, 1642

The Speaker came between 9 and 10 of the clock. I came into the house between 10 and 11. Before I came into the house, a pamphlet touching the late fighting at Sherborne Castle was complained of.[1] The clerk's assistant was reading articles of impeachment against the high sheriff of Shropshire, being engrossed in parchment, just as I came into the house.[2] One main charge against him was that he had been a chief actor in putting the commission of array in execution, and Sir Guy Palmes was nominated by the house to carry up the said impeachment to the lords. Divers other frivolous businesses were agitated in the house, which Mr. Moore took notes of. Amongst the rest the LORD RUTHIN delivered in a petition in the behalf of one Mr. Stampe, one of the Cavaliers, being in prison here, but it was rejected after it had been read.[3]

SIR GUY PALMES moved that we might admit Mr. Geoffrey Palmer into the house again, whom we had the other day disabled by vote to be of the house because he had neglected to return upon his being summoned, and he showed that being from home at the time when the summons were left at his house, he could not presently come because he had no notice of it but did come as soon as he had notice. But we all agreed that having once discomposed a member, we could not admit him again without a new election.[4] I went out of the house between eleven and twelve of the clock whilst this was in debate. See Mr. Moore's journal, who was present this day in the house.[5]

1. The pamphlet purported to be a "true Relation" of the proceedings of the king's army at Sherborne. *CJ*, II, 769. Wing, M 2876.
2. On 29 August Wilde and Glyn had been ordered to prepare an impeachment against Sheriff John Weld. See *CJ*, II, 743, 768, 770, 774.
3. However, it was ordered that an impeachment should be prepared by Miles Corbet against both Timothy Stampe and William Stampe. See 25 July, nn. 9, 10; and *CJ*, II, 768.
4. This action does not appear in *CJ*.
5. For proceedings omitted by D'Ewes, see *CJ*, II, 768–70.

D'EWES

September 17, Saturday, 1642

The Speaker came between 9 and 10 of the clock in the morning. After prayers SIR HARBOTTLE GRIMSTON delivered in a petition for the delivery of a poor [man] out of prison, who had spoken some scandalous words of the parliament, but MR. GURDON did very hotly oppose it and to little purpose, for in the issue it was granted upon the question.[1]

MR. PYM then made report from the committee of lords and commons appointed for the safety of the kingdom of several informations which they had received by intercepted letters and otherwise touching his majesty['s] proceedings in Nottinghamshire and Derbyshire. And then was delivered up a letter to the clerk who read it, bearing date at Derby September 15, 1642, and had been sent from Sir Edward Nicholas, one of his majesty's principal secretaries,[2] in which he showed that he had written to him on Monday last from Nottingham. That on Tuesday last (viz., September 13) his majesty marched from Nottingham to Derby with 500 horse and five regiments of foot and ten[3] pieces of artillery. That his majesty's army was well ordered but that under the Earl of Essex mutinous, and that was the reason why he stayed still at Northampton. That the trained bands of Derbyshire met the king at [blank] Bridge 7 miles from Nottingham (it was at Stapleford Bridge,[4] being but 5 miles from Nottingham and 7 from Derby), and that 500 of them had offered their service to his majesty. That they had received a new relation of a second victory obtained by the Marquess of Hertford at Sherborne Castle against the Earl of Bedford and the parliament's forces, in which young Mr. Stawell had killed Mr. Balfour, and that 200[5] of the parliament's forces besides were slain (both which were notorious falsehoods, for Mr. Balfour was never hurt and but 5 or 6 others at the

---

1. It was ordered that the petitioner, Ellis Coleman of Ipswich, should be released from the King's Bench prison. *CJ*, II, 770.

2. For the letter, directed to Sir William Boswell, ambassador to the United Provinces, see *CSPD, 1641–43*, pp. 389–90. Wing, E 3312.

3. Twelve pieces in *CSPD*.

4. Cavendish Bridge in *CSPD*.

5. Above 100 in *CSPD*. Contemporary pamphlets give widely varying accounts of the numbers killed. For example, Wing, B 1672, R 811, S 4647.

most slain), with other particulars of less moment,[6] and in the conclusion showed that there were two ships come with arms and other ammunition out of the Low Countries to the parliament, which he was very sorry for to see that they had supply sent them from so near allies. Some few spake after these letters and observed Secretary Nicholas his good inclination to the parliament that was sorry to see any relief sent to them.[7]

Then were some other informations read touching the plundering of houses by the king's forces in Nottinghamshire and that he had taken away the arms of divers of the trained bands of that county against their wills, with other particulars which were witnessed by Joshua Hill, being examined before the Earl of Essex the 14th day of this instant September. There was also the certificate of one Augustine Harper read bearing date September 9, 1642, in which he showed that his mare, saddle, and bridle with his money in his purse had been taken from him by the Cavaliers. Both these are in print.[8]

[f. 372b] I withdrew out of the house about eleven of the clock, and awhile after my going out they fell upon great and dangerous disputes which took up their time till about three of the clock in the afternoon, at which time the house rose. The debates were about a petition to be preferred to the king to return to the parliament and what the chief motives or pretenses should be for the Earl of Essex to proceed with his army,[9] and MR. PYM moved that there should be a new seal cut to be used and kept by the authority of both houses.[10] I was told by some of the house that during these agitations they desired to have heard how far

6. This encounter took place on 7 September. Edward Stawell and Balfour were sons to Sir John Stawell and Sir William Balfour. Subsequently the castle fell into parliamentarian hands and on 19 September was evacuated by Hertford, who then retreated to Wales. See 12 September, n. 2; and Underdown, *Somerset,* pp. 42–43.

7. Perhaps D'Ewes, in this enigmatic sentence, was saying that though Nicholas was believed by some to have a good inclination toward parliament, he was nevertheless sorry to see this aid sent to them.

8. Wing, E 3719.

9. The house ordered Essex "to advance, with all convenient Speed, towards his Majesty" with this petition, one head of which was to be "That his Majesty will be pleased to come to his Parliament." Instructions for Essex were also being formulated, which were agreed to by both houses on 22 September. See *CJ,* II, 769–70, 771, 776. For the texts of the petition and instructions, see *CJ,* II, 776, 778.

10. In May, just prior to Lord Keeper Littleton's departure for York, the great seal had been taken from him by Thomas Elliott and delivered to the king. In a letter of 30 August to Thomas Willis, clerk of the crown, Littleton complained of not having access to the seal. As a result a committee was named on 8 September to consider "the Inconvenience by having the Great Seal out of the Custody of the sworn Officer." The committee was also to consider the commons' problem of apprehending delinquents and of issuing writs for new elections when such documents could not be sealed. However, a new seal for the use of parliament was not provided until 30 November 1643. See *PJ,* 2: 367, n. 15, and 373, n. 15; *CJ,* II, 754–55, 759, 771; and *LJ,* VI, 315, 318.

any of these particulars could have been warranted by record and therefore wanted my company there, which if they did it was well, that so they might consider how undeservedly and ungratefully they had rewarded all my services by their malicious dealing with me on July 23, Saturday, last past.[11]

11. For proceedings omitted by D'Ewes, see *CJ,* II, 771.

MINUTE BOOK OF THE COMMISSIONERS
FOR IRISH AFFAIRS

[p. 67]   *Die Martis, viz., 7° Junii* 1642

Present[1]

Lord Admiral	Sir Walter Erle	Mr. Marten
Earl of Holland	Sir Henry Vane	Mr. Pym
Lord Mandeville	Sir Robert Cooke	Mr. Reynolds
Sir Robert Harley	Sir John Evelyn	

Mr. Chambers to take notice of money for Ireland[2]

It is ordered that it be added to a former order of the lords and others his majesty's commissioners for the affairs of Ireland dated the last day of May that Mr. Chambers do also take notice of all money that hath been issued out of those several offices to any person whatsoever for the service of Ireland.[3]

Mr. Aldworth of Bristol to send 8000 ells of cloth to Munster

Whereas by an order of the 27th day of May last[4] it was ordered by the lords and others his majesty's commissioners for the affairs of Ireland amongst other thing concerning the delivery and paying for 30,000 ells of lockram for making of shirts for the soldiers in Ireland, which the said commissioners had contracted for with Richard Aldworth of Bristol and Richard Wollaston of London[5] after the rate of elevenpence the ell, that they should cause the 8000 ells thereof intended for Munster to be shipped from Bristol and consigned to the lord president of Munster at Cork to be disposed of by his lordship for the use of the soldiers in Munster, according to such directions as shall be given by these commissioners for the apportionment of the said several parcels of cloth, making them into shirts and the soldiers paying for them as they shall need them, it

---

1. On this day the following commissioners from the House of Lords were absent: Essex, Pembroke, Say and Sele, Robartes; and from the House of Commons: Cave, Cromwell, Holles, Meyrick, Parkhurst, Wallop. Hereafter the daily attendance record will not be included; instead it appears at the end of the minute book in a chart compiled by the editors. Pagination of the minute book has been added by the editors.

2. All headings actually appear in the left margin of the minute book.

3. For the earlier order see *PJ*, 2: 465–66. Robert Chambers was auditor for the commission for Irish affairs.

4. See *PJ*, 2: 461–62.

5. Aldworth was a merchant and alderman, Wollaston a linen draper. See *PJ*, 2: 448, n. 3; and *LJ*, V, 347.

is now further ordered by the said commissioners that in regard the 8000 ells of lockram intended for Munster is already at Bristol, packed up by the said Mr. Aldworth dwelling there, be desired to cause the same to be shipped and sent away with all speed to Cork in Ireland directed to the lord president of Munster and to Richard Ward, gentleman, commissary of the musters in that province, who shall receive instructions from these commissioners for disposing thereof as aforesaid. And upon certificate sent unto these commissioners of the shipping thereof, payment shall be made according to the former contract of the money arising by the price of elevenpence the ell, and also of such other sums of money as the said Mr. Aldworth shall lay out or agree for towards the shipping and freight thereof from Bristol to Cork.

Order for disengaging the Lord Dungarvan of the 2 companies at Youghal

Whereas the lords and others his majesty's commissioners for the affairs of Ireland have been this day informed that a garrison [p. 68] of 200 men being raised and maintained in the town of Youghal until March last by the right honorable the Earl of Cork at his own charge, and since that time continued there by the engagement of the Lord Dungarvan, it is now thought fit and ordered by the said commissioners that Mr. Pym be desired to move the House [of] Commons to take upon them the payment of the said 200 men since the beginning of March last and so discharge the said Lord Dungarvan and to continue the payment of them for such further time as they shall think convenient.[6]

Sir William Balfour, 600£

Whereas upon report of Mr. Pym to the House of Commons that the lords and others his majesty's commissioners for the affairs of Ireland had thought fit that a troop of 60 horse should be raised for Sir William Balfour, Knight, who is appointed to command the regiment of horse which is to accompany the Scottish army in Ireland, and that a sum of money be allowed for doing the same, it was upon the last day of April last resolved upon the question and ordered by that house that 600£ should be imprested to him for the raising of the said troop of horse,[7] it is now therefore ordered by the said commissioners that the lord lieutenant of Ireland be desired to give order unto Mr. Nicholas Loftus, deputy treasurer at wars for that kingdom, to imprest unto the said Sir William Balfour the said sum of six hundred pounds for the raising of a troop consisting of 60 horse for the service aforesaid.

---

6. On 9 June the house agreed to assume the payment of the garrison from 1 March until 1 July at the rate of 3s. 6d. a week for each man. *CJ*, II, 614.

7. See *PJ*, 2: 252.

Sir William Balfour for his pay, conduct, transport,
and saddles for his troop

Whereas Sir William Balfour, Knight, hath this day presented to the lords
and others his majesty's commissioners for the affairs of Ireland these his
humble desires, first, that his pay may begin from the day of his nomination in
the House of Commons, viz., *19°* April 1642, he having ever since provided
both horse and men, secondly, that such conduct moneys as shall be thought
fitting for transportations of the officers and soldiers of his troop hence into
Ireland may be ordained in like manner, and thirdly, that order may be given for
such a proportion of arms and saddles as the ten troops appointed to attend the
Scottish army stand in need of, they being defective of all necessaries for that
service, as Captain Hill lately come over can give more particular information,
it is for answer hereunto ordered: First, that though the commissioners are [p.
69] very willing to comply with the desires of Sir William Balfour in what may
stand with the convenience of this service, yet in regard that his first desire (if
granted) may be of ill consequence in respect of others, it is thought fit that he
receive pay as other captains from the date of his commission.[8] Secondly, that
for his conduct to the seaside where he intendeth to ship his horses and for his
transportation, forty shillings for every horse and such other accommodations
shall be allowed him as hath been given to others in like cases. Thirdly, that 500
new saddles with bits, stirrups, and all other necessaries thereunto belonging
shall be provided according unto such pattern as the said Sir William Balfour
shall prescribe for his own troop and for the rest of the troops according to such
fashion and pattern as the commissioners shall think fit. And it is further
ordered that Mr. Payler and Mr. Greene, gentlemen of the horse to the lord
admiral and the Earl of Holland, with Mr. Chambers, auditor to this commission, be appointed to provide and agree for so many saddles with their[9] furniture as together with those provided by Sir William Balfour will make up the
number of 500 aforesaid.

Mr. Frost, 1500£ imprest

It is this day ordered by the lords and others his majesty's commissioners for
the affairs of Ireland that the lord lieutenant of Ireland be desired to give order to
Mr. Nicholas Loftus, deputy treasurer at wars for Ireland, to pay by way of
imprest upon account unto Walter Frost, gentleman, commissary of victual in
this kingdom, the sum of 1500£ more than he hath formerly received towards
his further provision of corn and victual for supply of his majesty's magazine at

8. In other words Balfour's pay was granted from 1 June rather than 19 April. See *PJ*, 2: 187–
88, 467.
9. MS: *they.*

Dublin, which sum of 1500£ is to be paid unto him as soon as the said Mr. Loftus shall have sufficient moneys in his hands for doing the same.

[p. 70]   *Die Jovis, viz., 9° Junii* 1642

Lord Cromwell's petition for 500£ to be advanced upon his troop's pay

Whereas the lords and others his majesty's commissioners for the affairs of Ireland have this day taken into consideration the petition of the Lord Cromwell for the sum of 600£ to be advanced to him in part of payment of what is due unto him, his officers, and troop for the 6 months they have been in actual service, to be discounted out of his entertainment when it shall be resolved by the House of Commons from what time the whole army shall enter into their pay, whereby his lordship shall be enabled to do that service which he is ambitious to perform, and without which sum (his estate being in the rebels' hands)[1] he cannot keep his troop serviceable, they having no means to subsist by for three half years past but what came out of his purse, it is now ordered by the said commissioners that Mr. Pym be desired to report to the House of Commons that these commissioners think fit that the sum of 500£ be advanced to him towards such enablement of him and his troop, there being more due as appears by the certificate of Mr. Chambers, and that defalcation thereof may be made as is offered out of the first money that shall be coming to his lordship with the rest of the army.

Mr. Chichester and Mr. Hill, petition

Whereas the humble petition of Arthur Chichester, commander of a regiment of foot, and of Arthur Hill, Esquire, commander of a regiment of horse now in garrison in Belfast and other parts of the county of Antrim, was this day read unto the lords and others his majesty's commissioners for the affairs of Ireland, they thinking the same very much worthy of due consideration, both for the matter therein contained and for the testimony that hath been given of the [p. 71] merits of the said Mr. Hill, have thought fit and ordered that Mr. Pym be desired to report the said petition to the House of Commons together with the Lord Conway's letters[2] and other testimonies of their well deservings in the province of Ulster that such consideration may be had thereof as that house shall think fit.

Petitions of commanders in Ulster

It is this day ordered that the petitions and demands of such as have commands in the province of Ulster be taken into consideration on Saturday next in the afternoon, and the lords and others his majesty's commissioners for the affairs for Ireland will meet for the same purpose at that time.[3]

---

1. See *PJ*, 2: 410–11.
2. A letter from Conway in support of Hill had already been read in the house. See D, 4 June. For Pym's report of these petitions to the house, see D, 14 June.
3. However, no action was taken on the petitions until the following week.

Gunners and drummers for Londonderry

Whereas the lords and others his majesty's commissioners for the affairs of Ireland have been this day moved by Sir Thomas Staples, Captain Newburgh, Captain Beresford, and Captain Hartwell, captains now appointed to raise four new companies for the garrison of Londonderry,[4] that in regard there are many pieces of ordnance alread[y] and now lately more sent to that city by the companies of London, they may have allowed them two able gunners for the use of those pieces of ordnance in this time of action, and also an allowance of four partisans, eight halberds, and eight drums for the four new companies now to be raised by them, it is ordered by the said commissioners that Pym be desired to move the House of Commons for allowance to be given to a gunner and his mate for the service aforesaid, and that provision may be made of partisans, halberds, and drums for these companies as for others.

Londonderry, 653£ 6s. 8d. and 500 pair of shoes

It is this day ordered by the lords and others his majesty's commissioners for the affairs of Ireland that the old company of the standing army in Ireland now commanded by Sir John Vaughan in Londonderry to be made up a 100 men and the four new companies now to be raised by the said Sir Thomas Staples, Captain Newburgh, Captain Beresford, and Captain Hartwell shall have a month's pay advanced to them, that is to say, for the captains and their officers from the date of their commissions given them for their new companies and for the soldiers of each of the five companies from the time of their musters. And the lord lieutenant of Ireland is desired to give order unto Mr. Nicholas Loftus, deputy treasurer at wars for that kingdom, with the money which by order of parliament he receiveth from the poll office in London,[5] being given by some companies of London for the use of [p. 72] Londonderry, and out of such other moneys as he hath in his hands by the same order, to pay unto Sir Thomas Staples, Captain Newburgh, Captain Beresford, and Captain Hartwell by way of advance for Sir John Vaughan and themselves the sum of 653£ 06s. 08d. for the payment of the said five companies, consisting each of 100 soldiers besides officers, one month's pay as aforesaid. And also to deliver unto them 500 pair of shoes of those that are now ready made here in London by agreement with him, to be carried to Londonderry and equally divided among the common soldiers of these five companies (every company alike), the prices whereof being made known unto them, they are to defalk[6] the same out of the pay of such soldiers as

---

4. See *PJ*, 2: 289–90.

5. For an order of 7 June concerning payment of the garrison at Londonderry, see *CJ*, II, 610–11.

6. To allow a deduction. *NED*.

shall need to receive those shoes and stand accountable for so much as the shoes shall amount unto, together with the money advanced to them as aforesaid.

Mr. Pennoyer, 1000£ in part of his account

Whereas Mr. William Pennoyer of London, merchant,[7] hath this day presented unto the lords and others his majesty's commissioners for the affairs of Ireland an account and certificate of a quantity of powder and match, delivered by him in pursuit of an agreement made with the said commissioners 22th of April last, on shipboard the *Ruth* at Bristol,[8] and for some quantities of match sent to Chester and some carriages provided by him for Minehead as appeareth by the said account, which is yet depending before the said commissioners, the said commissioners have now ordered that the lord lieutenant of Ireland be desired to give order unto Mr. Nicholas Loftus, deputy treasurer at wars for that kingdom, for the present payment of the sum of 1000£ unto the said Mr. Pennoyer in part of satisfaction of what shall appear to be due unto him upon that account for the services aforesaid, it shall be allowed after more full examination.

692£ 10s. for the officers and artificers of the train of artillery, doctors, apothecaries, and surgeons, a month's pay

Whereas it was this day moved to the lords and others his majesty's commissioners for the affairs of Ireland by the lord lieutenant of that kingdom that the officers and artificers belonging to the train of artillery, part of them being ready to embark at Chester and the rest giving attendance here to receive the ordnance, arms, and ammunition which are to be sent into Ireland, may receive one month's pay more from the 29th day of May last to the 25th of June, the whole sum amounting to 692£ 10s., it is now ordered that the lord lieutenant of Ireland be desired to give order unto Mr. Nicholas Loftus, deputy treasurer at wars for that kingdom, to pay the said sum of 692£ 10s. unto such persons as the said lord lieutenant of Ireland [p. 73] shall appoint to receive the same for the payment of the said officers and artificers belonging to the train of artillery and the said doctors, surgeons,[9] and apothecaries for their pay of one month beginning and ending respectively as aforesaid.

2 battery pieces for Munster with furniture and equipage

Whereas an order of parliament was brought to the lords and others his majesty's commissioners for the affairs of Ireland this day dated the 8th of June 1642 in these words:

---

7. For Pennoyer see Greaves and Zaller, *Dictionary of British Radicals*, III, 28–29.
8. See *PJ*, 2: 423–24 and passim.
9. MS: *chirurgeons*. The seventeenth-century spelling is frequently used in the minute book.

Die Mercurii, 8° Junii 1642. Ordered by the lords and commons in parliament assembled, that two pieces of battery with their furniture and equipage be forthwith sent over into the province of Munster in Ireland for the defense of that province.

Subsc., John Browne, *Cleric. Parliamentor.*[10]

It is now ordered by the said commissioners that these words following should be underwritten in the same paper: It is this day ordered by the lords and others his majesty's commissioners for the affairs of Ireland that those persons who have the charge of the ordnance, arms, and ammunition which were lately in the ships that came from Hull shall deliver as many of these particulars hereafter mentioned as are in their charge and custody unto such persons as the lord lieutenant of Ireland shall appoint to receive the same in pursuance of the above-written order of parliament for the 2 pieces of battery with their furniture and equipage to be sent into Munster for the defense of that province.[11] And that the officers of his majesty's ordnance do likewise deliver the residue of those particulars out of his majesty's stores within the Tower of London in pursuance of the said order of parliament and for the service aforesaid:[12] one culverin drake and another drake of 12-pound bullet mounted upon their carriages complete to march withal, spare carriage wheels for them four, spare rammers, tampions[13] of each four, spare forecarriage wheels two, spare axletrees two, ladles, sponges each four, beds of each sort two, coins of each sort four, budge barrels four, spare linchpins 6, levers and crows ten, shot for them each 100 rounds,[14] a gin complete, a hand screw or miche, thill horse harness four, trace horse harness twenty-four.

Train of artillery

Whereas the lords and others his majesty's commissioners were this day moved by the lord lieutenant of Ireland that a list of ordnance, arms, and ammunition agreed on to be sent [to] Dublin as for a train of artillery for his lordship may be furnished and prepared, it is ordered by the lords and others his majesty's commissioners for the affairs of Ireland that as many of the several natures and particulars in the said list as are in the ships that brought the arms and ammunition from Hull shall be taken thence towards the furnishing thereof, and what is wanting in those ships shall be furnished out of the stores in the Tower of London as far as those stores will supply the same.

10. For the order see *LJ*, V, 119.

11. The commissioners were apparently acting on the commons' vote. See D, 7 June, n. 4. The list which follows was presented to both houses on 24 June. See *CJ*, II, 637, and *LJ*, V, 159–60.

12. Terms pertaining to tactical weaponry of the seventeenth century are defined in the Glossary of Military Terms which follows the CIA minute book.

13. MS: *tomkins.*

14. MS: *£.*

[p. 74]   *Die Lunae, 13° Junii* 1642

Lord president of Munster's allowance of 3£ per diem

Whereas the lords and others his majesty's commissioners for the affairs of Ireland have this day taken into their consideration the good services done by the lord president of Munster, who now commandeth in chief the forces that are in that province without any allowance for his labor and charges in that command, they have thought fit that Mr. Pym be desired to move the House of Commons that for the better support and encouragement of the said lord president of Munster, an allowance of three pounds sterling per diem may be made unto him from the first day of this instant June during such time as he shall command in chief the forces in that province, but during the time of this allowance such pay as was formerly allowed him as sergeant major general of the army is[1] to cease.

Lord Conway's and Sir John Clotworthy's regiments

Whereas it hath this day been reported unto the lords and others his majesty's commissioners for the affairs of Ireland by Mr. Pym from the House of Commons that that house was willing to provide some supply of moneys to the Lord Conway and Sir John Clotworthy for the payment of their regiments in Ulster if these commissioners would set down what sum might be fit for that purpose,[2] it is now ordered that Mr. Pym be desired to return to the House of Commons the opinion of these commissioners that 6000£ may be a fit sum to send to the Lord Conway and Sir John Clotworthy to pay their regiments and that the money be provided with as much convenient speed as may be.[3]

Lieutenant Colonel Mervin, Mr. Hamilton, et al., petitions

Whereas the petition of Lieutenant Colonel Mervin was this day read to the lords and others his majesty's commissioners for the affairs of Ireland and he heard to speak thereunto, the said commissioners have thought fit that the said petition, with the petition of Mr. Hamilton on the behalf of the Lord Clandeboye, his father, the petition of the Lord Viscount Montgomery of Ards, and of Sir James Montgomery, who have by his majesty's commissions raised several regiments of foot and troops of horse, should by Mr. Pym be reported to the House of Commons to give such order therein as they shall think fit.[4]

1. MS: *his.* For the order see D, 15 June.
2. For the petitions from Ulster, see above, 9 June. For the commons' order of 13 June, now reported to the commissioners by Pym, see *CJ,* II, 622.
3. For the action taken by the commons, see D, 14 and 15 June. On 4 July the house ordered Loftus to make the payment of £6000 to Clotworthy. *CJ,* II, 649.
4. For Sir James Montgomery's role in the Irish rebellion, see *CSP Ire., 1633–1647,* p. 468. On 4 July the house referred the petition submitted by Sir James and Viscount Montgomery to the committee for the Chichester petition. See D, 14 June, and *CJ,* II, 650.

[p. 75] Lord Dungarvan, 800£ for draft and carriage horses

Whereas the lords and others his majesty's commissioners for the affairs of Ireland have taken into consideration what good use may be made of draft and carriage horses for the service of the army in Munster, they have this day ordered that out of the 10,000£ now ordered by the houses of parliament to be sent into that province,[5] the sum of 800£ be imprested upon account unto the Lord Dungarvan for providing of 100 draft and carriage horses (not exceeding the price of eight pounds a horse) to be employed for drawing the two pieces of battery and the four fieldpieces appointed for the service of that army and for other carriages and use requisite. And it is further thought fit and ordered that one man shall be allowed at the rate of eightpence per diem for the keeping of every three of these horses and 12d. per diem for the meat of every horse.

Lord president of Munster to pay the 200 men at Youghal
and disengage the Lord Dungarvan

Whereas it appeareth by an order of the House of Commons dated the 9th day of this instant June[6] that the house being informed that a garrison of 200 men was raised and maintained in the town of Youghal until March last by the right honorable the Earl of Cork at his own charge, and since that time continued there by the engagement of the Lord Dungarvan, they therefore thought fit and so ordered that the House of Commons do take upon them the payment of the said 200 men since the beginning of March last after the rate of three shillings and sixpence a week by the man and so disengage the Lord Dungarvan and continue the payment of them till the first of July next, it is now thought fit by the lords and others his majesty's commissioners for the affairs of Ireland that the lord president of Munster be desired (out of the 10,000£ now ordered by the parliament to be sent unto him for the payment of the forces in that province) to make payment unto the said 200 men in garrison at Youghal for the time mentioned and according to the rate aforesaid, and so to discharge them of that service.

Materials for the train of artillery, 3000£

Whereas the lord lieutenant of Ireland hath this day presented to the lords and others his majesty's commissioners for the affairs of Ireland a list of such materials and utensils for the train of artillery which are wanting, both in the ships that brought the ordnance, arms, and ammunition from Hull and also in the stores of the Tower of London, to make up and complete the train of artillery required of the lord lieutenant of Ireland and allowed by the said commissioners,[7] the charge whereof by estimation may amount to the sum of 3737£, it

5. See D, 7 June, n.8.
6. For the order see *CJ*, II, 614.
7. For the order see above, 9 June.

is now ordered by the said commissioners that the said lord lieutenant of Ireland be desired to give order to Mr. Nicholas Loftus, deputy treasurer at wars for that kingdom of Ireland, to pay by way of imprest upon account unto such person as the lord lieutenant of Ireland shall authorize [p. 76] to receive the same sum of 3000£ for the provision of the said materials and utensils or so many of them as the lord lieutenant shall direct.

Captain St. John's petition concerning the Lord Grandison's troop

Upon reading of the petition of Captain St. John, the lords and others his majesty's commissioners for the affairs of Ireland thought fit that the lord lieutenant should have time given to write to the Lord Viscount Grandison and to receive his answer whether he would relinquish his troop of horse in the standing army in Ireland or not, that accordingly the lord lieutenant might proceed to give a commission to the said Captain St. John as the commissioners desired or some other course might be taken as should be advised.[8]

Train of artillery, 612 horse, 4896£

Whereas the lord lieutenant of Ireland presented to the lords and others his majesty's commissioners for the affairs of Ireland certain demands requisite for the train of artillery to be sent into Leinster, viz., that there might be an allowance of wagons for the officers of the train, an allowance of horse for the gentlemen of the ordnance and the conductors which might be on horseback, and an allowance for buying of draft horses for the ordnance and carriages, that is to say, wagons for the officers of the train, the general three wagons, the lieutenant general two wagons, controller one wagon, two commissaries one wagon, two engineers one wagon, two fireworkers and two petardiers one wagon, the chaplain and surgeon one wagon, quartermaster and marshal one wagon, commissary of the draft horses and paymaster one wagon, six gentlemen of the ordnance two wagons, captain of the pioneers and captain of the matrosses one wagon, the master gunner, wagon master, and four gunners' mates one wagon, in all sixteen wagons, draft horses for the ordnance and carriages 598, six gentlemen of the ordnance six horses, and eight conductors eight horses, in all 612 horses, which at the rate of eight pound every horse will come to 4896£, it is now ordered by the lords and others his majesty's commissioners aforesaid that for and towards the provision of those horses the lord lieutenant of Ireland be desired to give order to Mr. Nicholas Loftus, deputy treasurer at wars for that kingdom, to pay by way of imprest upon account to such person as the lord lieutenant shall appoint to receive the same the said sum of 4896£. And it is also thought fit and ordered by the said commissioners that one man by the rate of eightpence by the day shall be allowed unto every three

8. For this issue see *PJ*, 2: 294.

horses of the said number to dress, feed, and drive them, and that twelvepence by the day shall be allowed to every horse for his meat and litter.

[p. 77] Punts and arms for the matrosses, 698£ 6s. 8d.

Whereas the lord lieutenant of Ireland hath delivered unto the lords and others his majesty's commissioners for the affairs of that kingdom an estimate of the charge of 18 flat bottom punts 21 foot long, six foot broad, and two foot high of oaken wood with 30 anchors and cables, with joists and rafters, planks, and all necessaries belonging to two bridges, one of 444 foot long and 12 foot broad, which may cost about 425£, and also of the charge of carriages belonging to the 18 punts and bridges which may cost 220£, and whereas by the same estimate is required arms for the matrosses, that is to say, half-pikes twelve foot long with iron feet, a hundred at 20d. apiece, 8£ 6s. 8d., and short swords and belts, 100 at nine shillings apiece, 45£, the total of which punts, carriages, half-pikes, and swords doth amount to 698£ 6s. 8d., forasmuch as the said commissioners do conceive that the said punts and other particulars above-mentioned are of good use for the service and fit to be furnished, it is now ordered by them that the lord lieutenant of Ireland be desired to give order to Mr. Nicholas Loftus, deputy treasurer at wars for that kingdom, to pay unto such person as the lord lieutenant shall appoint to receive the same the said sum of 698£ 6s. 8d. imprest upon account of provision of the said punts, carriages, and arms at the most reasonable rates and as may be most convenient for the service.

A warrant *pro* ordnance out of the ships which came from Hull

Whereas we understand by a list showed unto us that towards the supply of the train of artillery which is intended for the province of Leinster in Ireland, there remaineth in the ships that brought the ordnance, arms, and ammunition from Hull to London these particulars following, viz., ordnance 34, carriages 42, spare wheels 24, round shot 2860, match 5 fat containing two ton and a half, barrels of powder 282 containing 12 last, and ladles and sponges 118, and that towards the supply of the stores of Dublin there are in the said ships these particulars following, viz., powder 480 barrels containing 20 last, match in fats 53, in packs four, and in bundles half a ton, amounting in all to 29 ton, muskets 3500, pikes 1500, bandoliers 3500, swords 1500, pistols 500 pair, carbines 500, horse arm 200, holster 700 pair, fats with soldiers' tents four, in all 200 tents, we his majesty's commissioners for the affairs of Ireland do hereby will and require you forthwith to deliver unto such person as the lord lieutenant of Ireland shall nominate and appoint to receive the same all the aforementioned particulars according to the numbers and quantities herein expressed to be employed for the service aforesaid, for which this together with his indenture or acquittance that receiveth the same by order abovesaid shall be your sufficient. Star Chamber, the 13th day of June 1642.

[p. 78] To our very loving friends, Solomon Smith, Walter Baylisse, for the Admiralty, and to all others who it shall or may concern.[9]

A warrant *pro* divers particulars belonging to the 34 brasses
to be delivered out of the office of the ordnance

Whereas we understand by a list showed unto us that towards the supply of the train of artillery which is intended for the province of Leinster in Ireland there remaineth in his majesty's stores within the office of the ordnance the particulars following, viz., wadhooks 50, handspikes 40, lever crows 40, gins complete three, screws or miches six, commanders 20, tilts of hair 20, tilts of canvas 20, trace horse harness 168, thill horse harness 46, cart saddles 20, heads and rammers 12 pair, rammers for one man 34, rakes for cleansing skidgates 12, blinds 10, pulleys double and single 15 pair, dark fire beacons 10, molds for musket, carbine, and pistol shot 24, iron brand marks 12, horseshoes 1500, nails for them [*blank*],[10] shovels and spades 4000, cramp spades 10, pickaxes 500, wheelbarrows 1000, handbarrows 50, scoops 50, oozing[11] vessels 20, hand hatchets 100, felling axes 100, two-hand axes 100, hedging bills 100, crows of iron 50, oaken planks 30 ton, oaken timber for joists, etc., 30 ton, roweling bridges to fasten petards three, scaling ladders 40, palisados 1000, long stakes with iron at both ends 1000, field hasples six, supporters for blinders 30, barricados with iron work 10, baskets of several sorts 400, tents two, elm plank 3650, wagons eight, whereof four to be repaired, fare carts three, tumbrels seven, we his majesty's commissioners for the affairs of Ireland do hereby will and require forthwith to deliver unto such person as the lord lieutenant of Ireland shall nominate and appoint to receive the same all the particulars above-mentioned according to the number and quantity herein expressed to be employed for the service aforesaid, for which this together with his indenture or acquittance that receiveth the same by order abovesaid shall be your sufficient warrant. Star Chamber, 13th of June 1642.
To our loving friends, Sir John Heydon, Knight, lieutenant
of the ordnance, and to the rest of his majesty's officers
in that office whom it shall or may concern.

The ships at sea victualed

Whereas the lord high admiral of England presented this day to the lords and others his majesty's commissioners for the affairs of Ireland [p. 79] a list of the victualing of his majesty's ships set forth to sea this present year to the end

---

9. The above list, as well as the one that follows, was presented to both houses of parliament on 24 June. See *CJ*, II, 637, and *LJ*, V, 159.

10. 12,500. *LJ*, V, 159.

11. MS: *owsing*.

direction might be given for further continuance of them, if resolution were[12] taken to continue the said ships in further service, it is now thought fit that the same list being entered here should be reported to the House of Commons to be by them considered of and ordered as shall be thought fit.[13]

A LIST OF THE VICTUALING OF HIS MAJESTY'S SHIPS
SET FORTH TO SEA THIS PRESENT YEAR 1642

Ships	Men	Days	Beginning	Ending
For the guard of Ireland:				
Swallow	150	224	1 January 1641[14]	12 August 1642
Bonaventure	170	224	27 January 1641	7 September 1642
Entrance	160 ⎫	224	7 February 1641	28 September 1642[15]
Providence	100 ⎭			
Total	580			
For the guard of the narrow seas:				
Rainbow	240 ⎫	168	22 March 1641	5 September 1642
Garland	170 ⎭			
St. George	260	168	28 March 1642	11 September 1642
Victory	260 ⎫	168	1 April 1642	15 September 1642
Antelope	160 ⎭			
James	260	168	9 April 1642	23 September 1642
Unicorn	250 ⎫	168	13 April 1642	27 September 1642
Charles	250 ⎭			
Henrietta Maria	250 ⎫	168	19 April 1642	3 October 1642
Reformation	250 ⎭			
Vanguard	250	168	21 April 1642	5 October 1642
Mary Rose	100	112	9 May 1642	28 August 1642
Greyhound	50	112	12 May 1642	31 August 1642
Lion	170	112	15 May 1642	3 September 1642[16]
Expedition	100	112	25 May 1642	13 September 1642
Total	3020			
Crescent	50 ⎫	112	3 June 1642	22 September 1642
Lily	35 ⎭			

12. MS: *where.*

13. On 20 June the commons ordered that this list be submitted to the committee for the navy. *CJ,* II, 634. On 9 July the list appears in *LJ,* V, 194. For additional statistics about the ships, see the "1642 Fleet Survey by William Batten," in John Tucker and Lewis S. Winstock, eds., *The English Civil War: A Military Handbook* (London, 1972), p. 77.

14. I.e., 1641/42. Months have been changed by the editors from Latin to English.

15. The date is 18 September in *LJ,* V, 194.

16. The date is 7 September in *LJ.*

[p. 80]   *Die Mercurii, viz., 15° Junii* 1642

Sir Hardress Waller

Whereas a letter was this day read directed from[1] the lord president of Munster unto the lords and others his majesty's commissioners for the affairs of Ireland in favor of Sir Hardress Waller, Knight, lieutenant colonel under him in the province of Munster, and showing his great affection to the service, it is now answered by the said commissioners unto Sir William Waller (who presented the said letter unto them) and also by the lord lieutenant of Ireland now present that Sir Hardress Waller should be remembered upon any fit occasion that should be offered for his reward and encouragement.[2]

Mr. St. John's command of a troop

The lords and others his majesty's commissioners for the affairs of Ireland, taking into consideration the petition of John St. John, Esquire, and the intent of the House of Commons concerning his having the command and benefit of the troop of horse in the standing army of Ireland, whereof the Lord Viscount Grandison hath been captain and he lieutenant, and which he hath divers times recruited since the rebellion and paid for these two last years past at his own charge, have thought fit and ordered that the said Mr. St. John do forthwith go into Ireland and take upon him the command of the troop [of] horse that was the Lord Viscount Grandison['s], and that he shall receive and have to his own use the captain's pay thereunto belonging thereunto. And if the said Lord Viscount Grandison do come into Ireland and challenge the command of the said troop during the time that it is in the pay of this state, the pay thereof is to cease. But if he do not come to attend the service of the said troop, he is to be cashiered according to an order of parliament made in such cases. And then the lord lieutenant of Ireland is desired to make forth a commission or to give warrant for entering the said Mr. St. John into the muster roll of the standing army in that kingdom as captain of the said troop with all the rights and privileges thereunto belonging.

Mr. St. John, to recruit[3] his troop, 360£ and a month's advance

It is this day ordered by the lords and others his majesty's commissioners for the affairs of Ireland that the lord lieutenant of Ireland be desired [p. 81] to give order to Mr. Nicholas Loftus, deputy treasurer at wars for that kingdom, to pay

---

1. MS: *to.*

2. Sir Hardress Waller, formerly of Kent and first cousin to Sir William, had lost much of his property in the counties of Limerick and Tipperary at the outbreak of the rebellion. For this letter, a certificate of Waller's losses, and his subsequent service under Lord Inchiquin, see Hogan, *Irish Rebellion,* pp. 24–25, 33–34, 60–63. *DNB.*

3. MS: *receive.* The correction is from the list of "Orders made by the . . . commissioners for the affairs of Ireland," which follows the minutes for daily proceedings in the CIA minute book.

unto John St. John, Esquire, who hath now the command of the troop of horse that was the Lord Viscount Grandison's in the standing army in Ireland, the sum of 360£ to buy 30 horses for the recruiting of the said troop and making it up 60 and to advance unto him a month's pay for the said troop according to the number of 60 horse to be afterwards defalked out of such pay as shall be first due unto that troop and payable with the rest of the standing army in that kingdom.

Mr. Lucy

Whereas the lords and others his majesty's commissioners for the affairs of Ireland have this day been moved by the petition of Lucas Lucy of London, merchant, that he having for some years past traded in several merchandises to and from Limerick in Ireland, where at present he hath to his great loss a great part of his estate remaining in cote seed, butter, tallow, beef, hides, and other merchandise, which is yet preserved by reason Jacob Van Hoogarden, a Dutchman, his factor there, hath kept these goods as his own chattels, and the better to get all merchandises thence, the petitioner hath freighted one hoy named the *John* of Hamburg, whereof John Henson is master, and another vessel named the *William and Judith* of Ipswich, whereof Nicholas Golsweny is master, and to the end that those vessels which go with any lading to Limerick may without any interruption pass to and from thence with the said merchandise, which will be seized by the rebels and so lost if they be discovered to be the petitioner's goods, he humbly prayeth the said commissioners to be pleased to grant him warrants that the said vessels with the said merchandises may pass and go to and from Limerick without any interruptions of any ships appointed by the parliament for our king and kingdom's service. It is now therefore ordered that the lord high admiral of England be desired to give warrant and command to the captains of his majesty's ships and other ship now in the service of this state and all other whom it doth or may concern to permit and suffer the beforementioned hoy and vessel, with the goods and merchandises of the said Lucas Lucy therein laden, to have free passage by them both to and from the said city of Limerick without any their lets and hindrances and to be aiding and assisting those that are employed in the performance of this service.

Sir Adam Loftus for 3d. upon the pound

Whereas the lords and others his majesty's commissioners for the affairs of Ireland have been this day moved on the behalf of Sir Adam Loftus, Knight, treasurer at wars for the kingdom of Ireland, that according to an order of the commons house of parliament, which was directed to the late committee for Irish affairs,[4] these commissioners would be pleased to lay down such al-

---

4. For the discussion on 8 March of Loftus's allowance, see *PJ*, 2: 13.

lowance as shall be thought fit for execution [p. 82] of treasurer at wars for Ireland, both for himself, deputies, and clerks, and therein to consider the great burden, charge, and hazard which he must undergo in keeping an agent and servants here in London and of sending of the treasurers from London to Dublin, Youghal, Carrickfergus, and divers other places in Ireland where the several armies shall go, having consideration of such allowances as other treasurers at wars have had formerly in this kingdom and what further addition of allowances they would be pleased to make him in respect the burden, charge, and hazard will be much more for this present service of Ireland than was or could be in the discharge and execution of that office in the kingdom of England, it is now thought fit and ordered that from the time of these wars in Ireland first began, which was in November last, the said Sir Adam Loftus, Knight, shall be allowed as treasurer at wars for that kingdom the sum of 3d. upon every 20s. sterling of all such moneys as shall come upon his account for those wars during the time that the armies shall continue in the pay of this state. And it is also ordered that he shall not take any other fee or expect any allowance whatsoever for himself, his deputies, clerks, or servants or for portage or other conveyance of the moneys designed for the wars of that kingdom but only this fee of 3d. in the pound of money as aforesaid.

Lord Blayney's company and all the old companies in Ireland

The lords and others his majesty's commissioners for the affairs of Ireland having taken this day into consideration the petition of the Lord Blayney[5] exhibited to the House [of] Commons in parliament, whereby he showeth that his foot company in the standing army in Ireland being cut off and so dispersed by the rebels that he could not find them out towards the raising them to 100 men besides officers, although he had full power from the lord justices and commission from the lieutenant general of the army[6] there so to do, and because that number cannot be raised there with officers and arms both for his want of means and the scarcity of supplies, he desireth that commission may be given to Arthur Savile, his lieutenant, and reasonable means allowed him for the raising of the said men and officers. The said commissioners have thought fit (in favor of the said Lord Blayney and do intend that this shall be a rule for all the rest of the old companies of the standing army in Ireland) hereby to order that old company of the said Lord Blayney shall be taken into the pay of this state according to the number thereof from the 2d day of February last, and that the new levies added thereunto that were mustered and in actual service shall be taken into pay from the first of April last, and the Lord Blayney is to recruit and

5. The estate of Lord Blayney in Co. Monaghan had been destroyed by the Irish rebels in 1641. GEC, *Peerage*.
6. The Earl of Ormonde.

make up this his company with such men as may be raised in Ireland as other captains of the standing army have done.

[p. 83] Lord Cromwell, 500£ advanced

Whereas the lords and others his majesty's commissioners for the affairs of Ireland have formerly thought fit that the sum of 500£ should be advanced to the Lord Cromwell towards the better enablement of him and his troop in the present wars of Ireland, which hath been since ordered by the commons house of parliament,[7] it is now ordered by the said commissioners that the lord lieutenant of Ireland be desired to give order to Mr. Nicholas Loftus, deputy treasurer at wars for that kingdom, to pay by way of advance unto the said Lord Cromwell the said sum of 500£ as aforesaid to be afterwards defalked out of the first money that shall be coming to his lordship with the rest of the standing army in that kingdom.

Fisher's offer of 150 dozen of shirts

Whereas Christopher Fisher of London, seamster, hath offered to the lords and others his majesty's commissioners for the affairs of Ireland to provide a 150 dozen of shirts for the soldiers in Ireland according to a pattern left with Mr. Willis[8] but without wristbands at the rate of four thirty shillings a dozen, to be brought within one month after this day and to be paid one third of the money at the delivery of the first 100 dozen and the rest at two three months next after the delivery of them, the said commissioners have thought fit to accept of the offer and upon bringing of the said shirts will take order payment to be made accordingly.

Lord lieutenant to recruit his troop of horse, 240£

The lord lieutenant of Ireland having this day moved the lords and others his majesty's commissioners for the affairs of Ireland that his lordship's [troop] in the standing army in Ireland having ever since the rebellion been in actual service, 20 of the horse have troop [sic] have been lost, it is now thought fit by the said commissioners and accordingly ordered that the lord lieutenant of Ireland do give order to Mr. Nicholas Loftus, deputy treasurer at wars for that kingdom, to pay unto such persons as the lord lieutenant shall appoint to receive the same the sum of 240£ for the providing and transporting of 20 horse into that kingdom for recruiting that his lordship's troop as is desired.

Goodyeare for 906 barrels of wheat delivered at Dublin 957£

Whereas it appeareth by a certificate this day presented to the lords and others his majesty's commissioners for the affairs of Ireland under the hands of the lord

---

7. See D, 15 June. This order was repeated on 3 September. See *CJ*, II, 751.

8. Richard Willis was responsible for keeping "the door, paper, books, ink, fire, and other necessaries" for the commissioners. See *PJ*, 2: 408.

justices and council of Ireland dated the 20th day of May 1642 that commissaries at Dublin had bought of Moses Goodyeare of Plymouth, merchant, 906 barrel of wheat, which was laid into [p. 84] his majesty's stores in Dublin in May 1642 and agreed for by the said commissaries at the rate of 22s. the barrel, which comes to in money 996£ 12s., whereof paid in money for discharge of freight 39£ 12s., so rest [sic] 957£, which he desires might be paid in London to him the said Moses Goodyeare or his assigns thirty days after the sight of this their certificate, their second not being paid, which payment the lord justices prayed might be made to the order of parliament, it is now ordered by the said commissioners that the lord lieutenant of Ireland be desired to give order to Mr. Nicholas Loftus, deputy treasurer at wars for that kingdom, to pay unto the said Moses Goodyeare or his assigns the said sum of 957£ upon the 15th day of July next in discharge of the 906 barrels of wheat so delivered as is certified and according to the order of parliament in that behalf.

Medford for 352 barrels of wheat 396£ delivered at Dublin

Whereas it appeareth by the certificate of Sir Philip Percivall, Knight, commissary general for the victual in Ireland, dated the 20th day of May and testified by Sir Adam Loftus, Knight, vice treasurer and treasurer at wars for that kingdom, this day presented to the lords and others his majesty's commissioners for the affairs of Ireland that Richard[9] Medford of Barnstaple, merchant, hath brought into the port of Dublin 352 barrels of good and wholesome wheat for the subsistence of his majesty's army, which the said Sir Philip Percivall agreed for and received into his majesty's stores at the price of 22s. 6d. per barrel, amounting to the sum of 396£ English money to be paid unto Richard Medford of Barnstaple, aforesaid merchant, or his assigns out of the Chamber of London by those who are or shall be thereunto assigned within 30 days after producing this first certificate, the second not being paid, according to the order of the high court of parliament in that behalf published in print, it is now ordered by the said commissioners that the lord lieutenant of Ireland be desired to give order to Mr. Nicholas Loftus, deputy treasurer at wars for that kingdom, to pay unto the said Richard Medford or his assigns the said sum of 396£ upon the 15th day of July next in discharge of the said wheat so delivered as is certified and according to the order of parliament in that behalf.

Warner for corn 268£ delivered at Dublin; Castell

Whereas it appeareth by a certificate this day presented to the lords and others his majesty's commissioners for the affairs of Ireland under the hands of the lord justices and council of that kingdom [p. 85] dated the 12th day of May 1642 that Robert Warner, merchant, hath delivered into his majesty's granaries at Dublin

9. MS: *George*. See below.

220 barrels of wheat at the rate agreed upon by the commissaries, which was 22s. for every barrel, and 26 barrels of peas at 20s. the barrel, the whole amounting to 268£ sterling, the value whereof the said Robert Warner hath acknowledged to have received of Mr. Abraham Rickesis, merchant in Dublin, by way of exchange, and he desireth the like sum of 268£ may be paid unto Mr. Michael Castell, merchant in London, or his assigns 30 days after sight of this second certificate, the first not being paid, which payment the lord justices pray may be made according to the order of parliament, it is now ordered by the said commissioners that the lord lieutenant of Ireland be desired to give order unto Mr. Nicholas Loftus, deputy treasurer at wars for that kingdom, to pay unto the said Mr. Michael Castell or his assigns the said sum of 268£ upon the 15th day of July next in discharge of the said wheat and peas so delivered as is certified and according to the order of parliament in that behalf.

Rickesis for corn 2617£ 4s. delivered at Dublin; Castell

Whereas it appeareth by a certificate presented this day to the lords and others his majesty's commissioners for the affairs of Ireland under the hands of the lord justices and council of Ireland dated the 24th day of May 1642 that the commissaries of Dublin had bought of Mr. Abraham Rickesis and Daniel Hutchinson, merchants, 1324 barrels of beef agreed for by the commissaries at the rate of 25s. per barrel, 1156 barrels of full herrings at 20s. per barrel, 50 barrels of herrings swimmers at 18s. the barrel, 264 barrels of herrings shotters[10] at 16s. per barrel, amounting in the whole to the sum of 3067£ 04s., all which provision were brought into his majesty's stores at Dublin, of which said sum of 3067£ 4s. the said Mr. Rickesis and Daniel Hutchinson have acknowledged to have received 450£, the remainder being 2617£ 04s. they desire may be paid unto Mr. Michael Castell, merchant in London, or his assigns 30 days after sight of this their second certificate, their first being not paid, which payment the said lord justices prayed might be made according to the order of parliament, it is now ordered by the said commissioners that the lord lieutenant of Ireland be desired to give order unto Mr. Nicholas Loftus, deputy treasurer at wars for that kingdom, to pay unto the said Michael Castell or his assigns the said sum of 2617£ 04s. upon the 15th day of July next in discharge of the said beef and herrings so delivered as is certified and according to the order of parliament in that behalf.

[p. 86] Dowde for corn 192£ 17s. delivered at Dublin; Castell

Whereas it appeareth by a certificate presented to the lords and others his majesty's commissioners for the affairs of Ireland under the hands of the lord justices and council of Ireland dated the 20th of May 1642 that the commis-

10. I.e., shotten, meaning a fish (esp. herring) that has spawned. *NED.*

saries of Dublin have bought of Francis Dowde, merchant, 144 barrels of French wheat and 53 barrels of beans, which were laid into his majesty's stores in Dublin in April 1642 and agreed for by the said commissioners to have for his wheat at the rate of 22s. the barrel and for his beans at the rate of 13s. the barrel, which comes to in money 192£ 17s., the value whereof the said Francis Dowde hath acknowledg[ed] to have received of Mr. Abraham Rickesis, merchant, and of Daniel Hutchinson for the said Mr. Rickesis by way of exchange, which said sum of 192£ 17s. he desires may be paid in London to Michael Castell, merchant, or his assigns 30 days after sight of this their first certificate, their 2d being not paid, which payment the lord justices prayed might be made according to an[11] order of parliament, it is now ordered by the said commissioners that the lord lieutenant of Ireland be desired to give order unto Mr. Nicholas Loftus, deputy treasurer at wars for that kingdom, to pay unto the said Michael Castell or his assigns the said sum of 192£ 17s. upon the 15th day of July next in discharge of the said wheat and beans so delivered as is certified and according to the order of parliament in that behalf.

Memorandum: That this day a certificate was brought to the lords and others his majesty's commissioners for the affairs of Ireland dated the 14th of May 1642 under the common seal of Londonderry, that the 10th day of that month Edward Clemens, master of the good ship called the *Anne* of London, arrived at Londonderry with sixty-four London barrels of peas, eighteen hogsheads of wheat meal, 192 quarters of wheat, which as Mr. Vassall of London affirmed was a free gift from the City of London to the inhabitants of Londonderry.

[p. 87]   *Die Veneris, viz., 17° Junii* 1642

Letters of lord justices, etc., to be reported to the House of Commons

It is this day ordered by the lords and others his majesty's commissioners for the affairs of Ireland that the letters of the lord justices and council of Ireland this day presented to these commissioners shall be reported and read in the House of Commons tomorrow morning with the observation of the most considerable points thereof.[1] And that after immediately reading of the said letters, that house be moved by Mr. Pym to take the lord lieutenant of Ireland's desires into consideration and to hasten his lordship's dispatch into Ireland, than which these commissioners think nothing more important for the safety and service of that kingdom.[2]

11. MS: *and.*

1. For a letter from the lord justices read at a conference, see D, 20 June, n. 13.
2. For the commons' actions concerning the lord lieutenant, see D, 13 and 20 June.

Sir Thomas Staples et al. to provide drums, cases, etc., 24£

It is this day ordered, etc., according to the resolution of the House of Commons,[3] that the lord lieutenant of Ireland be desired to give order unto Mr. Nicholas Loftus, deputy treasurer at wars for that kingdom, for payment unto Sir Thomas Staples, Captain Newburgh, Captain Beresford, and Captain Hartwell, who are to command the four new companies in Londonderry, the sum of 24£ for provision of eight drums, eight cases, eight heads with cords, eight halberds, and four partisans for their said companies at the rate of 35s. each drum, 5s. each case, 5s. 8d. each drumhead, 8s. each halberd, and 14s. each partisan.

Symonds and Ford, 2 gunners for Londonderry

Whereas it is ordered by the House of Commons in parliament that a gunner and his mate shall be allowed in the garrison of Londonderry in Ireland, where there are many pieces of ordnance mounted for the defense of that city, have provided two gunners for that service, viz., John Symonds and John Ford, who are certified by Sir John Conyers, Knight, to be men sufficient and serviceable, it is now ordered by the lords and others his majesty's commissioners for the affairs of Ireland that allowance shall be made unto the said John Symonds as master gunner of that garrison of 3s. per diem and to the said John Ford as gunner's mate 2s. per diem, and that these allowances be entered into the list of the former establishment. And the lord lieutenant of Ireland is desired to give order that according to their allowances they may have advanced unto them a month's pay.

Mr. Turner et al., 7000 coats and 7000 pair of stockings

Whereas Mr. Turner and others of London have this day informed the lords and others his majesty's commissioners for the affairs of Ireland tha[t] according to agreement made with the commissioners[4] they have provided and delivered at several [p. 88] times towards the clothing of the soldiers sent hence to Dublin 7000 coats and 7000 pair of stockings, as appeareth by an account thereof by them delivered, it is now ordered by the said commissioners that the auditor[5] attending this commission shall cast up what the said 7000 coats and 7000 pair of stockings at the rate of eight shillings sixpence every coat and 12d. every pair of stockings shall amount unto, having also respect to the several times of the delivery of them. And that Mr. Pym be desire[d] to move the House of Commons that the money which these coats and stockings shall amount unto may by order of that house be secured unto them and payment made thereof as shall be thought fit and agreed.

---

3. See above, 9 June. For the order of 15 June, see *CJ*, II, 626.
4. For the agreement made with Richard Turner, a woolen draper, see *PJ*, 2: 442–43.
5. Robert Chambers.

Die Martis, viz., 21° Junii 1642

A list to be made of what arms are fit to be required
from his majesty's stores

　　Whereas the lords and others his majesty's commissioners for the affairs of
Ireland, having formerly sent unto the officers of his majesty's ordnance an[1]
order of parliament and another order of these commissioners thereupon for the
delivery of some ordnance, arms, and ammunition requisite for the service of
Ireland, have received this day from them an answer in writing that they were
prohibited by his majesty to deliver out of his stores any things of those natures
without special warrant under his sign manual, it is now ordered by the said
commissioners that a list shall be made of such ordnance, arms, and ammunition, and necessaries thereunto belonging as are to be had out of any his
majesty's stores in the Tower of London or elsewhere for the service of that
kingdom. And that Mr. Pym be desired to move the House of Commons that his
majesty may be sent unto and desired to give warrant for the delivery of them
out of any his majesty's magazines or stores.[2]

Lord justices' letters touching the protection of Galway

　　Whereas divers letters and other papers were this day presented unto the lords
and others his majesty's commissioners for the affairs of Ireland from the lord
justices and council of that kingdom concerning the city of Galway's being
taken into his majesty's protection by the Earl [p. 89] of St. Albans and
Clanricarde, it is thought fit and ordered by the commissioners aforesaid that
Mr. Pym be desired to report the letters and other papers to the House of
Commons[3] with this opinion of these commissioners, that this form of protection as it is granted to that city is against the act of parliament lately made,
against the declaration of parliament touching the advancement of Protestant
religion in that kingdom, against the peace and settlement intended to be had
there, and the satisfaction which the inhabitants of that city ought to make to
those his majesty's subjects that have received losses and injuries by them.

---

　　1. MS: *and.* For the order and an earlier response from the officers of the ordnance, see D, 3
June, n. 20, and 7 June.

　　2. For the earlier lists see above, 9 and 13 June. On 24 June, when these lists were presented to
both houses, it was ordered: "That His Majesty be desired . . . to grant His Warrant to the Masters
and Officers of the Ordnance, for the issuing out of such Ordnance, Ammunition, Arms, and
Necessaries, as are requisite for the Train of Artillery" for Ireland. See *CJ,* II, 637, and *LJ,* V, 159–
60. For the king's negative response, see D, 7 July.

　　3. The matter of Galway occupied the house for several days. For the letters see D, 23 June, and
G and H, 24 June.

Mr. Terence, 385£ 19s. 2d. for beef delivered at Dublin
by Frederick Pankard

Whereas it appeareth by the certificate of Sir Philip Percivall, Knight, commissary general for the victual in the kingdom of Ireland, dated 20th day of May 1642 and testified by Sir Adam Loftus, Knight, vice treasurer and treasurer at wars for that kingdom, this day presented to the lords and others his majesty's commissioners for the affairs of Ireland that Frederick Pankard, merchant, hath delivered into his majesty's stores in Dublin 295 barrels of beef at 26s. 2d. the barrel, amounting in the whole to the sum of 385£ 19[s.] 2d., to be paid in London to Mr. Anthony Terence, merchant, or his assigns out of the Chamber of London by those who are or shall be thereunto assigned within thirty days after sight of this second certificate, his first being not paid according to an order of parliament in that behalf published in print, it is now ordered by the said commissioners that the lord lieutenant of Ireland be desired to give order to Mr. Nicholas Loftus, deputy treasurer at wars for that kingdom, to pay unto the said Anthony Terence or his assigns the said sum of 385£ 19s. 2d. upon the 22th day of July next ensuing the date hereof in discharge of the price of the said beef so delivered as is certified and according to the order of parliament in that behalf.

Mr. Kirle, 300£

Whereas Anthony Kirle is appointed by the lords and others his majesty's commissioners for the affairs of Ireland to make divers provisions of corn and victual in the northern parts of this kingdom to be sent for the relief of his majesty's army in Ireland and hath in that service laid out great sums of money, towards which by his letters to Mr. Pym he hath desired that the sum of 300£ may upon his account be paid to John Biles, merchant, dwelling in Mincing Lane, London, to be by him paid over to Mr. Hildiard in discharge of a bill of exchange drawn upon him, it is this day ordered by the commissioners that the lord lieutenant of Ireland be desired to give order [p. 90] to Mr. Nicholas Loftus, deputy treasurer at wars for that kingdom, to pay unto the said John Biles the sum of 300£ upon the 27th day of June instant upon the account of the said Anthony Kirle to be deducted out of such demands as he shall make upon the service he hath in hand.

Die Mercurii, viz., 22° Junii 1642

Mr. Hill and Mr. Chichester

It being this day moved to the lords and others his majesty's commissioners for the affairs of Ireland by Mr. Hill that some course be taken for the keeping together Mr. Chichester's regiment of foot and the said Mr. Hill's regiment of horse in the north of Ireland, it is now thought fit by the said commissioners that in regard the great affairs of this kingdom will not yet admit of the resolving upon the petitions of the said Mr. Hill and Mr. Chichester, and that their regiments have done good service a long time and yet continue therein, Mr. Pym be desired to recommend from these commissioners to that house that the commissary of Carrickfergus may deliver to the soldiers of those regiments that are mustered and in actual service to the value of 2s. 4d. a man every week in victual to keep them together in the service, to be taken unto them by way of imprest from this day and so continued until the House of Commons shall take some resolution concerning their entertainment and pay.[1]

Lord Blayney's company

The petition of Arthur Savile, lieutenant of the Lord Blayney's company, being this day read to the lords and others his majesty's commissioners for the affairs of Ireland, it is by them answered that as soon as commission is granted from his majesty for raising further number of men, order will be taken for recruiting his company in this kingdom and transporting them from Chester into Ireland.

[p. 91] Recruits for Ireland

It is this day thought fit by the lords and others his majesty's commissioners for the affairs of Ireland that the lord lieutenant of that kingdom be desired to write to Sir Edward Nicholas, Knight, his majesty's principal secretary, for moving his majesty for to give warrant and commission to the said lord lieutenant to raise 4000 men volunteers in this kingdom needful for the service of Ireland, whereof 2000 are earnestly desired by the lord justices and the council to recruit the companies already sent hence into that kingdom.

A physician and apothecary for Munster, 130£ 10[s.]

Whereas it hath been ordered by the House of Commons the first day of this instant June that 5s. per diem should be allowed to a physician and 2s. 6d. per diem to an apothecary to be sent into Munster to attend the army there,[2] forasmuch as the lords and others his majesty's commissioners for the affairs of Ireland have given order therein accordingly and do further think fit that respective allowances also made unto them of a month's advance upon their pay for the physician's transportation and the apothecary's provision of medicaments, it is this day ordered that the lord lieutenant of Ireland be desired to give order unto Mr. Nicholas Loftus, deputy treasurer at wars for that kingdom, to pay unto Dr. Meashier, physician appointed for that service, the sum of 20£ without

1. See D, 23 June.
2. For the order see *PJ*, 2: 466–67.

account for his transportation and the advance of one month's pay according to the establishment, and also to pay unto Charles Kynaston, apothecary appointed for that service, the like advance of a month's pay according to the establishment and also the sum of 100£ upon account for provision and carriage of medicaments for the service of the army in that province.

Sir William Balfour, 159£ 12s.

Whereas Sir William Balfour, Knight, commissary general of the horse which are to be joined with the Scottish army in Ireland, hath this day moved the lords and others his majesty's commissioners for the affairs of Ireland that allowance may be given him for the conduct and transportation of 60 horses appointed him formerly for his own troop at the rate of forty shillings a horse, and that a smith and a saddler may also be allowed amongst the number of the 12 officers of his said troop and money allowed them for providing and transporting of each of them a horse at the rate of 12£ apiece, and that allowance may be given for a minister and a chaplain to attend the said regiment and money allowed for a surgeon's chest as are allowed to other regiments, it is this day ordered by the said commissioners that the lord lieutenant of Ireland be desired to give order to Mr. Nicholas Loftus, deputy treasurer at wars for that kingdom, to pay unto the said Sir William Balfour the sum of 120£ for the conduct and [p. 92] transportation of the 60 horses formerly appointed for his troop,[3] the sum of 24£ for providing and transporting two horses for the smith and the saddler to be added to the number of his officers of his troop, and the sum of 10£ for a surgeon's chest of medicaments, and also for payment of such allowance to a chaplain for that regiment as is given to the chaplain of other regiments of that condition.

Paman and Hunt, 479£ 3s. 4d.

Whereas it appeareth by the acquittance of George Wood, appointed to receive divers clothes for the soldiers and to send them into Ireland, that Henry Paman and Edmund Hunt having according to agreement made with the lords and others his majesty's commissioners for the affairs of Ireland the 27th of May last[4] delivered unto him 5000 caps according to the patterns and at the rate of 23s. the dozen as was then agreed on, it is now ordered by the said commissioners that the lord lieutenant of Ireland be desired to give order to Mr. Nicholas Loftus, deputy treasurer at wars for that kingdom, to pay unto the said Henry Paman and Edmund Hunt the sum of 479£ 3s. 04d. to be equally divided betwixt them in full satisfaction of the said 5000 caps so delivered by them and in performance of the said agreement in that respect.

3. For the order of 30 April, see *PJ*, 2: 252.
4. See *PJ*, 2: 461.

Shoemakers of London

Whereas Edward Johnson, John Jones, Bartholomew Helby, and Edward Poole of London, cordwainers, have under their hands by a note dated the 18th of this instant June promised and undertaken to the lords and others his majesty's commissioners for the affairs of Ireland to deliver 10,000 pair of well-conditioned neat's leather shoes (some black and some russet) of four sizes, viz., nines, tens, elevens, and twelves, the one half to be with three soles and the other with two soles according to the patterns left with Mr. Willis, for which they are to be paid upon the delivery of each 1000 pair at the rate of 2s. 5d. for the dry leather shoes and 2s. 6d. for those that are liquored, and further agreed that but 500 pair of the shoes above-mentioned shall be of the nines and 500 pair of thirteens, it is now ordered by the said commissioners that Mr. Nicholas Loftus, deputy treasurer at wars for the kingdom of Ireland, shall see indentures to be drawn up and seised[5] according to the particulars abovesaid by the parties aforenamed on the one part and him the said Mr. Loftus on the other. And that he take order out of such mone[y]s as shall from time to time remain in his hands for the service of Ireland for performance of what is on his part to be performed, and that he receive the other part whereby the shoemakers are obliged to perform the service therein mentioned by them to [p. 93] be performed. And that a clause be inserted in the said indentures that the master and wardens of the Company of Cordwainers of London shall have the view and approbation of these shoes to be good and serviceable.

Harvey

The lords and others his majesty's commissioners for the affairs of Ireland, having this day received the petition of James Harvey, ensign of the foot company under the command of Captain Anthony Willoughby in the fort of Galway in Ireland, have thought fit to recommend the petitioner and his petition to the committee for distributions to consider of his service pay and his present wants and to recommend him to the committee of adventurers for some fit employment in the expedition from the City of London for Ireland according to his condition and quality.

Mr. Frost, 1000£

It is this day ordered by the lords and others his majesty's commissioners for the affairs of Ireland that the lord lieutenant of Ireland be desired to give order to Mr. Nicholas Loftus, deputy treasurer at wars for that kingdom, to pay by way of imprest upon account unto Walter Frost, gentleman, commissary for providing victual in this kingdom for the supply of the magazine at Dublin, the sum of 1000£ more than hath been formerly ordered towards the further provision of

5. Put in possession, invested with the fee simple of. *NED*.

corn and victual for his majesty's army in that kingdom according to directions given him by these commissioners.

Whitcomb

Whereas Benjamin Whitcomb of London, merchant, craveth allowance of the lords and others his majesty's commissioners for the affairs of Ireland of the sum of 356£ 15s. 05d. for sundry provisions made by their order at Bristol for the victualing of several forts in Ireland,[6] in which sum is included the sum of 64£ 5s. 2d. for 25 tuns of beer and cask which he shipped and sent away without direction of the said commissioners, it is now ordered that he shall receive the full sum of 356£ 15s. 05d. if he will give security that if in case the beer and vessels so sent away by him be not delivered to some hand that may give account for it, he will repay so much as the vessel and beer do come to. And he is to set down what doth expect for his labor in this service.

Saddlers, 225£ imprest

Whereas it is concluded and agreed upon by Edward Payler, John Greene, Thomas Lloyd, and Robert Chambers,[7] gentlemen, for and on the behalf (and by the order) of the lords and others his majesty's commissioners for the affairs of Ireland with Benjamin Potter, Daniel Holdenby, Daniel Potter, and Ellis Parry of London, saddlers, that the said saddlers will provide 400 trooping saddles complete according to a pattern produced before the said commissioners the 18th of this instant June, viz., a great saddle with bridle [*illegible*] and crupper, stirrups and stirrup leathers, three strong pack nets, [p. 94] girths with iron staples and straps before and behind for the pistols and knapsacks, to be delivered for the service of the state in manner and form following, viz., 100 of them at or upon the 27th day of this instant June and so on every Monday following the number of 100 more until the full number of 400 saddles be delivered into such place as the said commissioners shall appoint for which the said Edward Payler, John Greene, Thomas Lloyd, and Robert Chambers have agreed, that the said Benjamin Potter and the rest that be allowed and paid the sum 225£ for each 100 of saddles so to be made and delivered, whereof they are to have by way of imprest the sum of 225£ in present for the first 100 and the like sum upon the delivery of every other 100 saddles until the number agreed for shall be complete, the lords and others his majesty's commissioners aforesaid have this day thought fit to accept of this agreement. And the lord lieutenant of Ireland is desired to give order unto Mr. Nicholas Loftus, deputy treasurer at wars for that kingdom, to make present payment by way of imprest of the sum of 225[£] to the said Benjamin Potter, Daniel Holdenby, Daniel Potter, and Ellis

6. For the order of 28 April, see *PJ*, 2: 427.
7. Doubtless the auditor for the commissioners.

Parry for the first 100 saddles to be by them made and delivered in according to this agreement. And upon the delivery of the rest of the said saddles, the commissioners will take order that due payment shall be also made as is above expressed.

Castell, 1231£ 8s. for corn at Dublin

Whereas it appeareth by the certificate of Sir Philip Percivall, Knight, commissary general for the victual in the kingdom of Ireland, dated the 26th day of May 1642 and testified by Sir Adam Loftus, Knight, vice treasurer and treasurer at wars for that kingdom, this day presented to the lords and others his majesty's commissioners for the affairs of Ireland, that Mr. Abraham Rickesis, merchant, hath delivered into his majesty's stores in Dublin 463 barrels of wheat, which the said Sir Philip Percivall agreed for at the rate 24s. a barrel, 433 barrels of rye at the rate of 16s. the barrel, and 366 barrels of maslin[8] at the rate of 18s. the barrel, amounting in the whole to the sum of 1231£ 8s., to be [paid] in London to Michael Castell, merchant, or his assigns out of the Chamber of London by those who are or shall be thereunto assigned within thirty day[s] after his producing this his first certificate, his second being paid, according to the order of parliament in that behalf.

[p. 95] Mr. Castell, 1115£ 6s. for corn delivered at Dublin

Whereas it appeareth by the certificate of the lord justices and council of Ireland bearing date the 26th day of May 1642 this day presented to the lords and others his majesty's commissioners for the affairs of Ireland that Mr. Abraham Rickesis, merchant, hath delivered into his majesty's magazine at Dublin 626 barrels of French wheat the commissaries there agreed for at the rate of 24s. the barrel, amounting in all at the prices abovesaid to the sum of 1115£ 06s., to be paid in London to Michael Castell, merchant, or his assigns out of the Chamber of London by those who are or shall be thereunto assigned within 30 days after producing their first certificate, their second not being paid, according to the order of parliament in that behalf published in print, it is now ordered by the said commissioners that the lord lieutenant of Ireland be desired to give order to Mr. Nicholas Loftus, deputy treasurer at wars for that kingdom, to pay unto the said Michael Castell or his assigns the said sum of 1115£ 6s. upon the 22th day of July next ensuing the date hereof in discharge of the said wheat so delivered as is certified and according to the order of parliament in that behalf.

Bitmaker, 25£ imprest

Whereas it is agreed upon and concluded between John Greene, Thomas Lloyd, and Robert Chambers, gentlemen, for and on the behalf (and by the

---

8. Mixed grain, especially rye mixed with wheat. *NED*.

order) of the lords and others his majesty's commissioners for the affairs of Ireland on the one part and John Savage, Nicholas Holton, and John Milborne of London, lorimers and bitmakers, on the other part that the said bitmakers will forthwith provide 400 good and serviceable bits cannon with a rising plane cannon and million[9] to be delivered in manner following, viz., 100 of them at or upon the 27th day of this instant June and upon every Monday following 100 more until the said number be complete, for which they are to receive the sum of 25£ for every 100 of bits upon the delivery of them according to the lords and others his majesty's commissioners, and 25£ imprest towards the said work, the said commissioners have this day thought fit to accept of this agreement. And the lord lieutenant of Ireland is desired to give order unto Mr. Nicholas Loftus, deputy treasurer at wars for that kingdom, to make present payment by way of imprest of the sum of 25£ unto the said John Savage, Nicholas Holton, and John Milborne for the first 100 bits to be by them made and delivered in according to agreement, and upon the delivery in of the residue of the said bits, the commissioners will take order that due payment shall be also made as is above expressed.

[p. 96]   Die Lunae, viz., 27° Junii 1642

Corn for Coleraine

Whereas upon the reading of the petition of Griffith Haward,[1] agent here for the town of Coleraine, the lords and others his majesty's commissioners for the affairs of Ireland have taken into consideration the seasonable relief of the inhabitants thereof, it is now ordered by the said commissioners that Mr. Pym be desired to move the House of Commons that 500£ worth of corn may forthwith be sent unto them before the winter comes on, it being a place that cannot be relieved in the winter season.

Mr. Chichester and Mr. Hill's soldiers

It is also thought fit by the lord commissioners for the affairs of Ireland, upon the motion of Arthur Hill, Esquire, and according to an order of the House of Commons dated the 23th day of June 1642,[2] have this day ordered that the commissary of victual at Carrickfergus for the time being do deliver out of such stores as shall from time to time remain in his charge and custody unto the 1000 soldiers of the foot regiment and the 300 soldiers of the regiment of horse raised by Mr. Chichester and Mr. Hill, which shall be mustered and continue in actual

9. Possibly *bit mollet*. See Glossary.

---

1. Griffin in *CJ*. On 30 June the house ordered that the corn be sent to Coleraine. On 11 July Haward's petition, along with several others from Ulster, was referred to the committee for the Chichester petition. *CJ*, II, 645, 664.

2. See D, 23 June.

service, the value of 2s. 4d. a man every week in victual for the better keeping of them together in the service, to be taken unto them from the 23th day of this instant June by way of imprest upon account and continued until the House of Commons shall take some further resolution concerning their pay and entertainment and the sum be made known unto the said commissary.[3]

50,000£ to go into Ireland for the soldiers in Leinster

It is also thought fit by the said commissioners that the sum of 50,000£ may be prepared to be sent into Ireland when the lord lieutenant of that kingdom shall go thither for payment of the soldiers in Leinster, and that Mr. Pym do move the House of Commons to take order for the same.[4]

[p. 97] Clothes for the soldiers at Dublin, Carrickfergus, and Munster

It is this day thought fit and ordered by the lords and others his majesty's commissioners for the affairs of Ireland that provision shall be made and added to what is already bespoken, provided, and sent away of so many cassocks, suits of clothes, shirts, caps, stockings, and shoes as will make up the several numbers hereafter expressed for the soldiers in those places, viz.: 2000 suits of clothes (that is to say, doublets, cassocks, and breeches), 4000 shirts, 4000 pair of shoes, 4000 pair of stockings, and 2000 caps for the soldiers of the English regiments under the Lord Conway and Sir John Clotworthy in Ulster, the prices of which as they cost here together with the charges of carriage and transportation is to be defalked out of the pay of such soldiers as shall receive the same. 7000 caps, 7000 cassocks, 7000 pair of stockings, and 7000 pair of shoes for the soldiers sent out of England to Dublin, which are to be given them in discharge of a promise made unto them by the parliament of one cap, one cassock, one pair of stockings, and one pair of shoes to every common soldier so sent out of England to Dublin, and 3000 cassocks more, 10,000 suits of apparel as aforesaid, 20,000 pair of shoes, 20,000 pair of stockings, and 24,000 shirts to furnish a magazine of apparel at Dublin to be delivered to the soldiers, and the prices as they cost here with the charge of carriage and transportation to be likewise defalked upon the pay of such soldiers as shall receive them. And lastly 3000 cassocks, 3000 caps, 3000 pair of shoes, and 3000 pair of stockings to be sent to the lord president of Munster to be given to the three regiments of English soldiers sent into Munster in discharge of a promise made unto them by the parliament of a cap, a cassock, a pair of shoes, and a pair of stockings to every soldier, and 3000 suits more consisting of cassocks, doublets, and breeches, 6000 pair of shoes, 6000 pair of stockings, and 6000 shirts to furnish a magazine of apparel at Cork to supply the wants of the soldiers, and the prices

3. For the subsequent action taken by the House of Commons, see D, 9 July, n. 4.
4. On 30 June the house resolved that £50,000 should be sent to Leinster out of the £100,000 to be lent by the City. *CJ*, II, 645. For the loan see D, 3 June.

as they cost here with the charge of carriage and transportation to be likewise defalked upon the pay of such soldiers as shall receive them.

3000£ to be imprested to the lord lieutenant
and 5000£ for incident charges

Whereas upon the reading of the desires of the right honorable the Earl of Leicester, lord lieutenant of Ireland, presented to the lords and others his majesty's commissioners for the affairs of Ireland and by them to the House of Commons in parliament, the first being for 3000£ [p. 98] to be allowed him for preparation of necessaries for his journey, it was by the house resolved upon the question the 20th day of this instant June 1642 after debate had thereof that 3000£ shall be imprested to the said lord lieutenant upon account, it is this day ordered by the aforesaid commissioners that a warrant be prepared for authorizing and requiring Mr. Nicholas Loftus, deputy treasurer at wars for that kingdom, to pay by way of imprest unto the said lord lieutenant the said sum of 3000£ according to the resolution of that house. And it is also ordered that according to another resolution of the House of Commons the same day another warrant be prepared for authorizing and requiring the treasurer at wars for the kingdom of Ireland and his deputy that, of such moneys as shall come into their hands by order of parliament for the wars of Ireland, to reserve and lay apart in their custody upon account the sum of 5000£ to be issued out upon the said lord lieutenant's warrants for such incident charges and services as may require the same.[5]

Gunter, 278£ 7s. 6d. for corn delivered at Dublin

Whereas it appeareth by the certificate of Sir Philip Percivall, Knight, commissary general for the victual in the kingdom of Ireland, dated the 20th day of May 1642 and testified by Sir Adam Loftus, Knight, vice treasurer and treasurer at wars for that kingdom, this day presented to the lords and others his majesty's commissioners for the affairs of Ireland that Thomas Gaskell, merchant, hath delivered into his majesty's stores 255 barrels of barley malt, which the said Sir Philip Percivall agreed for at the rate of 16s. the barrel, and 85 barrels of wheat at the rate of 17s. 6d. the barrel, amounting in the whole to the sum of 278£ 7s. 6d., to be paid unto John Gunter of Lamphey Court in the county of Pembroke, Esquire, or his assigns out of the Chamber of London by those who are or shall be thereunto assigned within 30 days after producing the first certificate (his 2d not being paid) according to the order of parliament in that behalf published in print, it is now ordered by the said commissioners that the lord lieutenant of Ireland be desired to give order to Mr. Nicholas Loftus, deputy treasurer at wars for that kingdom, to pay unto the said John Gunter or to

5. See D, 20 June.

his assigns the sum of 278£ 7s. 6d. upon the 27th day of July next ensuing the date hereof in discharge of the said barley malt and wheat so delivered as is certified and according to the order of parliament in that behalf.

[p. 99] Jones, 874£ 17s. for cheese[6] delivered at Dublin

Whereas it appeareth by the certificate of Sir Philip Percivall, Knight, commissary general of the victual in the kingdom of Ireland dated the 28th day of May 1642 and testified by Sir Adam Loftus, Knight, vice treasurer and treasurer at wars for that kingdom, this day presented to the lords and others his majesty's commissioners for the affairs of Ireland that John Owen, gentleman, hath delivered into his majesty's stores four hundred eighty-nine hundred one quarter and twenty-four pounds of cheese, which the said Sir Philip Percivall agreed for at the rate of 35s. 6d. the 100, and 300 one quarter and 21 pounds of bacon at 35s. 6d. the 100, amounting in the whole to the sum of 874£ 17s. sterling, to be paid in London to Cadwallador Jones, gentleman, or his assigns out of the Chamber of London by those who are or shall be thereunto appointed within 30 days after sight of his second certificate (his first not being paid) according to the order of parliament in that behalf published in print, it is now ordered by the said commissioners that the lord lieutenant of Ireland be desired to give order to Mr. Nicholas Loftus, deputy treasurer at wars for that kingdom, to pay unto the said Cadwallador Jones or his assigns the said sum of 874£ 17s. upon the 27th day of July next ensuing the date hereof in full discharge of the said cheese and bacon so delivered as is certified and according to the order of parliament in that behalf.

Castell, 1050£

Whereas it appeareth by the certificate of John Davies, major[7] of Carrickfergus and victualler of the forces there, attested under the hands and seal of the Lord Conway, Sergeant Major General Monro,[8] and others the 10th day of May last that one Thomas Cullen, master of the ship called the *Peter and Thomas* of Dover, hath delivered unto the said John Davies for the supply of the stores of victual in that town 500 barrels of wheat at 24s. the barrel and 30,000 weight of flour at 14s. the 100 weight, 400 barrels of barley at 12s. the barrel, amounting in the whole to the sum of 1050£, which he desired might according to the ordinance of parliament be paid here in London unto Michael Castell, merchant, proprietor of the said wheat, barley, and meal, it is now ordered by the lords and others his majesty's commissioners for the affairs of Ireland that

6. MS: *corn*. The correction is from the list of "Orders" which follows the daily proceedings in the minute book.

7. It seems likely that William Hawkins, secretary to the commissioners, intended to write *merchant*. For Davies see *PJ*, 1: 459.

8. Robert Monro was second in command of the Scots forces in Carrickfergus.

the lord lieutenant of Ireland be desired to give order to Mr. Nicholas Loftus, deputy treasurer at wars for that kingdom, to pay unto the said Michael Castell or his assigns the said sum of 1050£ upon the 27th day of July next ensuing the date hereof in full satisfaction of the said wheat, barley, and flour so delivered as is certified and according to the order of parliament in that behalf.

[p. 100] Mr. Chambers to see how much of the 100,000£
is received and expended

It is this day ordered by the lords and others his majesty's commissioners for the affairs of Ireland that Mr. Chambers, auditor to the commission, do inform himself from those that collect the 100,000£ now lent by the City of London for the supply of the service in Ireland how much money of that sum is already come unto their hands and how much thereof they have paid out by order of parliament.

Die Lunae, viz., 11° Julii 1642

Mr. St. John, 266£ 14s.

Whereas upon the 15th day of June last it was ordered (amongst other things) by the lords and others his majesty's commissioners for the affairs of Ireland that a month's pay should be advanced to John St. John, Esquire, who hath the command of that troop of horse in the kingdom of Ireland that was the Lord Viscount Grandison's, according to the number of 60 horse for that troop,[1] it is now thought fit and ordered by the lords and others his majesty's commissioners for the affairs of Ireland for explanation of that former order that the month's advance so mentioned in that order shall be extended to the number of 60 horses and all the officers belonging to that troop (except the lieutenant whose pay is to cease until further order be given concerning the same). And the lord lieutenant of Ireland is desired to give order to Mr. Nicholas Loftus, deputy treasurer at wars for that kingdom, to make payment of the month's advance unto the said Mr. St. John or his assigns accordingly.

Wollaston and Aldworth, 1375£ 11s.

Whereas, in performance of a contract made by the lords and others his majesty's commissioners for the affairs of Ireland with Richard Wollaston of London and Richard Aldworth of Bristol the 17th day of May last,[2] the said Richard Wollaston and Richard Aldworth have upon the first day of June last past delivered 30,012 ells of lockram for the making of 11,250 shirts for the soldiers in Ireland at the rate of 11d. the ell, amounting in the whole to the sum of 1375£ 11s., which sum by that contract is to be paid [p. 101] unto them, the

1. See above, 15 June.
2. See *PJ*, 2: 453–54.

one half at the end of four months after the delivery of the cloth and the other half at the end of the next four months after that, it is now ordered by the said commissioners that Mr. Pym be desired to move the House of Commons in parliament that the said sum of 1375£ 11s. may by order of that house be secured unto them and paid at the time so agreed on.[3]

Moneys in Munster to be issued by the council of war

Whereas the lords and others his majesty's commissioners for the affairs of Ireland have been moved by Nicholas Loftus, Esquire, deputy treasurer at wars for the kingdom of Ireland, to give directions and order (now the lord president of Munster is dead) how those moneys sent into that province for payment of the officers and soldiers and other incident charges should for the future be issued forth and disposed of and upon whose warrant, it is now ordered by the said commissioners that all such money as now are or hereafter shall be put into the hands of the treasurer at wars or his deputies for payment of the army in the province of Munster shall be by them issued out upon the warrant of the lord Dungarvan, Lord Inchiquin, Sir Charles Vavasour, Sir William Ogle, and Mr. Jephson, who are of the council of war there, or any three of them, for payment of the officers and soldiers and other necessary charges according to such orders and establishments as are or shall be settled in that behalf.

Kirle, 400£, 300[£]

Whereas Anthony Kirle [is designated] by the lords and others his majesty's commissioners for the affairs of Ireland to make divers provisions of corn and victuals in the northern part of this kingdom to be sent for relief of his majesty's army in Ireland and hath in that service laid out divers sums of money, as appeareth by his letter of advice to Mr. Pym, one of the said commissioners, dated this first day of this instant July, in discharge of a bill of exchange drawn by the said Anthony Kirle the first day of this month upon Mr. Nicholas Loftus for value received in Hull of Peregrine Pelham, and whereas by the said letter he also desireth that 300£ more may upon his account of the service aforesaid be paid unto Mr. Henry Crone[4] of London in lieu of so much which the said Anthony Kirle hath disbursed of Mr. Crone's money at Hull, it is this day ordered by the said commissioners that the lord lieutenant of Ireland be desired to give order to Mr. Nicholas Loftus, deputy treasurer at wars for that kingdom, to pay upon the account of the said Anthony Kirle unto the said James Whitehall or his assigns upon the 11th day of this instant July the sum of 400£ in discharge of that bill of exchange so drawn upon himself and to take up the bill of exchange into his own hands, [p. 102] and also to pay unto the said Henry Crone upon the account of the said Anthony Kirle the sum of 300£ according to his

3. For the order dated 14 July, see *LJ*, V, 213.
4. A London vintner. *CSPD, 1640–41*, p. 261.

directions in the above-mentioned letter for moneys used of the said Mr. Crone's at Hull, both which sums of 400£ and 300£ are to be charged upon the said Anthony Kirle as moneys imprested unto him for the service aforesaid.

Kirle, 100£

Whereas it appeareth by a deed of charter party[5] dated the 4th of this instant July that Henry Crone of London hath hired of John Warner[6] a ship called the *Friendship* of Yarmouth of the burden of 160 ton or thereabouts for carriage of corn and provision from the town of Kingston upon Hull to Carrickfergus in Ireland at the rate of 28s. per ton, of which the said Henry Crone hath already paid in hand the sum of 100£, it is now ordered by the lords and others his majesty's commissioners for the affairs of Ireland that the lord lieutenant of Ireland be desired to give order unto Mr. Nicholas Loftus, deputy treasurer at wars for that kingdom, for payment of the said sum of 100£ unto the said Henry Crone in full of so much by him paid according to the said charter party towards the hire of the said ship, which sum is to be put upon the account of Anthony Kirle together with the rest of the charges of the voyage and the provisions made by him by order of these commissioners.

Mr. Frost, 4000£

It is this day ordered by the lords and others his majesty's commissioners for the affairs of Ireland that the lord lieutenant of Ireland be desired to give order unto Mr. Nicholas Loftus, deputy treasurer at wars for the kingdom of Ireland, to pay by way of imprest upon account unto Mr. Frost, gentleman, commissary of victual in this kingdom, the sum of 4000£ more than he hath formerly received towards his further provision of corn and victual for supply of his majesty's magazines at Dublin and Carrickfergus according to such directions as shall be given him for the quantities to be sent to either of these places.

Wood, 140£

It is this day ordered by the lords and others his majesty's commissioners for the affairs of Ireland that the lord lieutenant of Ireland be desired to give order unto Mr. Nicholas Loftus, deputy treasurer at wars for that kingdom, forthwith to pay unto George Wood imprest upon his account the sum of 140£ more than he hath formerly received for the defraying of the charges of packing up and carriage from London and Northampton to Chester and Minehead [p. 103] such clothes, stockings, shoes, shirts, and other necessaries for the soldiers in those places as are or shall be provided and consigned according to directions given him by the said commissioners.

5. The charter or deed made between owners and merchants for hire of a ship and safe delivery of the cargo. *NED*.

6. Doubtless the London alderman and member of the London militia committee.

MacCarthy

The lords and others his majesty's commissioners for the affairs of Ireland, having taken into consideration the petition of Daniel MacCarthy[7] whereby he complaineth of the present want he, his wife, and family are brought into, have thought fit to recommend him to the committee for contributions in the lords house of parliament, and that their lordships be desired to give order that 30£ of that contribution money may be set apart in the clerk of the crown's hands to be by him given to the said Daniel MacCarthy by 3£ a month.

Ford et al., 862£ 4s. for wheat delivered at Cork

Whereas it appeareth by the certificate of the right honorable Richard, Earl of Cork, lord high treasurer of Ireland, dated the 29th day of May last past, that upon the letter and entreaty of the lord president of Munster the said earl bought of one Henry Baily, factor or agent for Thomas Ford, Richard Ford, John Levering, Thomas Pytt, and John Butler of the city of Exon, merchants, 958 barrels of French wheat, which by the lord president of Munster's order and direction was delivered on land at the city of Cork where the greater part of his majesty's army of that province was then quartered, at the rate of 18s. the barrel, amounting in the whole to the sum of 862[£] 4s., which sum the said earl desireth that when the owners of the said corn or any of them or their assigns shall tender the certificate hereof for payment to be made according to the order of parliament made in that behalf, they may be fully and faithfully paid, it is this day ordered by the lords and others his majesty's commissioners for the affairs of Ireland that the lord lieutenant of Ireland be desired to give order unto Mr. Nicholas Loftus, deputy treasurer at wars for that kingdom, to pay unto the said Thomas Ford, Richard Ford, John Levering, Thomas Pytt, and John Butler or their assigns the said sum of 862£ 4s. upon the last day of this instant July in full satisfaction of the said wheat so delivered as is certified and according to the order of parliament in that behalf.

Wollaston and Aldworth for 4000 shirts more

Whereas Richard Aldworth and Richard Wollaston have upon the 7th day of this instant July offered themselves to the lords and others his majesty's commissioners for the affairs of Ireland to provide 4000 fine Osnaburg[8] shirts more than they have already contracted for, which shall be white and well conditioned for the use of [p. 104] the soldiers in Ireland, suitable to a pattern for the size and goodness showed and remaining to be seen at the rate of 2s. 9d. the shirt, three shirts containing eight ells, and to deliver 2000 of them within 14 days and 2000 more within 14 days next after or sooner, the said 4000 shirts

7. His father, Florence MacCarthy, had been deprived of his lands in Ireland. See *PJ*, 2: 430.

8. MS: *Oxenbridge*. A kind of coarse linen originally made in Osnabrück, North Germany. *NED*. For the earlier contract see *PJ*, 2: 468.

amounting at that rate to the sum of 550£, they desire their payment may be for one half thereof at the end of three months next after the delivery of the said shirts and for the other half at the end of other three months next after 1st offer the lords and others his majesty's commissioners aforesaid have accepted of, and upon the delivery of the said shirts to such persons as shall be appointed to receive them, they will give order for payment as is desired.

Lord Moore

Upon reading the letters of the lord justices and council of Ireland on the behalf of the Lord Viscount Moore,[9] it is answered by the lords and others his majesty's commissioners for the affairs of Ireland that they will take all occasions to express their good esteem and approbation of the services done by the said Lord Moore.

Sir Robert King's letters

Upon reading the letters of Sir Robert King[10] to the right honorable the Earl of Essex and Mr. Pym concerning the late march of the army at Dublin to Athlone and their return, it is ordered by the lords and others his majesty's commissioners for the affairs of Ireland that Mr. Pym be desired to report those letters to the House of Commons.[11]

Propositions *pro* recovering of Limerick

Whereas certain propositions were this day produced by Mr. Pym concerning the drawing some forces out of Ulster towards Limerick for the better recovery thereof,[12] it was this day ordered that the Earl of Northumberland be desired to communicate them to the lord lieutenant of Ireland to be considered of to the end that if his lordship approve thereof, order may be given to the forces in Ulster accordingly.

Wollaston and Aldworth

Whereas, in performance of a contract made by the lords and others his majesty's commissioners for the affairs of Ireland with Richard Wollaston of London and Richard Aldworth of Bristol the first day of June last past, the said Richard Wollaston and Richard Aldworth have on the 7th day of this instant July delivered 4000 fine Osnaburg shirts, white and well conditioned, for the use [p. 105] of the soldiers in Ireland at the rate of 2s. 9d. a shirt, eight ells being allowed to three shirts, the said 4000 shirts amounting at the rate to the sum of

9. For this letter of 20 June commending Lord Moore for his role in the defense of Drogheda, see Hogan, *Irish Rebellion*, pp. 43–44.

10. Commissary general of the musters for Ireland. See *PJ*, 2: 2, n. 7.

11. For a letter from the lord justices describing this march, see Hogan, *Irish Rebellion*, pp. 68–70.

12. See D, 9 July, n. 6, and 16 July, n. 6.

550£, which sum by that contract is to be paid unto them the one half at the end of three months next after the said delivery of those shirts and the other half at the end of other three months next after that, it is now ordered by the said commissioners that Mr. Pym be desired to move the House of Commons in parliament that the said sum of 550£ may by order of that house be secured unto them and paid at the time so agreed on.[13]

Harris for corn delivered at Londonderry, 1009£

Whereas it appeareth to the lords and others his majesty's commissioners for the affairs of Ireland by the humble petition and certificate of Sir John Vaughan, Knight, Robert Thornton, mayor of the city of Londonderry, Henry Vaughan,[14] Dudley Phillips, and Thomas Dutton, Esquires, trusted with the government of that city, dated the 29th day of April and directed to the right honorable the lords and commons assembled in parliament in England, that the forces in that city and town of Coleraine, being at that time in such distress for want of victuals that they were not longer able to subsist, they then bought out of a ship called the *Jonathan* of Bristol of William Harris, factor for some merchants of Bristol, six barrels of powder at eight pound per barrel, 600 weight of lead at 15s. the 100, 110 barrels of white peas at 24s. the barrel, 49 barrels of wheat at 28s. the barrel, 123 barrels of malt at 20s. the barrel, 154 ells of dowlas[15] in bags at 14d. the ell, 1475 pounds of bacon at 6d. the pound, 240 barrels of beer at eighteen shilling the barrel, 11 butts of sherry sack at 20£ the butt, eight and thirty yards and three quarters of red cloth at 15s. 6d. the yard, 36 yards and a quarter of red cloth at eleven shillings the yard, 153 yards of coarse kerseys at 5s. the yard, 22 yards of Spanish cloth at 20s. the yard, and 46 100 and a half and 17 pounds of wheat meal at 18s. the 100, amounting in the whole to the sum of 1009£ 11s., part of which commodities we sent in two barks to relieve Coleraine. Other proportions were delivered to the regiments of Sir William and Sir Robert Stewart and the regiment of Sir Ralph Gore,[16] and the remainder left in the [p. 106] hands of the mayor of Londonderry, and which sum they desired might be paid unto the said William Harris by virtue of an order of parliament made in that behalf. Although according to the tenor of that order, there being no victual appointed for that port, the goods were so received and certified by them, it is now ordered by the said commissioners that the lord lieutenant of Ireland be desired to give order unto Mr. Nicholas Loftus, deputy treasurer at wars for that kingdom, to pay unto the said William Harris or his assigns for the use of

13. For the order dated 14 July, see *LJ*, V, 213.
14. Henry Vaughan was probably brother to Sir John. See *CJ*, III, 37.
15. A coarse kind of linen. *NED*.
16. The Stewarts—brothers, professional soldiers, and former members of the Irish parliament—were serving with the Scots troops in Ulster. Bagwell, *Ireland under the Stuarts*, II, 17. *DNB*. Gore had died about two months earlier. See *PJ*, 2: 449.

Richard Vickris, George Lane, Philip Love, William Clare, Richard Ditts, and John Knight, merchants of Bristol and proprietors of the said goods, the aforementioned sum of 1009£ 11s. upon the 28th day of this instant July in full discharge of the said goods and according to the order of parliament made in that behalf.

Fisher for shirts, 85£

Whereas in performance of a contract made by the lords and others his majesty's commissioners for the affairs of Ireland the 15th day of June last past with Christopher Fisher of London, seamster,[17] the said Christopher Fisher hath upon the 8th day of this instant July delivered 100 dozen of shirts for the service of the soldiers in Ireland in part of 150 dozen which at the rate of 34s. the dozen he was to make and deliver according to that contract for which he is to have payment of the sum of 255£ in the manner following, viz., one third of that money at the delivery of the first 100 dozen and the rest at two three months next after the delivery of the rest, it is now ordered by the said commissioners that the lord lieutenant of Ireland be desired to give order to Mr. Nicholas Loftus, deputy treasurer at wars for that kingdom, to pay unto the said Christopher Fisher the sum of 85£, being the one third part of the said sum of 255£ so coming to him by the said contract and in discharge of so much thereof.

[p. 107]   *Die Jovis, viz., 14° Julii* 1642

Arms and ammunition for Sir William Balfour

It is this day ordered by the lords and others his majesty's commissioners for the affairs of Ireland that Mr. Pym be desired to move the House of Commons that order of parliament may be given for delivering unto such person as the lord lieutenant of Ireland shall appoint to receive the same out of the ships that brought the arms and ammunition 560 pair of pistols, 560 carbines, and 560 back and breasts with pots[1] to them to be carried to Chester and delivered over to Sir William Balfour, Knight, towards the arming of the ten horse troops (whereof the troop now commanded by Mr. St. John to be one) that are appointed to join with the Scottish army in the province of Ulster.[2]

400 saddles for Sir William Balfour's regiment, 675£

It is also this day ordered by the lords and others his majesty's commissioners for the affairs of Ireland that Benjamin Potter, Daniel Holdenby, Daniel Potter, and Ellis Parry of London, saddlers, who have on the 22th of June last con-

17. See above, 15 June.

---

1. These arms had been brought from Hull. *CJ,* II, 675.
2. For the order passed by the house, see G, 16 July.

tracted with the said commissioners to provide and deliver 400 trooping saddles complete according to a pattern for the service of the state at the rate of 45 shillings apiece, shall deliver unto such person as the lord lieutenant shall appoint to receive the same said 400 saddles as they are or shall be made ready and allowed of according to the pattern mentioned in that contract to be forthwith sent to Chester and to be delivered unto Sir William Balfour, Knight, commissaries [*sic*] general for the troops of horse that are to join with the Scottish army in Ulster towards the arming and completing of those troops; and that the lord lieutenant of Ireland be desired to give order to Mr. Nicholas Loftus, deputy treasurer at wars for that kingdom, to pay unto the said Benjamin Potter, Daniel Holdenby, Daniel Potter, and Ellis Parry the sum of 675£ upon [p. 108] the delivery of the said 400 saddles as aforesaid, which sum with 225£ imprested upon them by a former order is in full of the price agreed on by the said contract.

400 bits for Sir William Balfour's regiment, 75£

It is this day also ordered by the said commissioners that John Savage, Nicholas Holton, and John Milborne of London, bitmakers, who have on the 22th day of June last contracted with the said commissioners to make and deliver 400 good and serviceable bits cannon with a rising plane cannon and million[3] at the rate of 25£ the 100 shall deliver unto such person as the lord lieutenant of Ireland shall appoint to receive the same the said 400 bits as they are or shall be made ready and allowed according to the contract to be forthwith sent to Chester and delivered over unto Sir William Balfour, Knight, commissary for the troop of horse that are to join with the Scottish army in Ireland towards the furnishing of those troops, and that the said lord lieutenant of Ireland be desired to give order unto Mr. Nicholas Loftus, deputy treasurer at wars for that kingdom, to pay unto the said John Savage, Nicholas Holton, and John Milborne the sum of 75£ upon the delivery of the said 400 bits as aforesaid, which sum together with 25£ imprested unto them by an former order is in full of the price agreed on by the said contract.

Shelston, 92£ 16s. 04d.

Whereas it appeareth by the certificate of Sir Philip Percivall, Knight, commissary general for the victual in Ireland, dated last day of May 1642 and testified by Sir Adam Loftus, Knight, vice treasurer and treasurer at wars for that kingdom, this day presented to the lords and others his majesty's commissioners for the affairs of Ireland that Mr. George Shelston hath delivered into his majesty's stores in Dublin 130 flitches of bacon weighing 5569 pounds neat at the rate of 4d. per pound, amounting to the sum of 92£ 16s. 04d., to be paid in

3. Possibly *bit mollet*. See Glossary.

London to the said Mr. George Shelston or his assigns out of the Chamber of London by those who are or shall be thereunto appointed within 30 days after sight of this his first certificate (his second not being paid) according to the order of parliament in that behalf published in print, it is now ordered by the said commissioners that the lord lieutenant of Ireland be desired to give or[der] unto Mr. [p. 109] Nicholas Loftus, deputy treasurer at wars for that kingdom, to pay unto the said George Shelston or his assigns the said sum of 92£ 16s. 04d. upon the 13th day of August next ensuing the date hereof in full discharge of the said bacon so delivered as is certified and according to order of parliament in that behalf.

Whitcomb, 370[£] 2s. 1d.

Whereas Benjamin Whitcomb of London, merchant, desireth allowance of the lords and others his majesty's commissioners for the affairs of Ireland of the sum of 356£ 15s. 05d. for sundry provisions made by him by their order at Bristol for the victualing of several forts in Ireland[4] as appeareth by a bill of the particulars, amongst which he demandeth the allowance of 64£ 5s. 2d. for 25 tun of beer and cask, which he shipped and sent away without direction of the said commissioners and which he hath given caution to repay in case the said beer and cask be not delivered into hands that may be accountable, and whereas the said commissioners think fit to allow him for his pains and charges and the disbursement of his money the sum of 13£ 6s. 8d. more than the sum so disbursed, it is now ordered by the said commissioners that the lord lieutenant of Ireland be desired to give order unto Mr. Nicholas Loftus, deputy treasurer at wars for that kingdom, to pay unto the said Benjamin Whitcomb as well the sum of 356£ 15s. 05d. in full discharge of all the provisions so made by him including the said beer and cask, as also the sum of 13£ 6s. 8d. for his labor and forbearance of his money laid out in the service.

Officers and artificers of the train of artillery, 492£ 8s.

It is this day ordered that the lord lieutenant of Ireland be desired to give order to Mr. Nicholas Loftus, deputy treasurer at wars for that kingdom, to pay unto such person as shall be by his lordship authorized to receive the same the sum of 492£ and eight shillings for a month's pay for the officers and artificers of the train of artillery, that is to say from the 26th day of June last past to the 23th day of July next inclusive.

Officers of the lord lieutenant's train, 220£ 19s. 4d.

It is this day ordered that the lord lieutenant of Ireland be desired to give order to Mr. Nicholas Loftus, deputy treasurer at wars for that kingdom, to pay unto such person as the lord lieutenant of Ireland shall think fit to receive the same

4. See above, 22 June.

the sum of 220£ 19s. 4d. for one month's pay for some officers [p. 110] and others belonging to the said lord lieutenant's train as lord general of the army according to computation thereof made by Mr. Chambers, auditor to this commission, to commence from the 26th of June last past and to end the 23d day of July 1642 inclusive.

Savage, petition for Bandonbridge

It is this day ordered by the lords and others his majesty's commissioners for the affairs of Ireland that Mr. Pym be desired to move the House of Commons that the petition of Abram Savage on the behalf of the town of Bandonbridge may be read and taken into their consideration.[5]

Train of artillery

It is this day ordered by the lords and others his majesty's commissioners for the affairs of Ireland that a warrant shall be prepared in form following: Whereas it hath been resolved by the House of Commons in parliament that such things as were by a list formerly required out of the office of his majesty's ordnance for making up the train of artillery to be sent to Dublin should now be bought with ready money and have therefore ordered the 13th day of this instant July that according to the prices of the particulars mentioned in that list, the sum of 1790£ 16s. 01d. should be imprested for the buying thereof,[6] these are to will and require you forthwith to pay unto the lord lieutenant of Ireland or whom his lordship shall appoint to receive the same the said sum of 1790£ 16s. 01d. imprest upon account for buying and providing the said materials and necessaries mentioned in the said list, for which this shall be your warrant. Star Chamber, the 14th day of July 1642.
To our loving friend, Nicholas Loftus, Esquire,
deputy treasurer at wars for that kingdom.

Recruits for the old army in Leinster

Whereas the lords and others his majesty's commissioners for the affairs of Ireland have taken into consideration the recruiting of the companies of the standing army in Ireland and make them up 100 soldiers each besides officers, and whereas the lord lieutenant of Ireland hath received his majesty's warrant for the raising of 4000 soldiers by the beating of th[e] drum of such as will voluntarily undertake the service for the supply of the forces that are already levied and transported into Ireland,[7] it is now ordered by the lords and others his majesty's commissioners for the affairs of Ireland [p. 111] that the lord lieuten-

5. On 16 July the house referred the petition to the committee for Irish adventurers. *CJ*, II, 675.
6. For the order, following Pym's presentation of the list of artillery to the commons on 13 July, see *CJ*, II, 670.
7. The Earl of Leicester had informed the lords of this warrant on 19 May. *LJ*, V, 73.

ant of Ireland be desired to give commissions and warrants according to the power given him by his majesty to such persons as his lordship shall think fit to raise in such parts of this kingdom as are most convenient for their transportation the number of 2000 men and for conducting them to West Chester to the end they may be transported into Leinster and other parts of Ireland for recruiting and making up the old companies the number of 100 soldiers besides officers. And if any be to spare after the old companies are so made up, the residue are to be employed for recruiting the new companies lately sent over unto Leinster as need shall require. And the said commissioners will allow after the rate of 20s. for every soldier so to be raised and brought to West Chester, the rate allowed upon former levies.

Mr. Dalbier

Whereas Sir William Balfour, commissary general for the troops of horse that are to join with the Scottish army in Ireland, desired the lords and others his majesty's commissioners for the affairs of Ireland that John Dalbier, Esquire,[8] might receive commission to quartermaster general for those troops, notwithstanding the lord lieutenant of Ireland now declared some exceptions against the said Mr. Dalbier, yet upon the desire of these commissioners and Sir William Balfour's undertaking for him in all particulars, the lord lieutenant of Ireland hath assented to Mr. Dalbier's having that place and promised to give him his commission forthwith.

Pennoyer, 694[£] 0[s.] 4[d.]

Whereas there appeareth to the lords and others his majesty's commissioners for the affairs of Ireland by the account of William Pennoyer of London, merchant, remaining with the auditor attending the commission for powder and match by him furnished and for carriage of arms and ammunition from London to Chester and Minehead the sum of 694£ 0s. 4d. clear without any exception over and above the sum of 1000£ by him already received thereupon by a former order,[9] it is now ordered by the said commissioners that the lord lieutenant of Ireland be desired to give order to Mr. Nicholas Loftus, deputy treasurer at wars for that kingdom, to pay unto the said Mr. William Pennoyer the said sum of six hundred ninety-four pounds and fourpence towards the further clearing of that his account and his satisfaction of his demands thereupon.

[p. 112] Adams

Upon the petition of Thomas Adams to be commissary for victual in the city of Londonderry in Ireland, it is this day ordered by the lords and others his

---

8. An experienced Dutch soldier who served in the Thirty Years War and subsequently under the Earl of Essex. Snow, *Essex,* pp. 314, 316.

9. See above, 9 June.

majesty's commissioners for the affairs of Ireland that he attend the lord lieutenant of Ireland, who is desired to take such order therein as may be for admitting
him thereunto if he find him a fit man to be employed in that service.

Die Martis, viz., 19° Julii 1642

White, 25£ 7s. 6d.

Whereas it appeareth by the warrant of Captain Kettleby and the certificate of
the officers of the port of Minehead that John White, master of the ship called
the *Curteen* of London, did by order of the said Captain Kettleby upon the third
day of April last receive on board the said ship at Kinsale and set on shore at
Minehead 145 poor distressed people, which at the rate of 3s. 6d. apiece, the
price agreed on for freight, amounting to 25£ 7s. 6d. the lords and others his
majesty's commissioners for the affairs of Ireland upon the petition of the said
White have thought fit should be paid unto him, it is now ordered by the said
commissioners that the lord lieutenant of Ireland be desired to give order to Mr.
Nicholas Loftus, deputy treasurer at wars for that kingdom, to pay unto the said
John White or his assigns the sum of 25£ 7s. 6d. in full of his demand and in
satisfaction of the service aforesaid.

Sir William Balfour, 400£

Whereas Sir William Balfour, Knight, commissary general for the troops of
horse that are to join with the Scottish army in Ireland, hath agreed with Daniel
Potter for 160 trooping saddles completely furnished for the service of those
troops at the rate of 45s. the saddle, amounting in the whole to the sum of 360£,
it is now ordered by the lords and others his majesty's commissioners for the
affairs of Ireland that the lord lieutenant of Ireland be desired to give order to
Mr. Nicholas Loftus, deputy treasurer at wars for that kingdom, to pay upon [p.
113] delivery of the said saddles unto the said Daniel Potter the sum 360£[1] in
full discharge of those saddles. And whereas the said Sir William Balfour hath
likewise agreed with John Milborne, bitmaker, for 160 bits for the same
service at the rate of 5s. apiece, it is now likewise ordered that the said lord
lieutenant do give order also to Mr. Loftus for the payment of the sum of 40£
unto the said John Milborne in full discharge of those bits upon the delivery of
them.

Fort of Duncannon

Whereas amongst other things tending to the defense of the fort of Duncannon in Leinster in the kingdom of Ireland and the ports adjacent it is desired by
the Lord Esmonde and other captains now in garrison and in that fort that a ship

---

1. MS: *160£.*

of war and a small pinnace be appointed always to attend that fort and river for the better preventing of bringing in of arms and ammunition into that harbor, which is daily expected by the enemy in Waterford, Ross, and the rest of the corporations, it is now thought fit by the lords and others his majesty's commissioners for the affairs of Ireland that Mr. Pym be de[sired] to move the House of Commons that order of parliament may be given to the Earl of Warwick to send one of his majesty's ships now at sea under his lordship's command that may best be spared, whereunto being joined one of the ten small pinnaces, to be both victualed and appointed to ride in the harbor mouth of Waterford near the fort of Duncannon for the assistance thereof.[2]

Earl of Thomond, letter

It is also ordered by the said commissioners that Mr. Pym be desired to report unto the House of Commons a letter of the Earl of Thomond dated the 25th of June last to the commissioners with this their opinion that his lordship, being a person of honor and great integrity and having deserved well since the rebellion, may by some addition of forces under his command be better enabled for his own defense and the English about him and that such a proportion of arms and ammunition may be sent him as that house shall think fit.[3]

Train of artillery

It is also ordered by the said commissioners that Mr. Pym be desired to move the House of Commons that a message may be sent to the lords house to desire their lordships to join in an order brought up unto them for the delivery of the ordnance, [p. 114] arms, and ammunition out of the ships which come from Hull which are required for the furnishing of the train of artillery which is to be sent unto Dublin and the supplying the stores there, as also for arming the troops of horse that are under the command of Sir William Balfour, Knight, to join with the Scottish army in Ulster.[4]

T[w]o whole cannon for Dublin

It is further ordered by the said commissioners that Mr. Pym be desired to move the House of Commons that in regard the lord justices and council of Ireland have written earnestly that two whole cannon with their carriage and equipage may be sent unto them from hence for the more speedy taking in some strong castles and holds, which these commissioners think fit they should be furnished withal, and for that there are no whole cannon in the ships that

2. For the order see D, 20 July, n. 7. For an additional action taken by the house, see D, 21 July, n. 8, and G, 22 July.

3. For Pym's report of this letter, see D, 20 July.

4. On 20 July Sir Henry Mildmay carried the message to the lords concerning the arms for Balfour. *CJ,* II, 682, 683.

brought the arms and ammunition from Hull, that that house would be pleased to give some direction therein.[5]

Mr. Frost, 3000£

It is this day ordered by the lords and others his majesty's commissioners for the affairs of Ireland that the lord lieutenant of Ireland be desired to give order to Mr. Nicholas Loftus, deputy treasurer at wars for that kingdom, forthwith to imprest upon account unto Walter Frost, gentleman, commissary of victual in this kingdom, to supply the magazine at Dublin and Carrickfergus the sum of 3000£ more than he hath formerly received for further provision of corn and victual for those places.

Lord Conway, etc., letter for Henry Le Squire

Upon reading the letter of the Lord Viscount Conway, Sergeant Major General Monro, and Sir John Clotworthy, Knight, dated the 11th day of June last past, this day presented to the lords and others his majesty's commissioners for the affairs of Ireland,[6] it is this day ordered by the said commissioners that the lord lieutenant of Ireland be desired to appoint and authorize by commission Henry Le Squire of Belfast to be commissary for keeping, carrying, and distributing of the victual provided for the army in Ulster under their command when it marcheth, and that he be allowed six shillings per diem for himself, two shillings apiece for two clerks, and such other allowances for other necessary servants as are made unto others in like cases.

[p. 115] 2 ships to transport ordnance into Ireland

It is this day ordered by the lords and others his majesty's commissioners for the affairs of Ireland that 400 ton of shipping or thereabouts in two ships be hired in the river of Thames for the transporting from hence of the ordnance, arms, ammunition, and materials requisite for the service of that kingdom to such ports of Ireland as shall be directed by the said commissioners or the lord lieutenant of Ireland. And Mr. Alexander Bence, one of the members of the House of Commons, is desired by these commissioners to take order for the hiring and providing of such ships for more speedy accommodation of this service.[7]

---

5. The lord justices had made this request to the commissioners in a letter dated 8 July. On 20 July the commons ordered that the cannons and equipment be supplied from the stores in the Tower. See Hogan, *Irish Rebellion*, p. 73; and *CJ*, II, 683.

6. For this letter, which recommended Le Squire for the position of commissary based on his previous experience, see Hogan, *Irish Rebellion*, pp. 41–42.

7. Bence was co-owner of several ships sailing from Aldeburgh and London and was recognized by the commons as an authority on naval matters. Keeler, p. 106.

Mr. Willis, 7£ 17s. 01d.

Whereas Richard Willis, Esquire, hath desired allowance of the lords and others his majesty's commissioners for the affairs of Ireland for divers necessaries by him provided and delivered for the service of the commission the sum of 7£ 17s. 01d., as appeareth by a bill of the particulars examined by Mr. Chambers, auditor to the said commission, it is now ordered by the said commissioners that the lord lieutenant of Ireland be desired to give order to Mr. Nicholas Loftus, deputy treasurer at wars for that kingdom, to pay unto the said Richard Willis the said sum of 7£ 17s. 01[d.] in full of the said bill of disbursements by him made betwixt the 6th of April 1642 and the 6th of July then next following and now last past.

Earl of Antrim to be sent for

It is this day thought fit and ordered by the lords and others his majesty's commissioners for the affairs of Ireland that the commissioners of this kingdom[8] appointed to treat with the commissioners of Scotland be desired to move those commissioners that order may be given to those that command in chief the Scottish army in Ulster to send from thence in sure custody unto the parliament of this kingdom the body of the Earl of Antrim to be landed to London by the first and most convenient shipping that may be gotten in those parts.[9]

Wood, 100£

It is this day ordered by the lords and others his majesty's commissioners for the affairs [of Ireland] that the lord lieutenant of Ireland be desired to give order unto Mr. Nicholas Loftus, deputy treasurer at wars for that kingdom, to imprest upon account unto George Wood the sum of 100£ more than he hath formerly received towards the packing up and carriage of divers clothes, linen, and [p. 116] shoes from London and Northampton to Chester and Bristol as he is or shall be directed for the use of the soldiers in Ireland.

Sir William Courtenay, 360£

Whereas the lords and others his majesty's commissioners for the affairs of Ireland have been this day moved by the petition of Sir William Courtenay, Knight,[10] that in regard that he at the beginning of the rebellion had raised a troop of horse in the province of Munster at his own charge and kept them together until the first of April last, when they were taken into the pay of this

---

8. The committee for Scottish negotiations.

9. The Earl of Antrim had been in custody in Carrickfergus since mid-June. *CJ*, II, 631. For subsequent action by the commons, see D, 12 September.

10. Probably Sir William Courtenay of Newcastle, Co. Limerick. See *Roy. Off.*, p. 89.

state, in which time hath lost many of his horses being forced to serve against the enemies with slender or no arms, it is now ordered by the said commissioners that the lord lieutenant of Ireland be desired to give order to Mr. Nicholas Loftus, deputy treasurer at wars for that kingdom, to pay unto the said Sir William Courtenay the sum of 360£ imprest upon account to be laid out by him for the buying and conducting to the seaside of 30 horses (the number alleged to be lost) at the rate of 12£ the horse for the recreating of his said troop. And it is further thought fit and ordered that it shall be made appear by certificate of the commissary of the musters that the said Sir William Courtenay did lose so many horses in actual service, then he shall be acquitted and discharged of this sum now imprested unto him, 30 horse being bought therewith and brought to the service. But if the same shall not be made appear as aforesaid, defalcation shall be made of so much money as the horse so lost shall appear to be in number less worth after that rate.

Supply for the fort of Duncannon

Whereas there hath been this day presented unto the lords and others his majesty's commissioners for the affairs of Ireland by one Mr. [Bunbury][11] on the behalf of the Lord Esmonde, Captain Weldon, and Captain Aston certain desires of theirs for the better defense of the fort of Duncannon[12] and a commendation of them and the soldiers now engarrisoned there:

1. First, that supply of moneys, 6 months' victual, and clothing for the three captains there may be sent in due season before the 3 months now in being be expired, whereupon it was now ordered by the said commissioners that the sum of 336£ shall be [p. 117] forthwith sent thither to pay the officers of the said three companies from the 23th of April to the 16th day of this instant July. That 65£ 2s. shall be sent thither to pay the artificers there for the same time. And that the sum of 840£, the pay of the common soldiers for three months, viz., from the 21th of May last to the 13th of August next, shall be sent unto them in manner following, that is to say 140£ (being half a month's at 4d. per diem in money) and the residue being 700£ in victual for 5 months at the rate of 4d. a man each day.

2. Secondly, that supply of powder, match, and bullet proportionable may be sent, whereupon it was ordered that 10 barrels of powder with bullet and match proportionable shall be forthwith sent to the Lord Esmonde, who is to be written unto by the said commissioners and advertised what hath been already sent to

11. In a letter of 4 June to the commissioners, Lord Esmonde indicated that John Bunbury was to serve as his agent to present the needs of Duncannon Fort to the parliament. Hogan, *Irish Rebellion*, p. 39.

12. For events at the fort during June, see Thomas Aston, *A brief relation* (1642). Wing, A 4080. Aston's death on 20 July is described in Hogan, *Irish Rebellion*, pp. 92–93. For Anthony Weldon see *PJ*, 2: 186.

him by this state that his lordship may make return unto them whether he hath received it and how far it hath lasted.

3. Thirdly, that a supply of deal boards may be sent and such other necessaries as belong to hutting and sentinel houses for the south, whereupon it was ordered that 50£ shall be issued for providing of timber boards and nails at Bristol and sending them to Duncannon for that purpose.

4. Fourthly, that rugs or caddows[13] may be allowed for the poor soldiers to cover them in the winter, they having no other manner of lodging, whereupon it was ordered that such rugs shall be provided by some person appointed by the said commissioners and sent unto the soldiers speedily.

5. Fifthly, whereas some question is made whether the 14s. a man formerly sent for clothing of the soldiers in coats be given them or deducted out of their pay by the captains, it is now declared by the said commissioners that the said 14s. a man for coats, etc., is freely given to those soldiers sent out of England.

6. Sixthly, whereas it is demanded how the captains, officers, ministers, surgeons, gunners, and artificers are to be victualed and desired that some provisions may be sent for them, it is answered by the said commissioners and accordingly ordered that directions shall be given to William Dobbins, gentleman, commissary at Bristol for victual, to supply the magazines in the western part of Ireland (and to whom the Lord Esmonde and the captains in that fort of Duncannon are to give directions for such victual as are appointed them) to provide and send the public officers and artificers such victual and other accommodation of that kind as they will require so as they pay for them.

[p. 118] 7. Seventhly, that a ship of war and small pinnace be appointed to attend always that fort and river for the better preventing the bringing in of arms or ammunition into that harbor, it is now ordered that Mr. Pym be desired to move the House [of] Commons that order of parliament may be given to the Earl of Warwick to send one of his majesty's ships now at sea under his lordship's command that may best be spared, and that thereunto being joined one of the ten small pinnaces, they may be both victualed and appointed to ride in the harbor mouth of Waterford near the fort of Duncannon for[14] the assistance thereof.

8. Eight[h]ly, that there may be some salary of sixpence per diem or the like granted to one man of each company at their captain's appointment to be clerk of the company to take care and deliver out the said provisions of victual as they shall be required, whereupon it is ordered that such allowance of 6d. per diem apiece shall be allowed and paid to 3 soldiers whom the several captains shall appoint for the service aforesaid.

---

13. Rough woolen coverings. *NED*.
14. MS: *of*. For the order see above, n. 2.

9. Ninthly, that it may be considered how necessary firing will be for the soldiers in the court of guard for the winter season, whereupon it is ordered that 50 ton of coals shall be speedily sent to the said fort and delivered unto the Lord Esmonde for that purpose.

10. To the tenth concerning the reparation of that fort by arching of the port and sally port and raising of an outwall or facing the foot of the rampire at 12 or 14 foot high and repairing of the drawbridge and mending the lower platform ruined by the seawater, which is supposed will cost little more than 200£ sterling, it is answered and accordingly ordered by the said commissioners that 100£ shall be imprested upon the said Lord Esmonde toward the said reparations and work. And upon his lordship's account given in at the finishing thereof, the residue, not exceeding in the whole 200£ with the sum imprested, shall be paid unto him as it shall appear to be expended.

11. To the eleventh for a supply of the surgeon's chest with medicaments, it is answered and accordingly ordered that the sum of 10£ shall be allowed for the same.

12. To the twelfth for the sending over of a dozen of scythes and 40 sickles to spoil or reap the enemy's corn near the fort, it is answered and ordered that the number of scythes and sickles desired shall be forthwith sent.

[p. 119] 13. To the thirteenth for a pair or two of smith's bellows and an anvil or two, and for stones and timber to make an horse mill within the fort, it [is] ordered that those particulars be provided so that the charge thereof exceed not above 20£.

And whereas the said Mr. Bunbury produced to the said commissioners a letter of the Lord Esmonde's whereby his lordship desired for the advancement of the service upon the sallies of the soldiers out of the fort that 60 snaphances may be sent unto him, it is now ordered that they shall be provided and sent as is desired, the charge whereof being estimated to be under 60£. And lastly it is ordered by the said commissioners that Mr. Chambers, auditor to this commission, do make an estimate of the charge of all the before-mentioned particulars to be bought and provided for this service that order may thereupon be given for the issuing of moneys for the same.

Dobbins, 3000£

It is this day ordered by the lords and others his majesty's commissioners for the affairs of Ireland that the lord lieutenant of Ireland be desired to give order unto Mr. Nicholas Loftus, deputy treasurer at wars for that kingdom, to pay unto William Dobbins, gentleman, commissary for providing victual in the western parts of that kingdom, for furnishing the magazine in Munster by way of imprest upon account the sum of 3000£ more than he hath formerly received for the further provision of victuals for the service aforesaid.

Die Martis, viz., 26° Julii 1642

Lord Kerry's regiment

It is this day ordered by the lords and others his majesty's commissioners for the affairs of Ireland that the House of Commons may be moved to pass an ordinance of parliament for transporting the regiment raised in this kingdom under the command of the Lord of Kerry into the kingdom of Ireland, there to be employed against the rebels and for the aid of the Earl of Ormonde. And Mr. Reynolds is desired to draw up and prepare such an ordinance to be presented to the houses of parliament.[1]

[p. 120] 32,000£ to be borrowed of the adventurers

Whereas it hath been formerly resolved by the House of Commons, upon the motion of the lords and others his majesty's commissioners for the affairs of Ireland presented to that house by Mr. Pym, that 50,000£ should be provided for the lord lieutenant of Ireland to carry over with him to pay the soldiers there and 5000£ more to be put into the hands of treasurer at wars for that kingdom to be issued out upon the lord lieutenant's warrant for incident charges,[2] of which sums the said commissioners are informed that 23,000£ are already sent to Chester, it is now ordered by the said commissioners that Mr. Pym be desired to move the House of Commons to procure from the adventurers the sum of 32,000£ yet wanting to make up that sum fo[r] the purpose aforesaid.[3]

Die Jovis, viz., 28° Julii 1642

Captain Kettleby

Upon reading the petition of Captain Kettleby concerning his disbursements for the repair of the fort of Castlepark near Kinsale and the charge he has been at for the raising of a company of 50 soldiers besides officers for the securing of that place and keeping them together in that service ever since, and also for the raising of 70 men more who are since discharged but their entertainments yet unpaid for the respective time of their service, it is now ordered by the lords and others his majesty's commissioners for the affairs of Ireland that the said Cap-

1. Cf. D, 20 July, n. 7. For subsequent orders concerning Kerry and for the approval of the ordinance by both houses in early September, see *CJ*, II, 729, 736, 742, 758, and *LJ*, V, 346. For the text of the ordinance, see *LJ*, V, 347.

2. See above, 27 June.

3. On 2 August the commons ordered that these sums of money should be sent to Ireland; the lords agreed to £27,000 but not the additional £5000, which they would consider when "the Lord Lieutenant be at Chester." A few days later the commons further ordered that "in regard of the Obstructions," the magazine and provisions at Chester should immediately be sent to Dublin and that Augustine Skinner should go over with the £23,000 and see to its proper disposition. However, on 18 August both houses agreed that the entire £28,000 should be "deposited in the Hands of the Lord Mayor Elect" (Isaac Penington), until they were assured of the lord lieutenant's "going over into Ireland." See *CJ*, II, 700, 709, 725; and *LJ*, V, 260, 262, 294.

tain Kettleby do make appear unto them by what warrant the said soldiers were raised and how long they were continued in service and upon what entertainment and pay, whereupon they will take some order that due allowance may be given him.

[p. 121] Captain Smith, etc.

Whereas a petition of one Captain Smith, Lieutenant Cosby, and Lieutenant Barnard hath been read to the lords and others his majesty's commissioners for the affairs of Ireland, wherein they acknowledge 100£ to be imprested unto them towards their charges in bringing over the Lord Maguire, Captain Mac-Mahon, and Captain Reade from Dublin to London and desire that some further allowance may be given them for that service,[1] it is now ordered by the said commissioners that they shall present unto them a bill of their charges expended and they will consider of such further allowance and reward as shall be thought fit.

Mr. Loftus

Whereas the lords and others his majesty's commissioners for the affairs of Ireland have been this day moved by Mr. Nicholas Loftus, deputy treasurer at wars for that kingdom, for leave to return into Ireland upon some occasions of his own, the said commissioners have assented unto that his desire upon his promise and assurance that he will leave a sufficient person here in London to attend the commission and to undertake the charge and duty of the office of deputy treasurer at wars for Ireland during his absence, which person he is to nominate unto these commissioners and to have their approbation before he go hence.

List of the army

It is this day ordered by the lords and others his majesty's commissioners for the affairs of Ireland that a perfect list and establishment of the commanders, officers, and soldiers employed in the wars of Ireland, as they now stand in the pay of this state, be forthwith prepared for these commissioners to allow and sign to the end the same may be sent to the lord lieutenant of Ireland that accordingly warrants for pay may be issued out from time to time during the service.

Mr. Walley et al., accounts

It is also ordered by the lords and others his majesty's commissioners for the

---

1. The lord justices' letter of 10 June urged Leicester to recompense Captain Henry Smith, Lieutenant Arnold Cosby, and Lieutenant John Barnard "for their travel and charge in this service" and to find employment for them, as they had "suffered in their estates by the rebels." See 20 June, n. 13; and *HMC, Ormonde MSS*, n.s., II, 151–52.

affairs of Ireland that Mr. Chambers do take the account of Mr. Walley[2] and others at Chester for such moneys as have been issued by them at Chester out of the moneys sent by Mr. Loftus thither upon the warrants of the lord lieutenant of Ireland.

[p. 122] Lord lieutenant's guard

It is this day ordered by the lords and others his majesty's commissioners for the affairs of Ireland upon the motion of the lord lieutenant of that kingdom that 6d. per diem be added to the pay of every halberdiers of the 30 halberdiers appointed by the establishment to attend as a guard to the said lord lieutenant, whereby the 12d. per diem is to be made up 18d., and that the same be so entered upon the establishment and paid accordingly from the 22th of this present July, the day when it was moved.

Scottish treaty

Whereas it is thought requisite that the articles of treaty agreed on by the commissioners of England and Scotland on the behalf of both kingdoms and approved of in parliament should upon any occasions be resorted to for the better dispatch of the affairs of Ireland and managing the wars there, it is this day ordered by the lords and others his majesty's commissioners for the affairs of Ireland that the commissioners appointed to treat with those of Scotland be desired that two authentic copies of the said articles so agreed on and approved of may be delivered to these commissioners, one of them to be kept here for their own use and the other sent to the lord lieutenant of Ireland to be made use of by him upon all occasions in that kingdom.[3]

Train of artillery, etc.

Whereas the lord lieutenant of Ireland, at his last being with the lords and others his majesty's commissioners for the affairs of Ireland, did earnestly press them that the troop of artillery long since resolved on by the House of Commons and since that ordered by these commissioners might be completed and sent away, divers sums of money having been already issued for that purpose, it is now ordered by the said commissioners that the Earl of Northumberland be desired to move the House of Lords that the list for ordnance, arms, ammunition, and other materials thereunto belonging, which are desired by the House of Commons to be delivered out of the stores that came from Hull to make up the train of artillery and to furnish the stores at Dublin, and also the list of the arms for the troops that are to join with the Scottish army in Ulster, which are

2. Charles Walley was the agent at Chester and Liverpool responsible for transporting soldiers, as well as supplies and money, to Ireland. See *PJ*, 2: 376, n. 5.

3. See D, 2 August, n. 4.

already ordered and sent up by the House of Commons to the lords in parliament, may receive their lordships' approbation and speedy order.[4]

[p. 123] 25 July, lord lieutenant went for Ireland

Memorandum: That the Earl of Leicester, lord lieutenant of Ireland, did set forward from the City of London towards the kingdom of Ireland to take upon him the execution of the offices of lord lieutenant of that kingdom and general of the army there upon Monday, being the 25th of July 1642.[5]

Commissioners to sign warrants for issuing of moneys

Whereas the lords and others his majesty's commissioners for the affairs of Ireland have directed their orders for the issuing of moneys unto the lord lieutenant of that kingdom and desired his lordship to give order to Mr. Nicholas Loftus, deputy treasurer at wars, to make payment accordingly, forasmuch as the said lord lieutenant is now gone for Ireland, it is thought fit and ordered that from henceforth upon all occasions for issuing of moneys the said commissioners be moved to sign warrants with their own hands which shall be directed to the treasurer at wars for Ireland or to his deputy, which warrants being prepared by the secretary to the commission and signed by a full number of the said commissioners shall be a sufficient warrant to the treasurer at wars to issue thereupon the respective sums so ordered and required.

Stone, 30£ *pro* 30 halberds

It is this day ordered by us the lords and others his majesty's commissioners for the affairs of Ireland that Mr. Nicholas Loftus, deputy treasurer at wars for that kingdom, do forthwith pay unto Benjamin Stone or his assigns the sum of 30£ in full satisfaction of the price of 30 halberds sold and delivered by him for the arming of the guard of the lord lieutenant of Ireland.

Saddles and bits for Sir William Balfour's troops

It is this day ordered by the lords and others his majesty's commissioners for the affairs of Ireland that Mr. Payler, Mr. Greene, and Mr. Lloyd, gentlemen of the horse to the right honorable the Earl[s]of Northumberland, Pembroke, and Holland, and Mr. Chambers, auditor to these commissioners, who formerly contracted with Benjamin Potter, Daniel Holdenby, Daniel Potter, and Ellis Parry of London, saddlers, for 400 trooping saddles, and with John Savage,

---

4. For previous actions see above, 21 June and 19 July. On 30 July the House of Commons urged the lords "to give Expedition to the List for Ammunition and Arms to be sent into Ireland, being of great Importance." On 8 August, upon complaint of William Gilbert, secretary to the Earl of Leicester, that the officers of the train of artillery "remain still in Town," it was ordered that they should "Repair by Land to Chester, and so to Dublin." See *LJ, V,* 249; and *CJ, II,* 710.

5. See D, 25 July, n. 3.

Nicholas Holton, and John Milborne of London, bitmakers, for 400 bits,[6] do forthwith view the said saddles which are now made and compare them with the patterns left for the fashion and goodness, and that the same saddles and bits being allowed of by them may be delivered over to George Wood to be sent unto Chester and there delivered unto such person as Sir William Balfour, Knight, shall appoint to receive the same for the service of those troops that are appointed under his command to be joined with the Scottish army in Ulster.

[p. 124] 3 months' pay for the troops in Ulster to be joined
with the Scottish army

It is this day ordered by the lords and others his majesty's commissioners for the affairs of Ireland that Mr. Pym be desired to move the House of Commons, as a thing thought fit by these commissioners, that the troops in Ulster that are to be joined with the Scottish army which have been in actual service may be paid according to their musters for 3 months past, and that Sir William Balfour's troop which is newly raised may be paid according to agreement from the date of this commission.[7]

Sir William Courtenay

Whereas the lords and others his majesty's commissioners for the affairs of Ireland have this day thought fit that Sir Williams Courtenay, Knight, who in the beginning of the rebellion in Ireland raised a troop of horse in the province of Munster at his own charge and kept them together till the first of April last, when they were taken into the pay of this state, in which time he lost many of his horses being forced to serve against the enemy with slender or no arms, should now be supplied with 30 pair of pistols, 20 carbines, and 40 great saddles out of his majesty's stores for his better accommodation and encouragement in the service, the said commissioners have ordered that before any further resolution be taken therein it be recommended to the consideration of the lords and others the committee of both houses of parliament for the safety of this kingdom whether the said arm[s] and saddles may be spared out of his majesty's stores for the supply of Sir William Courtenay as aforesaid.

Clothworkers of London to bring in their subscription money, in all 5500£

Whereas amongst other companies in the City of London the Company of Clothworkers have been apportioned and subscribed to the sum 5500£, in part of the 100,000£ lent by the City unto the parliament for the service and relief of Ireland, it is now ordered by the lords and others his majesty's commissioners for the affairs of Ireland that the master, wardens, and assistants of that com-

6. See above, 14 July.
7. It was so ordered by the house on 2 August. See *CJ*, II, 700.

pany be hereby required to certify them forthwith the names of such persons of their society as have subscribed or have been thought fit amongst themselves to be contributors towards the raising of that sum and who of them have not brought in their money according to the subscriptions and rates and to give all possible assistance for the speedy bringing in thereof, the present occasions so much requiring it.[8]

[p. 125] Captain Chichester et al. for their troops of horse
to be harquebusiers

Whereas it appeareth by an order of both houses of parliament dated the 21th day of this instant July[9] reciting that: Whereas upon report of Sir Robert Crane, Knight, it was ordered *die Sabbati, 9° Julii* 1642, that Captain Arthur Chichester, Mr. Hill, Lord Viscount Montgomery, Lord Viscount Clandeboye, Sir James Montgomery, Sir William Stewart, Sir Robert Stewart, Sir William Cole,[10] and Audley Mervin shall be received into pay from the first of July for their several troops and regiments of horse and foot, and that 600 horse now informed by their several petitions to be in service in Ulster shall be formed into troops of dragooners of 100 in each troop (which 600 horse are distinct from the ten troop[s] assigned to attend the Scottish army), it was then ordered by the lords and commons in parliament assembled that it should be referred to the consideration of the commissioners for Irish affairs, who are thereby authorized to form the said troop[s] either into nine troops of harquebusiers or six troops of dragooners, as they should find most advantageous for the present service, and to enter them into pay according to the first order. Forasmuch as the lords and others his majesty's commissioners for the affairs of Ireland, having heard what was alleged by the said Sir James Montgomery, Mr. Hill, and Mr. Mervin on the behalf of themselves and the rest and taken into consideration both the difference in point of charge and point of service betwixt those troops as harquebusiers and as dragooners, did at last make this offer, that if the charge of forming those troops into serviceable harquebusiers both for horse and arms now wanting might appear not to be very great but rather such as these commissioners should allow of, that charge should for the present be undertaken by this state and money issued for the buying of such arms as are now wanting, so that the same might be again defalked after the rate of sixpence a man per diem out of every soldier's pay as a harquebusier that should receive arms or saddle to

8. For the loan from the City, see D, 3 and 4 June. On 2 August the house ordered the master and wardens of the Clothworkers to explain why their proportion of the £100,000 had not been brought in; on 4 August their excuses were accepted. See *CJ*, II, 700, 702–03.

9. For the order see *CJ*, II, 662–63, 678; and *LJ*, V, 228.

10. Cole, a former member of the Irish parliament, was governor of Enniskillen and commander of a foot troop in Ulster. For a letter telling of his accomplishments, see *HMC, Ormonde MSS*, n.s., II, 301–02. *DNB*.

furnish himself for that quality, which after was accepted of and assented unto by the said Mr. Hill.

Fort of Duncannon

It is this day ordered by the lords and others his majesty's commissioners for the affairs of Ireland that a warrant be prepared to be signed by them for issuing of such sums of money as are already resolved on by an order of the 19th of this instant July for paying the officers and soldiers of the fort of Duncannon and for such reparations and accommodations as in the said order are already agreed on and thought fit by the said commissioners.

[p. 126] Taylor *pro* hire of ships, 100£ 14s. 03d. ½

It is also ordered, etc., that a warrant be prepared for them to sign for payment unto [*blank*] Taylor[11] of Bristol according to the direction of that city of the sum of 100£ 14s. 03d. ½ for the hire of 2 ships contracted for by the said mayor[12] by order of the Earl of Northumberland, then lord admiral of England, who was desired thereunto by these commissioners.

Fisher, 170£

It is ordered by the lords and others his majesty's commissioners for the affairs of Ireland that a warrant be prepared to be signed by them for the payment of 170£ unto Christopher Fisher of London, seamster, upon delivery of 50 dozen of shirts, which according to contract made the 15th of June last he hath upon the 22th of this instant July delivered at the [rate] of 34s.[13] the dozen, that is to say, 85£[14] upon the 22th day of [October and][15] January then next following, which sum of 170£ together with 85£ paid him already upon a former order is in full of the contract made with him for 150 dozen of shirts at that rate.

Hunt, 359£ 7s. 6d.

Ordered, etc., that a like warrant be prepared for the payment of 359[£] 7s. 6d. unto Edmund Hunt for 3750 Monmouth caps by him delivered accordingly to a contract made the 27th day of May last at the rate of 23s. the dozen, which sum is in full of the said caps so delivered by him.[16]

---

11. Possibly John Taylor, MP, who was part owner of the *Mary Rose*. See Appendix A.

12. John Locke.

13. MS: *24s.*

14. MS: *82£.*

15. This portion has been corrected to correspond with the agreement made with Fisher. See above, 15 June and 11 July.

16. This order for payment was reported to the house by Pym on 3 September. See *CJ*, II, 751. For an earlier order see above, 22 June.

Sir Hugh Owen, 56£, corn delivered Dublin

Ordered, etc., that a warrant be prepared for payment of 56£ unto Sir Hugh Owen, Knight and Baronet, according to an order of parliament for corn delivered into the stores of Dublin by William Bevan, merchant, as appears by the certificate of Sir Philip Percivall, Knight, testified by Sir Adam Loftus dated the tenth of this instant July.

Gunter, 255£ 12s., corn delivered at Dublin

Ordered, etc., that a warrant be prepared for payment of 255[£] 12s. unto John Gunter, Esquire, according to an order of parliament for corn delivered into the stores of Dublin by Thomas Gaskell as appeareth by a certificate of Sir Philip Percivall attested by Sir Adam Loftus the 4th day of this instant July.

400£ for wagon horses

Ordered, etc., that a warrant be prepared for payment of 400£ by way of imprest upon account unto the lord lieutenant of Ireland for the charges of transportation and sending at sea of the wagon horses which are to be sent to Dublin, whereunto the said commissioners were[17] move[d] before his lordship's going hence.

[p. 127] Allen, 146£ 16s.

Ordered, etc., that a warrant be prepared for a payment of 146£ 16s. unto Nehemiah Allen, linen draper, according to an order of parliament for herrings delivered into his majesty's stores at Dublin by Tobias Norris and William Aubrey, merchants, appeareth by a certificate of the lord justices and council of that kingdom date the 28th of June last.

Captain Kettleby, 349£ 14s. 01d., 300[£] 0[s.] 0[d.]

Ordered, etc., that a warrant be prepared for payment as well of the sum of 349£ 14s. 01d. unto Captain Thomas Kettleby in full of his demands for the reparation of the fort of Castlepark near Kinsale, as appears by his account avouch[ed] by the late lord president of Munster's letter remaining with the auditor, as also the sum of 300£ towards the sum of 669£ 7s. 10d. alleged to be by him paid for the entertainment and victuals of 120 men taken by him into that fort, some by warrant and some without warrant, for the defense thereof until the account concerning the same be perfected and certified to the commissioners.

Hamilton's order for a letter

Ordered, etc., that a letter be prepared for the commissioners to sign recommending the petition of Andrew Hamilton as a matter worthy the lord lieutenant of Ireland's consideration for the petitioner's relief.

17. MS: *where.*

Lord Loftus of Ely's order for a letter

Ordered, etc., that a letter be prepared for the commissioners to sign on the behalf of the Lord Viscount Loftus of Ely that the lord lieutenant of Ireland at his coming into that kingdom would take order for a fit gavel[18] for his lordship's house and payment thereof.

Die Martis, viz., 2° August 1642[1]

Powder, match, etc., for Duncannon

It is this day ordered by the lords and others his majesty's commissioners for the affairs of Ireland that in pursuance of an order of theirs made the 19th of July last concerning the better defense and supply of the fort of Duncannon, wherein amongst other things it was ordered that ten barrels of powder with match and bullet proportionable and also 60 snaphances should be sent thither, the right honorable the Earl of Essex, lord general of the forces designed[2] [p. 128] by the parliament for the safety of his majesty and this kingdom, be desired that out of the stores of this kingdom that quantity of powder with match and bullet proportionable and also 60 snaphances (if any such be there) may be delivered unto John Bunbury, agent to the Lord Esmonde and other captains in that fort, to be by him amongst other provisions speedily sent thither for the supply and better defense thereof.[3]

A convoy for Mr. Frost's six ships

Whereas it was this day moved by Walter Frost, gentleman, commissary for victual, to store the magazines in Leinster and Ulster, that in regard he had now laden 6 ships in the river of Thames with corn and victual for that service which were to put to sea, some ships of strength might be appointed for the guard and convoy of them, it is now ordered by the lords and others his majesty's commissioners for the affairs of Ireland that the right honorable the Earl Warwick be desired to appoint some good ships of burden and strength to convoy the said six

18. Rent. *NED*. After his fall as lord chancellor, Viscount Loftus lived in Yorkshire until his death in 1643 but apparently retained property in Ireland. The commissioners' action may have been prompted by the lords' reversal on 3 May of all decrees against Loftus. On 6 August parliament ordered that £200 be paid to him. *LJ*, V, 38–39, 270. *DNB*.

1. There is no attendance list on this day.

2. Marginal note: *Memorandum. This powder with shot and match was delivered by warrant of the lord general out of the stores in the charge of Captain Duboys and delivered to Mr. Wood to be sent to Bristol 23 August.*

3. On 17 August Essex informed the lords that the officers of the ordnance refused to issue out any such provisions for Ireland because of a warrant from the king commanding them not to do so without his express warrant. *LJ*, V, 298–99. Meanwhile further action concerning the fort was taken on 5 August when the House of Commons ordered that one hundred soldiers be recruited in Bristol to guard it. For details of this order, approved by the lords on 10 August, see *CJ*, II, 705, and *LJ*, V, 279.

ships along the coasts as far as shall be thought fit, and that a letter be prepared for the commissioners to sign for that purpose.[4]

4000 pair of shoes and 600 pair of boots to be indented for

It is this day ordered by the lords and others his majesty's commissioners for the affairs of Ireland that Mr. Nicholas Loftus do indent with [blank] Johnson and others, shoemakers of Northampton, for four thousand pair of shoes at the rate of 2s. 4d. the pair and 600 pair of boots at 7s. the pair, with such usual advances, clauses, and conditions as have been formerly made and allowed in like indentures for the manner of delivery of the said shoes and boots and the payment for them.

[p. 129]   [*Die Jovis, viz., 18° Augusti* 1642][1]

Hence all the orders are passed by the commissioners in the number of a committee and authorized by both houses, dated the 16th August 1642, and reported to the house for approbation and determination.[2]

Troops and regiments in Ulster

Whereas it appeareth by several resolutions and orders of both houses of parliament dated the 21 of July last past[3] that the several troops of horse and foot commanded by Captain Arthur Chichester, Mr. Hill, Viscount Montgomery, Sir James Montgomery, Sir William Cole, and Audley Mervin, which are forces distinct from those troops which are to join with the Scottish army, shall be taken into pay from the first day of that instant July, that those 600 horse informed to be in service in Ulster shall be either formed into nine troops of harquebusiers or six troops of dragooners as the commissioners for the affairs of Ireland shall find most advantageous for the present service, and that they shall accordingly be entered into pay from the time aforementioned, that there shall be a month's pay for each regiment advanced for themselves and companies and

---

4. On 2 September the house ordered Warwick to send two ships to secure the seas from pirates "and others that interrupt the Intercourse betwixt the Kingdoms." See *CJ*, II, 749.

---

1. There is no date or attendance list on this day. From the entry which follows, it appears that the probable date is 18 August, for the order originated in the commons on the 16th and was approved by the lords on the 18th.

2. When the commission for Irish affairs was originally constituted, the quorum required was eight commoners and three lords. However, on 16 August the House of Commons ordered that hereafter "those Members of this House that are in the Commission for Ireland, or any Four of them, shall meet, as a Committee for the Affairs of Ireland," along with a proportionable number (i.e., two or more) of the commissioners from the House of Lords, "to prepare and consider of Things necessary for Ireland; and to present the same to both Houses; in regard the Commissioners cannot meet, by reason that divers of them are out of Town, in the Service of the Parliament." The lords agreed to this order on 18 August. See *PJ*, 2: 403–04; *CJ*, II, 721, 723; and *LJ*, V, 303.

3. See above, 28 July.

the money to pay them shall be taken out of the contribution money for Ireland, the lords and others his majesty's commissioners for the affairs of Ireland, having this day taken the said orders and resolutions into consideration and having heard what was alleged by the said Sir James Montgomery, Mr. Hill, and Mr. Mervin on the behalf of themselves and the rest, do hereby order that Captain Arthur Chichester, Mr. Hill, Viscount Montgomery, Sir James Montgomery, Lord Viscount Clandeboye, Sir William Stewart, Sir Robert Stewart, Sir William Cole, and Mr. Mervin be forthwith entered upon the list of the army now in the pay of this state in Ireland as colonels of their respective numbers and paid for themselves and their several troops and regiments of horse and foot as other troops and regiments are from the first day of July last past. That the horse troops of these forces making (as is informed) six hundred horse be formed into nine troops of harquebusiers consisting of 60 apiece besides officers and so listed and paid from the said first day of July last past. That the charge of such arms and saddles as are requisite to make them complete harquebusiers, being estimated and cast up by the auditor to these commissioners, shall be [p. 130] provided and delivered to those that are defective to be defalked after the rate of six[pence] a man per diem out of their pay as harquebusiers. That a month's pay respectively for every regiment of foot and troop of horse with their several officers be cast up by the auditor according to their musters, warrants be prepared for the commissioners for the payment of the same to the several colonels of the regiments of foot and captains of the troops of horse to be received here in this kingdom from the deputy treasurer at wars for Ireland by as many of the said colonels and captains or their agents as are here and shall desire the same. That the commissary general for victuals and those under him that are employed for the victualing of the army do provide from time to time for the supply of these numbers of men with necessary victual and other accommodations as of other forces in other parts of that kingdom. That warrants be prepared for the commissioners to sign for payment of such sums of money unto the said colonels and captains for the furnishing of surgeons' chests to each regiment of foot and troop of horse as have been allowed to others in like cases. And that Mr. Pym be desired to move the House of Commons that according to their former order the total of these payments may be issued out of the contribution moneys for Ireland. And in case there be not sufficient of these moneys, that house will provide either the whole or so much thereof as shall be wanting to be paid out of some other place.

Clothes for the soldiers in Ulster now taken into pay

It is this day ordered by the lords and others his majesty's commissioners for the affairs of Ireland that such clothes as shall be set down in writing by Sir James Montgomery, Mr. Hill, and Mr. Mervin and thought requisite by these commissioners for the clothing of the soldiers in the before-mentioned troops and regiments shall be provided and sent unto them under such prices and payments as are set upon others in like cases.

Scottish army to be removed into Munster

Whereas it hath been this day reported to the lords and others his majesty's commissioners for the affairs of Ireland from the committee of both houses of parliament for the safety of this kingdom by Mr. Pym that, for the better reducing of the rebels in Ireland to their due obedience, it is considered by [p. 131] that committee, now that the province of Ulster is some good measure cleared of those rebels and that the forces there now in the pay of this state is greater than service doth require, the whole body of the Scottish army may be removed towards the city of Limerick and other parts of Munster where the heat of the war now is and the defense weakest,[4] it is now ordered by these commissioners that Mr. Pym be desired to report the same likewise to the House of Commons as the opinion of these commissioners also to the end such course may be taken for accomplishment thereof as both houses of parliament shall think fit.

Earl of Thomond

Whereas, by an order of the House of Commons in parliament the 3d day of this instant August, it is referred to the lords and others his majesty's commissioners for the affairs of Ireland to consider speedily what way there may be 1000 men sent for the relief of the Earl of Thomond out of the north of Ireland or elsewhere by sea, and whereas it is then also ordered that Mr. Loftus shall pay one month's pay due to the Earl of Thomond for one company of foot and a troop of horse from the first of July last and one month's advance,[5] these commissioners are very ready to take order therein so that money may be provided to effect the same.

Bishop of Raphoe

Whereas the petition of the Bishop of Raphoe was this day read together with his majesty's reference thereupon and the order of the House of Commons,[6] it was answered at the present here was not a full commission,[7] but the commis-

4. On 16 August both houses had agreed to this action. See *LJ*, V, 294.

5. For these orders see *CJ*, II, 702. See also D, 20 July.

6. On 16 July the house had received a petition from the Protestant Bishop of Raphoe referred to them by the king. The king's message stated that he believed the petitioner's plea for relief of the barony of Raphoe (in Co. Donegal, Ulster) to be reasonable but that he would not take "all that concerns the Rebellion in Ireland . . . out of their Hands." On 15 August the house had referred the bishop's petition to the commissioners "as to a Committee." See *CJ*, II, 675–76, 721. *DNB*.

7. There was not a quorum; therefore, they could not act as a commission. This conclusion seems to be confirmed by the absence of attendance lists on 2 and 18 August.

sioners conceived that they, apprehending it a matter which concerned his own particular and that which would draw on a new charge, they could not determine anything till they had communicated it unto the House of Commons and received their order.[8]

Captain Cosby, account

It is this day ordered by the lords and others, etc., that the account of Captain Cosby[9] be examined and certified by Mr. Chambers, the auditor to this commission, against the next sitting.

[p. 132]   *Die Martis, viz., 23° Augusti* 1642[1]

Lord lieutenant's letter; Lord Inchiquin's letter; lord justices, etc., letter

It is this day thought fit by the lords and others his majesty's commissioners for the affairs of Ireland (in a number authorized by the house of parliament as a committee) that the letter of the lord lieutenant of Ireland directed to these commissioners and now read unto them, as also the letter of the Lord Inchiquin on the behalf of Captain Peasly[2] and his petition, and another letter of the lord justices and council of Ireland be reported by Sir Robert Harley, Knight of the Bath, to the House of Commons.

A letter to be drawn to the lord justices, etc., and Earl of Ormonde

That a letter be drawn to be signed by these commissioners to be directed to the lord justices and council of Ireland and to the lieutenant general of the army there, that seeing there are men enough in Leinster and Ulster to reduce the rebels in these several provinces, and that by relation of Sir William Ogle Munster is in great danger and distress for want of men,[3] the great numbers in the other provinces be so distributed and disposed of in such a way as it shall seem best by them now being upon the place or may be for the succor of the small numbers in Munster and regaining thereof from the rebels.[4]

8. On 7 September the bishop's petition was read in the House of Commons and referred to the committee for Irish adventurers "to consider what is fit to be done with the Castle of Raphoe, built at his Charge; and likewise . . . what present Relief is fit to be afforded unto him." *CJ,* II, 757.
9. See above, 28 July.

---

1. At this and the two subsequent meetings, the joint committee for Irish affairs continued to act on behalf of the commissioners. There were enough members present to constitute a quorum as a committee but not as a commission. See above, 18 August, n. 2, and the attendance record following the minute book.
2. In the ordinance of 10 September to raise two thousand foot soldiers for Munster, William Peasly was named to serve as sergeant major under Lord Kerry. See above, 26 July; and *LJ,* V, 347.
3. Two letters from Lord Inchiquin concerning affairs in Munster had been brought to the House of Commons by Sir William Ogle. See *CJ,* II, 733, 735.
4. This letter from the commissioners to Borlase, Parsons, and Ormonde was subsequently approved by both houses. For this and other resolutions, which followed a report from the commit-

Lord Conway, 100 barrels of powder

That the House of Commons be moved[5] by Sir Robert Harley that in regard the store of powder sent to Carrickfergus for the supply of the garrisons and forces of the English regiments in those parts are taken for supply of the Scottish army there, another quantity of an 100 barrels may forthwith be sent to the Lord Viscount Conway for the use of his lordship's regiment, that of Sir John Clotworthy, and the other regiments lately taken into the pay of this state.

[p. 133] Lord Conway, 3 months' pay for his troop

That the House of Commons be likewise moved by Sir Robert Harley that in regard the Lord Viscount Conway's troop of horse (being one of the troops of the old army in that kingdom) hath been in actual service ever since the beginning of the rebellion and is taken into pay with the rest from the first of February last but hath not yet received any pay, his lordship may now receive three months' pay for his said troop to be paid to him or assigns in part of what shall appear to be due for the time since that troop was taken into the pay of this state.

Lord Conway's pay as marshal of Ireland

That the House of Commons be likewise moved to give order that the Lord Conway may receive at Dublin out [of] 27,000£ intended to be sent thither to pay the army such part of his pay due to him as marshal of Ireland as shall be proportionable to that which is received by other officers of the army there.[6]

Mr. Pennoyer

That the House of Commons be moved by Mr. Pym from these commissioners to give order for payment of 50£ unto Mr. Pennoyer of London, merchant, in full of all demands by him made upon account of his for providing powder and match and sending the same to Bristol, Chester, and Minehead by agreement with these commissioners and in consideration of his readiness and great care used in that service.

tee for Irish adventurers, see *CJ*, II, 736. For the letter see *LJ*, V, 322. A response dated 13 September explained the near impossibility of sending forces to Munster. Meanwhile, however, an order was formulated on 5 September "for sending, out of the Lord Conwaye's Command in Ulster, One Thousand Men into Munster, by Sea." See Hogan, *Irish Rebellion*, pp. 127–33; and *LJ*, V, 338.

    5. MS: *removed*. The resolution which follows was reported to the commons on 3 September, whereupon the house ordered that the Earl of Essex should give directions for furnishing the powder. See *CJ*, II, 751.

    6. For this and several other orders passed by the house on 3 September, following Pym's report from the committee for Irish affairs (acting for the commissioners), see *CJ*, II, 751.

Orders *pro* the troops and regiments of Captain Chichester, Mr. Hill, etc.[7]

Whereas it appeareth by several resolutions and orders of both houses of parliament dated the 21th day of July last past that the several regiments of horse and foot commanded by Captain Arthur Chichester, Mr. Hill, Lord Viscount Montgomery, Sir James Montgomery, Lord Viscount Clandeboye, Sir William Stewart, Sir Robert Stewart, Sir William Cole, and Audley Mervin, which are forces distinct from the ten troops designed to join with the Scottish army, shall be taken into pay from the first day of that instant July, that those 600 horse informed to be in Ulster shall be either formed into nine troops of harquebusiers or six troops of dragooners as the commissioners for the affairs of Ireland shall find most advantageous for the present service, and that they shall accordingly be entered into pay from the time before mentioned, that there shall be a month's pay for each regiment advanced for themselves and companies [p. 134] and that the money to pay them shall be taken out of the contribution money for Ireland, the lords and others his majesty's commissioners for the affairs of Ireland being by an order of both houses of parliament authorized as a committee,[8] having this day taken the said orders and resolutions into consideration and having heard what was alleged by the said Sir James Montgomery, Mr. Hill, and Mr. Mervin on the behalf of themselves and the rest, have thought fit that it be reported to the House of Commons as the opinion of this committee that Captain Arthur Chichester, Mr. Hill, Lord Viscount Montgomery, Sir James Montgomery, Lord Viscount Clandeboye, Sir William Stewart, Sir Robert Stewart, Sir William Cole, and Mr. Mervin be forthwith entered upon the list of the army now in the pay of this state in Ireland as colonels of their respective numbers and paid for themselves and their several troops and regiments of horse and foot as other troops and regiments are from the first day of July last past. That the horse troops of their forces making (as is informed) 600 horse be formed into nine troops of harquebusiers consisting of 60 apiece besides officers and so listed and paid from the first day of July last past. That the charges of such arms and saddles as are requisite to make them complete harquebusiers, being estimated and cast up by the auditor to these commissioners amounting to the sum of 4853£ 14s. 0d., be provided and delivered to those that are defective to be again defalked after the rate of 6d. per diem a man out of their pay as harquebusiers. That a full month's pay respectively for every regiment of foot and horse with their several officers, being cast up by the auditor amounting to 11,109£ for the regiments of foot and 2742£ 8s.

---

7. The order which follows contains additional financial details. Cf. the earlier version of 18 August.

8. This phrase does not appear in the earlier version of the order.

4d. for Mr. Hill's regiment of horse and 5 other troops, may be imprested unto the several colonels of the regiments aforesaid and captains of the troops of horse to be received from this kingdom from the deputy treasurer at wars for Ireland by as many of the said colonels and captains or their agents as are here and shall desire the same. And if the said colonels and captains shall not produce and make appear that they have [p. 135] mustered and kept their full numbers, defalcation to be made out of their respective entertainments that shall next grow due, that the commissary general for victual and those under him that are employed for the victualing of the army do provide from time to time for the supply of these numbers of men with necessary victual and other accommodations as of other forces in other parts of that kingdom. That allowance be made of such sums of money unto the said colonels and captains for furnishing of surgeons' chests, that is to say, to each regiment of foot at the rate of 25£ the chest and to each troop of horse at the rate of 10£ the chest as have been allowed to others in like cases, making in the whole 290£. And Mr. Pym is desired to move the House of Commons that according to their former order the total of these payments may be issued out of the contribution moneys for Ireland. And in case there be not sufficient of these moneys, that house will provide either the whole or so much thereof as shall be wanting to be paid out of some other place.

Clothing for the soldiers in Ulster last taken into pay[9]

Whereas the lords and others his majesty's commissioners for the affairs of Ireland, authorized thereunto as a committee of both houses of parliament, have (amongst other things) taken into consideration the clothing of the regiments of horse and foot last taken into pay in the province of Ulster, they think fit that it be reported as their opinions to the House of Commons that 7500 suits of clothes, viz., caps, doublets, cassocks, breeches, two pair of stockings, two pair of shoes, and two shirts for every soldier, are thought fit to be provided and sent to these regiments of foot, that is to say, 4000 complete suits as aforesaid to be landed at Belfast and the rest at Londonderry or to the officers or their agents here, the charge whereof amounting to 15,937£ 10s. at the rate of 2£ 2s. 6d. the suit to be afterward defalked upon the pay of every soldier at the rate of 2d. per diem. That some merchants, citizens of London, may be dealt with for the furnishing of such clothes for the captains and other inferior officers of these regiments and troops as will amount unto one month's pay for the captains and 2 months' pay for the inferior officers, [p. 136] the whole making 8236£ 05s. 04d. to be secured by the parliament to be paid unto the said merchants at the end of six months after the delivery of those clothes and to be taken again out of the full pay of those captains and officers that shall first become due after the

9. For the genesis of this order, see above, 18 August.

first month's pay herein before mentioned, and that the same course may be held for provision and furnishing of such clothes for the ordinary troopers of the aforesaid nine troops of harquebusiers as will amount to one month's pay, the whole making 3024£ to be secured by the parliament as aforesaid and taken again out of the full pay of those troopers that shall first become [due] after the first month's pay already ordered to be paid. And Mr. Pym is desired to report this to the House of Commons to give such further orders herein as they shall think fit.[10]

3 months' pay for the troops appointed to join
with the Scottish army in Ulster

Whereas it was resolved upon the second of this instant August by the commons now assembled in parliament that 3 months' pay should be forthwith paid to the ten troops of horse which are appointed to join with the Scottish army in Ulster for 3 months past,[11] the lords and others his majesty's commissioners for the affairs of Ireland, being by an[12] order of both houses of parliament authorized as a committee, have thought fit that it be reported as their opinion to the House of Commons that the pay of those troops which have been mustered being six troops, viz., Captain Arthur Chichester's, the Lord Viscount Montgomery's, the Lord Viscount Clandeboye's, Sir James Montgomery's, Mr. Arthur Hill's, and Captain Upton's, amounting for 3 months past according to their numbers to the sum of 5321£ 08s., may be paid to the respective captains of those troops or their agents here. That for Sir William Cole's troop, in regard that it could not be mustered by the muster master when the rest were, there may be paid unto him by way of imprest upon account the sum of 886£ 10s., the pay of 3 months to be afterwards defalked or allowed as his musters shall be made appear. And that for Sir Robert Adair's troop,[13] which was levied since the rest and his musters not yet appearing, that the sum of 295£ 12s. 08d. be likewise paid unto him by way of imprest upon account to be afterward defalked or allowed as his musters shall be made appear. That they also think fit that the allowance of 10£ be [p. 137] made to each troop of these nine for surgeons' chests as hath been allowed to other troops, making in the whole 90£, and because the arms for the ten troops cannot be had out of the stores of this kingdom as was formerly resolved, that order may given for the sum 3540£ 12s. to provide al[l] sorts of arms and furniture for them except saddles and bits, which being already contracted for by these commissioners and part of the

10. This order concerning clothing, which had apparently received the commons' assent, was agreed to by the lords on 10 September. *CJ*, II, 758; *LJ*, V, 345. For the text see *LJ*, V, 347.

11. For this order see above, 28 July, n. 7.

12. MS: *and*.

13. For the order giving Adair command of a horse troop, see *PJ*, 2: 449, 450.

money paid may also be ordered to be accordingly delivered for this service, and defalcation of these arms and saddles to be made out of the soldiers' pay as is usual with the rest of the army in that kingdom. And Mr. Pym is desired to report this to the House of Commons that according to their former order some course may be taken for their providing of money to discharge these payments.

Pennoyer, 80£ 3s. 7d.

Whereas William Pennoyer of London, merchant, in pursuance of a contract made with the lords and others his majesty's commissioners for the affairs of Ireland the 22th of April last,[14] having disbursed and demanded as appeareth by his accounts several sums of money amounting to 1809£ 07s. 10d. for provision of powder and match and for carriage of the same and other ammunition and arms to Bristol, Minehead, and Chester for the service of Ireland, towards which he hath received already by several orders the sum of 1694£ 0s. 4d., forasmuch as it appeared to the commissioners this day that by the said contract and account certified by Mr. Chambers, auditor to this commission, there is clearly due unto the said William Pennoyer more than he hath received the sum of 36£ 3s. 7d., the residue being disputable, it is now thought fit by the said commissioners that the said sum of 36£ 3s. 7d. so clearly due as aforesaid together with 50£ more in consideration of his labors, charges, and expenses in that service, making in the whole 86£ 3s. 7d., be paid unto him in full of all demands upon that account. And that Mr. Pym be desired to move the House of Commons that order may be given for payment thereof unto him accordingly.

[p. 138]   *Die Veneris, viz., 16° September* 1642

Sir William Hamilton

Whereas the petition of Sir William Hamilton, Knight, presented by him to the House of Commons and by them referred to the lords and others commissioners for the affairs of Ireland,[1] was this day taken into consideration whereby he allegeth that by virtue of a commission to the commissioner for the north of Ireland, who was authorized by the lord justices and council of that kingdom, he was appointed by commission dated the *26° Martii* 1642 to raise a regiment of 1000 foot and to be colonel thereof, and in pursuance of that commission he hath raised as yet only three companies, each consisting of 100 men which he hath ever since armed, paid, and victualed at his own charge after the loss of his estate worth 1000£ per annum in that kingdom and hath in his own person and with the commands of these men much advantaged the service, and therefore prays that the said commission granted unto him might be approved of and

14. See *PJ,* 2: 423–24.

---

1. Hamilton's petition had been referred to the commissioners on 29 July. *CJ,* II, 695.

confirmed as well as others and that he might be satisfied in his arrears and entertained into the new list and pay, it is now thought fit by the said commissioners in the number of a committee of both house[s] of parliament that the said Sir William Hamilton, having a commission as a colonel and three hundred men actually in service, who deserved as well as others already taken into pay, be recommended by Mr. Pym from these commissioners to the House of Commons to have a colonel's pay for himself and pay for his 300 soldiers with captains and officers in three companies according to establishment but not to be allowed any lieutenant colonel, sergeant major, or other officer [p. 139] of the staff until the regiment be filled up unto the number of 1000 and further order given by the houses of parliament for their receiving into pay.[2]

Sir Hardress Waller

It is this day thought fit by the lords and others his majesty's commissioners for the affairs of Ireland in number of a committee of both houses of parliament that a letter be prepared for them to sign to recommend Sir Hardress Waller, Knight, to the lord lieutenant of Ireland to be colonel of that regiment of foot which was [commanded] by the late lord president of Munster and to which he was lieutenant colonel, his good services and merits being attested by the letters of the said lord president in his lifetime and his losses appearing to be very great by the certificate of the commissioners that were appointed to examine them.[3]

Mris. Hunkes, 40£

Upon reading the petition of Mris. Frances Hunkes, wife of Captain Hercules Hunkes in the Lord Conway's regiment in Ireland, it is this day thought fit and ordered that a warrant be prepared for the commissioners to sign for payment of 40£ unto her here by the deputy treasurer at wars for Ireland upon her said husband's account to be afterwards defalked out of such moneys as are already or hereafter shall be due unto him for the service and become payable with the rest of that regiment.

Mr. Hawkins, Mr. Chambers, and Mr. Willis, allowances

Whereas William Hawkins, Robert Chambers, and Richard Willis, Esquires, servants appointed to attend his majesty's commission for the affairs of Ireland, have this day humbly desired that allowance might be made unto them for their constant attendance of that commission from the 6th day of April 1642 unto this present day inclusive being 163 days, the lords and others his maj-

2. It was so ordered by the commons. The committee for Irish adventurers was to consider out of what money Hamilton and his companies should be paid. This and the actions which follow were taken by the commons on 24 September as a result of Pym's report from the commissioners for Irish affairs (acting as a committee). See *CJ*, II, 781.

3. See above, 15 June. The commons referred Waller's petition to the Earl of Leicester.

esty's commissioners for the affairs of Ireland have thought fit that the several and respective allowances be made unto them, viz., unto the said William Hawkins for his labor and attendance as secretary for the number of days aforesaid at the rate of 8s. per diem 65£ 04s., unto the [said] Robert Chambers for his labor and attendance as auditor the like number of days at the same rate of 8s. per diem 65£ 4s., and to the said Richard Willis for his attendance by himself and his servants the same number of days at the rate of 5s. per diem 40£ 15s. And that Mr. Pym be desired to report the [p. 140] same to the House of Commons as the opinion of these commissioners that order may be given for payment unto them of those sums respectively by the treasurer at wars for the kingdom of Ireland.[4]

Carter, petition

Whereas the petition of Arthur Carter, gentleman, was this day presented to the lords and others his majesty's commissioners for the affairs of Ireland whereby he showeth that his parents and he having of late been spoiled by the rebels in Ireland of all their estate to the value of 1000£, the petitioner was employed thence into England to the parliament by the Earl of Cork, where after his dispatch returning he obtained the charitable benevolence of some of his friends to the sum of 18£ in money, but endeavoring to embark himself therewith, he was stayed by the searcher of the port of Minehead and his said money taken from him there. Until some order be given for the delivery and transportation thereof, it is now thought fit by the said commissioners that Mr. Pym be desired to report the said petition to the House of Commons as a thing worthy of their consideration and order.[5]

Wither and Waylet

Upon reading the petition of John Wither and John Waylet, surgeons, showing that they, being employed for Ireland as surgeon and surgeon's mate to the artillery, were robbed and pillaged upon the way to Coventry by one Captain Middleton, a party with his majesty, whereby the petitioner Wither lost his chest of surgery, linen, clothes, books, and goods to the value of 50£ or thereabouts and the other petitioner's ware about 10£, by which means they are not only disabled to proceed in their employment but are utterly undone if not righted and relieved, it is this day thought fit that Mr. Pym be desired to report the said petition unto the House of Commons as a matter thought fit by these commissioners for the petitioners to be relieved in.[6]

4. It was so ordered by the commons. The committee for Irish adventurers was to consider out of what money these sums should be paid.

5. The commons ordered that the £18 should be returned to Carter and that he might transport it to Ireland.

6. The commons referred the matter of reparation to the committee for Irish adventurers.

Moneys due upon certificate and for corn, victual, and clothes, etc.

Whereas divers sums of money are become due and payable unto several persons for certain quantities of corn, victual, clothing, and other necessaries delivered by them for the service of his majesty's armies in Ireland unto several commissaries and shopkeepers for [p. 141] that kingdom, part whereof are delivered by the printed order of both houses of parliament for payment to be made within thirty days after certificate returned of the delivery thereof, and part are delivered in clothing and other necessaries of the soldiers within the carriage of them to the places w[h]ere they were to be used, the particulars whereof hereafter mentioned and amount to the sum of 11,339£ 12s. 06d., as appeareth by the certificates and bills remaining with the lords and others commissioners for the affairs of Ireland, the said commissioners in number of a committee of both house[s] of parliament have this day taken the same into their consideration and, thinking it most just that those sums should be discharged, have ordered that Mr. Pym be desired to move the House of Commons that out of the remainder 27,000£,[7] which was designed to be sent [to] Dublin to pay the soldiers there but is yet remaining here in the deputy treasurer at wars his charge, the said sum of 11,339£ 12s. 06d. may [be] in the first place presently and entirely paid unto those respective persons to whom this sum is due.[8] And that the lords and others his majesty's commissioners for the affairs of Ireland in the number that is appointed for a committee of both houses may issue forth several warrants to the deputy treasurer at wars for the payment thereof accordingly.

		£	s.	d.
Ford	To Thomas Ford and others for 958 barrels of French wheat delivered at Cork payable the last of July 1642.	0802	04	00
Jenkenson, etc.	To Mathew Jenkenson, William Lisset, or John Sampson for 336 barrels of rye and 175 barrels of wheat delivered at Dublin and payable the third of September 1642.	0514	01	00
Lort	To Mr. John Lort for 58 barrels of wheat and 40 barrels of beans delivered at Dublin payable the 10th September 1642.	0082	00	00
Ellis	To Henry Ellis for 400 barrels of barley malt delivered at Dublin and payable the 15th September 1642.	0371	05	00
Castell	To Michael Castell for 817 barrels and ½ of			

7. For this sum see above, 26 July, n. 3. On 23 September the house resolved that this money should be conveyed to Dublin and that the committee being sent to Ireland should oversee its distribution to the soldiers there. See *CJ*, II, 779.

8. The commons ordered that the committee for Irish adventurers consider out of what money this sum should be paid.

	wheat delivered at Dublin and payable 16 September 1642.	0919	13	09
Tibbet	To Mathew Tibbet for 80 bushels of peas delivered at Cork and payable the 29th September 1642.	0016	00	00
[p. 142]				
Castell	To the said Michael Castell for 1200 barrels of wheat, 60,000 weight of flour, 1000 barrels of wheat, 4000 weight of flour, 600 barrels of wheat, and 300 barrels of wheat delivered at Carrickfergus payable 26th September 1642.	4161	13	04
Castell	To the said Michael Castell for 495 barrels and ¾ of wheat delivered at Dublin and payable 27th September 1642.	0557	14	00
Captain Partridge	For victual delivered to Captain Hall out of Captain Partridge's ship by order of Mr. Fountaine payable presently.	0022	01	00
Bennet	To Richard Bennet for provand,[9] suits, shirts, and stockings delivered at Dublin payable ult. August 1642.	0198	13	00
Wybrants	To Peter Wybrants for 1824 pair of shoes delivered at Dublin and payable the 22th of September 1642.	0273	12	00
Paman	To Henry Paman for 3750 Monmouth caps payable forthwith.	0359	07	00
Roberts	To Nicholas Roberts for scythes and sickles with their appurtenances.	0103	17	07
Githin	To Mr. Githin and others in part of 16,799£ 10s. for clothes for the soldiers payable presently.	2000	00	00
Wollaston	To Mr. Wollaston in part of 4500£ for doublets for the soldiers payable presently.	0500	00	00
Wood	To Mr. Wood for money laid out upon his account for boats and the carriage of clothes payable presently.	0432	10	04
		11,339	12	06

Pay for the 8 regiments and nine troops in Ulster

Whereas it appeareth by an order and resolution of the House of Commons in parliament dated the 29th day of August last past, grounded upon former reports of several committees and orders of both houses of parliament,[10] that the several regiments of foot under the command [p. 143] of Captain Arthur

9. Food and provisions, especially for an army. *NED.*
10. See above, 23 August.

Chichester, Lord Viscount Montgomery, Sir James Montgomery, Lord Viscount Clandeboye, Sir William Stewart, Sir Robert Stewart, Sir William Cole, and Mr. Mervin, consisting of 7500 men besides of officers and Mr. Hill's regiment and the other troops of harquebusiers, making nine troops of horse of 60 apiece besides officers, being listed and taken into pay by this state for their respective numbers from the first day of July last, and that amongst other things it is ordered that a full month's pay for every regiment of foot and troop of horse with the several officers, amounting to 11,109£ for all the said regiments of foot and 2742£ 08s. 04d. for Mr. Hill's regiment of horse and 5 other troops, shall be imprested unto the several colonels of the regiments aforesaid and captains of the troops of horse to be received here in this kingdom from the deputy treasurer at wars for Ireland by as many of the said colonels and captains or their agents as are here and shall desire the same with this proviso, that if the said colonels and captains shall not afterward produce and make appear that they have maintained and kept their full numbers, defalcation is to be made out of their respective entertainments that shall next grow due, and also that 290£ shall be paid unto them for providing surgeons' chests at the rate of 25£ for every regiment of foot and 10£ for every troop of horse, the several sums so ordered making 14,141£ 08s. 04.

Pay for 8 of the 10 troops that are to join with the Scots

And whereas also upon former resolution and order of the several house of parliament it was the same day likewise ordered by the House of Commons in parliament that the month's pay due the 2d of August last past should be forthwith paid unto six of the ten troops that are to join with the Scottish army in Ireland,[11] viz., Captain Arthur Chichester's, the Lord Viscount Montgomery's, the Lord Viscount Clandeboye's, Sir James Montgomery['s], Mr. Arthur Hill's, and Mr. Upton's troops, who having been mustered their pay according to their numbers for that amounteth to the sum of 5321£ 8s., and that 886£ 18s. should be imprested upon account unto Sir William Cole, Knight, for 3 months past in regard his troop had not been mustered, to be afterwards defalked or allowed as his musters shall be made appear, and further that 295£ 12s. 08d. being a month's [pay] should likewise be imprested to Sir Robert Adair, Knight, for his troop which was raised since the rest and his musters not yet appearing to be afterwards also defalked or allowed upon his musters, and that after the rate of 10£ for a surgeon's chest to each of nine of the troops, the sum of 90£ be also paid unto them with several sums for their troops which are to join with the Scottish army, making [p. 144] 6593£ 18s. 08 be added to the former, making the whole 20,735£ 07s., the lords and others his majesty's commissioners for

11. See above, 23 August.

the affairs of Ireland in the number of a committee of both houses of parliament have thought fit and ordered that Mr. Pym be desired to report it as their opinion to the House of Commons that what shall be remaining in the hands of the deputy treasurer at wars for Ireland of the 27,000£ which was heretofore designed to be sent to Dublin to pay the soldiers there, after 11,339£ 12s. 06d. is paid for corn, victuals, clothes and other necessaries according to the particulars this day presented, the same may be paid unto Sir James Montgomery, Knight, and Arthur Hill, Esquire, in part of the said 20,735£ 7s. so ordered as aforesaid, and that the residue may be paid unto them out of the moneys which are not yet brought in of the 100,000£ lent by the City of London towards the wars of Ireland, all which to be by them paid unto the several colonels of the said regiments of foot and colonels and captains of regiments and troops of horse or their agents or assigns proportionably according to the rate set down and ordered in this and the former order, and to move the house that warrants may be issued by the lords and others his majesty's commissioners for the affairs of Ireland in the number of a committee of both houses to the deputy treasurer at wars for paying of the said moneys accordingly.

Commissions for Captain Chichester

It is this day ordered and thought fit by the lords and others his majesty's commissioners for the affairs of Ireland in the number of a committee of both house[s] of parliament that a letter be prepared for them to sign to desire the lord lieutenant of Ireland that now the regiment of horse of Mr. Arthur Hill, the troop of horse commanded by Captain Dudley Phillips, and the regiments of foot of Captain Chichester and Captain Audley Mervin are listed and taken into the pay of this state, amongst the other forces in Ulster, his lordship would grant them as colonels and their captains and officers commissions authorizing them to proceed in the service as other commanders and officers that have already received commissions.

[p. 145]   *Die Mercurii*, viz., XII October 1642[1]

Jones his ship hired by Captain Constable

Whereas it appeareth by the certificate of Captain Robert Constable, captain of the ship called the *Ruth*, who was employed by order of these commissioners for the carriage of ammunition, victual, and men from Bristol about the end of April last for the relief of the town of Kinsale and the forts of Limerick and Galway in Ireland[2] that he did hire the ship called the *Amity* of Elmore of the

1. This day's minutes are included, though they fall outside the scope of this volume, because they represent the last meeting of the commissioners recorded in the minute book. Meanwhile a new select committee for Irish affairs had superseded the commission. See D, 3 September.
2. See *PJ*, 2: 418, 427.

burden of 60 tons or thereabouts of John Jones, mariner and master of the said ship, to carry part of those victuals and provisions and to accompany him in the service at the rate of 42£ a month, and that there is due and owing unto the said John Jones for the service of that ship in that voyage the sum of 120£, which the said Captain Constable hath appointed him to demand of the lords and others his majesty's commissioners for the affairs of Ireland according to an order of theirs remaining with the mayor of the city of Bristol, the said lords and others his majesty's commissioners in regard they gave order by their letter of the 29th of April last to John Locke, Esquire,[3] then mayor of that city, to give his assistance in contracting for and hiring such a ship for that service and did promise that upon the said mayor's signification unto them of the price agreed on and performance of the service they would take order for due payment, have thought fit the said sum of 120£ be paid unto the said John Jones or his assigns in full of his demands for the said ship and according to the certificate of the said Captain Constable, and Mr. Pym is desired to move the House of Commons that order may be given for payment thereof. But because it doth not yet appear by any certificate from the mayor of Bristol at what rate the said ship was hired and when she entered into the service and returned from the same, it is further thought fit and ordered that a letter be prepared for them to sign requiring the said mayor to send them such certificate. And the committee for the navy of this kingdom are desired that if it shall appear that the service of that ship according to the rate agreed on shall not amount unto the sum of 120£, deduction and defalcation may be made out of the pay that shall be due and coming to Captain Constable for his present service of this state of so much as the said Jones shall hereby be overpaid.

Captain Conway, petition

It is this day ordered by the lords and others his majesty's commissioners for the affairs of Ireland in the number of a committee of both houses of parliament that Mr. Pym be desired to report to the House of Commons the petition of Captain Henry Conway and the certificate thereunto annexed as a matter worthy of their consideration and the petitioner's relief.

3. See *PJ*, 2: 428.

COMMISSIONERS FOR IRISH AFFAIRS ATTENDANCE RECORD

	Je 7	9	13	15	17	21	22	27	*Jl* 11	14	19	26	28	*Ag* 2	18[1]	23	*Sp* 16	*Oc* 12
Northumberland	x	x	x	x	x	x	x	x	x	x	x	x	x			x	x	x
Essex		x	x		x	x	x	x	x	x								
Pembroke		x	x	x	x	x			x	x	x		x					
Holland	x		x	x	x	x	x									x	x	x
Say and Sele				x	x	x	x	x				x	x			x		
Kimbolton (Mandeville)	x	x	x	x	x	x	x	x	x	x	x	x	x			x		
Robartes														No attendance list.	No attendance list.			
Cave																		
Cooke	x	x	x	x	x	x		x				x	x					
Cromwell		x	x	x	x		x	x	x	x	x	x	x			x		
Erle	x	x	x	x	x	x	x	x			x	x	x					x
Evelyn of Wilts	x	x	x	x	x	x	x	x	x	x		x	x					
Harley	x	x		x	x			x	x	x	x		x			x	x	
Holles			x	x	x	x	x			x			x				x	
Marten	x	x						x	x			x	x			x	x	
Meyrick		x	x	x	x	x	x	x	x	x	x							
Parkhurst				x			x			x	x	x	x			x		
Pym	x	x	x	x	x	x	x	x	x	x	x	x	x			x	x	x
Reynolds	x		x	x	x	x	x	x	x	x	x	x	x			x	x	
Vane, Jr.	x			x	x	x		x	x								x	x
Wallop									x	x	x	x	x					x

Note: An x indicates attendance.

1. The commission was henceforth to act as a joint committee. See above, 18 August, n. 2.

GLOSSARY OF MILITARY TERMS

The technical or military terms defined below occur in the Minute Book of the Commissioners for Irish Affairs. Definitions are principally from the *NED* and several military dictionaries.

bandolier	a broad belt worn over the shoulder and across the breast to support the musket, with twelve cases for the musket charge attached
barricado	a hastily formed rampart thrown up to obstruct the advance of an enemy
bed	that portion of a gun carriage upon which the gun rests
bit cannon	a smooth, round bit
bit mollet	a studded or toothed bit
blind	a screenlike structure used in fortification to give protection from enemy fire
budge barrel	a small tin barrel for carrying powder
carbine	a kind of firearm, shorter than a musket, used by cavalry and other troops
coin	a wedge used for raising and lowering pieces of ordnance
commander	a large wooden mallet; a rammer
conductor	a driver of artillery or ammunition wagons
crow	a grappling hook or crowbar
crupper	a leather strap buckled to the back of the saddle and passing under the horse's tail
culverin	a large cannon
dragooner	a mounted infantry soldier who fought on foot, carrying a dragoon or short musket
drake	a small cannon
engineer	one who designed or constructed military works for attack or defense
fat	a cask or barrel to contain dry things
fireworker	an artillery officer concerned with explosives
gin	an instrument for casting stones or other missiles
halberd	a weapon combining spear and battle-ax, mounted on a long handle
halberdier	a soldier armed with a halberd

half-pike	a small pike with a shaft about half the length of the full-sized one
hand screw	an engine used to cant beams or other weighty timbers
handspike	a wooden bar used as a lever or crow, especially in artillery service
harquebus	a portable gun, varying in size from a small cannon to a musket, fired from a support
harquebusier	a lightly armed cavalry soldier, formerly carrying a harquebus, which by 1642 had been replaced by a carbine
hedging bill	an implement with a long blade and long handle, used in cutting and trimming hedges
ladle	an instrument for charging with loose powder or for removing the shot from a cannon
match	a wick or cord prepared so as not to be easily extinguished when lighted, used for firing cannon and other firearms
matross	a soldier next in rank below the gunner in a train of artillery, who acted as assistant or mate
miche	a wedge for sighting a cannon
Monmouth cap	a flat, round knit cap worn by soldiers and sailors
musket	the standard firearm of the infantry, five feet in length
pack net	presumably equipment for carrying packs or bundles on a horse
palisado	a strong, pointed wooden stake, a number of which, when fixed deeply in the ground in a close row, form a defense
partisan	a weapon having a broad, flat blade with projections on either side, used by officers of foot
petard	a metal pot or box containing an explosive, used to breach a door, gate, or wall
petardier	a soldier who managed and fired a petard
pike	the standard weapon of the infantry, sixteen to eighteen feet in length, consisting of a wooden shaft with a pointed head of iron or steel
pioneer	one of a body of foot soldiers who marched in advance of a regiment with spades, pickaxes, etc., to clear the way
pot	a steel cap or small helmet worn by both infantry and cavalry
rammer	a cylindrical block of wood fixed at the end of a staff, used to drive home the charge of a gun or cannon
rampire	rampart

roweling bridge	a wheeled bridge used by the petardier to span a moat
sally port	an opening in a fortified place for the passage of troops making a sally
snaphance	a musket fitted with an early form of flintlock
sponge	a mop or swab for cleaning a cannon bore after firing
tampion	a block of wood fitting into the muzzle of a gun
thill (horse harness)	the pole or shaft by which a wagon or cart is attached to the animal drawing it
tilt	an awning or cover for a cart or wagon
trace (horse harness)	one of the pair of ropes or leather straps by which the collar of a draft animal is connected with the splinter bar of the vehicle
trooping saddle	a cavalry saddle
tumbrel	a two-wheeled covered cart used for carrying ammunition, tools, etc., for an army
wad	a plug of tow or cloth, or a disk of felt or cardboard, to retain the powder and shot in position in charging a gun or cartridge
wadhook	a spiral tool for withdrawing wads or charges from guns

APPENDIXES

APPENDIX A

Changes in the Composition of the House of Commons
2 June–17 September 1642[1]

Deaths[2]

Sir Arthur Ingram   Sir John Jennings
24 August   July

Henry Tulse
summer

Disablements[3]

Date		MP	Constituency	Source CJ, II
Ag	4	Robert Hyde	Salisbury, Wilts	703
	5	Sir Ralph Hopton	Wells, Somerset	704
		Thomas Smith	Bridgwater, Somerset	704
		John Digby	Milborne Port, Somerset	704
	8	Sir John Poulett	Somerset	708
		Sir John Stawell	Somerset	708
	9	Sir Nicholas Slanning	Penryn, Cornwall	711
	10	John Griffith	Caernarvonshire	712
	11	Edward Hyde	Saltash, Cornwall	715
		Robert Holborne	Mitchell, Cornwall	715
		Sir William Pennyman	Richmond, Yorks	715
		Edward Kirton	Milborne Port, Somerset	715
	12	John Coventry	Evesham, Worcs	716
		Sir Edward Rodney	Wells, Somerset	716
	16	Nicholas Weston	Newton, I. of W.	723
		George Goring	Portsmouth, Hants	723
	20	Sir Henry Herbert	Bewdley, Worcs	729
		Samuel Sandys	Droitwich, Worcs	729
		Sir John Pakington	Aylesbury, Bucks	729
	22	Gervase Holles	Grimsby, Lincs	730
	26	Sir William Widdrington	Northumberland	738
		Sir William Carnaby	Morpeth, Northumb	738
	29	Roger Kirkby	Lancashire	742
		Orlando Bridgeman	Wigan, Lancs	742

(*continued*)

Date		MP	Constituency	*Source* *CJ, II*
	30	Sir Richard Cave	Lichfield, Staffs	744
Sp	2	Christopher Lewknor	Chichester, Sussex	750
	6	Sir William Savile	Old Sarum, Wilts	754
		Henry Belasyse	Yorkshire	754
		John Belasyse	Thirsk, Yorks	754
		Sir Henry Slingsby	Knaresborough, Yorks	754
		Sir Thomas Danby	Richmond, Yorks	754
		Sir George Wentworth[4]	Pontefract, Yorks	754
		Sir Thomas Ingram	Thirsk, Yorks	754
		William Mallory	Ripon, Yorks	754
		Richard Aldborough	Aldborough, Yorks	754
		Sir John Strangways	Weymouth and Melcombe Regis, Yorks	754
		Sir Richard Lee	Shropshire	755
		Sir Robert Howard	Bishop's Castle, Salop	755
	7	Sir Christopher Hatton	Higham Ferrers, Northants	755
		Sir Robert Hatton	Castle Rising, Norfolk	755
		Geoffrey Palmer	Stamford, Lincs	755
		Henry Coke	Dunwich, Suffolk	756
		Sir Thomas Fanshawe	Hertford, Herts	756
	12	Richard Rogers	Dorset	762
		Richard Herbert	Montgomery, Mont	762
	16	Thomas Chicheley	Cambridgeshire	769

1. For the complete list of MPs in January 1642 and changes between March and June, see *PJ,* 1: 520–33, and 2: 473.

2. For the deaths of Ingram and Jennings, see Anthony F. Upton, *Sir Arthur Ingram* (Oxford, 1961), p. 258; and History of Parliament Trust, MS biography of Sir John Jennings. Tulse's death must have occurred between 13 June, when he pledged £20 for defense, and 21 September, when a writ for a new election was ordered. See Appendix F, and *CJ,* II, 775.

3. Though in some cases writs for new elections were issued, none of these MPs were replaced until sometime after 21 August 1645. On that day several orders for new elections appear in *CJ,* IV, 249. For information concerning Recruiters (members elected after this date), see Brunton and Pennington, *Members,* pp. 21–22. See also Godfrey Davies and Edith Lucile Klotz, "List of Members Expelled from the Long Parliament," *Huntington Library Quarterly,* 2 (1939): 479–81; and R. N. Kershaw, "The Recruiting of the Long Parliament, 1645–7," *History,* 8 (1923): 169–79.

4. Identified in *CJ* as "of Wolley" and therefore cousin to the Earl of Strafford.

New Members of Parliament[5]

Constable, Sir William, Bart.
  Knaresborough, Yorks
  Vice: Henry Benson

Jennings, Richard
  St. Albans, Herts
  Vice: Sir John Jennings

5. Biographical information follows. For further comments about the new MPs, see pp. xv–xvi.

Glanville, Sir John
  Bristol, Glos
  Vice: Humphrey Hooke or
    Richard Long
Hanham, Thomas
  Minehead, Somerset
  Vice: Alexander Luttrell

Scudamore, James
  Hereford, Herefs
  Vice: Richard Weaver
Taylor, John
  Bristol, Glos
  Vice: Humphrey Hooke or
    Richard Long

SIR WILLIAM CONSTABLE,[6] Bart. (c. 1580–1655), of Flamborough and Holme, Yorks, was son and heir to Sir Robert Constable (d. 1601) by Anne, daughter and heir to John Hussey of Duffield, Yorks.

Constable served under the 2d Earl of Essex in Ireland, by whom he was knighted in 1599. Though involved in the Essex conspiracy of 1601, he was subsequently bailed. In 1608 he married Dorothy, daughter to Thomas, Lord Fairfax, and sister to Ferdinando, Lord Fairfax, MP for Yorkshire in the Long Parliament. In 1611 Constable purchased a baronetcy.

A leading Puritan, Constable served in parliament for Yorkshire (1626) and Scarborough (1628). Meanwhile in 1627 he was imprisoned for a time for refusing to contribute to the forced loan. Continually in debt because of his extravagant life-style, he was forced to sell the family estates, though in 1650 he recovered Holme. Doubtless both his financial plight and his Calvinist convictions encouraged him to emigrate to Holland in 1637, where he remained until 1641.

When Henry Benson, MP for Knaresborough, Yorks, in the Long Parliament, was disabled to sit in November 1641 for selling protections, an election dispute resulted between William Dearlove, Benson's son-in-law, and Sir William Constable. This dispute, though brought to the attention of the House of Commons on 19 March 1642, was not finally settled in Constable's favor until 17 August. Though it is not clear when he took his seat, the warrant from the sheriff of Yorkshire for amending the return was presented to the house on 8 November. The next day Constable was named to a committee "to consider how a Body of Horse may be raised . . . And . . . any thing else . . . necessary for the Safety of the Kingdom." Clearly he was in the house on 8 February 1643, when he was among those who "declared in Affirmative to the Vote of adhering to my Lord of Essex in this Cause."

Meanwhile in Yorkshire, Constable, a deputy lieutenant, actively promoted the parliamentary cause and on 4 October 1642 was named by the House of Commons as one of the commissioners for raising money, horse, and plate in

6. *DNB*. Foster, *Pedigrees of Yorkshire*, II, n.p. Pink MS 299, ff. 557–58. *M of P*, I, 473, 479, 497. *CJ*, II, 301, 334, 488, 725, 792–93, 839, 841, 958; III, 209, 374–75; V, 108. Keeler, pp. 75, 107–08. Coates, pp. 66, 242–43. *PJ*, 2: 61, 63, 323.

his county, and subsequently in several other counties as well. Upon the outbreak of the civil war, he became an officer in the parliamentary army under the 3d Earl of Essex, serving at Edgehill in October 1642 and in other engagements, but was deprived of his command by the self-denying ordinance of April 1645. Because of his distinguished service and his precarious finances, his nephew Sir Thomas Fairfax, commander-in-chief of the New Model Army, persuaded parliament in 1647 to grant Constable £1984 out of sequestration moneys.

Between 1645 and 1649 Constable served on a number of committees, including several related to Yorkshire. In the quarrel between the army and parliament in 1647, Constable as an Independent sided with the army. In January 1648 he assisted in guarding King Charles at Carisbrooke Castle and subsequently was governor of Gloucester until 1651. In January 1649 he was named one of the king's judges by the House of Commons; he attended the trial regularly and signed the king's death warrant.

Having remained a member of parliament after Pride's Purge (December 1648), Constable continued to be politically active during the Interregnum, serving on three of the Councils of State. He died without an heir in June 1655 and, following a state funeral, was buried in Westminster Abbey. However, at the Restoration his remains were disinterred.

SIR JOHN GLANVILLE,[7] the younger (1586–1661), of Broad Hinton, Wilts, was the second son of Sir John Glanville, the elder (d. 1600), by Alice, daughter of John Skerret of Tavistock, Devon. The elder Glanville had been both an MP and a justice of the Common Pleas. About 1615 the younger Glanville married Winifred, daughter of William Bouchier of Barnsley, Glos, by whom he had seven children.

Having been admitted to Lincoln's Inn in 1603, Glanville was called to the bar about 1610 and in the 1630s became a reader and a bencher there. He was made a serjeant-at-law in 1637, a king's serjeant in 1640, and was knighted at Whitehall in 1641. In addition, he served as recorder first of Plymouth (1614) and later of Bristol.

In his early parliamentary career, beginning in 1614 (MP for Liskeard, Cornwall) and continuing through the next five parliaments (MP for Plymouth), Glanville was a conspicuous opponent of the crown and friend of Sir John Eliot. In the Short Parliament (April–May 1640) he sat for Bristol and was elected

7. *DNB*. J. L. Vivian, *The Visitations of the County of Devon* [Harleian Society Publications] (Exeter, 1895), I, 411. Pink MS 302, ff. 125–26. Foss, *Judges*, VI, 230–31; VII, 31. W. R. Williams, *The Parliamentary History of the County of Gloucester* (Hereford, 1898), p. 114. *M of P*, I (Index), xxxvii; I, 489, 507. *PJ*, 2: 310. *CJ*, II, 567–68; III, 536–37; IV, 285; V, 648, 662. *LJ*, V, 667. *CAM*, I, 408–11. Keeler, pp. 163, 186.

Speaker. By this time, despite his opposition to ship money, he had become a
supporter of the king and in November 1640 was not elected to the Long
Parliament.

On 12 May 1642 the House of Commons called for the election of two
burgesses for Bristol following the disabling of Richard Long and Humphrey
Hooke as wine monopolists. Though the election of Sir John Glanville and John
Taylor took place in June, it is not clear whether Glanville ever took his seat. As
a king's serjeant he had frequently served as messenger from the lords to the
commons since the early days of the Long Parliament. Despite the Bristol
election he continued in this role until given leave by the House of Lords on 24
March 1643 to go to his house in the country. Soon thereafter he joined the king
at Oxford, where he received the degree of DCL and sat in the Oxford parliament.

In June 1644 Glanville was committed to the Tower for deserting the parliament and for serving on a commission which had indicted various members of
both houses of high treason. In consequence, it was ordered that an impeachment be prepared. When he appeared before the Committee for Advance of
Money in January 1645 to compound for his delinquency, he stated that "He did
not desert Parliament, but going away by leave, on his return, was taken
prisoner and carried to Oxford, where he did all the good offices in his power."
Nevertheless, on 25 September 1645 he was disabled to sit as a member of
parliament.

Upon his release from the Tower in 1648, Glanville's fine and composition
were accepted and his delinquency was pardoned. He subsequently retired to
Hampshire. In 1659 he served briefly in parliament for St. Germans, Cornwall,
until declared "not qualified" and at the Restoration was again appointed a
king's serjeant. Upon his death in October 1661, he was buried at Broad
Hinton, and his son William succeeded to his estates. William, along with
Glanville's son-in-law Piers Edgcombe, was MP for Camelford, Cornwall, in
the Long Parliament.

THOMAS HANHAM[8] (c. 1617–1650) of Dean's Court, Wimborne Minster,
Dorset, was the second son of Thomas Hanham (c. 1576–1652) by Elizabeth,
daughter and heir to Robert Broughton of Somerset and widow of William
Frampton. His grandfather Thomas Hanham (d. 1593) had married Penelope,

---

8. John Hutchins, *The History and Antiquities of the County of Dorset* (London, 1861–70),
III, 231–32. Keeler, pp. 140, 263, 310, 319. *AO,* II, 644. *CJ,* II, 604, 713, 762, 763, 766, 769, 840;
III, 562; IV, 32, 313, 565, 727. *M of P,* I (Index), xliv. Pink MS 303, f. 74. *CCC,* II, 942–43. *CAM,*
II, 785–86. The information in Pink, *CCC,* and *CAM* does not wholly agree with that in the other
sources cited. The evidence seems, however, to indicate that the younger Hanham was the MP, not
his father.

daughter to Sir John Popham, lord chief justice. Through them the younger Hanham was related to several members of the Long Parliament: William Constantine and John Pyne (Poole, Dorset), Alexander Luttrell and Sir Francis Popham (Minehead, Somerset), and Alexander Popham (Bath, Somerset).

Thomas Hanham was admitted to Queen's College, Oxford, in 1634 and to the Middle Temple in 1637. In 1645 he was called to the bar. The date of his marriage to Margaret, eldest daughter to Sir William Doddington of Bremer, Hants, is uncertain.

Following the death of Alexander Luttrell in the spring of 1642, a new election was called for on 3 June. Though the election was referred to the committee for privileges on 10 August, by 12 September Hanham had taken his seat as the new MP for Minehead. On that day he pledged £50 "for the Service of the King and Parliament" and brought in his pledge four days later. He was named to two committees in September and to a third in November.

Subsequently Hanham joined the king and attended the Oxford parliament in January 1644. In consequence he was soon thereafter disabled by the House of Commons and apparently imprisoned for a time. In October 1645 he was referred to the Committee for Compounding, and the following June the house accepted his composition. An ordinance pardoning his delinquency and discharging the sequestration of his estate was formulated but was not sent up to the lords until November 1646.

When Hanham died in 1650, his widow erected a monument in the church of St. Cuthberga at Wimborne Minster. He left no heir.

RICHARD JENNINGS[9] (c. 1619–1668) of Sandridge, near St. Albans, Herts, was son and heir to Sir John Jennings, K.B. (d. July 1642), by Alice, daughter to Sir Richard Spencer of Offley, Herts. Sir John, who had been sheriff and justice of the peace, sat for St. Albans in both the Short and Long Parliaments.

In 1634 Richard Jennings was admitted to the Inner Temple and from 1637 to 1640 traveled abroad. He married Frances, daughter and heir to Sir Gifford Thornhurst, Bart., of Agnes Court, Old Romney, Kent, in 1643.

Following the death of Sir John Jennings and the call for a new election on 5 August, Richard Jennings was chosen to succeed his father. It is uncertain how soon he took his seat. However, he subscribed to the parliamentary oath and covenant in June 1643 and to the solemn league and covenant in September 1643. He seems not to have had an active role in parliament and was named to

9. Greaves and Zaller, *Dictionary of British Radicals,* II, 139. Pink MS 305, f. 46. Keeler, pp. 233–34. *CJ,* II, 704, 736; III, 118; IV, 177, 410, 413. Rushworth, V, 481. *M of P,* I, 508, 523. In addition, the editors are grateful for having access to the biographies (in MS) of Sir John and Richard Jennings prepared by Eleanor Reid of the History of Parliament Trust.

only a few committees. He was apparently more active in local affairs, serving on a number of county committees related to Hertfordshire and subsequently as a justice of the peace.

In the conflict between king and parliament, Jennings sided with the parliament, as had his father. On 25 August 1642 he was named by the House of Commons as a deputy lieutenant for Hertfordshire. In January 1646 he and his wife were taken prisoner by the king's forces at Faringdon, Berks; soon thereafter the House of Commons approved of their exchange for a royalist prisoner.

Between 1645 and 1648 Jennings was much absent from the house and did not sit after Pride's Purge. However, he again represented St. Albans from 1659 until his death in 1668. He was buried in the abbey church of St. Albans. Of his five surviving children, the youngest daughter was the well-known Sarah, who in 1678 married John Churchill, Duke of Marlborough.

JAMES SCUDAMORE[10] (1624–1668) of Holme Lacy, Herefs, was son to John, Viscount Scudamore of Sligo (d. 1671), by Elizabeth, daughter and heir to Sir Arthur Porter of Llanthony, Glos. The elder Scudamore, who had been MP for both Hereford and Herefordshire, was ambassador to France in the 1630s. James Scudamore, having spent some time in Paris with his father, matriculated at St. John's College, Oxford, in 1640. In 1642–44 he was a justice of the peace in Herefordshire.

Following the death of Richard Weaver on 16 May 1642, the House of Commons ordered that a new burgess be elected for Hereford. Though the return electing James Scudamore was dated 26 July, it is not certain when he took his seat. His career in the Long Parliament was brief, for on 8 May 1643 he was disabled "for bearing Arms, and being in actual War, against the Parliament." He was also among those disabled on 22 January 1644 "for deserting the Service of the House, and being in the King's Quarters, and adhering to that Party."

Both Scudamore and his father supported the royalist cause, and the latter was imprisoned in London by the parliament from 1643 to 1647. Because of the forced sale of his goods, sequestrations, and gifts to the royal cause, Viscount Scudamore experienced heavy losses during the civil war. In September 1648 the House of Commons accepted a fine of £2690 and pardoned both father and son.

10. *DNB*. W. R. Williams, *The Parliamentary History of the County of Hereford* (Brecknock, 1896), pp. 55–56. *PJ*, 2: 360. *CJ*, II, 582; III, 75, 374; VI, 21. *M of P*, I, 489, 523. GEC, *Peerage*. *CCC*, III, 1643. *An Inventory of the Historical Monuments in Herefordshire*, I (London, 1931), 146–47. Basil Duke Henning, *The History of Parliament: The House of Commons 1660–1690* (London, 1983), III, 407–08.

Meanwhile in 1647 James Scudamore went abroad for further education and in 1648 married Jane, daughter and heir to Richard Bennet of Kew, Surrey. Because of debts he spent much of the Interregnum abroad. In 1661 he was again elected to parliament, this time for Herefordshire, and served until his death in June 1668. He was buried at Holme Lacy, where there is a monument to him and his wife in the church of St. Cuthbert. When his father died in 1671, James Scudamore's eldest son John succeeded as viscount and was subsequently MP for Hereford and for Herefordshire.

JOHN TAYLOR[11] (c. 1585–1645) of Bristol, Glos, son to John Taylor of Lichfield, Staffs, was apprenticed to a Bristol merchant in 1600 and was made a burgess in 1609. In the 1620s he served as warden and later treasurer of the Merchant Venturers. Part owner of several ships, including the *Mary Rose* (with Richard Long), he was involved in trade with Newfoundland and New England. He also had a financial interest in the ironworks of the forest of Dean. The date of his marriage to Mary, daughter of Alderman Henry Yate, a Bristol soap manufacturer, is uncertain.

Having earlier served as sheriff, Taylor was an alderman for Bristol from 1640 to 1645 and mayor in 1640–41. In June 1642 he was elected along with Sir John Glanville as MP for Bristol, replacing Humphrey Hooke and Richard Long, who had been disabled on 12 May 1642 as wine monopolists. Taylor apparently took his seat not long after the election, for on 9 August the house requested him to thank the gentlemen of Bristol for their services on behalf of parliament during an encounter at Chewton Mendip, Somerset. On 5 September he was given leave to go to the country for three weeks.

Though ultimately Taylor supported the royalist cause, for a time he vacillated in his loyalty. On 13 October he subscribed £50 toward the needs of parliament and promised more if needed. Shortly thereafter the house requested him to send copies of the propositions to Bristol with an accompanying letter encouraging subscriptions of money, horse, and plate. In the spring of 1643, while Bristol was in parliamentary hands, he was implicated in an unsuccessful plot to admit Prince Rupert. Yet in June he subscribed to the parliamentary oath and covenant in the House of Commons. However, when Bristol fell to Rupert

11. H. E. Nott, ed., *The Deposition Books of Bristol, 1643–1647* [Bristol Record Society], I (Bristol, 1935), 254–55. Patrick McGrath, ed., *Merchants and Merchandise in Seventeenth-Century Bristol* [Bristol Record Society, XIX] (Bristol, 1955), pp. 111–13, 213, 236. *PJ*, 2: 310. *CJ*, II, 567–68, 711, 752, 759, 806, 820; III, 118, 389. *M of P*, I, 489. John Latimer, *The Annals of Bristol in the Seventeenth Century* (Bristol, 1900), pp. 156–57, 189. Bryan Little, *The City and County of Bristol* (Bristol, 1954), pp. 124–32. Bristol Record Office, P/StJB/R/1(a). The date of Taylor's birth is from the list of MPs for 1640–60 compiled by the staff of the History of Parliament Trust.

in July, Taylor joined the king at Oxford. In consequence, he was disabled to serve in parliament on 5 February 1644.

In September 1645 Taylor, by then a member of the royalist forces, was killed during the siege of Bristol, which resulted in its surrender to parliament. He was buried in the crypt of St. John's Church. He was survived only briefly by his son John (1641–48).

APPENDIX B

Leaves Granted to Members of Parliament
2 June–17 September 1642[1]

Date		MP	Constituency	Source CJ, II
Je	2	Robert Scawen	Berwick-on-Tweed, Northumb	600
	4	Sir Gervase Clifton	East Retford, Notts	605
	6	Edward Exton	Southampton, Hants	607
	7	Sir Samuel Luke	Bedford, Beds	611
	9	Richard Boyle, Viscount Dungarvan	Appleby, Westmor	614
	11	Sir Thomas Smith	Chester, Cheshire	621
	13	Sir Neville Poole[2]	Malmesbury, Wilts	
	16	Sir John Strangways	Weymouth and Melcombe Regis, Dorset	626
	17	Sir George Wentworth[3]	Pontefract, Yorks	628
		Sir Robert Hatton	Castle Rising, Norfolk	628
		Sir Thomas Cheeke	Harwich, Essex	628
	18	Francis Newport	Shrewsbury, Salop	631
		Sir William Uvedale	Petersfield, Hants	631
	20	Sir Robert Cooke	Tewkesbury, Glos	633
		John Polwhele	Tregony, Cornwall	633
	21	Richard Ferris	Barnstaple, Devon	634
		William Bassett	Bath, Somerset	634
		Sir Roger North	Eye, Suffolk	634
	22	Henry Brett	Gloucester, Glos	635
		Sir Edward Master	Canterbury, Kent	636
		Augustine Skinner	Kent	636
		John Dutton	Gloucestershire	636
	27	Hugh Potter	Plympton, Devon	641
		Edward Stephens or Nathaniel Stephens	Tewkesbury, Glos, or Gloucestershire	641

(continued)

1. Leaves granted to MPs for military purposes—for example, executing the militia ordinance in their counties; collecting subscriptions for money, horse, and plate; joining the lord general—are not included. In some cases, however, the purpose of the leave is not clear.
2. This leave is not noted in *CJ;* however, see 13 June, n. 12.
3. Cousin to the Earl of Strafford.

Date		MP	Constituency	Source CJ, II
	28	Sir Ralph Sydenham	Bossiney, Cornwall	643
		George Fane	Callington, Cornwall	643
		John White[4]	Rye, Cinque Port	643
		Sir Patrick Curwen	Cumberland	643
		Sir John Fenwick	Northumberland	643
		John Fenwick	Morpeth, Northumb	643
Jl	1	Sir Walter Erle	Weymouth and Melcombe Regis, Dorset	648
		John Cowcher	Worcester, Worcs	648
	2	Sir James Thynne[5]	Wiltshire	648
	4	Sir Roger Palmer	Newton, Lancs	649
	9	Sir William Dalston	Carlisle, Cumb	662
	11	Matthew Davies	Christchurch, Hants	664
	12	Francis Lloyd[6]	Carmarthen, Carm	668
		Thomas Pury	Gloucester, Glos	668
	16	Sir Thomas Whitmore	Bridgnorth, Salop	675
	19	Sir John Hippisley	Cockermouth, Cumb	680
	20	Piers Edgcombe	Camelford, Cornwall	682
	21	Sir Samuel Rolle	Devonshire	684
	22	Robert Goodwin	East Grinstead, Sussex	685
		Sir Thomas Widdrington	Berwick-on-Tweed, Northumb	686
	25	Sir Edmund Moundeford	Norfolk	689
	29	William Wheeler	Westbury, Wilts	696
Ag	6	Sir William Allanson	York, Yorks	706
		William Cage	Ipswich, Suffolk	706
	8	Augustine Skinner	Kent	709
		Sir Benjamin Rudyard	Wilton, Wilts	709
	10	Richard Shuckburgh	Warwickshire	713
		Sir Hugh Owen	Pembroke, Pemb	713
	16	John Trenchard	Wareham, Dorset	723
	20	Thomas Pury	Gloucester, Glos	729
	27	Edmund Prideaux	Lyme Regis, Dorset	740
Sp	3	Roger Hill	Bridport, Dorset	751
	5	John Taylor	Bristol, Glos	752

4. Probably the John White who had royalist sympathies. He was to go to York "concerning the Payment of the Prince's Servants."

5. Thynne's leave is noted on 30 June in D'Ewes.

6. Doubtless Francis Lloyd, for Walter Lloyd was present in the house on 21 July according to D'Ewes.

APPENDIX C

Bills before the House of Commons: 2 June–17 September 1642[1]

Name of Bill	1st Reading	2d Reading C: Committed	3d Reading A: Assented	To the Lords	Lords' Vote A: Assented	Royal Disposition
Pluralities	10 Mr 1641 CJ, II, 100	16 Mr 1641 CJ, II, 105 C	19 Je 1641 CJ, II, 181 A	19 Je 1641 CJ, II, 181	4 My 1642 LJ, V, 43 A	No action 23 Jl 1642 LJ, V, 211, 234
Scandalous ministers	23 Je 1641 CJ, II, 183	24 Je 1641 CJ, II, 184 C	7 Ap 1642 CJ, II, 516 A	12 Ap 1642 CJ, II, 523	30 Ja 1643 LJ, V, 578 A	No action
Sir Thomas Dawes	19 Nv 1641 CJ, II, 320	18 Dc 1641 CJ, II, 348 C	6, 11 Ag 1642 CJ, II, 706, 714 A	13 Ag 1642 CJ, II, 718		
Earl of Pembroke	3 Ja 1642 CJ, II, 366	7 Ap 1642 CJ, II, 515 C	8 Sp 1642 CJ, II, 758 A	8 Sp 1642 CJ, II, 758	20 Dc 1641[2] LJ, IV, 482 A	No action HMC, 4th Rpt., p. 108
Innovations in churches	16 Fb 1642 CJ, II, 436	17 Fb 1642 CJ, II, 437 C	23 Mr 1642 CJ, II, 493 A	23 Mr 1642 CJ, II, 494	16 Jl 1642 LJ, V, 214 A	No action
Soap boilers, restitution	7 Ap 1642 CJ, II, 515	12 Ap 1642 CJ, II, 523 C				
Westminster Assembly (1)	9 My 1642 CJ, II, 564	9 My 1642 CJ, II, 564 C	19 My 1642 CJ, II, 579 A	19 My 1642 CJ, II, 579	3 Je 1642 LJ, V, 101 A	No action 23 Jl 1642 LJ, V, 211, 234

						Royal Assent
Ireland, reducing rebels (subscriptions)	12 My 1642 *CJ*, II, 569	12 My 1642 *CJ*, II, 569 C	3 Je 1642 *CJ*, II, 603 A	3 Je 1642 *CJ*, II, 603	8 Je 1642 *LJ*, V, 117 A	22 Je 1642 *LJ*, V, 154 c. 37
Draining of great level	31 My 1642 *CJ*, II, 596	3 Je 1642 *CJ*, II, 603 C				
Sir Robert Coke	9 Je 1642[3] *CJ*, II, 616				12 My 1642[2] *LJ*, V, 61 A	
Tonnage and poundage:[4] 1 Jl 1642–1 Mr 1643			25 Je 1642 *CJ*, II, 639 A	25 Je 1642 *CJ*, II, 639	27 Je 1642 *LJ*, V, 166 A	No action 23 Jl 1642 *LJ*, V, 211, 234
Militia	9 Jl 1642 *CJ*, II, 663	9 Jl 1642 *CJ*, II, 663 C				
Westminster Assembly (2)	15 Jl 1642 *CJ*, II, 673	15 Jl 1642 *CJ*, II, 673 C				
Fast days	4 Ag 1642 *CJ*, II, 702	4 Ag 1642 *CJ*, II, 702 C				
Peers, restraining	7 Sp 1642[5] *CJ*, II, 755				14 My 1642[2] *LJ*, V, 64 A	

1. For other references to these bills during this period, see the Index.
2. This bill originated in the House of Lords.
3. This bill is not noted in the private journals on this day. For an earlier reference see *PJ*, 2: 361.
4. There is no indication in *CJ* as to when the bill received its first two readings.
5. This bill is not noted in the private journals on this day. For an earlier reference see *PJ*, 2: 318.

APPENDIX D

The King's Proclamation
concerning the Militia[1]

By the King:

A Proclamation, forbidding all his Majesty's Subjects, belonging to the Trained Bands or Militia of this Kingdom, to rise, march, muster, or exercise, by virtue of any Order or Ordinance of one or both Houses of Parliament, without Consent or Warrant from His Majesty, upon Pain of Punishment according to the Laws.

Whereas, by the Statute made in the Seventh Year of King Edward the First, the Prelates, Earls, Barons, and Commonalty of the Realm, affirmed in Parliament, That to the King it belongeth, and His Part it is by His Royal Segniory, straightly to defend wearing of Armour, and all other Force against the Peace, at all Times when it shall please Him, and to punish them which do the contrary according to the Laws and Usages of the Realm; and hereunto all Subjects are bound to aid the King, as their Sovereign Lord, at all Seasons when need shall be: And whereas We understand that, expressly contrary to the said Statute, and other good Laws of this Our Kingdom, under Colour and Pretence of an Ordinance of Parliament, without Our Consent, or any Commission or Warrant from Us, the Trained Bands and Militia of the Kingdom have been lately, and are intended to be, put in Arms, and drawn into Companies, in a Warlike Manner, whereby the Peace and Quiet of Our Subjects is, or may be, disturbed: We, being desirous, by all gracious and fair Admonitions, to prevent that some Malignant Persons in this Our Kingdom do not by Degrees seduce Our good Subjects from their due Obedience to Us and the Laws of this Our Kingdom, subtily endeavouring, by a general Combustion or Confusion, to hide their mischievous Designs and Intentions against the Peace of this Our Kingdom, and, under a specious Pretence of putting Our Trained Bands into a Posture, draw and engage Our good Subjects in a Warlike Opposition against Us, as Our Town of Hull is already by the Treason of Sir John Hotham, who at first pretended to put a Garrison into the same only for Our Security and Service;

We do therefore, by this Our Proclamation, expressly charge and command

1. *LJ*, V, 111–12 (6 June 1642).

all Our Sheriffs, and all Colonels, Lieutenant Colonels, Serjeant Majors, Captains, Officers, and Soldiers, belonging to the Trained Bands of this Our Kingdom, and likewise all High and Petty Constables, and other Our Officers and Subjects whatsoever, upon their Allegiance, and as they tender the Peace of this Our Kingdom, not to muster, levy, raise, or march, or to summon or warn, upon any Warrant, Order, or Ordinance, from one or both our Houses of Parliament (whereto We have not, or shall not, give Our express Consent), any of Our Trained Bands, or other Forces, to rise, muster, march, or exercise, without express Warrant under Our Hand, or Warrant from Our Sheriff of the County, grounded upon a particular Writ to that Purpose under Our Great Seal: And in case any of Our Trained Bands shall rise or gather together contrary to this Our Command, We shall then call them in due Time to a strict Account, and proceed legally against them, as Violators of the Laws, and Disturbers of the Peace of the Kingdom.

Given at Our Court at Yorke, the 27th Day of May, 1642.

Parliament's Response[2]

A Declaration of the Lords and Commons in Parliament, concerning His Majesty's Proclamation, the 27th of May, 1642.

The Lords and Commons, having perused His Majesty's Proclamation, forbidding all His Majesty's Subjects, belonging to the Trained Bands or Militia of this Kingdom, to rise, march, muster, or exercise, by virtue of any Order or Ordinance of one or both Houses of Parliament, without Consent or Warrant from His Majesty, upon Pain of Punishment according to the Laws;

Do thereupon Declare, That neither the Statute of the 7th of Edward the First, therein vouched, nor any other Law of this Kingdom, doth restrain or make void the Ordinance agreed upon by both Houses of Parliament, for the ordering and disposing the Militia of the Kingdom, in this Time of extreme and imminent Danger, nor expose His Majesty's Subjects to any Punishment for obeying the same, notwithstanding that His Majesty hath refused to give His Consent to that Ordinance, but ought to be obeyed by the fundamental Laws of this Kingdom.

The Declaration of 7 Ed. I, quoted in His Majesty's Proclamation, runneth thus:

The King to the Justices of His Bench sendeth Greeting. Whereas of late, before certain Persons deputed to treat upon sundry Debates had between Us and certain Great Men of Our Realm, amongst other Things, it was accorded, That, in Our next Parliament, after Provision shall be made by Us, and the Common Assent of Prelates, Earls, and Barons, That, in all Parliaments, Treaties, and other Assemblies, which should be made in the Realm of England forever, that every Man shall come, without all Force and Armour,

2. *LJ*, V, 112–13 (6 June 1642).

well and peaceably, to the Honour of Us and Our Realm; and now, in Our next Parliament at Westm. after the said Treaties, the Prelates, Earls, Barons, and the Commonalty of Our Realm, there assembled to take Advice of this Business, have said, That to Us it belongeth, and Our Part is, through Our Royal Segniory, straightly to defend Force of Armour, and all other Force against Our Peace, at all Times when it shall please Us, and to punish them which shall do contrary, according to Our Laws and Usages of Our Realm.

And hereunto they are bound to aid Us, as their Sovereign Lord, at all Seasons when Need shall be: We command you, that you cause these Things to be read afore you in the said Bench, and there to be inrolled.

Given at Westm. the 30th Day of October.

The Occasion of this Declaration was, for the Restraint of armed Men from coming to the Parliament, to disturb the Peace of it, and is very improperly alledged for the Maintenance of such Levies as are now raised against the Parliament, the Title of the Statute being thus, *To all Parliaments and Treaties every Man shall come without Force and Arms*; so that the Question is not, whether it belong to the King or no, to restrain such Force; but, if the King shall refuse to discharge that Duty and Trust, whether there is not a Power in the Two Houses to provide for the Safety of the Parliament and Peace of the Kingdom, which is the End for which the Ordinance concerning the Militia was made, and, being agreeable to the Scope and Purpose of the Law, cannot in Reason be adjudged to be contrary to it; for, although the Law do affirm it to be in the King, yet it doth not exclude those in whom the Law hath placed a Power for that Purpose, as, in the Courts of Justice, the Sheriffs and other Officers and Ministers of those Courts: And as their Power is derived from the King by his Patents, yet cannot it be restrained by His Majesty's Command, by His Great Seal, or otherwise; much less can the Power of Parliament by concluded by His Majesty's Command, because the Authority thereof is of a higher and more eminent Nature than any of those Courts.

It is acknowledged, that the King is the Fountain of Justice and Protection; but the Acts of Justice and Protection are not exercised in His own Person, nor depend upon His Pleasure, but by His Courts, and by His Ministers, who must do their Duty therein, though the King in His own Person should forbid them; and therefore, if Judgements should be given by them against the King's Will and Personal Command, yet are they the King's Judgements.

The High Court of Parliament is not only a Court of Judicature, enabled by the Laws to adjudge and determine the Rights and Liberties of the Kingdom, against such Patents and Grants of His Majesty as are prejudicial thereunto, although strengthened both by His Personal Command and by His Proclamation under the Great Seal; but it is likewise a Council, to provide for the Necessities, prevent the imminent Dangers, and preserve the Public Peace and Safety, of the Kingdom, and to declare the King's Pleasure in those Things as are requisite thereunto; and what they do herein hath the Stamp of Royal Authority, although His Majesty, seduced by evil Counsel, do, in His own Person, oppose or interrupt the same; for the King's Supreme and Royal Pleasure is exercised and declared, in this High Court of Law and Council, after a more eminent and obligatory Manner than it can be by Personal Act or Resolution of His own.

Seeing, therefore, the Lords and Commons, which are His Majesty's Great and High Council, have Ordained, That, for the present and necessary Defence of the Realm, the Trained Bands and Militia of the Kingdom should be Ordered according to that Ordinance, and that the Town of Hull should be committed to the Custody of Sir John Hotham, to be preserved from the Attempts of Papists and other malignant Persons, who thereby might put the Kingdom into a Combustion, which is so far from being a Force against the King's Peace, that it is necessary for the keeping and securing thereof, and for that End alone is intended; and all His Majesty's loving Subjects, as well by that Law as by other Laws, are bound to be obedient thereunto; and what they do therein is (according to that Law) to be interpreted to be done in Aid of the King, in Discharge of that Trust which He is tied to perform; and it is so far from being liable to Punishment, that, if they should refuse to do it, or be persuaded by any Commission or Command of His Majesty to do the contrary, they might justly be punished for the same, according to the Laws and Usages of the Realm; for the King, by His Sovereignty, is not enabled to destroy His People, but to protect and defend them; and the High Court of Parliament, and all other His Majesty's Officers and Ministers, ought to be subservient to that Power and Authority, which the Law hath placed in His Majesty to that Purpose, though He Himself, in His own Person, should neglect the same.

Wherefore the Lords and Commons do declare the said Proclamation to be void in Law, and of none Effect; for that, by the Constitution and Policy of this Kingdom, the King by His Proclamation cannot declare the Law contrary to the Judgement and Resolution of any of the Inferior Courts of Justice, much less against the High Court of Parliament; for, if it were admitted that the King, by His Proclamation, may declare a Law, thereby His Proclamations will in Effect become Laws, which would turn to the subverting of the Law of the Land and the Rights and Liberties of the Subjects.

And the Lords and Commons do require and command all Constables, Petty Constables, and all other His Majesty's Officers and Subjects whatsoever, to muster, levy, raise, march, and exercise, or to summon or warn any, upon Warrants from the Lieutenants, Deputy Lieutenants, Captains, or other Officers of the Trained Bands, and all others, according to the said Ordinance of both Houses; and shall not presume to muster, levy, raise, march, or exercise, by virtue of any Commission or other Authority whatsoever, as they will answer the contrary at their Perils; and in their so doing, they do further declare that they shall be protected by the Power and Authority of both Houses of Parliament; and that whosoever shall oppose, question, or hinder them, in the Execution of the said Ordinance, shall be proceeded against as Violators of the Laws, and Disturbers of the Peace of the Kingdom.

APPENDIX E

Propositions for Defense of the Kingdom[1]

Whereas it appears that the King, seduced by wicked Counsel, intends to make War against his Parliament; and, in pursuance thereof, under Pretence of a Guard for his Person, hath actually begun to levy Forces, both of Horse and Foot; and sent out Summons, throughout the County of York, for the Calling together of great Numbers; and some ill-affected Persons have been employed in other Parts to raise Troops, under the Colour of his Majesty's Service, making large Offers of Reward and Preferment to such as will come in: And that his Majesty doth with a high and forcible Hand, protect and keep away Delinquents; not permitting them to make their Appearance, to answer such Affronts and Injuries as have been by them offered unto the Parliament: And those Messengers which have been sent from the Houses for them, have been abused, beaten, and imprisoned; so as the Orders of Parliament, which is the highest Court of Justice in this Realm, are not obeyed; and the Authority of it is altogether scorned and vilified; and such Persons as stand well affected to it, and declare themselves sensible of these publick Calamities, and of the Violations of the Privilege of Parliament, and common Liberty of the Subject, are baffled and injured by several Sorts of malignant Men, who are about the King; some whereof, under the Name of Cavaliers, without having Respect to the Laws of the Land, or any Fear either of God or Man, are ready to commit all Manner of Outrage and Violence; which must needs tend to the Dissolution of this Government, the Destroying of Religion, Laws, Liberty, and Property; all which will be exposed to the Malice and Violence of such desperate Persons as must be employed in so horrid and unnatural an Act, as the Overthrowing of a Parliament by Force, which is the Support and Preservation of them all: Which being duly considered by the Lords and Commons, and how great an Obligation lies upon them, in Honour, Conscience, and Duty, according to the high Trust reposed in them, to use all possible Means, in such Cases, for the timely Prevention of so great and irrecoverable Evils, they have thought fit to publish their Sense and Approbation of this imminent Danger; thereby to excite all well-affected Persons, to contribute their best Assistance, according to their solemn Vow and Protestation, to the Preparations necessary for the Opposing and Suppressing of the traiterous Attempts of these wicked and malignant Coun-

1. *CJ*, II, 618–19 (10 June 1642).

sellors, who seek to engage the King in so dangerous and destructive an Enter-prize, and the whole Kingdom in a Civil War, and destroy the Privileges and Being of Parliaments; This Recourse to the good Affections of those that tender their Religion, and just Liberties, and the Enjoyments of the blessed Fruits of this present Parliament, which were almost ready to be reaped, and are now as ready to be ruined by those wicked Hands, being the only Remedy left them under God, and without which they are no longer able to preserve themselves, or those by whom they are intrusted.

1. They the said Lords and Commons do Declare, That whosoever shall bring in any Proportion of ready Money or Plate, or shall underwrite to furnish and maintain any Number of Horse, Horsemen, and Arms, for the Preservation of the publick Peace, and for the Defence of the King, and both Houses of Parliament, from Force and Violence, and to uphold the Power and Privileges of Parliament according to his Protestation, it shall be held a good and accept-able Service to the Commonwealth, and a Testimony of his good Affection to the Protestant Religion, the Laws, Liberties, and Peace of this Kingdom, and to the Parliament and Privileges thereof.

And, because a considerable Aid cannot be raised by few Hands, and the Condition of all Mens Estates and Occasions is not always proportionable to their Affection, the Lords and Commons do Declare, That no Man's Affection shall be measured according to the Proportion of his Offer, so that he express his good Will to this Service in any Proportion whatsoever.

2. And it is further Declared, by the Lords and Commons in Parliament, that whosoever shall bring in any Money or Plate, or shall furnish or maintain any Horse, Horsemen, and Arms, for the Purposes aforesaid, shall have their Money repaid with the Interest, according to Eight Pounds per Cent. and the full Value of their Plate, with Consideration for the Fashion, not exceeding One Shilling per Ounce; and shall have full Recompence for all their Charge, in Finding, Furnishing, and Maintaining of Horse, Horsemen, and Arms: And for this both Houses of Parliament do engage the Publick Faith.

3. And it is Ordained, That Sir John Wollaston, Knight and Alderman, Alderman Towse, Alderman Warner, and Alderman Andrews, shall be the Treasurers to receive all such Monies and Plate as shall be brought in for the Purposes aforesaid: And that Acquittances of them, or any Two of them, for the Receipt of the same, shall be a sufficient Ground for the Party so lending Money or Plate, to demand the same again, with the Interest, and likewise Consideration for the Fashion of the Plate.

4. It is Ordered, That [*blank*] shall be Commissaries, to value the Horse and Arms that shall be furnished for this Service; and that a Signification under the Hand of them, or any Two of them, of such Values of Horse and Arms, and of the time when they were first brought in, shall be a Warrant to demand Satisfac-

tion, according to the said Values: And they shall keep an Account of the Time, from the first Inrollment of any such Horse and Horsemen, that such as find and maintain them, may be repaid, according to the Rate of Two Shillings and Sixpence per Diem, for so long time as they have maintained them in this Service: And the Commissioners are to attend at Guildhall, for the Receiving and Inrolling of such Numbers of Horse, as shall be brought in.

5. It is Ordered, That whosoever shall bring in Money, or Plate, or shall provide and maintain Horse, Horsemen, and Arms, for this Service, shall do according to their Duty therein: And the Lords and Commons do engage the Power and Authority of Parliament to save them harmless from all Prejudice and Inconvenience that may befal them by Occasion thereof.

6. It is Ordered, That the Members of either House who are present, shall be desired to declare in their Houses respectively, what Money or Plate they will bring in, or what Horse, Horsemen, and Arms, they will find and maintain.

7. It is desired, That all such as have their Residence in or about London, or within Eighty Miles, will bring in their Money, Plate, or Horse, within a Fortnight after Notice; and they that dwell further off within Three Weeks.

8. And, because every Person may not be provided with present Money, or with Horse, or not have his Plate with him, which he means to bring in; and yet resolves to contribute his Part within the Time limited; and that it is necessary it should be presently known what the Provision will be for the Effecting of this great and important Service; It is Ordered, That the Committees of either House appointed for that Purpose, respectively, shall receive the Subscriptions of such Member of each House, as have not declared themselves in the House, or are absent upon the publick Service, or for their private Occasions. 2. That the Committee of London, intrusted with the Militia, shall receive the Subscriptions in London and Middlesex. 3. That some Persons nominated by the Knights and Burgesses of each County, and approved by both Houses, shall be appointed to receive the Subscriptions in the several Counties.

9. And lastly, it is Declared, That whatsoever is brought in, shall not at all be employed upon any other Occasion, than to the Purposes aforesaid; which are, to maintain the Protestant Religion, the King's Authority, and his Person in his Royal Dignity, the free Course of Justice, the Laws of the Land, the Peace of the Kingdom, and the Privilege of Parliament, against any Force which shall oppose them; and this by the Direction of both Houses of Parliament.

APPENDIX F

[f. 61v] Book of the Names of the Members of the House of Commons
That Advance Horse, Money, and Plate for Defense of the
Parliament, June the 10th, 11th, etc., 1642[1]

[f. 51r]   *Veneris, x° Junii 1642*

Sir John Evelyn, Jr.	[Ludgershall, Wilts]	will bring in four horses, two hundred pounds in present money.
Mr. [Walter] Long	[Ludgershall, Wilts]	four horses, 2 hundred pounds in plate or money.
Sir Peter Wentworth	[Tamworth, Staffs]	three horses, hundred pounds in present money.
Mr. [Thomas] Tomkins [R][2]	[Weobley, Herefs]	two horses freely at his own charge.
Mr. Arthur Goodwin	[Buckinghamshire]	one hundred pounds in ready money and will maintain four horses at his own charge.
Mr. William Strode	[Bere Alston, Devon]	will maintain two horses at his own charge and will bring in fifty pounds and some plate.
Mr. [Denzil] Holles	[Dorchester, Dorset]	will bring in three hundred pounds and maintain four horses and set them forth in buff coats and p/
Sir Samuel Rolle	[Devonshire]	will maintain the pay of twelve horses.
Mr. [Benjamin] Valentine	[St. Germans, Cornwall]	will bring in and maintain 2 horses.
Mr. [Henry] Marten	[Berkshire]	will bring in and maintain six horses at his own charge.
Mr. Serjeant [John] Wilde	[Worcestershire]	will bring in and maintain two horses at his own charge.
Sir John Northcote	[Ashburton, Devon]	will bring in two horses and men presently and

466

[f. 53r] Sir Gilbert Gerard	[Middlesex]	four more so soon as he can have them out of the country and a hundred pounds in mone[y].
		will bring in four horses and maintain them at his own charge.
Sir John Franklin	[Middlesex]	will do the like.
Mr. [John] Hampden	[Buckinghamshire]	will bring in two hundred pounds in plate and bring in and maintain three horses.
Mr. [John] Crew	[Brackley, Northants]	will bring in two hundred pounds in plate and maintain four horses.
Mr. [William] Pierrepont	[Much Wenlock, Salop]	will bring in and maintain two horses and bring in an hundred pounds in money or plate.
Mr. [John] Pym	[Tavistock, Devon]	will bring in and maintain two horses and one hundred pounds either in plate or moneys.
Mr. Nathaniel Fiennes	[Banbury, Oxon]	will find one horse and bring in an hundred pounds in money.
Sir Robert Pye	[Woodstock, Oxon]	will bring in and maintain 4 horses and lay down, either in money or plate, two hundred pounds.
Mr. Henry Darley	[Northallerton, Yorks]	will bring in two hundred pounds.
Sir Robert Cooke	[Tewkesbury, Glos]	will bring in and maintain two horses and bring in one hundred pounds in money or plate. He offers the like for Sir Samuel Luke [Bedford, Beds].
Sir Benjamin Rudyard	[Wilton, Wilts]	an hundred pounds freely without interest for defense of king, kingdom, and parliament conjunctively.
[f. 54r] Sir Francis Knollys, Sr.	[Reading, Berks]	will bring in and maintain two horses for himself and two for his son [Sir Francis Knollys, Jr., Reading, Berks].

(continued)

Mr. [John] Browne	of Dorset	will bring in and maintain one horse and bring in an hundred pounds.
Sir William Brereton	[Cheshire]	will bring in four horses and send them up as speedily as he can and bring in an hundred pounds in ready money or plate.
Mr. John Ashe	[Westbury, Wilts]	will contribute weekly ten pounds towards the maintaining of horse so long as the service shall continue.
Mr. Edward Ashe	[Heytesbury, Wilts]	will bring in four horses and maintain them at his own charge and, if there be occasion to march, will have five hundred pounds ready at an hour's warning for the service.
Sir William Lytton	[Hertfordshire]	will bring in two horses and an hundred pounds.
Mr. [Richard] Winwood	[New Windsor, Berks]	will bring in six horse and six more if there be need.
Mr. [Valentine] Walton	[Huntingdonshire]	will bring in two horse and an hundred pounds in money.
Sir Nathaniel Barnardiston	[Suffolk]	will bring in two horse and continue the five hundred pounds he has formerly lent.
Sir Thomas Dacres	[Hertfordshire]	will bring in two horses and, either in money or plate, two hundred pounds.
Sir Edmund Fowell	[Ashburton, Devon]	will bring in two horses for king, kingdom, and parliament conjunctively.
Mr. [William] Heveningham	[Stockbridge, Hants]	will bring in three horses and one hundred pounds in plate or money.
Mr. [Anthony] Nicoll	[Bodmin, Cornwall]	will bring in two horses.

Alderman [Isaac] Penington	[London, Middx]	will bring two hundred pounds in money.
[f. 55r] Sir John Harrison [R]	[Lancaster, Lancs]	will bring in four horses for himself and his son [William Harrison (R), Queenborough, Kent].
Sir Edmund Moundeford	[Norfolk]	will bring in two horses and maintain them.
Sir Harbottle Grimston	[Harwich, Essex]	will bring in an horse and will give twenty pounds freely.
Mr. [John] Rolle	[Truro, Cornwall]	will bring in an hundred pounds.
Sir Roger North	[Eye, Suffolk]	will bring in, in plate, an hundred pounds and give it freely to this service.
Sir Thomas Wodehouse	[Thetford, Norfolk]	will bring in two horses and two hundred pounds in plate or money.
Sir Edward Hungerford	[Chippenham, Wilts]	will bring in 6 horses.
Sir Dudley North	[Cambridgeshire]	will freely give 60 pounds.
Sir Richard Buller	[Fowey, Cornwall]	will bring in three horses for himself and his son, Francis Buller [East Looe, Cornwall].
Mr. Richard Trev[?]³	of Plymouth [Devon]	will the next week pay in five hundred pounds lent by the town and five hundred pounds more which he lends to this service. Sir Richard Buller is appointed to return him thanks.
Mr. [John] Glyn	[Westminster, Middx]	will maintain an horse and bring in an hundred pounds in money or plate.
Sir William Drake	[Amersham, Bucks]	will maintain two horses and bring in two hundred pounds in money or plate for the king and parliament conjunctively.
Mr. [Francis] Drake	[Amersham, Bucks]	will bring in an hundred pound in plate and have in readiness an horse.
Mr. Speaker [William Lenthall]	[Woodstock, Oxon]	will maintain an horse and give fifty pounds in money or plate.

(continued)

469

[f. 56r] Mr. [Robert] Jenner	[Cricklade, Wilts]	will maintain two horses so long as this/
Sir Richard Onslow	[Surrey]	will maintain four horses for himself and his son [Arthur Onslow, Bramber, Sussex].
Sir Samuel Owfield	[Gatton, Surrey]	will maintain four horses and do more if occasion shall be.
Mr. Henry Pelham	[Grantham, Lincs]	will bring an hundred pounds.
Mr. [Bulstrode] Whitelocke	[Marlow, Bucks]	will maintain two horses.
Mr. [Samuel] Vassall	[London, Middx]	will maintain one horse and, if occasion be, two more.
Mr. [John] Venn	[London, Middx]	will bring in an hundred pounds in money and will have a horse ready for himself to serve always upon.
Sir Henry Heyman	[Hythe, Cinque Port]	will bring in an hundred pounds in plate or money and two horses for defense of the king, kingdom, and privileges of parliament and liberties of the subject.
Mr. [Nathaniel] Stephens	[Gloucestershire]	will furnish two horses completely.
Mr. Robert Goodwin	[East Grinstead, Sussex]	will bring in one horse and fifty pounds in money or plate.
Mr. John Goodwin	[Haslemere, Surrey]	will bring in one horse and fifty pounds in plate or money.
Sir Gilbert Pickering	[Northamptonshire]	will bring in four horses and one hundred and fifty pounds in money or plate.
Mr. [Richard] Browne	of Kent [New Romney, Cinque Port]	will bring in an hundred pounds in money or plate.
Captain [Augustine] Skinner	[Kent]	will bring in two horses.

470

Sir Thomas Walsingham	[Rochester, Kent]	will bring in an hundred pounds in money or plate and have two horses always ready at four and twenty hours' warning.
Sir Robert Harley	[Herefordshire]	will furnish two horses.
Mr. [Thomas] Pury	[Gloucester, Glos]	will furnish one horse.
[f. 57r] Mr. [Giles] Green	[Corfe Castle, Dorset]	will furnish one horse and bring in fifty pounds in plate or money.
Sir Edward Boys	[Dover, Cinque Port]	will furnish two horses where there shall be occasion and bring in fifty pounds in plate or money.
Mr. [Edmund] Prideaux	[Lyme Regis, Dorset]	will bring in an hundred pounds.
Mr. [Henry] Lucas	[Cambridge University]	will bring in fifty pounds in money and one horse.
Mr. [George] Peard	[Barnstaple, Devon]	will bring in an hundred pounds and expect no interest.
Mr. [Alexander] Rigby	[Wigan, Lancs]	will send up one horse completely furnished if his county be in peace nine days after he comes down.
Mr. [Edward] Bagshaw [R]	[Southwark, Surrey]	will bring in fifty pounds and expect no interest for the preservation of the king and parliament according to his Protestation, Oath of Supremacy and Allegiance, conjunctively and not divided and in no other manner.
Mr. [Robert] Reynolds	[Hindon, Wilts]	will furnish out two horses and bring in an hundred pounds in plate.
Mr. [Richard] Knightley	[Northampton, Northants]	will bring in an hundred pounds in money and furnish two horses.
Mr. [Thomas] Grantham	[Lincoln, Lincs]	will furnish out two horses.
Sir John Meyrick	[Newcastle-under-Lyme, Staffs]	will furnish two horses.
Mr. [Michael] Oldisworth	[Salisbury, Wilts]	will subscribe fifty pounds and furnish an horse.

(continued)

Mr. [Walter] Kyrle	[Leominster, Herefs]	will furnish one horse.
Mr. [Oliver] Cromwell	[Cambridge, Cambs]	will bring in five hundred pounds.
Mr. [Ralph] Ashton	[Clitheroe, Lancs]	will bring in two horses.
Mr. John Moore	[Liverpool, Lancs]	will bring in two horse.
Sir Beauchamp St. John	[Bedford, Beds]	will bring in two horses.
Mr. [Zouch] Tate	[Northampton, Northants]	will bring in two horses and maintain them.
Mr. [Peregrine] Hoby	[Marlow, Bucks]	will find two horses.
Sir John Holland	[Castle Rising, Norfolk]	will bring in two horses ready furnished and an hundred pounds in money or plate for maintenance of the true Protestant religion, the defense of the king's person, his royal authority and dignity, our laws, liberties, and privileges conjunctive[ly].
[f. 58r] Mr. Samuel Browne	[Dartmouth, Devon]	will bring in an hundred pounds.
Sir Thomas Soame	[London, Middx]	will bring in two horses completely furnished.
Sir Edward Master	[Canterbury, Kent]	will bring in an hundred pound presently and an hundred pounds a month hence.
Mr. Thomas Moore	[Heytesbury, Wilts]	will furnish two horses.
Mr. Cornelius Holland	[New Windsor, Berks]	will furnish two horses.
Mr. [John] White	[Southwark, Surrey]	will bring in an hundred pounds and expect no interest.
Mr. Lawrence Whitaker	[Okehampton, Devon]	will freely give twenty pounds.
Mr. [Roger] Matthew [R]	[Dartmouth, Devon]	will find one horse and furnish fifty pounds in plate or money.
Mr. [John] Downes	[Arundel, Sussex]	will bring in fifty pounds.
Mr. [Gilbert] Millington	[Nottingham, Notts]	will for the present bring in fifty pounds.

472

Mr. [Michael] Noble	[Lichfield, Staffs]	will bring in one hundred pounds.
Mr. Henry Herbert	[Monmouthshire]	will furnish one horse.
Mr. Edward Montagu	[Huntingdon, Hunts]	will bring in an hundred pounds in plate or money for defense of the king and parliament conjunctively and not divided.
Mr. Thomas Lane[4]	[Chipping Wycombe, Bucks]	will furnish one horse.
Mr. [Thomas] Fountain	[Wendover, Bucks]	will bring in one horse.
Mr. [John] Harris	[Launceston, Cornwall]	will give fifty pounds
Mr. George Buller	[Saltash, Cornwall]	will furnish one horse.
Mr. Thomas Arundell	[West Looe, Cornwall]	will furnish one horse.
Mr. Richard Barwis	[Carlisle, Cumb]	will furnish fifty pounds.
Sir John Hippisley	[Cockermouth, Cumb]	will completely furnish three horses. [5]
Sir John Curzon	[Derbyshire]	will furnish two horses.
Sir John Yonge	[Plymouth, Devon]	will furnish with a free loan of two hundred pounds.
Mr. [Richard] Ferris [R]	[Barnstaple, Devon]	will lend fifty pounds freely.
Mr. [Edward] Thomas	[Okehampton, Devon]	will lend fifty pounds freely.
Mr. [William] Constantine [R]	[Poole, Dorset]	will furnish one horse.
[f. 59r] Sir Walter Erle	[Weymouth and Melcombe Regis, Dorset]	will furnish four horses for himself and his son [Thomas Erle, Wareham, Dorset].
Mr. Roger Hill	[Bridport, Dorset]	will bring in an hundred pounds. [6]
Mr. [William] Ellis	[Boston, Lincs]	will bring in an hundred pounds.
Mr. [William] Ashurst	[Newton, Lancs]	will bring in one horse.
Mr. Ralph Ashton	[Lancashire]	will bring in two hundred and fifty pounds.
Mr. [Richard] Harman	[Norwich, Norfolk]	will bring in one horse.
Mr. [Miles] Corbet	[Great Yarmouth, Norfolk]	will bring in fifty pounds.
Mr. [Edward] Owner	[Great Yarmouth, Norfolk]	will lend fifty pounds freely.
Sir John Fenwick	[Northumberland]	will furnish two horses.

(continued)

473

Mr. [John] Blakiston	[Newcastle-on-Tyne, Northumb]	will bring in fifty pounds.
Mr. Thomas Sandys	[Gatton, Surrey]	will bring in an horse.
Mr. [William] Spurstow	[Shrewsbury, Salop]	will bring in two hundred pounds.
Sir Peter Wroth	[Bridgwater, Somerset]	will furnish an horse.
Mr. [Robert] Hunt [R]	[Ilchester, Somerset]	will furnish one horse.
Mr. Henry Shelley	[Lewes, Sussex]	will bring in fifty pounds.
Mr. Robert Nicholas	[Devizes, Wilts]	will give twenty pounds freely.
Mr. John Franklin	[Marlborough, Wilts]	will bring in fifty pounds.
Mr. [Humphrey] Salway	[Worcestershire]	will bring in and maintain one horse.
Serjeant [Richard] Cresheld	[Evesham, Worcs]	will bring in one hundred pounds.
Mr. [John] Barker	[Coventry, Warks]	will bring in fifty pounds.
Mr. [Godfrey] Bosvile	[Warwick, Warks]	will either bring in one horse or an hundred pounds.
Mr. William Thomas [R]	[Caernarvon, Caern]	will bring in one horse.
Mr. John Wogan	[Pembrokeshire]	will send in one horse well furnished.
Sir Hugh Owen	[Pembroke, Pemb]	will find two horses.
Mr. [John] Lowry	[Cambridge, Cambs]	will find a horse ready furnished.

Sabbathi, xi° Junii 1642

Sir Henry Ludlow	[Wiltshire]	will find three horses ready furnished and, if occasion be, three more.
Sir Henry Vane, [Jr.][7]	[Hull, Yorks]	will find two horses ready furnished and maintain them.
Mr. [Richard] Lee	[Rochester, Kent]	will find one horse ready furnished and maintain it.
[f. 59v] Mr. [George] Searle	[Taunton, Somerset]	will presently bring in 50£.
Mr. [Nathaniel] Hallowes	[Derby, Derbs]	will presently bring in 50£.
Mr. [Edward] Dowse	[Portsmouth, Hants]	will presently bring in 50£.

474

Mr. [John] Percival and Mr. [Thomas] Toll	[King's Lynn, Norfolk]	will presently bring in 50£ apiece.
Colonel [George] Goring [R]	[Portsmouth, Hants]	will (as soon as his month's pay, due to him as governor of Portsmouth, comes in) express what he will do in this service to which he hath so much affection.
Mr. [Richard] Shuttleworth	[Preston, Lancs]	will bring in 100£ for himself and his son [Richard Shuttleworth, Clitheroe, Lancs].
Sir Robert Crane	[Sudbury, Suffolk]	will bring in 4 horses for the defense of king and parliament not divided.
Mr. [John] Gurdon	[Ipswich, Suffolk]	will lend 100£ freely.
Mr. Philip Smith	[Marlborough, Wilts]	will lend 40£ freely.

Luna, xiii° Junii

Sir Neville Poole[8]	[Malmesbury, Wilts]	undertakes to bring in four horses for himself and his son [Edward Poole, Wootton Bassett, Wilts].
Sir John Finch	[Winchelsea, Cinque Port]	undertakes to bring in two horses.
Sir Ambrose Browne	[Surrey]	will find two horses well furnished.
Mr. [William] Hay	[Rye, Cinque Port]	will bring in 100£ toward this service to be lent freely.
Mr. George Lowe [R]	of Colne [Wilts]	will bring in 100£.
Mr. [Framlingham] Gawdy	[Thetford, Norfolk]	will lend fifty pounds freely.
Sir John Price [R]	[Montgomeryshire]	will bring in two horses, having convenient time given.
Mr. [Thomas] Hodges	[Cricklade, Wilts]	will bring in two horses or one horse and fifty pounds.
Sir Francis Barnham	[Maidstone, Kent]	will lend an hundred pounds freely.
[f. 60r] Sir William Waller	[Andover, Hants]	will find 4 horse and bring in 100£.

(*continued*)

Mr. [John] Trenchard	[Wareham, Dorset]	will find one horse.
Sir Roger Burgoyne	[Bedfordshire]	will find two horses.
Sir Thomas Barrington[9]	[Colchester, Essex]	will underwrite for 4 horses and bring in 500£.
Sir William Masham	[Essex]	will bring in 4 horses.
Sir Martin Lumley	[Essex]	the like.
Mr. Herbert Morley	[Lewes, Sussex]	two horses.
Mr. [Walter] Yonge	[Honiton, Devon]	100£.
Mr. [Henry] Tulse	[Christchurch, Hants]	will give freely 20£.
Mr. [Anthony] Stapley	[Sussex]	2 horses.
Mr. [Alexander] Bence	[Aldeburgh, Suffolk]	1 horse.
Captain [Squire] Bence	[Aldeburgh, Suffolk]	50£.
Mr. [James] Fiennes, Sr.	[Oxfordshire]	2 horse.
Sir Christopher Yelverton	[Bossiney, Cornwall]	4 horse, 200£.[10]
Sir John Evelyn	[Blechingley, Surrey]	2 horse.
Mr. [Anthony] Hungerford [R]	[Malmesbury, Wilts]	2 horse.
Sir William Playters	[Orford, Suffolk]	2 horse.
Sir Thomas Jervoise	[Whitchurch, Hants]	2 horse.
Sir Henry Wallop [and]	[Hampshire]	8 horse.
Mr. [Robert] Wallop	[Andover, Hants]	
Mr. [Richard] Whitehead	[Hampshire]	2 horse.
Mr. [Henry] Campion	[Lymington, Hants]	1 horse.
Sir John Potts	[Norfolk]	100£.
Mr. [John] George [R]	[Cirencester, Glos]	1 horse.
Mr. [Edmund] Dunch	[Wallingford, Berks]	4 horse.

Additional List of Pledges: 14 June–31 December 1642

Date	Name	Constituency	Pledge	Source CJ, II
Je 20	Henry Darley (Je 10)[11]	Northallerton, Yorks	* 4 horses	D'Ewes[12]
Jl 22	Thomas Moore (Je 10)	Heytesbury, Wilts	* £100	685
Sp 7	Sir William Morley [R][13]	Chichester, Sussex	6 horses, £200	757
	Thomas Eden	Cambridge University	£200	757
12	Thomas Hanham [R]	Minehead, Somerset	£50	762
14	Sir William Morley (Sp 7)	Chichester, Sussex	* £400, 2 horses	765
16	Hall Ravenscroft	Horsham, Sussex	£50	769
	John Waddon	Plymouth, Devon	200 oz. of plate	769
19	Sir William Ogle [R]	Winchester, Hants	£100	772
	Sir Thomas Hutchinson	Nottinghamshire	£100 in money or plate	772
	Sir John Wray	Lincolnshire	£100, 200 marks in plate	772
	Sir William Strickland	Hedon, Yorks	£100 instead of 4 horses[14]	772
	Sir Edward Partridge	Sandwich, Cinque Port	£50 in plate	772
	Sir John Leigh	Yarmouth, I. of W.	£50	772
	Dennis Bond	Dorchester, Dorset	£100	772
	John Dutton [R]	Gloucestershire	10 or 20 horses	772
	Sir Thomas Bowyer [R]	Bramber, Sussex	£50 in money or plate	772
	Sir George Stonehouse [R]	Abingdon, Berks	4 horses	772
	John Fettiplace [R]	Berkshire	4 horses	772
	Squire Bence (Je 13)	Aldeburgh, Suffolk	# £50	772
	Sir Edward Ayscough[15]	Lincolnshire	money and horses	772

(continued)

APPENDIX F (*Continued*)

Date	Name	Constituency	Pledge	Source CJ, II
	Sir William Armine	Grantham, Lincs	money and horses, all his plate	772
	Sir Christopher Wray	Grimsby, Lincs	money and horses	772
	Thomas Hatcher	Stamford, Lincs	money and horses	772
	John Broxholme	Lincoln, Lincs	money and horses	772
	Sir Anthony Irby	Boston, Lincs	money and horses	772
	Henry Brett [R]	Gloucester, Glos	£50 in money or plate	772
	Sir Robert Harley (Je 10)	Herefordshire	# £500 in plate	772
	John Nash	Worcester, Worcs	£40	772
	Robert Scawen	Berwick, Northumb	£30 in money or plate	772
	William Smith [R]	Winchelsea, Cinque Port	will pledge at committee	772
	Richard More	Bishop's Castle, Salop	£120 in plate	772, 774
20	Sir Thomas Cheeke	Harwich, Essex	3 horses, £200 in money or plate	774
26	Sir Poynings Moore	Haslemere, Surrey	2 horses	783
	Sir John Bampfield	Penryn, Cornwall	£100	783
	Sir Norton Knatchbull	New Romney, Cinque Port	£100 in plate	783
	Sir Alexander Denton [R]	Buckingham, Bucks	2 horses	783
	John Alford	Shoreham, Sussex	£100	783
	William Jesson	Coventry, Warks	100 marks	783
	Sir Peter Wroth (Je 10)	Bridgwater, Somerset	* £50	783
27	Sir John Meux [R]	Newtown, I. of W.	2 horses	784
29	Sir Henry Worsley	Newport, I. of W.	£100 in money or plate	787
	Sir Thomas Pelham	Sussex	£200	787
	Sir Guy Palmes [R]	Rutland	4 horses	787

Oc 4	Thomas Leedes [R]	Steyning, Sussex	£50	792
	Thomas Heblethwaite [R]	New Malton, Yorks	£40	792
8	Sir John Harrison (Je 10)	Lancaster, Lancs	* £200	801
8	Sir John Evelyn (Je 13)	Blechingley, Surrey	# £200	801
10	Sir Thomas Eversfield [R]	Hastings, Cinque Port	£100	802
11	Sir Simonds D'Ewes	Sudbury, Suffolk	£100	803
13	John Taylor [R]	Bristol, Glos	£50	806
15	Thomas Middleton	Horsham, Sussex	£50	810
25	Sir John Evelyn (Oc 8)	Blechingley, Surrey	# £100	822
29	Edmund Waller [R]	St. Ives, Cornwall	£250	827
Nv 2	John Maynard	Totnes, Devon	£40	832
8	Sir John Coke	Derbyshire	2 horses	840
Dc 12	William Allestry [R]	Derby, Derbs	£50	884
26	Sir Thomas Jermyn [R][16]	Bury St. Edmunds, Suffolk	100 marks	902

1. This list is preserved in the Bodleian Library, Oxford, Tanner MS 63. Several corrections have been made to the list as "faithfully transcribed from an original (MS.) parliamentary minute-book of the period" by F. Kyffin Lenthall in *Notes and Queries*, 1st series, 12 (1855): 337–38, 358–60. The handwriting in the MS appears to be that of Henry Elsynge, occasionally interpersed with John Rushworth's hand.

The editors have followed their usual practice of modernization, including spelling out abbreviated first names. In addition, first names and constituencies not appearing in the MS have been supplied in brackets. Where identification of MPs with similar names has been difficult, the editors have relied on M. F. Keeler's *The Long Parliament*. This volume has also been useful in correcting several errors in the *N and Q* article. Of the 193 pledgers fourteen were present or potential royalists [R] according to the classification in Brunton and Pennington, *Members*, pp. 225–45.

3. This name is puzzling as well as illegible. It is rendered as "Trench" in *N and Q*, 1st series, 12: 358. However, there was no MP by that name in June 1642. The MPs for Plymouth were John Waddon and Sir John Yonge. The latter had replaced Sir Robert Trelawney, who had been disabled in March.

4. From this point until the end of the day, the house was called alphabetically by counties. See 10 June, n. 9.

5. Crossed out in MS: *so long as he continue.*

6. Crossed out in MS: *Mr. St. John. Mr. Wingate.*

7. Probably Vane, Jr., for by June 1642 his father was taking a less active role.

8. The pledges of Poole, Hay, Gawdy, Price, and Hodges which follow appear also in brief notes of committee proceedings dated 11 June. See HMC, *Fifth Report*, p. 28. At the committee two MPs refused to pledge:

(continued)

Mr. Shughburgh declared that he hath horses in readiness to defend the King, the Commonwealth, the laws, and the Parliament. Noted, Nihil. Sir Nicholas Slanning, that when the King and both Houses of Parliament shall command it he shall be ready to serve them with his life and fortune, till then he desires not to intermeddle. Noted, Nihil.

9. The pledges of Barrington and Masham which follow are recorded on 17 June in D'Ewes.
10. It is not clear from the MS whether £200 was part of Yelverton's pledge.
11. The date following a few names indicates an earlier pledge to which the MP made an alteration [*] or an addition [#].
12. This change appears in D'Ewes but not in *CJ*.
13. This list contains forty-nine new pledgers, of whom nineteen were royalists [R] according to the classification in Brunton and Pennington.
14. However, the earlier pledge was not recorded.
15. Ayscough and the following five MPs pledged in Lincolnshire while serving as members of the parliamentary committee there.
16. The small number of pledges in November and December may perhaps be accounted for by the fact that the house was already proposing a new program of taxation.

480

APPENDIX G

Members of Parliament Absent without Leave[1]
16 June 1642

Aldborough, Richard
  Aldborough, Yorks
Alford, Sir Edward
  Arundel, Sussex
Anderson, Sir Henry
  Newcastle-on-Tyne, Northumb
Arundell, John
  Bodmin, Cornwall
Ashburnham, John
  Hastings, Cinque Port
Belasyse, Henry
  Yorkshire
Belayse, John
  Thirsk, Yorks
Bridgeman, Orlando
  Wigan, Lancs
Cary, Lucius, Viscount Falkland
  Newport, I. of W.
Cave, Sir Richard
  Lichfield, Staffs
Cavendish, Charles, Viscount Mansfield
  East Retford, Notts
Chicheley, Thomas
  Cambridgeshire
Colepeper, Sir John
  Kent
Fanshawe, Sir Thomas
  Hertford, Herts
Gerard, Francis
  Seaford, Cinque Port
Grenville, Sir Bevil
  Cornwall
Griffith, John
  Caernarvonshire
Harding, Richard
  Great Bedwin, Wilts

Hartnoll, George
  Tiverton, Devon
Hatton, Sir Christopher
  Higham Ferrers, Northants
Heblethwaite, Thomas
  New Malton, Yorks
Herbert, William
  Cardiff, Glam, or Monmouthshire
Holborne, Robert
  Mitchell, Cornwall
Holles, Gervase
  Grimsby, Lincs
Hopton, Sir Ralph
  Wells, Somerset
Howard, Thomas
  Wallingford, Berks
Hyde, Edward
  Saltash, Cornwall
Ingram, Sir Thomas
  Thirsk, Yorks
Jane, Joseph
  Liskeard, Cornwall
Jermyn, Thomas
  Bury St. Edmunds, Suffolk
Kirton, Edward
  Milborne Port, Somerset
Leigh, Sir John
  Yarmouth, I. of W.
Mallory, Sir John
  Ripon, Yorks
Pakington, Sir John
  Aylesbury, Bucks
Pennyman, Sir William
  Richmond, Yorks
Porter, Endymion
  Droitwich, Worcs

Price, Herbert
  Brecon, Brec
Rashleigh, Jonathan
  Fowey, Cornwall
Rose, Richard[2]
  Lyme Regis, Dorset
Savile, Sir William
  Old Sarum, Wilts
Slingsby, Sir Henry
  Knaresborough, Yorks

Strickland, Sir Robert
  Aldborough, Yorks
Trevanion, John
  Lostwithiel, Cornwall
Turner, Samuel
  Shaftesbury, Dorset
Warwick, Philip
  Radnor, Rad

Absentees subsequently excused:

16 June	Temple, Sir Peter	*CJ*, II, 628
	Buckingham, Bucks	
	Mauleverer, Sir Thomas	
	Boroughbridge, Yorks	
30 June	Erisey, Richard	*CJ*, II, 644
	St. Mawes, Cornwall	
	Godolphin[3]	
	Helston or St. Ives, Cornwall	
	Manaton, Ambrose	
	Launceston, Cornwall	
12 July	Hele, Sir Thomas	*CJ*, II, 666
	Plympton, Devon	

---

1. The following list of MPs appears in *CJ*, II, 626. It is preceded by the notation: "*Die Jovis 16° Junii* 1642. The House called; and those Members underwritten were absent." Spelling has been modernized, the list alphabetized, and a few first names plus all constituencies have been added. Most of the absentees were royalists according to the classification in Brunton and Pennington, *Members*, pp. 225–45.

2. Since Rose had been given leave on 1 June "to go into the Country," it is possible that this name should be Richard Rogers of Dorset. On 22 July both men were summoned by the house. *CJ*, II, 597, 685.

3. It is not possible to tell which of the Godolphins who sat for Cornwall was excused: Francis (St. Ives), Francis (Helston), or Sidney (Helston).

APPENDIX H

The Commission of Array
5 H. IV, nn. 24, 25[1]

Also, touching the Commission of Array: there were many forfeitures and other different clauses and words contained within it which were grievous, damaging, and perilous, for the commissioners named in the commissions to different shires of England. Therefore, a copy was delivered to the said commons, for their consideration concerning it, and in order that they might correct it according to their intent.

The same commons have had deliberation and consideration on this matter, and caused certain clauses and words contained in the Commission to be cancelled. And they pray the king that in future no Commission of Array should issue otherwise, and in no other words, than is contained in the said copy. . . .

Which prayer our lord the king, with the advice of the lords, and having on this matter communication with the judges of the realm, most graciously heard in parliament. The tenor of this copy follows in these words:

The king to his beloved and faithful Thomas Sackvill [and a long list of names] and to our sheriff of Buckingham, greeting.

Know that when certain enemies of ours have now recently entered our realm of England in hostile manner, with no small power, notwithstanding the present truces, and would have burned in various parts of the same realm.

Wishing to dispose and ordain, as we are bound to do, so that we may, by the favour of divine grace resist the malice of these invaders, if they shall presume to invade our kingdom again, *quod absit,* and for the salvation and defence of us and of our realm aforesaid and of our lieges:

We have assigned you, singly and collectively, to array and inspect all and singular men at arms, and armed men, and archers who reside in the said shire, within liberties and outside. And you are to cause to be armed all those who are able in body and fit to be armed; those who have of their own possession the means whereby they can arm themselves, that is to say, each one of them according to his estate and ability. And you are to assign and apportion them according to your advisement and discretion.

---

1. *RP,* III, 526–27. The English translation, used by permission, is from B. Wilkinson, *Constitutional History of England in the Fifteenth Century (1399–1485)* (New York, 1964), pp. 366–67.

And also, you are to distrain all those who are able in lands and goods, but are unable on account of debility of body to bear the physical burden, to find arms for the men-at-arms and armed men, and bows and arrows, to the extent to which they can reasonably bear, according to their estate. So that those who shall remain, or can be kept, in their own homes, in their own districts, for the defence of the same against our enemies if danger shall arise, shall not receive wages or expenses for their stay at their own homes.

And you are to cause the said men-at-arms and armed men and archers thus arrayed and armed to be placed and held continuously in array, in thousands, hundreds, and scores, or otherwise as shall be convenient and necessary.

And you are to command them, and direct them to the sea coast, or to any other place where there shall be need (and as often as there shall be) in order to expel, defeat and destroy our said enemies, from time to time when any danger threatens.

And you are diligently to make and survey, from time to time, whenever there is need, muster or parade of those men-at-arms and armed men and archers. And also you are to proclaim, ordain, and diligently examine, to see that all and singular of the men-at-arms, armed men, and archers, should appear armed in the muster of their own kind of equipment and not in a different kind, under penalty of loss of the same; excepting however those who ought to be armed, as aforesaid, at the expense of others.

And all and singular whom you shall find to be obstructive or rebellious in this matter you are to seize and arrest; and you are to commit them to our prisons, where they are to remain as a punishment until we shall be led to ordain otherwise. [And you are to muster them on certain days.]

And further, you will cause to be placed in the usual places the signs called Beacons by which the people of the district can be warned in suitable time of the arrival of our enemies; and you will cause the said men thus arrayed and mustered to be led, when danger threatens, in defence of the kingdom and district aforesaid, from time to time, both to the sea coast and to other places where there is great need.

So that no damage to the aforesaid district shall in any way come henceforth by our enemies in any way to the best of your power. [And the Commissioners are to be aided by the king's subjects and officers.]

APPENDIX I

The Petition of Peace[1]

May it please Your Majesty,

Although we, Your Majesty's most humble and faithful Subjects, the Lords and Commons in Parliament assembled, have been very unhappy in many former Petitions and Supplications to Your Majesty, wherein we have represented our most dutiful Affections, in advising and desiring those Things which we held most necessary for the Preservation of God's true Religion, Your Majesty's Safety and Honour, and the Peace of the Kingdom, and with much Sorrow do perceive that Your Majesty, incensed by many false Calumnies and Slanders, doth continue to raise Forces against us and Your other peaceable and loyal Subjects, and to make great Preparations for War, both in the Kingdom and from beyond the Seas, and by Arms and Violence to over-rule the Judgement and Advice of Your Great Council, and by Force to determine the Questions there depending, concerning the Government and Liberty of the Kingdom:

Yet, such is our earnest Desire of discharging our Duty to Your Majesty and the Kingdom, to preserve the Peace thereof, and to prevent the Miseries of Civil War amongst Your Subjects, that, notwithstanding we hold ourselves bound to use all the Means and Power, which, by the Laws and Constitutions of this Kingdom, we are trusted with, for Defence and Protection thereof, and of the Subjects from Force and Violence; we do, in this our humble and loyal Petition, prostrate ourselves at Your Majesty's Feet, beseeching Your Royal Majesty, that You will be pleased to forbear and remove all Preparations and Actions of War, particularly the Forces from about Hull, from Newcastle, Tynmouth, Lincolne, and Lincolneshire, and all other Places; and that Your Majesty will re-call the Commissions of Array, which are illegal, dismiss Troops and extraordinary Guards by You raised; that Your Majesty will come nearer to Your Parliament, and hearken to their faithful Advice and humble Petitions, which shall only tend to the Defence and Advancement of Religion, Your own Royal Honour and Safety, the Preservation of our Laws and Liberties; and we have been, and shall ever be, careful to prevent and punish all Tumults and seditious Actions, Speeches, and Writings, which may give Your Majesty just Cause of Distaste, or Apprehension of Danger; from which public Aims and Resolutions

1. *LJ*, V, 206–07 (12 July 1642).

no sinister or private Respect shall ever make us to decline: That Your Majesty will leave Delinquents to the due Course of Justice; and that nothing done or spoken in Parliament, or by any Person in Pursuance of the Command or Direction of both Houses of Parliament, be questioned any where but in Parliament; and we, for our Parts, shall be ready to lay down all those Preparations which we have been forced to make for our Defence: And for the Town of Hull, and the Ordinance concerning the Militia, as we have in both these Particulars only sought the Preservation of the Peace of the Kingdom, and the Defence of the Parliament, from Force and Violence, so we shall most willingly leave the Town of Hull in the State it was before Sir John Hotham drew any Forces into it, delivering Your Majesty's Magazine into Your Tower of London, and supplying whatsoever hath been disposed by us for the Service of the Kingdom: We shall be ready to settle the Militia by a Bill, in such a Way as shall be honourable and safe for Your Majesty, most agreeable to the Duty of Parliament, and effectual for the Good of the Kingdom, that the Strength thereof be not employed against itself, and that such as ought to be for our Security [be not] applied to our Destruction; and that the Parliament, and those who profess and desire still to preserve the Protestant Religion, both in this Realm and in Ireland, may not be left naked and indefensible to the mischievous Designs and cruel Attempts of those who are the professed and confederated Enemies thereof, in Your Majesty's Dominions and other Neighbour Nations: To which if Your Majesty's Courses and Counsels shall from henceforth concur, we doubt not but we shall quickly make it appear to the World, by the most eminent Effects of Love and Duty, that Your Majesty's Personal Safety, Your Royal Honour and Greatness, are much dearer to us than our own Lives and Fortunes, which we do most heartily dedicate, and shall most willingly employ, for the Support and Maintenance thereof.

APPENDIX J

The Parliament's Commission to the Earl of Essex
to be Captain-General of their Army[1]

Whereas, upon serious Consideration of the present and imminent Dangers of Force and Violence, which, at this time, threaten the Parliament and the whole Kingdom, through the cunning practice of Papists, and malicious Counsels of divers ill-affected Persons, inciting his Majesty to raise men, make great Provisions for War, and place Garrisons in Towns and other Places of Importance within this Kingdom; and, by Terror of Arms, to compel his Subjects to submit to a Commission of Array, contrary to Law; whereby God's true Religion and the Liberty of the Kingdom are like to be suppressed, and the whole Frame of the antient and well-tempered Government of this Realm to be dissolved and destroyed, and the English Nation inthralled, in their Persons and Estates, to an arbitrary Power; The Lords and Commons in this present Parliament assembled, according to the Duty and Trust which lies upon them, for Prevention of these great Mischiefs and Preservation of the Safety of his Majesty's Person, the Peace of the Kingdom, and the Defence of the Parliament, resolved and ordained, That an Army be forthwith raised; and that the Trained Bands, and other Forces of the Kingdom, be put into a Posture and Condition fit to oppose any Force and Insurrection by Papists, or ill-affected Persons, against the Public Peace and Laws of the Kingdom, however countenanced by any pretended Commission or Authority from his Majesty, and finding it most necessary that some Persons of Honour, Wisdom, and Fidelity, should be appointed to command the said Army and Forces; and having had long Experience and certain Knowledge that Robert Earl of Essex is, every Way, qualified for a Trust of so high a Nature and Concernment, in regard of the Nobility of his Birth, his great Judgment in Martial Affairs, approved Integrity and Sufficiency in divers Honourable Employments and Commands in the said Public Service of this State; and in whom his Majesty reposed such Confidence, that, when he went into Scotland the last Summer, he left him General of all the South Parts of the Kingdom; and especially in regard of his Faithfulness and good Affections to the Liberty, Peace, and Prosperity of the Kingdom, in this present Parliament abundantly manifested; and of the great Honour and Confidence among the well-affected People of the Kingdom, which he hath hereby gained: The said

1. Firth and Rait, *Acts and Ordinances*, I, 14–16 (15 July 1642).

Lords and Commons do constitute and ordain him, the said Robert Earl of Essex, to be the Captain-General and Chief Commander of the Army appointed to be raised, and of all other Forces of the Kingdom, for the Ends and Purposes aforementioned; and that he the said Earl shall have and enjoy all Power, Titles, Preheminence, Authority, Jurisdiction, and Liberties, incident and belonging to the said Office of Captain-General, throughout the whole Kingdom of England and Dominion of Wales, in as large and ample a Manner as any other General of an Army in this Kingdom hath lawfully used, exercised, and enjoyed; to have, hold, and execute the Office of Captain-General, in such Manner, and according to such Instructions, as he shall, from Time to Time, receive from both Houses of Parliament.

And do further grant and ordain, That the said Earl shall have Power to raise and levy Forces, as well Men at Arms, as other Horsemen and Footmen of all kinds, and meet for the Wars, in all Counties, Cities, Boroughs, Towns Corporate, and other Places, of this Kingdom and Dominion of Wales, as well within Liberties as without; and them to conduct and lead against all and singular Enemies, Rebels, Traitors, and other like offenders, and every of their Adherents; and with them to fight, and them to invade, resist, repress, subdue, pursue, slay, and kill; to put in Execution all and singular other Things for the levying and governing of the said Forces, preserving the Safety of his Majesty's Person, Defence of the Parliament, and the Conservation of this Realm and the Subjects thereof in Peace, howsoever countenanced by any pretended Commission or Authority from his Majesty, or otherwise; and shall have Power to assign and appoint a Lieutenant-General under him, the said Earl, in his Stead to do and execute all and every the Powers and Authority granted to him, the said Earl, also to appoint a Lieutenant-General of the Troops of Horse and all such Commanders and Officers as shall be necessary and requisite for the Government and Command of the said Army; and likewise one Provost-Martial for the Execution of his Commands, according to this Ordinance.

And for the better Execution of the Premises, it is ordered and ordained, that the said Earl shall have Power to command all Forts and Castles, already fortified or to be fortified; and to remove, displace, or continue, the Captains, Lieutenants, and Soldiers: As likewise all Ships, Barks and Vessels, which he, the said Earl, shall think meet, from Time to Time, for the Use and Service of the said Army and Forces, under his Government and Command; likewise to give Rules, Instructions, and Directions, for the Governing, Leading, and Conducting the said Army; and for the Punishing of all Mutinies, Tumults, Rapines and other Crimes, and Misdemeanors of any Person whatsoever in the same, according to the Course and Custom of the Wars, and Law of the Land; and the same Rules and Instructions to cause to be proclaimed, performed and executed; straitly charging and requiring both the said Lieutenant-Generals,

Provost-Martial, and all other Officers and Soldiers, of the said Army; as likewise all Lieutenants of Counties, Sheriffs, Deputy Lieutenants, Officers of the Ordnance, Commanders of Forts, Justices of Peace, Mayors, Bailiffs, and other his Majesty's Officers and Subjects whatsoever, to be aiding and assisting, and obedient to him, the said Earl, in the Execution of the said Office of Captain-General, for the Ends and Purposes, and in the Manner aforesaid.

And do likewise ordain and declare, That the said Earl, the Commanders and Officers of the said Army, and all his Majesty's Officers and Subjects whatsoever, in the Execution of the Premises, shall be saved harmless, and defended by the Power and Authority of both Houses of Parliament.

APPENDIX K

Letters from Roger Hill
to Abigail Gurdon Hill

In the spring of 1641 Roger Hill (1605–1667), MP for Bridport, Dorset, married as his second wife Abigail Gurdon, daughter of Brampton Gurdon (d. 1649) of Assington Hall, Suffolk. Hill's first wife Katherine, daughter of Giles Green, MP, had died in 1638. Abigail, by whom he had several children, died in 1658.

A group of twenty-seven letters written by Roger Hill to Abigail between 1 January 1641 and 22 March 1654 is preserved in the British Library, Add. MS 46,500. While the letters are largely personal, there are occasional insights on current events. Of the seven letters written during 1642, three are included here because they touch on events occurring just prior to and during the period of this volume. Four others were written earlier in the year.

[f. 27a] My dearest Love,

How much I long to hear how thou dost thou mayst judge according to that thou thinkest of my estimation of thyself. Thou mayst believe me without an oath (because I never used it), there is nothing in the world that I can value equal with thee. If I did, let this rise up in judgment against me and condemn me as unworthy of so great a blessing. I should be glad to see thee here as soon as thou wilt. The fast is Wednesday next.[1] If conveniently thou mayst and thou shalt think it worthy thy pains, thou mayst come up before that day, and doubtless I may bring thee home again Whitsun Eve[2] by water or some other conveyance in case I can be spared. If not, I shall enjoy thee here.

My love, we fly higher every day, and we have good cause to prepare against a day of trial. Both houses have voted that it appears that the king intends to make war against his parliament.[3] 2. That whensoever he doth, it is a breach of the trust reposed in him by his people, contrary to his oath, and tending to the

---

1. For the fast observed on 25 May, see *PJ*, 2: 370.
2. 28 May.
3. This vote and the two that follow were passed by both houses on 20 May and sent to the king along with a message concerning his assembling forces at York. The king responded with his proclamation of 27 May against the militia. See *PJ*, 2: 348–53, 386; and Appendix D.

dissolution of this government. 3. That such as shall serve or assist him in such wars are traitors and have been so adjudged by two acts of parliament[4] and ought to suffer as traitors.

My dear, if thou dost come to town, thou mayst set down with thy sister Edward,[5] whereby thou shalt be satisfactory to them, nearer to me, and I shall desire it may be at our own charge. Troublesome we may be, but burdensome I would not be to any. Our little ones and friends at Poundisford[6] do newly remember thee in their letters. My dear, I thank thee for they cakes. I never had better, nor were any ever better accepted. Remember my best duty to my good mother.[7] I wish a happy increase of thy little great belly, and that thou mayst be a happy nursing mother[8] shall be the prayer of him that is dearest to thee and thy

Roger Hill

Inner Temple, May [21, 164]2[9]

[f. 28a] My sweetest Love,

It was better with me when thou wert at Assington,[10] for in this fortnight's distance since I saw thee, I should have received a brace of letters from thee, whereas now I cannot receive a line. My love, I am still inquiring how thou dost. I can find but the common answer, all is well. Were I so happy as to be informed by thee, it would be much satisfaction to me. Now I am betwixt hope and fear. I did conceive I should had [sic] seen thee here Monday or Tuesday last. I did take it for granted that this day thou wouldst come because I heard that you would send for the Lady Mildmay, which as it seems is not so. I cannot promise when to see Greenford.[11] I fear we shall run away too fast. The king increaseth in his strength, and the Earls of Salisbury, Devonshire, Northampton, and some other lords and some of our house stole away to York yesterday morning following the example of the lord keeper.[12] I shall say no more. I resolved long since not to trust one man. He that is my portion, let him

4. 11 R. II and 1 H. IV.

5. Abigail's brother Edward Gurdon and his wife apparently lived in London.

6. Hill was the son of William Hill of Poundisford, Somerset (near Taunton). The "little ones" may be Hill's son and daughter by his first wife. *DNB*.

7. The reference is doubtless to Abigail's mother.

8. Probably a reference to their son Roger subsequently born to them. *DNB*.

9. The page is torn here and part of the date obliterated, but it appears again on f. 27b.

10. MS: *Ason*. Hill frequently used this abbreviation.

11. Apparently Abigail was staying in Greenford, Middx, rather than at Assignton Hall, Suffolk, her parents' home.

12. For the departure of the lord keeper and other lords for York in late May, see *PJ*, 2: 367, 373, 386; and *LJ*, V, 92.

be thy God. Thy husband and all unto thee, in haste I bid thee farewell that am thy most endeared husband.

Roger Hill

Temple, May 26, 1642

Impart this to my good father,[13] and our other good friends with the tenders of what I owe them all.

[f. 29a] My dearest Love,

How much I was cheered (after a dozen hours attending at the house this day)[14] when I was twice told how well thou wert Wednesday last at Isleworth[15] and when I reviewed thy brother's letter which tells me how well thou hast been ever since I left thee. Some friends of ours can witness with me; I bless God for it, and my prayers shall never be wanting for the continuance of the same unto thee.

We have received another declaration this day published by his majesty,[16] wherein we are highly accused of those things that we are not authors of and I am confident was never in the thought of any of us. Many aspersions are laid at our doors which can never be owned by us. I shall forbear to enlarge in this because I presume my brother Gurdon[17] will send it to you and enlarge himself to my father of all our passages, else I would have troubled him with a letter. Only this much I dare inform thee, that the king is removing to Belvoir[18] Castle, which is 60 miles nearer London; but I should be sorry to see that which is feared by many, that he intends to visit us with a power before we expect him. We shall not be wanting[19] to defend his majesty, ourselves, and kingdom against that wicked brood that would destroy both prince and people and make both a prey unto themselves. Horse, money, and plate come in apace.[20] Peradventure Midsummer morning I may bring Sir John Yonge,[21] my aunt, and

13. Doubtless Abigail's father.
14. D'Ewes indicated that the session lasted only from 8 a.m. to 1 or 2 p.m. See 17 June. However, Hill was a member of numerous committees.
15. MS: *Thistleworth*. Not far from Greenford, Middx.
16. For this message from the king, see 17 June, n. 11.
17. Abigail's half-brother, John Gurdon, was MP for Ipswich, Suffolk, in both the Short and Long Parliaments. Brunton and Pennington, *Members*, p. 78.
18. MS: *Bever*. The king did not make this move to Belvoir Castle in Leicestershire, though in July his travels took him to Newark, Nottingham, and Leicester, all nearby.
19. I.e., lacking.
20. The initial pledging of money, horse, and plate had taken place on 10, 11, and 13 June. See Appendix F.
21. Sir John Yonge, MP, and Roger Hill were cousins, as Sir John's father Walter Yonge, MP, and Hill's mother Jane were brother and sister. *DNB*.

others to Greenford before you are stirring. They resolved once to have seen thee this week now past. Farewell my dearest Ab. Tendered my best duty to my father and mother Gurdon, my continued affections to my brother and sister Brampton[22] and with thanks for his letter, and I shall ever be thy most endeared husband.

Roger Hill

Temple, June 17, 1642

22. Abigail's brother Brampton Gurdon served in the parliamentary army and was subsequently a member of parliament. Brunton and Pennington, *Members*, p. 78.

INDEX

The following abbreviations are used in the Index:

CA	commission of array
CIA	Commission for Irish Affairs
com.	committee(s)
H. of C.	House of Commons
H. of L.	House of Lords
lord lieut.	lord lieutenant
mess.	messenger
MO	militia ordinance
pet.	petition(s)

ADAIR, Sir Robert, 429, 435

Aldworth, Richard, 363–64, 395, 398, 399

Alford, Sir Edward, MP (Arundel, Sussex), 478

Allanson, Sir William, MP (York, Yorks), 233, 455

Allen, Francis, 154, 155, 236

Allestry, William, MP (Derby, Derbs), 479

Alured, John, MP (Hedon, Yorks), 5n, 115, 170, 171, 196, 227, 228, 232

Alvey, Yeldard, 2n, 69n, 100n

Amsterdam, 54, 56, 63, 64, 85, 90

Andover, Viscount. See Howard, Charles

Andrewes, Thomas, 49n

Anhalt-Bernburg, Prince of (Christian II), 105, 108–09, 293

Antrim, Earl of. See MacDonnell, Randal

Armagh, Archbishop of (James Ussher), 72, 108

Armine, Sir William, MP (Grantham, Lincs), 5, 8, 114, 322, 348–49, 478

Army, parliamentarian, xxii–xxiii, xxix, 95n, 104n, 191, 193, 194, 202, 204, 216n, 262, 299, 301n, 308, 341, 343, 360; arms for, 185, 361. See also Hull, magazine

Army, royalist, 172, 173, 227, 232, 233n, 238–39, 251, 261, 282, 304, 324, 342, 347, 349, 350, 353, 360; arms for, 174, 283. See also York

Army plots, 54n, 160n, 170n, 280n

Arundel and Surrey, Earl of. See Howard, Thomas

Arundel, Sussex
mayor of (James Morris), 88

Arundell, Thomas, MP (West Looe, Cornwall), 473

Ashburnham, William, 54, 160n, 170, 172, 173n, 192, 204, 215

Ashe, MP, 151

Ashe, Edward, MP (Heytesbury, Wilts), 63n, 468

Ashe, John, MP (Westbury, Wilts), xx, 66, 67, 71, 287n, 468

Ashe, Simeon, 151

Ashton, Ralph, MP (Clitheroe, Lancs), 472

Ashton, Ralph, MP (Lancashire), 61n, 63, 198n, 199, 473

Ashurst, William, MP (Newton, Lancs), 473

Aston, Sir Thomas, 26, 54, 77n, 142, 159n, 199

Atkins, Thomas, 59

Audley, Sir Henry and Lady Anne, 337, 342

Aylesbury, Bucks, 126, 187, 231, 267n

Aylett, Robert, 58, 82, 94, 95, 96, 105, 107, 114, 127, 137, 158, 195, 197, 198, 206, 221, 222, 292, 294, 340, 343

Ayloff, William, 42, 43, 66, 80, 186

Ayscough, Sir Edward, MP (Lincolnshire), 5n, 12, 13–14, 22, 23, 56n, 170, 227, 247–48, 477

BAGSHAW, Edward, MP (Southwark, Surrey), 471

Bale, Sir John, 100, 103n, 141, 143, 182n, 185

Balfour, Sir William, 361n, 364–65, 387, 401–02, 405, 406, 407, 416–17

Ball, Peter, 219

Bampfield, Sir John, MP (Penryn, Cornwall), 478

Banks, Sir John, 51, 67, 70, 194

495